Lecture Notes in Computer Science 14323

Formal Methods

Subline of Lecture Notes in Computer Science

More information about this series at https://link.springer.com/bookseries/558

Carla Ferreira · Tim A. C. Willemse
Editors

Software Engineering and Formal Methods

21st International Conference, SEFM 2023
Eindhoven, The Netherlands, November 6–10, 2023
Proceedings

Springer

Editors
Carla Ferreira 🆔
NOVA University Lisbon
Caparica, Portugal

Tim A. C. Willemse 🆔
Eindhoven University of Technology
Eindhoven, The Netherlands

ISSN 0302-9743   ISSN 1611-3349   (electronic)
Lecture Notes in Computer Science
ISBN 978-3-031-47114-8   ISBN 978-3-031-47115-5   (eBook)
https://doi.org/10.1007/978-3-031-47115-5

Preface

This volume contains the papers presented at SEFM 2023, the 21st International Conference on Software Engineering and Formal Methods, held on November 6–10, 2023 in Eindhoven, The Netherlands.

The SEFM conference series aims to bring together researchers and practitioners from academia, industry and government, to advance the state of the art in formal methods, to facilitate their uptake in the software industry, and to encourage their integration within practical software engineering methods and tools.

Following the call for papers, there were 53 announced submissions of which 12 were retracted or not submitted in time. The 41 submissions that remained were each Single blind reviewed independently by at least three reviewers, and this was followed by a lively online discussion amongst the reviewers. The SEFM submissions were judged on their originality and quality. Only submissions that were unpublished, and not submitted concurrently for publication elsewhere were considered. Based on the reviewing results, the Programme Committee decided to accept 18 regular research papers and one tool paper for presentation at the conference and publication in this volume. The editors thank the members of the Programme Committee and the additional reviewers for their reviews and discussions. We also thank all authors for their submissions, whether accepted or not, and hope that they will keep contributing to future editions of this conference series.

This year, for the first time, SEFM invited the authors of accepted papers to submit their associated artefacts for evaluation against the EAPLS badging scheme. The artefact evaluation serves to enable future researchers to effectively build on and compare with previous work. The Artefact Evaluation Committee awarded the *Available* badge to eleven artefacts, the *Reusable* badge to six artefacts, and the *Functional* badge to five artefacts. We thank the members of the Artefact Evaluation Committee, chaired by Mário Pereira and Flip van Spaendonck, for their work.

The programme also includes the following three invited talks: Mira Mezzini (Technische Universität Darmstadt) reported on "Safe and Secure Programming Abstractions for Decentralized Software"; Reiner Hähnle (Technische Universität Darmstadt) spoke on "Context-aware Trace Contracts"; and Burcu Ozkan (Delft University of Technology) gave a talk titled "Randomized Testing of Distributed Systems". We thank the three invited speakers for their insights.

Associated with the main SEFM 2023 conference there were three workshops: OpenCERT 2023, CIFMA 2023, and DataMod 2023. We thank all organisers of these associated events for contributing to the success of SEFM. The proceedings of these events will appear in a separate LNCS volume.

We would like to thank the Steering Committee and their chair Antonio Cerone for their guidance and support. The event was only possible thanks to the SEFM Organising Committee members Jeroen Keiren and Thomas Neele, and the webmaster, Thomas Neele, for all their help with planning and organising the conference. Finally, we would like to thank NWO (the Dutch Research Council) for sponsoring this event, Springer's Lecture Notes in Computer Science team for their support and sponsorship, and EasyChair for providing the reviewing infrastructure.

November 2023   Carla Ferreira
                                                                Tim A. C. Willemse

Organization

Programme Chairs

Carla Ferreira   NOVA University Lisbon, Portugal
Tim A. C. Willemse   Eindhoven University of Technology, The Netherlands

Programme Committee

Mario Bravetti   University of Bologna, Italy
Julien Brunel   ONERA, France
Radu Calinescu   University of York, UK
Taolue Chen   Birkbeck, University of London, UK
Rance Cleaveland   University of Maryland, USA
Loek Cleophas   TU Eindhoven, The Netherlands
Alcino Cunha   University of Minho, Portugal
Rocco De Nicola   IMT - School for Advanced Studies Lucca, Italy
Adrian Francalanza   University of Malta, Malta
Hubert Garavel   Inria, France
Silvia Ghilezan   University of Novi Sad, Mathematical Institute SASA, Serbia
Mario Gleirscher   University of Bremen, Germany
Christian Johansen   Norwegian University of Science and Technology, Norway
Daniela Kaufmann   TU Wien, Austria
Burcu Kulahcioglu Ozkan   Delft University of Technology, The Netherlands
Zhiming Liu   Southwest University, China
Marjan Mernik   University of Maribor, Slovenia
Stephan Merz   Inria Nancy, France
Charles Morisset   Newcastle University, UK
Jovanka Pantovic   University of Novi Sad, Serbia
Gwen Salaün   University of Grenoble Alpes, France
Augusto Sampaio   Federal University of Pernambuco, Brazil
Pierre-Yves Schobbens   University of Namur, Belgium
Marjan Sirjani   Mälardalen University, Sweden
Ana Sokolova   University of Salzburg, Austria
Bernardo Toninho   Universidade Nova de Lisboa and NOVA-LINCS, Portugal
Rolando Trujillo   Universitat Rovira i Virgili, Spain
Peter Ölveczky   University of Oslo, Norway

Organizing Committee

Jeroen J. A. Keiren	Eindhoven University of Technology, The Netherlands
Thomas Neele	Eindhoven University of Technology, The Netherlands

Artefact Evaluation Committee

Mário Pereira	NOVA University of Lisbon, Portugal
Flip van Spaendonck	Eindhoven University of Technology, The Netherlands
Guillaume Bertholon	Université de Strasbourg, France
Jan Haltermann	University of Oldenburg, Germany
Manish Goyal	The University of North Carolina at Chapel Hill, USA
Daniel Pelsmaker	Delft University of Technology, The Netherlands
Maya Setyautami	Fakultas Ilmu Komputer Universitas Indonesia, Indonesia
Mohammad Rezaalipout	Università della Svizzera Italiana, Switzerland
Tiago Soares	NOVA School of Science and Technology, Portugal

Steering Committee

Radu Calinescu	University of York, UK
Antonio Cerone (Chair)	Nazarbayev University, Kazakhstan
Ming Chai	Beijing Jiaotong University, China
Rocco De Nicola	IMT - School for Advanced Studies Lucca, Italy
Gwen Salaün	University of Grenoble Alpes, France
Bernd-Holger Schlingloff	Fraunhofer FOKUS and Humboldt University of Berlin, Germany
Marjan Sirjani	Mälardalen University, Sweden

List of Additional Reviewers

Sara Abbaspour Asadollah	Bjørnar Luteberget
Filipe Arruda	Radu Mateescu
Duncan Paul Attard	Zahra Moezkarimi
Lorenzo Bacchiani	Thomas Neele
Buda Bajic	Vivek Nigam
Rodrigo Bonifacio	Quentin Nivon
Pierre Bouvier	Jiajie Peng
David Chemouil	Martin Rosso
Zhenbang Chen	Maghsood Salimi
João Costa Seco	Wendelin Serwe
Jovana Dedeic	Jacopo Soldani
Brendan Devlin-Hill	Clay Stevens
Xinwei Fang	Milan Todorovic
Ross Horne	Yedi Zhang
Jeroen J. A. Keiren	Yuanrui Zhang
Frédéric Lang	Liang Zhao

Randomized Testing of Distributed Systems (Abstract)

Burcu Kulahcioglu Ozkan (ID)

Delft University of Technology, Delft, The Netherlands
b.ozkan@tudelft.nl

Abstract. Distributed systems are prone to concurrency bugs due to the non-determinism in the interleavings of concurrent events. Detecting and diagnosing concurrency bugs in distributed systems is critical since unforeseen interleavings of concurrent messages, network, or process faults can result in unexpected, erroneous system behavior. However, concurrency bugs are hard to detect as they are triggered only in some subtle interleavings of the events.

Random testing offers a practical way of searching for bugs in large distributed systems. While naïve random stress testing is unlikely to discover rare bugs, our recent randomized testing methods present effective testing algorithms. The effectiveness of our methods lies in the mathematical characterization of concurrency bugs and sampling test cases from the set of executions that are likely to produce a buggy execution.

A significant advantage of our testing techniques is that they provide theoretical guarantees on the probability of detecting a bug.

Transferring the theoretical insight of formal methods and verification into the design of testing methods further improves the bug detection guarantees of randomized testing. Incorporating state space reduction strategies from model checking reduces the sample set of executions to explore, resulting in a higher probability of detecting bugs. Besides generic strategies, exploiting ideas from the verification of specific systems can lead to efficient testing of these systems. Our recent works exploit theoretical insights from the verification of distributed consensus algorithms, which are at the core of distributed databases and blockchain systems, to develop efficient methods for testing their implementations.

This talk overviews the key ideas in our randomized testing techniques for detecting concurrency bugs in distributed systems.

Keywords: Software testing · Concurrency · Distributed systems

Contents

Tool Papers

Invited Contribution

Herding CATs

Reiner Hähnle[1], Marco Scaletta[1(✉)], and Eduard Kamburjan[2]

[1] Technical University of Darmstadt, Darmstadt, Germany
{reiner.hahnle,marco.scaletta}@tu-darmstadt.de
[2] University of Oslo, Oslo, Norway
eduard@ifi.uio.no

Abstract. We illustrate the usage of *context-aware trace contracts* (for short: CATs) by way of an example. CATs are a systematic approach to specify non-procedure local behavior. Technically, they consist of symbolic expressions specifying the assumed behavior of the callers before a procedure enters its contract, the behavior a procedure guarantees, and the behavior expected to happen in the continuation after termination. This generalizes state-based, Hoare-style specification triples.

1 Introduction

Specification contracts are pivotal for deductive verification to scale [5], because they permit to verify a large program by tackling one procedure at a time. Given a procedure m, a *state contract* [7,8] is a pair $\langle \text{Pre}, \text{Post} \rangle$, where Pre is an expression specifying the execution states under which m enters the contract and Post specifies the execution states m must guarantee upon termination.

In many scenarios, however, notably in concurrent execution, state contracts are insufficient. For example, how to specify that at some point in time *before m* was called a certain action took place? Often, this is achieved with *ad hoc* ghost variables, leading to bloated and hard-to-read contracts. It is even more difficult to specify that *after* a call to m the *callers* must take some action, for example, a cleanup. To enable systematic specification of such *non-procedure local* properties it is desirable to have a generalized notion of contract that permits to specify the *context* wherein a procedure enters into a contract.

The technical basis for context-aware contracts is a recent generalization of state contracts to *trace contracts* [2]. Trace contracts generalize a pre-/post-condition pair $\langle \text{Pre}, \text{Post} \rangle$ to a *symbolic trace* θ, permitting to specify a set of execution traces a procedure m is expected to adhere to. This makes it possible to specify events taking place *during* execution of some code, hence, specification elements are not limited to the start or finish, as state contracts are.

Context-aware trace contracts (CATs, for short) [6] build upon trace contracts and specify the *non-local* behavior of a procedure m as a triple consisting of (i) a symbolic trace θ_{a_m} specifying the *assumptions* on the context, *before* m enters into its contract, (ii) a symbolic trace θ_{s_m} specifying the *guarantee* m gives about its internal behavior, and (iii) a symbolic trace θ_{c_m} specifying the expected *continuation* of the call context *after* m terminates.

C. Ferreira and T. A. C. Willemse (Eds.): SEFM 2023, LNCS 14323, pp. 3–8, 2023.
https://doi.org/10.1007/978-3-031-47115-5_1

We illustrate the usage of CATs *informally* by way of an example taken from the well-known *Casino Case Study*[1] used, for example, in [1,4]. We refer to [6] for the formal definition of CATs, the deduction system, and the soundness proofs.

2 CATs by Example

We introduce the general structure of a CAT, then we present a running example extracted from the Casino Case Study. We first define informal requirements on the behavior of procedures and their context. Then we illustrate how a formal specification with CATs can be done.

2.1 General Structure of a CAT

A *context-aware trace contract* [6] C_m for a procedure m consists of a triple of symbolic trace formulas [2]:

$$C_m = \ll \theta_{a_m} \mid \theta_{s_m} \mid \theta_{c_m} \gg$$

Here, θ_{s_m} is the *internal* behavior that m guarantees, while θ_{a_m} and θ_{c_m} specify the call context, wherein m enters into the contract: The *pre-trace* θ_{a_m} specifies the *assumptions* on what must have happened before executing m, and the *post-trace* θ_{c_m} specifies the requirements on how the computation must *continue* after the termination of m. We assume that the final state specified in θ_{a_m} is the state where θ_{s_m} starts, and similarly for θ_{s_m} and θ_{c_m}.

Trace formulas θ contain state formulas ψ as building blocks of the form $\lceil \psi \rceil$, denoting all singleton traces consisting of an execution state that satisfies ψ. Moreover, trace formulas can be composed by concatenation $\cdot$, conjunction $\wedge$ and disjunction $\vee$. We use the notation "$\cdot\cdot$" to denote an arbitrary finite trace[2], hence a traditional state contract $\langle \text{Pre}, \text{Post} \rangle$ corresponds to the trace formula $\lceil \text{Pre} \rceil \cdot\cdot \lceil \text{Post} \rceil$. Expression $\overset{\overline{m}}{\cdot\cdot}$ further restricts traces to those not containing any procedure call to an $m \in \overline{m}$.

2.2 Accessing the Program State: Observation Quantifiers

To restrict possible execution states of a specified program it is necessary to access the value of program variables at some point during execution. In state contracts it is obvious when a variable is observed in the pre- and postcondition: at the start and at the finish of a procedure, respectively. In a trace formula, however, such as $\theta \cdot \lceil i \geq 0 \rceil \cdot \theta' \cdot \lceil i \geq 0 \rceil \cdot \theta''$, two observations of program variable i refer to arbitrary different time points *during* execution.

To be able to compare the value of program variables at different states in a trace formula, it is necessary to capture the value and define a scope. This

---

[1] https://verifythis.github.io/02casino/.

[2] This constitutes a special case of a general smallest fixed point operator that is part of the definition of trace formulas, see [2] for details.

is done with an *observation quantifier*. An observation quantifier has the form $℧ x$ as $y.\theta(y)$, where x is a program variable whose current value is bound to the logical (first-order) variable y, which then can be accessed from the *scope* of the quantifier, the trace formula θ. For example, $℧ x$ as $y. (\lceil y > 0 \rceil \cdots)$ specifies the set of finite traces starting in a state, where x has positive value. We say y *observes* x at such a position. Logic variables are rigid, meaning their values are immutable: when y observes x at a certain instant of the computation it is immutably bound to the value x has at that instant. Therefore, $℧ x$ as $y. (\lceil y > 0 \rceil \cdots)$ is equivalent to $℧ x$ as $y. (\cdots \lceil y > 0 \rceil)$, the only difference being that the check whether x is positive in the beginning is now syntactically located at the end of the trace formula. The same programs are conforming to these two trace formulas.

Specifying Pre- and Postconditions. With observation quantifiers it easily possible to specify state preconditions, simply by placing the quantifier at the border between θ_{a_m} and θ_{s_m}, as for example in

$$\ll \theta'_{a_m} \cdot ℧ x \text{ as } y.\lceil y > 0 \rceil \mid \theta_{s_m} \mid \theta_{c_m} \gg .$$

It is important to observe that the scope of an observation quantifier occurring in a contract always includes all subsequent contract elements, here θ_{s_m} and θ_{c_m}. Postconditions are analogous. It is possible to observe the same program variable at different execution states and compare the values. For example, if we want to specify that m increases the value of x by one we can write

$$\ll \theta'_{a_m} \cdot ℧ x \text{ as } y.\lceil true \rceil \mid \theta'_{s_m} \cdot ℧ x \text{ as } y'.\lceil y' \doteq y + 1 \rceil \mid \theta_{c_m} \gg .$$

2.3 Running Example

To illustrate our approach we use an excerpt of the *Casino Case Study* mentioned in Sect. 1, where a player can place bets and, depending on the outcome, collect a win. Procedures placeBet and decideBet are shown in Fig. 1. We look at the following properties: (i) a game is either available and can be started with placeBet, or it is ongoing and can be terminated with decideBet (there is no *idle* state, i.e. no creation of the game is needed); (ii) we focus on the constraints on the player's wallet, ignoring the amount of money in the pot (infinite amount).

```
placeBet() {                    decideBet() {
    bet = amountToBet;              if (coinSide == guess) {
    playerWallet -= bet;               playerWallet += 2*bet;
    return;                        }
}                                  bet = 0;
                                   return;
                               }
```

Fig. 1. Code for placeBet and decideBet

2.4   Goal of Specification

We give an informal description of the requirements for the execution of `placeBet` and `decideBet`:

Requirements for `placeBet`. (Pre-trace): Before executing `placeBet` there cannot be any pending bet still to be decided. (Precondition): The amount the player bets must be positive and cannot exceed the amount of money in the wallet. (Internal behavior): Procedure `placeBet` does not call any other procedure.[3] (Postcondition): By betting, the wallet of the player is reduced by the amount of the bet. (Post-trace): After a bet is placed it must be decided upon.

Requirements for `decideBet`. (Pre-trace): Before executing `decideBet`, any pending bet still to be decided must have been placed. (Precondition): None. (Internal behavior): Procedure `decideBet` does not call any other procedure. (Postcondition): The wallet of the player is credited twice the amount of money only if the guess of the player was correct and the amount of the bet is reset to 0. (Post-trace): None.

2.5   CATs

We formalize the requirements stated in Sect. 2.4 in the CAT framework.

CAT for `placeBet` . We define the components for the CAT for `placeBet`:

$$C_{\text{placeBet}} = \ll \theta_{a_{\text{placeBet}}} \mid \theta_{s_{\text{placeBet}}} \mid \theta_{c_{\text{placeBet}}} \gg$$

(Pre-trace): The case that no pending bet is still being decided can occur in two situations: Either no bet has ever been placed, or the most recently placed bet was decided, i.e. no bet is placed after the most recent occurrence of `decideBet`. This can be specified with the trace formula:[4]

$$\theta'_{a_{\text{placeBet}}} = \overset{\text{placeBet}}{\cdots} \vee \cdots \text{pop}(\text{decideBet}, \_) \overset{\substack{\text{placeBet} \\ \text{decideBet}}}{\cdots} .$$

(Precondition): The trace formula for the precondition is straightforward, but we must observe the values of `amountToBet` and `playerWallet`:

$$\phi_{pre_{\text{placeBet}}} = \mho \, \texttt{amountToBet as } toBet.$$
$$\mho \, \texttt{playerWallet as } wallet. \lceil toBet > 0 \wedge toBet \leq wallet \rceil$$

Therefore the pre-trace for `placeBet` is $\theta_{a_{\text{placeBet}}} = \theta'_{a_{\text{placeBet}}} \cdot \phi_{pre_{\text{placeBet}}}$.

---

[3] This is a simplified form of a typical secure information flow property.

[4] An event of the form $\text{pop}(m, k)$ signifies that a call of procedure m with call identifier k has terminated, see [2] for details. There is also a dual event $\text{start}(m, k)$ used below.

(Internal Behavior): No procedure calls are allowed in the internal behavior of `placeBet`:

$$\theta'_{s_{\text{placeBet}}} = \overset{\substack{\text{placeBet}\\\text{decideBet}}}{\cdots}$$

(Postcondition): To specify requirements on the value of `playerWallet` at the end of the execution of `placeBet` we use another observation quantifier and refer to the observed variables in $\phi_{pre_{\text{placeBet}}}$:

$$\phi_{post_{\text{placeBet}}} = \mho\ \texttt{playerWallet as } wallet'.\lceil wallet' = wallet - toBet\rceil$$

So the internal behavior for `placeBet` is $\theta_{s_{\text{placeBet}}} = \theta'_{s_{\text{placeBet}}} \cdot \phi_{post_{\text{placeBet}}}$.

(Post-trace): The requirement that the continuation of execution must include a matching occurrence of `decideBet` can be specified by the trace formula:

$$\theta_{c_{\text{placeBet}}} = \overset{\substack{\text{placeBet}\\\text{decideBet}}}{\cdots} \texttt{start}(\texttt{decideBet}, \_) \cdots$$

CAT for `decideBet` . We define the components for the CAT for `decideBet`:

$$C_{\text{decideBet}} = \ll \theta_{a_{\text{decideBet}}} \mid \theta_{s_{\text{decideBet}}} \mid \theta_{c_{\text{decideBet}}} \gg$$

(Pre-trace): A bet can be decided only if it has been placed and it has not been decided yet:

$$\theta'_{a_{\text{decideBet}}} = \overset{\substack{\text{placeBet}}}{\cdots} \wedge \cdots \texttt{pop}(\texttt{placeBet}, \_) \overset{\substack{\text{placeBet}\\\text{decideBet}}}{\cdots}$$

(Precondition): Even though the precondition is trivial, we still need to observe the values of `coinSide`, `guess`, `playerWallet`, and `bet` in the beginning of the execution of `decideBet`, because the observed values are referred to in the postcondition:

$$\phi_{pre_{\text{decideBet}}} = \mho\ \texttt{coinSide as } c, \texttt{guess as } g,$$
$$\texttt{playerWallet as } wallet, \texttt{bet as } b.\lceil true \rceil$$

(Internal Behavior): No procedure calls are allowed in the internal behavior of `decideBet`: $\theta'_{s_{\text{decideBet}}}$ is specified analogous to $\theta'_{s_{\text{placeBet}}}$.

(Postcondition): To specify the postcondition we need an additional observation quantifier, to observe `playerWallet` and `bet` at the end of the computation:

$$\phi_{post_{\text{decideBet}}} = \mho\ \texttt{playerWallet as } wallet', \texttt{bet as } b'.$$
$$\lceil b' \doteq 0 \wedge (c \doteq g \rightarrow wallet' \doteq wallet + b)\rceil$$

So the internal behavior for `decideBet` is $\theta_{s_{\text{decideBet}}} = \theta'_{s_{\text{decideBet}}} \cdot \phi_{post_{\text{decideBet}}}$.

Post-trace. There is no requirement on how the execution must continue after the execution of `decideBet`, therefore, $\theta_{c_{\mathrm{decideBet}}} = \cdots$.

3 Wrapping Up

The paper [6] contains a sound calculus that can prove the contracts specified in Sect. 2.5 separately. Moreover, it is proven that validity of a set of contracts implies the validity of any proven program specified with those contracts. In consequence, the principle of *procedure-modular* verification carries over from state contracts to CATs.

What remains to be shown is how to incorporate concurrent execution—our case study is sequential. The above mentioned paper shows how CATs can be applied to asynchronous procedure calls in the style of cooperative scheduling [3]. More general programming models are future work.

References

1. Bliudze, S., van den Bos, P., Huisman, M., Rubbens, R., Safina, L.: JavaBIP meets VerCors: towards the safety of concurrent software systems in Java. In: Lambers, L., Uchitel, S. (eds.) Fundamental Approaches to Software Engineering, 26th International Conference, FASE, Paris, France, vol. 13991 of LNCS, pp. 143–150. Springer, Heidelberg (2023). https://doi.org/10.1007/978-3-031-30826-0_8
2. Bubel, R., Gurov, D., Hähnle, R., Scaletta, M.: Trace-based deductive verification. In: Piskac, R., Voronkov, A. (eds.) Proceedings 20th International Conference on Logic for Programming, Artificial Intelligence and Reasoning (LPAR), Manizales Colombia, EPiC Series in Computing. EasyChair (2023)
3. de Boer, F., et al. A survey of active object languages. ACM Comput. Surv. **50**(5), 76:1–76:39 (2017)
4. Ernst, G., Knapp, A., Murray, T.: A Hoare logic with regular behavioral specifications. In: Margaria, T., Steffen, B. (eds.) Leveraging Applications of Formal Methods, Verification and Validation, 11th International Symposium, ISoLA, Rhodes, Greece, Proceedings Part I, vol. 13701 of LNCS, pp. 45–64. Springer, Heidelberg (2022)
5. Hähnle, R., Huisman, M.: Deductive verification: from pen-and-paper proofs to industrial tools. In: Steffen, B., Woeginger, G. (eds.) Computing and Software Science: State of the Art and Perspectives. LNCS, vol. 10000, pp. 345–373. Springer, Cham (2019)
6. Hähnle, R., Kamburjan, E., Scaletta, M.: Context-aware trace contracts. In: De Boer, F., Damiani, F., Hähnle, R., Johnsen, E.B., Kamburjan, E. (eds.) Active Object Languages: Current Research Trends, vol. 14360 of LNCS. Springer, Cham (2023)
7. Hoare, C.A.R.: Procedures and parameters: an axiomatic approach. In: Engeler, E. (ed.) Symposium on Semantics of Algorithmic Languages. LNM, vol. 188, pp. 102–116. Springer, Heidelberg (1971). https://doi.org/10.1007/BFb0059696
8. Meyer, B.: Applying "design by contract". IEEE Comput. **25**(10), 40–51 (1992)

Regular Papers

Refinements for Open Automata

Rabéa Ameur-Boulifa[1]($\boxtimes$)(iD), Quentin Corradi[2](iD), Ludovic Henrio[2](iD),
and Eric Madelaine[3](iD)

[1] LTCI, Télécom Paris, Institut Polytechnique de Paris, Palaiseau, France
rabea.ameur-boulifa@telecom-paris.fr
[2] Université Lyon, EnsL, UCBL, CNRS, Inria, LIP, Lyon, France
{quentin.corradi,ludovic.henrio}@ens-lyon.fr
[3] INRIA Sophia Antipolis Méditérannée, UCA, Sophia Antipolis, France
eric.madelaine@inria.fr

Abstract. Establishing equivalence and refinement relations between
programs is an important mean for verifying their correctness. By establishing that the behaviours of a modified program simulate those of
the source one, simulation relations formalise the desired relationship
between a specification and an implementation, two equivalent implementations, or a program and its optimised implementation. This article
discusses a notion of simulation between *open automata*, which are symbolic behavioural models for communicating systems. Open automata
may have *holes* modelling elements of their context, and can be composed by instantiation of the holes. This allows for a compositional approach for verification of their behaviour.

We define a simulation between open automata that may or may not
have the same holes, and show under which conditions these refinements
are preserved by composition of open automata.

Keywords: Labelled transition systems · Simulation · Composition

1 Introduction

Compositional design is a highly convenient approach for specifying and verifying large systems. Automata are often used as the basic formalism for this
approach, but most automata definitions allow only the specifications of finite
closed systems. These systems can be verified efficiently, but programming often
consists in writing systems that should be interfaced with others, and with potentially unbound behaviours. We investigate in our works the reasoning on open
symbolic systems, with a strong focus on compositionality of properties. More
precisely, we say that a system is open if it contains a "hole" to be filled by
another system. Open systems are typically composition operators [17] or com-
ponentised systems where some of the components are yet to be provided [6].
This form of composition is more complex to handle than top-level interaction
usually found in process algebra, as the behaviour of each entity in the system
is parameterised both by classical symbolic variables and by process variables.

C. Ferreira and T. A. C. Willemse (Eds.): SEFM 2023, LNCS 14323, pp. 11–29, 2023.
https://doi.org/10.1007/978-3-031-47115-5_2

Symbolic systems and their bisimulation raises additional challenges [15,17]. Reasoning on a symbolic automaton allows one to represent an infinite system in a finite manner, but then the state of the system is not only characterised by an automaton state but also by the value of the different variables representing the system. In parameterised systems, it is necessary to guard state transitions depending on the system state and on the input values. This is why in previous works and in this article, it we extend the classical form of bisimulation relation: in a symbolic setting a bisimulation relation relates classically states of two systems but it is additionally parameterised by a formula that must be verified by the state variables. This has been introduced in details in previous works [6] and will be recalled briefly in Sect. 2.2. We have shown in previous works that open symbolic systems are particularly convenient to model process algebra operators and open component systems with infinite behaviour [6,17].

The refinement concept plays an important role in software engineering. In addition to helping to cope with the complexity of requirements and design, refinement provides a foundation for ensuring system correctness. The correctness of a system can be established by proving, that a system refines its specification with the idea that some properties of the specification are preserved in the refined system. Refinement entails that one system can be considered as a more precise version of another one that is considered to be the specification. The refined model features all the specified behaviours with more concrete details. From a formal point of view, refinement is a mathematical relations between a specification and its implementation, with trace inclusion or simulation being frequently used relations [20,22].

In this article, we design a simulation theory for open symbolic systems. We build a very generic theory that should allow us to reason on simulation-based verification for most concurrent systems, as our base theory merely relies on automata parameterised by both variables and processes. As we shall see, our composition of automata is also very generic to account for any interaction mechanism found in concurrent systems. While our contribution is theoretical, it establishes the foundations for to the verification of any compositionally designed system, like component systems, algorithmic skeletons.

Open automata (that we abbreviate OA) were defined as a way to provide a semantics for open parameterised hierarchical labelled transition systems (abbreviated LTS). They were proposed as a theoretical foundation for parametrised automata used in verification tools and called *pNets*. An OA [17] is similar to a classical automaton but with variables and holes. Variables make automata symbolic and allow them to encode infinite-state systems. Holes enable the composition of automata: an automaton with a hole is an operator that takes another automaton as parameter and reacts to the actions it emits; the composed automaton is an automaton where the behaviour of one "process parameter" of the main automaton has been provided. Due to their generic nature, the notion of OA model is quite abstract but we already illustrated previously how to derive OAs for process algebra operators [17] or for component systems [5,6].

In previous works [6,24] a bisimulation relation was defined for OA and open parameterised hierarchical LTSs. It exhibited good properties concerning bisimulation, but refinement relations were not studied. In this article we go further to define a theory of simulation for OA. The simulation relation we introduce in the paper is based on the notion of simulation, in a similar way to that defined in classical automata theory [8,21]. It possesses the common behaviour-preserving property: all the behaviour of the abstract specification must be followed by its (complex) implementation but additional behaviours may exist. However we also ensure that a whole scenario, made of several steps, of the specification can also be simulated by the refined system, which is slightly richer than the traditional simulation relation and allows us to obtain a compositionality result.

Our contribution in this paper is the definition of a simulation relation for OA that has the following characteristics:

- Classical simulation characterisation but also an additional criteria ensuring that simulation does not introduce deadlocks when following a trace from the simulated automaton.
- Good properties relatively to composition: we prove that composition preserves the simulation relation.
- Ability to take into account both composition and transitivity: this is a challenge because composition changes the set of holes of the OA and simulation takes into account the actions of the holes.

The simulation relation is introduced in two steps. First we define a simulation that relates two automata with the same holes, which allows us to focus on the automaton aspect. Second we introduce a relation that relates two automata with different sets of holes, which allows us to take into account the open nature of OA, and to deal with composition. Properties of the simulation are stated and proven on the second, more general version of the relation, thus also being valid for the first simpler simulation relation.

This paper is organized as follows. Section 2 recalls the definition of OA and defines their composition. We then define a simulation relation for OA, first only considering two automata with the same set of holes in Sect. 3 and generalize it to automata with a different set of holes in Sect. 4. Section 5 is dedicated to formalize and prove basic properties of the simulation defined, including the proof that simulation is a preorder and has nice composability properties. In Sect. 6 we review related works, and Sect. 7 concludes the paper.

2   Open Automata and Their Composition

This section presents our notations and the principles of automata. Except for minor changes in the notations, compared to previous works [6] the only new contribution is the definition of a composition operator for OA.

2.1 Preliminaries and Notations

Countable families of values (equivalent to maps) will be noted $x_i^{i \in I}$, $\{i {\mapsto} x_i \mid i \in I\}$, or $\{i \leftarrow x_i \mid i \in I\}$, depending on what is more convenient (e.g. $i \leftarrow x_i$ is used for maps that are used as substitution). Statements like $\exists c_j^{j \in J}$ defines both J and the mapping $j {\mapsto} c_j$. The disjoint union on sets is noted $\uplus$. Disjoint union is also used on maps. There are several ways of ensuring a union is disjoint, we will indifferently either suppose sets are disjoint or rename conflicting objects (useful for variables). In a formula, a quantifier followed by a finite set will be used as a shorthand for the quantification on every variable in the set: $\forall \{a_1, \ldots, a_n\}, \exists \{b_1, \ldots, b_m\}, P$ means $\forall a_1, \ldots, \forall a_n, \exists b_1, \ldots, \exists b_m, P$.

Our expression algebra E is the disjoint union of terms, actions, and formulas $E = \mathcal{T} \uplus \mathcal{A} \uplus \mathcal{F}$. $\mathcal{T}$ and $\mathcal{A}$ are term algebras. The set of formulas $\mathcal{F}$ contain at least first order formulas and equality[1] over $\mathcal{T}$ and $\mathcal{A}$. For $e \in E$, $vars(e)$ is the set of variables in e that are not bound by a binder. An expression is closed if $vars(e) = \varnothing$. The set $\mathcal{P}$ denotes values which is a subset of closed terms. $\mathcal{F}_V$ is the set of formulas f that only uses variables in V, i.e., the formulas such that $vars(f) \subseteq V$. The parallel substitution of variables in e by a map $\psi : V \to \mathcal{T}$ is denoted $e\{\!\{\psi\}\!\}$.

We suppose given a satisfiability relation on closed formulas, denoted $\models f$. We will use two variants of the satisfiability relation:

- The satisfiability of a formula $f \in \mathcal{F}$ under some valuation $\sigma : V \to \mathcal{P}$ is defined as follows: $\sigma \models f \iff\; \models \exists vars(f\{\!\{\sigma\}\!\}), f\{\!\{\sigma\}\!\}$
- The satisfiability of a formula $f \in \mathcal{F}$ with some variable set V as context is defined as follows: $V \models f \iff\; \models \forall V, \exists (vars(f) \setminus V), f$

2.2 Open Automata (OA)

OA are labelled transition systems with variables that can be used to compose other automata: they are made of transitions that are dependent on the actions of "holes", a composition operation consists in filling a hole with another automaton to obtain a more complex automaton. The variables makes the OA symbolic, and the holes allow for a partial definition of the behaviour.

Definition 1 (Open transition, Open automaton). *An* open automaton *is a tuple* $\langle S, s_0, V, \sigma_0, J, T \rangle$ *with* S *a set of states,* $s_0 \in S$ *the initial state,* V *the finite set of variable names,* $\sigma_0 : V \to \mathcal{P}$ *the initial valuation of variables,* J *the set of hole names and* T *the set of open transitions.*

An open transition *is a structure* $\dfrac{\beta_j^{j \in J'}, g, \psi}{s \xrightarrow{\alpha} s'}$ *made of several composing entities, equivalent to a tuple. In an open transition* $s, s' \in S$ *are the source and target states,* $\alpha \in \mathcal{A}$ *is the resulting action that can be observed from the outside,* $J' \subseteq J$ *are the holes involved in the transition,* $g \in \mathcal{F}$ *is the guard that may constraint the transition, and* $\psi : V \to \mathcal{T}$ *are the variable assignments that have*

---

[1] Equality does not need to be only syntactic.

an effect on the state of the automaton. Each $\beta_j \in \mathcal{A}$ is an action of the holes j, To be well-formed, an open transition should use only variables of the automaton and variables appearing in the involved actions, formally:

$$vars(g) \subseteq vars(\alpha) \cup \bigcup_{j \in J'} vars(\beta_j) \cup V$$

$$\forall v \in V.\, vars(\psi(v)) \subseteq vars(\alpha) \cup \bigcup_{j \in J'} vars(\beta_j) \cup V$$

A pair consisting of a state and a valuation is called a *configuration* (of the automaton). We use two operators to access pieces of information of the OA.

Definition 2 (Out-transition, Transition variables). *Let* $\langle S, s_0, V, \sigma_0, J, T \rangle$ *be an automaton and let* r *be a state in* S. *$\mathrm{OT}_T(r) \subset T$ are the transition outgoing from state* r^2. *The local variables of a transition* $vars(t)$ *are all variables appearing in transition* t *except the variables of the automaton. Outgoing transitions and variables are formally defined as follows.*

$$\mathrm{OT}_T(r) = \left\{ \left. \frac{\beta_j^{j \in J'},\, g,\, \psi}{s \xrightarrow{\alpha} s'} \in T \,\right|\, s = r \right\}$$

$$vars\left(\frac{\beta_j^{j \in J'},\, g,\, \psi}{s \xrightarrow{\alpha} s'} \right) = \left(vars(\alpha) \cup \bigcup_{j \in J'} vars(\beta_j) \right) \setminus V$$

Example 1 (prod-cons). As a running example, we consider a classical producer-consumer pair interacting through FIFO buffer, named `prod-cons`. Figure 1 reflects the overall structure of the system involving a producer process, a consumer process and an orchestrator that coordinates their activities.

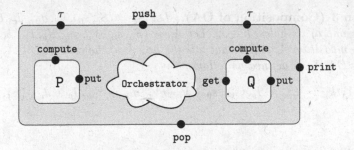

Fig. 1. Structure of the example. Each box corresponds to a process whose ports are the actions it can perform. The actions observable by the environment are `push`, which indicates the enqueuing of an element, `pop` which indicates the dequeuing, and `print` which indicates the production of results.

---

[2] When the set T is clear from the context, it will be omitted and we will use $\mathrm{OT}(r)$.

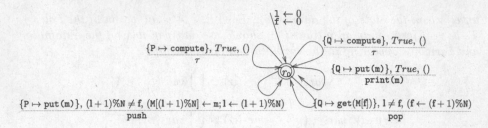

Fig. 2. OA for the `prod-cons` system using FIFO circular buffer.

The OA modelling the behaviour of such a system using an unbounded circular/ring buffer is depicted in Fig. 2. The automaton has a single state with two holes: P and Q that are the two interacting processes. l (as last) indicates the next available position for enqueuing an element and f (as first) is the position that contains the next element to be dequeued. The buffer reacts to a push from P and enqueues it. Similarly, whenever Q pops an element, it dequeues it. Additionally, whenever Q produces an item, it is exposed as an external observable **print** action. When any process do its internal computation, it is exposed externally as unobservable action τ.

The example uses several kinds of data. Variable m holds a message (we can leave the message type abstract here). We additionally use arrays of messages with a syntax of the form M[l] for array accesses; M is an array of N elements, from 0 to $N-1$. Finally we use addition and modulo operation (%) on integers.   □

Open Automata Composition. OA are partially specified automata, the partiality arises from the holes. A hole can be seen as a port in which we can plug an OA. The plugging operation is called composition. The composition of OA was already implicitly defined by the means of composition on pNets in previous work [17]. We provide here a (new) direct definition of composition for OA.

Definition 3 (Composition of OA). *Let* $A_c = \langle S_c, s_{0c}, V_c, \sigma_{0c}, J_c, T_c \rangle$ *be an OA and* k *one of its holes,* $k \in J_c$. *Let* $A_p = \langle S_p, s_{0p}, V_p, \sigma_{0p}, J_p, T_p \rangle$ *be another OA, the composition* $A_c[A_p/k]$ *that fills the hole* k *of the context OA* A_c *with the parameter OA* A_p *is defined as follows:*

$$A_c[A_p/k] ::= \langle S_c \times S_p, (s_{0c}, s_{0p}), V_c \uplus V_p, \sigma_{0c} \uplus \sigma_{0p}, J_p \uplus J_c \setminus \{k\}, T \rangle$$

with

$$T = \left\{ \frac{\beta_j^{j \in J'_p \uplus J'_c}, g_c \wedge g_p \wedge \alpha_p = \beta_k, \psi_c \uplus \psi_p}{(s_c, s_p) \xrightarrow{\alpha_c} (s'_c, s'_p)} \;\middle|\; \frac{\beta_j^{j \in J'_c \uplus \{k\}}, g_c, \psi_c}{s_c \xrightarrow{\alpha_c} s'_c} \in T_c, \frac{\beta_j^{j \in J'_p}, g_p, \psi_p}{s_p \xrightarrow{\alpha_p} s'_p} \in T_p \right\}$$

$$\cup \left\{ \frac{\beta_j^{j \in J'_c}, g_c, \psi_c}{(s_c, s_p) \xrightarrow{\alpha_c} (s'_c, s_p)} \;\middle|\; \frac{\beta_j^{j \in J'_c}, g_c, \psi_c}{s_c \xrightarrow{\alpha_c} s'_c} \in T_c, k \notin J'_c, s_p \in S_p \right\}$$

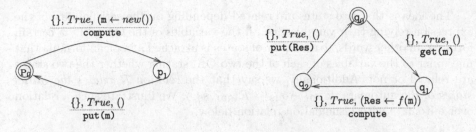

Fig. 3. (Left) A producer. It produces one item at a time and pushes it. (Right) A consumer. It pops an item, does some work and pushes the result.

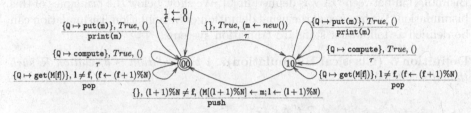

Fig. 4. OA for filling the hole P in prod-cons: prod-cons[P/producer].

The first OA decides when the second can evolve by involving its hole in a transition: the action emitted when A_p makes a transition is synchronised with the action of the hole k in transitions of A_c. The condition $\alpha_p = \beta_k$ ensures that the action emitted by the automaton A_p filling the hole is the one expected in the hole k of the open automaton A_c.

Example 2. Figure 3 shows a producer automaton and a consumer automaton that can be used to fill the holes P and Q of prod-cons defined in Example 1.

The OA on Fig. 4 is the composition of the system in Fig. 2 and the producer in Fig. 3 (left). The composition consists of two states (the product of the states of both automata). The transitions from one state to another come from the synchronisation of the transitions of the encompassing automaton with those of the producer filling the hole P, this is why there is no more action from hole P in the composed automaton. Only elements related to the hole P are changed and in particular, transitions involving Q remain unchanged. □

2.3   Relations Between Open Automata

Establishing semantic equivalences and simulation relations between different OA requires to compare their states. For this purpose, we suppose that the variables of the two OA are disjoint (a renaming of variables may have to be applied before comparing OA states).

Definition 4 (Relation on open automata configurations). *Suppose V_1 and V_2 are disjoint. A relation on configurations of two OA $\langle S_1, s_{01}, V_1, \sigma_{01}, J_1, T_1 \rangle$ and $\langle S_2, s_{02}, V_2, \sigma_{02}, J_2, T_2 \rangle$ is a function $\mathcal{R} : S_1 \times S_2 \to \mathcal{F}_{V_1 \uplus V_2}$.*

The idea is that two states are related depending on the satisfiability of the expression relying their variables, i.e., if the variables of the OA verify a certain formula. In other words, to each pair of states is attached a boolean formula that may refer to the variables of each of the two OA, stating whether the two states are related or not. Additionally, we say that the relation $\mathcal{R}$ *relates the initial states* of the automata if: $\sigma_{01} \uplus \sigma_{02} \models \mathcal{R}(s_{01}, s_{02})$. We illustrate such a relation over automata with bisimulation relation below.

2.4   A Bisimulation for Open Automata

Bisimulation between OA was defined in [6]. We show below the principles of this bisimulation. We first recall the usual definition of bisimulation. Bisimulation can be defined as follows for standard transition systems:

Definition 5 (Classical Bisimulation). *A bisimulation is a relation $\mathcal{R}$ such that if $s \ \mathcal{R} \ t$ then:*

$$\forall l \ s', \ s \xrightarrow{l} s' \implies \exists t'. \ s' \ \mathcal{R} \ t' \wedge t \xrightarrow{l} t'$$

and conversely

$$\forall l \ t', \ t \xrightarrow{l} t' \implies \exists s'. \ s' \ \mathcal{R} \ t' \wedge s \xrightarrow{l} s'$$

i.e.

$$\begin{array}{ccc} s & \mathcal{R} & t \\ l \downarrow & & \downarrow l \\ s' & \mathcal{R} & t' \end{array}$$

s and t are bisimilar, written $s \sim t$ iff there is a bisimulation relation $\mathcal{R}$ such that $s \ \mathcal{R} \ t$. If only the first one of the two implications above is verified, we say that s simulates t and denote it $s \leqslant t$.

A bisimulation relation relates pair of states and ensures that any behaviour of one automaton can be performed by the other one while staying in relation. We informally explain here the symbolic nature of the bisimulation for OA and the related complexity of its definition. The notion of symbolic bisimulation, as it was introduced in [15], is aimed at computing bisimulation of value-passing systems, i.e. systems made of processes exchanging data with their environment and between processes, where data are values from a possibly infinite domain. The presence of holes in fact raises no strong difficulty but the variables must be handled carefully. Consider the two following simple OA:

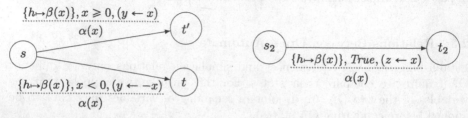

We should be able to consider these two OA as bisimilar. Both can input any $\beta(x)$ input on their hole and stores the value of x, emitting $\alpha(x)$ along the transition. The difference is the way x is stored. We can then define a configuration relation $\mathcal{R}$ such that $\mathcal{R}(s, s_2)$ is true and $\mathcal{R}(t, t_2)$ holds when $z \geqslant 0$ and

$y = z$, while $\mathcal{R}(t', t_2)$ holds when $z < 0$ and $y = -z$. This illustrates relation on configurations, but also shows that bisimulation on OA is more complex than in the classical case. Indeed, we need two transitions on the left OA to simulate a single one on the right OA. We should check that these two transitions cover all the cases accepted by the right hand side OA, and of course that destination states are in relation. Formally, FH-bisimulation is defined as follows [6]:

Definition 6 (Strong FH-bisimulation).

Suppose $\langle S_1, s_{01}, V_1, \sigma_{01}, J_1, T_1 \rangle$ *and* $\langle S_2, s_{02}, V_2, \sigma_{02}, J_2, T_2 \rangle$ *are OA with identical holes of the same sort, with disjoint sets of variables* $(V_1 \cap V_2 = \varnothing)$.

Then $\mathcal{R}$, *a relation on configurations of OA, is an FH-bisimulation if and only if for any states* $s \in S_1$ *and* $t \in S_2$, *we have the following:*

- *For any open transition OT in* T_1: $\dfrac{\beta_j^{j \in J'}, g_{OT}, \psi_{OT}}{s \xrightarrow{\alpha} s'}$ *there exists an indexed set of open transitions* $OT_x^{x \in X} \subseteq T_2$: $\dfrac{\beta_{jx}^{j \in J_x}, g_{OT_x}, \psi_{OT_x}}{t \xrightarrow{\alpha_x} t_x}$ *such that the following holds*

$$\mathcal{R}(s, t) \wedge g_{OT} \implies$$
$$\bigvee_{x \in X} (\forall j. \beta_j = \beta_{jx} \wedge g_{OT_x} \wedge \alpha = \alpha_x \wedge \mathcal{R}(s', t_x) \{\!\!\{\psi_{OT} \uplus \psi_{OT_x} \}\!\!\})$$

- *and symmetrically any open transition from* t *in* T_2 *can be covered by a set of transitions from* s *in* T_1.

Two automata are bisimilar if there exists a strong FH-bisimulation $\mathcal{R}$ *that relates their initial states.*

Note that this definition matches an open transition t_1 to a family of covering open transitions $t_{2x}^{x \in X}$. Intuitively, this means that for every pair of related states (s_1, s_2) of the two automata, and for every transition of the first automaton from s_1, there is a set of matching transitions of the second automaton from s_2 such that the produced action match, the actions of the same holes and the successors are related after variable update. Technically, the following sections do not rely on the definition of strong bisimulation on OA, but they follow the same principles and in particular the same way to faithfully simulate an open transition by a set of other open transitions.

2.5   Reachability

We finally define a new predicate abstracting state reachability for OA, it allows us to reason on reachable states in an automaton. It can be seen as an abstraction of the reachable states under the form of a predicate that must stay verified along the execution of the OA.

Definition 7 (Reachability). *For any OA* $A = \langle S, s_0, V, \sigma_0, J, T \rangle$, *a reachability predicate* $\checkmark_A : S \to \mathcal{F}_V$ *is any predicate on states that is valid on initial state, and preserved across transitions:*

$$\sigma_0 \models \checkmark_A(s_0) \quad \wedge \quad \forall t = \frac{\beta_j^{j \in J'}, g, \psi}{s \xrightarrow{\alpha} s'} \in T, vars(t) \models (\checkmark_A(s) \wedge g \implies \checkmark_A(s')\{\psi\})$$

Reachability takes into account all paths, and can over-approximate the reachable configurations. From an automation point of view, finding the most precise reachability predicate for a given automaton is not decidable because of the symbolic nature of OA, but only an over-approximation is necessary.

3   Simulation for Automata with the Same Holes

Similarly to FH-bisimulation [6] we are interested in finding simulation relations between configurations of two OA that contain variables and holes. When dealing with open systems it is common to define simulation in terms of a simulation relation. We rely on a classical notion of simulation and perform the same extension as in [6], i.e., we start from a simulation relation and add holes and symbolic. The idea is to consider two configurations related by a relation; if one state can do a transition, then the other can also make this transition. Like for bisimulation, a simulation relation characterises when two states are related, and this characterisation is expressed as a predicate on the variables of the two automata. Simulation defines conditions on a relation $\mathcal{R}$ such that $\mathcal{R}(s_1, s_2)$ is a predicate (possibly involving variables of the automata) that is true when the state s_1 of A_1 simulates the state s_2 of A_2.

However here we want to build a simulation relation that also guarantees that no deadlock is introduced when refining the automaton. This property is quite frequent in simulation relation, and referred to as *lack of new deadlocks* [20] or *complete simulation* [23]. The notion of deadlock should however be specialised to our OA. Indeed, it is not very useful to check the existence of a transition, instead it makes more sense to use the guards to check if a transition can be taken. We thus define a deadlock reduction criterion based on how the outgoing transitions are guarded. As such, a simulation does not introduce deadlocks if in the conditions where no transition is possible in the refined automaton, no transition were already possible in the more general one. More formally, for any pair of states s_1 and s_2 we introduce a criterion of the form:

$$\forall (s_1, s_2) \in S_1 \times S_2,$$

$$V_1 \uplus V_2 \models \left(\mathcal{R}(s_1, s_2) \wedge \neg \left(\bigvee_{t_1 \in \mathrm{OT}(s_1)} guard(t_1) \right) \implies \neg \left(\bigvee_{t_2 \in \mathrm{OT}(s_2)} guard(t_2) \right) \right)$$

Which can be rewritten as:

$$\forall (s_1, s_2) \in S_1 \times S_2, V_1 \uplus V_2 \models \left(\mathcal{R}(s_1, s_2) \implies \left(\bigvee_{t_1 \in \mathrm{OT}(s_1)} guard(t_1) \right) \vee \neg \left(\bigvee_{t_2 \in \mathrm{OT}(s_2)} guard(t_2) \right) \right)$$

Both statements being equivalent, as each of them may reveal more intuitive than the other in different situations, we use them interchangeably. We can now state the definition of simulation between OA that have the same set of holes.

Definition 8 (Hole-equal simulation). *Consider two OA with identical set of holes:* $A_1 = \langle S_1, s_{01}, V_1, \sigma_{01}, J, T_1 \rangle$ *and* $A_2 = \langle S_2, s_{02}, V_2, \sigma_{02}, J, T_2 \rangle$, *the relation on configurations* $\mathcal{R} : S_1 \times S_2 \to \mathcal{F}_{V_1 \uplus V_2}$ *is a hole-equal simulation from* A_1 *to* A_2 *if the following conditions hold :*

(1) $\sigma_{01} \uplus \sigma_{02} \models \mathcal{R}(s_{01}, s_{02})$

(2) $\forall (s_1, s_2) \in S_1 \times S_2,$

$$\forall t_1 = \frac{\beta_{1j}^{j \in J_1'}, g_1, \psi_1}{s_1 \xrightarrow{\alpha_1} s_1'} \in OT(s_1). \quad \exists \left(t_{2x} = \frac{\beta_{2xj}^{j \in J_{2x}'}, g_{2x}, \psi_{2x}}{s_2 \xrightarrow{\alpha_{2x}} s_{2x}'} \right)^{x \in X} \in OT(s_2).$$

$$\left(\forall x \in X, J_{2x}' = J_1' \right) \wedge$$

$$V_1 \uplus V_2 \uplus vars(t_1) \models \mathcal{R}(s_1, s_2) \wedge g_1 \implies \bigvee_{x \in X} \left(\begin{array}{c} \alpha_{2x} = \alpha_1 \wedge \bigwedge_{j \in J_1'} \beta_{2xj} = \beta_{1j} \wedge \\ g_{2x} \wedge \mathcal{R}(s_1', s_{2x}')\{\psi_{2x} \uplus \psi_1\} \end{array} \right)$$

(3) Deadlock reduction:

$$\forall (s_1, s_2) \in S_1 \times S_2, V_1 \uplus V_2 \models \left(\mathcal{R}(s_1, s_2) \implies \left(\bigvee_{t_1 \in OT(s_1)} guard(t_1) \right) \vee \neg \left(\bigvee_{t_2 \in OT(s_2)} guard(t_2) \right) \right)$$

If there is a hole-equal simulation from A_1 *to* A_2, *then we say that* A_2 *simulates* A_1; *we denote it* $A_2 \leqslant A_1$.

The first and second conditions coincide with the natural way to prove inductively that an automaton simulates another by starting with the initial state. The third condition ensures that simulation prevents the introduction of deadlocks. Similarly to bisimulation, the second condition states that, for any transition of the simulating automaton A_1, it corresponds to a transition of the automaton A_2 that does the same thing and ends up in a similar state. However a family is needed in A_2 because of the symbolic nature of transitions, and because depending on the values of the variables, t_1 may correspond to different transitions in A_2. Our definition captures a simple simulation for OA with the same holes that is more expressive than a strict simulation since it matches a transition with a family of transitions. For example, with such a relation we are able to check the simulation between two OA that differ by duplicated states, removed duplicated transitions, reinforced guards, different variables, etc. We will show in Sect. 5 that this simulation relation has good properties in terms of transitivity, compositionality, and reflexivity.

Example 3. To illustrate the simulation of OA, we consider a variation on the prod-cons example. Namely, we suppose that the two processes P and Q communicate through a one-place buffer. Figure 5 shows the OA modelling this simpler version of the system, that we refer to as simprod-cons. We can easily check that this automaton simulates the one of Fig. 2. Indeed, one can see that $\mathcal{R} = \{(r_0, s_0) \mapsto \mathbf{l} = \mathbf{f}, (r_0, s_1) \mapsto \mathbf{f} = \mathbf{l} + \mathbf{1}\%\mathbf{N}\}$ is a simulation relation. It follows that simprod-cons $\leqslant$ prod-cons. $\qquad\qquad$ □

The simulation relation defined above is insufficient in the setting of composition which is the main advantage of the OA-based approach. Indeed, it should be possible to refine an automaton by filling its hole, providing a concrete view of a part of the application that was not specified originally. More generally, it should be possible to relate automata that do not have the same holes because composition is a crucial part of system specification. However, filling holes can result in a system with more or less holes than the original system because the plugged subsystem can contain itself many holes. Next section defines a more powerful simulation relation able to reason on automata with different sets of holes.

4 A Simulation Relation that Takes Holes into Account

This section extends the preceding relation to automata where the set of holes is not the same. This is particularly useful to state whether the automaton after composition is a simulation of the original automaton or not. Indeed, when composing the set of holes changes. Being able to compare automata with only some of their holes in common seems useful in general.

One major challenge in the extension of simulation to different sets of holes is to maintain a form of transitivity while being able to take into account the actions of some of the holes. A naive definition of simulation would ensure that only the holes that are identical in the two OA are taken into account in the simulation. Unfortunately, considering all the common holes does not ensure transitivity of the simulation for the following reason. If A_1 simulates A_2 and A_2 simulates A_3, and one hole j appears in A_3 and in A_1 but not in A_2 then we have no guarantee on the way A_1 and A_3 take the actions of this hole into account, thus a simulation between and A_1 and A_3 would require conditions involving actions of the hole j which cannot be ensured. The way we solve this issue is to remember in the simulation relation which holes have been compared. This makes the relation parameterised by a subset of the set of holes that belong to

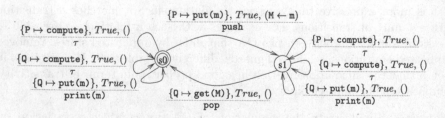

Fig. 5. The simprod-cons OA: the system using one-place buffer.

the two automata that we want to take into account. This way, in the example above, we would have no guarantee on actions the hole j by transitivity but can state a simulation relation with guarantees on the actions of the other holes.

In the following definition we add a parameter H which is the set of holes tracked by the simulation relation and adapt the definition by ignoring actions of the holes that are not in H.

Consequently, there is no guarantee related to the actions of the holes outside H. We provide compositionality properties when plugging an automaton inside a hole in H but cannot state anything when plugging an automaton outside H. The principle is that any property concerning holes that are not in H should be proven specifically for the considered automaton or the considered composition of automata.

Definition 9 (Hole-tracking simulation). *For two OA*
$A_1 = \langle S_1, s_{01}, V_1, \sigma_{01}, J_1, T_1 \rangle$ *and* $A_2 = \langle S_2, s_{02}, V_2, \sigma_{02}, J_2, T_2 \rangle$, A_1 *is a simulation of* A_2 *tracking holes* H, *noted* $A_1 \leqslant_H A_2$, *with* $H \subseteq J_1 \cap J_2$, *if there is a relation on configurations* $\mathcal{R} : (S_1 \times S_2) \to \mathcal{F}_{V_1 \uplus V_2}$ *such that[3]:*

(1) $\sigma_{01} \uplus \sigma_{02} \models \mathcal{R}(s_{01}, s_{02})$

(2) $\forall (s_1, s_2) \in S_1 \times S_2,$

$$\forall \frac{\beta_{1j}^{j \in J_1'}, g_1, \psi_1}{s_1 \xrightarrow{\alpha_1} s_1'} \in OT(s_1), \exists \left(\frac{\beta_{2xj}^{j \in J_{2x}'}, g_{2x}, \psi_{2x}}{s_2 \xrightarrow{\alpha_{2x}} s_{2x}'} \in OT(s_2) \right)^{x \in X},$$

$$(\forall x \in X, J_{2x}' \cap H = J_1' \cap H) \wedge$$
$$V_1 \uplus V_2 \uplus vars(t_1) \models$$

$$\left(\mathcal{R}(s_1, s_2) \wedge g_1 \implies \bigvee_{x \in X} \left(\begin{array}{l} \alpha_1 = \alpha_{2x} \wedge \bigwedge_{j \in J_1' \cap H} \beta_{1j} = \beta_{2xj} \wedge \\ g_{2x} \wedge \mathcal{R}(s_1', s_{2x}') \{\psi_1 \uplus \psi_{2x}\} \end{array} \right) \right)$$

(3) Deadlock reduction:

$$\forall (s_1, s_2) \in S_1 \times S_2, V_1 \uplus V_2 \models \left(\mathcal{R}(s_1, s_2) \implies \left(\bigvee_{t_1 \in OT(s_1)} guard(t_1) \right) \vee \neg \left(\bigvee_{t_2 \in OT(s_2)} guard(t_2) \right) \right)$$

Note that every action of the holes outside H is unconstrained according to the simulation relation.

Property 1 (Relating simulations). Hole-equal simulation is a particular case of hole-tracking simulation when $J_1 = J_2 = H$.

In particular, if an OA has no hole, the two definitions are equivalent and result in a "symbolic simulation", if additionally there is no variable in the OA, this corresponds to classical simulation.

---

[3] Note that the definition below is identical to the hole equal simulation except $\cap H$ is added in a few places.

Example 4. Consider the automata of Examples 1 and 3. As we saw above, simprod-cons ⩽ prod-cons, therefore prod-cons ⩽$_{\{P,Q\}}$ simprod-cons.

Property 2 (Tracked holes). By construction, if an automaton is the simulation of another one, it is also a simulation by tracking less holes.

$$A_1 \leqslant_H A_2 \wedge H' \subseteq H \implies A_1 \leqslant_{H'} A_2$$

Now that we have a simulation relation that takes both variable parameters and process parameters into account, we would like to ensure that it has properties one would expect for a simulation relation.

5 Properties of Our Simulation Relations

Before reasoning on the properties of simulation, we need to introduce one additional notion that characterises when the composition of two automata does not introduce new blocked transitions.

5.1 Non-blocking Composition

Unfortunately, the deadlock reduction property in the definition of simulation is not compositional: the composition operator can itself introduce a deadlock. In other words, when filling the hole of two related automata with a third one, even if there is a deadlock reduction between the two original automata, there might not be a deadlock reduction in the composed ones. The same problem may arise when two related automata are composed in the same hole of a third one.

This creates a conflict between deadlock reduction and the properties involving composition. We call *non-blocking composition* a composition that can safely be used to compose OA that are involved in a deadlock reducing relation.

Definition 10 (Non-blocking composition). *Consider two OA:*
$A_1 = \langle S_1, s_{01}, V_1, \sigma_{01}, J_1, T_1 \rangle$ *and* $A_2 = \langle S_2, s_{02}, V_2, \sigma_{02}, J_2, T_2 \rangle$. *Let A be the OA resulting from the composition* $A = A_1[A_2/k] = \langle S, s_0, V, \sigma_0, J, T \rangle$. *The composition* $A_1[A_2/k]$ *is non-blocking if A has a reachability predicate such that, for each reachable configuration, if there is a possible transition in A_1 then there is a possible transition in A:*

$$\forall s = (s_1, s_2) \in S, V \uplus \biguplus_{t \in \mathrm{OT}(s_1)} vars(t) \models \left(\checkmark_A(s) \wedge \bigvee_{t \in \mathrm{OT}(s_1)} guard(t) \implies \bigvee_{t \in \mathrm{OT}(s)} guard(t) \right)$$

Like in the definition of simulation (Definition 8) we use guards to ensure that the transition can occur. In general, one would not want to only consider non-blocking composition as it may reveal a bit restrictive, but it is the best necessary condition that we could identify for compositionality of simulation. It will be used to prove composition theorems given below. In absence of non-blocking composition, simulation may also be checked specifically for a given composed automaton.

5.2 Properties

We now state the properties of our simulation, their formal proofs can be found in the extended version of this paper [16]. We express these properties in terms of hole-tracking simulation because, thanks to Property 1 all the properties of hole-tracking simulation are also valid for hole-equal simulation. The first crucial theorem of simulation is that it is a preorder on the set of OA. This latter enables stepwise refinement.

Theorem 1 (Simulation is a preorder). *Hole-tracking simulation is reflexive and transitive: it is a preorder on the set of OA.*

Proof sketch. The relation $\leqslant_H$ is reflexive, $A \leqslant_H A$. This is shown by considering the relation $\mathcal{R}$ such that $\mathcal{R}(s_1, s_2) \triangleq s_1 = s_2 \wedge \bigwedge_{v \in vars(s_1)} v = v$ we can prove the conditions for Definition 9. In [16], we give proof of transitivity. It is done classically by identifying the relation between A_1 and A_3 that is a simulation. What is less classical is the definition of this relation because it is a boolean formula. For each couple of states s_1 and s_3 of A_1 and A_3 we build a formula that defines the simulation. To do this, we take the disjunction of formulas relating s_1 and s_3, and passing by all states s_2 of A_2. More precisely, we define a relation of the following form:

$$\mathcal{R}_{13}(s_1, s_3) = \bigvee_{s_2 \in S_2} (\mathcal{R}_{12}(s_1, s_2) \wedge \mathcal{R}_{23}(s_2, s_3))$$

We then prove that this relation is a simulation, according to Definition 9.   □

The next theorem states that if two automata are in simulation relation and the same automaton is placed in the same hole of the two automata, then the simulation is preserved. This is the first step toward proving that simulation is compositional in the sense that it is sufficient to prove simulation for the composed automata separately to obtain a simulation relation.

Theorem 2 (Context refinement). *Let A_1, A_2 and A_3 be three OA with $A_1 \leqslant_H A_2$. Let J_3 be the set of holes of A_3 and suppose that $k \in H$. Suppose additionally that $A_1[A_3/k]$ is non-blocking. We have:*

$$A_1[A_3/k] \leqslant_{J_3 \uplus H \setminus \{k\}} A_2[A_3/k]$$

Proof sketch. The proof relies on a simulation relation that we consider is the one that makes A_1 and A_2 similar, complemented with identity of configurations for A_3. Then, by construction, all transitions of the composed automaton $A_1[A_3/k]$ are specified by open transitions of A_1. For the transitions that do not involve hole k, the transition of $A_1[A_3/k]$ is the same and simulation between A_1 and A_2 allows us to conclude directly. If the hole k is involved the considered relation implies that valuations in A_3 are equal (i.e., the value for each variable are the same in both valuations), after a transition we should obtain "equal" valuations because post-conditions are deterministic. The requirement "$A_1[A_3/k]$ is non-blocking" ensures the deadlock reduction property holds. More precisely, if $A_1[A_3/k]$ is stuck, then A_1 is stuck, and thus $A_1[A_2/k]$ is also stuck.   □

Example 5. Consider again the `prod-cons` and `simprod-cons` automata given in the examples above. Since `prod-cons` $\leqslant_{\{P,Q\}}$ `simprod-cons`, then according to Theorem 2, `prod-cons[producer/P]` $\leqslant_{\{Q\}}$ `simprod-cons[producer/P]`. The automaton of `prod-cons[producer/P]` is shown in Fig. 4. The automaton resulting from the composition of `simprod-cons` and `producer` is bigger and not shown here.   □

Theorem 3 (Congruence). *Let A_1, A_2 and A_3 be three OA with $A_2 \leqslant_H A_3$. Let J_1 be the set of holes of A_1 and suppose that $k \in J_1$. Suppose additionally that the composition $A_1[A_2/k]$ is non-blocking. We have:*

$$A_1[A_2/k] \leqslant_{J_1 \uplus H \setminus \{k\}} A_1[A_3/k]$$

Consequently, as the simulation is transitive we can compose the previous theorems and state the following:

Theorem 4 (Composability). *Let A_1, A_2, A_3 and A_4 be four OA with $A_1 \leqslant_H A_2$ and $A_3 \leqslant_{H'} A_4$. Suppose that $k \in H$. We have:*

$$A_1[A_3/k] \leqslant_{H \uplus H' \setminus \{k\}} A_2[A_4/k]$$

Example 6. As an example of the use of this theorem, if we design a refined version of the producer process of Example 2 called `Refproducer`. According to Theorem 4, we have `prod-cons[producer/P]` $\leqslant_{\{Q\}}$ `simprod-cons[Refproducer/P]`.

Note that the substitution operation can be extended to a multiple substitution that fills several holes at the same time, and the theorems can be adapted accordingly.

6   Related Work

The origins of refinement are in the approach of programming that aims to provide solid foundations for building correct programs [12]. Many work contributed to the development of elaborated notions of refinement in various area (e.g. [1,7,8,10]). In the context of process algebra, refinement between processes can be defined in terms of simulations relation (e.g. ([19,22]). However, the concept of simulations presented so far has focused on the refinement of systems that are inherently closed, i.e., systems which are bounded and without environment,
    The simulation ensures the preservation of safety properties as deadlock-freeness and, more generally, all linear temporal logic properties [1,20]. The difference between the existing refinement principles have been studied in [13], for example the authors explain in what sense failure semantics is different from (bi)simulation in the compared systems and properties ensured. In this paper we particularly focus on the compositionality of simulation-based refinement.
    There are not a lot of works that study refinement for open systems. Defining refinement of open systems as trace inclusion is addressed as a notion of subtyping in type theory (e.g. [9,14]). The definition of refinement is based on

a connection between session types and communicating automata theories – a notion of session automata based on Communicating Finite-State Machines, that are used for modelling processes communicating through FIFO channels. The refinement of open systems is also defined in terms of alternating simulation [3,4]. Alternating simulation is originating from the game theory [2], it allows the study of relation between individual components by viewing them as alternating transition systems. In particular, a refinement of game-based automata expresses that the refined component can offer more services (input actions) and fewer service demands (output actions). However, the composition of such automata may lead to illegal states, where one automaton issues an output that is not acceptable as input in the other one. The theory of alternating simulation provides an optimistic approach to compute compatibility between automata based on the fact that each automaton expects the other to provide legal inputs, i.e., two components can be composed if there is an environment where they can work together. Our approach has some commonalities with the above mentioned simulation [3]: both are process-oriented approaches even if they are not based on the same notion of simulation, and both include in the model how to compose and interact with processes that are accepted as parameters. Nevertheless, they differ in that our approach focuses on the compositional properties of the simulation, and not on the fact that entities can be composed.

Previous works on OA focused on equivalence relations compatible with composition. In [18], a computable bisimulation is introduced, while in [6] a weak version of the bisimulation is introduced. In this paper we tackle the refinement relation in the form of simulation, as is the case for the corresponding relations on labelled transition systems [8]. Unlike the standard simulation we deal with symbolic and open models. In [25], the authors exploit transition systems to reason about the systems that are partially specified by using variables, making the state space potentially infinite.

Some work target component-based refinement with the concern of preserving deadlock freedom (e.g. [11,20]). These works are not concerned with the theory of open symbolic systems, and therefore do not focus on the same modularity as we do, in particular we provide preservation of refinement by composition.

7   Conclusion

In this article we investigated the notion of refinement for a symbolic and open model: open automata. OA are convenient for compositional software verification. Indeed, OA model parallel systems that are parameterised both by the use of variables and by the possibility to compose automata. The formalism supports compositional specification through the simulation paradigm. In this paper, we introduce a refinement relation between open automata. It relies on a simulation relation between the two automata; it specifies that the refined process must follow the behaviour of the simulated one. We finally showed that simulation is a preorder that is preserved by composition, both when filling a hole and when placing automata in comparable contexts.

References

1. Abrial, J.R.: The B-book - Assigning Programs to Meanings. Cambridge University Press, Cambridge (1996)
2. Alfaro, L.: Game models for open systems. In: Dershowitz, N. (ed.) Verification: Theory and Practice. LNCS, vol. 2772, pp. 269–289. Springer, Heidelberg (2003). https://doi.org/10.1007/978-3-540-39910-0_12
3. de Alfaro, L., Henzinger, T.A.: Interface automata. In: Tjoa, A.M., Gruhn, V. (eds.) Proceedings of the 8th European Software Engineering Conference held jointly with 9th ACM SIGSOFT International Symposium on Foundations of Software Engineering 2001, Vienna, Austria, September 10–14, 2001, pp. 109–120. ACM (2001). https://doi.org/10.1145/503209.503226
4. Alur, R., Henzinger, T.A., Kupferman, O., Vardi, M.Y.: Alternating refinement relations. In: Sangiorgi, D., de Simone, R. (eds.) CONCUR 1998. LNCS, vol. 1466, pp. 163–178. Springer, Heidelberg (1998). https://doi.org/10.1007/BFb0055622
5. Ameur-Boulifa, R., Henrio, L., Kulankhina, O., Madelaine, E., Savu, A.: Behavioural semantics for asynchronous components. J. Logical Algeb. Methods Program. **89**, 1–40 (2017). https://doi.org/10.1016/j.jlamp.2017.02.003, https://www.sciencedirect.com/science/article/pii/S2352220817300287
6. Ameur-Boulifa, R., Henrio, L., Madelaine, E.: Compositional equivalences based on Open pNets. J. Logical Algeb. Methods Program. **131**, 100842 (2023). https://doi.org/10.1016/j.jlamp.2022.100842, https://www.sciencedirect.com/science/article/pii/S2352220822000955
7. Back, R., Sere, K.: Stepwise refinement of parallel algorithms. Sci. Comput. Program. **13**(2), 133–180 (1990). https://doi.org/10.1016/0167-6423(90)90069-P, https://www.sciencedirect.com/science/article/pii/016764239090069P
8. Bellegarde, F., Julliand, J., Kouchnarenko, O.: Ready-simulation is not ready to express a modular refinement relation. In: Maibaum, T. (ed.) FASE 2000. LNCS, vol. 1783, pp. 266–283. Springer, Heidelberg (2000). https://doi.org/10.1007/3-540-46428-X_19
9. Bravetti, M., Zavattaro, G.: Asynchronous session subtyping as communicating automata refinement. Softw. Syst. Model. **20**(2), 311–333 (2021). https://doi.org/10.1007/s10270-020-00838-x
10. Butler, M.J., Grundy, J., Långbacka, T., Ruksenas, R., von Wright, J.: The refinement calculator: Proof support for program refinement. In: Groves, L., Reeves, S. (eds.) Proceedings of the Conference on Formal Methods Pacific 1997, Springer Series in Discrete Mathematics and Theoretical Computer Science, 01 January 1997, pp. 40–61 (1997). https://eprints.soton.ac.uk/250550/
11. Dihego, J., Sampaio, A., Oliveira, M.: A refinement checking based strategy for component-based systems evolution. J. Syst. Softw. **167**, 110598 (2020). https://doi.org/10.1016/j.jss.2020.110598
12. Dijkstra, E.W.: A Discipline of Programming. Prentice-Hall, Englewood Cliffs (1976)
13. Eshuis, R., Fokkinga, M.M.: Comparing refinements for failure and bisimulation semantics. Fundam. Inf. **52**(4), 297–321 (2002)
14. Gay, S.J., Hole, M.: Subtyping for session types in the pi calculus. Acta Informatica **42**(2–3), 191–225 (2005). https://doi.org/10.1007/s00236-005-0177-z
15. Hennessy, M., Lin, H.: Symbolic bisimulations. Theoretical Computer Science **138**(2), 353–389 (1995). https://doi.org/10.1016/0304-3975(94)00172-F, https://www.sciencedirect.com/science/article/pii/030439759400172F, meeting on the mathematical foundation of programing semantics

16. Henrio, L., Madelaine, E., Ameur-Boulifa, R., Corradi, Q.: Refinements for Open Automata (Extended Version). Technical report RR-9517, Inria - Research Centre Grenoble - Rhône-Alpes (2023), https://inria.hal.science/hal-04193421
17. Henrio, L., Madelaine, E., Zhang, M.: A theory for the composition of concurrent processes. In: Albert, E., Lanese, I. (eds.) FORTE 2016. LNCS, vol. 9688, pp. 175–194. Springer, Cham (2016). https://doi.org/10.1007/978-3-319-39570-8_12
18. Hou, Z., Madelaine, E.: Symbolic bisimulation for open and parameterized systems. In: Proceedings of the 2020 ACM SIGPLAN Workshop on Partial Evaluation and Program Manipulation, New York, NY, USA, pp. 14–26. PEPM 2020, Association for Computing Machinery (2020). https://doi.org/10.1145/3372884.3373161
19. Jifeng, H.: Process simulation and refinement. Form. Asp. Comput. 1(1), 229–241 (1989). https://doi.org/10.1007/BF01887207
20. Kouchnarenko, O., Lanoix, A.: How to verify and exploit a refinement of component-based systems. In: Virbitskaite, I., Voronkov, A. (eds.) PSI 2006. LNCS, vol. 4378, pp. 297–309. Springer, Heidelberg (2007). https://doi.org/10.1007/978-3-540-70881-0_26
21. Milner, R.: Communication and Concurrency. Prentice-Hall Inc, USA (1989)
22. Milner, R.: A Calculus of Communicating Systems, LNCS, vol. 92. Springer, Heidelberg (1980). https://doi.org/10.1007/3-540-10235-3
23. Sangiorgi, D.: Introduction to Bisimulation and Coinduction. Cambridge University Press, Cambridge (2012) https://hal.inria.fr/hal-00907026
24. Wang, B., Madelaine, E., Zhang, M.: Symbolic Weak Equivalences: Extension, Algorithms, and Minimization - Extended version. Research Report RR-9389, Inria & Université Cote d'Azur, CNRS, I3S, Sophia Antipolis, France; East China Normal University (Shanghai) (2021). https://hal.inria.fr/hal-03126313
25. Zhang, L., Meng, Q., Lo, K.: Compositional abstraction refinement for component-based systems. J. Appl. Math. 2014, 1–12 (2014). https://doi.org/10.1155/2014/703098

The Cubicle Fuzzy Loop: A Fuzzing-Based Extension for the Cubicle Model Checker

Sylvain Conchon[✉] and Alexandrina Korneva

Université Paris-Saclay, CNRS, ENS Paris-Saclay, Laboratoire Méthodes Formelles,
91190 Gif-sur-Yvette, France
sylvain.conchon@universite-paris-saclay.fr

Abstract. This paper presents the Cubicle Fuzzy Loop (CFL), a fuzzing-based extension for Cubicle, a model checker for parameterized systems.

To prove safety, Cubicle generates invariants, making use of forward exploration strategies like BFS or DFS on finite model instances. However, these standard algorithms are quickly faced with the state explosion problem due to Cubicle's purely nondeterministic semantics. This causes them to struggle at discovering critical states, hindering invariant generation.

CFL replaces this approach with a powerful DFS-like algorithm inspired by fuzzing. Cubicle's purely nondeterministic execution loop is modified to provide feedback on newly discovered states and visited transitions. This feedback is used by CFL to construct schedulers that guide the model exploration. Not only does this provide Cubicle with a bigger variety of states for generating invariants, it also quickly identifies unsafe models. As a bonus, it adds testing capabilities to Cubicle, such as the ability to detect deadlocks.

Our first experiments have yielded promising results. CFL effectively allows Cubicle to generate crucial invariants, useful to handle hierarchical systems, while also being able to trap bad states and deadlocks in hard-to-reach areas of such models.

Keywords: Fuzzing techniques · Model Checking · Parameterized Systems

1 Introduction

Cubicle [3,5] is a model checker for verifying safety properties of array-based systems. This is a syntactically restricted class of parametrized transition systems with states represented as arrays indexed by an arbitrary number of processes (or nodes) [6]. Distributed protocols, cache coherence, and mutual exclusion algorithms are typical examples of such systems.

Cubicle is based on the Model Checking Modulo Theory (MCMT) framework [7] where states and transitions are both represented as formulas in a particular fragment of first-order logic. To verify safety, Cubicle checks that unsafe states are not reachable using a symbolic backward reachability analysis: starting from a user-defined formula describing unsafe states, it iteratively computes its pre-image closure (understood as unreachable states), making use of an SMT back-end for termination and safety tests.

In order to speed up safety proofs, Cubicle supports invariant synthesis [4]. For that, it first computes a set $\mathcal{M}$ of reachable states using a *forward exploration* for a finite instance of the system (with a *fixed number* of processes). The current strategies implemented in Cubicle for this forward search are BFS and DFS (users can choose which strategy to use). Then, Cubicle performs a backward reachability analysis of the *parameterized* system. At each loop iteration, Cubicle computes an over-approximation of pre-images and checks that they represent states that are not in $\mathcal{M}$. All these approximations, which can be seen as *candidate invariants*, are model checked together with the original safety property. Sometimes approximations can be too coarse, leading to false positives known as spurious traces. When these occur, Cubicle is forced to backtrack in order to ensure completeness.

The strength of this method lies in the fact that finite instances are generally good oracles for guiding the choice of approximations, as they can be seen as concentrated knowledge of the system. However, the method only works if the set $\mathcal{M}$ is sufficiently large and contains crucial system states. If this is not the case, Cubicle will backtrack very often during its backward analysis, which will likely prevent it from completing its proof.

Unfortunately, the space of states $\mathcal{M}$ to be visited for a finite instance can grow exponentially, even for a small number of processes. This is the case, for example, for hierarchical systems such as cache coherence algorithms, where it is necessary to explore execution traces deep enough to visit significant states. For such systems, Cubicle's current exploration strategies are either unable to go deep enough into the system (BFS), or unable to explore subtle interleavings of component executions (DFS). In both cases, Cubicle is forced to backtrack often during its backward analysis.

In this paper, we describe an algorithm for a new forward exploration strategy for Cubicle inspired by fuzzing techniques [8,9,11]. This strategy not only makes it possible to explore very deep traces, but also to discover extremely rare events in a system, such as synchronization points resulting from highly improbable interleavings. The relevance of the states visited by this approach is such that it enables Cubicle to deduce invariants for systems that previously ranged from difficult to impossible to analyze. Furthermore, not only does this new exploration technique provide Cubicle with a bigger variety of states for inferring invariants, it also quickly identifies unsafe models. As a bonus, it adds testing capabilities to Cubicle, such as the ability to detect deadlocks.

To summarize, we make the following contributions:

1. We define the Cubicle Fuzzy Loop (CFL), a new (forward) exploration algorithm for Cubicle based on fuzzing techniques, for which we present and discuss different heuristics.

2. We have implemented CFL in a new prototype version of Cubicle. We are experimentally evaluating the benefits of CFL on representative examples of highly concurrent and hierarchical systems.
3. Finally, we demonstrate experimentally that CFL can be easily extended to detect deadlocks, which is not possible with the current version of Cubicle.

The rest of the paper is organized as follows: In Sect. 2, we recall the backward reachability algorithm of Cubicle and its (candidate) invariant inference mechanism. In Sect. 3, we illustrate how CFL works on a simple example that is representative of systems that are difficult for Cubicle to analyze. We formalize CFL in Sect. 4. We show and discuss experimental results in Sect. 5. We conclude and present related works in Sect. 6.

2   Backgound on Cubicle

Cubicle is based on MCMT, a declarative framework for parameterized systems in which (sets of) states, transitions and properties are expressed in a particular fragment of first order logic with enumerative data types. Systems expressible in this framework are called array-based transition systems, because their states can be seen as a set of unbounded arrays (denoted by capital letters $X, Y, \ldots$) whose indexes range over elements of a parameterized domain, called proc, of process identifiers (denoted by $i, j, \ldots$). Given an array variable X and a process variable i, we write $X[i]$ for an array access of X at index i. Systems may also contain variables but, from a theoretical point of view, a variable is seen as an array with the same value in all its cells. Arrays may contain integers or real numbers, booleans (or constructors from an enumerative user-defined datatype), or process identifiers.

A parameterized array-based system $\mathcal{S}$ is defined by a triplet $(\mathcal{X}, I, \tau)$ where $\mathcal{X}$ is a set of array symbols, I is a formula describing the initial states of the system and τ is a set of (possibly quantified) formulas, called *transitions*, relating states of $\mathcal{S}$. The formula I is a universal conjunction of literals of the form $\forall i. \bigwedge_n \ell_n$ which characterizes the values for some array entries. Each literal ℓ_n is a comparison ($=, \neq, <, \leq$) between two terms. A term can be a constant (integer, boolean, real, constructor), a process variable (i), an array access $X[i]$. A transition $t \in \tau$ is represented by a formula parameterized by the set of variables before and after the transition ($\mathcal{X}$ and $\mathcal{X}'$) and prefixed by the existentially quantified process variables involved in the transition:

$$t(\mathcal{X}, \mathcal{X}') = \exists i. \Delta(i) \wedge \gamma(i, \mathcal{X})$$
$$\wedge \bigwedge_{X' \in \mathcal{X}'} \forall k. \bigwedge_n (C_n(i, k, \mathcal{X}) \Rightarrow X'[k] = v_n(i, k, \mathcal{X}))$$

where $\Delta(i)$ is the conjunction of all disequations between the variables in i (to ensure that variables i denote distinct processes) the formula $\gamma(i, \mathcal{X})$ is a conjunction of literals that represents the transition's guard, *i.e.* the conditions that must be met for the transition to be triggered and the conjunction

$\bigwedge_n (C_n(i, k, \mathcal{X}) \Rightarrow \mathsf{X}'[k] = v_n(i, k, \mathcal{X}))$ represents the updated value of each array X defined by a case-split expression, where each conjunction of literals $C_n(i, k, \mathcal{X})$ and term $v_n(i, k, \mathcal{X})$ may depend on i, k and $\mathcal{X}$.

In Fig. 1, we give an example of an array-based system implementing a simple, slightly modified, Dekker mutual exclusion algorithm. The system keeps track of the status S[i] of a process i. A process can have one of three statuses:

- Idle: the process is not doing anything in particular
- Want: the process has requested access to the critical section
- Crit: the process has been granted access to the critical section

As denoted by the formula Init in Fig. 1, the status of every process i is Idle in the initial state of the system. There is also a variable Turn, keeping track of who among those who've requested access can enter the critical section (the content of Turn is not specified in the Init formula). The three transitions Req, Enter and Exit describe the behavior of any process i. For example, transition Enter should be read as: if there exists a process i such that S[i] = Want and Turn = i, then the new value of the array S, called S', is S[$i \leftarrow$ Crit] which succinctly denotes an array equal to S, except for cell i, which is now equal to Crit.

type t = Idle | Want | Crit
globals:
        Turn : proc
        S : (proc, t) array
	Req: $\exists i.$	S[i] = Idle $\wedge$ Turn = i $\wedge$
		S' = S[$i \leftarrow$ Want] $\wedge$ Turn = Turn'

Init: $\forall i.$ S[i] = Idle	Enter: $\exists i.$	S[i] = Want $\wedge$ Turn = i $\wedge$ S' = S[$i \leftarrow$ Crit] $\wedge$ Turn = Turn'
Unsafe: $\exists i,j.$ $i \neq j \wedge$ S[i] = Crit $\wedge$ S[j] = Crit	Exit: $\exists i,j.$	S[i] = Crit $\wedge$ S' = S[$i \leftarrow$ Idle] $\wedge$ Turn' = j

Fig. 1. Modified Dekker mutual exclusion algorithm

Safety properties to be verified on array-based systems are expressed in their negated form as formulas that represent unsafe states. Each unsafe formula $\varphi(\mathcal{X})$ must be a *cube*, i.e., have the form $\exists k.(\Delta(k) \wedge \bigwedge_m \ell_m(k, \mathcal{X}))$, where each literal $\ell_m(k, \mathcal{X})$ may depend on k and array symbols in $\mathcal{X}$. For example, the Unsafe formula in Fig. 1 describes the bad states of the Dekker algorithm, which correspond to states where two distinct processes have been granted access to the critical section simultaneously.

For a state formula φ and a transition $t \in \tau$, let $pre_t(\varphi)$ be the formula describing the set of states from which a φ-state can be reached in one t-step. The pre-image of a formula $\varphi(\mathcal{X})$ by a transition t is given by:

$$pre_t(\varphi)(\mathcal{X}) = \exists \mathcal{X}'. \, t(\mathcal{X}, \mathcal{X}') \wedge \varphi(\mathcal{X}')$$

The pre-image *closure* of φ w.r.t a set of transitions τ, denoted by $\mathrm{PRE}_\tau^*(\varphi)$, is defined as follows:

$$\begin{cases} \mathrm{PRE}_\tau^0(\varphi) \triangleq \varphi \\[2mm] \mathrm{PRE}_\tau^n(\varphi) \triangleq \bigcup \{ pre_t(\psi) \mid \psi \in \mathrm{PRE}_\tau^{n-1}(\varphi), t \in \tau \} \\[2mm] \mathrm{PRE}_\tau^*(\varphi) \triangleq \bigcup_{k \in \mathbb{N}} \mathrm{PRE}_\tau^k(\varphi) \end{cases}$$

and the pre-image of a set of formulas V is defined by $\mathrm{PRE}_\tau^*(V) = \bigcup_{\varphi \in V} \mathrm{PRE}_\tau^*(\varphi)$. We also write $\mathrm{PRE}_\tau(\varphi)$ for $\mathrm{PRE}_\tau^1(\varphi)$.

Given an array-based parameterized system $\mathcal{S} = (\mathcal{X}, I, \tau)$ and a set of unsafe states represented by a cube U, we say that U is *reachable* if and only if $\mathrm{PRE}_\tau^*(U) \wedge I$ satisfiable. In order to decide if U is reachable or not, Cubicle implements the symbolic backward reachability loop $\mathsf{Bwd}(\mathcal{S}, U, d_{max}, k)$ given in Algorithm 1. This function takes as input a parameterized system $\mathcal{S}$, a cube U, and two integers d_{max} and k. It starts by initializing a variable $\mathcal{M}$ with the set $\mathsf{FWD}(d_{max}, k)$ of reachable states constructed by a forward exploration of the reachability graph for k processes starting in a state defined by the formula $I(\#1) \wedge \cdots \wedge I(\#k)$ and limited to depth d_{max}. FWD is not fixed and can be any user-chosen forward exploration strategy (BFS, DFS, etc.).

Algorithm 1: Cubicle backward reachability loop

```
1  function Bwd(S, U, d_max, k) : begin
2  │   M := FWD(d_max, k);
3  │   V := ∅;
4  │   push(Q, U);
5  │   while not_empty(Q) do
6  │   │   φ := pop(Q);
7  │   │   if φ ∧ I satisfiable then
8  │   │   │   return unsafe
9  │   │   else if φ ⊭ V then
10 │   │   │   V := V ∪ {φ};
11 │   │   │   ψ := Approx(φ);
12 │   │   │   if M ⊭ ψ then
13 │   │   │   │   push(Q, Pre_τ(ψ))
14 │   │   │   else
15 │   │   │   │   push(Q, Pre_τ(φ))
16 │   return safe
```

Then, $\mathsf{Bwd}(\mathcal{S}, U, d_{max}, k)$ computes the pre-image closure of U by maintaining two collections of states:

- Q contains the (unsafe) states to visit (it is initialized with U)
- V is filled with the visited states (initially empty)

Each iteration of the loop performs the following operations:

1. (*pop*) retrieve and remove a formula φ from Q
2. (*safety test*) check the satisfiability of $\varphi \wedge I$, *i.e.* determine if the states described by φ intersect with the initial states I. If so, the system is declared as *unsafe*
3. (*fixpoint test*) check if $\varphi \models V$ is valid, *i.e.* determine if the states described by φ have already been visited. If so, discard φ and go back to 1
4. (*over-approximate*) call function `Approx` to find an over-approximation of φ. This step can be sophisticated or simple. For instance, one way to calculate an approximation is to remove a (or multiple) literal(s) of φ.
5. (*oracle test* and *pre-image*) if ψ represents states not in $\mathcal{M}$ ($\mathcal{M} \not\models \psi$), then compute the pre-image $\mathsf{Pre}_\tau(\psi)$ and add these new (set of) states to Q. When ψ appears in $\mathcal{M}$ (meaning it represents reachable states), then we keep φ, and add the result of $\mathsf{Pre}_\tau(\varphi)$ to Q.

If Q is empty at step 1, then all of the state space has been explored and the system is declared *safe*. Note that the (non-trivial) fixpoint and safety tests are discharged to an embedded SMT solver. Notice that the *correctness* of Bwd does not depend on the content of $\mathcal{M}$, which thus acts as an oracle and only impacts the completeness of the algorithm.

3   Motivation

Cubicle's current forward exploration strategies are extremely efficient, but have their limitations. In this section we show how and where Cubicle struggles.

If we consider real-life concurrent systems and how they are built, there are three prevailing features: (i) pipeline parallelism, (ii) synchronization barriers, and (iii) nondeterminism. Pipeline parallelism breaks up a task into a sequence of sub-tasks, where each one can be treated concurrently by the system. This is done to improve performance by leveraging parallel processing. It complicates system models, because it not only adds depth, since each sub-task becomes an independent transition, it also introduces more interleavings to check. Synchronization barriers are necessary to coordinate the multiple processes in a concurrent system. For example processes may be required to be in a certain configuration before gaining access to specific parts of the system. These conditions can be very precise, which can lead to them appearing rarely. Last but not least, nondeterminism is inherent to concurrent systems- processes can behave independently or run tasks in parallel, and the order in which they do this can differ from execution to execution, which again adds multiple branchings to a model.

We condense these features into a specific pattern, shown in Fig. 2. There we can see an initial node (at the top) with multiple arrows leading from it. This is to simulate branching and nondeterminism, since a process at that stage would be able to choose any of the arrows. After branching, we insert the pipeline - multiple transitions to represent a task. This adds depth to our models. Note that at any point, when a process gets finished with a sub-task, it can decide to either continue forward to the next task, or go back. All of this culminates with a synchronization barrier that demands processes behave a certain way to be activated. It is important to note that while we constructed our pattern in this order, in real life the elements can appear wherever and however often they want. This pattern can also repeat itself, leading to hierarchical systems.

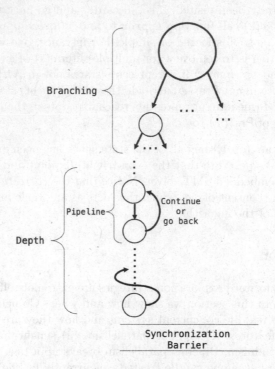

Fig. 2. Concurrent systems pattern

The problem is that this specific pattern and its repetition, so prevalent in concurrent systems, is exactly at the root of Cubicle's limitations. We converted our pattern to Cubicle types and transitions, shown in Fig. 3. The `branch` transitions are to give a process initial choices. The transitions `pipeline` and `task` simulate breaking up one task into multiple sub-tasks. Note that these transitions can be repeated many times to complicate the system. We give an example synchronization barrier transition `sync`. This transitions's guard can easily range from simple to more complex. When faced with this pattern, both of Cubicle's forward strategies face difficulties. BFS will be forced to run through every possible branching before being able to go down a level. The more branchings there are, combined with an elevated number of processes, the longer BFS has to spend

type branch = None $|$ A$_1$ $|$ ... $|$ A$_k$ $\qquad\qquad$ where $k, n, m \in \mathbb{N}$

type task = T$_{11}$ $|$ ... $|$ T$_{1n}$ $|$ T$_{21}$ $|$ ... $|$ T$_{2n}$ $|$ ... $|$ T$_{m1}$ $|$ ... $|$ T$_{mn}$

globals:
  Cmd: (proc,branch) array
  PC: (proc, task) array

Init: $\forall p.$ Cmd[p] = None $\wedge$ PC[p] = T$_{11}$

branch$_x$: $\exists p.$ $\begin{aligned}&\text{Cmd}[p] = \text{None} \wedge\\ &\text{Cmd}' = \text{Cmd}[p \leftarrow \text{A}_x]\end{aligned}$ $\qquad$ where $x \in [1, k]$

pipeline$_{xy}$: $\exists p.$ $\begin{aligned}&\text{Cmd}[p] = \text{A}_x \wedge \text{PC}[p] = \text{T}_{xy}\\ &\text{PC}' = \text{PC}[p \leftarrow \text{T}_{x(y+1)}]\end{aligned}$ $\quad$ where $x \in [1, m]$ and $y \in [1, n-1]$

task$_{xy}$: $\exists p.$ $\begin{aligned}&\text{PC}[p] = \text{T}_{xy}\\ &\text{PC}' = \text{PC}[p \leftarrow \text{T}_{(x+1)y}]\end{aligned}$ $\qquad$ where $x \in [1, m-1]$ and $y \in [1, n]$

sync: $\exists\, pqr.$ PC[p] = T$_{53}$ $\wedge$ PC[q] = T$_{42}$ $\wedge$ PC[r] = T$_{33}$ $\wedge$ $\forall i_{\neq p, q, r}.$ PC[i] = T$_{53}$

Fig. 3. Pattern as Cubicle transitions

checking every one. And as we stated, this pattern can repeat itself, so the interesting part of the system might be below the synchronization barrier, but BFS will visit countless states before it even gets close to it. DFS handles this specific problem better than BFS, as it privileges depth. But complicated interleavings and algorithms that do not loop slow it down and lower its efficiency.

For example, we take the previous pattern and create a model for three processes. We give a process four initial **branch** transitions (*i.e.* $k = 4$ in Fig. 3), as well as four tasks decomposed into three sub-tasks each (*i.e.* $m = 3$ and $n = 4$ in Fig. 3) and set a synchronization barrier that forces each of the three process to be doing different tasks in order to be activated. We let BFS and DFS each explore 1 000 000 states to see how often they visit the synchronization barrier. This is important because activating the barrier means having access to the potentially interesting transitions behind it. For 1 000 000 visited states, both BFS and DFS visited the **sync** transition two times. This means that any transitions that require **sync** to happen are barely ever visited.

We turn to fuzzing techniques to mitigate this problem. CFL's goal is to tackle this pattern by basically abandoning exhaustivity and skipping around the system. CFL abandons exhaustivity because it does not try to methodically explore every single path in the system - it tries to diversify the state space as much as possible. The reason it skips around the system is that anytime a state is visited by CFL, this state becomes an eligible initial state from which CFL can explore. This means that CFL has a higher chance of directly accessing crucial states and exploring from them. If we let CFL explore 1 000 000 states for the above example, it visits the `sync` transition approximately 150 times.

4   Fuzzing Cubicle

In this section we discuss and formalize CFL, detailing how we draw from fuzzing to create a new exploration strategy for Cubicle.

Fuzzing is essentially rapidly generating inputs for a program to see how it reacts. If an input leads to new code coverage, that input is retained and later mutated to generate new inputs that hopefully lead to more new code coverage. We retain two key notions – *new inputs* and *mutation* – both of which we want to incorporate into Cubicle. This is not straightforward, because Cubicle directly contradicts both these notions.

Cubicle's models have fixed initial states, meaning that any system exploration starts from there. We cannot randomly generate these states, since we cannot guarantee reachability. We also cannot take reachable states and mutate them for the same reasons. To fix the input problem, CFL takes already visited states and reuses them as the initial state. This guarantees that all initial states are reachable. It also allows us to diversify the explored state space: any visited state can become the initial state from which a system exploration is run.

However, setting the initial state isn't enough. When inputs are mutated in a fuzzer, the hope is that it will lead to new coverage and/or behavior fast. Simply setting new initial states in Cubicle does not lead to that if the exploration itself is not modified. The problem with the DFS and BFS strategies as they are now in Cubicle is that they are exhaustive and provide no feedback while they run, whereas we want something that might not provide exhaustivity, but will skip around the system trying to visit as many interesting new states as possible. This is why we have decided that since we cannot mutate states, we will *mutate the scheduler*, i.e. change exploration tactics while CFL runs. CFL has multiple exploration techniques, and each time an initial state is chosen, one of these techniques is run. Before going into detail on the techniques themselves, it is first necessary to describe how CFL treats states.

In CFL each state s is represented as a CFL node, a record containing the following fields:

- `state`: the explicit representation of s where variables (or arrays) are mapped to their values
- `count`: the number of times s has been visited
- `exit_num`: the number of *exit* transitions from s, *i.e.* the transitions with guards evaluating to true in s
- `exit_transitions`: an explicit representation of the *exit* transitions from s (represented by the name of the transitions and their arguments)
- `exits_taken`: which transitions have been taken from s
- `exit_count`: how many times each *exit* transition has been taken.

CFL essentially keeps track of two key pieces of information: a map V of visited explicit states mapped to their corresponding nodes, and a set P of potential initial fuzzer nodes. Any time a new explicit state is visited its calculated fuzzer node to is added to P and the mapping of the explicit state to the node is added to V.

The reason we keep track of *exit transitions* is because they decide when a node is no longer an interesting initial candidate. If every potential exit transition has been taken, then that node can no longer offer any new information and can be removed from P. The basic algorithm for CFL is given in Algorithm 2.

Algorithm 2: Basic CFL Algorithm

```
1  V := ∅ ;
2  P := ∅ ;
3  T := init_transitions(k);
4  U := all_unsafes(k);
5  Init := init_system(k);
6  P := P ∪ {Init};
7  while not_empty(P) do
8      n := choose_node(P);
9      explore := choose_strategy();
10     V,P := explore(n, U, T);
11 end
```

Initially, V and P start off empty. CFL explores the model for a given number of processes k. It calculates all possible transitions for all processes on line 3. For example if the model only contains a transition t(i) and CFL is run with three processes, T with contain t(#1), t(#2), and t(#3). It does the same for the unsafe formulas on line 4. The user-declared initial state is instantiated for k processes on line 5 and is then added to P.

CFL then takes the form of a while loop that runs as long as there are still potential initial nodes to process in P. During the loop, it first chooses a random node from P, chooses a random exploration technique (described below), and applies the technique to the node. Both V and P are modified as a result of this. When choosing a random exploration technique, CFL has the choice between six techniques, detailed below.

1. *Random exploration*: CFL chooses a number of steps and applies random transitions to the starting node for that many steps.
2. *Process sequences*: CFL selects a random process, picks a number of steps, and only moves that process forward for that amount of steps (or until it can't anymore)
3. *Weighted decision*: CFL grades potential steps using the following criteria
   - this step will lead me to a never visited state

- this step means taking a transition that has never been taken by anyone globally
- this step means taking a transition never taken from this node

These criteria are in order of importance - being able to visit a state that has never been visited will outweigh the rest.

4. *Maximizing randomness*: a certain percentage of the time, CFL picks steps that will give the most choices in the next step.
5. *Limited BFS*: runs a very limited depth BFS from the node
6. *Unused exit*: covers an exit that hasn't been taken yet

Each technique follows the same basic algorithm, shown in Algorithm 3. It first picks a random number s of steps (*bound* can be set by the user) to take and sets the current step *curr* to zero. The environment *env* is set to the chosen node, and all possible transitions from that node's explicit state are kept in *poss*. Then, while the current number of steps taken is less than the chosen s, each technique does the following: on line 5, it picks a transition from all possible transitions according to the current technique. So for example if the current technique is *Process sequences* and the chosen process is #1, technique will return a transition with #1 as an argument.

Algorithm 3: Basic exploration technique template

```
1 function explore(n, U, T) : begin
2     s := random_int(bound); curr := 0; env := n;
3     poss := env.exit_transitions;
4     while curr < s do
5         t := technique(poss);
6         clean_exits(env, t);
7         state := apply_transition(env, t);
8         check_unsafe(state, U);
9         try:
10            env := find(state, V);
11            env.count := env.count + 1;
12            poss := env.exit_transitions;
13            curr := curr + 1;
14        catch NotFound:
15            poss := all_possible_transitions(state, T);
16            env := init_node(state, poss);
17            V := add(env, state, V);
18            P := P ∪ {env};
19            curr := curr + 1;
20        end
21    end
22 end
```

CFL cleans the aforementioned *exit transitions* in the fuzzer node on line 6. For example if t is a transition that's never been taken, the exits_taken field will be modified in the node to include t. Then at line 7, the transition is applied to the node and a new explicit state, *state*, is calculated. Line 8 checks *state* against the unsafe formulas. How this is treated depends on how CFL is being run. Our implementation allows CFL to be run in two different manners: (i) as an oracle for the invariant generating algorithm and (ii) as a standalone fuzzer to explore models. If the algorithm is running as an oracle, then encountering an unsafe state immediately makes Cubicle return `Unsafe`. If CFL is running in a standalone fashion, it only shows a warning, but does not stop. Then (lines 9–18) the algorithm checks if a mapping from *state* to a node already exists in $\mathcal{V}$. If it does, then *env* is set to the existing node, with only its `count` being modified and *poss* is set to the possible exits from that node. If a mapping doesn't exist, then *poss* is calculated, a fuzzer node is created, a mapping is added to $\mathcal{V}$ and the node is added to $\mathcal{P}$. When a node is initialized, `count` is set to 1, `exit_num` is set to how many transitions are in *poss*, `exit_transitions` is set to *poss*, `exits_taken` is empty, and `exit_count` has 0 for every possible transition.

5   Experimental Results and Discussion

CFL is implemented in Cubicle[1]. As mentioned in Sect. 3, there is a specific recurring pattern in strongly concurrent and hierarchical models. We run our benchmarks on examples that were originally used to run Cubicle's benchmarks (available on `github`[1]). The difference is that we have modified them to include a layer of transitions as described in Fig. 2 and Fig. 3. All of our examples now have 25 extra transitions to represent depth, branching, and piplining, as well as one synchronization transition which requires that processes be in different configurations throughout the model.

We compare several forward exploration strategies with our new CFL heuristic: (i) Cubicle's existing BFS and DFS strategies, both optimized for speed, (ii) a random exploration strategy, i.e. one that starts at the initial state and randomly chooses transitions, and (iii) CMurphi, an enumerative model checker [12] developed on top of Murφ, only used here to efficiently visit the state space. The results of this comparison, excluding CMurphi, can be seen in Table 1. We discuss CMurphi separately further down.

Each strategy is run for three processes and has the same amount of time allocated for its forward exploration, noted in the Forward Time column. We then compare how many states were visited (States column) and whether Cubicle was able to prove safety before hitting the timeout criteria (Safe column). The total time (forward + proof) is noted in the Total Time column for each strategy. Each example was timed out after 5 min. This was chosen due to the time taken using CFL, as well as the number of proof nodes generated by Cubicle within those 5 min, compared in Table 2. The values underlined and in bold are where Cubicle was successful in proving safety. We can see that the number of nodes for the timed out examples is much higher than is necessary for Cubicle in the cases where it quickly proves safety.

---

[1] https://github.com/cubicle-model-checker/cubicle/tree/debugger.

Table 1. Comparing CFL with different forward strategies.

Model	Forward Time	BFS			DFS			Random			CFL		
		States	Safe	Total Time	States	Safe	Total Time	States	Safe	Total Time	States	Safe	Total Time
Dekker	10 s	466K	T.O	-	605K	Yes	12.72 s	266K	Yes	11.74 s	120K	Yes	10.61 s
Germanish	10 s	424K	T.O.	-	593K	Yes	12.91 s	261K	Yes	11.94 s	120K	Yes	10.78 s
Germanish2	10 s	315K	T.O.	-	515K	Yes	12.26 s	244K	Yes	11.92 s	115K	Yes	10.75 s
Germanish4	10 s	287K	T.O.	-	547K	Yes	14.54 s	186K	T.O.	-	110K	Yes	11 s
German	10 s	312K	T.O.	-	547K	Yes	16.25 s	207K	Yes	13.55	107K	Yes	12.23 s
German_Baukus	10 s	359K	T.O.	-	591L	Yes	14.82 s	207K	Yes	12.93 s	105K	Yes	12 s
German_CTC	50 s	1 429K	T.O.	-	2 010K	Yes	62.81 s	505K	T.O.	-	265K	Yes	55.17 s
German_pfs	10 s	416K	T.O.	-	431K	Yes	17.37 s	174K	Yes	12.69 s	100K	Yes	13.11 s
Szymanski_at	10 s	372K	T.O.	-	534K	T.O.	-	155K	Yes	11.92 s	105K	Yes	11.60 s
Szymanski_na	10 s	270K	T.O.	-	483K	T.O.	-	270K	T.O.	-	100K	Yes	12.50 s
Bakery_lamport	40 s	1 565K	T.O.	-	2038K	T.O.	-	650K	T.O.	-	230K	Yes	42.59 s
Flash_no_data	40 s	862K	T.O.	-	1 048K	T.O.	-	273K	T.O.	-	140K	Yes	43.32 s

Table 2. Number of generated proof nodes for each strategy

Model	BFS	DFS	Random	CFL
Dekker	6904	**4**	**4**	**4**
Germanish	889	**4**	**4**	**4**
Germanish2	1770	**4**	**4**	**4**
Germanish4	2415	**20**	3255	**20**
German	2862	**41**	**41**	**41**
German_Baukus	2170	**41**	**41**	**41**
German_CTC	1500	**61**	1231	**60**
German_pfs	1121	**44**	44	**44**
Szymanski_at	2861	174	**33**	**33**
Szymanski_na	2061	210	510	**43**
Bakery_lamport	779	2189	230	**16**
Flash_no_data	1329	61	1227	**37**

Another problem is that, when it comes to Cubicle, models following patterns like the one described above are a double-edged sword. When they are safe, a proof will take a long time, and when they are unsafe, a counter-example might also take a long time. Both of these things are impacted by the number of states visited during the forward exploration. More visited states does not necessarily imply a faster proof, since Cubicle will have to compare its invariant candidates to every state. The key is visiting fewer, but more important, states. Cubicle is designed to prove safety, and while it *will* give a counter-example should the system be unsafe, this can take an arbitrarily long time in huge systems. The forward and backward algorithm face the same problem in essence- huge safe models take too much time to explore forward, and huge unsafe models take too much time to trace backward. Running a time-and-calculation-heavy proof only to be hit with an "Unsafe" for trivial reasons is something we want to avoid. This problem is in the same family as trying to prove safety when the model deadlocks. When Cubicle says that a model is safe, it is safe - there is no way to get from the initial state to the unsafe state. However, the reason for that could be a correctly written model, or a model that deadlocks- it is natural that an unsafe state is unreachable if the model is incapable of taking any steps. The inclusion of CFL in Cubicle allows us to tackle both of these problems. We buried unsafe states deep within our test models and launched CFL against Cubicle's normal backward algorithm, without any additional forward strategies to accelerate invariant finding. The results can be seen in Table 3. Once again timeout was set to five minutes. Deadlocks were a bit harder to compare - while it was fairly easy to deadlock our models, it wasn't simple to pinpoint the specific state that could be classified as a deadlock. We provide deadlock detection results for CFL in Table 4 without comparing them to Cubicle.

Table 3. Unsafe: backward vs. CFL

Model	Backward	CFL
Dekker	T.O.	0.3 s
Germanish	T.O.	0.7 s
Germanish2	T.O.	0.2 s
Germanish4	T.O.	0.7 s
German	T.O.	0.4 s
German_Baukus	T.O.	0.4 s
German_CTC	T.O.	0.5 s
German_pfs	T.O.	0.3 s
Szymanski_at	T.O.	2 s
Szymanski_na	T.O.	2 s
Bakery_lamport	T.O.	1.5 s
Flash_no_data	T.O.	3 s

The reason CMurphi is excluded from Table 1 is due to the fact that we were unable to find an option that would force CMurphi to run for the allocated time. For each of our models, CMurphi raised the following error: "Internal Error: Too many active states." For the sake of fairness, we rerun CFL, manually setting the limit for each model to how many states were visited by CMurphi. The results for this are seen in Table 5.

Table 4. Deadlock detection

Model	CFL
Dekker	0.1ms
Germanish	0.5 s
Germanish2	0.2 s
Germanish4	0.5 s
German	0.4 s
German_Baukus	0.4 s
German_CTC	0.4 s
German_pfs	1 s
Szymanski_at	2 s
Szymanski_na	0.6 s
Bakery_lamport	2 s
Flash_no_data	4 s

This leads us to the discussion part of this section, namely concerning CFL's stability. As you can see in Table 5, the results for CFL all have the form X/Y. This is due to CFL's innate randomness. Two executions will not necessarily have the same results, especially if the allocated time/number of states to visit is low and the model is large. For example, in Table 5, Dekker was run 10 times, and all 10 times CFL managed to visit enough states to help Cubicle quickly prove safety. However, on a model like Germanish4, which is longer and more complex, running CFL 10 times only led to seven quick successes. This is due to CFL containing a fair amount of randomness in how it chooses execution strategies.

Table 5. Comparison with CMurphi

Model	CMurphi		CFL	
	States	Safe	States	Safe
Dekker	48K	T.O.	48K	10/10
Germanish	48K	T.O.	48K	10/10
Germanish2	39K	T.O.	39K	10/10
Germanish4	39K	T.O.	39K	7/10
German	33K	T.O.	33K	6/10
German_Baukus	33K	T.O.	33K	7/10
German_CTC	24K	T.O.	24K	0
German_pfs	33K	T.O.	33K	6/10
Szymanski_at	32K	T.O.	32K	3/10
Szymanski_na	26K	T.O.	26K	2/10
Bakery_lamport	32K	T.O.	32K	1/10
Flash_no_data	21K	T.O.	21K	3/10

6   Conclusion and Related Work

In this paper, we presented CFL, an algorithm for a new forward exploration strategy based on fuzzing for Cubicle. CFL not only serves as an oracle for Cubicle's invariant generation algorithm, but also adds new functionalities. We show that this strategy is effective and capable of tackling a class of models that Cubicle struggles with. We describe how CFL draws from fuzzing, but is adapted to Cubicle's semantics. We show how it uses multiple exploration techniques to cover the state space as diversely as possible, leading to the discovery of crucial states needed to terminate proofs. CFL also introduces quick debugging and deadlock detection to Cubicle, quickly capturing both unsafe and deadlocking states in complicated models.

There are two immediate lines of future work. The one we are currently working on is including parameterization. The goal is for CFL to be able to estimate how many processes it needs to efficiently explore a system. The other is CFL's stability. As mentioned earlier, CFL is nondeterministic by nature, and chooses its exploration techniques randomly. Fine-tuning how these choices are made could increase CFL's performance. We also think it is important to extend CFL and add more techniques, for example allowing processes to die randomly throughout an exploration. We would also like to incorporate liveness testing into CFL, since, like with deadlocks, this would add a new functionality to Cubicle.

Our work is inspired by fuzzing. Fuzzing is a simple technique designed to quickly explore a program's execution paths. The idea of mutating and generating inputs in our case was specifically inspired by AFL [14], a state-of-the-art fuzzer. Combining model checking with fuzzing is not new. For example, the authors in [13] use it for test case generation. In [10], it serves as the inspiration to test Linear-time Temporal Logic (LTL) properties for C++ programs. Bounded model checking (BMC) has been combined with fuzzing in multiple instances. For example in [2], BMC is used to generate paths that the fuzzer would not have found on its own. In [1], the authors combine BMC and Gray-Box Fuzzing to find vulnerabilities in concurrent programs. To our knowledge, no previous works combine fuzzing with parameterized model checking. Our end-goal also diverges, the above examples all dealing with actual code, whereas we want to focus on the model. We consider this to be a new line of research, perfectly suited for Cubicle, since Cubicle's invariant generation needs a forward exploration strategy that is not exhaustive (contrary to model checking) but is capable of exploring the state space efficiently.

References

1. Aljaafari, F.K., Menezes, R., Manino, E., Shmarov, F., Mustafa, M.A., Cordeiro, L.C.: Combining BMC and fuzzing techniques for finding software vulnerabilities in concurrent programs. IEEE Access 10, 121365–121384 (2022)
2. Alshmrany, K.M., Aldughaim, M., Bhayat, A., Cordeiro, L.C.: FuSeBMC v4: Smart Seed Generation for Hybrid Fuzzing. In: FASE 2022. LNCS, vol. 13241, pp. 336–340. Springer, Cham (2022). https://doi.org/10.1007/978-3-030-99429-7_19

3. Conchon, S., Goel, A., Krstić, S., Mebsout, A., Zaïdi, F.: Cubicle: a parallel SMT-based model checker for parameterized systems. In: Madhusudan, P., Seshia, S.A. (eds.) CAV 2012. LNCS, vol. 7358, pp. 718–724. Springer, Heidelberg (2012). https://doi.org/10.1007/978-3-642-31424-7_55

4. Conchon, S., Goel, A., Krstić, S., Mebsout, A., Zaïdi, F.: Invariants for finite instances and beyond. In: 2013 Formal Methods in Computer-Aided Design, pp. 61–68. IEEE (2013)

5. Conchon, S., Mebsout, A., Zaïdi, F.: Vérification de systèmes paramétrés avec Cubicle. In: JFLA. Aussois, France, February 2013. http://hal.inria.fr/hal-00778832

6. Ghilardi, S., Nicolini, E., Ranise, S., Zucchelli, D.: Towards SMT model checking of array-based systems. In: Armando, A., Baumgartner, P., Dowek, G. (eds.) Automated Reasoning. Lecture Notes in Computer Science, vol. 5195, pp. 67–82. Springer, Heidelberg (2008)

7. Ghilardi, S., Ranise, S.: MCMT: A model checker modulo theories. In: IJCAR, pp. 22–29 (2010)

8. Godefroid, P.: Fuzzing: hack, art, and science. Commun. ACM **63**(2), 70–76 (2020)

9. Manès, V.J., et al.: The art, science, and engineering of fuzzing: a survey. IEEE Trans. Softw. Eng. **47**(11), 2312–2331 (2019)

10. Meng, R., Dong, Z., Li, J., Beschastnikh, I., Roychoudhury, A.: Linear-time temporal logic guided greybox fuzzing. In: Proceedings of the 44th International Conference on Software Engineering, pp. 1343–1355 (2022)

11. Miller, B.P., Fredriksen, L., So, B.: An empirical study of the reliability of unix utilities. Commun. ACM **33**(12), 32–44 (1990)

12. Penna, G.D., Intrigila, B., Melatti, I., Tronci, E., Zilli, M.V.: Exploiting transition locality in automatic verification of finite-state concurrent systems. STTT **6**(4), 320–341 (2004)

13. Yang, Y.: Improve model testing by integrating bounded model checking and coverage guided fuzzing. Electronics **12**(7), 1573 (2023)

14. Zalewski, M.: American fuzzy lop-whitepaper (2016)

Guiding Symbolic Execution with A-Star

Theo De Castro Pinto[1,2]([✉]), Antoine Rollet[1]([✉]), Grégoire Sutre[1],
and Ireneusz Tobor[2]

[1] Univ. Bordeaux, CNRS, Bordeaux INP, LaBRI, UMR 5800, 33400 Talence, France
{theo.de-castro-pinto,antoine.rollet,gregoire.sutre}@labri.fr
[2] Serma Safety & Security, 33600 Pessac, France
{t.de-castro,i.tobor}@serma.com

Abstract. Symbolic execution is widely used to detect vulnerabilities
in software. The idea is to symbolically execute the program in order to
find an executable path to a target instruction. For the analysis to be
fully accurate, it must be performed on the binary code, which makes
the well-known issue of state explosion even more critical. In this paper,
we introduce a novel exploration strategy for symbolic execution aiming
to limit the number of explored paths. Our strategy is inspired from the
A^* algorithm and steered towards least explored parts of the program.
We compare our approach, using the Binsec tool, to three other classical strategies: depth-first (DFS), breadth-first (BFS) and non-uniform
random (NURS). Our experiments on real-size programs show that our
approach is promising.

Keywords: Symbolic execution · Program analysis · Binary code
analysis · A^* algorithm

1 Introduction

Context. Software verification is a crucial step during the development of programs permitting to discover potential failures. It consists not only in assessing
the correct behavior of the program but also in checking if vulnerabilities exist.
Software verification techniques include (automatic) formal proofs [15], testing [5], fuzzing [16], code review and program analysis [3,6–8,14]. This paper
deals with program analysis of binary code, more precisely with the problem
of efficiently finding an executable path to a target instruction (aka the line
reachability problem). The number of inputs of a program is usually very big,
inducing a huge number of possible paths. A popular technique used to handle
this problem is symbolic execution [14]. It is an exploration technique aiming to
find inputs of a program, with the help of a constraint solver, corresponding to
a target path of the program. More precisely, considering a target path π of the
program, a corresponding path predicate formula representing the constraints
over the input variables along π is sent to a constraint solver. If the formula is
satisfiable, then the path is executable, and a solution of the constraint system
corresponds to a possible input set of the program activating π. A major problem
of this approach is that it generally does not scale well on real-size programs. The

C. Ferreira and T. A. C. Willemse (Eds.): SEFM 2023, LNCS 14323, pp. 47–65, 2023.
https://doi.org/10.1007/978-3-031-47115-5_4

order of exploration is crucial and decided by the exploration strategy, which can be for instance depth-first (DFS), breadth-first (BFS) or non-uniform random (NURS). In this work, we consider binary code. Directly analyzing the binary code is necessary to verify that the compilation did not introduce new behaviors or vulnerabilities, but it is challenging. This stems from the fact that a lot of information is lost after the compilation and that binary code contains a lot more instructions than source code.

Contributions. In this paper, we introduce two novel exploration strategies for symbolic execution, inspired by the well-known A* algorithm [13]. A* is an efficient single-pair shortest path algorithm, therefore using it in order to quickly reach a target during symbolic execution makes sense. This key insight is at the core of Blondin et al.'s efficient explicit reachability analysis tool for Petri nets [4]. We first adapt the A* algorithm to symbolic execution of binary code, using a precomputed distance heuristic, which has never been done previously to our knowledge. We then improve this basic A*-like strategy to steer the exploration towards least explored parts of the program. The total number of explored paths is reduced, implying better performance.

We provide a formal description of our approach on transition systems, which makes it generic and then applicable in various contexts. Our strategies have been implemented in the binary code analysis tool Binsec, although dynamic jumps are not currently handled. We present an experimental evaluation of our two A*-like exploration strategies on seven programs, two of them being of real-size (Wookey's bootloader [1] and the NetBSD `leave` command). Our experiments show that our approach is promising. A replication package is available at Zenodo [10].

Related Work. Symbolic execution [14] is a powerful technique to analyze programs. It is used in many program analysis tools, for instance KLEE [5], MIASM [19], ANGR [24] and Binsec [11]. KLEE is a dynamic symbolic execution engine that is used on source code (translated to LLVM). MIASM and ANGR are binary analysis platforms that combine both static and dynamic symbolic execution. Binsec is a framework for binary code analysis based on formal approaches such as symbolic execution, abstract interpretation [8], SMT solving [9] and fuzzing [16]. The exploration strategies provided by Binsec are BFS, DFS and NURS. Common uses of symbolic execution include test case generation [5], input generation for fuzzing [25] or even vulnerability detection [12,23].

In 2021, Blondin et al. proposed an approach based on the A* algorithm [13] to perform reachability analysis on Petri nets [4]. Their results showed that using this approach outperforms existing state-of-the-art Petri nets tools. The idea is to use distance oracles to guide the exploration of Petri nets. Our approach generalizes this concept to any labeled transition system. We also propose some enhancements in order to reach targets more efficiently in real programs. Many strategies aiming to guide the exploration towards more promising paths have been proposed in the literature. Some of them prioritize paths that are closer

```
1  #define MAX_SIZE 10000000
2  #define EXPECTED_SIZE 100
3  void valid(int y) {
4      int x;
5      for (x = 0; x < MAX_SIZE; x++) {
6          if (!correct(y)) break;
7          y--;
8      }
9      if (x != EXPECTED_SIZE) trap();
10     critical();
11 }
```

Listing 1.1. C-style running example.

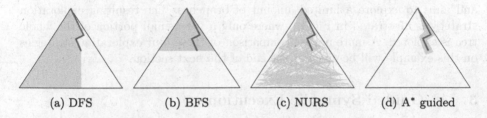

(a) DFS   (b) BFS   (c) NURS   (d) A* guided

Fig. 1. Illustration of different symbolic execution strategies.

to the target [2,18] while others prioritize paths that explore new parts of the program [17,26]. In both cases, only partial aspects of the A* algorithm are implemented. To our knowledge, none of them apply both strategies, and they are applied on source code. Our proposal combines both of these concepts into a novel exploration strategy, and applies it directly on binary code.

2 Running Example

The code given in Listing 1.1 is a simplified version of a security-critical code inspired from a real-life application. The parameter y of the function valid is a secret value that an attacker is not supposed to know. This value must satisfy a certain condition, namely that correct(n) returns true for all integers n with $y-99 \leq n \leq y$, and correct($y-100$) returns false. Note that the corresponding loop (lines 5–8) may, in fact, be traversed up to 10^7 times. If the above-mentioned condition on y is satisfied then the critical function is executed, otherwise a counter-measure, here trap, is triggered. For our discussion, the contents of these two functions does not matter, except that the trap function is an infinite loop whose body contains two small paths (corresponding to security measures). Our goal is to use symbolic execution to (efficiently) find an executable path from the start of the valid function to the target critical function.

Let us look qualitatively at the behavior of symbolic execution on this example regarding different exploration strategies. A depth-first (DFS) strategy either exits the loop early and ends up in the trap function, or executes the loop entirely and still ends up in the trap function. In both cases, it is highly inefficient, as a huge number of branches are explored in the trap function before the loop exits with the expected value of 100 for x. This behavior is illustrated in Fig. 1a, where the red branch is the only one leading to the target, and the gray zone represents the branches already explored. A breadth-first (BFS) strategy is also highly inefficient as it generates all branches of length lesser than the length of the branch reaching the target, including the ones that are stuck in the trap function. Its behavior is exhibited in Fig. 1b where a large part of the reachability tree is explored. A non-uniform random (NURS) strategy chooses randomly which branch to explore further (see Fig. 1c). Again, because of the trap function, a huge number of branches are generated on average before reaching the target. The approach proposed in this paper is inspired from the A* algorithm and aims to explore a limited amount of branches. The resulting exploration strategy is illustrated in Fig. 1d, where only a very small portion of the whole tree is explored. A more precise comparison of these four exploration strategies on this example will be given at the end of the next section.

3   A* Guided Symbolic Execution

Many verification questions, including vulnerability detection, can be phrased as reachability queries over a labeled transition system providing the operational semantics of the system under analysis. We start by recalling a few preliminary notions on reachability in labeled transition systems. The remainder of the section focuses on symbolic execution and discusses various exploration strategies.

Reachability in Labeled Transition Systems. A (non-deterministic) *labeled transition system* is a 5-tuple $S = (C, \Sigma, \rightarrow, I, F)$ where C is a possibly infinite set of *configurations*, Σ is a finite set of *actions*, $\rightarrow \subseteq C \times \Sigma \times C$ is a *labeled transition relation*, $I \subseteq C$ is a set of *initial configurations*, and $F \subseteq C$ is a set of *final configurations*. A *run* in S is an alternating sequence $\rho = (c_0, a_1, c_1, \ldots, a_n, c_n)$ of configurations $c_i \in C$ and actions $a_i \in \Sigma$ such that $c_{i-1} \xrightarrow{a_i} c_i$ for all i. We say that ρ is a run *from* c_0 *to* c_n and we write $\rho = c_0 \xrightarrow{a_1} c_1 \cdots \xrightarrow{a_n} c_n$. The word $a_1 \cdots a_n$ is called the *trace* of ρ. Given two configurations $c, c' \in C$ and a word $w \in \Sigma^*$, the notation $c \xrightarrow{w} c'$ means that there exists[1] a run from c to c' with trace w. The length of w is denoted by $|w|$. We say that c' is *reachable* from c, written $c \xrightarrow{*} c'$, when $c \xrightarrow{w} c'$ for some $w \in \Sigma^*$.

Our main objective is to determine whether there exists a run from an initial configuration to a final configuration. Formally, the *reachability problem* asks, given a LTS $S = (C, \Sigma, \rightarrow, I, F)$, whether there exists $c \in I$ and $c' \in F$ such that $c \xrightarrow{*} c'$. In theory, the reachability problem is only a decision problem.

---

[1] Due to non-determinism, there may be several runs from c to c' with trace w.

But, in practice, a trace $w \in \Sigma^*$ witnessing reachability $c \xrightarrow{w} c'$ should also be provided when the answer is positive.

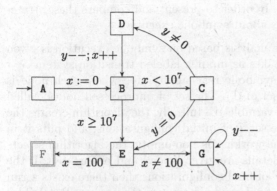

location	h(location)
A	3
B	2
C	2
D	3
E	1
F	0
G	$+\infty$

(a) States and transitions of the counter machine.

(b) Estimated distances to the final location F (so-called h values).

Fig. 2. Counter machine corresponding to the inlined code given in Listing 1.1, assuming that the `correct` function simply checks that its argument is nonzero.

Example 1. Consider the counter machine given in Fig. 2a. This machine is a translation of our running example where the `correct` function simply performs a nonzero test on its argument. All functions are inlined. The location F corresponds to the call to the `critical` function. The `trap` function is modeled in location G by two loops that are chosen non-deterministically (non-determinism typically comes in practice from inputs to the program).

Formally, this counter machine operates on two *counters*, namely x and y, that range over $\mathbb{Z}$. Its *locations* are A, B, ..., G and its *edges* are the arrows depicted in Fig. 2a. Each edge is labeled with an *action* over the counters. These actions are either guards or assignments. Let Σ denote the set of all counter actions appearing in Fig. 2a. The semantics $[\![a]\!]$ of an action $a \in \Sigma$ is defined, as expected, as a binary relation $[\![a]\!] \subseteq \mathbb{Z}^{\{x,y\}} \times \mathbb{Z}^{\{x,y\}}$ over valuations of the counters. The operational semantics of the counter machine is given by the labeled transition system $\mathcal{S} = (C, \Sigma, \rightarrow, I, F)$ defined as follows. The set of configurations C is the set of pairs (ℓ, v) where ℓ is a location and $v \in \mathbb{Z}^{\{x,y\}}$ is a valuation of the counters. The sets of initial and final configurations are $I = A \times \mathbb{Z}^{\{x,y\}}$ and $F = F \times \mathbb{Z}^{\{x,y\}}$. The labeled transition relation is the set of triples $(\ell, v) \xrightarrow{a} (\ell', v')$ such that $\ell \xrightarrow{a} \ell'$ is an edge depicted in Fig. 2a and $(v, v') \in [\![a]\!]$. Our goal can now be formally phrased as the reachability question for $\mathcal{S}$.   ◁

We present an algorithm for the reachability problem that is based on symbolic execution. Some additional notations are needed first. A *region* in a LTS $\mathcal{S} = (C, \Sigma, \rightarrow, I, F)$ is a subset $\varphi \subseteq C$ of configurations. Regions are often called symbolic states in the context of symbolic execution. We define the region transformer post : $2^C \times \Sigma \rightarrow 2^C$ as usual, by $\text{post}(\varphi, a) = \{c' \in C \mid \exists c \in \varphi : c \xrightarrow{a} c'\}$.

Symbolic Execution for Reachability Analysis. Symbolic execution has originally been proposed for program testing [14], but the technique can also be used for reachability analysis. Our main contribution concerns exploration strategies for symbolic execution. In order to present and compare these strategies, we first recall some elements about symbolic execution.

An algorithm for reachability analysis based on symbolic execution is given in Algorithm 1. This algorithm takes as input a labeled transition system $S = (C, \Sigma, \rightarrow, I, F)$ and computes a symbolic reachability tree where each node is labeled with a region (i.e., a subset of C). The set of unprocessed nodes, called the *worklist*, is maintained in the variable W. Initially, the algorithm creates the root of the tree, labeled with the set I of initial configurations, and puts it in the worklist. Then, as long as the worklist is non-empty, the algorithm selects a node from the worklist (more details are given below) and processes it. If the node's region intersects the set F of final configurations then there exists a run from an initial configuration to a final configuration, so the answer "Reachable" is returned. Note that a witnessing trace w can be obtained by collecting the actions along the branch (from the root to the node). Otherwise, the node is expanded, meaning that for each action $a \in \Sigma$, a child is created and labeled with the appropriate region according to the post transformer. This expansion is omitted if the node's region is empty. If the worklist becomes empty then all configurations reachable from an initial configuration have been explored, and none of them is final, so the algorithm returns "Unreachable".

Algorithm 1 SymbolicExecution(S, Prio)

Input: A LTS $S = (C, \Sigma, \rightarrow, I, F)$, a priority function Prio $: (\cdots) \rightarrow \mathbb{R} \cup \{+\infty\}$
Output: Either "Reachable" or "Unreachable"
1:   $r \leftarrow$ createRoot()
2:   $(r.\text{region}, r.\text{priority}) \leftarrow (I, \text{Prio}(S, r, \emptyset))$
3:   $W \leftarrow \{r\}$
4: **while** $W \neq \emptyset$ **do**
5:     $n \leftarrow \arg\min\{n.\text{priority} \mid n \in W\}$
6:     $W \leftarrow W \setminus \{n\}$
7:     $\varphi \leftarrow n.\text{region}$
8:     **if** $\varphi \cap F \neq \emptyset$ **then**
9:       **return** "Reachable"   ▷ *the branch provides a witnessing trace*
10:    **else if** $\varphi \neq \emptyset$ **then**
11:      **for all** $a \in \Sigma$ **do**
12:        $u \leftarrow$ createChild(n, a)
13:        $(u.\text{region}, u.\text{priority}) \leftarrow (\text{post}(\varphi, a), \text{Prio}(S, u, W))$
14:          $W \leftarrow W \cup \{u\}$
15:      **end for**
16:    **end if**
17: **end while**
18: **return** "Unreachable"

Remark 1. Algorithm 1 is correct in the sense that it either returns the correct answer to the reachability problem for the input LTS $\mathcal{S} = (C, \Sigma, \rightarrow, I, F)$, or loops forever. The proof is pretty standard. Let $\mathsf{post}^* : 2^C \rightarrow 2^C$ be defined as usual, by $\mathsf{post}^*(\varphi) = \{c' \in C \mid \exists c \in \varphi : c \xrightarrow{*} c'\}$. We introduce in Algorithm 1 a "ghost" variable N that maintains the set of constructed nodes. The correctness of the algorithm follows from the two following properties at line 4. First, $n.\mathtt{region}$ is disjoint from F for every node $n \in (N \setminus W)$. Second, $\mathsf{post}^*(I)$ is the union of the set $\bigcup_{n \in (N \setminus W)} n.\mathtt{region}$ and the set $\bigcup_{n \in W} \mathsf{post}^*(n.\mathtt{region})$. These two properties are routinely shown to be loop invariants at line 4.

In practice, symbolic execution implicitly assumes a maximum exploration depth. The potentially infinite symbolic reachability tree computed by Algorithm 1 is truncated at this maximum exploration depth (and the answer "Unreachable" is replaced by "Unknown" if the tree was truncated).

The order of exploration in Algorithm 1 can be customized via the priority function $\mathtt{Prio}$. This function takes three arguments, a LTS, a node and a worklist, and returns a priority in $\mathbb{R} \cup \{+\infty\}$. Each node is assigned a priority upon creation (lines 2 and 13) and this priority remains unchanged afterwards. When the algorithm picks an unprocessed node from the worklist, it picks one of minimal priority (see line 5).

Naturally, the classical search exploration strategies DFS, BFS and NURS can be encoded as priorities. The corresponding priority functions are given by:

$$\mathtt{PrioDFS}(\mathcal{S}, u, W) = \begin{cases} 0 & \text{if } W = \emptyset \\ \min\{n.\mathtt{priority} \mid n \in W\} - 1 & \text{otherwise} \end{cases}$$

$$\mathtt{PrioBFS}(\mathcal{S}, u, W) = \begin{cases} 0 & \text{if } W = \emptyset \\ \max\{n.\mathtt{priority} \mid n \in W\} + 1 & \text{otherwise} \end{cases}$$

$$\mathtt{PrioNURS}(\mathcal{S}, u, W) = \mathrm{random}(0, 1)$$

The depth-first (DFS) strategy is classically implemented with a last-in-first-out worklist. This strategy is encoded with priorities by ensuring that the last node added to the worklist receives a smaller priority than all other nodes in the worklist (see the $\mathtt{PrioDFS}$ function). Similarly, the breadth-first (BFS) strategy, which is classically implemented with a first-in-first-out worklist, is equivalent to using the $\mathtt{PrioBFS}$ function in Algorithm 1. Finally, the $\mathtt{PrioNURS}$ function provides a random priority for every node added to the worklist, which does correspond to a non-uniform random (NURS) exploration of the tree.

Remark 2. To implement Algorithm 1 in practice, regions have to be finitely representable, emptiness of a region and emptiness of the intersection of two regions have to be decidable, and the post transformer must be computable. In practice, regions are often encoded as SMT formulas.

Remark 3. As in classical symbolic execution, Algorithm 1 blindly expands a node regardless of whether its region has already been processed before. A computationally cheap inclusion test (i.e., a relation $\preceq$ on regions such that $r \preceq r' \implies r \subseteq r'$) could be used to partially truncate the exploration.

Exploration Strategy Inspired from A*. In addition to the classical strategies DFS, BFS and NURS, we provide a new exploration strategy for symbolic execution, inspired from the A* algorithm.

Recall that A* is a single-pair shortest path algorithm for nonnegatively weighted directed graphs. Assume that we are given such a graph together with a source vertex and a target vertex. Let V denote the set of vertices of the graph. The main idea of the A* algorithm is to guide the exploration using a heuristic function $h : V \rightarrow \mathbb{N} \cup \{+\infty\}$ that underestimates the (minimal) distance from any vertex to the target vertex. Note that $h(v)$ may be $+\infty$ if there is no path from v to the target vertex. When A* picks a vertex to process from its worklist, it chooses a vertex v that minimizes the sum $g(v) + h(v)$, where $g(v)$ is the weight of the shortest path *seen so far* from the source vertex to v. Let us see how to adapt this exploration strategy in our symbolic execution algorithm. In our context, edges are not weighted (they correspond to symbolic transitions $\varphi \xrightarrow{a} \varphi'$ where $\varphi' = \mathsf{post}(\varphi, a)$), so we assume a uniform weight of one. We first need to extend the notion of distance underapproximation to regions.

Definition 1. *A distance underapproximation for a LTS $\mathcal{S} = (C, \Sigma, \rightarrow, I, F)$ is a function $h_{\mathcal{S}} : 2^C \rightarrow \mathbb{N} \cup \{+\infty\}$ such that for every $i, c, f \in C$ and $w \in \Sigma^*$,*

$$i \in I \wedge i \xrightarrow{*} c \wedge c \in \varphi \wedge c \xrightarrow{w} f \wedge f \in F \implies h_{\mathcal{S}}(\varphi) \leq |w|$$

Informally, $h_{\mathcal{S}}(\varphi)$ returns an underapproximation of the distance between a given region $\varphi \subseteq C$ and the set of final configurations F. However, to facilitate the design of distance underapproximations, this condition on $h_{\mathcal{S}}(\varphi)$ is only required for the configurations $c \in \varphi$ that are reachable from an initial configuration.

To adapt the exploration strategy of A* in Algorithm 1, we assume that we are given a (computable) distance underapproximation $h_{\mathcal{S}}$ for the LTS $\mathcal{S}$ under analysis, and we use the priority function `PrioASTAR` defined as follows:

$$\mathtt{PrioASTAR}(\mathcal{S}, u, W, h_{\mathcal{S}}) = \mathrm{depth}(u) + h_{\mathcal{S}}(u.\mathtt{region})$$

where $\mathrm{depth}(u)$ denotes the depth of the node u in the symbolic reachability tree that is generated by Algorithm 1. Note that this is slightly different from A* since $\mathrm{depth}(u)$ only upper-bounds[2] the distance seen so far from the set of initial configurations to the region of u. This is not an issue as our primary goal is to quickly find an executable path, regardless of its length.

---

[2] To faithfully mimic A*, $\mathrm{depth}(u)$ should be compared with the depths of all processed nodes having the same region as u. But this would require checking equality between regions, which is computationally costly in general.

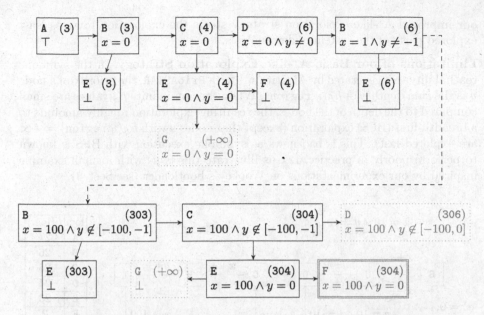

Fig. 3. Symbolic execution with `PrioASTAR` of the counter machine in Fig. 2.

Example 2. We illustrate this approach on our running example (see Example 1) by applying it on the LTS giving the semantics of the counter machine of Fig. 2a. The symbolic reachability tree generated by Algorithm 1 with the `PrioASTAR` function is (partially) depicted in Fig. 3. We use the distance underapproximation obtained by ignoring the counters, given in Fig. 2b. Each node in Fig. 3 is labeled with its region and its priority (in parentheses). The region is given by a location of the counter machine and a formula over its counters x, y. Recall that the priority of a node is the sum of its depth and of the h value of its location (given in Fig. 2b). The order of exploration is not explicitly shown but dotted/gray nodes have not yet been explored and are still in the worklist at the end of the exploration. Our approach explores about 600 nodes before reaching the final location.

In comparison, with a maximum exploration depth of 10000 nodes, at least 10^{270} nodes are explored with `PrioDFS`, assuming that actions are always taken in the same order at line 11 of Algorithm 1. About 10^{30} nodes are explored with `PrioBFS`, most of them stuck in location G (this location corresponds to the `trap` function). At least 10^{100} nodes are explored on average with `PrioNURS`.   ◁

4 Guiding the Exploration Towards the Unknown

This section presents an improvement of the A*-like exploration strategy presented in the previous section. We first exhibit some weaknesses of this exploration strategy and we then show how to tackle these weaknesses. In short, our improved A*-like exploration strategy steers the exploration towards least explored parts of the system under analysis.

Limitations of our Basic A*-like Exploration Strategy. In the symbolic reachability tree generated by Algorithm 1 with `PrioASTAR`, the priority of a node u is the sum $\text{depth}(u) + h_S(u.\text{region})$. When the non-infinite h_S values are small compared to the depth of the nodes, the resulting exploration roughly amounts to a breadth-first (BFS) exploration (except that nodes u with $h_S(u.\text{region}) = +\infty$ are explored last). This is bad news as symbolic execution with BFS is known to perform poorly in practice. Let us illustrate this issue with a small example inspired by our experimentations on Wookey's bootloader (see Sect. 6).

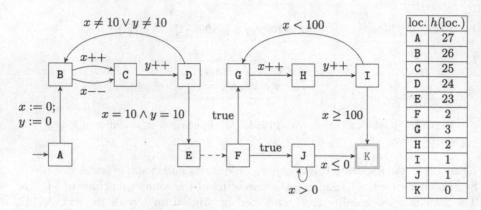

Fig. 4. Counter machine that illustrates some limitations of our basic A*-like exploration strategy induced by the priority function `PrioASTAR`. The distance underapproximation is shown on the right-hand side.

Example 3. Consider the counter machine given in Fig. 4. The two edges B $\xrightarrow{x++}$ C and B $\xrightarrow{x--}$ C model a non-deterministic choice from the location B. Similarly, the two edges originating from F are chosen non-deterministically. The dashed edge from E to F stands for 20 intermediate locations between E and F. This is reflected in the distance underapproximation values given in the table on the right hand-side of the figure. As before, this distance underapproximation is obtained by simply ignoring the counters.

The only run reaching the final location K takes the loop B–C–D exactly 10 times, each time choosing the B $\xrightarrow{x++}$ C edge so that x and y remain equal, and exits the loop in E with $x = y = 10$. It then moves to F and takes the edge F $\xrightarrow{true}$ G since K is not reachable from J with $x = 10$. Finally, the loop G–H–I is taken exactly 90 times before moving to K.

Symbolic execution with `PrioASTAR` first constructs all nodes obtained by taking the loop B–C–D exactly 9 times, so we end up with 2^9 copies of B in the worklist, each with the same depth $1 + 9 \cdot 3$, hence, the same priority 54. Then, the loop B–C–D is taken once more, and exactly one branch exits the loop. This branch reaches F, forks into G and J, and takes the loop on J twice. At this point, the worklist contains $2^{10} - 1$ copies of B with priority 57, one copy of G with priority 56, and one copy of J with priority 56. In order to reach the final location K, the exploration now needs to iterate the loop G–H–I exactly 90 times. But for each iteration of this loop, an additional iteration of the B–C–D loop is performed from each copy of B in the worklist, leading each time to twice as many copies of B in the worklist. This dramatically slows down the construction of the only branch leading to the final location K.   ◁

An Improved A*-like Exploration Strategy. As mentioned previously, the issue at hand arises when the sum $\mathrm{depth}(u) + h_{\mathcal{S}}(u.\mathtt{region})$ is dominated by $\mathrm{depth}(u)$, which is very common in real-size programs. To fix this issue, we propose to replace $\mathrm{depth}(u)$ by another measure that still accounts for the length of the branch from the root of the tree to u, but prioritizes nodes corresponding to parts of the system that have rarely been visited.

Remark 4. A tempting solution to the above-mentioned issue may be to simply replace $\mathrm{depth}(u)$ by zero, i.e., to let the priority of each node u be $h_{\mathcal{S}}(u.\mathtt{region})$. The resulting symbolic execution of the counter machine given in Fig. 4 is similar, at first, to the one detailed in Example 3. However, when the branch reaching F forks into G and J, the copy of G now has priority 3 and the copy of J now has priority 1. So the copy of G remains in the worklist and the loop on J is taken forever (or until the maximum exploration depth is reached).

Let us now define the priority function $\mathtt{PrioASTAR\text{-}2}$ inducing our improved A*-like exploration strategy. We first introduce the notion that we use to identify "parts of the system". An *observable* for a LTS $\mathcal{S} = (C, \Sigma, \rightarrow, I, F)$ is any subset of C. Given a finite set P of observables, we define the region observation function $\mathsf{obs} : 2^C \rightarrow 2^P$ by $\mathsf{obs}(\varphi) = \{p \in P \mid (\varphi \cap p) \neq \emptyset\}$. Given a sequence of regions $r_0, \ldots, r_n$, we let $\mathsf{obs}_{\neg\emptyset}(r_0, \ldots, r_n)$ denote the sequence obtained from $\mathsf{obs}(r_0), \ldots, \mathsf{obs}(r_n)$ by removing all occurrences of $\emptyset$.

Observables will be used to focus the exploration on specific properties of the system under analysis. On a given branch of the symbolic reachability tree, instead of looking at the sequence of regions $r_0, \ldots, r_n$ that have been visited along the branch, we will look at the sequence of observations $\mathsf{obs}_{\neg\emptyset}(r_0, \ldots, r_n)$. Typically, for counter machines and binary programs (see Sect. 5), we consider observables induced by specific locations. But we could use observables expressing properties on counters or registers.

Example 4. In the counter machine of Fig. 4, we focus on locations that are targets of branching instructions, i.e., locations in the set $T = \{\mathsf{B}, \mathsf{C}, \mathsf{E}, \mathsf{G}, \mathsf{J}, \mathsf{K}\}$. For each location $t \in T$, we define the observable $p_t = \{t\} \times \mathbb{Z}^{\{x,y\}}$.   ◁

The $\mathtt{PrioASTAR\text{-}2}$ function is defined in Algorithm 2. To simplify the presentation, we assume that the set I of initial configurations has a nonempty

---

Algorithm 2 `PrioASTAR-2`$(\mathcal{S}, u, W, h_{\mathcal{S}}, P, \lambda)$

Input: A LTS $\mathcal{S} = (C, \Sigma, \rightarrow, I, F)$, a node u, a worklist, a distance underapproximation $h_{\mathcal{S}}$ for $\mathcal{S}$, a finite set P of observables for $\mathcal{S}$, a function $\lambda : \mathbb{N} \rightarrow \mathbb{R}_{\geq 0}$
1: Let $u_0, \ldots, u_n$ denote the branch from the root $r = u_0$ to the node $u = u_n$
2: Let $obs_0, \ldots, obs_k = \mathtt{obs}_{\neg\emptyset}(u_0.\mathtt{region}, \ldots, u_n.\mathtt{region})$ $\triangleright k \geq 0$
3: Let $g = \mathrm{Card}\{obs_0, \ldots, obs_m\}$ where $m = \min\{i \in [0,k] \mid obs_i = obs_k\}$
4: Let $\mu = \mathrm{Card}\{i \in [0,n] \mid obs_i = obs_k\}$
5: **return** $g \cdot \lambda(\mu) + h_{\mathcal{S}}(u.\mathtt{region})$

---

observation. This guarantees that the sequence $obs_0, \ldots, obs_k$ defined at line 2 is nonempty. The priority returned by `PrioASTAR-2` is $g \cdot \lambda(\mu) + h_{\mathcal{S}}(u.\mathtt{region})$ where g and μ depend on the sequence $obs_0, \ldots, obs_k$ of nonempty observations seen along the branch. In words, g is the "elementary" length of this sequence, i.e., the number of distinct elements in the sequence $obs_0, \ldots, obs_m$ where obs_m is the first occurrence of obs_k, and μ is the number of times that obs_k occurs in the sequence $obs_0, \ldots, obs_k$. Intuitively, obs_k indicates which part of the system corresponds to the node u, so μ tells us how many times this part of the system has been visited along the branch. Observe that g only depends on the first occurrence of each observation in $obs_0, \ldots, obs_k$. We call g the *elementary depth* of the node u.

The function $\lambda : \mathbb{N} \rightarrow \mathbb{R}_{\geq 0}$ allows us to adjust the priority depending on the value of μ. The choice of a good λ function is crucial to guide the exploration properly. In order to steer the exploration towards least explored parts of the system, λ should be non-decreasing, and $\lambda(\mu)$ should be small when μ is small. According to our experiments, a λ function of the form

$$\lambda_\theta(\mu) = \begin{cases} 0 & \text{if } \mu < \theta \\ \log_{10}(\mu - \theta + 1) & \text{otherwise} \end{cases}$$

performs well in practice. Here, the parameter $\theta \in \mathbb{N}$ acts as a threshold (in our experiments, we use $\theta = 3$, see Sect. 6). The idea behind λ_θ is to give precedence to nodes that are in a part of the system that has rarely been visited (less than θ times) along the branch. Note that this function always returns zero or a small value. As mentioned before, we do this to prevent the elementary depth g from dominating $h_{\mathcal{S}}$. Note that this is just an example of a possible λ function that we designed during our experimentations. Different λ functions may also work, and even outperform this one.

Example 5. Consider again the counter machine given in Fig. 4. We take the same set of observables as in Example 4, and we use the function λ_θ defined above with $\theta = 3$. As with `PrioASTAR`, symbolic execution with `PrioASTAR-2` first constructs all nodes obtained by taking the loop B–C–D exactly 9 times. When the branch that exits the loop forks into G and J, the worklist contains $2^{10} - 1$ copies of B with priority $26 + 1 \cdot \log_{10}(8)$, one copy of G with priority 3, and one copy of J with priority 1. So the loop on J is iterated first, and the priority of the J copy in the worklist slowly increases. When this priority becomes larger than 3, the loop G–H–I is also iterated. The exploration then interleaves the construction of the two corresponding branches. After 90 iterations of the loop G–H–I, the worklist contains a copy of K with priority 0. This copy is then processed immediately, and the algorithm returns "Reachable". Let us estimate the number of iterations of the loop on J. Just before completion of the G–H–I loop, the last copy of G in the worklist has priority $3+4\cdot\log_{10}(90-1) < 3+4\cdot2 = 11$. Similarly, the last copies of H and I have priorities less than 8 and 7, respectively. After $k \geq 3$ iterations of the loop on J, the priority of the J copy is $1 + 4\cdot\log_{10}(k-1)$. Observe that $(1+4\cdot\log_{10}(k-1) > 11) \Leftrightarrow k > 317$. So the loop on J is iterated at most 318 times. Note also that the $2^{10} - 1$ copies of B have not left the worklist since their priority is larger than 26, hence, larger than 11.   ◁

5   Application to Binary Programs

We show in this section how to apply our approach to binary programs. Recall that our new A*-like exploration strategies require a distance underapproximation for the LTS under analysis. The main purpose of this section is to provide an efficiently computable distance underapproximation for binary programs. Before that, we need to define[3] the syntax and semantics of binary programs.

Syntax and Semantics. Consider a fixed set Req of *registers* and a fixed set $Addr$ of *addresses*. To account for instructions that do not impact the control-flow of the program, such as memory accesses and arithmetic operations on registers, we assume an a priori given set $\mathtt{Op}$ of *operations*. Each operation $\mathtt{op} \in \mathtt{Op}$ comes with its semantics $[\![\mathtt{op}]\!]$, given as a function from $\mathbb{Z}^{Reg} \times \mathbb{Z}^{Addr}$ to itself. A *binary program* is a finite sequence of instructions $(I_1,\ldots,I_n)$, where each *instruction* I_k is in the following set:

$$\mathtt{Op} \cup \{\mathtt{BR}\ r\ \ell \mid r \in Reg \wedge \ell \in [1,n]\} \cup \{\mathtt{CALL}\ \ell \mid \ell \in [1,n]\} \cup \{\mathtt{RET}\}$$

Here, BR stands for conditional branching, and CALL and RET stand for procedures call and return. A *location* of the binary program is any integer in $[1, n+1]$.

The operational semantics of a binary program $(I_1,\ldots,I_n)$, equipped with a final location $f \in [1, n+1]$, is given by the labeled transition system $\mathcal{S} = (C, \Sigma, \rightarrow, I, F)$ defined as follows. The set of actions Σ is the set of instructions of the programs, i.e., $\Sigma = \{I_1,\ldots,I_n\}$. The set of configurations C is the set of quadruples (ℓ, R, M, s) where $\ell \in [1, n+1]$ is a location, $R \in \mathbb{Z}^{Reg}$ and $M \in \mathbb{Z}^{Addr}$ are register and memory contents, and $s \in [1, n+1]^*$ is a stack contents. The sets of initial and final configurations are $I = \{(\ell, R, M, s) \in C \mid \ell = 1 \wedge s = \varepsilon\}$ and $F = \{(\ell, R, M, s) \in C \mid \ell = f\}$. The labeled transition relation $\rightarrow$ is defined by the rules given in Fig. 5. Note that each of these rules implicitly requires that $\ell \in [1, n]$ since I_ℓ must be defined.

---

[3] Similar definitions of the syntax and semantics of binary programs can be found in the literature. Our definition is intentionally simple and tailored to our purposes.

$$\frac{I_\ell = \mathtt{op} \in \mathtt{Op} \quad (R', M') = [\![\mathtt{op}]\!](R, M)}{(\ell, R, M, s) \xrightarrow{I_\ell} (\ell+1, R', M', s)}$$

$$\frac{I_\ell = \mathtt{BR}\ r\ \ell' \quad R(r) = 0}{(\ell, R, M, s) \xrightarrow{I_\ell} (\ell+1, R, M, s)} \qquad \frac{I_\ell = \mathtt{BR}\ r\ \ell' \quad R(r) \neq 0}{(\ell, R, M, s) \xrightarrow{I_\ell} (\ell', R, M, s)}$$

$$\frac{I_\ell = \mathtt{CALL}\ \ell'}{(\ell, R, M, s) \xrightarrow{I_\ell} (\ell', R, M, (\ell+1) \cdot s)} \qquad \frac{I_\ell = \mathtt{RET}}{(\ell, R, M, \ell' \cdot s) \xrightarrow{I_\ell} (\ell', R, M, s)}$$

Fig. 5. Operational semantics of binary programs.

Distance Underapproximation. Following the approach of Blondin et al. for Petri nets [4], we propose a distance underapproximation for binary programs that is based on an abstraction of the operational semantics defined above. This abstraction merely consists of ignoring the register and memory contents.

$$\frac{I_\ell = \mathtt{op} \in \mathtt{Op}}{(\ell, s) \xrightarrow{I_\ell}{}^\sharp (\ell+1, s)} \qquad \frac{I_\ell = \mathtt{BR}\ r\ \ell'}{(\ell, s) \xrightarrow{I_\ell}{}^\sharp (\ell+1, s)} \qquad \frac{I_\ell = \mathtt{BR}\ r\ \ell'}{(\ell, s) \xrightarrow{I_\ell}{}^\sharp (\ell', s)}$$

$$\frac{I_\ell = \mathtt{CALL}\ \ell'}{(\ell, s) \xrightarrow{I_\ell}{}^\sharp (\ell', (\ell+1) \cdot s)} \qquad \frac{I_\ell = \mathtt{RET}}{(\ell, \ell' \cdot s) \xrightarrow{I_\ell}{}^\sharp (\ell', s)}$$

Fig. 6. Abstract semantics of binary programs.

Formally, the abstract semantics of a binary program $(I_1, \ldots, I_n)$, equipped with a final location $f \in [1, n+1]$, is given by the labeled transition system $\mathcal{S}^\sharp = (C^\sharp, \Sigma, \rightarrow^\sharp, I^\sharp, F^\sharp)$ defined as follows. The set of actions Σ is the same as before, i.e., $\Sigma = \{I_1, \ldots, I_n\}$. The set of abstract configurations $C^\sharp$ is the set of pairs (ℓ, s) where $\ell \in [1, n+1]$ is a location and $s \in [1, n+1]^*$ is a stack contents. The sets of initial and final abstract configurations are $I^\sharp = \{(1, \varepsilon)\}$ and $F^\sharp = \{f\} \times [1, n+1]^*$. The labeled abstract transition relation $\rightarrow^\sharp$ is defined by the rules given in Fig. 6. Again, each of these rules implicitly requires that $\ell \in [1, n]$. Obviously, every run in $\mathcal{S}$ can be mimicked in $\mathcal{S}^\sharp$ by ignoring the register and memory contents. Formally, it holds that $(\ell, s) \xrightarrow{w}{}^\sharp (\ell', s')$ in $\mathcal{S}^\sharp$ when $(\ell, R, M, s) \xrightarrow{w} (\ell', R', M', s')$ in $\mathcal{S}$. So we can use $\mathcal{S}^\sharp$ to underestimate the distance in $\mathcal{S}$ between two (sets of) configurations.

For efficiency reasons, our distance underapproximation is based on the pre-computation of the distance in $\mathcal{S}^\sharp$ between pairs of locations $\ell, \ell' \in [1, n+1]$. However, if we start in ℓ with an arbitrary stack contents, then a RET instruction may directly lead to ℓ'. This would yield an extremely coarse distance under-approximation. So we restrict the stack contents to "legitimate" ones, in the sense that the stack starts with a valid return location. Formally, we say that an abstract configuration (ℓ, s) is *coherent* if s is empty or of the form $s = \ell' \cdot s'$ with $\ell' \in [1, n+1]$ such that $(\ell'', \varepsilon) \xrightarrow{*}^\sharp (\ell, \ell')$ for some $\ell'' \in [1, n+1]$. Note that every abstract configuration (ℓ, s) reachable in $\mathcal{S}^\sharp$ from $(1, \varepsilon)$ is coherent. A run in $\mathcal{S}^\sharp$ is called *coherent* when all abstract configurations visited by the run (including the first and last ones) are coherent. We write $(\ell, s) \xrightarrow{w}^\sharp_{\mathrm{co}} (\ell', s')$ when there exists a coherent run from (ℓ, s) to (ℓ', s') with trace w. Let $d^\sharp : [1, n+1] \times [1, n+1] \to \mathbb{N}$ be defined[4] by:

$$d^\sharp(\ell, \ell') \;=\; \inf\{|w| \mid \exists s, s' \in [1, n+1]^* : (\ell, s) \xrightarrow{w}^\sharp_{\mathrm{co}} (\ell', s')\}$$

The distance underapproximation $h_{\mathcal{S}}$ that we propose is defined as follows:

$$h_{\mathcal{S}}(\varphi) \;=\; \inf\{d^\sharp(\ell, f) \mid (\ell, R, M, s) \in \varphi\}$$

Intuitively, $h_{\mathcal{S}}(\varphi)$ is the minimal distance from the locations of φ to f in the abstract semantics $\mathcal{S}^\sharp$ restricted to coherent abstract configurations. It is readily seen that the function $h_{\mathcal{S}}$ satisfies the condition of Definition 1.

Remark 5. Our notion of coherence for abstract configurations only accounts for the top-most return location on the stack. The remainder of the stack may be arbitrary. However, for every coherent run $(\ell, \ell_1 \cdots \ell_k \cdot s) \xrightarrow{*}^\sharp_{\mathrm{co}} (\ell', s)$, the prefix $\ell_1 \cdots \ell_k$ of the stack that is popped in the run is "legitimate" in the sense that each ℓ_i is a valid return location for ℓ_{i-1} (formally, the abstract configurations (ℓ_{i-1}, ℓ_i) are coherent).

To compute $h_{\mathcal{S}}(\varphi)$, we need to compute $d^\sharp(\ell, f)$ for every location ℓ. First, we compute, for each instruction CALL ℓ appearing in the binary program, the ℓ-summary $\inf\{|w| \mid \exists \ell' : (\ell, \varepsilon) \xrightarrow{w}^\sharp (\ell', \varepsilon) \wedge I_{\ell'} = \mathrm{RET}\}$. Second, we compute the values $d^\sharp(\ell, f)$ by applying a single-source shortest path algorithm on $\mathcal{S}^\sharp$ augmented with summaries, starting from f and moving backwards on edges. The resulting algorithm is similar to the one described in [2].

Wrap Up. We now have the necessary ingredients to perform symbolic execution (see Algorithm 1) with our new A*-like exploration strategies. Regions use SMT formulas for register and memory contents, and an explicit representation for locations and stack contents. The post transformer is computed by following the operational semantics given in Fig. 6. The distance underapproximation provided to PrioASTAR and PrioASTAR-2 is the one presented in the previous subsection. Finally, the finite set P of observables given to PrioASTAR-2 is induced by the locations that are targets of control-flow instructions. Let T denote these locations, i.e., T is the set of all $t \in [1, n+1]$ such that there exists $\ell, \ell' \in [1, n]$ and $r \in Reg$ verifying $I_\ell \in \{\mathrm{BR}\ r\ \ell', \mathrm{CALL}\ \ell'\}$ and $t \in \{\ell', \ell+1\}$. Formally, P is the set of all subsets $p_t = \{t\} \times \mathbb{Z}^{Reg} \times \mathbb{Z}^{Addr} \times [1, n+1]^*$ where t ranges over T.

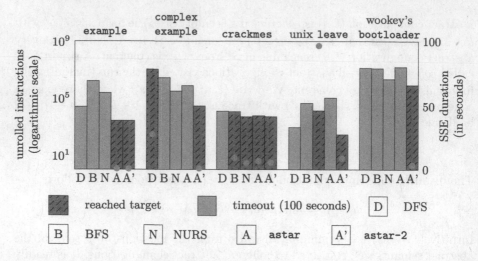

Fig. 7. Experimental results obtained with Binsec: bars represent the number of unrolled instructions in a logarithmic scale and dots represent the SSE duration in seconds.

6   Experimental Results

We evaluate our new approach on seven programs: the two running examples of the paper (Figs. 2 and 4), three "*crackme*" challenges [20–22] which are relatively easy to solve and with a reasonable size (around 200 instructions), and two "real-size" programs namely the Wookey bootloader [1] which is a popular software designed by the ANSSI[5] meant to be robust against various type of attacks (∼10K locations), and the `leave` command of NetBSD (∼100K locations). The programs are cross-compiled to pure THUMB-2 with target CPU *cortex-m3* and *armv7-m* architectures.

We use the symbolic execution tool Binsec (version 0.6), in which we have implemented our new strategies. The targets for the study are chosen arbitrarily but meant to be deep in the execution flow or difficult to reach. A time limit of 100 s is allowed for each experiment, beyond which we stop it and report a timeout (*t.o.*). In the Wookey bootloader and the `leave` programs, we have stubbed some parts of the code to accelerate the process. All benchmarks were ran on a AMD64 Oracle Linux Server (release 8.8) machine with an Intel(R) Xeon(R) Gold 6244 CPU (3.60 GHz) and with 256GiB of RAM. A replication package for our experiments (including the source code and the seven programs) is available at Zenodo [10].

We compare the approach based on `PrioASTAR-2` (named `astar-2` in the benchmarks) with the usual exploration strategies (`dfs`, `bfs` and `nurs`), and also

---

[4] Recall that inf X = min X for every non-empty subset $X \subseteq \mathbb{N}$ and that inf $\emptyset = +\infty$.
[5] French National Cybersecurity Agency.

with our basic A*-like approach, i.e., based on `PrioASTAR` (named `astar` in the benchmarks). In Fig. 7, we compare the number of unrolled instructions and the symbolic execution time for each exploration strategy on the different programs. The results of the three crackmes are summed up and displayed as one "program" named `crackmes`. In the case of NURS, the experiments are ran 10 times and the average for both metrics are displayed. The exploration strategies are on the X-axis, the number of unrolled instructions is on the left Y-axis and represented by the bars. Finally, the symbolic execution time is on the right Y-axis and displayed by green dots. For readability reasons, we use a logarithmic scale for the number of unrolled instructions. Clearly, our new exploration strategy `astar-2` always outperforms the classical strategies. Moreover, it also always outperforms the strategy solely based on `astar`, as expected. The `astar` exploration strategy is generally not powerful enough to reach the target on real programs (`leave`, Wookey's bootloader). Regarding the duration of the symbolic execution, the strategy `astar-2` also always outperforms the other strategies. Note that the number of unrolled instructions is not directly correlated to the execution time of symbolic execution. In fact, what really slows it down are satisfiability queries, which are made at conditional branching points.

The efficiency of the exploration depends on the maximum exploration depth. The perfect bound is not definable beforehand so we set it to 10^7 instructions for all programs. Finally, the results of our exploration strategy `astar-2` depend on the function λ (see Sect. 4). The best λ function is specific to each situation, nevertheless we chose to systematically use λ_θ with $\theta = 3$ in our experiments. Using a smaller parameter θ tends to steer the exploration towards a BFS, while a larger parameter θ steers the exploration towards a DFS. The best in-between value we found was $\theta = 3$.

7   Conclusion

In this paper, we have introduced a novel exploration strategy for symbolic execution inspired from the A* algorithm permitting to find efficiently an executable path to a target instruction. This approach orders the exploration of symbolic states by using heuristics permitting to visit in priority states that have been less explored. Consequently the number of paths to explore is smaller than in usual approaches such as DFS, BFS and NURS, implying better performance. Although some faulty execution may still remain difficult to catch, this approach shows promising results. Our key insight while designing this algorithm is to create a balanced mix between a DFS and a BFS. The strategy has been designed on generic transition systems, making it applicable in various situations. We have described how to apply it on binary code, and provided an experimental evaluation showing that our strategy outperforms the classical exploration strategies DFS, BFS and NURS and scales well on real-size programs. As future work, we intend to apply this technique to the detection of hardware vulnerabilities (i.e., vulnerabilities to fault injection attacks).

Acknowledgements. This work was supported by the French ANRT CIFRE 2021/1673 Project. We also would like to thank Guillaume Baud-Berthier, Julien Bernet and Michael Grand for their helpful discussions.

References

1. ANSSI: Wookey (2018). https://wookey-project.github.io/
2. Babić, D., Martignoni, L., McCamant, S., Song, D.: Statically-directed dynamic automated test generation. In: Proceedings of the 2011 International Symposium on Software Testing and Analysis, pp. 12–22 (2011)
3. Biere, A., Cimatti, A., Clarke, E.M., Strichman, O., Zhu, Y.: Bounded model checking. Handbook of satisfiability **185**(99), 457–481 (2009)
4. Blondin, M., Haase, C., Offtermatt, P.: Directed reachability for infinite-state systems. In: TACAS 2021. LNCS, vol. 12652, pp. 3–23. Springer, Cham (2021). https://doi.org/10.1007/978-3-030-72013-1_1
5. Cadar, C., Dunbar, D., Engler, D.R., et al.: Klee: unassisted and automatic generation of high-coverage tests for complex systems programs. In: OSDI, vol. 8, pp. 209–224 (2008)
6. Chess, B., McGraw, G.: Static analysis for security. IEEE Secur. Privacy **2**(6), 76–79 (2004)
7. Clarke Jr, E.M., Grumberg, O., Kroening, D., Peled, D., Veith, H.: Model checking. MIT press (2018)
8. Cousot, P.: Abstract interpretation. ACM Comput. Surv. (CSUR) **28**(2), 324–328 (1996)
9. David, R., et al.: Binsec/se: a dynamic symbolic execution toolkit for binary-level analysis. In: 2016 IEEE 23rd International Conference on Software Analysis, Evolution, and Reengineering (SANER), vol. 1, pp. 653–656. IEEE (2016)
10. De Castro Pinto, T., Rollet, A., Sutre, G., Tobor, I.: Replication package for "Guiding Symbolic Execution with A-star" (2023). DOI: https://doi.org/10.5281/zenodo.8169445
11. Djoudi, A., Bardin, S.: BINSEC: binary code analysis with low-level regions. In: Baier, C., Tinelli, C. (eds.) TACAS 2015. LNCS, vol. 9035, pp. 212–217. Springer, Heidelberg (2015). https://doi.org/10.1007/978-3-662-46681-0_17
12. Ducousso, S., Bardin, S., Potet, M.L.: Adversarial reachability for program-level security analysis. In: Programming Languages and Systems. LNCS, p. 59. (2023). https://doi.org/10.1007/978-3-031-30044-8_3
13. Hart, P.E., Nilsson, N.J., Raphael, B.: A formal basis for the heuristic determination of minimum cost paths. IEEE Trans. Syst. Sci. Cybern. **4**(2), 100–107 (1968)
14. King, J.C.: Symbolic execution and program testing. Commun. ACM **19**(7), 385–394 (1976)
15. Kirchner, F., Kosmatov, N., Prevosto, V., Signoles, J., Yakobowski, B.: Frama-c: a software analysis perspective. Formal Aspects Comput. **27**(3), 573–609 (2015)
16. Li, J., Zhao, B., Zhang, C.: Fuzzing: a survey. Cybersecurity **1**(1), 1–13 (2018)
17. Li, Y., Su, Z., Wang, L., Li, X.: Steering symbolic execution to less traveled paths. ACM SigPlan Notices **48**(10), 19–32 (2013)
18. Ma, K.-K., Yit Phang, K., Foster, J.S., Hicks, M.: Directed symbolic execution. In: Yahav, E. (ed.) SAS 2011. LNCS, vol. 6887, pp. 95–111. Springer, Heidelberg (2011). https://doi.org/10.1007/978-3-642-23702-7_11
19. MIASM: Cea-sec (2015). https://github.com/cea-sec/miasm

20. NoraCodes: crackmes (2017). https://github.com/NoraCodes/crackmes/blob/master/crackme03.c
21. NoraCodes: crackmes (2017). https://github.com/NoraCodes/crackmes/blob/master/crackme05.c
22. NoraCodes: crackmes (2017). https://github.com/NoraCodes/crackmes/blob/master/crackme09.c
23. Potet, M.L., Mounier, L., Puys, M., Dureuil, L.: Lazart: a symbolic approach for evaluation the robustness of secured codes against control flow injections. In: 2014 IEEE Seventh International Conference on Software Testing, Verification and Validation, pp. 213–222. IEEE (2014)
24. Shoshitaishvili, Y., et al.: SoK: (State of) the art of war: offensive techniques in binary analysis. In: IEEE Symposium on Security and Privacy (2016)
25. Stephens, N., et al.: Driller: augmenting fuzzing through selective symbolic execution. In: NDSS, vol. 16, pp. 1–16 (2016)
26. Xie, T., Tillmann, N., De Halleux, J., Schulte, W.: Fitness-guided path exploration in dynamic symbolic execution. In: 2009 IEEE/IFIP International Conference on Dependable Systems & Networks, pp. 359–368. IEEE (2009)

Robustness Testing of Software Verifiers

Florian Dyck, Cedric Richter$^{(\boxtimes)}$ ⓘ, and Heike Wehrheim ⓘ

University of Oldenburg, Department of Computing Science, Oldenburg, Germany
{florian.dyck,cedric.richter,heike.wehrheim}@uol.de

Abstract. Software verification tools fully automatically prove the correctness of verification tasks (i.e., programs with correctness specifications). With their increasing application on safety-critical software, the quality of such tools becomes of prime importance. This quality is typically assessed via *experimental evaluation*. In this paper, we present a novel approach for *robustness* testing of software verifiers. We consider tools to be robust if their output (for a given input task) does not change under small perturbations of the input. The core idea of our technique is to start with tasks of publicly available benchmarks and systematically apply small program transformations on them which *preserve* program semantics. As a consequence, the ground truth known from the benchmark (i.e., the correct outcome used as an *oracle* during testing) carries over to all of its perturbed versions. We experimentally evaluate robustness testing on three state-of-the-art software verifiers. To this end, we perturbate 778 tasks from the annual Competition on Software Verification via 8 transformations. Our evaluation shows that all three verifiers are non-robust, however, to different extents.

Keywords: Software Verification · Robustness · Testing

1 Introduction

The past years have seen enormous progress in software verification, partially due to novel approaches being developed and partially due to optimizations of existing techniques. Annual challenges (e.g., the RERS challenge [20]) as well as competitions (e.g., the Competition on Software Verification SV-COMP [1]) fuel novel developments. As automatic verification is also increasingly applied to industrial software, the quality of software verification tools (short: verifiers) is of prime importance. In competitions, verifiers are assessed on common benchmark sets. A benchmark case in such a set, a *verification task*, is typically a program (in some programming language) together with a specification of a property. In addition, benchmarks often contain information on the expected correct output, the *ground truth*, true or false, stating whether the property does or does not hold for the program. This assessment via benchmarks is the main form of quality assurance for software verifiers.

Partially funded by German Research Council DFG under grant number 418257054.

C. Ferreira and T. A. C. Willemse (Eds.): SEFM 2023, LNCS 14323, pp. 66–84, 2023.
https://doi.org/10.1007/978-3-031-47115-5_5

```
int main() {         int main(){          void function(int *i){
 int i = 0;           int i = 0;            while(*i < 5 &
 while (i < 5)        while (i < 5)              nondet())
     i++;                 while(i < 5 &            (*i)++;}
 if (i < 5)                   nondet())      int main(){
     error();             i++;               int i = 0;
 return 0; }          if (i < 5)             while(i < 5)
                          error();               function(&i);
                      return 0; }            if(i < 5) error();
                                             return 0; }
```

Fig. 1. Example program (left) and two versions obtained by transformation

In this paper, we propose an approach for *robustness testing* of software verifiers (for the C programming language). In general, robustness testing checks whether a system under test (SUT) – in our case a software verifier – is sensitive to small perturbations of the input – in our case a verification task. The small perturbations should be inconsequential, i.e. they should not change programs behavior or the expected verification outcome of a given verification task.

In particular, we would expect software verifiers to be robust under perturbations which *preserve program semantics*. Consequently, our robustness testing employs simple semantics-preserving program transformations and checks whether a software verifier computes the same results for a verification task and its transformed version. Conceptually, our testing approach is thus an instance of *metamorphic testing* [11] in which the SUT is supplied with a pair of inputs related by some metamorphic relation R_1 and the tester checks whether the corresponding outputs are related via a relation R_2. In our setting, relation R_1 is semantic equality and R_2 simply the identity. As R_2 is the identity (the same output should be computed for a verification task and its transformed version), the ground truth for a verification task stored in public benchmarks carries over to the transformed version and can also be used as an oracle during testing. This ultimately allows us to not only check the robustness of a verifier, but also provides us with further benchmarks for assessing its overall quality.

Example. As a first example, consider the program on the left of Fig. 1. The program represents a simple verification task. The software verifier has to prove that the function call `error` is not reachable, i.e., there does not exist an execution leading to the function call. The expected outcome for the task is true. Our robustness testing would now for instance apply the semantics preserving transformation loop deepening (giving the program in the middle) and further function encapsulation (giving the program on the right). Our testing approach then checks whether a software verifier computes the same outcome for the transformed versions and the original version.

Contributions. In this paper, we introduce a number of such transformations and employ them to systematically evaluate the robustness of three state-of-

68   F. Dyck et al.

$$v \in \mathcal{V} ::= z \in \mathbb{Z} \mid \mathbf{nondet}()$$
$$C \in \mathcal{C} ::= x := A \mid \mathbf{call}\ p \mid \mathbf{skip} \mid \mathrm{error} \mid$$
$$\quad \mathbf{if}\ B\ \mathbf{then}\ C_1\ \mathbf{else}\ C_2\ \mathbf{fi} \mid$$
$$\quad \mathbf{while}\ B\ \mathbf{do}\ C\ \mathbf{od} \mid C_1\ ;\ C_2$$
$$P \in \mathcal{P} ::= \mathbf{proc}\ p\ \mathbf{is}\ C\ \mathbf{end} \mid P_1\ ;\ P_2 \mid P\ ;\ C$$

$$B \in BExpr ::= v \mid x \in \mathcal{X} \mid \neg B \mid$$
$$B_1 \wedge B_2 \mid B_1 \vee B_2$$
$$A \in AExpr ::= v \mid x \in \mathcal{X} \mid \ominus A \mid$$
$$A_1 \oplus A_2$$
$$p \in PId$$

Fig. 2. Program syntax ($\mathcal{X}$ program variables, PId procedure identifiers)

the-art software verifiers. In summary, we make the following contributions on robustness testing of software verifiers.

- We propose several semantics-preserving transformations that concern the introduction of loops, branches, recursion and functions as well as new types of variables (pointers, arrays, structs).
- We provide a formalization of our notion of semantics preservation and prove eight of our transformations to be sound.
- We evaluate the effectiveness of robustness testing on three state-of-the-art software verifiers (and – to see the effect on specific verification algorithms – three additional specific configurations of one verifier). To this end, we have taken 778 verification tasks from the SV-COMP benchmark set and have transformed it via 8 transformations.
- Our evaluation shows that both verification tools and verification algorithms are not robust against semantic-preserving transformations. The degree of robustness highly depends on the type of the employed verifier.

The implementation of all semantic-preserving transformations introduced in this work are publicly available on Github[1] and can easily be adopted for testing of software verifiers. All experimental data and our open-source implementation are also archived and available in our supplementary artifact [17].

2 Background

We start by shortly introducing the syntax and semantics of programs[2] and formalizing the task of software verification.

Program Syntax and Semantics. To ease representation, we consider a simple programming language (see Fig. 2). We assume a set of program variables $\mathcal{X}$ and identifiers for procedures PId. Program values $v \in \mathcal{V}$ can only be numerical constants or random values returned by a function **nondet**. Booleans $B \in BExpr$ are also represented by numerical values (**0** for false and $v \neq \mathbf{0}$ for true) and can be negated and logically connected. Furthermore, values can be modified through

---

[1] https://github.com/FlorianDyck/semtransforms.
[2] For our formalization, we employ an artifical programming language; our implementation transforms C programs.

$$(\text{skip})\frac{}{(\textbf{skip},\phi)\xrightarrow{\tau}\phi}$$

$$(\text{assign})\frac{[\![A]\!]_\phi\ni v,\quad \alpha=(x:=A)}{(x:=A,\phi)\xrightarrow{\alpha}\phi[x\mapsto v]}$$

$$(\text{if1})\frac{[\![B]\!]_\phi\ni v, v\neq 0}{(\textbf{if } B \textbf{ then } C_1 \textbf{ else } C_2 \textbf{ fi},\phi)\xrightarrow{\tau}(C_1,\phi)}$$

$$(\text{if2})\frac{[\![B]\!]_\phi\ni 0}{(\textbf{if } B \textbf{ then } C_1 \textbf{ else } C_2 \textbf{ fi},\phi)\xrightarrow{\tau}(C_2,\phi)}$$

$$(\text{while1})\frac{[\![B]\!]_\phi\ni v, v\neq 0}{(\textbf{while } B \textbf{ do } C \textbf{ od },\phi)\xrightarrow{\tau}(C;\textbf{while } B \textbf{ do } C \textbf{ od },\phi)}$$

$$(\text{while2})\frac{[\![B]\!]_\phi\ni 0}{(\textbf{while } B \textbf{ do } C \textbf{ od },\phi)\xrightarrow{\tau}\phi}$$

$$(\text{seq1})\frac{(C_1,\phi)\xrightarrow{\alpha}(C_1',\phi')}{(C_1;C_2,\phi)\xrightarrow{\alpha}(C_1';C_2,\phi')}$$

$$(\text{seq2})\frac{(C_1,\phi)\xrightarrow{\alpha}\phi'}{(C_1;C_2,\phi)\xrightarrow{\alpha}(C_2,\phi')}$$

$$(\text{pdef})\frac{p\in\mathcal{P}Var}{(\textbf{proc } p \textbf{ is } C \textbf{ end },\phi)\xrightarrow{\tau}\phi[p\mapsto C]}$$

$$(\text{call})\frac{\phi[p]=C}{(\textbf{call } p,\phi)\xrightarrow{\tau}(C,\phi)}$$

$$(\text{pseq1})\frac{(P_1,\phi)\xrightarrow{\alpha}\phi'}{(P_1;P_2,\phi)\xrightarrow{\alpha}(P_2,\phi')}$$

$$(\text{pseq2})\frac{(P,\phi)\xrightarrow{\alpha}\phi'}{(P;C,\phi)\xrightarrow{\alpha}(C,\phi')}$$

$$(\text{err1})\frac{}{(\textbf{error},\phi)\xrightarrow{err}\phi_{\textbf{error}}}$$

$$(\text{err2})\frac{}{(\textbf{error};C_2,\phi)\xrightarrow{err}\phi_{\textbf{error}}}$$

Fig. 3. Operational semantics of programs

common unary and binary operators. Statements $C\in\mathcal{C}$ consists of assignments, branches, while loops, sequences and an error statement[3]. Altogether, a program $P\in\mathcal{P}$ consists of procedure definitions followed by statements.

The semantics of a program is defined by a state transition system consisting of an initial state (P,ϕ) and a transition relation $\rightarrow\ \subseteq(\mathcal{P}\times\Phi)\times Act\times(\mathcal{P}\times\Phi)$. In this, a program *state* is a tuple (P,ϕ) of the current program $P\in\mathcal{P}$ and a mapping $\phi:\mathcal{X}\cup PId\rightarrow\mathbb{Z}\cup\mathcal{C}^4$, $\mathcal{P}\times\Phi$ is the set of all such states and $Act:=\{err,\tau\}\cup\{x:=A\mid x\in\mathcal{X},A\in AExpr\}$ is the set of actions. An *execution trace* of a program P_1 and an initial mapping ϕ_1 is a (potentially infinite) sequence of program states $(P_1,\phi_1)\xrightarrow{\alpha_1}(P_2,\phi_2)\xrightarrow{\alpha_2}\ldots\xrightarrow{\alpha_{n-1}}(P_n,\phi_n)\xrightarrow{\alpha_n}\ldots$ such that $(P_i,\phi_i)\xrightarrow{\alpha_i}(P_{i+1},\phi_{i+1})$. If an execution trace ends, we denote this by eliding the current program and just giving the final mapping ϕ^*. The transition relation $\rightarrow$ is defined by the operational semantics shown in Fig. 3. Therein, $[\![\cdot]\!]_\phi:AExpr\cup BExpr\rightarrow 2^{\mathbb{Z}}$ defines the set of interpretations of a given expression with respect to ϕ. Programs are allowed to be non-deterministic represented by calling a random function **nondet**, i.e., $[\![\textbf{nondet}()]\!]_\phi=\mathbb{Z}$. Furthermore, we define the evaluation of the other operators as $[\![z]\!]_\phi=\{z\}$ for all $z\in\mathbb{Z}$, $[\![x]\!]_\phi=\{\phi(x)\}$ for $x\in\mathcal{X}$, $[\![\ominus A]\!]_\phi=\{\ominus z\mid z\in[\![A]\!]_\phi\}$ and $[\![A_1\oplus A_2]\!]_\phi=\{z_1\oplus z_2\mid z_1\in[\![A_1]\!]_\phi,z_2\in[\![A_2]\!]_\phi\}$. We let the set of all execution traces with initial state (P,ϕ) be $traces(P,\phi)$ and its *execution results* be $exec(P,\phi):=\{\phi^*\mid(P,\phi)\rightarrow^*\phi^*\}$. Execution results can also be restricted to subsets of variables $X\subseteq\mathcal{X}$ with $\phi_{|X}:=\{x\mapsto\phi(x)\mid x\in X\}$ and $exec_{|X}(P,\phi):=\{\phi_{|X}\mid\phi\in exec(P,\phi)\}$. Finally, the function computed by a program P for a given mapping ϕ can be represented by $f_P(\phi)=exec(P,\phi)$ which can be restricted to $f_{P|X}(\phi)=exec_{|X}(P,\phi)$.

Weak Bisimilarity of Program States. The transformations which we employ for robustness testing preserve the semantics of programs. We will prove

---

[3] In Fig. 1 we used an error-function to make it proper C syntax.

[4] To simplify the notation, the mapping ϕ stores both assignments to variables and procedure definitions.

such preservations by showing weak bisimilarity [24] between program's transition systems. Two program states (P_1, ϕ_1) and (P_2, ϕ_2) are *weak bisimilar* if they share the same *observable* behavior with respect to their state transition systems. For observability, we fix a set of program variables $X \subseteq \mathcal{X}$ that we are interested in for the particular transformation. Formally, for a given X we define any behavior as X-*observable* that changes the observable state ϕ of X (plus the error transition), i.e. any transition $\alpha \in \text{Act}_X := \{err\} \cup \{x := A \mid x \in X, A \in AExpr\}$. We consider any changes to procedure definitions and variables not defined in X as non-observable. Based on this, a relation $\mathcal{R} \subseteq (\mathcal{P} \times \Phi) \times (\mathcal{P} \times \Phi)$ is a *weak X-bisimulation*, $X \subseteq \mathcal{X}$, if the following holds for all $((P_1, \phi_1), (P_2, \phi_2)) \in \mathcal{R}$ and all $\alpha \in \text{Act}_X \cup \{\tau\}$:

1. $(P_1, \phi_1) \xrightarrow{\alpha} (P_1', \phi_1')$ implies
   $\exists (P_2', \phi_2') : (P_2, \phi_2) \xRightarrow{\alpha} (P_2', \phi_2')$ and $((P_1', \phi_1'), (P_2', \phi_2')) \in \mathcal{R}$,
2. $(P_2, \phi_2) \xrightarrow{\alpha} (P_2', \phi_2')$ implies
   $\exists (P_1', \phi_1') : (P_1, \phi_1) \xRightarrow{\alpha} (P_1', \phi_1')$ and $((P_1', \phi_1'), (P_2', \phi_2')) \in \mathcal{R}$.

where $\xRightarrow{\alpha} := \xrightarrow{\tau^* \alpha \tau^*}$ if $\alpha \in \text{Act}_X$ and $\xRightarrow{\alpha} := \xrightarrow{\tau^*}$ otherwise. Two states (P_1, ϕ_1) and (P_2, ϕ_2) are weak X-bisimilar $((P_1, \phi_1) \approx_X (P_2, \phi_2))$ if there exists a weak X-bisimulation $\mathcal{R}$ with $((P_1, \phi_1), (P_2, \phi_2)) \in \mathcal{R}$. Note that any two weak X-bisimilar states $(P_1, \phi_1) \approx_X (P_2, \phi_2)$ share the same observable behavior [15], i.e. $Obs_X(P_1, \phi_1) = Obs_X(P_2, \phi_2)$ where $Obs_X(P, \phi) := \{\alpha_1 \alpha_2 \cdots \alpha_n \in \text{Act}_X^* \mid (P, \phi) \xRightarrow{\alpha_1} (P_1, \phi_1) \xRightarrow{\alpha_2} \ldots \xRightarrow{\alpha_n} \phi_n \in traces(P, \phi)\}$.

Program Verification. The goal of program verification is to show that a program $P \in \mathcal{P}$ is safe with respect to some property φ (e.g., that a program is memory safe, terminates or avoids error statements). A program verifier (or software verifier) is a tool that proves or disproves that P satisfies φ. In the context of this work, we view program verifiers as functions $V_\varphi : \mathcal{P} \to \{\text{true}, \text{false}, \text{unk}\}$ which decide whether the property is satisfied ($V_\varphi(P) = \text{true}$), unsatisfied ($V_\varphi(P) = \text{false}$) or it fails to make a decision ($V_\varphi(P) = \text{unk}$). The *ground truth* $\mathbf{gt} \in \{\text{true}, \text{false}\}$ of a verification task (P, φ) defines whether P *truly* satisfies the property φ. Therefore, a verifier is said to be *correct* for a given verification task (P, φ) if the output of the verifier matches the ground truth $\mathbf{gt}$ (i.e. $V_\varphi(P) = \mathbf{gt}$). Finally, we will evaluate a verifier on verification benchmarks which are sets of verification tasks $(P, \varphi, \mathbf{gt})$ with a known ground truth.

The Unreachability Property. Here, we consider verification tasks with the unreachability property. We assume that safety properties are encoded in the program (e.g., as assertions) and the program verifier has to prove that error locations are unreachable. Formally, an error location inside a program P is unreachable iff there does not exist a state (P, ϕ) with

$$(P, \phi) \xrightarrow{\alpha_1} (P_1, \phi_1) \xrightarrow{\alpha_2} \ldots \xrightarrow{\alpha_n} \phi_{\text{error}},$$

or alternatively the error state is not contained in the execution result (i.e., $\forall \phi : \phi_{\text{error}} \notin exec(P, \phi)$). In this work, we specifically focus on unreachability verifiers which simplifies the notation: unreachability verifiers $V_{\text{unreach}} : \mathcal{P} \to \{true, false, unk\}$ are verifiers that are specialized to prove the unreachability property and unreachability benchmarks are sets of verification tasks $(P, \mathbf{gt})$.

3 Robustness Testing for Software Verification

Our goal is to evaluate the robustness of unreachability verifiers with respect to simple semantics-preserving program transformations. In the following, we start by defining robustness of verifiers in general and then show how the robustness of unreachability verifiers can be tested via semantics-preserving transformations.

3.1 Robustness of Software Verifiers

We start by defining the robustness of software verifiers with respect to some program transformation:

Definition 1. *A verifier* $V_\varphi : \mathcal{P} \to \{true, false, unk\}$ *is robust* with respect to a *program transformation* $\gamma : \mathcal{P} \to \mathcal{P}$ *iff:*

$$\forall P \in \mathcal{P} : \mathbf{gt}_P = \mathbf{gt}_{\gamma(P)} \Rightarrow V_\varphi(P) = V_\varphi(\gamma(P)),$$

where $\mathbf{gt}_P$ *and* $\mathbf{gt}_{\gamma(P)}$ *are the ground truths for the verification tasks* $(P, \varphi, \mathbf{gt}_P)$ *and* $(\gamma(P), \varphi, \mathbf{gt}_{\gamma(P)})$ *respectively.*

A verifier is said to be *non-robust* if there exists a program transformation $\gamma : \mathcal{P} \to \mathcal{P}$ such that the verifier is not robust with respect to γ.

Testing Robustness. Calculating the robustness of a verifier is highly challenging in practice as the verifier would have to be evaluated on all possible verification tasks and with all possible program transformations. Therefore, a common approach is to *test* for robustness. Here, the goal is to check whether there exists a verification task P and a transformation γ for which the verifier is non-robust:

$$\exists P \in \mathcal{P} : \mathbf{gt}_P = \mathbf{gt}_{\gamma(P)} \Rightarrow V_\varphi(P) \neq V_\varphi(\gamma(P)) .$$

In practice, this is often done by taking a set $S \subseteq \mathcal{P}$ of *seed* programs and checking whether the verifier is non-robust for any seed $s \in S$ and any transformation $\gamma : \mathcal{P} \to \mathcal{P}$ of a defined set of transformations. If a verifier is not robust for any of the seed programs and their transformed variants, then the verifier can be decided to be non-robust. Note however that checking whether the ground truth is preserved after the transformation is non-trivial. Therefore, in practice, property preserving program transformations are often employed, i.e., $\mathbf{gt}_P = \mathbf{gt}_{\gamma(P)}$ is guaranteed by design of γ.

3.2   Semantics-Preservation

To effectively test the robustness of software verifiers, we employ *semantics-preserving* transformations of programs. In the following, we will formally introduce semantics-preserving transformations and then show that they also preserve the ground truth for verification tasks with the unreachability property.

Semantics-Preserving Transformations. To begin with, we define two programs P_1 and P_2 as *semantically equivalent* if they compute the same function. Therefore, a program transformation is semantics-preserving if the resulting program is semantically equivalent to the original program. Formally, we can define a semantics-preserving program transformation as follows:

Definition 2. *A program transformation* $\gamma : \mathcal{P} \to \mathcal{P}$ *is* semantics-preserving *with respect to some $X \subseteq \mathcal{X}$ if for any program state (P, ϕ) the following holds:*

$$f_{P|X}(\phi) = f_{\gamma(P)|X}(\phi)$$

In other words, the programs P and $\gamma(P)$ compute the same function for all *result* variables $x \in X$. Here, the error state $\phi_{\mathbf{error}}$ is independent of X, i.e. $\phi_{\mathbf{error}|X} := \phi_{\mathbf{error}}$. Therefore, it is easy to show that any semantics-preserving program transformation also preserves the unreachability of error-statements:

Lemma 1. *Any semantics-preserving program transformation* $\gamma : \mathcal{P} \to \mathcal{P}$ *preserves the ground truth for unreachability tasks, i.e.*

$$\phi_{\mathbf{error}} \in f_{P|X}(\phi) \Leftrightarrow \phi_{\mathbf{error}} \in f_{\gamma(P)|X}(\phi)$$

Note that this is a direct consequence of Definition 2. Because semantics-preservation is more strict than unreachability-preservation for any $X \neq \emptyset$, it is often easier to show that a transformation is semantics-preserving for certain $X \subseteq \mathcal{X}$ than showing unreachability-preservation. In fact, in the remaining paper, we assume that the set of variables can be split into two distinct sets $\mathcal{X} = \mathcal{X}_{\mathcal{P}} \cup \mathcal{X}_{\Gamma}$ where $\mathcal{X}_{\mathcal{P}}$ is the set of variables modified in programs and $\mathcal{X}_{\Gamma}$ is a unique set of variables that can only be introduced by program transformations. Further, we assume that the introduced variables $x \in \mathcal{X}_{\Gamma}$ can never be shared between two transformations. In other words, we assume that $Var(\gamma_1(P_1)) \cap Var(\gamma_2(P_2)) \subseteq \mathcal{X}_{\mathcal{P}}$ for any two transformations γ_1, γ_2 and two programs P_1, P_2 where $Var : \mathcal{P} \to 2^{\mathcal{X}}$ gives the set of variables used in the program.

In the following, we introduce several program transformations that are semantics-preserving with respect to $\mathcal{X}_{\mathcal{P}}$ if not stated otherwise. For showing that they are semantics-preserving, we employ the following two lemmas:

Lemma 2. *Any program transformation* $\gamma : \mathcal{P} \to \mathcal{P}$ *is semantics-preserving with respect to $X \subseteq \mathcal{X}$ if all program states (P, ϕ) are weakly bisimilar to the transformed variant $(\gamma(P), \phi)$, i.e., $(P, \phi) \approx_X (\gamma(P), \phi)$.*

Proof: Assume that $(P, \phi) \approx_X (\gamma(P), \phi)$ is weakly bisimilar but the function $\gamma : \mathcal{P} \to \mathcal{P}$ is not semantics-preserving for $P \in \mathcal{P}$. Then, there either exists

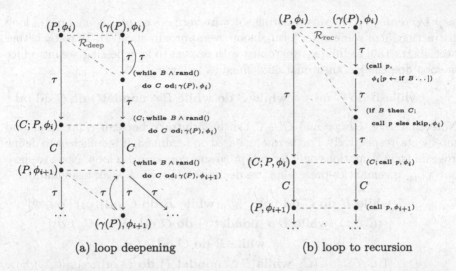

(a) loop deepening   (b) loop to recursion

Fig. 4. Weak bisimulation for loop deepening and loop to recursion (dashed lines represent the relation, early aborts of the while loop are not depicted)

$\phi^* \in f_P(\phi)$ such that there is no $\phi^\gamma \in f_{\gamma(P)}(\phi)$ with $\phi^*_{|X} = \phi^\gamma_{|X}$ or vice versa. W.l.o.g. we assume $\phi^* \in f_P(\phi)$ and $\phi^\gamma \notin f_{\gamma(P)}(\phi)$. Since $\phi^* \in f_P(\phi)$ there exists at least one observable trace $(P, \phi) \xrightarrow{\alpha_1} \dots \xrightarrow{\alpha_n} \phi'$ with $\phi'_{|X} = \phi^*_{|X}$. Since $(P, \phi) \approx_X (\gamma(P), \phi)$, there has to exist an observable trace $(\gamma(P), \phi) \xRightarrow{\alpha_1} \dots \xRightarrow{\alpha_n} \phi^\gamma$ with $\phi^\gamma_{|X} = \phi'_{|X} = \phi^*_{|X}$ and $\phi^\gamma \in f_{\gamma(P)}(\phi)$. Contradiction.

Lemma 3. *Any program transformation* $\gamma : \mathcal{P} \to \mathcal{P}$ *that transforms a part of a program P with a semantics-preserving transformation is also semantics-preserving with respect to $\mathcal{X}_\mathcal{P}$. In particular, the following program transformations are semantics-preserving:*

- *the identity* $id(P) := P$ *and* $\gamma_{seq}(C_1; C_2) := \gamma_1(C_1); \gamma_2(C_2)$,
- $\gamma_{branch}(\textbf{if } B \textbf{ then } C_1 \textbf{ else } C_2 \textbf{ fi}) :=$ **if** B **then** $\gamma_1(C_1)$ **else** $\gamma_2(C_2)$ **fi**,
- $\gamma_{loop}(\textbf{while } B \textbf{ do } C \textbf{ od}) :=$ **while** B **do** $\gamma_1(C)$ **od**,
- $\gamma_{proc}(\textbf{proc } p \textbf{ is } C \textbf{ end}) :=$ **proc** p **is** $\gamma_1(C)$ **end**,

where γ_1, γ_2 *are semantics-preserving transformations with respect to* $\mathcal{X}_\mathcal{P}$.

Due to lack of space we do not prove Lemma 3 here.

3.3   Transformations

In the following, we introduce eight different semantics-preserving transformations. Due to lack of space, we do not provide fully formal correctness proofs, but partly give and explain the weak bisimulation relations employed in proofs.

Control Flow Transformations. Three of our transformations alter the control flow of the program.

Loop Deepening (C1). Most existing software verifiers employ some type of loop abstraction [5] or some other form of loop overapproximation [7]. To test whether these abstraction techniques are robust with respect to loop nesting, we introduce the loop deepening transformation defined as follows:

$$\gamma_{deep}(\textbf{while } B \textbf{ do } C \textbf{ od}) := \textbf{while } B \textbf{ do while } B \wedge \textbf{nondet}() \textbf{ do } C \textbf{ od od}$$

Note that $B \in BExpr$ and $C \in \mathcal{C}$ can be arbitrary boolean expressions and statements, respectively. Furthermore, based on Lemma 3, it is sufficient to define program transformations only for sub-programs containing a loop. Now, to show that γ_{deep} is semantics-preserving, we define the following weak bisimulation:

$$\mathcal{R}_{deep} := \{((\textbf{while } B \textbf{ do } C \textbf{ od }, \phi), (\gamma_{\text{deep}}(\textbf{while } B \textbf{ do } C \textbf{ od}), \phi)) \mid \phi \in \Phi\}$$
$$\cup \{((C_w, \phi), (\textbf{while } B \wedge \textbf{ nondet }() \textbf{ do } C \textbf{ od }; \gamma_{\text{deep}}(C_w), \phi))$$
$$\mid \phi \in \Phi, C_w = \textbf{ while } B \textbf{ do } C \textbf{ od}\}$$
$$\cup \{((C; C_w, \phi), (C; \textbf{ while } B \wedge \textbf{ nondet }() \textbf{ do } C \textbf{ od }; \gamma_{\text{deep}}(C_w), \phi))$$
$$\mid \phi \in \Phi, C_w = \textbf{ while } B \textbf{ do } C \textbf{ od}\}$$
$$\cup \{((P, \phi), (P, \phi)) \mid P \in \mathcal{P}, \phi \in \Phi\} \cup \{(\phi, \phi) \mid \phi \in \Phi\}$$

We also depict the relation $\mathcal{R}_{\text{deep}}$ in Fig. 4a. Note that, since evaluating the loop condition has no effect on the variables, C is the only statement or sequence of statements that can modify the variables in ϕ. In addition, if the loop ever terminates (i.e. $[\![B]\!]_\phi = 0$), C either has to contain a modifying statement or the loop body will never execute. If the loop body is never executed, both the original program P and the transformed program $\gamma_{deep}(P)$ will end in the same state ϕ $((\phi, \phi) \in \mathcal{R}_{deep})$. Therefore, we focus in the following on the case that the loop body is executed at least once. To preserve weak bisimilarity over $\mathcal{X}_\mathcal{P}$, we hence have to guarantee that if C can be executed in P then C can also be executed in $\gamma_{deep}(P)$ and vice versa. In Fig. 4a, we can observe that this is possible for the program transformation γ_{deep}. The main difference is the τ loops that weak bisimulations abstract from. Since $\mathcal{R}_{deep}$ is a weak bisimulation and $((\textbf{while } B \textbf{ do } C \textbf{ od}, \phi), (\gamma_{\text{deep}}(\textbf{while } B \textbf{ do } C \textbf{ od}), \phi)) \in \mathcal{R}_{\text{deep}}$, we know that the program transformation γ_{deep} is semantics-preserving.

IF-encapsulation (C2). The branching width of a program can determine the complexity of a verification task. Therefore, we are interested in testing whether modern software verifiers are robust against increasing the branching width. For this, we introduce the if-encapsulation transformation:

$$\gamma_{\text{if-enc}}(C) := \textbf{if } 1 \textbf{ then } C \textbf{ else skip fi}$$

Dead error (C3). Unreachability verifiers are often designed to adjust their verification complexity with respect to the occurring error-statements [13]. The dead error transformation presents a way to inject additional such statements:

$$\gamma_{\text{dead-err}}(C) := \textbf{if } 0 \textbf{ then error else } C \textbf{ fi}$$

Both (C2) and (C3) are program transformations that map to the original program state after one execution step. In other words, for any program state (C, ϕ) the transformed variant has an additional step to map to the original program without changing any variable $((\gamma(C), \phi) \xrightarrow{\tau} (C, \phi))$. Therefore, both program transformation in (C2) and (C3) are semantics-preserving.

Indirected Transformations (I1) and (I2). Indirected transformations are transformations that redirect the data flow of a program without changing the semantics of the program. We implemented two types of indirected transformations: array indirection (I1) and pointer indirection (I2). Arrays and Pointers are often challenging for software verifiers. Introducing them with indirected transformations allows us to test the ability of verifiers to handle these data types.

In general, indirected transformations can be described in our semantics as follows:

$$\gamma_x(C) := px := x; C[x/px]; x := px,$$

where px is either (I1) a[0] of a newly introduced array or (I2) a pointer reference followed by a pointer dereference (*(& x)). Note that $[x/px]$ in C replaces all occurrences of some $x \in \mathcal{X}$ by px. The program transformation γ_x preserves the semantics of the program as we initialize px to be x and then perform the same operations on px as we would have done on x. Therefore, the resulting value of px is equivalent to resulting value of x in the original program. In the end, we map the resulting px back to x.

Function Transformations. So far, we mainly focused on local changes to the program code. However, changes to the procedural structure of the program can potentially have an impact on the verification process. Therefore, we are also interested how procedure (or function) changes impact the verification process.

Function encapsulation (F1). In function encapsulation, we encapsulate a part of the program inside a function and call this function in the previous context. This function encapsulation transformation can be represented as follows:

$$\gamma_{\text{f-enc}}(C) := \textbf{proc } p_{\text{new}} \textbf{ is } C \textbf{ end; call } p_{\text{new}}$$

According to our semantics, the transformed program ends in the original program after two non-observable execution steps. In other words, for any program state (C, ϕ) we can map $(\gamma_{\text{f-enc}}(C), \phi)$ to (C, ϕ') $((\gamma_{\text{f-enc}}(C), \phi) \xrightarrow{\tau} \xrightarrow{\tau} (C, \phi'))$ with $\phi_{|\mathcal{X}_\mathcal{P}} = \phi'_{|\mathcal{X}_\mathcal{P}}$. Note that for simplicity we allow that p_{new} is defined directly next to its call. When applied in the context of a larger transformation, we assume that p_{new} is appended to all other procedure definitions. Furthermore, we assume in our semantics that all variables are defined globally. This is not true in practice. In our implementation, we simulate access to "global variables" by providing access to all relevant local variables inside a code block via pointers. Since both caller and callee access and manipulate the same memory address for all relevant local variables in the caller context, both the original and the encapsulated code compute the same function.

Function inlining (F2). Inlining can be seen as the reverse operation to function encapsulation. Here, the function inlining transformation selects a random function call and replace it with its implementation:

$$\gamma_{\text{f-in}}(\textbf{call } p) := C,$$

where **proc** p **is** C **end** is defined in the program. Note that according to the semantics any state $(\textbf{call } p, \phi)$ maps to (C, ϕ) with $\phi[p] = C$. If $\phi[p] = C$ then **proc** p **is** C **end** must be defined in the program. Therefore, we know that $(\textbf{call } p, \phi) \xrightarrow{\tau} (\gamma_{\text{f-in}}(\textbf{call } p), \phi)$. As ϕ is not modified, the transformation is semantics-preserving. Again, we assume here that variables are accessed globally. In practice, we map formal parameters to actual parameters.

Loop to recursion (R1). Most software verifiers are effective in handling loops but fail for recursion. Therefore, to evaluate the robustness of software verifiers against recursion, we also introduce the loop to recursion transformation. The transformation is defined as follows:

$$\gamma_{\text{rec}}(\textbf{while } B \textbf{ do } C \textbf{ od}) := \textbf{proc } p_{\text{new}} \textbf{ is}$$
$$\textbf{if } B \textbf{ then } C;\ \textbf{call } p_{\text{new}} \textbf{ else skip fi}$$
$$\textbf{end; call } p_{\text{new}}$$

To show that γ_{rec} is semantics-preserving, we again define a weak bisimulation which we also depict in Fig. 4b.

$$\mathcal{R}_{\text{rec}} := \{((\textbf{while } B \textbf{ do } C \textbf{ od }, \phi), (\gamma_{\text{rec}}(\textbf{while } B \textbf{ do } C \textbf{ od}), \phi)) \mid \phi \in \Phi\}$$
$$\cup \{((\textbf{while } B \textbf{ do } C \textbf{ od }, \phi), (\textbf{call } p_{\text{new}}, \phi[p_{\text{new}} \mapsto \textbf{ if } B \ldots])) \mid \phi \in \Phi\}$$
$$\cup \{((\textbf{while } B \textbf{ do } C \textbf{ od }, \phi), (\textbf{if } B \textbf{ then } \ldots, \phi[p_{\text{new}} \mapsto \ldots])) \mid \phi \in \Phi\}$$
$$\cup \{((C;\ \textbf{while } B \textbf{ do } C \textbf{ od }, \phi), (C;\ \textbf{call } p_{\text{new}}, \phi[p_{\text{new}} \mapsto \ldots]))) \mid \phi \in \Phi\}$$
$$\cup \{(\phi, (\textbf{skip }, \phi[p_{\text{new}} \mapsto \ldots]))) \mid \phi \in \Phi\} \cup \{(\phi, \phi[p_{\text{new}} \mapsto \ldots])) \mid \phi \in \Phi\}$$
$$\cup \{((P, \phi), (P, \phi[p_{\text{new}} \mapsto \ldots])) \mid P \in \mathcal{P}, \phi \in \Phi\}$$

As soon as the function definition is handled, we can observe that the behavior of the while loop directly maps to the behavior of the recursive function call. In particular, the statement or statement sequence C can only be executed as often as in the recursive function. Since C can only include observable actions, the two state transition systems are weak bisimilar.

3.4 Robustness Testing Through Repeated Transformations

To evaluate the robustness of unreachability verifiers, we check whether there exists a seed program $P \in \mathcal{P}$ and a semantics-preserving transformation $\gamma : \mathcal{P} \to \mathcal{P}$ such that $V_{\text{unreach}}(P) \neq V_{\text{unreach}}(\gamma(P))$. Recall that since γ is semantics-preserving, it also preserves the ground truth of the seed program. Therefore, if our check succeeds for a combination of program and transformation we can

---

Algorithm 1 Robustness testing algorithm

$NR \leftarrow \emptyset$ ▷ non-robust transforms (pairs of seed and transformed seed)
for $S \in$ Seeds **do**
   $P \leftarrow S$
   for $k \leftarrow 1 \dots n$ **do**   ▷ apply n random transformations
      $\gamma \leftarrow$ random transformation
      $P \leftarrow \gamma(P)$
   if $V_{\text{unreach}}(S) \neq V_{\text{unreach}}(P)$ **then**
      $NR \leftarrow NR \cup \{(S, P)\}$

---

conclude that the verifier is non-robust. In practice, we apply Algorithm 1 and we vary the number of transformations applied to the seed program. This is sound since chains of semantics-preserving transformation are also semantics-preserving.

4 Evaluation

We implemented our testing approach and all semantics-preserving program transformations for testing unreachability software verifiers for C programs. In the evaluation, we are interested in answering the following research questions:

RQ1 Are software verification *tools* robust against semantics-preserving program transformations?
RQ2 Are software verification *algorithms* robust against semantics-preserving program transformations?
RQ3 Which transformations reveal non-robustness of software verification *algorithms*?

We designed individual experiments for answering our research questions.

4.1 Benchmark Setup

During our evaluation, we evaluate the robustness of verification tools as well as specific verification algorithms. For this, we transform existing verification tasks by applying our semantics-preserving transformations up to 100 times. Transformations are applied randomly and for answering RQ1 and RQ2 we apply all eight semantics-preserving transformations in addition to three helper transformations (`for2while`, `break2goto` and `add_compound`). The helper transformations perform only syntactic changes in C which will allow us to apply our technique on a wider range of verification tasks. For RQ3, we apply transformations of each transformation group (ControlFlow, Indirected, Functions and Recursion) individually to evaluate their impact on the robustness of verifiers. In our experiments, we measure two types of robustness: true-robustness and false-robustness. True-robustness is the percentage of verification tasks that were decided to be correct before and after the transformation. False-robustness is symmetrically

Table 1. Robustness results for verifiers on 778 tasks

	(a) CPAchecker after transformation					(b) ESBMC after transformation					(c) Symbiotic after transformation			
	true	false	unk	robust (%)		true	false	unk	robust (%)		true	false	unk.	robust (%)
true	136	43	168	39.2	true	139	3	148	47.9	true	318	0	87	78.5
before false	3	95	56	61.7	before false	0	112	50	69.1	before false	0	117	36	76.5
unk	33	50	194	70.0	unk	11	4	311	95.4	unk.	1	5	213	97.3

defined for tasks that are verified to be incorrect (false). A value below 100% means that the verifier is non-robust with respect to our transformations. Benchmarks were executed via BenchExec [8]. For RQ1, we use a 24-core machine with 128GB RAM. We limit the verifiers to 15GB RAM, a timelimit of 15min and 1 physical core (2 processing units) per task. The experiments for RQ2 and RQ3 were performed on a cluster of 4-core machines with 33GB RAM.

4.2   Experimental Results

For our experiments, we selected unreachability verification tasks from the benchmark set of the SV-COMP 2023 [1] as our seed programs. Included are all 778 tasks from the ReachSafety-Loops category.

RQ1. To answer RQ1, we evaluate the robustness of three of the most successful verifiers in the SV-COMP 2023 ReachSafety category [1]: CPAchecker [4], Symbiotic [10] and ESBMC [19]. CPAchecker composes several verification algorithms into verification strategies which are selected based on certain program features [2] (e.g. the occurrence of loops, arrays, floating point operations). Symbiotic employs program slicing [10] to remove parts of the program irrelevant for verification and then employs symbolic execution for the verification. ESBMC is built upon the bounded model checker CBMC [14] and uses k-induction [19] to infer loop invariants for the verification. Our results for the three verifiers are shown in Table 1 (showing the number of tasks with specific outcomes before and after transformation). The diagonals in the table give the number of tasks with the *same* outcome (i.e., on which the verifiers are robust). We can observe that no verification tool is robust with respect to all of our transformations, CPAchecker in particular having difficulties with true- and false-robustness and Symbiotic standing out with always achieving more than 70%-robustness. For obtaining an insight why these verification tools are non-robust, we reviewed the experiment logs for the individual verification tools. We found that CPAchecker has significant problems with programs that contain recursive function calls. This does not only lead to a low robustness score but also to high number of new (partially incorrect) true and false verdicts (see the last row of Table 1a). In the case of ESBMC and Symbiotic, the tools fail to verify a significant number of the transformed verification tasks due to timeouts and out-of-memory errors. It is unclear whether this is also caused by our loops to recursion-transformation.

Table 2. Robustness results for verification algorithms on 778 tasks

(a) Symbolic Execution					(b) Predicate Analysis					(c) k-Induction			
	after transformation					after transformation					after transformation		
	true	false	unk.	robust (%)		true	false	unk.	robust (%)		true	false	unk.	robust (%)
before true	5	0	254	1.9	before true	108	0	71	60.3	before true	105	0	147	41.7
false	0	76	66	53.5	false	0	51	9	85.0	false	0	105	20	84.0
unk.	0	2	375	99.5	unk.	18	0	521	96.7	unk.	9	8	384	95.8

Therefore, to avoid that the measured effect on the tool's robustness is dominated by recursion, we also evaluated the tools on verification tasks transformed via all transformations except loops to recursion. We find that CPAchecker is significantly more effective in avoiding incorrect results on verification tasks without recursion. However, surprisingly the tool performs even worse in terms of true- and false-robustness (with a score of 28.8% and 57.8% respectively). Interestingly, avoiding recursion in the transformation process has little to no influence on the robustness of the other tools. The only exception is the true-robustness of ESBMC which further decreases by 9.6%. Overall, we can conclude that:

> The tested verifiers are not robust against semantics-preserving transformations. The degree of robustness is highly dependent on the type of transformation applied during testing.

RQ2. As verifiers typically employ a mixture of different algorithms, we were also interested in the effect of the transformations on standalone algorithms. For RQ2, we thus evaluated the robustness of three verification algorithms implemented in CPAchecker[5]: (1) Symbolic Execution [6] using symbolic values to abstract the concrete program state, (2) Predicate Analysis [5] employing predicate abstraction, and (3) k-induction [3], an extension of bounded model checking with inductive invariants. Together all three algorithms cover a wide range of those used in state-of-the-art tools in SV-COMP [1]. The implementations of these algorithms however do not support programs with recursion. Therefore, we exclude transformation loop to recursion. Our results are shown in Fig. 2.

We can observe that verification algorithms are also not robust against the semantics-preserving transformations. Predicate analysis is the most robust algorithm with a true-robustness score of 60.3% and false-robustness of 85.0%. Symbolic Execution achieves the lowest robustness scores for both true-robustness and false-robustness. Overall, we find that the transformed tasks are significantly more challenging for the algorithms than the original tasks. In fact, for most of the tasks that they have previously solved, the algorithms fail on the transformed task because of a timeout or an out-of-memory error. Interestingly enough, there

---

[5] We chose CPAchecker for this purpose as it is the only verifier configurable to one particular algorithm.

Table 3. Robustness results for symbolic execution (SymEx), predicate analysis (Pred) and k-induction (kInd) per category (transformations applied 1, 10 or 100 times (subscript); reporting true robustness (%TRob), false robustness (%FRob) and total number of unknowns (#unk)).

	ControlFlow			Indirected			Functions			Recursion		
	%TRob	%FRob	#unk	%TRob	%FRob	#unk	%TRob	%FRob	#unk	%TRob	%FRob	#unk
SymEx$_1$	97.9	95.5	352	93.8	96.2	361	54.1	66.7	496	4.5	22.0	675
SymEx$_{10}$	56.6	89.1	456	3.3	60.6	627	54.1	66.7	496	0.0	14.4	696
SymEx$_{100}$	56.6	84.7	462	3.3	59.8	628	54.1	66.7	496	0.0	0.0	715
Pred$_1$	100.0	100.0	525	90.0	94.0	542	60.7	88.2	573	11.4	17.6	690
Pred$_{10}$	99.3	100.0	526	82.1	86.0	600	57.9	84.3	579	0.0	5.9	712
Pred$_{100}$	94.2	96.0	536	82.1	86.0	600	52.9	80.4	587	0.0	5.9	712
kInd$_1$	94.8	99.1	401	81.2	98.2	421	91.5	98.2	399	8.5	5.3	691
kInd$_{10}$	66.2	93.8	468	71.8	95.6	444	91.5	96.5	407	0.0	0.9	714
kInd$_{100}$	59.6	74.3	504	70.9	95.6	446	82.6	89.5	434	0.0	0.0	715

is a significant number of unknown results where the individual algorithms stop the verification of the transformed task without exceeding any resource limit. This is most evident in the symbolic execution. Here, the algorithm stops after a few seconds with an unknown result in 117 of the 320 cases. This could indicate that our transformations introduce program constructs that are not supported by the algorithm (see RQ3). Summarizing, we find that:

> Verification algorithms are not robust against semantics-preserving transformations. The degree of robustness and how much the verification complexity increases is highly dependent on the employed verification algorithm.

RQ3. For answering RQ3, we evaluate the robustness of the algorithms for the different transformation categories ControlFlow, Indirected, Functions and Recursion in isolation. We start from the same seed benchmark and apply 1, 10, 100 transformations of a category. We excluded tasks which cannot be transformed in at least one of the transformation categories (excluding 63 tasks without loops). The algorithms are again evaluated on the task before and after the transformation. Results are shown in Table 3.

As expected, loop to recursion has the highest negative impact on the verification performance. The verification algorithms usually abort and fail as soon as they discover a recursive function call. It is however surprising that some tasks can still be solved after the loop to recursion transformation was applied. Therefore, there are some tasks which can be solved without the need of processing the recursive function call. Apart from recursion, we find that the verification algorithms struggle to be robust for all transformation categories (with the exception of predicate analysis for a single application of control flow transformations).

In general, algorithms fail to be robust at least on a few tasks as soon as we apply multiple transformations. This is expected as we naturally increase the verification complexity by applying our transformation. It is however surprising that predicate analysis is the only algorithm that is nearly robust for control flow transformations while the other algorithms struggle in this category. The same also holds true for the Functions category where k-induction dominates in terms of robustness. Finally, our robustness results on individual transformation categories also allow us to identify the cause for the robustness problems of symbolic execution identified in RQ2. While symbolic execution is mostly robust for function and control flow transformations, it fails to be robust on most tasks after more than 10 applications of the indirected transformation. Upon closer inspection, we find that symbolic execution fails on these tasks by reporting an unknown or running into a timeout. From the tool's logs it is not clear why this happens, but we expect that symbolic execution either does not support arrays, pointers or combinations thereof. To validate this hypothesis, we also applied the Array indirected transformation and the Pointer indirected transformation independently (100 times each). We found that symbolic execution is significantly more robust against Array transformations (with a true-robustness of 90.3% and a false-robustness of 95.8%) than against Pointer transformations (with a true-robustness of 4.6% and a false-robustness of 62%). This indicates that symbolic execution as implemented in CPAchecker does not fully support the introduced pointers. Overall, this analysis demonstrate that robustness testing can be useful for identifying the individual weaknesses of verification algorithms. For RQ3, we thus get:

> Verification algorithms have different strengths and weaknesses which can be uncovered by robustness testing. Different transformation categories can reveal robustness problems of individual algorithms. By using transformations in isolation, it is possible to identify root causes for individual weaknesses of verifiers.

5 Related Work

Assessing the quality of software verifiers in general is an important problem [9] and many approaches have been proposed that address this problem by generating new benchmarks [16,25,26] and by transforming existing code [18,21,28]. For example, Chen and Furia [12] evaluated the robustness of intermediate verifiers by transforming existing Boogie programs with semantics-preserving transformations like swapping declarations or joining assertions. In contrast, we focused on semantics-preserving transformations for C code and we showed that complete verification tools are not robust against our transformations. Kapus and Cadar [21] evaluated the correctness of symbolic execution engines with semantics-preserving transformations. For this, they generated small deterministic C programs and then replaced constants with symbolic variables. The transformations are semantics-preserving as the symbolic variables are constrained to be equivalent to the replaced constants. While we also target C programs, our focus is more on the robustness of C verifiers in general. In fact, we showed that our transformations can be used to test the robustness of various unreachability verifiers. Zhang et al. [28] evaluated the correctness of unreachability verifiers by injecting arbitrary error locations into existing C code. As their transformations are not semantics-preserving, they had to rely on the execution of programs (with deterministically defined inputs) to determine the ground truth. Our approach works for arbitrary C programs and our transformations guarantee that the ground truth is preserved. Fink et al. [18] randomly generate artificial C code to benchmark software verifiers. For this, they use a template to generate various correct programs (so that the error location is unreachable) and employ *correctness*-preserving transformations on the generated code. In contrast, our transformations can be applied to correct and incorrect programs and we formally proved their soundness. While we mainly focused on testing the robustness of C software verifiers, evaluating software analyzers is also an issue in areas other than C software verification. For example, Dolan-Gavitt et al. [16] generate benchmarks for fuzz testing via bug injection into realistic code. Schott and Pauck [25] recombined existing benchmarks for evaluating taint analysis tools. Steffen et al. [26] generated benchmarks for evaluating C software verifiers. While our approach is not targeted at generating new benchmarks, it can be directly used to augment existing benchmarks with a known ground truth.

Finally, semantics-preserving transformations have also been applied for testing C compilers [22,23,27]. However, these works used a relaxation of semantics-preservation called Equivalence Modulo Input (EMI) [22]. Transformations that are semantics-preserving under EMI guarantee that program semantics are preserved for a restricted set of inputs. This allowed for example Le et al. [22] to drop certain statements which are never reached for a given set of inputs. In contrast, our transformations guarantee semantics-preservation for all possible inputs which is a necessity for testing software verifiers.

6   Conclusion

In this paper, we have proposed a new technique for testing the robustness of C software verifiers. We have employed this technique to test the robustness of entire verification tools as well as individual verification algorithms. Our evaluation has shown that most of the evaluated approaches are non-robust against the eight semantics-preserving transformations introduced in this work. In addition, it shows that the robustness against individual transformations is heavily dependent on the type of the employed verifier. While our technique is effective in uncovering robustness problems of software verifiers, identifying the root cause of the robustness problem is still challenging. For future work, we see the integration of search-based techniques that search for minimal modifications of the input that still trigger the non-robustness of the verifier. Minimal modifications – consisting of one or two types of transformations (such as the Pointer transformation in the case of symbolic execution) – are easier to interpret, which also makes it easier to isolate the cause of non-robustness. Finally, we believe that our insights in the robustness of software verifiers can potentially guide the development of more robust verifiers.

References

1. Beyer, D.: Competition on software verification and witness validation: SV-COMP 2023. In: TACAS. LNCS, vol. 13994, pp. 495–522. Springer, Cham (2023). https://doi.org/10.1007/978-3-031-30820-8_29

2. Beyer, D., Dangl, M.: Strategy selection for software verification based on Boolean features. In: Margaria, T., Steffen, B. (eds.) ISoLA 2018. LNCS, vol. 11245, pp. 144–159. Springer, Cham (2018). https://doi.org/10.1007/978-3-030-03421-4_11

3. Beyer, D., Dangl, M., Wendler, P.: Boosting k-induction with continuously-refined invariants. In: Kroening, D., Păsăreanu, C.S. (eds.) CAV 2015. LNCS, vol. 9206, pp. 622–640. Springer, Cham (2015). https://doi.org/10.1007/978-3-319-21690-4_42

4. Beyer, D., Keremoglu, M.E.: CPACHECKER: a tool for configurable software verification. In: Gopalakrishnan, G., Qadeer, S. (eds.) CAV 2011. LNCS, vol. 6806, pp. 184–190. Springer, Heidelberg (2011). https://doi.org/10.1007/978-3-642-22110-1_16

5. Beyer, D., Keremoglu, M.E., Wendler, P.: Predicate abstraction with adjustable-block encoding. In: Proceedings of 10th International Conference on Formal Methods in Computer-Aided Design, FMCAD 2010, Lugano, Switzerland, October 20–23, pp. 189–197. IEEE (2010). https://ieeexplore.ieee.org/document/5770949/

6. Beyer, D., Lemberger, T.: CPA-SymExec: efficient symbolic execution in CPAchecker. In: Proceedings of the 33rd ACM/IEEE International Conference on Automated Software Engineering, ASE 2018, Montpellier, France, September 3–7, 2018, pp. 900–903. ACM (2018). https://doi.org/10.1145/3238147.3240478

7. Beyer, D., Löwe, S.: Explicit-state software model checking based on CEGAR and interpolation. In: Cortellessa, V., Varró, D. (eds.) FASE 2013. LNCS, vol. 7793, pp. 146–162. Springer, Heidelberg (2013). https://doi.org/10.1007/978-3-642-37057-1_11

8. Beyer, D., Löwe, S., Wendler, P.: Reliable benchmarking: requirements and solutions. Int. J. Softw. Tools Technol. Transf. 21(1), 1–29 (2019). https://doi.org/10.1007/s10009-017-0469-y

9. Cadar, C., Donaldson, A.F.: Analysing the program analyser. In: ICSE, pp. 765–768. ACM (2016). https://doi.org/10.1145/2889160.2889206

10. Chalupa, M., Strejcek, J., Vitovská, M.: Joint forces for memory safety checking revisited. Int. J. Softw. Tools Technol. Transf. 22(2), 115–133 (2020). https://doi.org/10.1007/s10009-019-00526-2

11. Chen, T.Y., Kuo, F., Liu, H., Poon, P., Towey, D., Tse, T.H., Zhou, Z.Q.: Metamorphic testing: a review of challenges and opportunities. ACM Comput. Surv. 51(1), 4:1–4:27 (2018). https://doi.org/10.1145/3143561

12. Chen, Y.T., Furia, C.A.: Robustness testing of intermediate verifiers. In: Lahiri, S.K., Wang, C. (eds.) ATVA 2018. LNCS, vol. 11138, pp. 91–108. Springer, Cham (2018). https://doi.org/10.1007/978-3-030-01090-4_6

13. Clarke, E., Grumberg, O., Jha, S., Lu, Y., Veith, H.: Counterexample-guided abstraction refinement. In: Emerson, E.A., Sistla, A.P. (eds.) CAV 2000. LNCS, vol. 1855, pp. 154–169. Springer, Heidelberg (2000). https://doi.org/10.1007/10722167_15

14. Clarke, E., Kroening, D., Lerda, F.: A tool for checking ANSI-C programs. In: Jensen, K., Podelski, A. (eds.) TACAS 2004. LNCS, vol. 2988, pp. 168–176. Springer, Heidelberg (2004). https://doi.org/10.1007/978-3-540-24730-2_15
15. De Nicola, R.: Extensional equivalences for transition systems. Acta Informatica **24**(2), 211–237 (1987). https://doi.org/10.1007/BF00264365
16. Dolan-Gavitt, B., Hulin, P., Kirda, E., Leek, T., Mambretti, A., Robertson, W.K., Ulrich, F., Whelan, R.: LAVA: large-scale automated vulnerability addition. In: IEEE Symposium on Security and Privacy, SP 2016, pp. 110–121. IEEE Computer Society (2016). https://doi.org/10.1109/SP.2016.15
17. Dyck, F., Richter, C., Wehrheim, H.: Robustness testing of software verifiers (2023). https://doi.org/10.5281/zenodo.8186536
18. Fink, X., Berger, P., Katoen, J.: Configurable benchmarks for C model checkers. In: NFM. LNCS, vol. 13260, pp. 338–354. Springer, Cham (2022). https://doi.org/10.1007/978-3-031-06773-0_18
19. Gadelha, M.R., Monteiro, F., Cordeiro, L., Nicole, D.: ESBMC v6.0: verifying C programs using k-induction and invariant inference. In: Beyer, D., Huisman, M., Kordon, F., Steffen, B. (eds.) TACAS 2019. LNCS, vol. 11429, pp. 209–213. Springer, Cham (2019). https://doi.org/10.1007/978-3-030-17502-3_15
20. Howar, F., Jasper, M., Mues, M., Schmidt, D., Steffen, B.: The RERS challenge: towards controllable and scalable benchmark synthesis. Int. J. Softw. Tools Technol. Transf. **23**(6), 917–930 (2021). https://doi.org/10.1007/s10009-021-00617-z
21. Kapus, T., Cadar, C.: Automatic testing of symbolic execution engines via program generation and differential testing. In: ASE, pp. 590–600. IEEE Computer Society (2017). https://doi.org/10.1109/ASE.2017.8115669
22. Le, V., Afshari, M., Su, Z.: Compiler validation via equivalence modulo inputs. In: O'Boyle, M.F.P., Pingali, K. (eds.) PLDI '14, pp. 216–226. ACM (2014). https://doi.org/10.1145/2594291.2594334
23. Le, V., Sun, C., Su, Z.: Finding deep compiler bugs via guided stochastic program mutation. In: Aldrich, J., Eugster, P. (eds.) OOPSLA 2015, pp. 386–399. ACM (2015). https://doi.org/10.1145/2814270.2814319
24. Milner, R.: Communication and Concurrency. PHI Series in Computer Science, Prentice Hall (1989)
25. Schott, S., Pauck, F.: Benchmark fuzzing for android taint analyses. In: SCAM, pp. 12–23. IEEE (2022). https://doi.org/10.1109/SCAM55253.2022.00007
26. Steffen, B., Isberner, M., Naujokat, S., Margaria, T., Geske, M.: Property-driven benchmark generation: synthesizing programs of realistic structure. Int. J. Softw. Tools Technol. Transf. **16**(5), 465–479 (2014). https://doi.org/10.1007/s10009-014-0336-z
27. Sun, C., Le, V., Su, Z.: Finding compiler bugs via live code mutation. In: Visser, E., Smaragdakis, Y. (eds.) OOPSLA 2016, pp. 849–863. ACM (2016). https://doi.org/10.1145/2983990.2984038
28. Zhang, C., Su, T., Yan, Y., Zhang, F., Pu, G., Su, Z.: Finding and understanding bugs in software model checkers. In: ESEC/SIGSOFT FSE, pp. 763–773. ACM (2019). https://doi.org/10.1145/3338906.3338932

Decoupled Fitness Criteria for Reactive Systems

Derek Egolf$^{(\boxtimes)}$ and Stavros Tripakis

Northeastern University, Boston, MA, USA
{egolf.d,stavros}@northeastern.edu

Abstract. The correctness problem for reactive systems has been thoroughly explored and is well understood. Meanwhile, the efficiency problem for reactive systems has not received the same attention. Indeed, one correct system may be less fit than another correct system and determining this manually is challenging and often done ad hoc. We (1) propose a novel and general framework which automatically assigns comparable fitness scores to reactive systems using interpretable parameters that are decoupled from the system being evaluated, (2) state the computational problem of evaluating this fitness score and reduce this problem to a matrix analysis problem, (3) discuss symbolic and numerical methods for solving this matrix analysis problem, and (4) illustrate our approach by evaluating the fitness of nine systems across three case studies, including the Alternating Bit Protocol and Two Phase Commit.

Keywords: Formal methods · Verification · Reactive systems

1 Introduction

Correctness guarantees help us avoid irritating, costly, and, in some cases, deadly implementation bugs. However, two systems that both satisfy a correctness specification may differ with respect to efficiency. Inefficient systems result in real world consequences: delaying content delivery, using excess energy, and wasting clock cycles better spent elsewhere.

Much like reasoning about correctness, reasoning about efficiency is cognitively demanding, prone to errors, and requires expert insight. The framework proposed in this paper strives to eliminate this human burden, mitigate these errors, and capture the expert's insight and intentions in the parameters of the framework. The proposed framework accomplishes these goals by assigning a comparable *fitness score* to every system, such that we can decide between two systems on the basis of their score. Consider the following example.

Example 1. Consider the finite labeled transition systems (LTSs) depicted in Fig. 1. Labels s, a, t represent *send*, *acknowledge* (ack), and *timeout* respectively. The symbols !, ? (output, input) denote rendezvous communication in which a

C. Ferreira and T. A. C. Willemse (Eds.): SEFM 2023, LNCS 14323, pp. 85–105, 2023.
https://doi.org/10.1007/978-3-031-47115-5_6

! transition can only be taken in one LTS if the corresponding ? transition is taken in another LTS. Transitions with neither !, nor ?, can be taken freely.

LTS E represents a *sender* in the environment. LTSs G and B are 'good' and 'bad' receivers, respectively. B is 'bad' in the sense that it waits for two *send* actions before replying with an acknowledgement, whereas G replies right away. The synchronous products of the sender E with receivers G and B, denoted $E\|G$ and $E\|B$, are LTSs M and M', respectively. Both M and M' are *correct*, in the sense that they satisfy the specification *every s is eventually followed by an a* (given some fairness assumptions that prevent a from being ignored indefinitely). Because they both satisfy this specification, M and M' are indistinguishable from the perspective of traditional verification and synthesis. However, M is intuitively preferable to M' because G is a better receiver than B. As we will show in Sect. 5, our framework assigns fitness scores 0.25 and 0.14 to M and M', respectively, and thus distinguishes M as a better system.   □

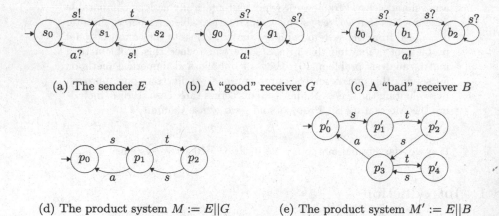

(a) The sender E (b) A "good" receiver G (c) A "bad" receiver B

(d) The product system $M := E\|G$ (e) The product system $M' := E\|B$

Fig. 1. A simple communication protocol modeled with finite LTSs.

The exact nature of the fitness score depends on the application domain. Our framework *decouples* the description of the system (e.g., the LTSs of Fig. 1) from a set of domain-specific *parameters* which capture user preferences.

By assigning fitness scores to systems, as in the example above, our framework can be used for performance evaluation. Our framework is additionally motivated by recent work in the synthesis of distributed protocols [5]. Unlike humans, synthesis tools typically ignore efficiency considerations. In some cases, these tools generate systems that are, strictly speaking, correct (i.e., they satisfy their logical specification), yet clearly unorthodox or even inefficient [6]. In such cases, we can use our framework to rank automatically generated systems according to their fitness score. In other cases, we may want to generate *all* correct systems [24], potentially with the aim of doing *fitness-optimal synthesis* (c.f. page 8).

In summary, the contributions of this paper are as follows: (1) We propose a novel and general framework for automatically assigning a comparable fitness score to a system; this framework uses interpretable parameters that are decoupled from the system being evaluated. (2) We provide an automated method for computing fitness scores; our method ultimately reduces the fitness-score computation problem to a matrix analysis problem. (3) We discuss symbolic and numerical methods for solving this matrix analysis problem. (4) We present an implementation and evaluation of our framework: our prototype tool allows, in a matter of seconds, to automatically compute the fitness of nine automatically synthesized systems.

We organize the rest of the paper as follows. Section 2 formalizes preliminary concepts. Section 3 presents our framework. Section 4 presents a method to compute fitness scores. Section 5 illustrates our approach on the communication protocol of Example 1, Two Phase Commit, and the Alternating Bit Protocol taken from [6]. Section 6 discusses related work. Section 7 concludes the paper.

2   Preliminaries

$\mathbb{N}$, $\mathbb{Q}$, $\mathbb{R}$, $\mathbb{R}_{\geq 0}$, and $\mathbb{B} = \{0, 1\}$ denote the sets of natural, rational, real, nonnegative real numbers, and booleans, respectively. A function $h : \mathbb{N}^d \to \mathbb{Q}$ is a *scalar arithmetic function* if h can be written in terms of basic scalar arithmetic operations $+, -, \times, /$, applied to its natural number arguments.

In traditional verification, we typically only consider the yes/no question: does the system produce any violating traces. While this question allows us to discard of the relative abundance of traces, the question of fitness is not so. All else equal, if a system is capable of producing the same 'unfit' trace by executing any one of many distinct runs, then that system is worse than a system that can produce the unfit trace in just one particular way. Toward this end, we require a notion of multisets.

A **multiset** X over domain D is a function $X : D \to \mathbb{N}$, where $X(x)$ represents the *multiplicity* of element x, i.e., how many times x occurs in X. $\mathcal{M}(D)$ denotes the class of all multisets over D, i.e., the set of all functions $X : D \to \mathbb{N}$. If $X(x) = m$, then we write $x \in_m X$ (possibly, $m = 0$). The *cardinality* of X, denoted $|X|$, is the sum of the multiplicities of all members of the domain D. We write multisets as $\{\!\!\{...\}\!\!\}$ to differentiate them from sets.

Example 2. We denote by $X = \{\!\!\{0, 0, 1, 1, 1\}\!\!\}$ the multiset where $0 \in_2 X$ and $1 \in_3 X$. Then: $|X| = 2 + 3 = 5$.   □

If $A \subseteq D$ and $X : D \to \mathbb{N}$ is a multiset, then X *restricted to* A is a new multiset, denoted $X|_A : D \to \mathbb{N}$ and defined as follows. If $x \notin A$, $X|_A(x) = 0$ and otherwise if $x \in A$, then $X|_A(x) = X(x)$. Let $X : D \to \mathbb{N}$ be a multiset and let $f : D \to D'$ be a function. Then intuitively, the *image of X by f* is a multiset denoted $f \odot X$ obtained by applying f to the members of X. E.g. if $f(x) = x^2$, then $f \odot \{\!\!\{2, -2, 3, 3, 3\}\!\!\} = \{\!\!\{4, 4, 9, 9, 9\}\!\!\}$. Formally, we define $f \odot X : D' \to \mathbb{N}$ as follows. $(f \odot X)(y) := |(X|_{D_y})|$, where $D_y := \{x \in D \mid f(x) = y\}$. We may treat a set as a multiset with all multiplicities as 0 or 1 and take its image by f to obtain a multiset. If $X \in \mathcal{M}(\mathbb{N}^d)$ and $1 \leqslant i \leqslant d$, then $sum(X, i) = \sum_{x \in_c X} cx_i$, where x_i is the ith component of $x \in \mathbb{N}^d$. E.g. $sum(\{\!\{(1,2),(1,2),(3,4)\}\!\}, 2) = 2 + 2 + 4$.

A **finite labeled transition system** (LTS) is a tuple $M = \langle \Sigma, Q, Q_0, \Delta \rangle$, where: Σ is a finite set of labels; Q is a finite set of states; $Q_0 \subseteq Q$ is the set of initial states; $\Delta \subseteq Q \times \Sigma \times Q$ is the transition relation. An n-length run of M is a sequence $t = q_0 \xrightarrow{a_1} q_1 \xrightarrow{a_2} q_2 ... \xrightarrow{a_n} q_n$ such that $q_0 \in Q_0$ and $(q_i, a_{i+1}, q_{i+1}) \in \Delta$ for all $i = 0, ..., n-1$. The *trace* of t, denoted $\mathrm{Lab}(t)$, is the sequence of labels $a_1 a_2 ... a_n$, while $\mathrm{Sts}(t) = q_0 q_1 ... q_n$ is the sequence of states visited during t. $[\![M]\!]_n$ denotes the set of all n-length runs of M. Two runs $t_1, t_2 \in [\![M]\!]_n$ may have equivalent traces, i.e., $\mathrm{Lab}(t_1) = \mathrm{Lab}(t_2)$. We denote the multiset of all n length traces of M as $M_n = Lab \odot [\![M]\!]_n$. We denote the 0 length trace as ε. Then $[\![M]\!]_0 = Q_0$ and M_0 is the multiset containing ε once for each state in Q_0.

Example 3 (Two Systems). We define two LTSs $M^{(1)}$ and $M^{(2)}$ over $\Sigma = \{0, \$\}$. We interpret the traces of these systems as follows: \$'s are money that we receive, and 0's are lapses in this income. Intuitively, we prefer behaviors that maximize the rate at which we receive \$'s.

Let $M^{(1)}$ be the LTS with one state and a self-loop with label \$. So $M_n^{(1)}$ contains one n length trace of multiplicity 1: $\$^n$. Let $M^{(2)}$ be the LTS that alternates between two states, outputting \$ when leaving the initial state and 0 when leaving the other. So $M_n^{(2)}$ contains one trace of multiplicity 1: $(\$0)^{\lfloor n/2 \rfloor} \$^{(n \bmod 2)}$, i.e., even length prefixes end in 0 and odd length prefixes end in \$.   □

A distributed system is typically modeled as the *product* of a set of LTSs. This product can be defined in the standard way, and is itself a monolithic LTS.

A **deterministic finite automaton** (DFA) is a tuple $M = \langle \Sigma, Q, q_0, Q_{acc}, \delta \rangle$, where: Σ is a finite alphabet; Q is a finite set of states; $q_0 \in Q$ is the single initial state; $Q_{acc} \subseteq Q$ is the set of accepting states; $\delta : Q \times \Sigma \to Q$ is the transition function. Unlike a generic LTS, every trace $w \in \Sigma^*$ corresponds to one and only one finite run of a DFA M.

3   A Formal Framework for Capturing Fitness

Our framework assigns a real number called a *fitness score* to every system. The key idea of our framework is that it *decouples* the description of the system from the following set of domain-specific framework parameters: (1) A finite alphabet Σ, e.g., $\{0, \$\}$. (2) A *fitness function*, $f : \Sigma^* \to \mathbb{N}^d$. This function measures some quantity of finite prefixes of infinite traces. (3) An *aggregate function*, $@ : \mathcal{M}(\mathbb{N}^d) \to \mathbb{Q}$. This function takes a multiset of fitness values, $X \in \mathcal{M}(\mathbb{N}^d)$, and compiles the values into a single value. Examples include min, max, average, etc. taken over arithmetic combinations of natural numbers.[1] In addition, the framework may also include: (4) A comparison relation, $\preccurlyeq$, used to compare the

---

[1] Slight generalizations to the framework, omitted here for the sake of simplicity, are able to capture, e.g., aggregates that output tuples of rational numbers [22].

fitness scores of two different systems. We next provide examples and formal definitions of these parameters.

Fitness Functions: The *rate* function is an example of a fitness function:

Definition 1 (Fitness Function: Rate of \$). *For* $\Sigma = \{0, \$\}$ *define* $rate_\$$ $(w) = (\#_\$(w), |w|)$, *where* $\#_\$(w)$ *is the number of \$'s in w and $|w|$ is the length of w. This fitness function treats a label as a unit of time.*   □

Example 4 (Rate of \$ Applied). Recall the systems $M_n^{(1)} = \{\!\{\$^n\}\!\}$ and $M_n^{(2)} = \{\!\{(\$0)^{\lfloor n/2 \rfloor}\$^{(n \bmod 2)}\}\!\}$ from Example 3. We apply $f := rate_\$$ to the n-length partial runs of these systems. Taking the image of $M^{(1)}$ and $M^{(2)}$ by f yields:

$$f \odot M_n^{(1)} = \{\!\{f(\$^n)\}\!\} = \{\!\{(n, n)\}\!\}$$
$$f \odot M_n^{(2)} = \{\!\{f((\$0)^{\lfloor n/2 \rfloor}\$^{(n \bmod 2)})\}\!\} = \{\!\{(\lceil n/2 \rceil, n)\}\!\}$$

□

We represent a fitness function $f : \Sigma^* \to \mathbb{N}^d$ by a d-tuple $\langle f_1, ..., f_d \rangle$, where each $f_i = \langle \Sigma, Q_i, q_i^0, Q_i^{acc}, \delta_i \rangle$ is a DFA. Specifically, consider an input $w \in \Sigma^*$. When the DFA f_i consumes w, it visits a sequence of states, $\hat{q} = q_i^0, q_i^1, ..., q_i^m$. Interpreting f_i as a function $f_i : \Sigma^* \to \mathbb{N}$, we define $f_i(w)$ as the number of times an accepting state is visited in $\hat{q}$. We then define the fitness function $f : \Sigma^* \to \mathbb{N}^d$ so that $f(w) = (f_1(w), ..., f_d(w))$. For instance, Fig. 2 depicts the DFA representation of $rate_\$$ from Definition 1 and, e.g., $f(\$0\$\$0) = (3, 5)$.

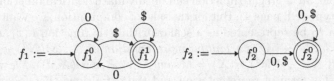

Fig. 2. The two DFA representing the $rate_\$$ fitness function: f_1 computes the number of \$'s in a word; f_2 computes the length of the word.

Aggregate Functions: The *average rate* function is one example of an aggregate function. The average rate function treats ordered pairs as fractions and takes the average value:

Definition 2 (Aggregate Function: Average Rate). *For $X \in \mathcal{M}(\mathbb{N}^2)$, let:*

$$@_{avg}(X) = \frac{1}{|X|} \sum_{(p,q) \in_m X} m \cdot \frac{p}{q}$$

□

Example 5. This example emphasizes the role of multiplicity in aggregates. For instance, if $X := \{\!\{(1,3),(1,3),(2,3)\}\!\}$, then the (1,3) term is counted twice:

$$@_{avg}(X) \;=\; \frac{1}{|X|} \sum_{(p,q)\in_m X} m \cdot \frac{p}{q} \;=\; \frac{1}{3}(2 \cdot \frac{1}{3} + \frac{2}{3}) \;=\; 4/9$$

□

Example 6. This example applies $@_{avg}$ to the running example (Example 3). The average is moot here as there is only one partial trace of each length. Recall from Example 4 that $f \odot M_n^{(1)} = \{\!\{(n,n)\}\!\}$ and $f \odot M_n^{(2)} = \{\!\{(\lceil n/2 \rceil, n)\}\!\}$, where $f := rate_\$$. We can apply average rate to these images: $@_{avg}(f \odot M_n^{(1)}) = n/n = 1$ and $@_{avg}(f \odot M_n^{(2)}) = \lceil n/2 \rceil / n$.   □

Another example of an aggregate function is the *maximum rate* function:

Definition 3 (Aggregate Function: Maximum Rate). *For $X \in \mathcal{M}(\mathbb{N}^2)$:*

$$@(X) = \max\{p/q \mid (p,q) \in X\}$$

□

Example 7. For instance, if $X := \{\!\{(1,3),(1,3),(2,3)\}\!\}$, then:

$$@(X) = \max\{1/3, 1/3, 2/3\} = 2/3$$

□

In principle, an aggregate function can be any mathematical function with the appropriate type (c.f. page 4). But for the sake of computation, we want an aggregate function to be represented as a scalar arithmetic function $h(x_1, x_2, ..., x_d)$. We say that $h : \mathbb{N}^d \to \mathbb{Q}$ is a *faithful representation* of $@ : \mathcal{M}(\mathbb{N}^d) \to \mathbb{Q}$ if and only if for all $X \in \mathcal{M}(\mathbb{N}^d), @(X) = h(sum(X,1), ..., sum(X,d))$. We will see in Sect. 4 that this form of representation and the definitions that follow are key, as the heart of our method is computing each $sum(X,i)$, where $X = f \odot M_n$. The importance should be clear by the time we state our primary correctness result, Theorem 1.

While h might not be a faithful representation of $@$ for all X, h may be a faithful representation assuming that X satisfies some condition. The fitness function may in turn guarantee that X satisfies that condition. Fortunately, this relationship holds between $@_{avg}$ (Def. 2) and $rate_\$$ (Def. 1). The following definition and lemmas capture this useful situation:

Definition 4 (Conditional Representation and Compatible). *Let Ψ be a predicate over $\mathcal{M}(\mathbb{N}^d)$, i.e., a mapping $\Psi : \mathcal{M}(\mathbb{N}^d) \to \mathbb{B}$. Additionally, let $@ : \mathcal{M}(\mathbb{N}^d) \to \mathbb{Q}$ be an aggregate function and $h : \mathbb{N}^d \to \mathbb{Q}$ be a scalar arithmetic function. Then h is a conditional representation of $@$ subject to Ψ if and only if for all $X \in \mathcal{M}(\mathbb{N}^d)$, if $\Psi(X)$ holds (i.e., $\Psi(X) = 1$), then $@(X) = h(sum(X,1), ..., sum(X,d))$.*

Let h be a conditional representation of the aggregate function @ subject to Ψ. Let f be a fitness function. We say that h and f are compatible when $\Psi(f \odot M_n)$ holds for any LTS M and any $n \in \mathbb{N}$. $\qquad\square$

Let predicate $\Psi_{rate}(X) :=$ 'If $(p,q),(p',q') \in X$, then $q = q'$.' Then we have the following two lemmas.

Lemma 1. *Let* $X \in \mathcal{M}(\mathbb{N}^2)$ *and suppose* $\Psi_{rate}(X)$ *holds. Then* $@_{avg}(X) = sum(X,1)/sum(X,2)$. *Therefore,* $@_{avg}$ *is conditionally represented by* $h(x_1,x_2) = x_1/x_2$, *subject to* Ψ_{rate}. $\qquad\square$

Lemma 2. *For all* $n \in \mathbb{N}$ *and all LTS M,* $\Psi_{rate}(rate_\$ \odot M_n)$ *holds. Hence,* $rate_\$$ *and* $h(x_1,x_2) = x_1/x_2$ *are compatible.* $\qquad\square$

Lemma 1 follows from the fact that the average of a multiset of fractions is equal to the sum of the numerators divided by the sum of the denominators when the denominators are all equal. Lemma 2 is immediate: if $w \in M_n$ and $rate_\$(w) = (p,q)$, then $q = n$. From Lemma 1 and 2 it follows that $@_{avg}$ and $rate_\$$ are compatible. Therefore, if the fitness function is $rate_\$$ we can represent $@_{avg}(X)$ with the expression $sum(X,1)/sum(X,2)$.

Note that fitness functions other than $rate_\$$ might not be compatible with $@_{avg}$. For instance, let $f(w) = (\#_\$(w), \#_0(w))$, which measures the number of \$'s per 0. f does not satisfy Ψ_{rate}, but it is a realistic fitness function. In the case of $rate_\$$, time is measured by the observation of any label from Σ. Now for f, time is measured using only 0. If \$ denotes a local action of a server and 0 an interaction between two servers, f captures communication complexity. We leave handling of such non-compatible fitness functions for future work.

Fitness Score: Given alphabet Σ, fitness function f, and aggregate function @, the *fitness score* of an LTS M, denoted $@_f M$, is defined to be the limit $@_f M := \lim_{n \to \infty} @(f \odot M_n)$. This limit is a value in $\mathbb{R}_{\geq 0} \cup \{\infty, \bot\}$. The limit either: converges to a value $v \in \mathbb{R}_{\geq 0}$, in which case the score is v; or increases without bound, in which case we assign the value ∞; or exhibits some other behavior such as oscillation, in which case we assign the ill-behaved value $\bot$.

Comparison Relations: A comparison relation $\preccurlyeq$ is a subset of $(\mathbb{R}_{\geq 0} \cup \{\infty, \bot\})^2$. If $(a,b) \in \preccurlyeq$, we write $a \preccurlyeq b$. If neither $a \preccurlyeq b$ nor $b \preccurlyeq a$, we say that a and b are *incomparable*. Ignoring ∞ and $\bot$ for the moment, $\preccurlyeq$ could be any one of $\leqslant, <, \geqslant$, or $>$ on $\mathbb{R}$. Extending this comparator to ∞ and $\bot$ would be up to the user. One choice is to have these values be incomparable to any other value. Note that, even though the aggregate @ maps to $\mathbb{Q}$, $\preccurlyeq$ needs to compare real (and not just rational) numbers because the fitness score involves taking a limit. The semantics of $a \preccurlyeq b$ are that a is preferrable to b.

Example 8. Concluding our analysis of Example 3, consider an instance of our framework with fitness function $rate_\$$ (Definition 1), aggregate function $@_{avg}$

(Definition 2), and comparison operator $\preccurlyeq \, := \, \geqslant$ (since we prefer high rates of income). We can then compare the two simple systems introduced in Example 3. Building on what we have presented so far (c.f. Examples 4 and 6), we have:

$$@_f M^{(1)} \;=\; \lim_{n\to\infty} @(f \odot M_n^{(1)}) \;=\; \lim_{n\to\infty} 1 \;=\; 1$$

$$@_f M^{(2)} \;=\; \lim_{n\to\infty} @(f \odot M_n^{(2)}) \;=\; \lim_{n\to\infty} \frac{\lceil n/2 \rceil}{n} \;=\; 1/2$$

Because $@_f M^{(1)} \geqslant @_f M^{(2)}$, we conclude $@_f M^{(1)} \preccurlyeq @_f M^{(2)}$ and therefore we prefer $M^{(1)}$ to $M^{(2)}$. This result aligns with our intuitions; we would rather receive a dollar every day than a dollar every other day.   □

Evaluation, Comparison, and Synthesis Problems: Within our framework, we can consider various types of computational problems. A basic problem is that of *evaluating* the fitness score of a given system: *Given a fitness function f, an aggregate function @, and a system M, compute $@_f M$.* Another problem is that of *comparing* two systems: *Given a fitness function f, an aggregate function @, a comparison relation $\preccurlyeq$, and two systems M_1, M_2, check whether $@_f M_1 \preccurlyeq @_f M_2$.* We can also consider *fitness-optimal synthesis* problems, which ask to find a system with the best fitness score, perhaps subject to some correctness constraint (e.g. an LTL formula). Of these problems, in the rest of this paper we will focus on the fitness evaluation problem:

Problem 1 (Fitness Evaluation Problem). Let $M = \langle \Sigma, Q, Q_0, \Delta \rangle$ be a finite LTS and let $f = \langle f_1, ..., f_d \rangle$, where each f_i is represented as a DFA. Let @ : $\mathcal{M}(\mathbb{N}^d) \to \mathbb{Q}$ be an aggregate function represented by the scalar arithmetic function $h : \mathbb{N}^d \to \mathbb{Q}$. Finally, suppose that h and f are compatible. The fitness evaluation problem is to compute the fitness score $@_f M$ of M, i.e., to compute $\lim_{n\to\infty} @(f \odot M_n)$.   □

4   Reducing Fitness Evaluation to Matrix Analysis

In this section we propose a method to solve Problem 1 that consists in the following steps (assuming the same notation and setup as in Problem 1):

1. Compute the product automaton $P_i = M \| f_i$, for each $i \in \{1, ..., d\}$.
2. For each P_i, compute a matrix-vector pair (ξ_i, v_i) representing a *recurrence relation*. We call the matrix ξ_i the *recurrence matrix* and the vector v_i the *initial condition vector*.
3. Solve the following matrix analysis problem:

Problem 2. Let $g_i(n) = (\xi_i^{n+1} v_i)_0$ for fixed square matrices $\xi_1, ..., \xi_d$ and vectors $v_1, ..., v_d$ with non-negative integer entries and where $(u)_0$ denotes the first entry of vector u. Let $h : \mathbb{N}^d \to \mathbb{Q}$ be a scalar arithmetic function. Compute $\lim_{n\to\infty} h(g_1(n), g_2(n), ..., g_d(n))$.   □

The motivation for the above steps follows. In step 1, the product P_i represented all simultaneous paths through M and f_i. I.e., a path through P_i corresponds to taking a path through M and handing the transition label encountered at each step to the automaton representing f_i. As mentioned, step 2 computes a recurrence relation, which is reasonable because the number of accepting states visited across $(n+1)$-length paths is related to certain quantities computed over the n-length paths. The exact relationship is explained in detail in Sect. 4.1.

The correctness of the reduction to Problem 2 (Corollary 1) hinges on the fact that $g_i(n) = sum(f \odot M_n, i)$, i.e., computing $sum(f \odot M_n, i)$ (which is then an input to the aggregate function) reduces to computing the nth term of a recurrence relation, which in turn reduces to taking a matrix power.

Step 1 of the method (computing automata products) is standard. Therefore, in the rest of this section, we focus on explaining Steps 2 and 3.

4.1   Step 2: Constructing the Recurrence Relation

We will first explain the recurrence relation construction by example and then give the general construction.

By Example: We skip the first step of the method and assume that we have a product $P_1 = M \| f_1$. In particular, we consider the automaton of Fig. 3.

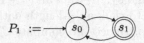

$$P_1 := \longrightarrow \; s_0 \;\; s_1$$

Fig. 3. A toy product $P_1 = M \| f_1$. P_1 has two states named s_0 and s_1. s_0 is the initial state and s_1 is the accepting state. The transition labels from Σ are not needed and hence are omitted.

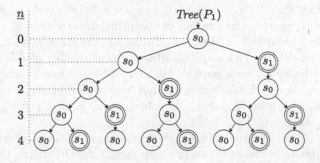

Fig. 4. Partial unfolding of the automaton of Fig. 3 into a tree up to depth 4. The column labeled n denotes the number of transitions taken.

From the automaton of Fig. 3 we extract the following recurrence relations:

$$\beta_{n+1}^{s_0} = \beta_n^{s_0} + \beta_n^{s_1}, \qquad\qquad \beta_0^{s_0} = 1 \qquad\qquad (1)$$

$$\beta_{n+1}^{s_1} = \beta_n^{s_0}, \qquad\qquad \beta_0^{s_1} = 0 \qquad\qquad (2)$$

$$\alpha_{n+1}^{s_0} = \alpha_n^{s_0} + \alpha_n^{s_1}, \qquad\qquad \alpha_0^{s_0} = 0 \qquad\qquad (3)$$

$$\alpha_{n+1}^{s_1} = \alpha_n^{s_0} + \beta_n^{s_0}, \qquad\qquad \alpha_0^{s_1} = 0 \qquad\qquad (4)$$

$$\alpha_n = \alpha_n^{s_0} + \alpha_n^{s_1}, \qquad\qquad \alpha_\varnothing = 0 \qquad\qquad (5)$$

where (as visual aid we provide Fig. 4, which displays the unfolding of P_1 of Fig. 3 into a tree containing all paths up to length 4):

- β_n^q is the total number of n-length paths through P_1 ending in state q, e.g., $\beta_0^{s_0} = 1$, $\beta_0^{s_1} = 0$, $\beta_3^{s_0} = 3$, $\beta_4^{s_1} = 3$.
- α_n^q is the total number of accepting states visited along all n-length paths through P_1 restricted to paths terminating in state q, e.g., $\alpha_1^{s_0} = 0$, $\alpha_1^{s_1} = 1$, $\alpha_3^{s_0} = 2$.
- α_n is the total number of accepting states visited along all n-length paths through P_1, e.g., $\alpha_0 = 0$, $\alpha_1 = 1$, $\alpha_2 = 2$, $\alpha_3 = 5$, $\alpha_4 = 10$.
- $\alpha_\varnothing$ is a dummy variable representing the initial condition of α_n. Notice that the α_n term of the recurrence is unique in that no other term depends on it.

We determine each equation of the example recurrence relation as follows:

Equations (1) capture the number of paths of a certain length ending in state s_0. The initial value $\beta_0^{s_0}$ is 1 because s_0 is an initial state. Otherwise, notice that s_0 has two predecessors: s_0 and s_1. To walk an $(n+1)$-length path ending in s_0, it is necessary and sufficient to walk an n-length path to one of its predecessors and then take one more step. Hence, we compute $\beta_{n+1}^{s_0}$ as the sum of $\beta_n^{s_0}$ and $\beta_n^{s_1}$. Analogous reasoning yields Equations (2); notice the initial value $\beta_0^{s_1}$ is 0 since s_1 is not an initial state.

Equations (3) capture the number of accepting states visited along all paths of a certain length ending in state s_0. Importantly, s_0 is not an accepting state. Therefore, adding it to an n-length path will not change the number of accepting states visited along that path. Hence, as with β, we can compute $\alpha_{n+1}^{s_0}$ as the sum of $\alpha_n^{s_0}$ and $\alpha_n^{s_1}$. The initial value $\alpha_0^{s_0}$ is 0 because s_0 is an initial state, but not an accepting state.

Equations (4) capture the number of accepting states visited along all paths of a certain length ending in state s_1. Unlike s_0, the state s_1 is an accepting state. Therefore, the $(n+1)$th step contributes to the number of accepting states visited, in particular for each path it will increase the count by one. There are $\beta_n^{s_0}$ such paths, hence the inclusion of that term in addition to the α of the predecessor s_0. The initial value $\alpha_0^{s_1}$ is 0 because s_1 is an accepting state, but not an initial state.

Equations (5) capture the accepting states along all paths of a certain length. The initial value $\alpha_\varnothing$ is irrelevant; we use 0 for simplicity. Otherwise, this equation merely captures the fact that we can partition the paths of length n based on which state they end in and take a sum over that partition to compute a value over all paths.

We can represent these recurrence relation as a matrix-vector pair (ξ_1, v_1), where:

$$
v_1 = \begin{bmatrix} \alpha_\varnothing \\ \alpha_0^{s_0} \\ \alpha_0^{s_1} \\ \beta_0^{s_0} \\ \beta_0^{s_1} \end{bmatrix} = \begin{bmatrix} 0 \\ 0 \\ 1 \\ 0 \\ 0 \end{bmatrix} \quad \text{and} \quad \xi_1 = \begin{bmatrix} 0\,1\,1\,0\,0 \\ 0\,1\,1\,0\,0 \\ 0\,1\,0\,1\,0 \\ 0\,0\,0\,1\,1 \\ 0\,0\,0\,1\,0 \end{bmatrix}
$$

E.g. row 1 of ξ_1 indicates which terms are required to compute α_n.

In General: The key to generalizing the above method is the set of predecessors for each state and how each term should be computed using the predecessor terms. Not shown in this example is the case where a state q is both an initial state and an accepting state. In that case α_0^q is 1. Also there is at most one transition between two states in this example. In general, there may be multiple transitions between two states (with different labels). In that case, the equations will include factors in front of the α and β terms. In particular,

$$
\beta_{n+1}^{q'} = \sum_{q \in Q} t_{q,q'} \cdot \beta_n^q
$$

where $t_{q,q'}$ is the number of transition labels that transition from q to q' (Note: $t_{q,q'}$ is 0 if q is not a predecessor of q'). Likewise:

$$
\alpha_{n+1}^{q'} = \sum_{q \in Q} (t_{q,q'} \cdot \alpha_n^q) + (t_{q,q'}^* \cdot \beta_n^q)
$$

where $t_{q,q'}^*$ is $t_{q,q'}$ when q' is an accepting state and 0 otherwise.

Now we explain the recurrence relation extraction algorithm in general. Let $P = M \| f$ be the synchronous product of some finite LTS M and some DFA f. We explain how to extract both the recurrence matrix ξ and the initial condition vector v from P.

In what follows, we assume that P has N states indexed by the set $\{1, ..., N\}$. We first define a matrix that encodes the transition relation of P:

Definition 5. *We define the $N \times N$ predecessor matrix, denoted* $\mathbf{D}$*, by its entries. We denote the entry in the ith row and jth column as* $\mathbf{D}_{ij}$*. Define* $\mathbf{D}_{ij}$ *to be the number of transitions from state j to state i in P.* □

Next, we define a matrix that encodes the accepting states of P:

Definition 6. *We define the $N \times N$ accepting matrix, denoted* $\mathbf{A}$*, so that* $\mathbf{A}_{ij} = \mathbf{D}_{ij}$ *if state i of P is an accepting state. Otherwise,* $\mathbf{A}_{ij} = 0$*.* □

We are now able to define the recurrence matrix ξ:

Definition 7. *The* recurrence matrix *of P is the $(2N + 1) \times (2N + 1)$ matrix*

$$
\xi = \begin{bmatrix} 0 & \hat{1} & \hat{0} \\ \hat{0} & \mathbf{D} & \mathbf{A} \\ \hat{0} & \mathbf{0} & \mathbf{D} \end{bmatrix}
$$

where $\hat{0}$ and $\hat{1}$ are n-dimensional vectors of 0's and 1's respectively and where $\mathbf{0}$ is an $n \times n$ matrix of 0's.   □

We now explain how to extract the initial condition vector v from P. We first introduce some notation. For convenience, we vectorize the α_n^q and β_n^q terms. Let $\hat{\alpha}_n := (\alpha_n^1, ..., \alpha_n^N)^T$ and $\hat{\beta}_n := (\beta_n^1, ..., \beta_n^N)^T$. Then, the two vectors $\hat{\alpha}_0$ and $\hat{\beta}_0$ capture the initial conditions of terms α_n^i and β_n^i in the recurrence relation, and we can construct the $2N+1$ dimensional vector v by combining $\hat{\alpha}_0$ and $\hat{\beta}_0$ along with $\alpha_\varnothing = 0$, namely, $v := (\alpha_\varnothing, \hat{\alpha}_0, \hat{\beta}_0)^T$.

The vectors $\hat{\alpha}_0$ and $\hat{\beta}_0$ are extracted from P as follows: (1) The ith entry of $\hat{\alpha}_0$ is 1 if and only if state i of P is both an accepting state and an initial state. Otherwise, that entry of $\hat{\alpha}_0$ is 0. (2) The ith entry of $\hat{\beta}_0$ is 1 if and only if state i of P is an initial state. Otherwise, that entry of $\hat{\beta}_0$ is 0.

The following two statements (proven in Appendix A.4 of [22]) capture the correctness of our reduction.

Theorem 1. *Let α and β be the recurrence relation terms for the product $M\|f_i$, as constructed above. Then for all $n \geqslant 0$, $\xi_i^{n+1} v_i = \begin{bmatrix} \alpha_n \\ \hat{\alpha}_{n+1} \\ \hat{\beta}_{n+1} \end{bmatrix}$. And hence*

$$(\xi_i^{n+1} v_i)_0 = \alpha_n = sum(f \odot M_n, i).$$ □

Corollary 1. *Let ξ_i and v_i be the recurrence matrices and initial condition vectors for the products $M\|f_i$, for $i = 1, ..., d$, as constructed above. Then*

$$@_f(M) = \lim_{n \to \infty} h((\xi_1^{n+1} v_1)_0, (\xi_2^{n+1} v_2)_0, ..., (\xi_d^{n+1} v_d)_0)$$

□

4.2   Step 3: Matrix Analysis

Next we will discuss two methods for solving the matrix analysis problem. One of these methods is *symbolic* and the other *numerical*. We illustrate them by continuing with the example of Fig. 3. We have constructed $g_1(n) = (\xi_1^{n+1} v_1)_0$. For sake of example, let us assume that $\xi_1 = \xi_2$ and that $v_2 = \xi_1 v_1$, so $g_2(n) = g_1(n + 1)$. Let us also assume that the aggregate function is represented by $h(x_1, x_2) = x_1/x_2$.

Symbolic Method: The first step of the symbolic method is to compute closed-form expressions for each g_i. Tools such as Mathematica can solve for this closed-form expression using Jordan decomposition [31]. We omit the details. The result in the case of the example is:

$$g_1(n) = \frac{1}{25 \cdot 2^{(1+n)}} \left(4\sqrt{5}k_1^n - 4\sqrt{5}c_1^n - 5k_1^n n + 5\sqrt{5}k_1^n n - 5c_1^n n - 5\sqrt{5}c_1^n n \right)$$

where $c_1 := 1 + \sqrt{5}$ and $k_1 := 1 - \sqrt{5}$. As mentioned, $g_2(n) = g_1(n + 1)$.

Once we have the closed-form expressions, we can ask Mathematica to solve the limit; it does so easily: $\lim_{n \to \infty} g_1(n)/g_2(n) = 2/(1 + \sqrt{5})$ (the reciprocal of the golden ratio). Tools such as Mathematica can solve a broad class of limits using, e.g., Gruntz's method [29].

Computing the Jordan decomposition is currently the bottleneck for the symbolic method. Our experiments with Mathematica suggest that it cannot compute the Jordan decomposition for even moderately sized matrices, the run-time being exponential in the dimension of the matrix. There have been several recent attempts to improve the state of the art in Jordan decomposition [28] and we are hopeful that this sub-problem will soon be feasible to compute for large matrices.

Numerical Method: In this method, we compute $h(g_1(K), g_2(K))$ for large K, which we call a K-*approximation*. Although we have not yet established an error bound on the difference between the K-approximation and the true value of the limit, the K-approximation appears to converge relatively quickly. For instance, in the case of Example 3, the K-approximation for $K = 15$ and $K = 20$ are 0.6180344 and 0.6180339 respectively, which do not differ until the seventh decimal place. Our current approach is to compute the K-approximation for, e.g., $K = 8192$ and $K = 9000$ and determine at which decimal place they differ to establish the precision of the K-approximation for $K = 9000$. We can also plot intermediate K-approximations against K.

A naive implementation of K-approximation does not scale. Instead, we use the standard *exponentiation by squaring* technique to quickly compute K-approximations for large K. For example, to compute ξ^{11} for some matrix ξ, it suffices to compute ξ^2, ξ^4, and ξ^8, since $\xi^{11} = \xi \cdot \xi^2 \cdot \xi^8$. Note that $\xi^4 = (\xi^2)^2$ and $\xi^8 = (\xi^4)^2$, hence the name *exponentiation by squaring*. We need only compute $\log K$ squares and combine them per the binary representation of K. Furthermore, in our implementation, we found that we needed large datatypes (128 bit) to represent the entries of the matrix. As matrix power for large datatypes appears to not be implemented in the linear algebra library we used (numpy), we implemented this operation ourselves.

Although the examples in this section used $h(x_1, x_2) = x_1/x_2$, our method generalizes to any aggregate conditionally represented by a scalar arithmetic function $h(x_1, x_2, ..., x_d)$. This generality holds because the g_i are constructed independently of one another and combined according to h. For instance, if we had $h(x_1, x_2, x_3) = (x_1 + x_2)/x_3$, we construct $g_3(n)$ as we did for g_1 and g_2. We then take the limit or approximation of $(g_1(n) + g_2(n))/g_3(n)$ rather than $g_1(n)/g_2(n)$.

Comparison: The symbolic method gives an exact, symbolic representation of the fitness score, but unfortunately does not yet scale well, as we shall see from the experiments in Sect. 5 that follows. The numerical approach on the other hand can compute in seconds an approximation of the fitness score. As we shall show, these approximations are precise enough to distinguish between systems of different fitness.

5   Case Studies

We evaluate our framework on three case studies, described in detail in the subsections that follow, and summarized in Table 1. The symbolic method did not terminate after an hour for the larger two case studies (2PC and ABP) due to limitations imposed by the state of the art in Jordan decomposition (c.f. Section 4.2). Therefore, Table 1 reports the results obtained by the numerical method.

In each case study we compute the fitness score for different system variants (column M). Column $|M|$ represents the size (total number of states) of the system being measured, which is the product of all distributed processes. Time refers to the total execution time, in seconds. Column $@_f(M_{8192})$ refers to the K-approximation of the fitness score with $K = 8192$, and likewise for $K = 9000$. As can be seen, the two approximations are very close within each row (identical up to at least the 3rd decimal point), which indicates convergence. The reason we report the fitness score for K = 8192 instead of another number, say K = 8000 or K = 8500, is efficiency: 8192 the largest power of two less than 9000, and in order to compute the fitness score for K = 9000 we need to compute it anyway for K = 8192. Our results can be reproduced using a publicly available artifact, which is structured, documented, and licensed for ease of repurposing [23].

Let us remark that in the 2PC and ABP case studies, the systems being measured were automatically generated by a distributed protocol synthesis tool, which is an improved version of the tool described in [5,6]. As our goal in this paper is fitness evaluation, we omit discussing the synthesis tool. But, as mentioned in the introduction, evaluation of automatically synthesized systems is a promising application of our framework.

All case studies use the $@_{avg}$ aggregate function. Additionally, we use three variations of the fitness function in Fig. 5. This parametric fitness function suggests the possibility of constructing a library of general, reusable fitness functions. Although it was straightforward to construct fitness functions for our purposes, this library would further reduce that burden for users.

In the rest of this section we provide further details on each case study. Some supporting figures and intermediate results are provided in Appendix A.5 of [22].

5.1   Case Study #1: Simple Communication Protocol

This section treats the communication protocol presented in Example 1. We instantiate the framework to measure the average rate at which send-ack sequences are executed and apply this instance of the framework to M and M' (Fig. 1). The python representations of all simple communication protocol

Table 1. A summary of the numerical method results of the three case studies.

case study	M	$|M|$	total time (sec.)	$@_f(M_{8192})$	$@_f(M_{9000})$
simple comm	good	3	0.0052	0.249970	0.249972
simple comm	bad	5	0.006	0.138165	0.138168
2PC	H	58	0.41	0.0833	0.0832
2PC	A1	30	0.25	0.07856	0.07857
2PC	A2	25	0.1	0.0833	0.0832
ABP	HH	144	9.1	0.016864	0.016859
ABP	HA	144	8.6	0.015435	0.015430
ABP	AH	144	8.7	0.015218	0.015212
ABP	AA	144	8.6	0.01391	0.01390

processes and fitness functions are available in `toy_automata.py` of the artifact [23].

Recall that $\Sigma = \{s, t, a\}$. Let $f_1(w) :=$ 'the number of send-ack sequences of the form st^*a in w'. For instance (brackets [and] added for emphasis), $f_1(aat[sa][sta]as[stta]stt[sa]) = 4$. Additionally, let $f_2(w) := |w|$ (the length of w) and let the fitness function be $f := \langle f_1, f_2 \rangle$. The functions f_1, f_2 can be represented as the DFA shown in Fig. 5, with $L = \{s\}$ and $R = \{a\}$. This fitness function is measuring the number of send-ack sequences per unit of discrete time, which is analogous to the traditional measure of throughput in distributed systems.

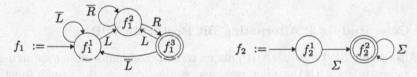

Fig. 5. The DFA representations of f_1 and f_2 for the case studies, parameterized by the set of labels Σ, as well as a set of *left endpoints* $L \subseteq \Sigma$ and *right endpoints* $R \subseteq \Sigma$. $\overline{L} = \Sigma \setminus L$ and likewise for $\overline{R}$.

As reported in Table 1, the system that uses the good receiver has a fitness score of about 0.25 and the system using the bad receiver a score of about 0.138. These scores are *interpretable* in that they have units: send-ack sequences per unit of discrete time. Hence, the framework deems the good receiver as more fit and this determination aligns with our intuitions. Because this example is relatively small, Mathematica was able to compute the exact fitness scores of these systems. The system that uses the good receiver has a fitness score of exactly 1/4 (obtained after 34 s) and the system that uses the bad receiver has a score of exactly $\frac{5-\sqrt{5}}{20} \approx 0.138$ (obtained after 563 s).

5.2   Case Study #2: Two Phase Commit (2PC)

Two phase commit (2PC) is a protocol for making transactional changes to a distributed database atomically; if one sub-operation of the transaction is aborted at one remote database, so too must the sub-operations at all other remote databases. Although each iteration of 2PC is terminating, it is typical to assume there will be infinitely many such iterations, and our model reflects this. In our model of 2PC, a user initiates a transaction by synchronizing with a *transaction manager* on the label x. The transaction is complete when the transaction manager synchronizes with the user on label *fail* or *succ*. We omit the details of the intermediate exchanges between the transaction manager and database managers. The python representations of all 2PC processes and fitness functions are available in _2pc_automata.py of the artifact [23].

The fitness function for this case study is as depicted in Fig. 5, with $L = \{x\}$, $R = \{fail, succ\}$, and Σ has a total of 18 labels. This fitness function measures the rate at which transactions are initiated and then completed.

We study three 2PC implementations, each using a different transaction manager LTS. The system labeled H in Table 1 uses a previously manually constructed transaction manager that the synthesis tool was also able to discover automatically, while the systems labeled A1 and A2 use new transaction managers generated by the synthesis tool. The automatically generated transaction managers have 12 states each and it is therefore hard to tell at a glance which will give rise to the most efficient protocol. Our tool automatically reports, in fractions of a second, a fitness score of about 0.083 for both systems H and A2, and a score of about 0.079 for system A1. These fitness scores have units: transactions per unit time. Hence, in the same amount of time, A1 completes about 5% fewer transactions than H or A2.

5.3   Case Study #3: Alternating Bit Protocol (ABP)

The Alternating Bit Protocol (ABP) allows reliable communication over an unreliable network. As with the prior two case studies, we use the fitness function depicted in Fig. 5, except with $L = \{send\}, R = \{done\}$, and Σ of size 12. Similar to case study #1 we are measuring the rate of send-done sequences. The python representations of all ABP processes and fitness functions are available in abp_automata.py of the artifact [23].

In [6], the authors present a method to automatically synthesize (distributed) ABP sender and receiver processes. Here, we evaluate the fitness of the ABP variants that use these various synthesized processes. Together the synthesized sender and receiver processes have 14 states, which again makes manual determinations about the fitness very challenging—even more so due to the distributed nature of the problem. It is no longer necessarily a question of which sender or receiver is better than the other sender or receiver, but a question of which combination of sender and receiver is best. Once again, our framework allows to automatically make this determination in a matter of seconds.

The systems are ranked by fitness in the following order: HH, HA, AH, AA. H stands for human-designed (and then also rediscovered during synthesis) and A stands for newly discovered during synthesis. The first position is for the sender process and the second for the receiver. In this case study, the newly discovered processes do worse than the manually constructed processes. The difference in fitness scores is meaningful: in the same amount of time, AA will complete about 18% fewer sequences on average. AH and HA will both complete about 8.5% fewer sequences than HH.

6   Related Work

Our work is broadly related to the field of performance analysis and evaluation. Mathematical models typically used there include Markov Chains, Markov Decision Processes, Markov Automata, queueing models, Petri nets, timed or hybrid automata, etc., e.g., see [9,15–17,25,34–36]. Our approach differs as our mathematical framework uses neither timed nor probabilistic models such as the ones above. Because we do not use stochastic models, our work is also different from the work on probabilistic verification, e.g., see [8–10,18,33]. Our work also differs from performance analysis approaches that use max-plus algebra based frameworks such as the real-time calculus, e.g., see [30,38,44,45].

Our work is also related to non-boolean interpretations of temporal semantics, such as the 5-valued robust temporal logic rLTL [7,43]. However, our motivation is performance comparisons rather than robustness. Our framework also differs from that of signal temporal logic (STL) [11,12,27,39–42], which is valued over real-time traces. Our framework is over discrete traces, although there have been recent STL extensions which handle both real and discrete time [26]. In addition, our framework is parameterized by generic quantitative concepts (the fitness and aggregate functions and the comparison relation) that are present neither in rLTL nor in STL or its variants.

Our work is closely related to the field of quantitative verification, synthesis, and games, e.g., see [1,2,13,14,19–21,32]. Typically, these works assign values to *weighted automata*. These automata blend in a single model both the description of the system and the description of any performance or fitness functions associated with the system. In comparison, our framework decouples the description of the system (e.g., a plain LTS without any weights) from the description of the fitness function (e.g., a DFA). These works support aggregates like sup while our framework is defined for more general aggregates, including averages.

Sensing cost [4] and propositional quality [3] are two other ways to measure the fitness of a system. Sensing cost is a specific measure of fitness, whereas our framework is a more general setting. The work on propositional quality is quite general, like our work, but it uses a quantitative variant of LTL to assign scores rather than DFA. This logic induces a sort of recursive computation that can never be captured by a DFA. The logic is limited though in that it can only characterize finite chunks of a trace at one time (and no limit is taken), whereas our characterization applies to the infinite trace after taking a limit. Hence propositional quality and our fitness evaluation are fundamentally distinct.

7   Conclusions and Future Work

We proposed a formal framework that assigns *fitness scores* to systems modeled as finite LTSs. The main novelty of our framework is that it *decouples* the description of the system from the set of domain-specific parameters such as fitness and aggregate functions, which determine the final fitness score. Furthermore, the user defines these fitness scores and aggregate functions over partial runs, which are easier for the user to reason about—our framework does the heavy lifting of extending this reasoning to infinite traces. This decoupling and finite reasoning make our framework more useable and its results more *interpretable*. Indeed, in all of our case studies the scores are not merely numbers; they have meaningful units, e.g., send-ack sequences per unit of time.

We used our framework to evaluate the automatically synthesized ABP protocols presented in [6] as well as our own automatically synthesized 2PC protocols. We showed that some of these protocols are better than others. Inspired by this application, we plan to investigate the use of our framework in protocol synthesis, specifically in synthesizing protocols that not only satisfy a given correctness specification but are also *optimal* with respect to a fitness score, i.e., *fitness-optimal synthesis* (c.f. page 8).

We are also actively exploring ways to improve the scalability of the symbolic method. In particular, we may be able to feasibly compute a simplified version of the recurrence matrix ξ_i without sacrificing the accuracy of the final computed limit. Additionally, we would like to generalize our method to aggregates like min / max, which do not have conditional representations, and to systems that cannot be represented as finite labeled transition systems. We suspect that best/worst-case analysis reduces to the minimal cost-to-time ratio problem [37], but in general aggregates with no conditional representation may be more challenging.

Acknowledgements. Derek Egolf's research has been initially supported by a Northeastern University PhD fellowship. This material is based upon work supported by the National Science Foundation Graduate Research Fellowship under Grant No. (1938052). Any opinion, findings, and conclusions or recommendations expressed in this material are those of the authors(s) and do not necessarily reflect the views of the National Science Foundation. We thank the anonymous reviewers for their helpful comments and feedback.

References

1. de Alfaro, L., Faella, M., Henzinger, T.A., Majumdar, R., Stoelinga, M.: Model checking discounted temporal properties. Theor. Comput. Sci. **345**(1), 139–170 (2005)
2. Almagor, S., Alur, R., Bansal, S.: Equilibria in quantitative concurrent games. eprint arXiv:1809.10503 (2018)

3. Almagor, S., Boker, U., Kupferman, O.: Formalizing and reasoning about quality. In: Fomin, F.V., Freivalds, R., Kwiatkowska, M., Peleg, D. (eds.) ICALP 2013. LNCS, vol. 7966, pp. 15–27. Springer, Heidelberg (2013). https://doi.org/10.1007/978-3-642-39212-2_3

4. Almagor, S., Kuperberg, D., Kupferman, O.: Regular sensing. In: FSTTCS. LIPIcs, vol. 29. Schloss Dagstuhl-Leibniz-Zentrum fuer Informatik (2014)

5. Alur, R., Martin, M., Raghothaman, M., Stergiou, C., Tripakis, S., Udupa, A.: Synthesizing finite-state protocols from scenarios and requirements. In: Yahav, E. (ed.) HVC 2014. LNCS, vol. 8855, pp. 75–91. Springer, Cham (2014). https://doi.org/10.1007/978-3-319-13338-6_7

6. Alur, R., Tripakis, S.: Automatic synthesis of distributed protocols. SIGACT News **48**(1), 55–90 (2017)

7. Anevlavis, T., Philippe, M., Neider, D., Tabuada, P.: Being correct is not enough: efficient verification using robust linear temporal logic. ACM Trans. Comput. Log. **23**(2), 8:1–8:39 (2022)

8. Baier, C., Haverkort, B.R., Hermanns, H., Katoen, J.P.: Performance evaluation and model checking join forces. Commun. ACM **53**(9), 76–85 (2010)

9. Baier, C., Katoen, J.P.: Principles of Model Checking. MIT Press, Cambridge (2008)

10. Baier, C., de Alfaro, L., Forejt, V., Kwiatkowska, M.: Model checking probabilistic systems. In: Handbook of Model Checking, pp. 963–999. Springer, Cham (2018). https://doi.org/10.1007/978-3-319-10575-8_28

11. Beg, O.A., Nguyen, L.V., Johnson, T.T., Davoudi, A.: Signal temporal logic-based attack detection in DC microgrids. IEEE Trans. Smart Grid **10**(4), 3585–3595 (2019)

12. Bortolussi, L., Gallo, G.M., Křetínský, J., Nenzi, L.: Learning model checking and the kernel trick for signal temporal logic on stochastic processes. In: Learning model checking and the kernel trick for signal temporal logic on stochastic processes. LNCS, vol. 13243, pp. 281–300. Springer, Cham (2022). https://doi.org/10.1007/978-3-030-99524-9_15

13. Bouyer, P., Gardy, P., Markey, N.: Quantitative verification of weighted kripke structures. In: Cassez, F., Raskin, J.-F. (eds.) ATVA 2014. LNCS, vol. 8837, pp. 64–80. Springer, Cham (2014). https://doi.org/10.1007/978-3-319-11936-6_6

14. Brihaye, T., Geeraerts, G., Haddad, A., Monmege, B., Pérez, G.A., Renault, G.: Quantitative games under failures. In: FSTTCS. Leibniz International Proceedings in Informatics (LIPIcs), vol. 45, pp. 293–306. Schloss Dagstuhl-Leibniz-Zentrum fuer Informatik (2015)

15. Bucci, G., Sassoli, L., Vicario, E.: A discrete time model for performance evaluation and correctness verification of real time systems. In: 10th International Workshop on Petri Nets and Performance Models, 2003. Proceedings, pp. 134–143 (2003)

16. Bucci, G., Sassoli, L., Vicario, E.: Correctness verification and performance analysis of real-time systems using stochastic preemptive time petri nets. IEEE Trans. Softw. Eng. **31**(11), 913–927 (2005)

17. Cassandras, C.G., Lafortune, S.: Introduction to Discrete Event Systems, 3rd edn. Springer (2021). https://doi.org/10.1007/978-0-387-68612-7

18. Cauchi, N., Hoque, K.A., Abate, A., Stoelinga, M.: Efficient probabilistic model checking of smart building maintenance using fault maintenance trees. eprint arXiv:1801.04263 (2018)

19. Černý, P., Chatterjee, K., Henzinger, T.A., Radhakrishna, A., Singh, R.: Quantitative synthesis for concurrent programs. In: Gopalakrishnan, G., Qadeer, S. (eds.)

CAV 2011. LNCS, vol. 6806, pp. 243–259. Springer, Heidelberg (2011). https://doi.org/10.1007/978-3-642-22110-1_20

20. Chatterjee, K., Doyen, L., Henzinger, T.A.: Quantitative languages. ACM Trans. Comput. Log. **11**(4) (2010)

21. Chatterjee, K., de Alfaro, L., Faella, M., Henzinger, T.A., Majumdar, R., Stoelinga, M.: Compositional quantitative reasoning. In: QEST, pp. 179–188. IEEE Computer Society (2006)

22. Egolf, D., Tripakis, S.: Decoupled fitness criteria for reactive systems. eprint arXiv: 2212.12455 (2023)

23. Egolf, D., Tripakis, S.: Decoupled Fitness Criteria for Reactive Systems (Artifact, SEFM 2023) (2023). https://doi.org/10.5281/zenodo.8168367

24. Egolf, D., Tripakis, S.: Synthesis of distributed protocols by enumeration modulo isomorphisms. In: ATVA. Springer (2023)

25. Fakih, M., Grüttner, K., Fränzle, M., Rettberg, A.: Towards performance analysis of SDFGs mapped to shared-bus architectures using model-checking. In: DATE, pp. 1167–1172. EDA Consortium San Jose, CA, USA/ACM DL (2013)

26. Ferrère, T., Maler, O., Ničković, D.: Mixed-time signal temporal logic. In: André, É., Stoelinga, M. (eds.) FORMATS 2019. LNCS, vol. 11750, pp. 59–75. Springer, Cham (2019). https://doi.org/10.1007/978-3-030-29662-9_4

27. Finkbeiner, B., Fränzle, M., Kohn, F., Kröger, P.: A truly robust signal temporal logic: monitoring safety properties of interacting cyber-physical systems under uncertain observation. Algorithms 15(4) (2022)

28. Ghabbour, R.R., Abdelgaliel, I.H., Hanna, M.T.: A directed graph and MATLAB generation of the Jordan canonical form for a class of zero-one matrices. In: ICENCO, vol. 1, pp. 86–91 (2022)

29. Gruntz, D.W.: On Computing Limits in a Symbolic Manipulation System. Ph.D. thesis (1996)

30. Guan, N., Yi, W.: Finitary real-time calculus: efficient performance analysis of distributed embedded systems. In: RTSS, pp. 330–339 (2013)

31. Hefferon, J.: Linear Algebra, pp. 440-463 (2020). https://hefferon.net/

32. Henzinger, T.A.: Quantitative reactive modeling and verification. Comput. Sci. Res. Dev. **28**(4), 331–344 (2013). https://doi.org/10.1007/s00450-013-0251-7

33. Jansen, N., et al.: Accelerating parametric probabilistic verification. In: Norman, G., Sanders, W. (eds.) QEST 2014. LNCS, vol. 8657, pp. 404–420. Springer, Cham (2014). https://doi.org/10.1007/978-3-319-10696-0_31

34. Kempf, J.-F., Bozga, M., Maler, O.: Performance evaluation of schedulers in a probabilistic setting. In: Fahrenberg, U., Tripakis, S. (eds.) FORMATS 2011. LNCS, vol. 6919, pp. 1–17. Springer, Heidelberg (2011). https://doi.org/10.1007/978-3-642-24310-3_1

35. Kwiatkowska, M.Z., Norman, G., Parker, D., Sproston, J.: Performance analysis of probabilistic timed automata using digital clocks. Formal Methods Syst. Des. **29**(1), 33–78 (2006)

36. Larsen, K.G.: Automatic verification, performance analysis, synthesis and optimization of timed systems. In: TIME, pp. 1–1 (2016)

37. Lawler, E.L.: Optimal cycles in graphs and the minimal cost-to-time ratio problem. Tech. Rep. UCB/ERL M343, EECS Department, UC, Berkeley (1972)

38. Lu, Q., Madsen, M., Milata, M., Ravn, S., Fahrenberg, U., Larsen, K.G.: Reachability analysis for timed automata using max-plus algebra. J. Logic Algebraic Program. **81**(3), 298–313 (2012)

39. Ničković, D., Lebeltel, O., Maler, O., Ferrère, T., Ulus, D.: AMT 2.0: qualitative and quantitative trace analysis with extended signal temporal logic. Int. J. Softw. Tools Technol. Transfer **22**(6), 741–758 (2020). https://doi.org/10.1007/s10009-020-00582-z
40. Prabhakar, P., Lal, R., Kapinski, J.: Automatic trace generation for signal temporal logic. In: RTSS, pp. 208–217 (2018)
41. Puranic, A.G., Deshmukh, J.V., Nikolaidis, S.: Learning from demonstrations using signal temporal logic. eprint arXiv:2102.07730 (2021)
42. Salamati, A., Soudjani, S., Zamani, M.: Data-driven verification of stochastic linear systems with signal temporal logic constraints. Automatica **131**, 109781 (2021)
43. Tabuada, P., Neider, D.: Robust linear temporal logic. In: EACSL, LIPIcs, vol. 62. Schloss Dagstuhl - Leibniz-Zentrum für Informatik (2016)
44. Thiele, L., Chakraborty, S., Naedele, M.: Real-time calculus for scheduling hard real-time systems. In: ISCAS, pp. 101–104 (2000)
45. Wandeler, E., Thiele, L.: Performance analysis of distributed embedded systems. In: Embedded Systems Handbook. CRC Press (2005)

Capturing Smart Contract Design
with DCR Graphs

Mojtaba Eshghie[1](✉)(iD), Wolfgang Ahrendt[2](iD), Cyrille Artho[1](iD),
Thomas Troels Hildebrandt[3](iD), and Gerardo Schneider[4](iD)

[1] KTH Royal Institute of Technology, Stockholm, Sweden
`eshghie@kth.se`, `artho@kth.se`
[2] Chalmers University of Technology, Gothenburg, Sweden
`ahrendt@chalmers.se`
[3] University of Copenhagen, Copenhagen, Denmark
`hilde@di.ku.dk`
[4] University of Gothenburg, Gothenburg, Sweden
`gerardo.schneider@gu.se`

Abstract. Smart contracts manage blockchain assets and embody business processes. However, mainstream smart contract programming languages such as Solidity lack explicit notions of roles, action dependencies, and time. Instead, these concepts are implemented in program code. This makes it very hard to design and analyze smart contracts.

We argue that DCR graphs are a suitable formalization tool for smart contracts because they explicitly and visually capture the mentioned features. We utilize this expressiveness to show that many common high-level design patterns representing the underlying business processes in smart-contract applications can be naturally modeled this way. Applying these patterns shows that DCR graphs facilitate the development and analysis of correct and reliable smart contracts by providing a clear and easy-to-understand specification.

Keywords: Smart Contract Modelling · DCR Graphs · Design
Patterns

1 Introduction

A *smart contract* is implemented as immutable code executed on a blockchain and may be seen as a special business process specifying a contractual agreement on actions to be carried out by different roles. While smart contracts offer advantages such as uncompromised (automated) execution even without a trusted party, they can also be complex and difficult to design and understand. This is even more problematic as they cannot be changed once deployed.

In a normal business process environment, different roles collaborate to achieve a common business goal. In contrast, different roles in a smart contract typically have adversarial interests. Therefore, smart contracts introduce

C. Ferreira and T. A. C. Willemse (Eds.): SEFM 2023, LNCS 14323, pp. 106–125, 2023.
https://doi.org/10.1007/978-3-031-47115-5_7

new types of patterns of behavior, which have so far only been informally described [19,30,50,52]. To provide an unambiguous understanding of the patterns that can also provide the basis for formal specifications, we set out to extend the study and formalization of process patterns to include these smart contract patterns.

Solutions to adversarial-interest problems often use time- or data-related constraints between actions cutting across the process and the more standard use of roles and sequential action dependencies. We find that a declarative notation involving data and time is appropriate for formalizing the new smart contract process patterns. Moreover, smart contract languages exhibit a transactional behavior of actions, where an action may be attempted but aborted if the required constraints for executing it are not fulfilled. This suggests that individual actions have a life cycle, like sub-processes.

For these reasons, we use DCR graphs [38,43], which are by now a well-established declarative business process notation that has been extended with data [38], time [38], and sub-processes [43]. DCR graphs visually capture important properties such as the partial ordering of events, roles of contract users, and temporal function attributes. Using DCR graphs, it is possible to represent a smart contract with a clear and concise model that is more expressive and comprehensive than other types of models. As the design patterns we model concern the *high-level* behavior of a smart contract under analysis, we elide technical details of the patterns' implementation and execution. Therefore, we use the term "high-level" design pattern for the patterns that DCR graphs capture well, as they represent the underlying business process of the contract. Further, DCR models are useful for analysis. We show that using DCR graphs facilitates the development of correct and reliable smart contracts by providing a clear and easy-to-understand specification. More concretely, our contributions are:

1. We systematically identify and distinguish high-level design patterns from low-level (implementation-specific) patterns in smart contracts (Table 1), and demonstrate how we model them with DCR graphs by going through four of the most complex ones (Sect. 3, Sect. 3, Sect. 3, and Sect. 3). The DCR models of the rest of the 19 patterns may be found in the accompanying repository [25].
2. We demonstrate how one can capture the design of a complete contract, not just a design pattern, with the help of DCR graphs (casino example in Sect. 4). The modeled contract has three of the design pattern models from this paper incorporated, which helps to demonstrate the combinability of pattern models to shape the final design of the contract.
3. As a result of a thorough analysis of real-world contracts, including popular contract libraries, we identify (and model) two new design patterns: *time incentivization* (Sect. 3) and *escapability* (Sect. 3). Both of these patterns are extensively used by the Solidity developer community but are not yet introduced as design patterns in research literature [30,42,50,52].

Our application of these formalized design patterns in Sect. 4 shows that using DCR graphs can facilitate the development of correct and reliable smart contracts by providing a clear and easy-to-understand specification. Moreover, DCR specifications can provide a basis for automated (dynamic or static) analysis of smart contracts, which we exemplified by preliminary runtime verification infrastructure and experiments in our tool paper [27].

Our usage of DCR graphs to model smart contracts and our focus on high-level rather than low-level properties allows us to capture the key semantics of the contract succinctly. We can verify properties (and likewise lack of vulnerabilities pertaining to these properties) related to roles and access control [4,5], partial ordering of actions (function calls and transaction execution) [6], as well as time-based vulnerabilities [7,9]. Furthermore, not being concerned with low-level patterns and properties lets our approach remain cross-platform and not tied to the features and limitations of a certain smart contract execution environment. We believe that these patterns provide a systematic classification of best practices for smart contracts in a similar way that software design patterns shaped the design of traditional software and established a nomenclature for it [31], while capturing aspects that are unique to smart contracts.

This paper is organized as follows: Sect. 2 introduces smart contracts and DCR graphs. Section 3 gives an overview of 19 smart contract design patterns, which we formalize as DCR graphs. Section 4 shows a case study on a casino smart contract. Section 5 covers related work, and Sect. 6 concludes.

2   Background

2.1   Smart Contracts: Ethereum and Solidity

Ethereum [51], with its built-in cryptocurrency Ether, is still the leading blockchain framework supporting smart contracts. In Ethereum, not only the users but also the contracts can receive, own, and send Ether. Ethereum miners look for transaction requests on the network, which contain the contract's address to be called, the call data, and the amount of Ether to be sent. Miners are paid for their efforts in (Ether priced) *gas,* to be paid by the initiator of the transaction.

A transaction is not always executed successfully. It can be reverted due to running out of gas, sending of unbacked funds, or failing runtime assertions. If a miner attempts to execute a transaction, a revert statement within the transaction's execution can *undo the entire transaction.* All the effects so far are undone (except for the paid gas), as if the original call had never happened.

The most popular programming language for Ethereum smart contracts is Solidity [17]. Solidity follows largely an object-oriented paradigm, with fields and methods, called 'state variables' and 'functions', respectively. Each external user and each contract instance has a unique `address`. Each `address` owns Ether (possibly 0), can receive Ether, and send Ether to other addresses. For instance, a.`transfer`(v) transfers an amount v from the caller to a.

The current caller, and the amount sent with the call, are always available via `msg.sender` and `msg.value`, respectively. Only `payable` functions accept payments. Fields marked `public` are read-public, not write-public. Solidity also offers some

```
1  contract Casino {
2    address public operator, player; bytes32 public hashedNumber;
3    enum State { IDLE, GAME_AVAILABLE, BET_PLACED };
4    State private state;  uint bet;  Coin guess;
5    function addToPot() public payable byOp {...}
6    function removeFromPot(uint amt) public byOp, noActiveBet {...}
7    function createGame(bytes32 hash) public byOp, inState(IDLE) {
8      hashedNumber = hash
9      state = GAME_AVAILABLE;}
10   function bet(Coin _guess) public payable inState(GAME_AVAILABLE) {
11     require (msg.sender != operator);
12     require (msg.value > 0 && msg.value <= pot);
13     player = msg.sender; bet = msg.value;
14     guess = _guess; state = BET_PLACED;}
15   function decideBet(uint secret) public byOp, inState(BET_PLACED) {
16     require (hashedNumber == keccak256(secret));
17     Coin secret = (secret% 2 == 0)? HEADS : TAILS;
18     if (secret==wager.guess) {playerWins();} else {operatorWins();}
19     state = IDLE;}
20 }
```

Fig. 1. Solidity-code for casino (some details are omitted)

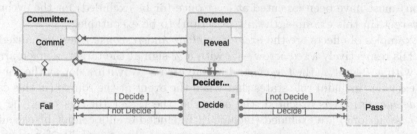

Fig. 2. Commit and reveal design pattern

cryptographic primitives, like keccak256 for computing a crypto-hash. require(b) checks the Boolean expression b, and reverts the transaction if b is false.

Solidity further features programmable *modifiers*. The contract in Fig. 1 uses the modifiers byOp, inState(s), and noActiveBet, whose implementation is omitted for brevity. These three modifiers expand to require(b), where b is msg.sender == operator, state == s, and state != BET_PLACED, respectively.

2.2 Dynamic Condition Response Graphs

A dynamic condition response (DCR) graph defines a dynamic process declaratively as a graph, defined formally in Definition 1 below and exemplified in Fig. 2. DCR graphs offer an alternative to state machines; instead of using transitions to represent events, DCR graphs represent events as nodes (boxes). Events in a DCR graph may be restricted to certain roles. Events can be enabled or disabled by other events, which is represented by different types of arrows.

The nodes of the graph constitute a set E of events labeled with roles and an action, visualized in Fig. 2 as boxes with the action label in the middle and the role label in the top bar. Nodes can be either input actions (denoted by a flipped paper corner in the top right of the box containing the action label; in this example, actions *commit* and *reveal*), computation actions (denoted by an =-sign in the top right of the box containing the action label; in this example, the *decide* action) or simple actions (in this example, the *fail* and *commit* actions). Input actions receive a value from the environment when the action is executed, which is associated with the event. Computation actions execute a computation expression (that may refer to the current value assigned to itself or other events) when the action is executed, which is then associated with the event. In this example, the computation assigned to the *decide* action is the Boolean expression *commit = hash(reveal)* (not shown graphically in Fig. 2), which refers to the values of the *commit* and the *reveal* actions.

The directed edges between nodes define rules for the execution of events. The rules can be constraints or effects. An example of a constraint is the condition rule, visualized in Fig. 2 as an orange arrow →• with a bullet at the target. It states that the event at the source of the edge (in this example, the commit action) must have been executed at least once (or be excluded) for the event at the target (in this example, the *reveal* action) to be executable.

Examples of effects are the *exclude*, *include* and *response* rules, visualized in Fig. 2 as respectively a red arrow →% with a %-sign at the target, a green arrow →+ with a +-sign at the target, and a blue arrow •→ with a dot at the source. The exclude (include) rule states that when the event at the source (in this case, the *decide* action) is executed, the events at the target (in this case, the *fail* and *pass* actions) are excluded (included). Excluded events cannot be executed and are also ignored when determining constraints. The possibility for an event to be excluded makes it easy to express *defeasible rules* [44]. For instance, in Fig. 4, the bank can give a fine a month after a loan, except if the client, in the meantime, pays the loan, in which case the event of the fine action is excluded.

In DCR graphs with data, rules may be guarded by Boolean expressions, determining whether a rule is to be considered in the current state of the graph. In this example, the guard *decide* of the exclude relation →% from *decide* to *fail* means that *fail* is excluded if and only if the value of *decide* is true, which is the case if the committed value provided when *commit* is executed is equal to the hash of the value provided when *reveal* is executed. The response rule •→ denotes that if the event at the source (e. g., the *commit* action in Fig. 2) is executed, then the event at the target (e. g., the *reveal* action in Fig. 2) must be executed or excluded in the future.

The execution state of a DCR graph is given by a marking, which assigns state information to each event. In the original version of DCR graphs [37], the marking of the graph assigned three Booleans to each event, denoting respectively if the event had been executed, if it is required to be executed (or excluded) in the future and if it is currently excluded. In this paper, we use an extended version of DCR graphs, allowing both data, time and nested sub-processes, which is supported by the online design tool.[1] This version of DCR graphs also adds two new effect rules: A *value relation* $\rightharpoonup=$, denoted by a grey arrow with an =-sign at the target, with the effect of updating the value of the target event when the source event is executed, and a *cancel relation* $\bullet\rightarrow\times$, denoted by a brown arrow with a ×-sign at the target, with the effect of removing a possible pending execution requirement (e. g., due to a previous activation of a response rule) of the target event when the source event is executed.

For a DCR graph with data, the marking assigns the current data value (if any) associated with each event, as exemplified above. For a DCR graph with time, the marking additionally assigns time information to events, concretely, how long ago an event was executed (if it has been executed) and a deadline for when it is required to be executed (if it is required to be executed in the future).

In Definition 1, we give the formal definition of timed DCR graphs with sub-processes and data. We combine timed DCR graphs with sub-processes [43] and timed DCR graphs with data [38] and add a new type of edge denoting a value effect, making it possible for one event to update the data of another event.

We assume a set of computation expressions $\mathsf{Exp_E}$, with $\mathsf{BExp_E} \subseteq \mathsf{Exp_E}$ being a subset of Boolean expressions. For every event $e \in E$, we assume an expression $e \in \mathsf{Exp_E}$ that denotes the current value of the event (as recorded in the marking). We also assume a discrete-time model (i. e., time is represented as time steps given as natural numbers) and let ω denote the natural numbers (including 0) and $\infty = \omega \cup \{\omega\}$, i. e., the natural numbers and ω (infinity).[2] Infinity is used to represent a non-fixed deadline of a required event, i. e., that an event must eventually be executed as known from classical liveness properties. This is the default deadline of a response relation if the deadline is not given, as it is the case for the two response relations in Fig. 2.

Definition 1. *A* timed DCR graph with sub-processes, data, and roles *G is given by a tuple $(E, sp, D, M, \rightarrow\bullet, \bullet\rightarrow, \bullet\rightarrow\times, \rightarrow\diamond, \rightarrow+, \rightarrow\%, \rightharpoonup=, L, l)$ where*

1. *E is a finite set of* events,
2. *$sp \in E \rightharpoonup E$ is an acyclic* sub-process *function, i. e., for all $k > 1$ $sp^k(e) \neq sp(e)$, if $sp(e)$ is defined.*
3. *$D : E \rightarrow \mathsf{Exp_E} \uplus \{?\}$ defines an event as either a computation event with expression $d \in \mathsf{Exp_E}$ or an input event ?,*
4. *$M = (\mathsf{Ex}, \mathsf{Re}, \mathsf{In}, \mathsf{Va}) \in ((E \rightharpoonup \omega) \times (E \rightharpoonup \infty) \times \mathcal{P}(E) \times (E \rightharpoonup V))$ is the timed marking with data,*
5. *$\rightarrow\bullet \subseteq E \times \omega \times \mathsf{BExp_E} \times E$, is the guarded timed condition relation,*
6. *$\bullet\rightarrow \subseteq E \times \infty \times \mathsf{BExp_E} \times E$, is the guarded timed response relation,*
7. *$\bullet\rightarrow\times, \rightarrow\diamond, \rightarrow+, \rightarrow\%, \rightharpoonup= \subseteq E \times \mathsf{BExp_E} \times E$ are the guarded cancel, milestone, include, exclude and value relations, respectively,*
8. *$L = \mathcal{P}(R) \times A$ is the set of labels, with R and A sets of roles and actions,*
9. *$l: E \rightarrow L$ is a labelling function between events and labels.*

---

[1] Available for free for academic use at dcrsolutions.net.
[2] The ISO 8601 standard (www.iso.org/iso-8601-date-and-time-format.html) is used in the design tool, allowing the use of years, months, days, and seconds.

The sub-process function $sp(e)$ defines a partial containment relation of events, which allows an event to be refined by a sub-process defined by the events contained in it. We call such a refined event a sub-process event. A sub-process event gets executed when an event contained in it is executed, and no events of the sub-process in the resulting marking are required to be executed in the future.

As already informally described above, the marking $M = (\text{Ex}, \text{Re}, \text{In}, \text{Va})$ defines the state of the process. Formally, the marking consists of three partial functions (Ex, Re, and Va) and a set In of events. $\text{Ex}(e)$, if defined, yields the time since event e was last **Ex***ecuted*. $\text{Re}(e)$, if defined, yields the deadline for when the event is **Re***quired* to happen (if it is included). The set In is the currently **In**cluded events. Finally, $\text{Va}(e)$, if defined, is the current value of an event.

Enabledness. The condition $\rightarrow\bullet$ and milestone $\rightarrow\diamond$ relations constrain the enabling of events and determine when events can be executed. As exemplified above, a condition $e' \rightarrow\bullet e$ means that e' must have been executed at least once or currently be excluded for e to be enabled. A milestone $e' \rightarrow\diamond e$ means that e' must either be currently excluded or not be pending for e to be enabled. In the example in Fig. 2, the milestone relations ensure that the *commit* action cannot be repeated as long as required executions of *reveal, decide, fail,* or *pass* are pending. Formally, an event e is enabled in marking $M = (\text{Ex}, \text{Re}, \text{In}, \text{Va})$ and can be executed by role $r \in R$, if $l(e) = (R', a)$ for $r \in R'$ and (1) e is included: $e \in \text{In}$, (2) all conditions for the event are met: $\forall e' \in E.(e', k, d, e) \in \rightarrow\bullet.(e' \in \text{In} \wedge [[d]]_M) \implies \text{Ex}(e') \geq k$ and (3) all milestones for the event are met: $\forall e' \in E.(e', k, d, e) \in \rightarrow\diamond.(e' \in \text{In} \wedge [[d]]_M) \implies \text{Re}(e')$ is undefined and (4) e is not contained in a sub-process event, or $sp(e)$ is enabled and can be executed by role r.

In the DCR graph in Fig. 2, the only enabled event is the event *commit*. It is enabled because it is included and the source events of the two milestone rules are not initially required to be executed. The *reveal* and *decide* events are blocked by condition rules, and the *fail* and *pass* events are disabled because they are initially excluded (marked by a dashed border).

We refer the reader to [38,43] for a more detailed definition and explanation of the execution semantics of timed DCR graphs with data and sub-processes.

3   Smart Contract Design Patterns as DCR Graphs

Due to the high stakes involved in applications, ensuring the safety and security of smart contracts is crucial. To address this, both the Solidity documentation and the developer and smart contract security community have put forth a range of recommendations. A considerable number of these recommendations are now known as *design patterns* [31], because they are widely adopted as a solution to recurring design problems. These patterns promote the creation of contracts that are designed with safety and security in mind, mitigating potential risks and safeguarding users' assets in the design phase.

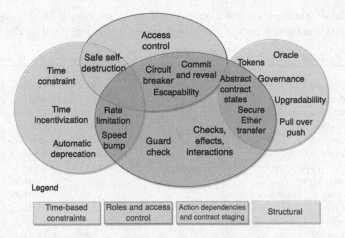

Fig. 3. Classification of smart contract high-level design patterns (upper part of Table 1)

We collected these design patterns from academic design pattern surveys [19,30,40,50,52], documentation of Solidity [17] and the Ethereum Foundation [15], and recommendations by a popular contract auditing company [22]. These design patterns are also confirmed by their occurrence in popular libraries and contracts such as OpenZeppelin, SolidState Solidity, and Aragon OSx [10,14,16, 45,48].

First, we identify the design patterns representing high-level behavior rather than implementation- and platform-specific patterns (Table 1). The latter concerns features inside a function (the execution of which we model as an event in DCR graphs). The analysis of low-level patterns is orthogonal to our work and can be handled, e. g., by runtime analysis of code [32]. We then classify the high-level patterns into the following four categories (see Fig. 3):

1. **Time-based constraints**: Time-based patterns impose constraints on when activities can be performed, which typically include deadlines and delays.
2. **Roles and access control**: Role-based access control [46] restricts access to given functions to predefined roles.
3. **Action dependencies and contract staging**: High-level design of a smart contract may impose an ordering on any pair of activities.
4. **Structural patterns**: These patterns impose a certain structure on the contract business process (and the implementation as a result) and are created by combining other design patterns.

Many patterns combine aspects of several categories; Fig. 3 depicts a classification of 19 design patterns we have identified. We elucidate these patterns further below. Also, we describe DCR graphs for selected design patterns here; the others are available on GitHub.[3] Table 1 gives an overview of references of the design patterns, libraries that implement them, and their respective DCR models.

---

[3] https://github.com/mojtaba-eshghie/SmartContractDesignPatternsInDCRGraphs.

Table 1. Smart contract design patterns and their respective DCR graph models. High-level patterns (upper part of the table) are further categorized in Fig. 3.

Design Pattern	Libraries	DCR Model
High-level Patterns		
Time constraint [19]	[45]	GitHub, §3
Time incentivization	[3, 8, 11, 12, 14]	GitHub, §3, §4
Automatic deprecation[52]	—	GitHub, §3
Rate limitation[50]	[22]	GitHub, §3
Speed bump[50]	[22]	GitHub, §3
Safe self-destruction[19, 52]	[45]	GitHub, §3
Ownership / Authorization / Access Control [19, 30, 52]	[10, 45, 48]	GitHub, §3, §4
Commit and reveal[52]	—	GitHub, §3, §4
Circuit breaker / Emergency stop[50]	—	GitHub, §3
Escapability	[1, 2, 33, 36]	GitHub, §3
Checks, effects, interactions[30, 50]	—	GitHub, §3
Guard check[30]	[29]	GitHub, §3
Abstract contract states[52]	[45]	GitHub, §3, §4
Secure Ether transfer[30]	—	GitHub, §3
Oracle [19, 52]	—	GitHub, §3
Token [19]	[45]	GitHub, §3
Pull over push[52]	[45]	GitHub, §3
Upgradability[42, 52]	[45]	GitHub, §3
Governance[19, 40]	[13, 21, 45]	GitHub, §3
Low-level Patterns		
Randomness [19, 30]	—	✗
Safe math operations[19]	[45]	✗
Variable Packing[30, 42]	[45]	✗
Avoiding on-chain data storage[42]	[45]	✗
Mutex[50]	[45]	✗
Freeing storage [42]	—	✗

[1] We identify these as design patterns since they have been used as a recurring solution in several real-world smart contracts but have not yet been considered a design pattern in the literature.

In the following subsections, we delve into each design pattern, highlighting its utility, and, for a chosen subset, offer the visual representation of their model and a succinct description of the associated DCR graph models. This study provides supplementary details and examples for each pattern, along with the DCR model semantics used, in our corresponding GitHub repository. We plan to focus on comprehensive guidelines for smart contract modeling in future research.

3.1 **Time Constraint.** In multi-stage business processes, code execution must adhere to specific stages. This can be achieved through time-based or action-based dependencies. The former denotes stages solely based on elapsed time [19]. This pattern prohibits calling a function until a specific time is reached on the blockchain, represented by a delayed condition relation in DCR graphs. The simplest form of this pattern is modeled directly using a delayed condition DCR relation. Modeling more complex time constraints where only part of a function should be executed or blocked based on time is

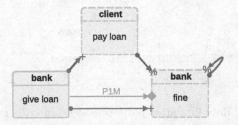

Fig. 4. DCR\model of time incentivization design pattern.

challenging and may require multiple guard conditions in DCR graphs. One approach is to interpret Solidity's **require** statements as guard conditions in DCR graphs, connecting multiple activities to shape the business logic.

3.2 **Time Incentivization.** In Ethereum, smart contracts work as a reactive system where specific function calls execute transactions. There are scenarios where certain actions should be performed at a specific time or when a specific condition is fulfilled. A lack of action may prevent progress, opening up adversarial behavior (e. g., the eternal locking of assets). The purpose of the *time incentivization* pattern is to motivate parties to cooperate even in the existence of conflicting interests. The incentivization is typically done by stipulating a deadline before which an actor shall make a move. The actor that misses the deadline can afterward be punished by other actors, e. g., by forfeiting the bets, as modeled in the casino contract (see Sect. 4).

To demonstrate this pattern, we use the simple example of giving a loan and then motivating the client to pay for the loan. Giving a loan is performed only by *bank* role. In Fig. 4, immediately after giving the loan, the bank includes →+ both the *pay loan* and *fine* activities. Without any more relationships, this would mean that the bank might increase the interest on the loan without giving the client enough time to pay for it. This issue is resolved by using the pre-condition arrow →• from *give loan* to activity *fine*. As this pre-condition arrow has a deadline attribute of P1M (one month), it will suspend the availability of *fine* to one month later. Without this pattern, the client could refuse to pay the loan by not participating in any further transaction.

Despite the widespread usage of this pattern in popular smart contracts such as Augur, MakerDAO, Compound, Aragon Court, and Synthetix [3,8,11,12, 14] to incentivize taking the next step by the actor(s), the current work is the first one classifying it as a design pattern and formalizing it using DCR graphs.

3.3 **Automatic Deprecation.** Automatic deprecation is the opposite of a time constraint, stipulating a deprecation time (block number) after which a function is not executable anymore [52]. In Solidity code, such functions are typically enabled by a *require* statement checking at the function entry point against the expiration. This means that a smart contract function can be called and reverted, which is different from DCR model semantics, where an activity is enabled only if it will successfully execute. We model this in DCR

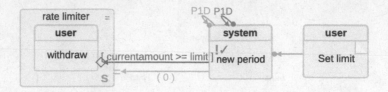

Fig. 5. Rate limitation pattern modeled in DCR graphs

by checking the deprecation condition on an exclusion arrow from another activity to the target activity subject to deprecation.

3.4 **Rate Limitation.** Rate limitation imposes a limit on the number of successful function calls by a participating user during a specific time period [22]. The more common type of this pattern that we analyze here explicitly limits the total amount of transfers allowed during the defined period.

To model this pattern, we assume the sensitive activity is the *withdraw* operation. We present the model in Fig. 5. When the model is simulated, the only included available activity to execute is *set limit*. The *new period* activity is initially *executed* (tick the on activity box). The gray arrow *valuerel* from *new period* to *rate limiter* copies value 0 to *rate limiter* every time *new period* is executed. Each execution of *new period* sets a deadline and delay of one day (P1D) for the given activity. Having such relationships (response and precondition) on *new period* and assigning an automatic agent to the *system* (when simulating the model) ensures that *new period* is indeed executed at exactly one-day intervals. In Fig. 5, labels P1D on the reflexive pre-condition →• and reflexive response •→ arrows of *new period* impose this periodic execution. Based on the purple milestone relation →◇, if the current period amount does not exceed the limit, role *user* can withdraw. Furthermore, having the milestone relation from *new period* to *rate limiter* occur periodically with *currentamount* ≥ *limit* ensures that if the current withdrawal of the period exceeds the limit, *withdraw* will not be executable until the next execution of *new period*. The new execution of *new period* resets the *currentamount* to 0 again.

3.5 **Timed Temporal Constraint (Speed Bump).** A *speed bump* is used to slow down critical operations such as the withdrawal of assets, authorization of significant actions, etc. [22]. It imposes a temporal barrier that gives enough time to a monitoring system to detect a problematic activity and mitigate it. This pattern is a specialized form of the time constraint pattern where the participating user can only execute an action after a predefined time period has passed (from the point the action request has been registered). The wait time is modeled using a *delay* on a condition arrow from the activity requesting the specified action to the actual action.

3.6 **Safe Self-Destruction.** It is possible to define a function in Solidity that uses `selfdestruct(address target)` to destroy the contract intentionally and send all Ether in the contract account to the target. Safe self-destruction is about limiting the execution of the function to specific roles such as the administrator. [19,52]. The simplest way to achieve this is to refine the access control pattern (Sect. 3). However, guard check and time constraint patterns (Sect. 3 and Sect. 3) can also be used to ensure safety.

3.7 **Access Control.** Access control restricts access to desired functions to only a subset of accounts calling them [19,30,52]. A common instance of this pattern is to initialize a variable *owner* to the contract deployer and only allow this account to successfully call certain functions. Here, we can nicely exploit that access control is built into DCR graphs as a first-class citizen, in the form of roles assigned to activities. Each activity in a DCR model can be limited to one or more specific roles. In simpler scenarios, roles are assigned statically to accounts when a contract is deployed on the blockchain. In general, however, access rights can be assigned dynamically. DCR graphs support this using *activity effects* from an external database source. This feature allows changing the roles of activities as a result of an activity being executed.

3.8 **Commit and Reveal.** In a public permissionless blockchain platform such as Ethereum, transaction data is public [52]. Therefore, if a secret is sent along with a transaction request, participants in the blockchain consensus protocol can see the secret value even before the transaction is finalized. On the other hand, the party holding the secret should commit to it before other parties act, so the secret cannot be changed after the fact. The commit and reveal pattern addresses this problem and works in two phases. In Phase 1, a piece of data is submitted that depends on the secret (which itself is not yet submitted). Often, that data is the crypto hash of the secret, such that the secret cannot be reconstructed. Phase 2 is the submission (and reveal) of the secret itself. We use a combination of condition, milestone, and response relations to enforce the ordering of actions in the commit and reveal pattern in Fig. 2. Here, the activity *reveal* is blocked initially by the condition relation from *commit* to *reveal* , and is enabled once a user commits. The commit makes *reveal* pending (by the response relation arrow). Finally, the milestone relation from the pending *reveal* to *commit* means that unless a reveal happens, no other commit is possible. The decision is then made using the *decide* activity based on committed and revealed values.

3.9 **Circuit Breaker (Emergency Stop).** This pattern enables the contract owner to temporarily halt the contract's normal operations until a manual or automatic investigation is performed [50]. Other contract functions, such as those based on timed temporal constraints (Sect. 3), can also trigger the circuit breaker. To model this design pattern, we categorize activities into two subsets: activities that are available in the normal execution of the contract and those that are only available when the circuit breaker is triggered. There is a milestone relationship $\rightarrow\!\diamond$ between circuit breaker grouping and all other DCR nodes. The existence of this milestone helps to disable the execution of all of these activities by making the circuit breaker pending. In Fig. 6, the activity *panic* executed by the *monitor* role makes the circuit breaker pending (*panic* $\bullet\!\rightarrow$ *circuit breaker*). This means unless *revive* activity in the circuit breaker group is executed, none of the *buy*, *sell*, *transfer*, and *panic* activities are executable. Executing *contingency* instead will enable a contingency plan (related to Sect. 3).

3.10 **Escapability.** There have been cases where a vulnerability in the contract triggered by a certain transaction led to funds being locked in the contract [36]. To prevent this, a smart contract can have a function whose logic is independent of the main contract logic; when triggered, it can withdraw all assets in the contract to a certain address. This new address can be the upgraded version of the contract that contains a patch for the vulnerability. Escapability is arguably the complementary pattern for the circuit breaker pattern (Sect. 3), as it concerns the functionality behind the *contingency* activity in Fig. 6 for the circuit breaker. This functionality often consists of transferring assets to an escape hatch. Despite being used by the community [1,2,36], the current work is the first one promoting it as a design pattern.

3.11 **Checks, Effects, Interactions.** This pattern is concerned with the order of certain activities, especially when interactions with other contracts (external calls) happen [30,50]. External calls can be risky, as call targets cannot necessarily be trusted. One risk is that the called contract calls back into the calling contract before returning, purposefully abusing the calling contract's logic [28]. To prevent such exploits, the caller first performs *checks* on its bookkeeping variables (variables keeping the balance of tokens, assets, etc.). Then, it modifies these bookkeeping variables based on the business logic *(effects)*. Last, there are *interactions* with (i.e., calls to) other contracts. In DCR graphs, we specify this strict ordering via inclusion/exclusion relations among the respective activities.

3.12 **Guard Check.** A guard check validates user inputs and checks bookkeeping variables and invariants before the execution of the function body (mainly as a *require* statement) [29]. This pattern is often applied using function modifiers in Solidity and represented using guard conditions on DCR relations.

3.13 **Abstract Contract States.** In most processes, action dependencies impose a partial order on action executions that a smart contract has to follow, as shown in the casino contract (Sect. 4). In Solidity, a state variable of type enumeration can mimic a finite state automaton [52], whose state transitions enforce the set of executable functions, encoding a partial order among action executions.

In DCR graphs, such dependencies (partial orderings of actions) can be represented explicitly. If the ordering between activities does not matter, no arrows are required. Therefore, DCR graphs can make contract states obsolete *at the modeling level*. If there is a strong reason for modeling the abstract contract states instead of the action dependencies they imply, it is still possible to model them using DCR graphs. This is done by grouping activities of the same state into the same group in DCR graphs and using arrows between state groupings to reflect state transitions of the system.

3.14 **Secure Ether Transfer.** This structural design pattern imposes a design choice between various ways of sending Ether from one contract to the other (via *send*, *transfer*, or *call*) [30]. Using each of them requires a distinct way of ensuring the target contract cannot harm the contract sending Ether. As a structural design pattern, Secure Ether Transfer imposes certain guard checks, mutual exclusions, and ordering of actions to ensure that an external call (especially to transfer Ether) is not exploitable by a malicious party. Therefore, this pattern can be represented in DCR graphs as action dependency relation in combination with the guard check (Sect. 3) and mutex (Table 1) design patterns.

3.15 **Oracle.** Oracles enable smart contracts to incorporate off-chain data in their execution and push information from a blockchain to external systems [19,52]. The oracle pattern employs an external call to another *service smart contract* (data source) to register the request for off-chain data. This registration call information should also be kept in bookkeeping variables inside the contract itself. When the data is ready in the service contract, it will inform the main contract about the result by calling a specific *callback* function. To model this, the callback function of the smart contract is excluded by default and is included when the smart contract calls an oracle.

3.16 **Token Design Patterns.** Tokens represent assets, their behavior, and manageability [19]. Ethereum smart contracts and token standards (such as ERC-20, ERC-721, and ERC-777) enable developers to use tokens according to specific requirements. DCR graphs can model both tokens and their interacting contracts. The ERC-20 token standard model included in the accompanying repository to this work involves inclusion/exclusion relations to model the partial ordering of activities. Tokens and contracts that use this model typically involve several other design patterns (most notably Sect. 3 and Sect. 3).

3.17 **Pull Over Push.** A contract might need to send a token or Ether to other accounts. The "pull over push" pattern discourages pushing tokens or Ether to the destination as a side-effect of calling a function. Rather, it encourages exposing a *withdraw* function that users of the contract can call [52] for this reason. This inclination towards pull is based on the fact that when sending Ether or tokens via any external call (even when adhering to patterns such as Sect. 3), the receiver may act unexpectedly before returning control. We model this pattern in a DCR graph by having an extra activity for the *withdraw* functionality.

3.18 **Upgradability.** This design pattern consists of up to five parts: (1) The proxy keeps addresses of referred contracts. (2) The data segregation part separates the logic and data layers by storing data in a separate smart contract. (3) The satellite part outsources functional units to separate satellite contracts and stores their addresses in a base contract, allowing the replacement of their functionality. (4) The register contract tracks different versions of a contract and points to the latest one. (5) While keeping the old contract address, the relay pattern uses a proxy contract to forward calls and data to the newest contract version [52]. Data segregation, satellite, and relay are platform-dependent low-level patterns, which we do not capture with our DCR graph model. Our upgradability pattern model (Table 1) instead explicitly includes activities for the register and proxy parts.

3.19 **Governance.** On-chain governance is a crucial component of decentralized protocols, allowing for decision-making on parameter changes, upgrades, and management [19,40]. The governance pattern is typically used to allow token holders or a group of privileged users to vote on proposals and make decisions that affect the contract's behavior. This pattern works in conjunction with other patterns, such as guard check (Sect. 3) and role-based access control (Sect. 3).

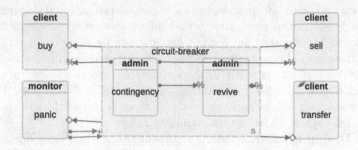

Fig. 6. Circuit breaker design pattern DCR model

4   Modeling and Analysis of a Casino Smart Contract

As an example of how patterns modeled in DCR graphs come into play when modeling a concrete smart contract scenario, we present a simple casino contract [26].[4] It uses four design patterns identified in Table 1: time incentivization, role-based access control, commit and reveal, and abstract contract states. This endeavor demonstrates how utilizing and combining the DCR model of several design patterns into one model captures the intended smart contract design.

The casino has two explicitly declared roles, *operator* and *player*. It also contains three abstract states (see Sect. 3): *IDLE*, *GAME_AVAILABLE*, and *BET_PLACED*. Three modifiers check the pre-conditions →• of each function based on the roles and the state the contract is in.

Figure 7 shows the DCR model of this contract. The activities all reflect functions of the same name, except subprocess *casino*, which everything is grouped under. This subprocess reflects the behavior of the deployed contract, which includes a suicidal *closeCasino* function that *selfdestructs*, shown by an exclusion arrow from *closeCasino* to the subprocess in Fig. 7. Without a subprocess, an exclusion arrow would go from *closeCasino* to all other activities, which is visually unappealing. Furthermore, we do not model the actual states of the contract, instead choosing to order the activities by inclusion →+ and exclusion →% arrows.

When the casino contract is deployed, it is in the *IDLE* abstract state. It is possible to create a game, add to the pot, remove from it, or self-destruct. Creating a game will change the abstract state to *GAME_AVAILABLE*, which enables anyone in the Ethereum network to place a bet and take the role of the

---

[4] The scenario was originally provided by Gordon Pace.

player (as a result). The function *decideBet* checks if the player is the winner by comparing the guess with the secret number. This gives both the player and the operator a 50 % chance of winning the game. In the model, a response arrow •→ from *placeBet* to *decideBet* emphasizes that *decideBet* has to execute at some point and should not block the game from continuing. However, since continuing the game at this point depends on the operator making a transaction, it is possible for a malicious operator or buggy reverted *decideBet* function to lock the funds the player puts in the game. Furthermore, after a player places the bet, the operator should not be able to change the actual secret stored. Therefore, three patterns are used in the model to provide the following functionality:

– A time incentivization pattern (Sect. 3) ensures that continuing the game is the favorable option for the casino operator. Figure 7 shows the required mechanism, where *timeoutBet* becomes available with a desirable delay (here P1D, one day) to provide the player with an option when the operator is unable or unwilling to make a transaction to *decideBet*. Calling this function after the timeout guarantees the player wins the game and motivates the operator to decide the game in time.
– A commit and reveal pattern (Sect. 3) is used to ensure when operator *createGame* is called, the operator commits to a secret without sending it. The revealing phase of this pattern is performed in *decideBet*, where the secret is submitted, checked, and compared to the player's guess.
– A role-based access control pattern (Sect. 3) to confine *player* and *operator* roles to their respective activities.

The abstract contract states pattern (Sect. 3) used in the implementation (Fig. 1) is not needed in the model (Fig. 7): The model's partial ordering provides the same semantics without the complications of abstract contract states.

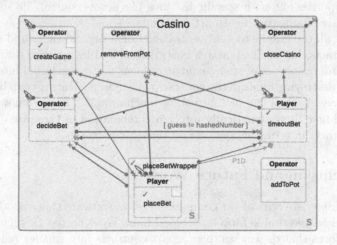

Fig. 7. Casino contract model.

As mentioned in Sect. 1, DCR specifications provide a basis for automated analysis, to *verify* that the implementation of the contracts adheres to their models.

We have implemented a runtime monitoring tool "Clawk" [27]. Clawk captures transactions from the Ethereum client and executes an instance of the DCR graph model in tandem. For each Ethereum transaction, Clawk checks if the DCR graph model permits a corresponding action in the model. If this is not the case, the tool reports a violation.

By leveraging runtime information, our framework enables automated runtime verification. While runtime verification in the blockchain domain is typically associated with the performance overhead of contract or platform instrumentation [32,34,41], we address this concern by placing the monitor off-chain. If any deviations from the specification are detected, Clawk generates alerts, which can be used to enhance the contract's implementation or enable a circuit breaker pattern in the contract implementation (cf. Sect. 3).

5   Related Work

Smart contracts often involve multiple dependent transactions, a challenge that has been addressed through various approaches. Sergey and Hobor discuss the non-deterministic nature of transaction ordering decided by miners [47], while other works focus on commutativity conditions to exploit interleavings [18] or identify serializable transactions in Ethereum [23]. These issues have also been modeled using finite state automata, which can lead to "bad states" in certain scenarios (e.g., when most of the actions are not accessible) [24]. DCR graphs offer a more elegant solution in such cases. Transactions and their dependencies can be graphically represented, as demonstrated by Chen et al., who use this to identify potential security issues [20]. Our work uniquely combines these general properties [49] with specific features like access control [39] to provide a comprehensive framework for smart contracts.

Chen et al. use graphs to analyze transactional dependencies and security in smart contracts, but their approach is statistical and less precise than ours [20]. While general properties of smart contracts focus on transactional integrity (not creating or destroying funds in the contract) [49], specific features can be modeled through access control [39] or finite-state machines [35]. To our knowledge, our work is the first to systematically apply a combination of these two aspects to smart contracts in terms of general and reusable patterns.

6   Conclusion and Future Work

Smart contracts are critical yet complex pieces of software that encode business processes in an executable form on a blockchain. We collected 19 smart contract design patterns that dissect complex smart contracts into smaller reusable components, making it easier to reason about them. DCR graphs are an ideal way to formally model the semantics of these patterns, supporting the concepts of time, data, and sub-processes. We demonstrate their usefulness on the casino smart contract that combines multiple patterns.

The contract DCR models serve as a repository of reusable templates for developing more secure and efficient smart contracts across various applications and smart contract execution platforms. This not only aids in the initial design phase but also has uses in monitoring the contract behavior, allowing for automated verification [27], which reduces the risk of vulnerabilities. Future directions of our research include an extensive evaluation of the Clawk tool, combinations of static or dynamic analysis of low-level patterns [32] with runtime monitoring against our high-level design patterns, as well as automated discovery of the models from the contract transaction history.

References

1. A decentralized escape hatch for DAOs. https://hackingdistributed.com/2016/07/11/decentralized-escape-hatches-for-smart-contracts/. Accessed 29 Aug 2023
2. Implement escape hatch mechanism contracts · Issue #1 · OpenZeppelin/openzeppelin-contracts. https://github.com/OpenZeppelin/openzeppelin-contracts/issues/1. Accessed 29 Aug 2023
3. The Maker Protocol White Paper — Feb (2020). https://makerdao.com/en. Accessed 29 Aug 2023
4. SWC-105 - Smart Contract Weakness Classification (SWC). https://swcregistry.io/docs/SWC-105/. Accessed 01 Sept 2023
5. SWC-106 - Smart Contract Weakness Classification (SWC). https://swcregistry.io/docs/SWC-106/. Accessed 01 Sept 2023
6. SWC-114 - Smart Contract Weakness Classification (SWC). https://swcregistry.io/docs/SWC-114/. Accessed 01 Sept 2023
7. SWC-116 - Smart Contract Weakness Classification (SWC). https://swcregistry.io/docs/SWC-116/#time_locksol. Accessed 01 Sept 2023
8. Synthetixio/synthetix: Synthetix Solidity smart contracts. https://github.com/Synthetixio/synthetix. Accessed 29 Aug 2023
9. Timestamp Dependence - Ethereum Smart Contract Best Practices. https://consensys.github.io/smart-contract-best-practices/development-recommendations/solidity-specific/timestamp-dependence/#avoid-using-blocknumber-as-a-timestamp. Accessed 01 Sept 2023
10. Aragon OSx Protocol (2023). https://github.com/aragon/osx. Accessed 29 Aug 2023
11. Aragon/aragon-court: Aragon (2023). Accessed 29 Aug 2023
12. Augur (2023). https://github.com/AugurProject/augur. Accessed 29 Aug 2023
13. Chainbridge-solidity (2023). https://github.com/ChainSafe/chainbridge-solidity. Accessed 29 Aug 2023
14. Compound Protocol: Compound (2023). Accessed 29 Aug 2023
15. Ethereum development documentation (2023). https://ethereum.org/en/developers/docs/. Accessed 29 Aug 2023
16. Smartcontractkit/chainlink (2023). https://github.com/smartcontractkit/chainlink. Accessed 29 Aug 2023
17. Solidity documentation (2023). https://docs.soliditylang.org/en/latest/. Accessed 29 Aug 2023

18. Bansal, K., Koskinen, E., Tripp, O.: Automatic generation of precise and useful commutativity conditions. In: Beyer, D., Huisman, M. (eds.) Tools and Algorithms for the Construction and Analysis of Systems, pp. 115–132. Lecture Notes in Computer Science, Springer International Publishing, Cham (2018). https://doi.org/10.1007/978-3-319-89960-2_7

19. Bartoletti, M., Pompianu, L.: An empirical analysis of smart contracts: platforms, applications, and design patterns. In: Brenner, M., et al. (eds.) FC 2017. LNCS, vol. 10323, pp. 494–509. Springer, Cham (2017). https://doi.org/10.1007/978-3-319-70278-0_31

20. Chen, T., et al.: Understanding Ethereum via graph analysis. ACM TOIT **20**(2), 1–32 (2020)

21. Compound: Compound v2 Governance. https://docs.compound.finance/v2/governance/. Accessed 29 Aug 2023

22. Consensys: ethereum smart contract best practices (2023). https://consensys.github.io/smart-contract-best-practices/development-recommendations/precautions/. Accessed 29 Aug 2023

23. Dickerson, T., Gazzillo, P., Herlihy, M., Koskinen, E.: Adding concurrency to smart contracts. In: PODC, pp. 303–312. ACM (2017)

24. Ellul, J., Pace, G.J.: Runtime verification of ethereum smart contracts. In: 2018 14th European Dependable Computing Conference (EDCC). IEEE (2018). https://doi.org/10.1109/EDCC.2018.00036

25. Eshghie, M.: A comprehensive collection of DCR graph model of business process-level (contract-level) design patterns in smart contracts (Aug 2023). https://github.com/mojtaba-eshghie/SmartContractDesignPatternsInDCRGraphs. Accessed 29 Aug 2023

26. Eshghie, M.: mojtaba-eshghie/CLawK (2023). https://github.com/mojtaba-eshghie/CLawK/blob/925bf9c9afe344c763963e0e40098c66420d1d6a/server/monitor/contracts/source/Casino.sol. Accessed 29 Aug 2023

27. Eshghie, M., Ahrendt, W., Artho, C., Hildebrandt, T.T., Schneider, G.: CLawK: Monitoring Business Processes in Smart Contracts (2023). https://doi.org/10.48550/arXiv.2305.08254. Accessed 29 Aug 2023

28. Eshghie, M., Artho, C., Gurov, D.: Dynamic vulnerability detection on smart contracts using machine learning. In: EASE 2021, pp. 305–312. ACM (2021)

29. etherscan.io: HOLDIT — Etherscan. http://etherscan.io/address/0x24021d38DB53A938446eCB0a31B1267764d9d63D. Accessed 29 Aug 2023

30. Fravoll: Solidity Patterns (2023). https://fravoll.github.io/solidity-patterns/. Accessed 29 Aug 2023

31. Gamma, E., Helm, R., Johnson, R., Johnson, R.E., Vlissides, J.: Design patterns: elements of reusable object-oriented software. Pearson Deutschland GmbH (1995)

32. Gao, J., Liu, H., Liu, C., Li, Q., Guan, Z., Chen, Z.: EASYFLOW: keep ethereum away from overflow. In: 2019 IEEE/ACM 41st International Conference on Software Engineering: Companion Proceedings (ICSE-Companion), pp. 23–26 (2019). https://doi.org/10.1109/ICSE-Companion.2019.00029, ISSN: 2574-1934

33. giveth.io: common-contract-deps (2021). https://github.com/Giveth/common-contract-deps/blob/094d36028eab30444314395016817735e57e9d77/contracts/Escapable.sol. Accessed 29 Aug 2023

34. Grossman, S., Abraham, I., Golan-Gueta, G., Michalevsky, Y., Rinetzky, N., Sagiv, M., Zohar, Y.: Online detection of effectively callback free objects with applications to smart contracts (2018). https://doi.org/10.48550/arXiv.1801.04032

35. Guth, F., Wüstholz, V., Christakis, M., Müller, P.: Specification mining for smart contracts with automatic abstraction tuning. arXiv:1807.07822 (2018)

36. Explained: The Akutars NFT Incident (2022) - Halborn Blockchain Security Firm: Ethical Hackers, Infosec & Pen Tests. https://halborn.com/blog/post/explained-the-akutars-nft-incident-april-2022. Accessed 29 Aug 2023

37. Hildebrandt, T.T., Mukkamala, R.R.: Declarative event-based workflow as distributed dynamic condition response graphs. In: Honda, K., Mycroft, A. (eds.) Proceedings Third Workshop on Programming Language Approaches to Concurrency and communication-cEntric Software, PLACES 2010, Paphos, Cyprus, 21st March 2010. EPTCS, vol. 69, pp. 59–73 (2010). https://doi.org/10.4204/EPTCS.69.5

38. Hildebrandt, T.T., Normann, H., Marquard, M., Debois, S., Slaats, T.: Decision modelling in timed dynamic condition response graphs with data. In: Marrella, A., Weber, B. (eds.) BPM 2021. LNBIP, vol. 436, pp. 362–374. Springer, Cham (2022). https://doi.org/10.1007/978-3-030-94343-1_28

39. Liu, Y., Li, Y., Lin, S.W., Artho, C.: Finding permission bugs in smart contracts with role mining. In: SIGSOFT ISSTA 2022, pp. 716–727. ACM (2022)

40. Liu, Y., Lu, Q., Zhu, L., Paik, H.Y., Staples, M.: A systematic literature review on blockchain governance. J. Syst. Softw. 197 (2023)

41. Ma, F., Fu, Y., Ren, M., Wang, M., Jiang, Y., Zhang, K., Li, H., Shi, X.: EVM: from offline detection to online reinforcement for ethereum virtual machine. In: 2019 IEEE 26th International Conference on Software Analysis, Evolution and Reengineering (SANER), pp. 554–558 (2019). https://doi.org/10.1109/SANER.2019.8668038, ISSN: 1534-5351

42. Marchesi, L., Marchesi, M., Destefanis, G., Barabino, G., Tigano, D.: Design patterns for gas optimization in Ethereum. In: IEEE IWBOSE, pp. 9–15 (2020)

43. Normann, H., Debois, S., Slaats, T., Hildebrandt, T.T.: Zoom and Enhance: action refinement via subprocesses in timed declarative processes. In: Polyvyanyy, A., Wynn, M.T., Van Looy, A., Reichert, M. (eds.) BPM 2021. LNCS, vol. 12875, pp. 161–178. Springer, Cham (2021). https://doi.org/10.1007/978-3-030-85469-0_12

44. Nute, D.: Handbook of logic in artificial intelligence and logic programming, vol. 3, chap. Defeasible Logic. Clarendon Press, Oxford University Press (1994)

45. OpenZeppelin: OpenZeppelin Contracts. https://github.com/OpenZeppelin/openzeppelin-contracts. Accessed 29 Aug 2023

46. Sandhu, R.S.: Role-based access control. In: Advances in Computers, vol. 46, pp. 237–286. Elsevier (1998)

47. Sergey, I., Hobor, A.: A concurrent perspective on smart contracts (2017). http://arxiv.org/abs/1702.05511

48. Solidstate: SolidState Solidity (2023). https://github.com/solidstate-network/solidstate-solidity/blob/de7c9545ac015f42a03aa3a678000ec1ec4c14a4/contracts/access/access_control/AccessControl.sol. Accessed 29 Aug 2023

49. Wang, H., et al.: Oracle-supported dynamic exploit generation for smart contracts. IEEE Trans. Dependable Secure Comput. 19(03), 1795–1809 (2022)

50. Wohrer, M., Zdun, U.: Smart contracts: security patterns in the Ethereum ecosystem and solidity. In: IEEE IWBOSE, pp. 2–8 (2018)

51. Wood, G.: Ethereum: a secure decentralised generalised transaction ledger. Ethereum Project Yellow Paper 151, 1–32 (2014)

52. Wöhrer, M., Zdun, U.: Design patterns for smart contracts in the Ethereum ecosystem. In: iThings/GreenCom/CPSCom/SmartData, pp. 1513–1520 (2018)

An Active Learning Approach to Synthesizing Program Contracts

Sandip Ghosal[1(✉)], Bengt Jonsson[1], and Philipp Rümmer[1,2]

[1] Uppsala University, Uppsala, Sweden
sandipsmit@gmail.com
[2] University of Regensburg, Regensburg, Germany

Abstract. Contracts capture assumptions (preconditions) and guarantees (postconditions) of functions in a software program, and are an important paradigm for documenting program code, for program understanding, and to enable modular program verification. In this paper, we focus on contracts for stateful software modules, for instance modules implementing data-structures like queues. Such modules offer different kinds of functions to their environment: *observers,* which are pure functions used to query the state of the module; and *mutators,* which can change the module state. We present a novel technique to synthesize contracts for the mutators of a module, in which pre- and postconditions are expressed as Boolean combinations of the observers. Our method builds on existing algorithms for active learning of register automata to model the possible behaviours of the stateful module. We then present techniques for synthesizing contracts from a learned register automaton. The entire method is fully black-box and automated. Based on our proposed approach, we develop a tool called `CoGent` that generates a set of contracts for a mutator from a given register automaton of a module. Finally, we evaluate our tool using the APIs for various data structures.

1 Introduction

The annotation of program functions with contracts, consisting of pre- and postconditions, serves several purposes. Contracts are an important form of documentation, and are as such widely used to describe the intended use of library and API functions. Contracts give rise to the Design-by-Contract (DbC) methodology [18], by stating both the assumptions made about the states in which a function may be called, and the guarantees established in return by the function. In formal verification, contracts are the main vehicle to decompose larger programs into smaller units that can be analysed in isolation (e.g., [6,7]).

It is non-trivial, however, to come up with correct contracts for a given function. In most of today's code bases, functions are documented only with unstructured text, or with informal contracts in which pre- and postconditions are stated in natural language. Like any kind of formal specification, the process of writing *formal* contracts (with pre- and postconditions being logical formulas) is an extremely time-consuming and error-prone process, and is in fact sometimes

C. Ferreira and T. A. C. Willemse (Eds.): SEFM 2023, LNCS 14323, pp. 126–144, 2023.
https://doi.org/10.1007/978-3-031-47115-5_8

considered the main bottleneck preventing application of formal methods in an industrial context.

Over the last years, researchers have therefore considered the automated inference of formal contracts from implementations (e.g., [1,2,4,5,13,19,20,22]). Such inferred contracts can serve as documentation of existing programs, and as auxiliary annotations in verification. However, although various approaches to contract inference have been proposed, methods that are (i) scalable enough to handle real-world code bases, (ii) precise enough to generate correct and complete contracts, (iii) refined enough to produce contracts that are human-readable so far remain elusive.

In this paper, we present a new approach to automatically infer contracts for software modules. Our approach starts with applying existing active black-box learning methods [8,9] to build a behavioural model of a program in the form of a finite-state register automaton. We then construct contracts for all mutator functions of the software module in terms of the available observer functions: for this, state transitions associated with a mutator are analysed, and the effects of the transitions are summarized using observers. Under certain assumptions on the shape of the automaton, the computed contracts are guaranteed to describe only the behaviour of the module that is reachable, i.e., they implicitly take module invariants into account. This is because the reachable states of the automaton correspond to the module states that are reachable from some designated initial state.

The *contributions* of this paper are:

- A new black-box framework for synthesizing program contracts for software modules (Sect. 4).
- An algorithm to extract program contracts from finite-state register automata (Sect. 4).
- An implementation of our approach in the tool CoGent (Sect. 5), and an evaluation of our method using software modules taken from the Java API (Sect. 6).

Outline: The remainder of this paper is structured as follows. Section 2 illustrates program contracts with an example of a stateful data structure that serves as a running example for this paper. Section 3 describes the semantics of program contract, and introduces to basic concepts and notations for dealing with register automata and active automata learning. Section 4 outlines the steps for synthesizing program contracts with illustrations using the running example. Section 5 describes the implementation details of our tool, CoGent, and Sect. 6 presents its evaluation on various data structures. Section 7 compares our approach with some of the earlier attempts for synthesizing program contracts in the literature, followed by the conclusions in Sect. 8.

2   Motivating Example

As an illustration, consider the Java class BoundedList in Fig. 1. It contains methods BoundedList() for constructing a list object, list, of maximum size

```
1    public class BoundedList {              18   public boolean contains(Integer e
2      private LinkedList<Integer> list;          ) {
3      private int maxSize;                   19     return list.contains(e);
4                                             20   }
5      public BoundedList(){                  21
6        maxSize = DEFAULT_SIZE;              22   public boolean isEmpty() {
7        list = new LinkedList<Integer        23     return (list.size == 0) ?
       >();                                          true: false;
8      }                                      24   }
9                                             25
10     public void push(Integer e) {         26   public boolean isFull() {
11       if(maxSize > list.size()) list.     27     return (list.size == maxSize) ?
       push(e);                                       true : false;
12     }                                      28   }
13                                            29 }
14     public int pop() {                     30
15       return list.pop();
16     }
17
```

Fig. 1. A module for a BoundedList (in Java)

$$\{(p = q) \land \neg\mathtt{isFull}()\} \quad \mathtt{push}(p) \quad \{\mathtt{contains}(q)\}$$

$$\left\{ \begin{array}{l} (\neg(p = q) \land \neg\mathtt{contains}(q)) \\ \lor (\mathtt{isFull}() \land \neg\mathtt{contains}(q)) \end{array} \right\} \quad \mathtt{push}(p) \quad \{\neg\mathtt{contains}(q)\}$$

Fig. 2. Contracts for the BoundedList module in Fig. 1

defined by maxSize. The class further contains the methods push and pop, which are mutators, and the observer methods contains, isEmpty, and isFull. The class BoundedList internally uses the LinkedList class available in JDK v1.8. The method push takes an integer as an input parameter and inserts the integer into the list. Method pop does not accept any parameter but removes an element from the list and outputs the removed integer. The method contains returns *True* if the argument passed in the method already exists in the list, and *False* otherwise. Methods isEmpty and isFull return *True* if the list is empty and full respectively, otherwise, *False*. The module serves as a running example for illustrating our proposed approach.

A contract relates a method call with the module states immediately before and after that call. Being in a black-box setting, we cannot refer directly to the internal module state. Instead we refer to the module state indirectly via the return values of calls to observer methods. An observer method does not modify the state of the module, and is used to extract information about the module state.

Let a *condition* be a Boolean combination of observer calls $f(r_1, \ldots, r_m)$, where $r_1, \ldots, r_m$ are variables of the appropriate types, and constraints formulated using the predicates from some background theory. In this paper, we define a *contract* for a method m with parameters $p_1, \ldots, p_n$ in a module to be of the form

$$\{P\} \ m(p_1, \ldots, p_n) \ \{Q\}$$

where P, called the *precondition* and Q, called the *postcondition*, are conditions. The conditions P, Q can contain variables $p_1, \ldots, p_n$, as well as further variables used to relate pre- and post-states. As a simplifying assumption, and without loss of generality, every variable in P or Q that does not occur among the $p_1, \ldots, p_n$ has to occur as an argument of some observer in P or Q. Let the *parameters* of the contract be $p_1, \ldots, p_n$ together with additional variables appearing in P, Q.

A contract $\{P\}\ m(p_1, \ldots, p_n)\ \{Q\}$ is *valid* if, for every valuation of variables occurring in the contract, whenever m is called in a reachable state of the module in which P is *True*, the method call $m(p_1, \ldots, p_n)$ terminates and leaves the module in a state in which Q is *True*.

As illustration, for the module `BoundedList` in Fig. 1, we aim to synthesize contracts for the mutators `push` and `pop`. The contracts may include the given Boolean observer methods `contains`, `isEmpty`, and `isFull`, as well as relations between the occurring parameters. To this end, we first compute a model of the module in terms of a register automaton. While the behaviour of a software module can in general not be described by a finite register automaton, such a finite automaton can be derived for data structures with bounded capacity. For `BoundedList` with `maxSize = 2`, for example, the computed automaton has four locations and two registers, see Fig. 3. The register automaton captures the reachable behaviour of both the mutators and the observers.

To generate contracts for a mutator m, we then consider the transitions that are associated with m. Such transitions describe how the return values of observer methods can change as a result of calling m: transitions can update the values of registers, and the observers are described by location-specific guards. We present an algorithm, which for each location generates a location-specific contract for m from its outgoing m-transitions; as a second step, the location-specific contracts are then combined to obtain an overall contract for m.

In general, we would like generated contracts to be both *valid* and *maximal*, by which we mean that the precondition cannot be weakened without making the contract invalid. Two example contracts for the `push` method are given in Fig. 2. We can observe that the first contract in Fig. 2 is valid, but it is not maximal, since the postcondition could also be established by assuming `contains`(q) already in the precondition. The second contract is both valid and maximal.

3 Background

In this section, we give background for the contract synthesis approach, described in Sect. 4. The synthesis approach works by using active automata learning to obtain a register automaton model of the stateful behaviour of the module. The register automaton then forms the basis for contract synthesis. In this section, we describe program contracts, register automata and active learning.

3.1   Contracts

Throughout the paper, we assume a *background theory*, i.e., a (many-sorted) first-order language with constant, function, and relation symbols, with fixed interpretation over the appropriate domains. Terms and formulas are constructed as usual from those symbols, as well as from variables taken from a set $\mathcal{V}$. A *valuation* μ is a mapping from variables $\mathcal{V}$ to their domains. Valuations are extended to terms and assertions in the usual way. We write $\mu \models \phi$ to express that ϕ evaluates to *True* in μ.

We assume a set $\mathcal{M}$ of *methods*, each with a signature that determines the number of input parameters, their types, and the return type of the method. We assume a distinguished subset of $\mathcal{M}$, the set of *observer methods*: an observer method is special in that it does not modify any state variables. Throughout the paper, we assume that each observer method returns a Boolean value. The other methods are called *mutators*.

A *method call* is a term of form $m(d_1, \ldots, d_n)$, where m is a method action and $d_1, \ldots, d_n$ are data values from the appropriate domains. A *parameterized method call* is a term of form $m(p_1, \ldots, p_n)$, where $p_1, \ldots, p_n$ are variables; in this context we sometimes call them *formal parameters* of the method call.

As mentioned in Sect. 2, a *condition* is a Boolean combination of observer calls $f(r_1, \ldots, r_m)$, where $r_1, \ldots, r_m$ are variables of the appropriate types, and constraints formulated using the predicates from the background theory. We say that a condition P *entails* condition Q, written $P \Rightarrow Q$, if the formula $P \to Q$ is valid when every observer method is considered as an uninterpreted first-order predicate.

A *contract* is a triple $\{P\}\ m(p_1, \ldots, p_n)\ \{Q\}$ consisting of a precondition P, a mutator call $m(p_1, \ldots, p_n)$, and a postcondition Q.

3.2   Register Automata

We assume a set of *registers* $x_1, x_2, \ldots$.

Definition 1 (Register automaton). *A register automaton (RA) is a tuple $\mathcal{A} = (L, l_0, \mathcal{X}, \Gamma)$, where L is a finite set of locations, $l_0 \in L$ is the initial location, $\mathcal{X}$ maps each location $l \in L$ to a finite set $\mathcal{X}(l)$ of registers, where in particular $\mathcal{X}(l_0) = \emptyset$, and Γ is a finite set of transitions. Each transition in Γ is of form*

$$\langle l, m(p_1, \ldots, p_n), g, e_{out}, x_{i_1} := e_{i_1}, \ldots, x_{i_m} := e_{i_m}, l' \rangle,$$

where $l \in L$ is a source location, $l' \in L$ is a target location, $m(p_1, \ldots, p_n)$ is a parameterized method call, g is a guard, i.e., a conjunction of negated and non-negated relations over $p_1, \ldots, p_n$ and $\mathcal{X}(l)$, e_{out} is an expression over $p_1, \ldots, p_n$ and $\mathcal{X}(l)$, and $x_{i_1} := e_{i_1}, \ldots, x_{i_m} := e_{i_m}$ is an assignment which updates the registers $x_{i_1}, \ldots, x_{i_m}$ in $\mathcal{X}(l')$ with the values of expressions $e_{i_1}, \ldots, e_{i_m}$. In this work, we assume that each expression e_{i_j} is either a register in $\mathcal{X}(l)$ or a formal parameter in $p_1, \ldots, p_n$. □

We write $\bar{x}$, $\bar{p}$, and $\bar{e}$ for tuples of registers, parameters, and expressions. Let us formalize the semantics of RAs. A *state* of an RA $\mathcal{A} = (L, l_0, \mathcal{X}, \Gamma)$ is a pair $\langle l, \mu \rangle$ where $l \in L$ and μ is a valuation over $\mathcal{X}(l)$, i.e., a mapping from $\mathcal{X}(l)$ to the appropriate domains. The *initial state* is the pair $\langle l_0, \mu_0 \rangle$ where μ_0 is the empty mapping. A *step* of $\mathcal{A}$, denoted $\langle l, \mu \rangle \xrightarrow{m(\bar{d})/\mu(e_{out})} \langle l', \mu' \rangle$, transfers $\mathcal{A}$ from $\langle l, \mu \rangle$ to $\langle l', \mu' \rangle$ on the method call $m(\bar{d})$, returning $\mu(e_{out})$, if there is a transition $\langle l, m(\bar{p}), g, e_{out}, x_{i_1} := e_{i_1}, \ldots, x_{i_m} := e_{i_m}, l' \rangle \in \Gamma$ such that

- $\mu \models g[\bar{d}/\bar{p}]$, i.e., $\bar{d}$ satisfies the guard g under the valuation μ, and
- μ' is the updated valuation which maps x_i to $\mu(e_i)$ when x_i is in $x_{i_1}, \ldots, x_{i_m}$, and maps other registers x_i in $\mathcal{X}(l')$ to $\mu(x_i)$.

A state $\langle l, \mu \rangle$ is *reachable* if there is a sequence of steps

$$\langle l_0, \mu_0 \rangle \xrightarrow{m_1(\overline{d_1})/o_1} \langle l_1, \mu_1 \rangle \quad \langle l_1, \mu_1 \rangle \xrightarrow{m_2(\overline{d_2})/o_2} \langle l_2, \mu_2 \rangle \quad \cdots \quad \langle l_{n-1}, \mu_{n-1} \rangle \xrightarrow{m_n(\overline{d_n})/o_n} \langle l, \mu \rangle$$

leading from the initial state $\langle l_0, \mu_0 \rangle$ to $\langle l, \mu \rangle$.

We can now define validity of a contract relative to a register automaton $\mathcal{A}$. Let P be a condition, let σ be a valuation of the variables in P, and let $\langle l, \mu \rangle$ be a state of $\mathcal{A}$. We say that P *is true in* $\langle l, \mu \rangle$ *under* σ, denoted $\langle l, \mu \rangle \models \sigma(P)$, if $\sigma(P)$ evaluates to true when each observer call in $\sigma(P)$, of form $obs(d_1, \ldots, d_n)$, is replaced by the value returned when calling $obs(d_1, \ldots, d_n)$ in $\langle l, \mu \rangle$.

Definition 2. *A contract* $\{P\}$ $m(p_1, \ldots, p_n)$ $\{Q\}$ *is valid for a RA* $\mathcal{A}$ *if for any assignment* σ *of values to the parameters of the contract, and any reachable state* $\langle l, \mu \rangle$ *of* $\mathcal{A}$ *with* $\langle l, \mu \rangle \models \sigma(P)$, *we have that*

- *there is an output* o *and state* $\langle l', \mu' \rangle$ *with* $\langle l, \mu \rangle \xrightarrow{m(\sigma(p_1, \ldots, p_n))/o} \langle l', \mu' \rangle$, *and*
- *for any such output* o *and state* $\langle l', \mu' \rangle$ *it holds that* $\langle l', \mu' \rangle \models \sigma(Q)$.

Example

Figure 3 showcases such a RA that serves as a model for capturing the behaviour of the BoundedList API (cf. Fig. 1) when the maximum capacity of the list is set to 2. The language for the model consists of sequences of API method calls. An execution of such a sequence may result in modifying the state of the list, causing state transitions, thereby producing an output sequence that adheres to the expected I/O behaviour of the methods within the sequence. The RA is composed of nodes, each representing a specific state of the list, and edges that signify state transitions. Each edge is labeled to denote the actions performed by a method during execution. In the following, we illustrate the labels corresponding to the edges for a mutator and an observer:

$$(i) \quad \frac{\text{pop()} \,[\!]\, true \to \{x_1 := x_2\}}{x_1} \qquad (ii) \quad \frac{\text{contains}(q) \,[\!]\, (x_1 = q) \vee (x_2 = q)}{true}$$

Consider a state ℓ_2 where the list has two elements stored in registers x_1 and x_2, with x_1 holding the most recently pushed element. In this state, a state

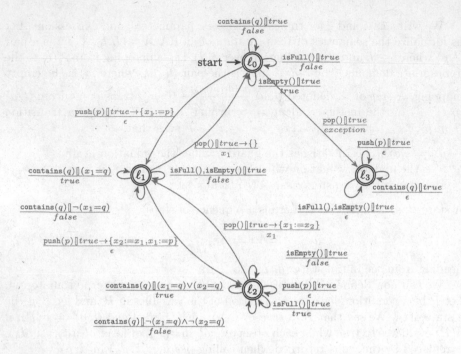

Fig. 3. Register automaton modeling a list (Fig. 1) with maximum capacity 2

transition occurs when the method **pop()** (a *mutator*) is invoked, as indicated by an edge labeled with (*i*). This label indicates that the method's guard condition is satisfied (*true*) and it outputs the recently pushed element stored into x_1 while moving the second element x_2 into x_1, thereby releases x_2. In fact, a call to **pop()** always outputs the last stored element unless the list is empty, in which case it throws an exception while leading to a trap state. The mutator **push**, however, in ℓ_2 does not change the state as the list has reached its maximum capacity. We use the notation ϵ to denote the **void** return type for method **push**. On the other hand, a method call **contains**(*q*) (an *observer*) in ℓ_2 checks if an element passed by the parameter *q* is present in the list, is labeled with (*ii*), meaning the method outputs *true* upon satisfying the condition $(x_1 = q) \vee (x_2 = q)$. Note that the label (*ii*) has no register assignments since observers do not modify register values and therefore, do not change the module state. In some cases we represent a single label for more than one method calls, method signature separated by comma (','), those exhibit similar behaviour.

3.3 Active Learning of Register Automata

The first step of our contract generation uses active automata learning (AAL) to automatically learn a register automaton model of the system under test (SUT). AAL is an automated black-box technique which *a priori* needs know only a module's methods and their signatures. Classical AAL learns finite automata or

Mealy machines from tests, using, e.g., the classic L^* algorithm [3] or the more recent TTT algorithm [16]. These, and other AAL algorithms are implemented in *LearnLib* [15]. Finite-state models do not capture how parameter values in method calls affect the module state and successive method calls. In order to capture data aspects of module behaviour, finite-state models can be, and commonly are, equipped with variables, sometimes called registers. Variables can store the values of data parameters; they can influence control flow by means of guards, and the control flow can cause variable updates. Finite state machines with variables are often called extended finite state machines (EFSMs). We will employ a specific such model, namely *register automata* (RAs), in which registers are used as variables. An extension of AAL to learning of RAs is SL^* [9], which has been implemented in RALib, an extension of LearnLib [8].

The SL^* algorithm must know the set of methods and their signatures. Like other AAL algorithms, it operates in two alternating phases: hypothesis construction and hypothesis validation. During hypothesis construction, sequences of method calls are submitted on the SUT, and the corresponding return values are observed to collect information about the module behaviour. When certain convergence criteria are met, the AAL algorithm constructs a *hypothesis*, which is a minimal deterministic RA that is consistent with the observations so far. To validate that the hypothesis agrees with the behaviour of the SUT, learning then moves to the validation phase, in which the SUT is subject to a conformance testing algorithm which aims to validate that the behaviour of the SUT agrees with the hypothesis. If conformance testing does not find any counterexample, learning terminates and returns the current hypothesis as the inferred model of the SUT. If a counterexample (i.e., a sequence of method calls on which the SUT and the hypothesis disagree) is found, the hypothesis construction phase is re-entered to build a more refined hypothesis. If the loop of hypothesis construction and validation does not terminate, this indicates that the behaviour of the SUT cannot be captured by a deterministic RA whose size and complexity is within reach of the employed learning algorithm. Still, even in these cases, the last constructed hypothesis can be used as an *approximate model* of the SUT.

4   Contract Synthesis

In this section, we describe our approach for inferring contracts for a module.

4.1   Learning a Behavioural Model

The first step of our approach is to obtain a register automaton model of the module. Sometimes, such an automaton model is readily available and can be supplied directly for generating contracts. Otherwise, such a register automaton can be learned using AAL as described in Sect. 3.3. Recall that AAL is fully automated and black-box, but may have practical limitations on the size of the learned model. For these reasons, we may modify the module so that its behaviour can be captured by an RA of modest size. A typical modification for container modules is to bound their capacity so that they become "full" for a small number of contained items: this will not change the set of valid contracts, as long as they do not count the number of contained items. For our running example such an automaton is shown in Fig. 3.

4.2   Generating Contracts from a Register Automaton

Given a register automaton model of our module, we present an algorithm for synthesizing contracts for each mutator method m. Recall that a contract is of form $\{P\}\, m(p_1, \ldots, p_n)\, \{Q\}$. Our methodology considers synthesizing contracts for one postcondition at a time. This means, our algorithm synthesizes contracts of the above form, given as input a postcondition Q, as well as a set $\mathcal{V}_{contr}$ of variables that can occur in P; the set $\mathcal{V}_{contr}$ should include $p_1, \ldots, p_n$ and the variables in Q. In our running example, a starting postcondition Q could be contains(q), where q is a parameter, or even ¬contains(q). In the following description, we will use generation of preconditions P in contracts of form

$$\{P\}\, \text{push}(p)\, \{\text{contains}(q)\}$$

to illustrate the successive steps in our algorithm. The generation of contracts proceeds through the following steps.

Step 1: Generating Weakest Preconditions: For each location l, we derive the weakest precondition $wp_l(m, Q)$, i.e., the weakest condition on the registers of l under which m will terminate and yield a state in which Q evaluates to true. This can be done using standard techniques (e.g., [11]). For each location l, let $[\![Q]\!]_l$ be the condition on the registers of l and parameters of Q under which Q evaluates to *True*. The condition $[\![Q]\!]_l$ can be obtained from Q by replacing each nonnegated observer call $obs(\overline{p})$ by the disjunction of the guards of transitions from l in which $obs(\overline{p})$ return *True*, and analogously for negated observer calls. Then, letting $t_1, \ldots, t_m$ be the outgoing transitions from l for method m, $wp_l(m, Q)$ is obtained as

$$wp_l(m, Q) = \bigvee_i g_i \;\wedge\; \bigwedge_i \left(g_i \to [\![Q]\!]_{l_i'}[e_{i_1}/x_{i_1}, \ldots, e_{i_m}/x_{i_m}]\right) \tag{1}$$

where g_i is the guard, l_i' is the target location, and $x_{i_1} := e_{i_1}, \ldots, x_{i_m} := e_{i_m}$ is the assignment of t_i.

Illustration: Let us illustrate the generation of the weakest precondition $wp_{l_1}(\text{push}(p), \text{contains}(q))$ for the method push(p) relative to the postcondition contains(q), where l_1 is the location in the RA fragment depicted in Fig. 4. Here, l_1 is the location representing a bounded list containing a single element stored in the register x_1. The transition from ℓ_1 to ℓ_2 is the only transition from l_1 for the method push. It inserts a second element into the list, causing two elements to be stored into the registers x_1 and x_2. We first obtain $[\![\text{contains}(q)]\!]_{l_2}$ as $(q = x_1 \vee q = x_2)$. Using Eq. (1), we then derive the weakest precondition

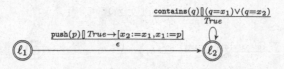

Fig. 4. The single transition for the method push from location ℓ_1, together with the transition for contains from location ℓ_2.

$wp_{l_1}(\text{push}(p), \text{contains}(q))$ as $(q = x_1 \vee q = x_2)[x_1/x_2, p/x_1]$, i.e., $(p = q) \vee (x_1 = q)$. $\quad\square$

Step 2: Generating Location-Specific Preconditions: The weakest precondition $wp_l(m, Q)$ is not adequate as a precondition, since in general it mentions registers, while a precondition can only refer to the module state through observer calls. Therefore, in each location l, we generate *location-specific* preconditions $Pre_l(m, Q)$ such that $[\![Pre_l(m, Q)]\!]_l$ implies $wp_l(m, Q)$. To this end, define the set $\mathcal{O}$ as containing all possible parameterized method calls $obs(\overline{p})$ whose parameters $\overline{p}$ are taken from $\mathcal{V}_{contr}$. Next, let $\mathcal{C}_l$ be the set of formulas, which are either (i) of form $[\![obs(\overline{p})]\!]_l$ or of form $[\![\neg obs(\overline{p})]\!]_l$ for a parameterized observer call $obs(\overline{p})$ in $\mathcal{O}$, or (ii) a (nonnegated or negated) relation between variables in $\mathcal{V}_{contr}$. We generate $Pre_l(m, Q)$ as a disjunction of conjunctions of formulas in $\mathcal{C}_l$, where each disjunct is obtained as a minimal conjunction of formulas in $\mathcal{C}_l$ which implies $wp_l(m, Q)$. The generation of $Pre_l(m, Q)$ can be performed using a SAT/SMT-solver by observing that the validity of

$$(c_1 \wedge \cdots \wedge c_k) \rightarrow wp_l(m, Q)$$

is equivalent to unsatisfiability of

$$(c_1 \wedge \cdots \wedge c_k) \wedge \neg wp_l(m, Q),$$

implying that we can obtain minimal conjunctions $c_1 \wedge \cdots \wedge c_k$ with the above properties by asking a SAT/SMT-solver to produce minimal unsatisfiable subsets (MUS) of formulas in $\mathcal{C}_l \cup \{(\neg wp_l(m, Q))\}$. From each of these we obtain a conjunction of formulas in $\mathcal{C}_l$ by first removing $\neg wp_l(m, Q)$, and replacing each conjunct of form $[\![obs(\overline{p})]\!]_l$ (or $[\![\neg obs(\overline{p})]\!]_l$) by the corresponding parameterized observer method call $obs(\overline{p})$ (or $\neg obs(\overline{p})$). We discard conjunctions, such as $obs(\overline{p}) \wedge \neg obs(\overline{p})$, which are syntactical contradictions. Since the generation of minimal unsatisfiable subsets may not explicitly generate the empty set of conjuncts (which is equivalent to *False*), we finally add, for each non-parameterized observer $obs()$ for which $[\![obs()]\!]_l$ is *True*, the disjunct $\neg obs()$; by symmetry we add the disjunct $\neg obs()$ if $[\![obs()]\!]_l$ is *False*. These disjuncts are redundant in the location-specific precondition at location l, but may be non-redundant in another location l' where $[\![obs()]\!]_{l'}$ is neither *True* nor *False*; in such a case they allow to form weaker global preconditions in Step 3. The result is our sought location-specific precondition $Pre_l(m, Q)$, structured as a disjunction of conjunctions over formulas in $\mathcal{O}$.

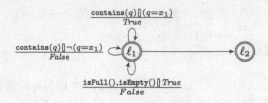

Fig. 5. Observers in location ℓ_1 in the automaton for BoundedList

Illustration: In Step 1, we obtained $wp_{l_1}(\texttt{push}(p), \texttt{contains}(q))$, the weakest precondition in location l_1, as $(p = q) \vee (x_1 = q)$. In Fig. 5, we show a fragment of the learned RA, showing calls to observers in location l_1. To construct $Pre_{l_1}(\texttt{push}(p), \texttt{contains}(q))$, we collect in $\mathcal{C}_l$ the guards for $\texttt{contains}(q)$ (i.e., $(q = x_1)$) and for $\neg\texttt{contains}(q)$ (i.e., $\neg(q = x_1)$) together with equalities and dis-equalities between occurring parameters. By interacting with a SAT/SMT solver, we identify the following minimal unsatisfiable subsets:

(i) $\{(p = q), \neg wp_{l_1}(\texttt{push}(p), \texttt{contains}(q))\}$
(ii) $\{(q = x_1), \neg wp_{l_1}(\texttt{push}(p), \texttt{contains}(q))\}$

which, after removing the negated weakest preconditions, yields the following two minimal disjuncts to be used in the precondition: (i) $(p = q)$, and (ii) $\texttt{contains}(q)$. Since none of these disjuncts entails the other, we use both when forming the formula in DNF, as $((p = q) \vee \texttt{contains}(q))$. As the final step, we consider unparameterized observer calls that always return *True* or *False* in location l_1. Considering that in l_1, the list contains one item, these are $\neg\texttt{isEmpty}()$ and $\neg\texttt{isFull}()$. Therefore, we add the two disjuncts $\texttt{isEmpty}()$ and $\texttt{isFull}()$. By making them antecedents in an implication, we can then write $Pre_{l_1}(\texttt{push}(p), \texttt{contains}(q))$ in the following way:

$$(\neg\texttt{isFull}() \wedge \neg\texttt{isEmpty}()) \rightarrow ((p = q) \vee \texttt{contains}(q)).$$

□

Step 3: Generating Global Preconditions: After obtaining location-specific preconditions, we can finally obtain a *location-agnostic* precondition $Pre(m, Q)$ as the conjunction

$$Pre(m, Q) = \bigwedge_{l \in L} Pre_l(m, Q) \tag{2}$$

over location-specific preconditions for all locations. The so obtained formula for $Pre(m, Q)$ is then simplified to a formula which is equivalent in each reachable location of the RA. The simplification transforms it into disjunctive normal form (DNF), and then pruning disjuncts that are either infeasible, i.e., evaluating to false in each location (this can be determined by inspecting the RA for the module), or redundant, i.e., entailed by some other disjunct.

Illustration: In Step 2, we obtained the following location-specific preconditions for postcondition $\texttt{contains}(q)$ while synthesizing contracts for method $\texttt{push}$:

location ℓ_0 (empty list): $\{(\neg\text{isFull}() \wedge \text{isEmpty}()) \to (p = q)\}$
location ℓ_n (full list): $\{(\text{isFull}() \wedge \neg\text{isEmpty}()) \to \text{contains}(q)\}$
other locations ℓ_i : $\{(\neg\text{isFull}() \wedge \neg\text{isEmpty}()) \to ((p = q) \vee \text{contains}(q))\}$

Then, taking the conjunction of the above preconditions and applying the simplification techniques described in Step 3, we obtain the global precondition as follows:

$$((p = q) \wedge \neg\text{isFull}()) \quad \vee \quad \text{contains}(q)$$

which is the sought precondition for our final contract.   □

4.3   Correctness and Optimality

In this section, we state and prove that our technique generates valid contracts (Theorem 1) which, under some conditions, are also maximal (Theorem 2).

Theorem 1 (Contract Validity). *If our method synthesizes a contract of form $\{P\}\ m(p_1, \ldots, p_n)\ \{Q\}$ for an RA $\mathcal{A}$, then this contract is valid for $\mathcal{A}$.*

Proof: The theorem follows by observing that the steps our methods produce results with the desired properties:

Step 1: For each location l, the generated weakest precondition $wp_l(m, Q)$ has the property to guarantee that a method call of form $m(p_1, \ldots, p_n)$ in location l is guaranteed to terminate and result in a state where Q evaluates to true. This follows by standard techniques for computing weakest preconditions.

Step 2: For each location l, the location-specific precondition $Pre_l(m, Q)$ generated in Step 2 has the property that $[\![Pre_l(m, Q)]\!]_l \to wp_l(m, Q)$. This follows from the observation that $[\![C_i]\!]_l \to wp_l(m, Q)$ for each disjunct C_i in $[\![Pre_l(m, Q)]\!]_l$.

Step 3: Since $Pre_l(m, Q)$ is a conjunct of $Pre(m, Q)$, it follows that $Pre(m, Q)$ entails $Pre_l(m, Q)$ for any l, hence $[\![Pre(m, Q)]\!]_l \to [\![Pre_l(m, Q)]\!]_l$. Thus, if $[\![Pre(m, Q)]\!]_l$ is true in l, then a method call of form $m(p_1, \ldots, p_n)$ in l is guaranteed to terminate and result in a state where Q evaluates to true. Since l is arbitrary, the theorem follows.   □

We say that an RA is *fully reachable* if for each location l and valuation μ of the registers $\mathcal{X}(l)$ of l, the state $\langle l, \mu \rangle$ is reachable.

Theorem 2 (Synthesis of Maximal Contracts). *Let $\mathcal{A}$ be a fully reachable RA, let m be a method, let the condition Q and set of variables $\mathcal{V}_{contr}$ be the input to our contract generation. If the condition R is such that its parameters are in $\mathcal{V}_{contr}$ and the contract $\{R\}\ m(p_1, \ldots, p_n)\ \{Q\}$ is valid for $\mathcal{A}$, then our method synthesizes a contract of form $\{P\}\ m(p_1, \ldots, p_n)\ \{Q\}$ such that $R \Rightarrow P$.*

Proof: Let R be a condition as above. Put R in DNF. Assume that $c_1 \wedge \cdots \wedge c_k$ is a disjunct of R. Consider a location l of $\mathcal{A}$. Since $\{R\}\ m(p_1, \ldots, p_n)\ \{Q\}$ is valid for $\mathcal{A}$, the corresponding condition $[\![c_1]\!]_l \wedge \cdots \wedge [\![c_k]\!]_l$ guarantees that calling $m(p_1, \ldots, p_n)$ in l is guaranteed to terminate and result in a state in which Q holds. Since $wp_l(m(p_1, \ldots, p_n), Q)$ is the weakest formula with such a property, it follows that $[\![c_1]\!]_l \wedge \cdots \wedge [\![c_k]\!]_l$ implies $wp_l(m(p_1, \ldots, p_n), Q)$. If none of $[\![c_1]\!]_l$, $\ldots$, $[\![c_k]\!]_l$ is *False*, our MUS generation will then find a subset of $[\![c_1]\!]_l, \ldots, [\![c_k]\!]_l$ which implies $wp_l(m(p_1, \ldots, p_n), Q)$, and generate the conjunction of the corresponding subset of $c_1, \ldots, c_k$ as a disjunct of $Pre_l(m, Q)$. If some $[\![c_i]\!]_l$ is *False*, then c_i will be added as a disjunct of $Pre_l(m, Q)$. In both cases, the result is that $Pre_l(m, Q)$ is entailed by R. Since P is obtained as the conjunction of the different $Pre_l(m, Q)$ for $l \in L$, this implies that also P is entailed by R.   □

The condition that $\mathcal{A}$ be fully reachable in Theorem 2 shows that our technique may generate unnecessarily strong preconditions if some states are not reachable in $\mathcal{A}$. This deficiency can be addressed by adding a procedure for generating invariant, which for each location l generates a characterization Inv_l of the valuations μ such that $\langle l, \mu \rangle$ is reachable. The formulas Inv_l are then used in Step 2, but generating minimal disjuncts $c_1 \wedge \cdots \wedge c_k$ such that

$$(c_1 \wedge \cdots \wedge c_k \wedge Inv_l) \rightarrow wp_l(m, Q)$$

is valid. We leave this extension as future work.

5   Implementation

We implement the strategies outlined in Sect. 4 in a Python tool called CoGent, abbreviation of **Co**ntract **Gen**erator. We build CoGent in integration with z3 SAT/SMT solver [10] for checking SAT/UNSAT of logical entailments and identifying minimal unsatisfiable subsets. For this purpose, we use z3 Python library, z3py [12], as the constraint solver. In addition, we have used the Python library Sympy [24] for simplification of Boolean expressions to conversion to DNF.

In our work, we first learn the RA model of the target API using the tool RAlib [8,9]. RAlib utilizes a given test harness tailored to the target API in order to learn the automaton. The test harness maps each method from the API to a symbol for learning the model. Next, we operate CoGent by giving inputs an XML representation of the automaton model and the target mutator for which we are interested in synthesizing contracts. The tool automatically identifies the observers (following the observer semantics) present in the API and generates pre and postconditions for the mutator. These conditions are quantifier-free first-order logic expressed in terms of Boolean valuations of observers and relation between input parameters. Thus the tools RAlib and CoGent in combine offer a comprehensive solution to synthesizing contracts for the mutators from an API.

Figure 6 shows the architecture of our tool where each step described in this paper is represented as a Python module (depicted as a box). The module Driver runs the contract synthesis engine by operating modules for performing steps 1

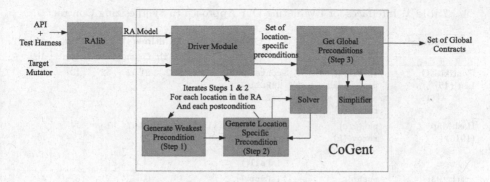

Fig. 6. Architecture of Contract Synthesis Engine

and 2 in rounds for every location in the automaton and each possible post-condition. While in step 2, the module `Solver` utilizes `z3py` API for checking SAT/UNSAT and eventually deriving MUSes that yield the set of preconditions. Once the module `Driver` accumulates all location-specific preconditions for a mutator, it delegates the task of synthesizing global contracts to a module that merges the preconditions wrt. each postcondition. Additionally, it simplifies the merged contract with the help of `Simplifier`, which inherits some of the functions provided by `Sympy`.

6 Evaluation

We evaluate our contract generation tool by synthesizing contracts for some of the modules from Java SEv8, and the Contiki-NG OS. We generate contracts for the mutators from those modules using the supplied Boolean observers including `isFull` and `isEmpty` methods for handling size bounds. The maximum size for each data structure is set to 3. Table 1 outlines the details of our tool evaluation. For each module, the number of non-whitespace, non-comment lines of code is mentioned within brackets. The average running time (in seconds) for model learning and synthesizing contract for a mutator are recorded in columns 4 and 5, respectively, using `RAlib` and `CoGent` tools. In `RAlib`, the maximum number of attempts to find counterexamples is set to 1000 per hypothesis. Column 6 shows the number of locations in the automaton, and column 7 indicates the total number of contracts generated by the tool. The final column specifies maximum number of disjuncts obtained after simplifying the preconditions for the contracts generated by our tool for each module. Following we illustrate a few contracts generated for two mutators from Contiki-NG list module.

Contiki-NG, a widely used open-source OS for IoT, includes a critical list module, which has unique characteristics compared to typical list implementations. This module is designed to be highly resource-constrained, where the API allocates a memory block by releasing it if it has been pre-allocated. Additionally, the list can function as both a stack and a queue, but storing a block in either way requires removing it first if it already exists in the list.

Table 1. Interfaces for Evaluating Our Approach to Synthesizing Contract

Modules	Mutators	Observers	Runtime(s)		#	#	max.
			RAlib	CoGent	locs.	cont.	disj.
Contiki-NG List (45)	insert(e_1, e_2), pop(), push(e_1), add(e), remove(e)	contains(e), isFull(), isEmpty()	51.2	21.02	52	19	3
HashMap (1916)	put(k, v), remove(k)	containsKey(k), containsValue(v), isEmpty(), isFull()	3.33	12.07	15	14	7
Stack (93)	push(e), pop()	isEmpty(), isFull(), contains()	1.6	0.6	21	8	3
PriorityQueue (704)	add(e), remove(e), poll()	isEmpty(), isFull(), contains()	5.4	11.7	53	21	5
BoundedList (43)	push(e), pop(), insert(e_1, e_2)	isEmpty(), isFull(), contains()	15.74	0.97	21	12	3

To evaluate this module, we create a Java class that simulates the behaviour of the Contiki-NG list module, treating memory blocks as integer elements, and generate contracts for the mutators. In the following, we discuss the contracts generated for two specific mutators: add and insert, which establish the aforementioned behaviour. The add method takes an input element through p, removes it if it already exists in the list, and then appends the element at the end. On the other hand, the insert method receives two parameters: p_1 and p_2. It removes p_2 if it is present in the list and inserts it again after p_1.

Here are two of the contracts generated for the add and insert methods:

i $\{$isEmpty() $\lor$ (contains(p) $\land$ ¬isFull())$\}$ add(p) $\{$¬isFull()$\}$
ii $\{$isEmpty() $\lor$ (contains(p_2) $\land$ ¬isFull())$\}$ insert(p_1, p_2) $\{$¬isFull()$\}$

Contract (i) for method add demonstrates that adding an element that is already present in the list will not result in the list becoming full. This is because the method removes the element before adding it again. Similarly, contract (ii) shows that the list cannot become full if the parameter p_2 is already present in the list.

Contract Validation: Next, we validate the synthesized contracts for the mutators listed in Table 1 leveraging symbolic execution [17], a program verification technique that explores different execution paths to test the validity of the contracts. Symbolic execution treats inputs as symbols representing arbitrary values and systematically explores feasible code paths with symbolic input values.

To validate contract for a mutator, we generate an arbitrary pre-state that can be reached after a bounded-length sequence of calls to mutators with symbolic parameters. Symbolic execution is then performed on the targeted mutator, under the assumption correspond to the precondition from synthesized contract. The postcondition is treated as an assertion checked after symbolic execution to identify any execution paths that fail to satisfy the postcondition for certain parameter values. If the postcondition remains valid throughout symbolic execution, the contract is considered to be valid for all module states. We utilize the Symbolic(Java) PathFinder tool (SPF) [21] to facilitate contract validation. Using the above setup, we successfully validated all contracts obtained through our proposed method, confirming that none of them are invalid. For a detailed implementation for contract validation, we encourage to refer to [14].

7 Related Work

We give an overview of the most related areas of research. For a broader survey of existing contract synthesis approaches, we refer the reader to [2].

Our work can be seen as an approach to *precondition inference:* given a method m with a given postcondition Q, produce a precondition P which guarantees that Q will hold when the method returns. Data-driven approaches to this problem (e.g., [22]) start from a set of *features*, i.e., predicates over m's inputs; they collect "good" test inputs (causing Q to be satisfied) as well as "bad" test inputs (causing Q to be falsified), which induce *feature vectors* (valuations of the features) for "good" and for "bad" inputs. A classification algorithm can then be used to separate "good" from "bad" inputs, producing a precondition. Padhi et al. [20] augment this technique by the ability to learn new features, when the existing ones are not sufficient to separate "good" from "bad" inputs. Astorga et al. [4,5] further build on this technique to be able to give guarantees relative to a given test input generator: a precondition is *safe* if the test generator cannot find a test input that satisfies the precondition and violates the postcondition; it is *maximal* if it includes all inputs found by the test generator that satisfy the postcondition. Our method is data-driven as well, as active automata learning is a black-box method and works by executing test cases. Our method differs from existing inference methods in the intermediate step of constructing a register automaton, and is, thus, able to discover which states of a system are reachable.

Molina et al. [19] use an analogous technique for generating postconditions for a given precondition, in which the method is executed with an exhaustive set of inputs, and postconditions are generated from the observed outputs using a genetic algorithm. Dynamic methods have also been used to infer program invariants. Ernst et al. [13] developed the Daikon system, which infers likely invariants by observing program executions. The obtained invariants are restricted to conjunctive Boolean expressions. The approach has later also been extended to generate likely program contracts. At the moment, it is not clear whether our method can be extended to synthesise postconditions, although this is an interesting avenue of future research.

There are also several white-box approaches to synthesize contracts. Alpuente et al. [1] apply a symbolic execution engine, which explores program paths reachable for given a precondition P. For each path, the engine produces a path condition and symbolic values of program variables, from which corresponding postconditions are synthesized. Singleton et al. [23] present an algorithm, based on symbolic execution, to extract human-readable concise contracts from strongest postconditions. Alshnakat et al. [2] use solvers for constrained Horn clauses (i.e., model checkers) to generate program contracts that are sufficient to verify given properties of a program. It remains to be investigated how our approach compares, in terms of the required runtime and readability of contracts, to white-box approaches.

8   Conclusion

We have presented a novel approach to synthesizing method contracts for stateful software modules, specifically those implementing data structures like stacks, queues, etc. Assuming that the modules are equipped with observer methods for querying the module state, and mutators for modifying it, our technique synthesizes contracts for the mutators, where pre- and postconditions are expressed as Boolean combinations of observer calls together with equalities between parameters to observers and mutators. Our proposed technique first learns a model of the module's behaviour, utilizing existing algorithms for active learning of register automata. On the basis of the learned model, our technique automatically synthesizes preconditions for any given postcondition. We prove that, under some assumptions, the obtained preconditions are the weakest possible. We have developed a tool called CoGent based on our approach, which generates contracts for mutators from a given register automaton where the contracts cover reachable behaviours (module locations). Our implementation provides evidence that this approach can successfully synthesize contracts for various stateful Java modules. As additional evidence, we validate obtained contracts using symbolic execution.

In future work, we plan to extend our approach to handle non-Boolean observers and inequalities between input parameters and registers during the model learning phase. This extension will enable the inference of preconditions in a more expressive language. In addition, we will enhance contract synthesis with location-specific invariant generation, to handle some cases in which invariants about registers are needed to prevent the synthesis of unnecessarily strong preconditions (see Sect. 4.3).

Acknowledgments. This research was partially funded by the Swedish Foundation for Strategic Research through projects aSSIsT and WebSec, the Swedish Research Council (Vetenskapsrådet), and the Knut and Alice Wallenberg Foundation through project UPDATE. We also thank the SEFM 2023 reviewers for comments and questions that have improved the presentation of our work.

References

1. Alpuente, M., Pardo, D., Villanueva, A.: Abstract contract synthesis and verification in the symbolic K framework. Fundam. Informaticae **177**(3–4), 235–273 (2020). https://doi.org/10.3233/FI-2020-1989
2. Alshnakat, A., Gurov, D., Lidström, C., Rümmer, P.: Constraint-based contract inference for deductive verification. In: Ahrendt, W., Beckert, B., Bubel, R., Hähnle, R., Ulbrich, M. (eds.) Deductive Software Verification: Future Perspectives. LNCS, vol. 12345, pp. 149–176. Springer, Cham (2020). https://doi.org/10.1007/978-3-030-64354-6_6
3. Angluin, D.: Learning regular sets from queries and counterexamples. Inf. Comput. **75**(2), 87–106 (1987)
4. Astorga, A., Madhusudan, P., Saha, S., Wang, S., Xie, T.: Learning stateful preconditions modulo a test generator. In: McKinley, K.S., Fisher, K. (eds.) Proceedings of the 40th ACM SIGPLAN Conference on Programming Language Design and Implementation, PLDI 2019, Phoenix, AZ, USA, 22–26 June 2019, pp. 775–787. ACM (2019). https://doi.org/10.1145/3314221.3314641
5. Astorga, A., Saha, S., Dinkins, A., Wang, F., Madhusudan, P., Xie, T.: Synthesizing contracts correct modulo a test generator. In: Proceedings of ACM Programming Languages, vol. 5, no. OOPSLA, pp. 1–27 (2021). https://doi.org/10.1145/3485481
6. Baudin, P., Filliâtre, J.-C., Marché, C., Monate, B., Moy, Y., Prevosto, V.: ACSL: ANSI/ISO C Specification Language. http://frama-c.com/acsl.html
7. Burdy, L., et al.: An overview of JML tools and applications. Int. J. Softw. Tools Technol. Transfer **7**(3), 212–232 (2004). https://doi.org/10.1007/s10009-004-0167-4
8. Cassel, S., Howar, F., Jonsson, B.: RALib: a LearnLib extension for inferring EFSMs. In: DIFTS 2015 (2015). https://www.faculty.ece.vt.edu/chaowang/difts2015/papers/paper_5.pdf
9. Cassel, S., Howar, F., Jonsson, B., Steffen, B.: Active learning for extended finite state machines. Formal Aspects Comput. **28**(2), 233–263 (2016). https://doi.org/10.1007/s00165-016-0355-5
10. De Moura, L., Bjørner, N.: Z3: an efficient SMT solver. In: Ramakrishnan, C.R., Rehof, J. (eds.) Proceedings of 14th International Conference on Tools and Algorithms for the Construction and Analysis of Systems (TACAS), ser. LNCS, vol. 4963, pp. 337–340. Springer, Cham (2008). https://doi.org/10.1007/978-3-540-78800-3_24
11. Dijkstra, E.W.: A constructive approach to the problem of program correctness. BIT Numer. Math. **8**(3), 174–186 (1968). https://doi.org/10.1007/BF01933419
12. Dutcher, A., Bjorner, N.: z3-solver 4.12.2.0 (2023). https://pypi.org/project/z3-solver/
13. Ernst, M.D., et al.: The Daikon system for dynamic detection of likely invariants. Sci. Comput. Program. **69**(1–3), 35–45 (2007)
14. Ghosal, S., Jonsson, B., Rümmer, P.: An active learning approach to synthesizing program contracts, July 2023. https://doi.org/10.5281/zenodo.8169860
15. Isberner, M., Howar, F., Steffen, B.: The open-source LearnLib. In: Kroening, D., Păsăreanu, C.S. (eds.) CAV 2015. LNCS, vol. 9206, pp. 487–495. Springer, Cham (2015). https://doi.org/10.1007/978-3-319-21690-4_32
16. Isberner, M., Howar, F., Steffen, B.: The TTT algorithm: a redundancy-free approach to active automata learning. In: Bonakdarpour, B., Smolka, S.A. (eds.) RV 2014. LNCS, vol. 8734, pp. 307–322. Springer, Cham (2014). https://doi.org/10.1007/978-3-319-11164-3_26

17. King, J.C.: Symbolic execution and program testing. Commun. ACM **19**(7), 385–394 (1976). https://doi.org/10.1145/360248.360252
18. Meyer, B.: Applying "design by contract". IEEE Comput. **25**(10), 40–51 (1992). https://doi.org/10.1109/2.161279
19. Molina, F., Ponzio, P., Aguirre, N., Frias, M.F.: EvoSpex: an evolutionary algorithm for learning postconditions. In: 43rd IEEE/ACM International Conference on Software Engineering, ICSE 2021, Madrid, Spain, 22–30 May 2021, pp. 1223–1235. IEEE (2021). https://doi.org/10.1109/ICSE43902.2021.00112
20. Padhi, S., Sharma, R., Millstein, T.D.: Data-driven precondition inference with learned features. In: Krintz, C., Berger, E.D. (eds.) Proceedings of the 37th ACM SIGPLAN Conference on Programming Language Design and Implementation, PLDI 2016, Santa Barbara, CA, USA, 13–17 June 2016, pp. 42–56. ACM (2016). https://doi.org/10.1145/2908080.2908099
21. Păsăreanu, C.S., et al.: Combining unit-level symbolic execution and system-level concrete execution for testing NASA software. In: Proceedings of the 2008 International Symposium on Software Testing and Analysis ISSTA, pp. 15–26 (2008). https://doi.org/10.1145/1390630.1390635
22. Sankaranarayanan, S., Chaudhuri, S., Ivancic, F., Gupta, A.: Dynamic inference of likely data preconditions over predicates by tree learning. In: Ryder, B.G., Zeller, A. (eds.) Proceedings of the ACM/SIGSOFT International Symposium on Software Testing and Analysis, ISSTA 2008, Seattle, WA, USA, 20–24 July 2008, pp. 295–306. ACM (2008). https://doi.org/10.1145/1390630.1390666
23. Singleton, J.L., Leavens, G.T., Rajan, H., Cok, D.R.: Inferring concise specifications of APIs. CoRR, abs/1905.06847 (2019). http://arxiv.org/abs/1905.06847
24. S. D. Team: Sympy 1.12 (2023). https://www.sympy.org/en/index.html

Ranged Program Analysis via Instrumentation

Jan Haltermann[1]([⊠]) [iD], Marie-Christine Jakobs[2] [iD], Cedric Richter[1] [iD], and Heike Wehrheim[1] [iD]

[1] Department of Computing Science, University of Oldenburg, Oldenburg, Germany
{jan.haltermann,cedric.richter,heike.wehrheim}@uol.de
[2] LMU Munich, Munich, Germany
m.jakobs@lmu.de

Abstract. *Ranged program analysis* has recently been proposed as a means to scale a single analysis and to define parallel cooperation of different analyses.

To this end, ranged program analysis first splits a program's paths into different parts. Then, it runs one analysis instance per part, thereby restricting the instance to analyze only the paths of the respective part. To achieve the restriction, the analysis is combined with a so-called *range reduction* component responsible for excluding the paths outside of the part.

So far, ranged program analysis and in particular the range reduction component have been defined in the framework of configurable program analysis (CPA). In this paper, we suggest *program instrumentation* as an alternative for achieving the analysis restriction, which allows us to use *arbitrary analyzers* in ranged program analysis. Our evaluation on programs from the SV-COMP benchmark shows that ranged program analysis with instrumentation performs comparably to the CPA-based version and that the evaluation results for the CPA-based ranged program analysis carry over to the instrumentation-based version.

Keywords: Software verification · ranged program analysis · program instrumentation

1 Introduction

Assessing whether developed software meets given quality criteria is an integral part of the development process. Software verification, which aims to prove whether software satisfies user-specified correctness properties like assertions, is one means to assess the quality. Today, many different automatic software verification tools exist, which employ different verification approaches and, thus, have different strengths and weaknesses. Instead of enhancing existing or developing new verification approaches, another option for improving on state-of-the-art verification technology is to combine the strengths of existing approaches. One strategy is to apply the idea of the divide-and-conquer principle and let different verification approaches or tools jointly solve a verification task.

This principle has already been put into practice in several combinations [3,14,19,24] including combinations of testing and verification tools [2,17]. However, the combinations studied therein mostly work in a *sequential* manner: tools alternate in working on the task, either cyclically or in sequence. Thereby, the task to be solved is successively getting smaller with every run of a verifier until solved. Splitting the verification task into different parts and then jointly working on these parts in *parallel* may reduce the overall time after which the result becomes available. Although this type of parallel approach can also be used for scaling verification, it has mostly been used to scale symbolic execution [28,30,32,33,36].

Recently, Haltermann et al. [20] proposed *ranged program analysis* to generalize the idea of ranged symbolic execution [30], one of the techniques used to scale symbolic execution. Like ranged symbolic execution, ranged program analysis splits the program paths to be analyzed into different parts (so-called *ranges*). To this end, an ordering $\leq$ on program paths is defined and a range $[\pi_1, \pi_2]$ fixed to be the set of paths such that $\pi_1 \leq \pi \leq \pi_2$ holds for each path π in the set. In contrast to ranged symbolic execution, ranged program analysis allows using analyses other than symbolic execution to inspect a range and in particular also permits using different analysis approaches for different ranges. To restrict an analysis to inspect the paths of its range only, ranged program analysis combines the analysis with a so-called *range reduction* component. It is synchronously executed with the "real" analysis and is responsible for excluding the paths outside the range.

So far, ranged program analysis and in particular the range reduction component have been defined in the framework of configurable program analysis (CPA) [7], which limits the applicability of the approach. In this paper, we further generalize the concept of ranged program analysis and make it applicable to arbitrary, off-the-shelf verification tools running arbitrary analyses. To this end, we propose *range instrumentation* as an alternative to restricting an analysis to a range and implement it as a standalone tool. The idea of our range instrumentation is to encode the input range into the program by adding additional statements to the program. Afterward, the resulting *range program* only contains the paths specified in the input range given to the range instrumentation. As a range program is syntactically just a normal program, we can give it to any verification tool for analysis.

We experimentally evaluate our instrumentation-based ranged program analysis on tasks from SV-COMP using the off-the-shelf verifiers Klee [11], Symbiotic [12] and Ultimate Automizer [22] as well as the CPA-based symbolic execution CPASE implemented in CPACHECKER [8], which we require to compare instrumentation-based ranged program analysis with the CPA-based one from [20]. Our evaluation reveals that instrumentation-based ranged program analysis performs comparably to CPA-based ranged program analysis and that the results for instrumentation-based ranged program analysis are in line with

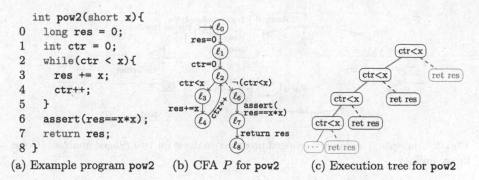

```
     int pow2(short x){
0      long res = 0;
1      int ctr = 0;
2      while(ctr < x){
3        res += x;
4        ctr++;
5      }
6      assert(res==x*x);
7      return res;
8    }
```

(a) Example program pow2   (b) CFA P for pow2   (c) Execution tree for pow2

Fig. 1. Example program pow2, the corresponding CFA and execution tree. (Color figure online)

the previous observations for CPA-based ranged analysis. In addition, we show that our instrumentation-based approach outperforms the approach based on residual program generation [3], which Haltermann et al. [20] originally mentioned as a way to generalize ranged program analysis to an arbitrary verifier.

2 Background

In this work, we aim to verify programs written in C. To explain the employed concepts of ranged program analysis, we start by introducing notations on programs and by defining (path) ranges.

2.1 Program Syntax and Semantics

To ease representation, we consider in this paper C-programs with numeric variables only[1]. Formally, we use a *control flow automaton (CFA)* $P = (L, \ell_0, G)$ to model a program, where L is a set of program locations, with initial location $\ell_0 \in L$, and $G \subseteq L \times Ops \times L$ are the control flow edges. A control-flow edge $g = (\ell_i, g, \ell_j)$ describes the statement $g \in Ops$ that is executed at location ℓ_i thereby leading to location ℓ_j. The set Ops contains all possible operations (on integer variables from a set Var), like assume-statements (boolean operations over the integer variables, denoted $BExpr$) or assignments. We assume that programs are deterministic except for the input values and that branches only occur at assume-statements. To be able to later define an ordering on paths, we employ an *indicator function* $B_P : G \rightarrow \{T, F, N\}$ on control-flow edges indicating for each $g \in G$ whether g is an assume-statement representing the T(rue) branch, the F(alse) branch or N(o) branch (in case g is not an assume statement).

Figure 1a shows our running example program pow2, which calculates the square (x^2) of the input x using addition. It contains an error (i.e., the assertion at line 8 is not always fulfilled) as the result for every negative number x is 0.

---

[1] The implementation covers the GNU C-standard.

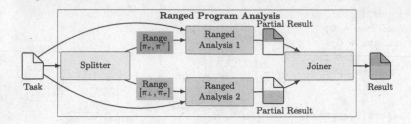

Fig. 2. Conceptual overview of ranged program analysis for two ranged analyses (Color figure online)

Figure 1b contains the corresponding CFA, where we draw assume-statements g with $B_P(g) = F$ dashed and all other edges solid.

In this work, we focus only on the syntactic paths of the program: A syntactical program *path* $\pi = \ell_0 \xrightarrow{g_1} \ell_1 \xrightarrow{g_2} \ldots \xrightarrow{g_n} \ell_n$ is a sequence of program statements, such that (1) it starts at the beginning of P in ℓ_0 and (2) adheres to the control-flow (i.e., $\ell_{i-1} \xrightarrow{g_i} \ell_i \in G$). We denote the set of all program paths of a CFA P by $Paths(P)$.

2.2 Program Ranges

The goal of ranged program analysis is to divide the program into so-called path *ranges*, such that each range can be analyzed individually and in particular also in parallel. Ranges are intervals of paths. To fix the paths inside a range, we first need an *ordering* $\leq$ on execution paths. Intuitively, we order paths with respect to their branch decisions, where an edge representing the true branch (of an assume statement) is smaller than the edge representing the false branch. Formally, for two paths $\pi = \ell_0 \xrightarrow{g_1} \ell_1 \xrightarrow{g_2} \ldots \xrightarrow{g_n} \ell_n$ and $\pi' = \ell'_0 \xrightarrow{g'_1} \ell'_1 \xrightarrow{g'_2} \ldots \xrightarrow{g'_m} \ell'_m \in Paths(P)$, we define $\pi \leq \pi'$, if $\exists 0 \leq k \leq n : \forall 1 \leq i \leq k : g_i = g'_i \wedge ((n = k \wedge m \geq n) \vee (m > k \wedge n > k \wedge B_P(g_{k+1}) = T \wedge B_P(g'_{k+1}) = F))$. Using this ordering, we can also represent the program paths as an *execution tree*. An execution tree is a tree where nodes are labeled with the assume operations of the program and the paths in the tree are ordered w.r.t. $\leq$. We depict a part of the execution tree of the example program in Fig. 1c.

Using the ordering on paths, we define a *range* $[\pi_l, \pi_u]$ as the set of paths s.t. $\forall \pi \in [\pi_l, \pi_u] : \pi_l \leq \pi \leq \pi_u$ holds. To be able to describe (partially) unbounded ranges, we use the two additional paths $\pi_\perp, \pi^\top \notin Paths(P)$, s.t. $\forall \pi \in Paths(P) : \pi_\perp \leq \pi \leq \pi^\top$ holds. Consequently, $[\pi_\perp, \pi^\top] = Paths(P)$. As previously stated, programs are expected to be deterministic except for the input. Hence, a *test case* τ, $\tau : Var \to Val$ mapping all (input) variables to concrete values of *Val*, *induces* a path $\pi_\tau \in Paths(P)$, obtained by executing the program using the test inputs. Now, we can define a range by two test cases τ_1 and τ_2, using the induced paths π_{τ_1} and π_{τ_2}. Therefore, we may write $[\tau_1, \tau_2]$ instead of $[\pi_{\tau_1}, \pi_{\tau_2}]$. In Fig. 1c, we highlight the path π_{τ_1} induced by $\tau_1 = \{x \mapsto 3\}$ in green and π_{τ_2}

induced by $\tau_2 = \{x \mapsto 0\}$ in blue. The range $[\pi_{\tau_1}, \pi_{\tau_2}]$ contains the paths to the blue, green, and black leaves. Note that $[\pi_{\tau_1}, \pi_{\tau_2}] = [\pi_{\tau_1}, \pi^\top]$.

2.3   Ranged Program Analysis

The idea of *ranged program analysis*, first proposed for symbolic execution [30] and then generalized in [20], is to split the program to be verified in ranges and analyze each range in parallel. A conceptual overview of the ranged program analysis, which considers two ranges, is given in Fig. 2. First, a set of ranges is generated by the Splitter. In the example, a path that can be generated by a Splitter is π_{τ_1}, highlighted in green in Fig. 1c. Using this test case, we can divide the program into two ranges $[\pi_\perp, \pi_{\tau_1}]$ and $[\pi_{\tau_1}, \pi^\top]$. Next, two ranged analyses verify both ranges of the program in parallel. Finally, when both analyses completed their tasks, the partial verification results are *joined* by a Joiner to a final answer. In case one analysis reports a property violation, the other is stopped, and the violation is reported as the final answer. As the program from Fig. 1a violates the assertion for any negative number, Ranged Analysis 2, which analyzes the range containing the error, reports a counter-example.

3   Ranged Program Analysis via Instrumentation

The concept of a parallel composition of different ranged analyses (as proposed in [20]) currently has the following major limitation: The range reduction, used to restrict a program analysis to a certain range, is defined for configurable program analyses only. Hence, using off-the-shelf tools for a ranged program analysis is currently not possible. To address this shortcoming, we propose using *program instrumentation* to encode the ranges directly into the program.

3.1   Instrumenting Programs with Ranges

For instrumentation, we semantically encode range constraints into the program. For this, we add additional constraints to the program execution to exclude execution paths that are out of range. However, execution paths cannot be excluded in hindsight (i.e. we cannot decide not to take a branch after we have taken it). Thus, our instrumentation has to exclude out-of-range paths *before* the branch is taken. To be able to exclude execution paths early, we make the following three observations for a given range $[\pi_{\tau_1}, \pi_{\tau_2}]$ and a finite prefix $\hat{\pi}$ of $\pi \in Paths(P)$:

1. *It is necessary to track whether $\hat{\pi}$ is a prefix of π_{τ_1} or π_{τ_2}.* If there exists a finite prefix $\hat{\pi}_{\tau_1}$ of π_{τ_1} (or a prefix $\hat{\pi}_{\tau_2}$ of π_{τ_2}), such that $\hat{\pi} = \hat{\pi}_{\tau_1}$ (or $\hat{\pi} = \hat{\pi}_{\tau_2}$), then π is potentially included in $[\pi_{\tau_1}, \pi_{\tau_2}]$.
2. *Only local branching decisions matter.* Let $\hat{\pi} = \ell_0 \xrightarrow{g_1} \ldots \xrightarrow{g_{n-1}} \ell_{n-1} \xrightarrow{g_n} \ell_n$ and let $\hat{\pi}_\tau = \ell_0 \xrightarrow{g_1} \ldots \xrightarrow{g_{n-1}} \ell_{n-1} \xrightarrow{g_{\tau,n}} \ell_{\tau,n}$ be a finite prefix of an arbitrary bound π_τ. If $B_P(g_{\tau,n}) = T$ and $B_P(g_n) = F$, then for all continuations π of $\hat{\pi}$ we have $\pi_\tau \leq \pi$. If $B_P(g_n) = T$ and $B_P(g_{\tau,n}) = F$, then $\pi \leq \pi_\tau$. Symmetrically, if $\pi_\tau \not\leq \hat{\pi}$ (or $\hat{\pi} \not\leq \pi_\tau$, resp.) then $\pi_\tau \not\leq \pi$ (or $\pi \not\leq \pi_\tau$ resp.).

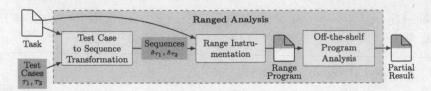

Fig. 3. Construction of a ranged analysis from an off-the-shelf program analysis for a range $[\pi_{\tau_1}, \pi_{\tau_2}]$ defined by two test cases τ_1, τ_2

3. *Inclusion is early decidable.* If $\pi_{\tau_1} \not\preceq \hat{\pi}$ or $\hat{\pi} \not\preceq \pi_{\tau_2}$, then π cannot be included in $[\pi_{\tau_1}, \pi_{\tau_2}]$ (as there exists no continuation of $\hat{\pi}$ included in the range).

Note that as soon as $\pi_{\tau_1} \not\preceq \hat{\pi}$ or $\hat{\pi} \not\preceq \pi_{\tau_2}$ for a prefix $\hat{\pi}$ we can safely abort the execution of the complete path π since the path cannot be in the range (observation 3). In addition, as soon as we can decide that $\pi_{\tau_1} \preceq \pi$ and $\pi \preceq \pi_{\tau_2}$ (observation 2) we do not have to restrict the execution any further. In the following, we exploit these observations to instrument relevant branching points (such as loops and branches) in the program by adding additional range constraints.

3.2 From Test Cases to Branching Decisions

Computing π_τ for a given test case τ requires an execution of the program or a semantical analysis of P. However, as soon as we derived π_τ, the decision of whether a path is in a given range is purely syntactical. In fact, based on our observations in Sect. 3.1, it is sufficient to decide whether the current execution path performs the same *branching decisions* as the path induced by the test case for the lower or upper bound. To simplify the instrumentation process, we, therefore, transform test cases τ into *sequences of branching decisions* s_τ taken when following π_τ and describing the same syntactic path π_τ. Now, to compute the sequence s_τ of branching decisions, we start by computing π_τ for a given test case τ provided by the splitter. Then, we generate the sequence s_τ by applying the recursively defined function $\mathcal{T}_P : Paths(P) \to \{T, F\}^*$:

$$\mathcal{T}_P(\ell_i \xrightarrow{g_i} \ell_j \xrightarrow{g_j} \cdots) = \begin{cases} x \circ \mathcal{T}_P(\ell_j \xrightarrow{g_j} \cdots) & \text{if } x = B_P(g_i) \in \{T, F\} \\ \mathcal{T}_P(\ell_j \xrightarrow{g_j} \cdots) & \text{otherwise} \end{cases}$$

For a given range $[\tau_1, \tau_2]$, we apply the sequence generator to the test case for the upper and lower bound to generate the sequences s_{τ_1} and s_{τ_2}. The generated sequences are then used for instrumentation.

Example. Let us consider our example program in Fig. 1 with the given range $[\tau_1, \tau_2]$ ($\tau_1 = \{x \mapsto 3\}$ and $\tau_2 = \{x \mapsto 0\}$). Based on the induced paths shown in Fig. 1c, the sequence generator generates two sequences $\mathcal{T}_P(\pi_{\tau_1}) = s_{\tau_1} = (T, T, T, F)$ and $\mathcal{T}_P(\pi_{\tau_2}) = s_{\tau_2} = (F)$ for the lower and upper bound respectively.

3.3   Instrumentation-Based Ranged Analysis

Using the observations of Sect. 3.1 and our sequence generator, we now instrument the program for a given range $[\tau_1, \tau_2]$ as shown in Fig. 3: We start by transforming the range bounds τ_1, τ_2 into sequences of branching decisions s_{τ_1} and s_{τ_2} respectively. Then, we instrument the program independently for both the lower and upper bound explained next.

Readout. Based on the given sequences of branching decisions $s_\tau = (b_0, b_1, \ldots, b_n)$ with $b_i \in \{T, F\}$, we define a *readout* function $R_{s_\tau} : \mathbb{N} \to \{T, F\}$ as follows:

$$R_{s_\tau}(x) = \bigvee_{b_i = T} (x = i) \vee x > n,$$

which is T if the predicate in the function evaluates to true and F otherwise. During instrumentation, we use function R_{s_τ} to read out the branching decision of the bound at the current branching point (e.g., a loop head or an if statement). To keep track of the branching decisions taken by the path induced by the lower (upper) bound at the current branching point, we introduce new counter variable lcounter (ucounter) for the lower (upper) bound. The counters are incremented for each branching decision taken in the program.

Keeping Track of Branching Decision. To keep track of whether the execution path is on the lower path π_{τ_1} or upper path π_{τ_2}, we introduce two new Boolean variables on_lpath and on_upath for the lower and upper path, respectively. Now, as soon as the execution path leaves the lower or upper path at a branching point, the execution is either aborted (since the path can never be in range) or we disable all instrumentations for the lower or upper path, respectively. For this, we guard our instrumentation using the two variables. This allows us to disable the instrumentation by setting on_lpath (or on_upath) to false. We abort the execution with a special abort function.

We instrument the code independently for both the upper and lower bound. During instrumentation, we instrument all branching points[2] represented by two edges $\ell_{i-1} \xrightarrow{g_i} \ell_i$ and $\ell_{i-1} \xrightarrow{g_j} \ell_j$ with $B_P(g_i) = T$ and $B_P(g_j) = F$.

Leaving the Lower Bound s_{τ_1}. For the lower bound, we handle the following two cases: (1) the execution path leaves the lower path with $B_P(g_i) = T$ and $R_{s_\tau}(\text{lcounter}) = F$ and (2) the execution leaves the lower path with $B_P(g_j) = F$ and $R_{s_\tau}(\text{lcounter}) = T$. For handling the former case, we add the following instrumentation directly after the branching decision g_i:

```
if(on_lpath) { if([[ R_{s_{\tau_1}}(lcounter) = F ]]) abort(); lcounter++; }
```

In other words, if the execution path branches to the true side with $B_P(g_i) = T$ and the lower path follows the false side (i.e. $R_{s_{\tau_1}}(\text{lcounter}) = F$) then any continuation of the execution path is smaller than the lower path and we abort the execution. Now, if the execution path leaves the lower path with $B_P(g_j) = F$

---

[2] In our implementation, we only instrument branching points that occur on the paths induced by the lower bound or upper bound.

```
 1  unsigned int on_lpath = 1;              1  unsigned int on_upath = 1;
 2  unsigned int lcounter = 0;              2  unsigned int ucounter = 0;
 3  int pow2(short x){                       3  int pow2(short x){
 4    long res = 0;                          4    long res = 0;
 5    int ctr = 0;                           5    int ctr = 0;
 6    while(ctr < x){                        6    while(ctr < x){
 7      if(on_lpath){                        7      if(on_upath){
 8        if(lcounter == 3) abort();         8        on_upath = (ucounter != 0);
 9        lcounter++;                        9        ucounter++;
10      }                                   10      }
11      res += x;                           11      res += x;
12      ctr++;                              12      ctr++;
13    }                                     13    }
14    if(on_lpath){                         14    if(on_upath){
15      on_lpath = (lcounter == 3);         15      if(ucounter != 0) abort();
16      lcounter++;                         16      ucounter++;
17    }                                     17    }
18    assert(res == x * x);                 18    assert(res == x * x);
19    return res;                           19    return res;
20  }                                       20  }
```

(a) A lower bound instrumentation   (b) An upper bound instrumentation

Fig. 4. Range programs generated using instrumentation for pow2

and $R_{s_{\tau_1}}(\texttt{lcounter}) = T$, all continuations of the execution path will be greater than the lower path and, therefore, we can safely disable the instrumentation for the lower bound by setting on_lpath = 0. We instrument the false branch after g_j accordingly. Finally, as a result of our lower bound instrumentation, all execution paths are aborted that are not in $[\pi_{\tau_1}, \pi^\top]$.

Leaving the Upper Bound s_{τ_2}. For the upper bound, we abort the execution if the execution path leaves the upper path with $R_{s_{\tau_2}}(\texttt{ucounter}) = T$ and $B_P(g_j) = F$. For this, we add the following instrumentation after g_j:

$$\texttt{if(on\_upath) \{ if([[} R_{s_{\tau_2}}(\texttt{ucounter}) = T \texttt{]]) abort(); ucounter++; \}}$$

If the execution path leaves the upper path with $R_{s_{\tau_2}}(\texttt{ucounter}) = F$ and $B_P(g_i) = T$, all continuations of the execution path will be smaller than the upper path and, therefore, we can disable the upper bound instrumentation by setting on_upath = 0. Now, by instrumenting a program with our upper bound instrumentation, all execution paths are aborted that are not in $[\pi_\bot, \pi_{\tau_2}]$.

To restrict the set of execution paths to $[\pi_{\tau_1}, \pi_{\tau_2}] = [\pi_{\tau_1}, \pi^\top] \cap [\pi_\bot, \pi_{\tau_2}]$ and therefore create a range program with the range $[\tau_1, \tau_2]$, we apply both the lower and upper bound instrumentation one after another.

Example. Let us again consider the example in Fig. 1 with the given range $[\tau_1, \tau_2]$ and corresponding sequences $s_{\tau_1} = (T, T, T, F)$ and $s_{\tau_2} = (F)$. For obtaining the range program, we apply both the lower bound and upper bound instrumentation. For brevity, we only show the program P instrumented independently for the lower bound $[\pi_{\tau_1}, \pi^\top]$ (using the sequence s_{τ_1}) in Fig. 4a and the upper bound $[\pi_\bot, \pi_{\tau_2}]$ (using s_{τ_2}) in Fig. 4b. Note that we perform some optimizations on the code. For example, lcounter==3 is equivalent to $R_{s_{\tau_1}}(\texttt{lcounter}) = F$ and ucounter!=0 is equivalent to $R_{s_{\tau_2}}(\texttt{ucounter}) = T$.

3.4   Handling Underspecified Bounds

In practice, C programs can contain other sources of non-determinism besides inputs, e.g. user inputs via scanf() or other functions like srand(). We handle them analogously to inputs, as the (random) values returned by these external functions can also be contained in a test case. We call a test case τ underspecified if it does not provide concrete values for all sources of randomness or inputs, and thus, τ induces a set $\mathcal{P}_\tau$ of paths. In [20], underspecified test cases representing a range bound are handled by splitting at the smallest path $min(\mathcal{P}_\tau)$. To accommodate for this splitting behavior, we adapt our instrumentation to handle underspecified bounds: $\mathcal{T}$ generates a sequence s_τ for the common prefix of all paths in $\mathcal{P}_\tau$ for an underspecified bound represented by a test case τ. During instrumentation, if we are still on the common prefix path of $\mathcal{P}(\tau)$, we check whether the next branching decision is specified in s_τ. If not, we abort if it is an upper bound or deactivate all checks by setting on_1path=0 for a lower bound.

4   Implementation

To show that we can use off-the-shelf tools in ranged program analysis, we realize the instrumentation described in Sect. 3. We also extend the existing implementation from [20] to support the use of range programs as exchange format instead of ranges. For the evaluation, we employ the best-performing splitter from [20], namely LB3. We implemented the transformation from test cases to sequences explained in Sect. 3.2 within the splitter to generate the correct input format needed for the instrumentation.

Instrumentation. We implement the instrumentation as a standalone component in Python. First, we use an AST parser[3] to identify all branching points in the program. Then, we instrument the program as defined in Sect. 3.3, using the sequences generated for the test cases. Our implementation supports the instrumentation of (GNU) C programs except for switch-statements.

Reduction for Generating Range Programs. Instead of instrumentation, Haltermann et al. proposed to use *residual program generation* [3] for generating a range program [20]. To compare the proposed idea with the instrumentation, we build a standalone component called *Reducer*. We realized this idea by modifying the range reduction from [20] to take a range described by two sequences as input and used the existing residual program generator [3] to generate a range program, containing all paths within the given range.

Verifiers. For the evaluation of our instrumentation-based ranged analysis technique, we need off-the-shelf verifiers for the analysis of the instrumented programs. As off-the-shelf verifiers, we selected the last two winners of the software verification competition [5,6]: SYMBIOTIC and ULTIMATEAUTOMIZER. SYMBIOTIC [12] combines slicing [34] with a sequential portfolio of three symbolic

---

[3] https://tree-sitter.github.io/tree-sitter/.

executions performed by KLEE [11], Slowbeast's [13] backward symbolic execution with loop folding, and Slowbeast's forward symbolic execution. ULTI-MATEAUTOMIZER (UAUTOMIZER) [22,23] applies counterexample guided abstraction refinement to iteratively refine an overapproximation of a program's error paths, which is represented by an automaton. In each iteration, the approach picks an error path from the current overapproximation. If the path is infeasible, UAUTOMIZER constructs a Floyd-Hoare automaton [23] explaining the infeasibility of that and similar paths and then removes all paths accepted by the Floyd-Hoare automaton from the current overapproximation. The approach stops if a feasible counterexample is found or the overapproximation becomes empty.

Besides the two verification approaches that make use of abstraction techniques, we also use two different tools employing symbolic execution: We employ KLEE [11] as a standalone tool and use the symbolic execution from CPA-CHECKER [8] (already used in [20]) to be able to compare the CPA-based and the instrumentation-based ranged program analyses.

5   Evaluation

The evaluation presented in [20] shows that CPA-based analyses can benefit from being used within ranged program analysis. With range instrumentation and range reduction, we can now employ off-the-shelf verifiers in ranged program analysis. We thus want to investigate whether CPASE, KLEE, SYMBIOTIC, and UAUTOMIZER also benefit from an application within a ranged program analysis. To this end, we study the following three research questions:

RQ1 How does instrumentation-based ranged program analysis compare to the CPA-based version?

RQ2 How does range instrumentation compare to range reduction?

RQ3 Do off-the-shelf analyses benefit from using instrumentation-based ranged analyses?

5.1   Evaluation Setup

All experiments were run on machines with an Intel Xeon E3-1230 v5 @ 3.40 GHz (8 cores), 33 GB of memory, and Ubuntu 22.04 LTS with Linux kernel 5.15.0. To increase the reproducibility of our results, we employ BENCHEXEC [9] for the execution of our experiments. Each tool is given a task (a program plus specification) per verification run. It either computes a proof (program fulfills specification) or raises an alarm (program violates specification). Each run is limited to 15 GB of memory, 4 CPU cores, and 15 min of CPU time, which yields a setup comparable to the one used in SV-COMP. We used all tasks from the SV-BENCHMARKS for the specification reach-safety used in the SV-COMP [15], in total 10 229 tasks. The specification reach-safety is fulfilled by a program, if all calls to the function reach_error are unreachable[4].

---

[4] In the benchmark, reach_error is called whenever an assert is violated, cf. Fig. 1.

Table 1. Results of CPACHECKER's symbolic execution used in CPA-based and instrumentation-based ranged program analysis.

	correct			incorrect	
	overall	proof	alarm	proof	alarm
CPASE(CPA)	1 648	584	1 064	5	57
CPASE(Instrument)	1 612	583	1 029	5	58

5.2 RQ1: Comparison of the CPA-Based and Instrumentation-Based Ranged Program Analysis

Evaluation Plan. To analyze the performance of the instrumentation- and the CPA-based approach, we compare the effectiveness (number of correctly solved tasks) and efficiency (time taken to compute an answer), of the CPA-based ranged program analysis for symbolic execution (CPASE(CPA)) from [20] with CPASE(Instrument). CPASE(Instrument) uses the instrumentation to generate range programs given to CPACHECKER's symbolic execution employed as an off-the-shelf tool. For efficiency, we are interested in the time consumed overall (*wall time*), as the consumed CPU time is not that meaningful in our setting, where several analyses run in parallel.

Effectiveness. Table 1 shows the number of correct answers given overall, also splits it into the number of correct proofs and alarms. In addition, it provides the number of incorrect proofs and alarms. We first observe that employing CPA-CHECKER's symbolic execution as an off-the-shelf tool on a range program does not decrease the overall effectiveness drastically. Compared to CPASE(CPA), it computes in total only 36 fewer correct answers. There are 73 tasks correctly solved by CPASE(CPA), for which CPASE(Instrument) exhausts the resource limits. We also observe that there are 37 tasks, where CPASE(Instrument) can compute the correct answer, but CPASE(CPA) runs into a timeout. Nearly all of these tasks contain a specification violation. Intuitively, there exist some tasks for which the instrumentation impedes the exploration of the violating path, but also other cases where it eases their exploration.

Efficiency. To analyze the efficiency of instrumentation-based ranged analysis compared to CPA-based, we compare the wall time taken by both to compute a correct answer, in case a range is generated. For each of these tasks, the log-scale scatter plot in Fig. 5 contains a data point that compares the time taken by CPASE(CPA) (x-axis) and the time taken by CPASE-(Instrument) (y-axis). The solid, diagonal line means that both analyses take the same time, while the dashed lines below and above indicate that one analysis takes twice as long as the other. The most

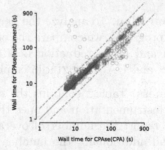

Fig. 5. Wall time of CPASE(CPA) and CPASE(Instrument)

Table 2. Results of CPASE, KLEE, SYMBIOTIC, and UAUTOMIZER used in instrumentation- and reduction-based ranged program analysis.

	correct			incorrect		
	overall	proof	alarm	unique	proof	alarm
CPASE(Instrument)	**1612**	583	1029	185	5	58
CPASE(Reduce)	1515	566	949	88	5	60
KLEE(Instrument)	**2968**	1293	1675	192	77	2
KLEE(Reduce)	2783	1283	1500	7	77	3
SYMBIOTIC(Instrument)	**3881**	2185	1696	235	95	1
SYMBIOTIC(Reduce)	3765	2217	1548	119	80	5
UAUTOMIZER(Instrument)	**3964**	2925	1039	562	22	0
UAUTOMIZER(Reduce)	3483	2557	926	81	20	1

important observation is that CPASE(Instrument) has a comparable overall execution time to the CPA-based approach for the vast majority of all tasks.

Having a closer look, we realize that for complex tasks, where CPASE(CPA) takes more than 100 s, CPASE(Instrument) is slightly faster, as it takes in the median only the 0.92-times of the runtime. The runtime decrease is based on the fact that we do not need to run the range reduction analysis in parallel when using the instrumentation for generating a range program. The additional overhead caused by generating the ranged programs is negligible, as the instrumentation takes in most cases less than a second.

> Based on the experimental results, we conclude that using instrumentation-based ranged program analysis instead of the CPA-based approach causes only a little overhead.

5.3   RQ2: Comparing Range Instrumentation and Range Reduction

Evaluation Plan. To analyze the performance of both approaches for generating range programs, we compare the effectiveness and efficiency of range instrumentation and range reduction of CPACHECKER's symbolic execution, KLEE, SYMBIOTIC, and UAUTOMIZER in combination as ranged program analyses.

Effectiveness. Table 2 contains the computed answers of the four tools, once using the instrumentation and once the reduction to generate the reduced program. We report the number of overall correct answers, of correct proofs and alarms, and additionally the number of tasks solved uniquely by using range instrumentation or range reduction. It also contains the number of incorrect proofs and alarms. First and foremost, we observe that using instrumentation to generate the range program increases the number of overall correctly solved tasks for all four tools. The increase ranges from 6.4% for CPASE to 13.8%

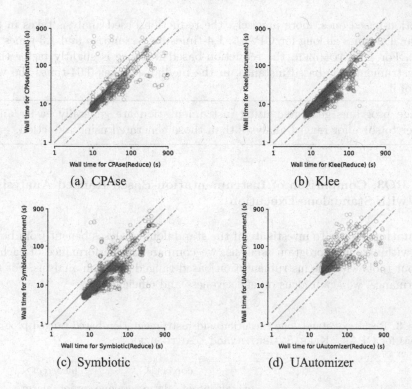

(a) CPAse

(b) Klee

(c) Symbiotic

(d) UAutomizer

Fig. 6. Scatter Plots comparing the wall time of instrumentation- and reduction-based ranged analysis

for UAUTOMIZER. The number of incorrect answers does not change for KLEE and CPASE, but decreases when using SYMBIOTIC(Reduce) or UAUTOMIZER-(Reduce). For SYMBIOTIC(Reduce) and most cases of UAUTOMIZER(Reduce), the decrease lies in the fact that the tools do not compute an answer.

We observe the largest difference in the effectiveness of reduction and instrumentation for UAUTOMIZER. The majority of tasks solvable by UAUTOMIZER-(Instrument) but not by UAUTOMIZER(Reduce) belong to the category called `eca` (383/562). Due to the task's artificial structure in that category, the size of the range program generated using the reducer increases by several orders of magnitude. The version of UAUTOMIZER employed in the experiments fails to process those large range programs and does not compute a result. Here, we observe one major advantage of instrumentation compared to reduction: The size of the range program generated is bounded by a constant factor and does not depend on the range.

Efficiency. To compare the efficiency of instrumentation- and reduction-based ranged analyses, we depict in Fig. 6 the scatter plots comparing the overall time taken to compute the solution for the four tools. For CPASE, SYMBIOTIC, and KLEE, we notice that versions using instrumentation are faster than the reduction-based ones, more precisely, the reduction-based analysis takes in the median 1.2-times as long for CPASE, 1.4-times for SYMBIOTIC and 1.3-times for KLEE. For UAUTOMIZER, the reduction-based instance is slightly faster than the instrumentation-based instance, in the median it takes 0.94-times the wall time of it.

> Range programs generated using instrumentation are generally easier and faster to solve for ranged analyses than those generated using reduction.

5.4   RQ3: Comparison of Instrumentation-Based Ranged Analysis with Standalone Execution

Evaluation Plan. To investigate, if the standalone analyses benefit from being used within ranged program analysis, we compare the performance of each of the four tools with the instrumentation-based ranged program analysis. For the performance, we again focus on effectiveness and efficiency.

Table 3. Results of standalone execution and instrumentation-based ranged program analysis for CPASE, KLEE, SYMBIOTIC and UAUTOMIZER.

		correct			incorrect	
	overall	proof	alarm	unique	proof	alarm
CPASE	1597	585	1012	–	5	27
CPASE(Instrument)	1612	583	1029	86	5	58
KLEE	2982	1294	1688	–	77	3
KLEE(Instrument)	2968	1293	1675	7	77	2
SYMBIOTIC	3917	2232	1685	–	77	1
SYMBIOTIC(Instrument)	3881	2185	1696	79	95	1
UAUTOMIZER	4240	3096	1144	–	23	0
UAUTOMIZER(Instrument)	3964	2925	1039	24	22	0

Effectiveness. In Table 3, we summarize the results for the standalone analyses and the ranged program analyses using instrumentation. Again, we report correct and incorrect proofs and alarms. In addition, Table 3 contains for each of the ranged analyses the number of uniquely solved tasks, i.e. the number of tasks only solved by the ranged analysis and not by the standalone analysis.

Taking a look at CPASE, we observe that it benefits from being used as a ranged analysis, as the number of overall solved tasks increases by 15 tasks. Moreover, CPASE(Instrument) can solve 86 tasks that are not solved by CPASE standalone. The incorrect alarms additionally raised by CPASE(Instrument) are most likely not caused by an error in the instrumentation, as we can also observe

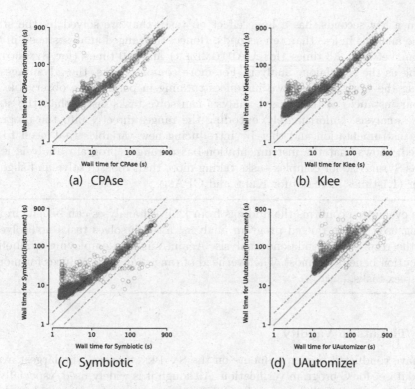

(a) CPAse

(b) Klee

(c) Symbiotic

(d) UAutomizer

Fig. 7. Scatter Plots comparing the wall time of instrumentation-based ranged analysis and the standalone analysis for different tools

additionally raised incorrect alarms for the same tasks for the CPA-based and reduction-based ranged analysis (c.f. Table 1 and Table 2).

For KLEE, the second symbolic execution, we observe a comparable effectiveness. The tasks that are only solved by KLEE standalone could not be solved by KLEE(Instrument) within the given resource limits. If we double these limits, all of them could be solved. There are 7 tasks uniquely solved by KLEE(Instrument). In all cases, KLEE(Instrument) detects the property violation within the given resource limits, as using a ranged program analysis allows it to search in different parts of the program in parallel.

SYMBIOTIC and UAUTOMIZER, the two techniques that aim for finding abstractions, perform not as well as the tools employing symbolic execution. In total, they compute 36 resp. 276 fewer correct answers. Again, we observe that the instrumentation-based ranged program analysis can compute 79 correct proofs and alarms for SYMBIOTIC and 24 for UAUTOMIZER that are not reported by the tools standalone. We thus confirm the findings from the previous work.

Efficiency. In Fig. 7, we compare the wall time of the four tools running standalone on the x-axis to the ranged analyses using instrumentation on the y-axis. The overhead of generating the sequences and the range program, completed within a few seconds, has a huge effect on tasks that are solved by the standalone analysis in less than ten seconds. Hence, the ranged analyses need in the median between 2.3-times (for UAUTOMIZER) and 3.0-times (for SYMBIOTIC) as long as the standalone analysis. For more complex tasks, the advantages of sharing the work between two instances running in parallel are observable, as all four instances of the ranged analysis can solve tasks faster than the standalone analysis. Unfortunately, encoding the ranges directly into the program using instrumentation and thereby introducing new variables that need to be tracked, shows that the instrumentation-based ranged program analysis is as fast as SYMBIOTIC for complex tasks taking more than 100 s to solve and slightly slower (1.1-times increase) for KLEE and CPASE.

> The evaluation confirms the findings from [20]: All analyses can benefit from being used within ranged program analysis, as each solves tasks not solved by the respective standalone analysis. Again, analyses employing symbolic execution benefit the most. The overhead of ranged analysis reduces for more complex tasks.

5.5   Threats to Validity

We have conducted the experiments on the SV-BENCHMARKS, the largest available dataset for C program verification. Although it is widely used, especially in the SV-COMP, our findings may not completely carry over to other real-world C programs. Currently, the instrumentation does not cover concurrent programs. Moreover, we do not support external functions, as the source code is needed for instrumentation.

It is unlikely that the implementation suffers from bugs, as the findings from [20] carry over to our evaluation. The additional incorrect answers for CPASE(Instrument) are also observable for CPASE(CPA), and we randomly selected and analyzed tasks where SYMBIOTIC(Instrument) computes additional incorrect proofs manually, validated that the range program contains a property violation, and cross-verified them using UAUTOMIZER and KLEE.

The fact that the performance of CPASE(CPA) and CPASE(Instrument) are comparable may be caused by using different formats for defining ranges. To account for this, we also have analyzed if there is a performance difference caused by the use of different formats. As the instrumentation requires a sequence as input, we updated CPASE(CPA) to also be able to process sequences as input and compared it with CPASE(CPA), observing no significant difference (cf. [21]).

The data collected may deviate in a reproduction study due to a different experimental setup or environment. To account for small, expected measurement errors, we restrict the presentation of our data to two significant digits.

6   Related Work

While there are several strategies for combining different verification approaches, we focus on combinations that like us divide the search space and let different verification approaches check different parts of the search space. Combinations like CoDiDroid [27], distributed assertion checking [35], or the compositional tester sketched in conditional testing [4] statically decompose the verification task into separate subtasks, which can be executed in parallel. Furthermore, several sequential or interleaved cooperation approaches restrict the subsequent verifiers to the yet uncovered search space, e.g., not yet covered test goals [4], open proof obligations [24], or yet unexplored program paths [1–3,14,16,17,19]. Like us, several of those approaches [3,4,14,16,19] encode the restriction within the program. Instead of forwarding the not yet explored state space, some techniques split the program paths in advance and then run different instances of the same analysis in parallel on different parts of the state space. For example, conditional static analysis [29] considers program branches to realize the split of program paths while concurrent bounded model checking techniques [25,26] rely on thread interleavings, but only Nguyen et al. [26] encode the split result as programs. In contrast, Yin et al. [37] dynamically split the input space if the abstract interpreter returns an inconclusive result and parallelly analyzes the different input partitions with the abstract interpreter. Meanwhile, parallel symbolic execution approaches [28,30,32,33,36] and ranged model checking [18] split execution paths. Often, they partition the execution tree, thereby relying on input constraints [32], path prefixes [31], or ranges [18,28,30,36] to describe the partitions. In contrast, GenSym [33] divides the execution tree into linear path segments, i.e., it splits at every branching point. The partitions themselves are generated dynamically based on the already explored symbolic execution tree [10,28,30,33,38] or statically from an initial shallow symbolic execution [31,32] or tests [28,30,36]. While most symbolic execution approaches symbolically interpret the program, GenSym [33] compiles the symbolic execution of a program P into a new program. Recently, Haltermann et al. [20] took on the idea to split program paths into ranges and analyzing those ranges in parallel. Instead of only supporting symbolic execution, their approach supports arbitrary configurable program analyses during the parallel analysis. To restrict a configurable analysis to the paths in a range, they suggest combining that configurable program analysis with a range reduction component. In this paper, we propose an even more general solution that can be applied to arbitrary off-the-shelf analysis tools. To this end, we encode the restriction to ranges into the program code, the language understood by analysis tools.

7   Conclusion

Ranged program analysis is a technique for analyzing different program parts (so-called ranges) with different verifiers or verifier instances in parallel. The original, CPA-based approach is limited to verifiers specified in the framework of configurable program analysis [7]. This paper lifts ranged program analysis to support arbitrary verifiers. Instead of restricting a verifier to its range during its execution, we instrument the restriction into the program code before running the verifier. Our evaluation demonstrates that instrumentation indeed allows us to plug existing verifiers into ranged program analysis. Furthermore, it shows that ranged program analysis with instrumentation performs comparably to the CPA-based approach and that the findings for CPA-based ranged program analysis also apply to ranged program analysis with instrumentation. In addition, it reveals that ranged program analysis with instrumentation is superior to reducer-based ranged program analysis, which Haltermann et al. [20] mention for lifting ranged program analysis to arbitrary verifiers.

Data Availability Statement. All experimental data and our open-source implementation are archived and available in our supplementary artifact [21].

References

1. Beyer, D., Henzinger, T.A., Keremoglu, M.E., Wendler, P.: Conditional model checking: a technique to pass information between verifiers. In: Proceedings of FSE. ACM (2012)
2. Beyer, D., Jakobs, M.-C.: CoVeriTest: cooperative verifier-based testing. In: Hähnle, R., van der Aalst, W. (eds.) FASE 2019. LNCS, vol. 11424, pp. 389–408. Springer, Cham (2019). https://doi.org/10.1007/978-3-030-16722-6_23
3. Beyer, D., Jakobs, M.-C., Lemberger, T., Wehrheim, H.: Reducer-based construction of conditional verifiers. In: Proceedings of ICSE, pp. 1182–1193. ACM (2018)
4. Beyer, D., Lemberger, T.: Conditional testing. In: Chen, Y.-F., Cheng, C.-H., Esparza, J. (eds.) ATVA 2019. LNCS, vol. 11781, pp. 189–208. Springer, Cham (2019). https://doi.org/10.1007/978-3-030-31784-3_11
5. Beyer, D.: Progress on software verification: SV-COMP 2022. In: Fisman, D., Rosu, G. (eds.) TACAS 2022. LNCS, vol. 13244, pp. 375–402. Springer, Cham (2022). https://doi.org/10.1007/978-3-030-99527-0_20
6. Beyer, D.: Competition on software verification and witness validation: SV-COMP 2023. In: Sankaranarayanan, S., Sharygina, N. (eds.) TACAS 2023. LNCS, vol. 13994, pp. 495–522. Springer, Cham (2023). https://doi.org/10.1007/978-3-031-30820-8_29
7. Beyer, D., Henzinger, T.A., Théoduloz, G.: Configurable software verification: concretizing the convergence of model checking and program analysis. In: Damm, W., Hermanns, H. (eds.) CAV 2007. LNCS, vol. 4590, pp. 504–518. Springer, Heidelberg (2007). https://doi.org/10.1007/978-3-540-73368-3_51
8. Beyer, D., Keremoglu, M.E.: CPACHECKER: a tool for configurable software verification. In: Gopalakrishnan, G., Qadeer, S. (eds.) CAV 2011. LNCS, vol. 6806, pp. 184–190. Springer, Heidelberg (2011). https://doi.org/10.1007/978-3-642-22110-1_16
9. Beyer, D., Löwe, S., Wendler, P.: Reliable benchmarking: requirements and solutions. STTT **21**(1), 1–29 (2019)
10. Bucur, S., Ureche, V., Zamfir, C., Candea, G.: Parallel symbolic execution for automated real-world software testing. In: Proceedings of EuroSys, pp. 183–198. ACM (2011)

11. Cadar, C., Dunbar, D., Engler, D.R.: KLEE: unassisted and automatic generation of high-coverage tests for complex systems programs. In: Proceedings of OSDI, pp. 209–224. USENIX Association (2008)

12. Chalupa, M., Mihalkovič, V., Řechtáčková, A., Zaoral, L., Strejček, J.: SYMBIOTIC 9: string analysis and backward symbolic execution with loop folding. In: Fisman, D., Rosu, G. (eds.) TACAS 2022. LNCS, vol. 13244, pp. 462–467. Springer, Cham (2022). https://doi.org/10.1007/978-3-030-99527-0_32

13. Chalupa, M., Strejček, J.: Backward symbolic execution with loop folding. In: Drăgoi, C., Mukherjee, S., Namjoshi, K. (eds.) SAS 2021. LNCS, vol. 12913, pp. 49–76. Springer, Cham (2021). https://doi.org/10.1007/978-3-030-88806-0_3

14. Christakis, M., Müller, P., Wüstholz, V.: Collaborative verification and testing with explicit assumptions. In: Giannakopoulou, D., Méry, D. (eds.) FM 2012. LNCS, vol. 7436, pp. 132–146. Springer, Heidelberg (2012). https://doi.org/10.1007/978-3-642-32759-9_13

15. SV-Benchmarks Community: SV-Benchmarks (2023). https://gitlab.com/sosy-lab/benchmarking/sv-benchmarks/-/tree/svcomp23

16. Czech, M., Jakobs, M.-C., Wehrheim, H.: Just test what you cannot verify! In: Egyed, A., Schaefer, I. (eds.) FASE 2015. LNCS, vol. 9033, pp. 100–114. Springer, Heidelberg (2015). https://doi.org/10.1007/978-3-662-46675-9_7

17. Daca, P., Gupta, A., Henzinger, T.A.: Abstraction-driven concolic testing. In: Jobstmann, B., Leino, K.R.M. (eds.) VMCAI 2016. LNCS, vol. 9583, pp. 328–347. Springer, Heidelberg (2016). https://doi.org/10.1007/978-3-662-49122-5_16

18. Funes, D., Siddiqui, J.H., Khurshid, S.: Ranged model checking. ACM SIGSOFT Softw. Eng. Notes **37**(6), 1–5 (2012)

19. Gerrard, M.J., Dwyer, M.B.: ALPACA: a large portfolio-based alternating conditional analysis. In: Proceedings of ICSE, pp. 35–38. IEEE/ACM (2019)

20. Haltermann, J., Jakobs, M., Richter, C., Wehrheim, H.: Parallel program analysis via range splitting. In: Lambers, L., Uchitel, S. (eds.) FASE 2023. LNCS, vol. 13991, pp. 195–219. Springer, Cham (2023). https://doi.org/10.1007/978-3-031-30826-0_11

21. Haltermann, J., Jakobs, M., Richter, C., Wehrheim, H.: Replication package for article 'Ranged Program Analysis via Instrumentation', June 2023. https://doi.org/10.5281/zenodo.8065229

22. Heizmann, M., et al.: Ultimate automizer and the CommuHash normal form - (competition contribution). In: Sankaranarayanan, S., Sharygina, N. (eds.) Proceedings of TACAS. LNCS, vol. 13994, pp. 577–581. Springer, Cham (2023). https://doi.org/10.1007/978-3-031-30820-8_39

23. Heizmann, M., Hoenicke, J., Podelski, A.: Software model checking for people who love automata. In: Sharygina, N., Veith, H. (eds.) CAV 2013. LNCS, vol. 8044, pp. 36–52. Springer, Heidelberg (2013). https://doi.org/10.1007/978-3-642-39799-8_2

24. Huster, S., Ströbele, J., Ruf, J., Kropf, T., Rosenstiel, W.: Using robustness testing to handle incomplete verification results when combining verification and testing techniques. In: Yevtushenko, N., Cavalli, A.R., Yenigün, H. (eds.) ICTSS 2017. LNCS, vol. 10533, pp. 54–70. Springer, Cham (2017). https://doi.org/10.1007/978-3-319-67549-7_4

25. Inverso, O., Trubiani, C.: Parallel and distributed bounded model checking of multi-threaded programs. In: Proceedings of PPoPP, pp. 202–216. ACM (2020)

26. Nguyen, T.L., Schrammel, P., Fischer, B., La Torre, S., Parlato, G.: Parallel bug-finding in concurrent programs via reduced interleaving instances. In: Proceedings of ASE, pp. 753–764. IEEE (2017)

27. Pauck, F., Wehrheim, H.: Together strong: cooperative android app analysis. In: Proceedings of ESEC/FSE, pp. 374–384. ACM (2019)

28. Qiu, R., Khurshid, S., Păsăreanu, C.S., Wen, J., Yang, G.: Using test ranges to improve symbolic execution. In: Dutle, A., Muñoz, C., Narkawicz, A. (eds.) NFM 2018. LNCS, vol. 10811, pp. 416–434. Springer, Cham (2018). https://doi.org/10.1007/978-3-319-77935-5_28

29. Sherman, E., Dwyer, M.B.: Structurally defined conditional data-flow static analysis. In: Beyer, D., Huisman, M. (eds.) TACAS 2018. LNCS, vol. 10806, pp. 249–265. Springer, Cham (2018). https://doi.org/10.1007/978-3-319-89963-3_15

30. Siddiqui, J.H., Khurshid, S.: Scaling symbolic execution using ranged analysis. In: Proceedings of SPLASH, pp. 523–536. ACM (2012)

31. Singh, S., Khurshid, S.: Parallel chopped symbolic execution. In: Lin, S.-W., Hou, Z., Mahony, B. (eds.) ICFEM 2020. LNCS, vol. 12531, pp. 107–125. Springer, Cham (2020). https://doi.org/10.1007/978-3-030-63406-3_7

32. Staats, M., Pasareanu, S.S.: Parallel symbolic execution for structural test generation. In: Proceedings of ISSTA, pp. 183–194. ACM (2010)

33. Wei, G., et al.: Compiling parallel symbolic execution with continuations. In: ICSE, pp. 1316–1328. IEEE (2023)

34. Weiser, M.D.: Program slicing. IEEE TSE 10(4), 352–357 (1984)

35. Yang, G., Do, Q.C.D., Wen, J.: Distributed assertion checking using symbolic execution. ACM SIGSOFT Softw. Eng. Notes 40(6), 1–5 (2015)

36. Yang, G., Qiu, R., Khurshid, S., Pasareanu, C.S., Wen, J.: A synergistic approach to improving symbolic execution using test ranges. Innov. Syst. Softw. Eng. 15(3-4), 325–342 (2019)

37. Yin, B., Chen, L., Liu, J., Wang, J., Cousot, P.: Verifying numerical programs via iterative abstract testing. In: Chang, B.-Y.E. (ed.) SAS 2019. LNCS, vol. 11822, pp. 247–267. Springer, Cham (2019). https://doi.org/10.1007/978-3-030-32304-2_13

38. Zhou, L., Gan, S., Qin, X., Han, W.: SECloud: binary analyzing using symbolic execution in the cloud. In: Proceedings of CBD, pp. 58–63. IEEE (2013)

Attack Time Analysis in Dynamic Attack Trees via Integer Linear Programming

Milan Lopuhaä-Zwakenberg[1(✉)] and Mariëlle Stoelinga[1,2]

[1] University of Twente, Enschede, the Netherlands
{m.a.lopuhaa,m.i.a.stoelinga}@utwente.nl
[2] Radboud University, Nijmegen, the Netherlands

Abstract. Attack trees (ATs) are an important tool in security analysis, and an important part of AT analysis is computing metrics. However, metric computation is NP-complete in general. In this paper, we showcase the use of mixed integer linear programming (MILP) as a tool for quantitative analysis. Specifically, we use MILP to solve the open problem of calculating the *min time* metric of dynamic ATs, i.e., the minimal time to attack a system. We also present two other tools to further improve our MILP method: First, we show how the computation can be sped up by identifying the modules of an AT, i.e. subtrees connected to the rest of the AT via only one node. Second, we define a general semantics for dynamic ATs that significantly relaxes the restrictions on attack trees compared to earlier work, allowing us to apply our methods to a wide variety of ATs. Experiments on a synthetic testing set of large ATs verify that both the integer linear programming approach and modular analysis considerably decrease the computation time of attack time analysis.

Keywords: Attack trees · Quantitative analysis · Optimization · Mixed integer linear programming

1 Introduction

(Dynamic) Attack Trees. Attack trees (ATs) are a prominent methodology in security analysis. They facilitate security specialists in identifying, documenting, analyzing and prioritizing (cyber) risks. An AT is a hierarchical diagram that describes a system's vulnerabilities to an adversary's attacks. Despite their name, ATs are rooted directed acyclic graphs. Roots of ATs represent the adversary's goal, while the leaves represent basic attack steps (BAS) undertaken by the adversary. Each internal root is labeled with a gate, determining how its activation depends on that of its children. Standard ATs (SATs) feature only OR and AND gates, but many extensions have been introduced to describe more elaborate attack scenarios [16]. One

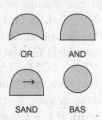

This research has been partially funded by ERC Consolidator grant 864075 CAESAR and the European Union's Horizon 2020 research and innovation programme under the Marie Skłodowska-Curie grant agreement No. 101008233.

of the most prominent extensions are *dynamic ATs* (DATs) [14]. DATs introduce a SAND (sequential AND) gate, which is activated only when its children are activated sequentially in the correct order. By contrast, an AND-node's children can be activated in parallel. An example is given in Fig. 1.

Quantitative Analysis. Quantitative analysis aims at computing *AT metrics*. Such metrics formalize how well a system performs in terms of security, and are essential when comparing alternatives or making trade-offs. Many such metrics exist, such as the minimal cost, minimal required skill, or maximal damage of a successful attack. This paper focuses on *min time*: the minimal time the adversary needs to perform a successful attack, given the duration of each BAS. This is important, since attack success crucially depends on time: attacks that take too long are not viable. Insight in timing behaviors of attacks is therefore a key to devising effective countermeasures. For instance, a security operations centre is interested in the time difference between the fastest viable attack and its average response time [1]. *Min time* is especially relevant in the context of DATs: On many metrics, such as cost/probability/skill, SAND and AND gates

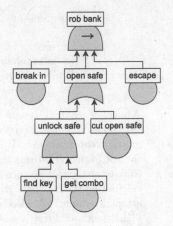

Fig. 1. A DAT for a bank robbery [4]. To rob a bank, attackers must break in, open the safe, and escape (in that order). The safe is opened by cutting it open, or by unlocking via obtaining the key and combination.

behave identically. Thus, to compute those metrics, algorithms for SATs immediately generalize to DATs. It is in the timing behavior that the difference between SAND and AND manifests itself, so that novel computation algorithms are needed.

Existing Algorithms for *min time*. The naive approach to calculating *min time* is to list all attacks that reach the root, and to find the one that takes the least time; clearly this is computationally prohibitive for larger ATs. A tree-shaped DAT can be computed via a bottom-up (BU) algorithm [14,23]. This algorithm works for general attributes (e.g. cost, probability, time), by using appropriate operators

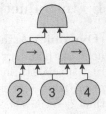

at each gate. For DAG-shaped ATs, the BU algorithm does not always work, because the values in different branches are no longer independent. For SATs this is not a problem because the relevant operators are idempotent [17]. In the DAT above, however, the BU algorithm of [14] calculates *min time* as $\max(2+3, 3+4) = 7$. However, the only successful attack is the one that activates the three BAS sequentially, and so *min time* equals $2+3+4 = 9$. Thus to find *min time* for DAG-shaped DATs new approaches are needed; in [5], efficient computation for DAG-shaped DATs is left as an open problem.

Integer Linear Programming. In this paper, we present a novel method to calculate *min time* for general DATs based on MILP. We translate calculating *min time* into a real-valued optimization problem, with a set of nonlinear constraints. We rewrite these into linear constraints by introducing auxiliary integer variables at each gate; for SAND-gates this is nontrivial and requires a careful analysis of the semantics, beyond the current literature (see below). Since dedicated solvers exist for MILP, translating attack time analysis into MILP speeds up computation time considerably.

Modular Analysis. To improve performance, we combine MILP with modular analysis [9]: we identify *modules* in a DAT, i.e., subDATs whose only connections to the rest of the DAT go via their root. We prove that *min time* can be computed by analyzing the modules separately; this requires a detailed comparison of the attacks on the larger DAT to the attacks on its modules. If a module is tree-shaped or static, then we can deploy the bottom-up algorithm to further decrease computation time. We integrate these modifications into our MILP algorithm.

Generalized Semantics. Another point we settle in this paper are generalized semantics for DATs. As SAND-gates require their children to be executed consecutively, different branches in the DAT may impose conflicting restrictions on the execution orders. To rule out these conflicts, [5] imposed well-formedness criteria at the cost of ruling out some satisfiable DATs. Furthermore, the corresponding attack definition was overly restrictive, with some fastest attacks not being recognized. This leads to an overestimation of *min time*. In this work we extend the definition of a (successful) attack so *min time* is correctly defined. This new definition applies to all DATs, not just the well-formed ones.

Experimental Validation. For confidentiality reasons industrial DATs are typically not disclosed to the general public [7, 26]. Therefore, we create a testing suite of 2400 synthetic DATs, obtained by combining smaller DATs from the literature via standard DAT composition methods, and we compare the performance of four methods (modular versus nonmodular and enumerative versus MILP). The experiments show that on larger DATs MILP outperforms enumerative, and modular outperforms nonmodular. The code for the experiments, the generated DATs and the experimental results are available in [22], and a version with proofs is available at [21].

Contributions. Summarized our main contributions are:

1. A generalization of the poset semantics of [5] that significantly relaxes the syntactic constraints on the use of SAND-gates.
2. A novel algorithm to calculate *min time* for general DATs based on Mixed Integer Linear Programming.
3. A modularization approach that yields significant speed ups by separately handling fragments of the DAT that are static or tree-shaped.
4. Extensive experimental validation to evaluate the performance of the algorithms.

2   Related Work

Dynamic ATs were first formally defined in [14], with series-parallel graphs semantics. These assume that each node must be activated separately for each of its parents. Effectively, this makes any DAT tree-shaped, which limits the range of scenarios that can be modeled.

Poset-semantics for DATs are used in [5]; here each node can be activated only once, allowing more scenarios to be modeled. The calculation of time-related metrics such as *min time* on DAG-shaped DATs is left as an open problem.

In [2,3,18,19,31] DATs are modeled as priced-timed automata. This allows for a detailed analysis, including *min time* calculation, by activating nodes from the root either in parallel or sequentially, depending on gate type. However, this approach does not consider satisfiability; hence the *min time* found via this method can correspond to a non-existing attack. As such, this method only calculates a lower bound to the actual *min time*.

Cyber security risks are also analyzed via *time-to-compromise* [24]. This assigns an (exponential) probability distribution to the failure time of each component, from which one finds the system failure pdf. This approach can be extended to consider different attack scenarios [28]. The current paper's DAT approach allows for a more systematic way of studying different attack scenarios, but we do not consider probabilistic data. Another way to incorporate stochastics is to consider *Bayesian fault trees* [12,25], in which a node's activation depends probabilistically on that of its children. This allows for more detailed modelling, but analysis is considerably more complicated: instead of a single *min time* metric, there is a Pareto front of attack time and attack success probability. Incorporating probability in these manners would be interesting for future work.

Time analysis of DATs falls into the wider framework of quantitative analysis on ATs. Existing approaches either focus on a single metric [4,6,7] or they develop methods that apply to general classes of metrics [5,17,23]. The latter case typically use algebraic structures like semirings, defining the metric in terms of operators which are assumed to have certain properties.

3   Dynamic Attack Trees

This section reviews the definition of DATs, and develops their semantics and the *min time* metric. The notation introduced throughout the paper is summarized in Table 1. The following definition of a DAT is from [5].

Definition 1. *A dynamic attack tree (DAT) is a rooted directed acyclic graph* $T = (N, E)$ *where each node* $v \in N$ *has a type* $\gamma(v) \in \{\texttt{BAS}, \texttt{OR}, \texttt{AND}, \texttt{SAND}\}$ *such that* $\gamma(v) = \texttt{BAS}$ *if and only if* v *is a leaf, and every node* v *with* $\gamma(v) = \texttt{SAND}$ *has an ordering of its set of children.*

Note that a DAT is not necessarily a tree. If it is, we call it *tree-shaped*. The root is denoted R_T. For $\gamma \in \{\texttt{BAS}, \texttt{OR}, \texttt{AND}, \texttt{SAND}\}$, we write N_γ for the set of nodes v with $\gamma(v) = \gamma$. The (po)set of children of v is denoted $\text{ch}(v)$. If $\gamma(v) = \texttt{SAND}$ and v has (ordered) children $v_1, \ldots, v_n$, we write $v = \texttt{SAND}(v_1, \ldots, v_n)$ for

Table 1. Notation used in this paper.

Notation	Meaning	Section	Notation	Meaning	Section
$T = (N, E)$	Dynamic attack tree	Sect. 3	$\mathrm{mt}(T, d), \mathrm{mt}(T)$	*min time* of DAT T	Sect. 3.2
$\gamma(v)$	Type of v	Sect. 3	$\mathcal{F}_T$	Time assignments of T	Sect. 4
R_T	Root of T	Sect. 3	M	*min time* upper bound	Sect. 4
N_{BAS}	$\{v \in N \mid \gamma(v) = \mathsf{BAS}\}$	Sect. 3	$Z_{\tilde{v}}^v$	Consecutive BAS pairs	Sect. 4
T_v	subDAT with root v	Sect. 3	$x_i^v, y^v, z_{i,a,a'}^v$	Auxiliary MILP variables	Sect. 4
B_v	Set of BAS of T_v	Sect. 3	n_v	Number of children of v	Sect. 4
$(\mathcal{A}_T, \leq)$	Poset of attacks on T	Sect. 3.1	T_v	Sub-DAT with root v	Sect. 5
$\mathcal{S}_T$	Successful attacks	Sect. 3.1	$\tilde{v}$	BAS replacement for T_v	Sect. 5
$\mathrm{t}(\mathcal{O}, d), \mathrm{t}(\mathcal{O})$	Time of attack $\mathcal{O}$	Sect. 3.2	T^v	T with T_v replaced by $\tilde{v}$	Sect. 5

convenience. We do the same for OR and AND, where the ordering of the children does not matter. We write T_v for the subDAG consisting of all *descendants* of v, i.e. all v' for which there is a path from v to v', including v itself. Furthermore, we let B_v be the set of descendants of v in N_{BAS}. DATs can be represented graphically as in Fig. 1.

A dynamic attack tree codifies the ways an attacker can make a system fail by executing the *basic attack steps*, i.e., the nodes in N_{BAS}. A non-BAS node is reached depending on its children, where OR and AND have the expected meaning, and a SAND-node is reached if all children are reached in their given order. The adversary's goal is to reach R_T. These semantics are defined in Sect. 3.1.

In the literature, two interpretations of nodes with multiple parent nodes exist, affecting both semantics and metrics. In the first interpretation, *multiple activation* (MA), [14,23,32] each BAS can be activated multiple times, and every parent of a node requires its own activation of that node. Thus SAND(a, a) succeeds only if a is activated twice consecutively. By adding a copy of each node for each of its parents, any DAT can be transformed into a tree-shaped one with equivalent semantics and metrics. As a result, metrics can be calculated quickly via a bottom-up algorithm [10], but MA cannot adequately model systems in which one action has multiple independent consequences.

In *single activation* (SA) [5,15] each BAS is executed at most once, and a node only needs to be activated once to count as an input for all its parents. In SA SAND(a, a) cannot be satisfied, because a cannot be activated before itself. SA is able to describe a much wider range of systems; although every SA representation can be turned into an equivalent MA representation, this process is both computationally expensive as it is done by writing the corresponding boolean function in disjunctive normal form. This rewriting also loses the meaning of the intermediate nodes in the DAT, which typically represent intermediate attacker goals. We therefore choose to analyze DATs under the SA interpretation; since every DAT is equivalent to a tree-shaped one under MA and MA and SA coincide on trees, SA can model every scenario that MA can.

3.1 Semantics

We discuss DAT semantics, extending [5]. An attack consists of a set A of attacker-activated BAS, and a strict partial order $\prec$, where $a \prec a'$ means a is executed before a'.

Definition 2. *The set $\mathcal{A}_T$ of attacks on T is the set of strictly partially ordered sets $\mathcal{O} = (A, \prec)$, where $A \subseteq N_{\text{BAS}}$. This set has a partial order $\leq$ given by $\mathcal{O} \leq \mathcal{O}'$, for $\mathcal{O} = (A, \prec)$ and $\mathcal{O}' = (A', \prec')$, if and only if $A \subseteq A'$ and $\prec \subseteq \prec'$.*

We are interested in successful attacks, i.e., attacks that manage to reach the root. Successful attacks, and the semantics of T, are defined as follows:

Definition 3. *Let v be a node. We say that an attack $\mathcal{O} = (A, \prec)$ reaches v if:*

1. *$v \in N_{\text{BAS}}$ and $v \in A$;*
2. *$v = \text{OR}(v_1, \ldots, v_n)$ and $\mathcal{O}$ reaches at least one of the v_i;*
3. *$v = \text{AND}(v_1, \ldots, v_n)$ and $\mathcal{O}$ reaches all of the v_i;*
4. *$v = \text{SAND}(v_1, \ldots, v_n)$ and $\mathcal{O}$ reaches all of the v_i, and for all $a \in A \cap B_{v_i}$, $a' \in A \cap B_{v_{i+1}}$ one has $a \prec a'$.*

A is successful *if it reaches R_T. The semantics of T is the set $\mathcal{S}_T$ of successful attacks on T.*

A SAND-gate $v = \text{SAND}(v_1, \ldots, v_n)$ is only reached if all of the BAS of v_i have been (successfully) executed before any of the BAS of v_{i+1} has started. By contrast, an AND-gate allows its children to be executed in parallel. Contrary to the static case (without SAND-gates), it is possible that $\mathcal{S}_T = \varnothing$. For example, $\mathcal{S}_{\text{SAND}(a,a)} = \varnothing$. Also, being successful is *not* 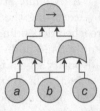 monotonous on the set of attacks, i.e., it is possible that $\mathcal{O}$ is successful while $\mathcal{O}'$ is not, even if $\mathcal{O} \leq \mathcal{O}'$. For instance, in the DAT above $(\{a, c\}, \{(a, c)\})$ is a successful attack, but $(\{a, b, c\}, \{(a, c)\})$ is not. Note that unlike the situation for SATs, a gate's activation does not simply depend on the activation of its children, but also on the relative order on the BAS associated to these children; this encodes the timing information essential to DATs.

Definition 3 is not the only way one might define the semantics of DATs. In fact, our semantics are based on those of [5], but differ on certain DATs; see Sect. 3.3. We have chosen to interpret the SAND-gate in a strict matter, so that it is activated only if the entirety of the attack on v_i has finished before the attack on v_{i+1} is started; in particular, v_i and v_{i+1} cannot share activated BAS, which may be considered unwanted behaviour. There are also other approaches, which unfortunately have other problems. 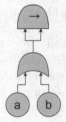 For instance, one could define succesful attacks bottom-up in a compositional fashion, defining $\mathcal{O}$ to reach $\text{SAND}(v_1, v_2)$ if there exists attacks $\mathcal{O}_1, \mathcal{O}_2$ such that $\mathcal{O}$ is the parallel composition of $\mathcal{O}_1$ and $\mathcal{O}_2$. However, under such a definition the AT above $(\{a, b\}, \{(a, b)\})$ is a succesful attack, whereas in our opinion this AT should not be considered satisfiable. Yet another approach would be to assign a starting and finishing time to each node, similar to what we do in Definition 5, but this has the disadvantage of being more convoluted as an attack is now a function $N \to \mathbb{R}$.

3.2 The *Min Time* Metric

Min time is the minimal time it takes to perform a successful attack on a given DAT. While other metrics exist for DATs, *min time* is a fundamental time metric, and calculating it efficiently for non-tree-shaped DATs is an open problem [5].

Min time is defined as follows: There is a *duration function* $d\colon N_{\text{BAS}} \to \mathbb{R}_{\geq 0}$, with $d(a)$ denoting the time it takes to execute a. If $a \prec a'$, then the BAS a' can only be started once a has been completed, while a and a' can be activated in parallel if such a relation does not exist. As such, we can define the total duration of an attack $t(\mathcal{O}, d)$ and *min time* $\mathrm{mt}(T, d)$ as

$$t(\mathcal{O}, d) = \max_{\substack{C \text{ max. chain} \\ \text{in } \mathcal{O}}} \sum_{a \in C} d(a), \qquad \mathrm{mt}(T, d) = \min_{\mathcal{O} \in \mathcal{S}_T} t(\mathcal{O}, d)$$

where the maximum is taken over the maximal chains (i.e., maximal linearly ordered subsets) of the strict poset $\mathcal{O}$. We will often omit d from the notation and write $t(\mathcal{O})$ if there is no confusion. Note that t is monotonous: if $\mathcal{O} \leq \mathcal{O}'$ one has $t(\mathcal{O}) \leq t(\mathcal{O}')$. Furthermore, $\mathrm{mt}(T) = \infty$ if $\mathcal{S}_T = \varnothing$.

Example 1. Figure 2 depicts the bank robbery DAT of Fig. 1 augmented with durations for the BAS (we take the expected durations from the distributions given in [4]). To calculate $\mathrm{mt}(T)$ one would first need to find $\mathcal{S}_T$. While this set is quite large, because of the monotonicity of t, the minimum is attained at one of the minimal elements of the poset $(\mathcal{S}_T, \leq)$. There are two minimal attacks, depending on whether the attackers choose to cut open the safe, or unlock it. Abbreviating BAS names, we can represent these minimal attacks as sets of chains as $\mathcal{O}_1 = \{bi \prec cos \prec e\}$ and $\mathcal{O}_2 = \{bi \prec fk \prec e, bi \prec gc \prec e\}$. These have duration $t(\mathcal{O}_1) = 1.00 + 0.67 + 0.20 = 1.87$ and $t(\mathcal{O}_2) = \max(1.00 + 0.50 + 0.20, 1.00 + 1.00 + 0.20) = \max(1.70, 2.20) = 2.20$. It follows that $\mathrm{mt}(T) = \min(1.87, 2.20) = 1.87$.

In the multiple activation scenario, *min time* can be calculated by reshaping a DAT into its canonical form [14], from which *min time* is easily calculated. However, this technique does not carry over to our formalism, as in the single activation scenario a canonical form does not exist.

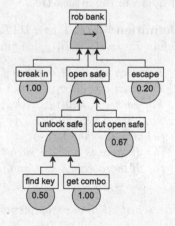

3.3 Relation to Semantics of [5]

In [5] attacks are called attacks only if they satisfy the ordering constraints imposed by *all* SAND-gates. This is defined only for *well-formed* DATs, i.e., all these constraints are simultaneously satisfiable. More formally, that work only considers attacks that we call *full* in the following definition.

Fig. 2. The bank robbery DAT of Fig. 1 augmented with durations.

Definition 4. *Let T be a DAT. Define a relation $\sqsubseteq'$ on N_{BAS} by $a \sqsubseteq' a'$ iff there exists a node $v = \text{SAND}(v_1, \ldots, v_n)$ and an $i < n$ such that $a \in B_{v_i}$ and $a' \in B_{v_{i+1}}$. Let $\sqsubseteq$ be the transitive closure of $\sqsubseteq'$. Then T is well-formed if $\sqsubseteq$ is a strict partial order. An attack $(A, \prec)$ on a well-formed DAT is full if $\prec = \sqsubseteq|_A$, the restriction of $\sqsubseteq$ to A.*

However, not all attacks will be full, because an attack may not need to reach all SAND-nodes in order to reach the root, and non-reached nodes should not put restrictions on attacks. Consider the well-formed DAT on the right. Only $(\{a, b\}, \{(a, b)\})$ is a full successful attack. However, $(\{a, b\}, \varnothing)$ is a successful attack as well. Hence non-full attacks are needed to fully describe the semantics of well-formed DATs, which motivates Definition 2.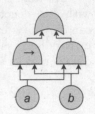
Furthermore, our definition defines the semantics of general DATs, not just the well-formed ones.

4   An MILP Approach to *Min Time*

This section describes a novel method to compute $\text{mt}(T)$ based on mixed-integer linear programming (MILP). Although MILP is NP-complete, a number of good heuristics and solvers exist specifically for MILP, which can result in a low computation time. We first show that *min time* can be found by solving an optimization problem in Theorem 1, and then we describe how that optimization problem can be rewritten into the MILP framework.

The building block of the new approach is the notion of *time assignment*, which assigns to each node a completion time f_v that respects all timing constraints in the DAT. If $f_v = \infty$ then v is not reached at all. The formal definition is stated below; recall that B_v is the set of BAS-descendants of v, and N the set of nodes in the attack tree.

Definition 5. *Let T be a DAT. For a node v with children $v_1, \ldots, v_n$ and $i < n$, define $Z_i^v := B_{v_i} \times B_{v_{i+1}}$. A time assignment is a vector $f \in [0, \infty]^N$ satisfying:*

1. *For each $a \in N_{\text{BAS}}$ one has $f_a \geq d(a)$;*
2. *For each $v = \text{OR}(v_1, \ldots, v_n)$ one has $f_v \geq \min_i f_{v_i}$;*
3. *For each $v = \text{AND}(v_1, \ldots, v_n)$ one has $f_v \geq \max_i f_{v_i}$;*
4. *For each $v = \text{SAND}(v_1, \ldots, v_n)$, the following must hold:*
   (a) it holds that $f_v \geq f_{v_n}$;
   (b) If there is a $i \leq n$ such that $f_{v_i} = \infty$, then $f_v = \infty$;
   (c) If there exist $i < n$ and $(a, a') \in Z_i^v$ such that $f_{a'} - d(a') < f_a < \infty$, then $f_v = \infty$.

The set of all time assignments for T is denoted $\mathcal{F}_T$.

The SAND-conditions can be understood as follows. 4a) tells us that v cannot be reached before v_n, and 4b) tells us that v cannot be reached if any of its children is not reached. 4c) conveys that whenever there is an $a \in B_{v_i}$ that is activated (i.e., $f_a < \infty$), then in order for v to be activated, one must have $f_{a'} - d(a') \geq f_a$ for all $a' \in B_{v_{i+1}}$. Since $f_{a'} - d(a')$ is the starting time of a', this means that a' must be started after a is finished activating. It is more subtle than simply requiring $f_{a'} - d(a') \geq f_a$ for all $(a, a') \in Z_i^v$; that would ensure that all SAND-gates impose ordering restrictions, not just those that are activated.

Note that $f_{a'} - d(a')$ is the starting time of a BAS a', so 4c) tells us that v is only reached if the BAS-descendants of v_{i+1} are started once those of v_i have been completed. We allow for a delay in completing node v, even when enough of its children have been completed. Time assignments relate to *min time*:

Theorem 1. $\mathrm{mt}(T) = \min_{f \in \mathcal{F}_T} f_{\mathrm{R}_T}$.

This result allows us to calculate $\mathrm{mt}(T)$ by solving the following optimization problem.

$$\text{minimize}_{f \in [0,\infty]^N} \ \& f_{\mathrm{R}_T} \qquad \text{s.t.} \quad f \in \mathcal{F}_T. \qquad (1)$$

This is not a linear problem, due to the nonlinear constraints of Definition 5. We use auxiliary integer variables to linearize these constraints. First, we need to get rid of the ∞ in Definition 5, which we do by replacing it with a suitably large real number. Define the constant $M = 1 + \sum_{a \in N_{\mathrm{BAS}}} d(a)$. The following lemma shows that if T is satisfiable, then to minimize (1) one can focus on the $\hat{f}$ with $f_v \in [0, M-1] \cup \infty$.

Lemma 1. *There is an f minimizing* (1) *for which* $\forall v\colon f_v \in [0, M-1] \cup \infty$.

This shows that we can use M to play the role of ∞ where necessary. We enforce this by demanding $f_v \in [0, M]$, and we interpret $f_v = M$ to mean that v is not reached. For a node v, let n_v be its number of children, which are denoted $v_1, \ldots, v_{n_v}$. We then use standard MILP techniques [8] to rewrite Definition 5.

To rewrite the OR-condition, we introduce an auxiliary binary variable x_i^v for each $v \in N_{\mathrm{OR}}$ and each $i \leq n_v$. The purpose of x_i^v is to represent the truthfulness of the statement "$i = \arg\min_{i'} f_{v_{i'}}$". We can then represent $f_v \geq \min_i f_{v_i}$ by

$$\sum_{i \leq n_v} x_i^v \geq 1, \qquad\qquad \forall i \leq n_v\colon f_v \geq f_{v_i} + M(x_i^v - 1).$$

The latter is automatically satisfied if $x_i^v = 0$, and reduces to $f_v \geq f_{v_i}$ if $x_i^v = 1$. The former ensures that the latter must happen for at least one i, so together these encode $f_v \geq \min_i f_{v_i}$. The condition for AND-gates can be rewritten as $\forall i \leq n_v\colon f_v \geq f_{v_i}$.

Finally, we consider SAND-gates. For $v \in N_{\mathrm{SAND}}$, we introduce an auxiliary binary variable y^v that encodes "$\exists i < n\colon f_{v_i} = \infty$ or $\exists i \exists (a, a') \in Z_i^v\colon f_{a'} - d(a') < f_a < \infty$." Then we can write Definition 5.4 as $f_v \geq f_{v_{n_v}}, f_v \geq My^v$. To ensure $y^v = 1$ whenever one of the f_{v_i} equals ∞, we add the constraint $\forall i < n_v\colon y^v \geq \frac{1 + f_{v_i} - M}{M}$, which forces $y^v = 1$ only when $f_{v_i} > M - 1$. Furthermore, to ensure $y^v = 1$ whenever some a, a' satisfy $f_{a'} - d(a') < f_a$, we would like to add the constraint

$$\forall i < n_v \forall (a, a') \in Z_i^v : y^v \geq \min \left\{ \frac{f_a - f_{a'} + d(a')}{M}, \frac{M - f_a}{M} \right\}. \tag{2}$$

This forces $y^v = 1$ only when both $f_{a'} - d(a') < f_a$ and $f_a < M$. To get rid of the minimum, we introduce an auxiliary variable $z_{i,a,a'}^v$ for each $i < n_v$ and $(a, a') \in Z_i^v$ as we did for the OR-condition. We then replace (2) with

$$\forall i < n_v \forall (a, a') \in Z_i^v : y^v \geq \frac{f_a - f_{a'} + d(a')}{M} - z_{i,a,a'}^v, \quad y^v \geq \frac{M - f_a}{M} - (1 - z_{i,a,a'}^v).$$

Taking all of this together, it can be shown that the constraint $f_v \in [0, M]$ holds automatically for all 'reasonable' f (i.e., if this does not hold for f, then f will not minimize f_{R_T}) and can be replaced by $f_v \in \mathbb{R}$. We then find that the optimization problem (1) can be rewritten into the following MILP problem of Fig. 3. Note that this optimization returns an f with $f_{R_T} \leq M - 1$ if and only if $\mathcal{S}_T \neq \varnothing$. Hence this optimization can also be used to determine whether T can successfully be attacked.

We note that this is not the only way to encode *min time* analysis into a MILP problem; for instance, instead of using the constant M, one could introduce an additional binary variable per node that denotes whether the node is activated or not. We chose for this approach since this ensures we need fewer optimization variables, even though this means that some equations such as (2) are less intuitive. Note that we get quadratically many constraints above, which is a consequence of the fact that we get a constraint for every pair (a, a') in Definition 3.4.

minimize f_{R_T} subject to:

$\forall v \in N$	$: f_v \in \mathbb{R},$
$\forall a \in N_{\mathrm{BAS}}$	$: f_a \geq d(a),$
$\forall v \in N_{\mathrm{OR}}, \ \forall i \leq n_v$	$: x_i^v \in \{0, 1\},$
$\forall v \in N_{\mathrm{OR}}, \ \forall i \leq n_v$	$: f_v \geq f_{v_i} + M(x_i^v - 1),$
$\forall v \in N_{\mathrm{OR}}$	$: \sum_{i \leq n_v} x_i^v \geq 1,$
$\forall v \in N_{\mathrm{AND}}, \ \forall i \leq n_v$	$: f_v \geq f_{v_i},$
$\forall v \in N_{\mathrm{SAND}}$	$: y^v \in \{0, 1\},$
$\forall v \in N_{\mathrm{SAND}}, \ \forall i < n_v, \ \forall (a, a') \in Z_i^v$	$: z_{i,a,a'}^v \in \{0, 1\},$
$\forall v \in N_{\mathrm{SAND}}$	$: f_v \geq f_{v_{n_v}},$
$\forall v \in N_{\mathrm{SAND}}$	$: f_v \geq M y^v,$
$\forall v \in N_{\mathrm{SAND}}, \ \forall i < n_v$	$: y^v \geq \frac{1 + f_{v_i} - M}{M},$
$\forall v \in N_{\mathrm{SAND}}, \ \forall i < n_v, \ \forall (a, a') \in Z_i^v$	$: y^v \geq \frac{f_a - f_{a'} + d(a')}{M} - z_{i,a,a'}^v,$
$\forall v \in N_{\mathrm{SAND}}, \ \forall i < n_v, \ \forall (a, a') \in Z_i^v$	$: y^v \geq \frac{M - f_a + 1}{M} + z_{i,a,a'}^v - 1.$

Fig. 3. The MILP problem for calculating *min time*.

5   Computation Time Reduction

In this section, we introduce an algorithm reducing the complexity of computing $mt(T)$. The algorithm consists of two components: First, we show that a bottom-up algorithm from [14] can be used to calculate *min time* for static (no SAND-gates) and tree-shaped DATs. As the state of the art method, based on binary decision diagrams [5], has exponential complexity, and the bottom-up algorithm has linear complexity, this is a big improvement. Second, we split up the calculation of *min time* into parts by identifying the *modules* of a DAT, i.e. subDAGs that are connected to the rest of the DAT via only one node.

5.1   Bottom-Up Computation

An important tool is the algorithm MT-BU introduced in [14] presented in Algorithm 4. It attempts to calculate $mt(T)$ by traversing T bottom-up, which only has linear time complexity and is significantly faster than the MILP approach of Fig. 3. For tree-shaped T it calculates *min time* correctly, but for DAGs it fails to account for the fact that two children of a node may share BAS, which may be counted double. However, this double counting is only an issue for SAND-gates, as the operators min/max of OR/AND-gates are idempotent, i.e., $\min(x,x) = \max(x,x) = x$. This was first realized in [17], for attack-defense trees under different semantics. However, *min time* based on these *set semantics* can be proven to be equivalent to our definition in Sect. 3.2, yielding the following result (Fig. 4):

Input: Dynamic attack tree T, duration vector $d \in \mathbb{R}^{N_{BAS}}$
Output: Potential min time $mt(T, d)$.

if $\gamma(v) = \mathtt{BAS}$ **then**
  | **return** $d(v)$
else if $\gamma(v) = \mathtt{OR}$ **then**
  | **return** $\min_{v' \in \mathrm{ch}(v)} \mathtt{MT\text{-}BU}(T_{v'}, d|_{B_{v'}})$
else if $\gamma(v) = \mathtt{AND}$ **then**
  | **return**
  | $\quad \max_{v' \in \mathrm{ch}(v)} \mathtt{MT\text{-}BU}(T_{v'}, d|_{B_{v'}})$
else // $\gamma(v) = \mathtt{SAND}$
  | **return** $\sum_{v' \in \mathrm{ch}(v)} \mathtt{MT\text{-}BU}(T_{v'}, d|_{B_{v'}})$

Fig. 4. MT-BU for a DAT T.

Theorem 2 [14,17]. *If T is tree-shaped or static, then* MT-BU *calculates* $mt(T)$.

5.2   Modular Analysis

Algorithm 4 only reduces complexity in the two relatively rare cases where the DAT is static or tree-shaped. However, it is possible to also reduce complexity when T is only partially static and/or tree-shaped. A well-established method in studying DATs is to consider the *modules* of T:

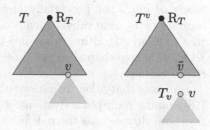

Fig. 5. Modular analysis.

Definition 6 [9]. *A module is a node $v \in N \setminus N_{BAS}$ such that all paths from $T \setminus T_v$ to T_v pass through v.*

The root of T is always a module. If v is a module, then v is the only node within T_v with parents outside of T_v. Hence we can create a tree T^v by replacing T_v within T by a new single BAS $\tilde{v}$; the parents of $\tilde{v}$ in T^v are the parents of v in T. Theorem 3 shows that *min time* can be calculated for T by first calculating it for T_v, and then for T^v. This is depicted in Fig. 5.

Theorem 3. *Let T be a DAT, and let v be a module of T. Let T^v be the node obtained by removing v and replacing v itself with a new BAS $\tilde{v}$. Then $\mathrm{mt}(T, d) = \mathrm{mt}(T^v, d^v)$ where d^v is a duration function for T^v given by*

$$d^v(a) = \begin{cases} d(a), & \text{if } a \in N_{BAS} \setminus B_v, \\ \mathrm{mt}(T_v, d|_{B_v}), & \text{if } a = \tilde{v}. \end{cases}$$

While the statement seems intuitively true, the proof requires quite a bit of work as one needs to develop machinery to relate attacks on T (and their minimal chains) to attacks on T_v and T^v. Theorem 3 reduces complexity in two ways: We split the tree into two parts whose total size is the same as the original tree. Since MILP is NP-hard, this can impact computation time. Furthermore, the smaller DAT T_v can be static or tree-shaped, in which case we can use MT-BU (Fig. 6).

The resulting algorithm is displayed in Algorithm 6. Here `Module` refers to an algorithm that finds the modules of T; this can be done with linear time complexity [9]. Algorithm $\mathcal{A}_{Mod}$ makes use of an algorithm $\mathcal{A}$ that

Input: Dynamic AT T, duration vector $d \in \mathbb{R}^{N_{BAS}}$, Algorithm $\mathcal{A}$ to calculate *min time*
Output: Min time $\mathrm{mt}(T)$.

$\mathcal{V} \leftarrow \mathtt{Module}(T)$;
while $\mathcal{V} \neq \varnothing$ **do**
  Pick $v \in \mathcal{V}$ of minimal height;
  if T_v *is static* **then**
    $d^v(\tilde{v}) \leftarrow \mathtt{MT\text{-}BU}(T_v, d|_{B_v})$;
  else
    $d^v(\tilde{v}) \leftarrow \mathcal{A}(T_v, d|_{B_v})$;
  for $a \in N_{BAS} \setminus B_v$ **do**
    $d^v(a) \leftarrow d(a)$;
  $(T, d) \leftarrow (T^v, d^v)$;
  $\mathcal{V} \leftarrow \mathcal{V} \setminus \{v\}$;
return $d(R_T)$ // R_T is a BAS now

Fig. 6. $\mathcal{A}_{Mod}$ for a DAT T. The notation T^v, d^v is from Theorem 3.

calculates *min time*. For this, one can use naive enumeration or the MILP approach of Fig. 3, or potentially any new algorithm. Since the calculation of a module's *min time* value depends on its own modules, we act on the lower modules first, so Algorithm 6 handles the modules by ascending height. Note that when T is tree-shaped, every inner node is a module, so $\mathcal{A}_{Mod}$ is equivalent to MT-BU for any $\mathcal{A}$.

We note that other definitions of *min time*, such as the automata-approach of [18] and the multiple-activation definition of [14], also allow for modular decomposition. However, as these definitions are not compatible with ours, we cannot directly use these results, and we require a novel proof for Theorem 3.

6   Experiments

This section evaluates the performance of our methods. We compare the MILP approach of Fig. 3 (MT-MILP) to the enumerative approach (MT-Enum). For the latter, rather than exhaustively generating all succesful attacks, we generate bottom-up a set of candidate attacks that include all minimal succesful attacks, hence certainly the optimal attack by the monotonicity of t. For this we generalize the set semantics of [17] to dynamic ATs. We also compare MT-MILP and MT-Enum to their modular counterparts.

Existing methods in the literature are based on series-parallel graphs [14] and priced timed automata [18]. Their definitions of *min time* are not equivalent to ours. In our view, methods with different definitions of *min time* can only be compared with respect to computation time if one of them is designed to be an approximation or bound of the other; then one can compare the gain in computation time versus the loss in accuracy. However, this is not the case here: the multiple activation definition is fundamentally different, and a DAT constructed under this model represents a system different from the same DAT in the single activation model. Therefore, we cannot directly compare performance to that of existing approaches.

Source	$|N|$	tree	Durations
[18] Fig. 1	12	no	unknown
[18] Fig. 8	20	no	unknown
[18] Fig. 9	12	no	unknown
[3] Fig. 1	16	yes	unknown
[4] Fig. 3	8	yes	known
[4] Fig. 5	21	yes	known
[4] Fig. 7	25	yes	known
[11] Fig. 2	20	yes	unknown
[17] Fig. 1	15	yes	unknown

Fig. 7. DATs from the literature used as building blocks. Trees from [11,17] are adapted from attack-defense Tree.

In practice, attack trees can be very large [26,30]; however, for confidentiality reasons these are typically not disclosed to the general public [7,26]. Hence to our knowledge no established benchmark suites of DATs exist, and the existing literature typically considers test cases with only ≤ 25 nodes [4,18]. For such small DATs, the computation of *min time* takes less than a second no matter which algorithm is being used, which makes them unsuitable for testing difference in algorithm performance. To address the deficiency of a benchmark suite of large DATs, we create a synthetic set of testing DATs. These are created by combining DATs from the literature into larger ones. Then, we compare (1) the MILP method MT-MILP to the enumerative algorithm MT-Enum and (2) the effect of modular analysis on performance time.

All experiments are performed on a PC with an Intel Core i7-10750HQ 2.8 GHz processor and 16 GB memory. All algorithms are implemented in Matlab, and for MILP we use the YALMIP environment [20] to translate the optimization problem into the Gurobi solver [13], a state-of-the-art optimizer that can handle MILP problems. The code and results are available in [22].

6.1   Generation of Testing DATs

To create a testing suite large enough for a meaningful performance comparison, we do the following. As building blocks, we use a selection of DATs from

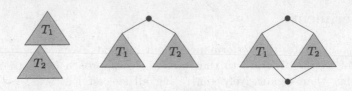

Fig. 8. The three ways of combining DATs.

the literature, shown in Fig. 7. For some, the duration of the BAS are random variables, and we take the expected value for the duration; otherwise we take a random duration from $\{1, 2, \ldots, 10\}$. We use three methods for combining two DATs T_1, T_2 into a larger one (see Fig. 8):

1. We take a random BAS v from T_1 and consider the modular composition by replacing v in T_1 by T_2. This represents a larger system, in which one subsystem, represented by v in T_1, is given its own DAT for more fine-grained analysis.
2. We introduce a new root node v with a random label, and add edges (v, R_{T_1}) and (v, R_{T_2}). This represents a system consisting of two separate subsystems.
3. We introduce a new root node v with a random label, and add edges (v, R_{T_1}) and (v, R_{T_2}); we then pick random BAS b_1 from T_1 and b_2 from T_2 and identify them (with a new random duration in $\{1, 2, \ldots, 10\}$). This represents a system consisting of two subsystems that have a shared attack step.

These are not the only ways by which multiple DATs can be combined; for instance, T_1 and T_2 could share multiple BAS. We selected these three methods to capture some of the common ways DATs are created by experts. Creating a benchmark suite of large DATs that resemble DATs from industry is an important avenue for further research, but beyond the scope of this paper.

We create two suites of testing DATs by combining the DATs from Fig. 7. For the first suite, $\mathcal{A}$, we combine DATs using one of the three methods above (drawn randomly) until the result has a given number of nodes. The resulting will have many modules, as T_1 is a module under the first method, and both T_1 and T_2 are modules under the second method. Therefore, we expect the modular approaches to be very fast on the DATs in $\mathcal{A}$. To also study DATs with less modules, we create the second suite, $\mathcal{B}$, by combining DATs using only the third method. Again, one could assign other weights to the three combination methods to obtain yet different testing suites, but $\mathcal{A}$ and $\mathcal{B}$ represent two of the extremes of what DATs can look like.

For a given $n_{\min}$, we combine DATs randomly drawn from Fig. 7 (either via randomly drawn methods from the 3 above, or by method 3 only) until $|N| \geq n_{\min}$. We do this 5 times for each $1 \leq n_{\min} \leq 240$, giving us two testing sets $\mathcal{A}, \mathcal{B}$ of 1200 DATs with $8 \leq |N| \leq 262$. On average 26.6% of the nodes of ATs in $\mathcal{A}$, and 16.5% of the nodes of ATs in $\mathcal{B}$ are modules. Furthermore 54.2% of the nodes of ATs in $\mathcal{A}$, and 52.5% of the nodes of ATs in $\mathcal{B}$ are BAS.

Table 2. Summary of the results. All times are in seconds. *Failure* denotes failure to compute within 10^4 seconds. $\mathcal{A}_{small}$ contains 754 DATs with ≤ 160 nodes, and $\mathcal{A}$ contains 1200 DATs with ≤ 262 nodes (including those of $\mathcal{A}_{small}$). The sets $\mathcal{B}_{small}$ and $\mathcal{B}$ hold the same amount of DATs of the same size; they are designed to contain less modules.

	$\mathcal{A}_{small}$				$\mathcal{A}$		
	MT-Enum	MT-MILP	MT-Enum$_{Mod}$	MT-MILP$_{Mod}$	MT-MILP	MT-Enum$_{Mod}$	MT-MILP$_{Mod}$
Median time	1.234	0.906	1.461	1.680	1.422	2.797	3.070
Max time	10000	7.984	12.656	6.656	19.125	10000	30.469
Failure	3.71%	0%	0%	0%	0%	0.08%	0%
	$\mathcal{B}_{small}$				$\mathcal{B}$		
Median time	1.391	0.938	1.469	1.656	1.266	3.203	2.773
Max time	10000	4.75	2326	9.484	4.75	10000	9.484
Failure	3.81%	0%	0%	0%	0%	3.08%	0%

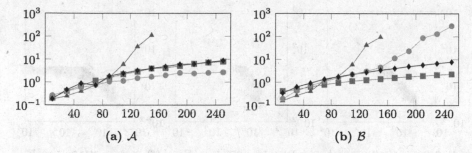

(a) $\mathcal{A}$ (b) $\mathcal{B}$

Fig. 9. Median time (in seconds) of —▲— MT-Enum, —■— MT-MILP, —●— MT-Enum$_{Mod}$, —◆— MT-MILP$_{Mod}$, grouped by the number of nodes $|N|$.

6.2 Time Comparisons

We measure the computation time of the four algorithms on the testing set; we cap computation time per DAT at 10^4 s. We group the DATs depending on their value of $\lceil |N|/20 \rceil$ and calculate the median per group: these are presented in Fig. 9. We use the median because it allows us to incorporate the computations that were cancelled after 10^4 s. Since already 21.3% of the DATs of $\mathcal{A}$, and 13.8% of DATs of $\mathcal{B}$, with $141 \leq |N| \leq 160$ fail to compute for MT-Enum, we do not continue testing this method for larger DATs. The subsets of $\mathcal{A}, \mathcal{B}$ of DATs with $|N| \leq 160$ is called $\mathcal{A}_{small}, \mathcal{B}_{small}$, and consist of 754 resp. 761 DATs. The results are also summarized in Table 2, and pairwise comparisons are presented in Fig. 10.

On the testing set $\mathcal{A}$, we see from Fig. 9 that MT-Enum is by far the slowest method, while MT-MILP is the fastest; the two modular approaches are slightly slower than MT-MILP and have similar efficiency. While the inefficiency of MT-Enum is to be expected, it is surprising that modular analysis for MILP has a net negative effect on computation time. One possible reason is that the Gurobi solver, which we treat as a black box, might incorporate strategies to reduce the MILP problem complexity that are equivalent to modular analysis on the DAT side. At any rate, the enumerative approach clearly shows the advantage of incorporating the modular approach. These results are also reflected in Fig. 10(a)–(d).

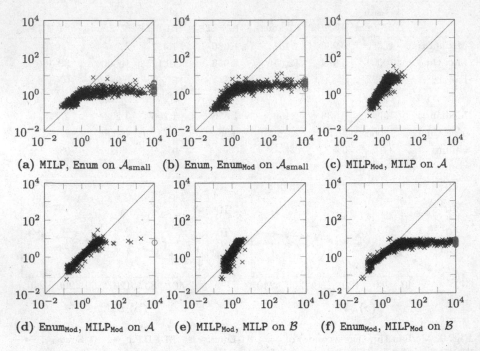

(a) MILP, Enum on $\mathcal{A}_{small}$ (b) Enum, Enum$_{Mod}$ on $\mathcal{A}_{small}$ (c) MILP$_{Mod}$, MILP on $\mathcal{A}$

(d) Enum$_{Mod}$, MILP$_{Mod}$ on $\mathcal{A}$ (e) MILP$_{Mod}$, MILP on $\mathcal{B}$ (f) Enum$_{Mod}$, MILP$_{Mod}$ on $\mathcal{B}$

Fig. 10. Pairwise computation time comparisons of the four algorithms. The first algorithm is the vertical axis while the second is the horizontal axis. Each mark is a DAT; purple circles are computations aborted for exceeding 10^4 s. (Color figure online)

Interestingly, the difference in median computation time between MT-Enum and MT-MILP disappears when considering the modular versions of these algorithms, although the worst-case behaviour of MT-Enum$_{Mod}$ is considerably worse than that of MT-MILP$_{Mod}$ (see Table 2). We hypothesize that this is due to the fact that the DATs of $\mathcal{A}$ contain many modules. As a result, the 'indecomposable' sub-DATs on which the algorithms MT-Enum and MT-MILP are called will typically be small. Since the difference in computation time between these algorithms only appears for larger DATs, we do not see it in these experiments.

For testing set $\mathcal{B}$, we again see that MT-Enum is by far the slowest. Furthermore, for larger DATs MT-MILP$_{Mod}$ outpaces MT-Enum$_{Mod}$ considerably; see also Fig. 10(f). This shows that also in a modular setting the MILP approach significantly speeds up calculations for large enough DATs. This is to be expected from our results on set $\mathcal{A}$ as for larger DATs the 'indecomposable' subDATs on which MT-MILP is invoked will be larger as well. Interestingly, on this dataset MT-MILP is slightly faster than MT-MILP$_{\text{Mod}}$, as can also be seen from Fig. 10(e). This might be due to the fact that on wide DATs, the MILP methods of Gurobi are more efficient at splitting up DATs into modules than our Matlab implementation of the modular decomposition algorithm. A detailed study into this difference in performance would entail a comprehensive analysis into Gurobi's Matlab implementation, which is beyond the scope of this paper.

Taking $\mathcal{A}$ and $\mathcal{B}$ together, we can conclude that both the MILP approach and modular analysis create a large decrease in computation time. While these methods are slightly slower for small DATs, computation time for such DATs only takes a few seconds anyway. By contrast, for larger DATs the difference in computation time can go up to a factor 10^3. For DATs with large modules, MT-Enum$_{\text{Mod}}$ loses out against MT-MILP and MT-MILP$_{\text{Mod}}$, which behave similarly.

7   Conclusion and Discussion

This paper introduced two novel tools to calculate *min time* for DATs. First, we introduced a novel MILP-based approach that finds *min time* by phrasing it as an optimization problem. Second, we show how modular analysis can be used to reduce the computation time of any *min time* calculation algorithm. In the experiments, we compared these to the enumerative method. The experiments show that for large DATs both MILP and modular analysis can have a big impact on computation time. In particular, the MILP approach is consistently fast on any input DAT, making it a reliable tool for quantitative DAT analysis in practice.

There are several directions in which this work can be expanded. First, a benchmark suite of DATs is needed. For this it is important to find out what sizes and properties are typical for DATs used in industry, even if industry DATs themselves may not be published due to confidentiality reasons.

Second, modular analysis can also be used for other metrics, as has been done for fault trees [27, 29]. Since modular analysis is a very general idea, a good approach would be to develop an axiomatization of metrics that can be handled via modular analysis, so that the method can be applied to a large set of metrics at once. Such a result is probably not hard to prove for metrics that are defined bottom-up as in [17]; the challenge lies in metrics that are defined directly from the semantics as in [5].

Third, our MILP approach can be combined with a Monte Carlo approach in a stochastic setting where the precise BAS values are unknown. A more thorough investigation can explore what guarantees such simulations can give for *min time*. As Monte Carlo methods involve sampling a large sample, performance of the *min time* calculation algorithm is important in such a study.

References

1. Agyepong, E., Cherdantseva, Y., Reinecke, P., Burnap, P.: Challenges and performance metrics for security operations center analysts: a systematic review. J. Cyber Secur. Technol. **4**(3), 125–152 (2020)
2. Ali, A.T., Gruska, D.P.: Attack trees with time constraints. In: CS&P, pp. 93–105 (2021)
3. Arnold, F., Guck, D., Kumar, R., Stoelinga, M.: Sequential and parallel attack tree modelling. In: Koornneef, F., van Gulijk, C. (eds.) SAFECOMP 2015. LNCS, vol. 9338, pp. 291–299. Springer, Cham (2015). https://doi.org/10.1007/978-3-319-24249-1_25
4. Arnold, F., Hermanns, H., Pulungan, R., Stoelinga, M.: Time-dependent analysis of attacks. In: Abadi, M., Kremer, S. (eds.) POST 2014. LNCS, vol. 8414, pp. 285–305. Springer, Heidelberg (2014). https://doi.org/10.1007/978-3-642-54792-8_16
5. Budde, C.E., Stoelinga, M.: Efficient algorithms for quantitative attack tree analysis. In: 2021 IEEE 34th Computer Security Foundations Symposium (CSF), pp. 1–15 (2021). https://doi.org/10.1109/CSF51468.2021.00041
6. Buldas, A., Laud, P., Priisalu, J., Saarepera, M., Willemson, J.: Rational choice of security measures via multi-parameter attack trees. In: Lopez, J. (ed.) CRITIS 2006. LNCS, vol. 4347, pp. 235–248. Springer, Heidelberg (2006). https://doi.org/10.1007/11962977_19
7. Byres, E.J., Franz, M., Miller, D.: The use of attack trees in assessing vulnerabilities in SCADA systems. In: Proceedings of the International Infrastructure Survivability Workshop, pp. 3–10. Citeseer (2004)
8. Chen, D.S., Batson, R.G., Dang, Y.: Applied Integer Programming: Modeling and Solution. Wiley, New York (2011)
9. Dutuit, Y., Rauzy, A.: A linear-time algorithm to find modules of fault trees. IEEE Trans. Reliab. **45**(3), 422–425 (1996)
10. Fila, B., Wideł, W.: Exploiting attack-defense trees to find an optimal set of countermeasures. In: 2020 IEEE 33rd Computer Security Foundations Symposium (CSF), pp. 395–410. IEEE (2020)
11. Fraile, M., Ford, M., Gadyatskaya, O., Kumar, R., Stoelinga, M., Trujillo-Rasua, R.: Using attack-defense trees to analyze threats and countermeasures in an ATM: a case study. In: Horkoff, J., Jeusfeld, M.A., Persson, A. (eds.) PoEM 2016. LNBIP, vol. 267, pp. 326–334. Springer, Cham (2016). https://doi.org/10.1007/978-3-319-48393-1_24
12. François-Xavier, A., Olivier, B., Grégory, B., Vania, C., Hervé, D.: Bayesian attack model for dynamic risk assessment. arXiv:1606.09042 (2016). Preprint
13. Gurobi Optimization, LLC: Gurobi Optimizer Reference Manual (2022). https://www.gurobi.com
14. Jhawar, R., Kordy, B., Mauw, S., Radomirović, S., Trujillo-Rasua, R.: Attack trees with sequential conjunction. In: Federrath, H., Gollmann, D. (eds.) SEC 2015. IAICT, vol. 455, pp. 339–353. Springer, Cham (2015). https://doi.org/10.1007/978-3-319-18467-8_23
15. Jürgenson, A., Willemson, J.: Computing exact outcomes of multi-parameter attack trees. In: Meersman, R., Tari, Z. (eds.) OTM 2008. LNCS, vol. 5332, pp. 1036–1051. Springer, Heidelberg (2008). https://doi.org/10.1007/978-3-540-88873-4_8

16. Kordy, B., Piètre-Cambacédès, L., Schweitzer, P.: DAG-based attack and defense modeling: don't miss the forest for the attack trees. Comput. Sci. Rev. **13**, 1–38 (2014)

17. Kordy, B., Wideł, W.: On quantitative analysis of attack–defense trees with repeated labels. In: Bauer, L., Küsters, R. (eds.) POST 2018. LNCS, vol. 10804, pp. 325–346. Springer, Cham (2018). https://doi.org/10.1007/978-3-319-89722-6_14

18. Kumar, R., Ruijters, E., Stoelinga, M.: Quantitative attack tree analysis via priced timed automata. In: Sankaranarayanan, S., Vicario, E. (eds.) FORMATS 2015. LNCS, vol. 9268, pp. 156–171. Springer, Cham (2015). https://doi.org/10.1007/978-3-319-22975-1_11

19. Kumar, R., et al.: Effective analysis of attack trees: a model-driven approach. In: Russo, A., Schürr, A. (eds.) FASE 2018. LNCS, vol. 10802, pp. 56–73. Springer, Cham (2018). https://doi.org/10.1007/978-3-319-89363-1_4

20. Lofberg, J.: YALMIP: a toolbox for modeling and optimization in MATLAB. In: 2004 IEEE International Conference on Robotics and Automation (IEEE Cat. No. 04CH37508), pp. 284–289. IEEE (2004)

21. Lopuhaä-Zwakenberg, M., Stoelinga, M.: Attack time analysis in dynamic attack trees via integer linear programming. arXiv:2111.05114 (2021). Preprint

22. Lopuhaä-Zwakenberg, M.: Attack time analysis in dynamic attack trees via integer linear programming (2023). https://zenodo.org/record/8173951

23. Mauw, S., Oostdijk, M.: Foundations of attack trees. In: Won, D.H., Kim, S. (eds.) ICISC 2005. LNCS, vol. 3935, pp. 186–198. Springer, Heidelberg (2006). https://doi.org/10.1007/11734727_17

24. McQueen, M.A., Boyer, W.F., Flynn, M.A., Beitel, G.A.: Time-to-compromise model for cyber risk reduction estimation. In: Gollmann, D., Massacci, F., Yautsiukhin, A. (eds.) Quality of Protection. Advances in Information Security, vol. 23, pp. 49–64. Springer, Cham (2006). https://doi.org/10.1007/978-0-387-36584-8_5

25. Meyur, R.: A Bayesian attack tree based approach to assess cyber-physical security of power system. In: 2020 IEEE Texas Power and Energy Conference (TPEC), pp. 1–6. IEEE (2020)

26. Paul, S.: Towards automating the construction & maintenance of attack trees: a feasibility study. arXiv:1404.1986 (2014). Preprint

27. Reay, K.A., Andrews, J.D.: A fault tree analysis strategy using binary decision diagrams. Reliab. Eng. Syst. Saf. **78**(1), 45–56 (2002)

28. Rencelj Ling, E., Ekstedt, M.: Estimating the time-to-compromise of exploiting industrial control system vulnerabilities. In: 8th International Conference on Information Systems Security and Privacy-ICISSP, vol. 1, pp. 96–107 (2022)

29. Ruijters, E., Stoelinga, M.: Fault tree analysis: a survey of the state-of-the-art in modeling, analysis and tools. Comput. Sci. Rev. **15**, 29–62 (2015)

30. Vigo, R., Nielson, F., Nielson, H.R.: Automated generation of attack trees. In: 2014 IEEE 27th Computer Security Foundations Symposium, pp. 337–350. IEEE (2014)

31. Vitkus, D., Salter, J., Goranin, N., Čeponis, D.: Method for attack tree data transformation and import into it risk analysis expert systems. Appl. Sci. **10**(23), 8423 (2020)

32. Wideł, W., Audinot, M., Fila, B., Pinchinat, S.: Beyond 2014: formal methods for attack tree-based security modeling. ACM Comput. Surv. (CSUR) **52**(4), 1–36 (2019)

SSCalc:
A Calculus for Solidity Smart Contracts

Diego Marmsoler$^{(\boxtimes)}$ and Billy Thornton

University of Exeter, Exeter, UK
{d.marmsoler,b.thornton}@exeter.ac.uk

Abstract. Smart contracts are programs stored on the blockchain, often developed in a high-level programming language, the most popular of which is Solidity. Smart contracts are used to automate financial transactions and thus bugs can lead to large financial losses. With this paper, we address this problem by describing a verification environment for Solidity in Isabelle/HOL. To this end, we first describe a calculus to reason about Solidity smart contracts. The calculus is formalized in Isabelle/HOL and its soundness is mechanically verified. Then, we describe a Verification Condition Generator to automate the use of the calculus. Our approach can be used to verify the functional correctness of Solidity smart contracts. To demonstrate this, we use it to verify a simple token implemented in Solidity. Our results show that the framework has the potential to significantly reduce the verification effort compared to verifying directly from the semantics.

Keywords: Smart Contracts · Solidity · Program Verification · Isabelle/Solidity

1 Introduction

Blockchain [33] is a novel technology for storing data in a decentralized manner, providing *transparency*, *security*, and *trust*. Although the technology was originally invented to enable cryptocurrencies, it quickly found applications in several other domains, such as *finance* [24], *healthcare* [5], *land management* [12], and even *identity management* [43]. According to McKinsey, blockchain had a market capitalization of more than \$150B in 2018 [8] and Gartner predicts its business value to be \$3.1T by 2030 [19].

One important innovation that comes with blockchains are so-called *smart contracts*. These are digital contracts that are automatically executed once certain conditions are met and that are used to automate transactions on the blockchain. For instance, a payment for an item might be released instantly once the buyer and seller have met all specified parameters for a deal. Every day, hundreds of thousands of new contracts are deployed managing millions of dollars' worth of transactions [42].

Technically, a smart contract is code that is deployed to a blockchain and that can be executed by sending special transactions to it. Smart contracts are usually developed in a high-level programming language, the most popular of which

C. Ferreira and T. A. C. Willemse (Eds.): SEFM 2023, LNCS 14323, pp. 184–204, 2023.
https://doi.org/10.1007/978-3-031-47115-5_11

is *Solidity* [18]. Solidity is based on the Ethereum Virtual Machine (EVM) and thus it works on all EVM-based smart contract platforms, such as Ethereum, Avalanche, Moonbeam, Polygon, BSC, and more. As of today, 85% of all smart contracts are developed using Solidity [25] and according to a 2019 survey, Solidity is by far the most popular language used by blockchain developers (in fact it outranked the second most popular language by 100%) [38].

As for every computer program, *smart contracts may contain bugs that can be exploited*. However, since smart contracts are often used to automate financial transactions, such exploits may result in huge economic losses. For example, in 2016 a vulnerability in an Ethereum smart contract was exploited resulting in a loss of approximately $60M [6]. More recently, hackers exploited a vulnerability in the DeFi-platform Poly Network to steal $600M [34]. As another example, an incorrectly initialized contract was the root cause of the Parity Wallet bug that froze $280M [36]. In general, it is estimated that since 2019, more than $5B was stolen due to vulnerabilities in smart contracts [13].

The high impact of vulnerabilities in smart contracts together with the fact that once deployed to the blockchain, they cannot be updated or removed easily, makes it important to "get them right" before they are deployed. As a result, there has been a growing amount of work to verify smart contracts (see [2] for an overview). Most of the existing work focuses on the automatic detection of certain types of vulnerabilities, such as *re-entrancy*, *integer overflow/underflow*, or *call-stack depth limit*. However, they do not allow for the verification of general *functional correctness*.

Thus, in the following paper, we present SSCalc, a framework for the verification of the functional correctness of Solidity smart contracts. To this end, the contributions of this paper are twofold. First, we describe a calculus to reason about Solidity smart contracts. Our calculus extends traditional calculi, used to reason about sequential and object-oriented programs [3], with new rules to capture the characteristics of smart contracts. We formalized the calculus in Isabelle/HOL [35] and verified its soundness mechanically from the formal semantics of Solidity developed in previous work [26]. Second, we developed a verification condition generator (VCG) to automate the use of the calculus. The VCG is implemented in Isabelle/Eisbach [30] and consists of a set of proof methods, which can be used to verify contract invariants and pre-/postconditions for (internal) methods.

To evaluate our approach, we verified a basic implementation of a token [39] in Solidity with and without using the calculus. Our results show that the calculus has the potential to significantly reduce the effort required to verify a Solidity smart contract. Without the calculus, verification required ca. 3250 lines of Isabelle/Isar code whereas using the calculus reduced it to ca. 700 lines.

2   Background

Our calculus is based on the denotational semantics of a subset of Solidity described in [26–28]. Our subset supports the following features of Solidity:

- *Fixed-size integer types* of various lengths with *support for overflow* and corresponding arithmetic.
- Domain-specific primitives to *transfer funds* and *query balances*.
- Different types of stores, such as *storage, memory, calldata,* and *stack.*
- Complex data types, such as *hash-maps* and *arrays.*
- *Assignment with different semantics,* depending on the location of the involved data types (deep vs. shallow copy of complex data types).
- An abstract *gas model* that can be instantiated with concrete gas costs for each statement.
- *Internal* and *external method declarations* and the ability to *transfer funds* with external method calls.
- Declaration of *fallback methods* which are implicitly executed with monetary transfers.

2.1 Inductive Data Types

Our semantics is formalized in higher-order logic using inductive data types [9]. To this end, we use **bold** font for types and Roman font for type constructors.

For a datatype

$$\mathbf{nat} \ \stackrel{\text{def}}{=} \ \mathrm{Zero}() \mid \mathrm{Suc}(\mathbf{nat})$$

we shall often use the case construct to match a variable against constructors:

$$\mathrm{dec}(x) \ \stackrel{\text{def}}{=} \ \mathrm{case}\ x\ \mathrm{of} \begin{cases} \mathrm{Zero}() & \Rightarrow \mathrm{Zero}() \\ \mathrm{Suc}(n) & \Rightarrow n \end{cases}$$

We shall also use

$$\mathbf{type}_\perp \ \stackrel{\text{def}}{=} \ \perp \cup \{x_\perp \mid x \in \mathbf{type}\}$$

to denote the type that adds a *distinct* element $\perp$ to the elements of **type**.

2.2 State Monad

Our semantics is defined using the concept of a state monad [14,40]. To this end we first define a result type as follows:

$$\mathbf{result}(n, e) \ \stackrel{\text{def}}{=} \ \mathrm{N}(n) \mid \mathrm{E}(e)$$

The type **result** is defined over two type parameters, n, and e, which denote the type for normal and erroneous return values, respectively.

We can then define a state monad as follows:

$$\mathbf{sm}(a, e, s) \ \stackrel{\text{def}}{=} \ s \rightarrow \mathbf{result}(a \times s, e)$$

The monad requires three type parameters: type a for return values, type e for exceptions, and type s for states. Such a monad either updates state s and returns an element of type a or returns an exception of type e.

2.3 State

In Solidity users and contracts are identified by *addresses* with associated balances. Moreover, a contract operates over different types of stores: a *stack* and *memory* to keep volatile data, as well as *storage* to keep persistent data. Finally, in Solidity computation consumes so-called *gas*. Thus, a state is defined as follows:

$$\textbf{state} \stackrel{\text{def}}{=} \textbf{accounts} \times \textbf{stack} \times \textbf{memory} \times (\textbf{address} \to \textbf{storage}) \times \textbf{nat}$$

where **accounts** map addresses to balances and **nat** represents the available gas. Data types **stack, memory,** and **storage** represent the different types of stores and map locations to values (note also that each address has its private storage). In the following, we use $\text{acc}(st)$, $\text{sck}(st)$, $\text{mem}(st)$, $\text{sto}(st)$, and $\text{gas}(st)$ to access the account, stack, memory, storage, and gas components of state st. Moreover, we shall use

$$st (\!| \text{gas} := g, \text{acc} := a, \text{sck} := k, \text{mem} := m, \text{sto} := s |\!)$$

to update the gas, account, stack, memory, and storage of state st to g, a, k, m, and s, respectively.

2.4 Exceptions

In the following, we distinguish between two types of exceptions to signal erroneous executions. Thus, we define the following type for exceptions:

$$\textbf{error} \stackrel{\text{def}}{=} \text{Gas}() \mid \text{Err}()$$

An exception Gas occurs whenever a computation runs out of gas. All other erroneous situations are captured by exception Err.

3 Calculus

In the following, we describe a *weakest precondition* calculus [17] to reason about Solidity. To this end, we fix the following four parameters:

- ep: A *procedure environment* assigning contracts to their addresses.
- ad: The *address* of the contract to be verified.
- contract: The *implementation* of *methods* of the contract to be verified.
- fb: The *implementation* of the *fallback* method of the contract to be verified.

In addition, we assume that the procedure environment ep associates the address ad of the contract to be verified with its implementation contract and fb:

$$\text{ep}(\text{ad}) = (\text{contract}, \text{fb})_\perp$$

We can then define the weakest precondition for our state monad as follows:

$$\mathrm{wp} : \mathbf{sm}((), \mathbf{error}, \mathbf{state}) \times (\mathbf{state} \rightarrow \mathbf{b}) \times (\mathbf{error} \rightarrow \mathbf{b}) \rightarrow \mathbf{state} \rightarrow \mathbf{b}$$

$$\mathrm{wp}(f, P, E) \stackrel{\mathrm{def}}{=} \lambda st.\ \mathrm{case}\ f(st)\ \mathrm{of} \begin{cases} \mathrm{N}(\_, st') & \Rightarrow P(st') \\ \mathrm{E}(e) & \Rightarrow E(e) \end{cases}$$

where () denotes the unit type (the type with only one element ()) and $\mathbf{b}$ is the boolean type. It defines the weakest precondition of statement f, state predicate P, and exception predicate E. If f, executed in state st, terminates successfully with state st', the weakest precondition equals P evaluated over st'. On the other hand, if the statement throws an exception e, the weakest precondition equals E evaluated over e.

A user usually prefers to specify correctness criteria using Hoare triples instead of weakest preconditions. Thus, we further introduce the validity of a Hoare triple for a statement. To this end, we first specify the notion of a state predicate and an exception predicate:

$$\mathbf{spred} \stackrel{\mathrm{def}}{=} \mathbf{accounts} \times \mathbf{stack} \times \mathbf{memory} \times (\mathbf{address} \rightarrow \mathbf{storage}) \rightarrow \mathbf{b}$$

$$\mathbf{epred} \stackrel{\mathrm{def}}{=} \mathbf{error} \rightarrow \mathbf{b}$$

Now we can define validity as follows:

$$\{\_\} \_ \{\_\}\{\_\} : \mathbf{spred} \times \mathbf{sm}((), \mathbf{error}, \mathbf{state}) \times \mathbf{spred} \times \mathbf{epred} \rightarrow \mathbf{b}$$

$$\{P\}\ f\ \{Q\}\{E\} \stackrel{\mathrm{def}}{=} \forall st.\ P(\mathrm{acc}(st), \mathrm{sck}(st), \mathrm{mem}(st), \mathrm{sto}(st))$$

$$\implies \mathrm{case}\ f(st)\ \mathrm{of} \begin{cases} \mathrm{N}(\_, st') & \Rightarrow \begin{aligned} &\mathrm{gas}(st') \le \mathrm{gas}(st)\ \wedge \\ &Q(\mathrm{acc}(st'), \mathrm{sck}(st'), \mathrm{mem}(st'), \mathrm{sto}(st')) \end{aligned} \\ \mathrm{E}(e) & \Rightarrow E(e) \end{cases}$$

A Hoare triple $\{P\}\ f\ \{Q\}\{E\}$ is valid if for every state st that satisfies the state predicate P, statement f either terminates in a state st' that satisfies state predicate Q or leads to an error e that satisfies error predicate E. Note that we also require that execution does not increase the amount of available gas.

To validate our definitions, we proved the following lemma about the relationship between the validity of Hoare triples and weakest preconditions:

Lemma 1.

$$\{P\}\ f\ \{Q\}\{E\} \iff \begin{aligned} &\forall s.\ P(\mathrm{acc}(s), \mathrm{sck}(s), \mathrm{mem}(s), \mathrm{sto}(s)) \\ &\implies \mathrm{wp}(f, (\lambda s.\ Q(\mathrm{acc}(s), \mathrm{sck}(s), \mathrm{mem}(s), \mathrm{sto}(s))), E, s) \end{aligned}$$

3.1 Basic Rules

Our calculus includes rules for all the basic statements: WP_SKIP for the empty statement, WP_ASSIGN for assignments, WP_COMP for compositions, WP_ITE for conditionals, and WP_WHILE for while loops (which require the specification of an invariant). These rules are mostly standard; and thus, they are not discussed further here.

There are, however, two particularities worth mentioning. First, each rule needs to deal with the case that there might not be enough gas available to execute a statement. Second, assignments are somewhat special in Solidity because the semantics of assignments depend on the location of the expression on the left and right. Each side may evaluate to a location on either stack, calldata, memory, or storage. Thus, when verifying an assignment in Solidity, we must consider 16 different cases and two additional error cases.

3.2   Method Invocation

In Solidity, a contract may have two types of methods. *Internal* methods can only be called internally from within the same contract. *External* methods, on the other hand, can only be called by other contracts. In addition, a Solidity contract has a designated *fallback* method. This method is invoked whenever the contract receives some payments or if a method is called that does not exist.

The following rule allows us to verify (recursive) method calls:

WP_EXTERNAL_INVOKE_TRANSFER
$$\frac{\forall st'.\; \text{gas } st' \leq \text{gas } st \implies P(i,p,p',p_f,p'_f,st') \;\vdash\; Q(i,p,p',p_f,p'_f,st)}{P(i,p,p',p_f,p'_f,st')}$$

where predicates P and Q are defined below and $A \vdash C$ denotes that C is derivable from A in our calculus.

The rule requires the specification of several parameters:

- i: An invariant for the contract's private storage and balance.
- p, p': Pre/postconditions for each internal method.
- p_f, p'_f: One pre/postcondition for the contract's fallback method.

We can then use the rule to establish a predicate P for an arbitrary state st' by proving Q for an arbitrary state st. While proving Q, the rule allows us to assume P for all states st' with less (or equal) gas than st.

In the following, we are going to discuss predicates P and Q in more detail.

Predicate P. This predicate is defined as follows:

$$P(i,p,p',p_f,p'_f,st) \stackrel{\text{def}}{=} P_{\text{e}}(i,st) \wedge P_{\text{i}}(p,p',st) \wedge P_{\text{fi}}(p_f,p'_f,st) \wedge P_{\text{fe}}(i,st)$$

It *establishes the weakest precondition* for method *calls* and *transfer* statements.

$P_{\text{e}}(iv,st)$. This predicate establishes the weakest precondition for *external method calls*. In Solidity, external method calls can be used to invoke methods of other contracts deployed to the blockchain. Moreover, it is possible to transfer funds from the caller to the callee with each call. In the following, we use External(ad',i,xe,val) to denote an external method call where

- ad' is an expression denoting the address of the called contract.
- i is the identifier of the method to be called.
- xe is a list containing actual parameters for the method.
- val is an expression denoting the amount of funds sent with the call.

Predicate $P_e(iv, st)$ can now be defined as in Fig. 1, where $address(ev)$ denotes the address associated with an environment ev, $expr(ex, ev, cd, st, g)$ evaluates an expression ex using an environment ev and calldata cd in a state st, ng is the updated gas value $gas(st) - costs(External(ad', i, xe, val), ev, cd, st)$, $\lceil x \rceil$ converts a string to an integer, and E denotes the exception predicate $\lambda e.\ e = \text{Gas} \vee e = \text{Err}$.

$$
\begin{aligned}
&\forall ev, ad', i, xe, val, cd. \\
&\quad address(ev) = \text{ad} \wedge \tag{1} \\
&\quad (\forall adv, g, v, t, g'.\ adv \neq \text{ad} \wedge adv \in \text{dom(ep)} \wedge \\
&\qquad expr(ad', ev, cd, st(\![\text{gas} := \text{ng}]\!), \text{ng}) = \text{N}((\text{V}(adv), \text{V}(\text{TAddr})), g) \wedge \\
&\qquad expr(val, ev, cd, st(\![\text{gas} := g]\!), g) = \text{N}((\text{V}(v), \text{V}(t)), g') \\
&\quad \Longrightarrow iv(\text{sto}(st)(\text{ad}),\ \lceil \text{acc}(st)(\text{ad}) \rceil - \lceil v \rceil)) \tag{2} \\
&\Longrightarrow \text{wp}(\text{stmt}(External(ad', i, xe, val), ev, cd), \\
&\qquad \lambda st.\ iv(\text{sto}(st)(\text{ad}), \lceil \text{acc}(st)(\text{ad}) \rceil), \text{E}, st) \tag{3}
\end{aligned}
$$

Fig. 1. Definition of $P_e(iv, st)$.

Equation 3 establishes the weakest precondition of invariant iv and error predicate E for an external method call executed in state st. Equation 1 ensures that the address of the currently executing contract is indeed address ad of the contract to be verified (fixed at the beginning of Sect. 3). Equation 2 requires that the invariant holds before executing the call. However, note that we require the invariant to hold on a modified version of the balance. In particular, value v (which is obtained by evaluating expression val) is deduced from the actual balance of the contract. This is because the actual call transfers v funds from the caller to the callee. Thus, to ensure that the invariant holds after the call, we must ensure that the invariant holds on a balance in which the value is already deduced.

$P_i(pre, post, st)$. This predicate establishes the weakest precondition for *internal method calls*. In Solidity, internal method calls can only invoke internal methods of the currently executing contract. In the following, we use $\text{Invoke}(i, xe)$ to denote a call to an internal method i with actual parameters xe. $P_i(pre, post, st)$ can now be defined as in Fig. 2, where $load(cp, fp, xe, nev, cd', sck', mem', ev, cd, st)$ initializes formal parameters fp

$$\forall ev, i, xe, cd.$$
$$\quad \text{address}(ev) = \text{ad} \,\wedge \tag{4}$$
$$\quad (\forall fp, e_l, cd_l, k_l, m_l, g.$$
$$\quad\quad \text{load}(\text{False}, fp, xe, \text{nev}, \emptyset, \emptyset, \text{mem}(st), ev, cd, st(\!|\text{gas} := \text{ng}|\!), \text{ng}) =$$
$$\quad\quad \text{N}((e_l, cd_l, k_l, m_l), g)$$
$$\quad\quad \implies pre(\lceil \text{acc}(st)(\text{ad}) \rceil, \text{sto}(st)(\text{ad}), e_l, cd_l, k_l, m_l)) \tag{5}$$
$$\quad \implies \text{wp}(\text{stmt}(\text{Invoke}(i, xe), ev, cd),$$
$$\quad\quad\quad \lambda st.\ post(i)(\lceil \text{acc}(st)(\text{ad}) \rceil, \text{sto}(st)(\text{ad})), \text{E}, st) \tag{6}$$

Fig. 2. Definition of $P_i(pre, post, st)$.

with actual parameters xe, nev is a fresh environment for the execution of the method body, and ng is the updated gas value $\text{gas}(st) - \text{costs}(\text{Invoke}(i, xe), ev, cd, st)$.

Equation 6 establishes the weakest precondition of the method's postcondition $post(i)$ and error predicate E for an internal method call executed in state st. Again, Eq. 4 ensures that the currently executing contract is the one to be verified (with address ad). Equation 5, however, requires that the method's precondition holds before the execution of the call. Note that the precondition is a predicate over 6 parameters: the current contracts balance and private store, as well as the environment created by loading the actual parameters (environment e_l, calldata cd_l, stack k_l, and memory m_l).

$P_{\text{fe}}(iv, st)$. This predicate establishes the weakest precondition for external transfers. In Solidity, transfer statements can be used to transfer funds from contracts to accounts. In the following, we use $\text{Transfer}(ad', ex)$ to denote a transfer statement in which

- ad' is an expression denoting the address of the receiver, and
- ex is an expression denoting the amount to be transferred.

Note that, if the receiving address belongs to a contract, a transfer implicitly triggers the execution of a so-called fallback method. Thus, $P_{\text{fe}}(iv, st)$ can be defined as in Fig. 3, where ng is the updated gas value $\text{gas}(st) - \text{costs}(\text{Transfer}(ad', ex), ev, cd, st)$.

$$\forall ev, ex, ad', cd.$$
$$\text{address}(ev) = \text{ad} \land \tag{7}$$
$$(\forall adv, g.\ \text{expr}(ad', ev, cd, st(\!\text{gas} := \text{ng}\!), \text{ng}) = \text{N}((\text{V}(adv), \text{V}(\text{TAddr})), g)$$
$$\implies adv \neq \text{ad}) \land \tag{8}$$
$$(\forall adv, g, v, t, g'.\ adv \neq \text{ad} \land$$
$$\text{expr}(ad', ev, cd, st(\!\text{gas} := \text{ng}\!), \text{ng}) = \text{N}((\text{V}(adv), \text{V}(\text{TAddr})), g) \land$$
$$\text{expr}(ex, ev, cd, st(\!\text{gas} := g\!), g) = \text{N}((\text{V}(v), \text{V}(t)), g')$$
$$\implies iv(\text{sto}(st)(\text{ad}), \lceil \text{acc}(st)(\text{ad}) \rceil - \lceil v \rceil\ )) \tag{9}$$
$$\implies \text{wp}(\text{stmt}(\text{Transfer}(ad', ex), ev, cd),$$
$$\lambda st.\ iv(\text{sto}(st)(\text{ad}), \lceil \text{acc}(st)(\text{ad}) \rceil), \text{E}, st) \tag{10}$$

Fig. 3. Definition of $P_{\text{fe}}(iv, st)$.

Equation 10 establishes the weakest precondition of invariant iv and error predicate E for a transfer statement executed in state st. Again, Eq. 7 ensures that the currently executing contract is the one we want to verify (on address ad). In addition, Eq. 8 requires that the receiving contract is different from the executing contract (because for self-transfers we have a different rule). Finally, Eq. 9 requires the invariant to hold before the transfer statement is executed. Again, we require that the invariant holds on a balance in which the value is already deduced from the balance of the currently executing contract.

$P_{\text{fi}}(pre_f, post_f, st)$. This predicate establishes the weakest precondition for internal transfers. The rule is similar to P_{fe}, but since control is not passed on to an external contract we may use pre-/post-conditions instead of an invariant. Thus, the definition of P_{fi} is the same as that of P_{fe} (shown in Fig. 3) with the following changes:

- Eq. 8 is changed to $adv = \text{ad}$.
- In Eq. 9 $iv(\dots)$ is replaced with $pre_f(\text{sto}(st)(\text{ad}), \lceil \text{acc}(st)(\text{ad}) \rceil)$.
- In Eq. 10 $iv(\dots)$ is replaced with $post_f(\text{sto}(st)(\text{ad}), \lceil \text{acc}(st)(\text{ad}) \rceil)$.

Note that we require pre_f to hold for the original balance $\text{acc}(st)(\text{ad})$ and *not* for the modified version as in Eq. 9. This is because an internal transfer does not modify the current contract's balance, because the amount is first deduced from it but then added again.

Predicate Q. This predicate is defined as follows:

$$Q(i, p, p', p_f, p'_f, st) \stackrel{\text{def}}{=} Q_e(i, st) \wedge Q_i(p, p', st) \wedge Q_{fi}(p_f, p'_f, st) \wedge Q_{fe}(p_f, p'_f, st)$$

It denotes *proof obligations* for different types of methods.

$Q_e(iv, st)$. This predicate denotes proof obligations for external methods; that is, it tells us what we need to verify to establish the weakest precondition of an invariant for an external method. It is defined in Fig. 4 where ng is the updated gas value gas(st') − costs(External($adex, mid, xe, val$), ev, cd, st'), nev is a fresh environment for the execution of the method body, and transfer(s, r, v, a) is used to transfer funds of value v from sending address s to receiving address r for accounts a.

Equation 15 shows the actual statement we need to verify, i.e., that the weakest precondition of invariant iv and error predicate E for method body f holds in state st' with gas g'', accounts acc, stack k_l, and memory m_l. The statement needs to be verified only for external methods invoked from a context outside the contract to be verified. Thus, Eq. 11 requires that f is indeed the body of an external method mid of the contract to be verified (contract) and Eq. 12 ensures that the method is invoked from outside (i.e. an address different from the contract to be verified).

To verify Eq. 15 we can assume that the invariant holds for the state in which f will be executed (Eq. 14). This is because we know that the invariant holds when control leaves the current contract. Thus, if another contract is to call back into the current contract the invariant must still hold. Note, however, that the invariant holds only on a modified balance for contract ad. This is because the calling contract may send some funds v with the method call which are then transferred to the receiving contract ad. Thus, since we know that the invariant holds before transferring the funds, we need to deduce v from the balance of ad after the transfer.

When verifying Eq. 15 we can also assume that the current level of gas is less than or equal to the original amount of gas (Eq. 13). This is an important property because it allows us to use all P predicates from WP_EXTERNAL_INVOKE_TRANSFER, which, according to the rule, can only be assumed for states with less or equal gas than the original state.

$\forall mid, fp, f, ev.$

$\quad$ contract$(mid) = $ Method$(fp, \text{True}, f)_\perp \wedge$ $\hspace{4cm}$ (11)

$\quad$ address$(ev) \neq$ ad $\hspace{6.5cm}$ (12)

$\implies (\forall adex, cd, st', xe, val, g, v, t, g', e_l, cd_l, k_l, m_l, g'', acc.$

$\quad\quad$ expr$(adex, ev, cd, st'(\!|\text{gas} := \text{ng}|\!), \text{ng}) = \text{N}((\text{V}(\text{ad}), \text{V}(\text{TAddr})), g) \wedge$

$\quad\quad$ expr$(val, ev, cd, st'(\!|\text{gas} := g|\!), g) = \text{N}((\text{V}(v), \text{V}(t)), g') \wedge$

$\quad\quad$ load$(\text{True}, fp, xe, \text{nev}, \emptyset, \emptyset, \emptyset, ev, cd, st'(\!|\text{gas} := g'|\!), g') =$

$\quad\quad\quad \text{N}((e_l, cd_l, k_l, m_l), g'')$

$\quad\quad g'' \leq \text{gas}(st) \wedge$ $\hspace{6cm}$ (13)

$\quad\quad$ transfer$(\text{address}(ev), \text{ad}, v, \text{acc}(st'(\!|\text{gas} := g''|\!))) = acc_\perp \wedge$

$\quad\quad iv(\text{sto}(st')(\text{ad}), \lceil acc(\text{ad}) \rceil - \lceil v \rceil)$ $\hspace{4cm}$ (14)

$\quad\implies$ wp$(\text{stmt}(f, e_l, cd_l), \lambda st. \ iv(\text{sto}(st)(\text{ad}), \lceil acc(st)(\text{ad}) \rceil), \text{E},$

$\quad\quad st'(\!|\text{gas} := g'', \text{acc} := acc, \text{sck} := k_l, \text{mem} := m_l|\!)))$ $\hspace{2cm}$ (15)

Fig. 4. Definition of $Q_e(iv, st)$.

$Q_i(pre, post, st)$. This predicate denotes proof obligations for internal methods, i.e., it tells us what we need to verify to establish the weakest precondition of a method's postcondition from its precondition. In Fig. 5 ng is the updated gas value gas$(st') - \text{costs}(\text{Invoke}(i, xe), ev, cd, st')$ and nev is a fresh environment for the execution of the method body.

Equation 20 states what we need to verify, i.e., that the weakest precondition of the postcondition $post(mid)$ associated with method mid and error predicate E for method body f holds in state st' with gas g, stack k_l, and memory m_l. The statement needs to be verified only for internal methods invoked from a context inside the contract to be verified. Thus, Eq. 16 requires that f is indeed the body of an internal method mid of the contract to be verified (contract) and Eq. 17 ensures that the method is invoked from inside (i.e., from address ad).

Again, when verifying Eq. 20, we can assume that the available gas is less or equal to the original amount of gas (Eq. 18). Moreover, we can also assume that the methods precondition holds for the environment in which method body f will be executed (Eq. 19). The statement needs to be verified only for external methods invoked from a context outside the contract to be verified. Thus, Eq. 11 requires that f is indeed the body of an external method mid of the contract to be verified (contract) and Eq. 12 ensures that the method is invoked from outside (i.e., an address different from the contract to be verified).

$Q_{\text{fe}}(iv, st)$. This predicate denotes proof obligations to establish the weakest precondition of an invariant for fallback methods executed as a result of an external

$$\forall mid, fp, f, ev.$$
$$\text{contract}(mid) = \text{Method}(fp, \text{False}, f)_{\perp} \wedge \tag{16}$$
$$\text{address}(ev) = \text{ad} \tag{17}$$
$$\implies (\forall cd, st', i, xe, e_l, cd_l, k_l, m_l, g.$$
$$\text{load}(\text{False}, fp, xe, \text{nev}, \emptyset, \emptyset, \text{mem}(st'), ev, cd, st'(\!| \text{gas} := ng |\!), ng) =$$
$$\text{N}((e_l, cd_l, k_l, m_l), g) \wedge$$
$$g \le \text{gas}(st) \wedge \tag{18}$$
$$pre(mid)(\lceil \text{acc}(st')(\text{ad}) \rceil, \text{sto}(st')(\text{ad}), e_l, cd_l, k_l, m_l) \tag{19}$$
$$\implies \text{wp}(\text{stmt}(f, e_l, cd_l), \lambda st.\, post(mid)(\lceil \text{acc}(st)(\text{ad}) \rceil, \text{sto}(st)(\text{ad})), \text{E},$$
$$st'(\!| \text{gas} := g, \text{sck} := k_l, \text{mem} := m_l |\!))) \tag{20}$$

Fig. 5. Definition of $Q_i(pre, post, st)$.

transfer. It is defined in Fig. 6 where ng is the updated gas value $\text{gas}(st') - c$ and nev is a fresh environment for the execution of the fallback method.

$$\forall ev.\, \text{address}(ev) \neq \text{ad} \tag{21}$$
$$\implies (\forall ex, cd, st', adex, v, t, g, g', acc, c.$$
$$\text{expr}(adex, ev, cd, st'(\!| \text{gas} := ng |\!), ng) = \text{N}((\text{V}(\text{ad}), \text{V}(\text{TAddr})), g) \wedge$$
$$\text{expr}(ex, ev, cd, st'(\!| \text{gas} := g |\!), g) = \text{N}((\text{V}(v), \text{V}(t)), g') \wedge$$
$$g' \le \text{gas}(st) \wedge \tag{22}$$
$$\text{transfer}(\text{address}(ev), \text{ad}, v, \text{acc}(st')) = acc_{\perp} \wedge$$
$$iv(\text{sto}(st')(\text{ad}), \lceil acc(\text{ad}) \rceil - \lceil v \rceil) \tag{23}$$
$$\implies \text{wp}(\text{stmt}(\text{fb}, \text{nev}, \emptyset), \lambda st.\, iv(\text{sto}(st)(\text{ad}), \lceil \text{acc}(st)(\text{ad}) \rceil), \text{E},$$
$$st'(\!| \text{gas} := g', \text{sck} := \emptyset, \text{acc} := acc, \text{mem} := \emptyset |\!))) \tag{24}$$

Fig. 6. Definition of $Q_{\text{fe}}(iv, st)$.

Equation 24 states what we need to verify, i.e., that the weakest precondition of the invariant iv and error predicate E for our contracts fallback method fb holds in state st' with gas g', a fresh stack and memory, and account acc. Since it only needs to be verified for external transfers, Eq. 21 ensures that the transfer statement is issued externally.

Again, when verifying Eq. 24, we can assume that the current level of gas is less than or equal to the original level (Eq. 22). Moreover, we know that the invariant holds when the transfer occurs. Thus, since the transfer adds v funds to the balance of contract ad, we can assume that the invariant holds when we deduce v again.

$Q_{fi}(pre_f, post_f, st)$. This predicate denotes proof obligations for internal transfers, i.e., it tells us what we need to verify to establish the weakest precondition of the postcondition of the fallback method from its precondition. Its definition is similar to that of Q_{fe}, with modifications similar to those required for P_{fi} above.

4   Formalization in Isabelle/HOL

The complete calculus is formalized in Isabelle/HOL, and its soundness is mechanically verified[1] from our semantics.

4.1   Verification of Soundness

The verification of soundness of our rules is mostly standard, except for rule WP_EXTERNAL_INVOKE_TRANSFER. In particular, external method calls and transfer statements transfer control to another contract. Thus, we must ensure that other contracts can never change the validity of an invariant. To this end, we prove the following lemma:

$$\forall st'.\ \text{address}(ev) \neq \text{ad} \land \tag{25}$$
$$iv(\text{sto}(st)(\text{ad}), \lceil \text{acc}(st)(\text{ad})\rceil) \land \tag{26}$$
$$\text{stmt}(f, ev, cd, st) = \text{N}((), st') \land \tag{27}$$
$$\forall st'.\ \text{gas}(st') < \text{gas}(st) \implies Q_e(iv, st') \land \tag{28}$$
$$\forall st'.\ \text{gas}(st') < \text{gas}(st) \implies Q_{fe}(iv, st') \tag{29}$$
$$\implies iv(\text{sto}(st')(\text{ad}), \lceil \text{acc}(st')(\text{ad})\rceil) \tag{30}$$

With this lemma we verified that an invariant iv for the storage and balance of contract ad is preserved (Eq. 26 and Eq. 30) by the execution of arbitrary statements f (Eq. 27) executed in a different context from that of ad (Eq. 25), given that the external methods (Eq. 28) and the fallback method (Eq. 29) of contract ad preserve the invariant. Equation 28 and Eq. 29 are particularly important here because f may contain statements that call back to ad and thus execute code that may potentially impact iv.

Since our semantics is formalized as a deep embedding in Isabelle/HOL, the statement above can be easily proven by structural induction on f.

4.2   Automation

To support users in applying the calculus for the verification of Solidity smart contracts we implemented a verification condition generator (VCG). The VCG automates the use of the calculus and leaves the user with a so-called verification condition that needs to be discharged to ensure the correctness of the contract. The VCG is implemented in Isabelle/Eisbach [30] and consists of different methods to support the verification of different types of statements[2].

---

[1] Theory Weakest_Precondition.thy from the accompanying artefact [29].
[2] Section "Verification Condition Generator" in Weakest_Precondition.thy [29].

5   Methodology

In the following section, we demonstrate our approach using a simple example. To this end, consider the contract depicted in Listing 1.1, which stores an unsigned integer x (and possibly other variables not shown). Moreover, it provides an internal method int1, which calls an external method ext() of a contract with address ad1 and sends 1 ether with it. It also provides another internal method int2, which calls int1. In addition, it provides an external method ext, which transfers 1 ether to a contract with address ad2 and another 1 ether to itself. Finally, it also has a fallback method which does not have a name.

```
1  contract Example {
2    uint x;
3    ...
4    function int1(uint y, ...) internal {
5      ...
6      ad1.call.value(1 ether)(abi.encodeWithSignature("ext()"));
7      ...
8    }
9    function int2(int y, ....) internal {
10     ...
11     int1(5, ...);
12     ...
13   }
14   function ext() external {
15     ...
16     ad2.transfer(1 ether);
17     ...
18     address(this).transfer(1 ether);
19     ...
20   }
21   function () external payable {
22     ...
23   }
24 }
```

Listing 1.1. A simple example contract.

To verify the contract using our calculus, we first need to specify the following:

- An *invariant*: A predicate over the contract's member variables (including, for example, x) and the contract's balance.
- *Preconditions* for internal methods int1 and int2: Predicates over the method's formal parameters (including, for example, y), the contract's member variables (including, for example, x), and the contract's balance.
- *Postconditions* for internal methods int1 and int2: Predicates over the contract's member variables and the contract's balance.
- A *precondition* and *postcondition* for the contract's fallback method: A predicate over the contract's member variables and the contract's balance.

We then need to verify the following:

- Executing the body of int1 (Ln. 5 - Ln. 7) in a state in which its precondition holds, leads to a state in which its postcondition holds.
- Executing the body of int2 (Ln. 10 - Ln. 12) in a state in which its precondition holds, leads to a state in which its postcondition holds.
- Executing the body of ext (Ln. 15 - Ln. 19) in a state in which the invariant holds, leads to a state in which the invariant holds again.
- Executing the body of the fallback method (Ln. 22) in a state in which its precondition holds, leads to a state in which its postcondition holds, and executing the body in a state in which the invariant holds, leads to a state in which the invariant holds again.

To verify the above proof obligations we can use the rules of the calculus and the following assumptions:

- If the invariant holds before executing Ln. 6, then it holds also after executing it.
- If the precondition associated with int1 holds before the execution of Ln. 11, then the corresponding postcondition holds after executing Ln. 11.
- If the invariant holds before executing Ln. 16, then it holds also after executing it.
- If the fallback methods precondition holds before the execution of Ln. 18, then its postcondition holds after executing Ln. 18.

6 Case Study: Verified Banking

In the following, we use our calculus to verify a contract that implements a simple banking system.

6.1 The Contract

The contract should allow users to deposit funds and later withdraw them. A possible implementation is provided by the contract shown in Listing 1.2.

```
1   contract Bank {
2     mapping(address => uint256) balances;
3
4     function deposit() external payable {
5       balances[msg.sender] = balances[msg.sender] + msg.value;
6     }
7
8     function withdraw() external {
9       uint256 bal = balances[msg.sender];
10      balances[msg.sender] = 0;
11      msg.sender.transfer(bal);
12    }
13  }
```

Listing 1.2. A simple banking contract.

The contract has one member variable `balances` to keep track of all the balances. Moreover, it provides two methods to deposit and withdraw funds. When a contract calls `deposit` with some funds, the funds are transferred to the Bank contract and the amount is kept in `msg.value`. Thus, method `deposit` simply adds the value to the balance of the calling contract to keep track of how much each contract contributed to the funds of the banking contract. A contract can call `withdraw` to get its funds back. To this end, the banking contract first sets the caller's internal balance to 0 (Ln. 10) and then returns the corresponding funds (Ln. 11). Note that it is important to *first* update the internal balance before transferring the money. Thus, the contract is secure against so-called re-entrancy attacks [4]. However, the question remains whether the contract is indeed functionally correct or if it is exposed to other vulnerabilities.

6.2 Formalizing the Contract

To answer this question, we first need to formalize the contract in our semantics. To this end, we need to provide definitions for the parameters of our calculus described at the beginning of Sect. 3:

$$
\text{contract} = \begin{cases} \text{``}balances\text{''} & \mapsto & \text{Var}(\text{STMap}(\text{TAddr}, \text{STValue}(\text{TUInt}(256)))) \\ \text{``}deposit\text{''} & \mapsto & \text{Method}([], \text{True}, \text{deposit}) \\ \text{``}withdraw\text{''} & \mapsto & \text{Method}([], \text{True}, \text{withdraw}) \end{cases}
$$
$$
\text{fb} = \text{Skip}
$$

The contract is formalized as a mapping from identifiers to corresponding members. While "*balances*" refers to a variable, "*deposit*" and "*withdraw*" refer to *external* methods with body deposit and withdraw defined as in Listing 1.2. The contract does not define a fallback method; thus fb is defined as Skip.

6.3 Specification of Properties

The property we want to verify for our contract is that the relationship between the sum of all stored balances and the internal balance of the contract is preserved through the execution of each external method.

Thus, we first formalize the following invariant:

$$
\text{iv}(bal, s, a) \stackrel{\text{def}}{=} a - \text{sum}(s) \geq bal \wedge bal \geq 0 \wedge \text{pos}(s)
$$
$$
\text{sum}(s) \stackrel{\text{def}}{=} \sum_{\{(ad,x) \mid s(ad+\text{``.''}+\text{``}balances\text{''})=x_\perp\}} \lceil x \rceil
$$
$$
\text{pos}(s) \stackrel{\text{def}}{=} \forall ad, x.\ s(ad + \text{``.''} + \text{``}balances\text{''}) = x_\perp \implies \lceil x \rceil \geq 0
$$

The important part here is the first conjunction in the definition of iv: $a - \text{sum}(s) \geq bal$. Here, a represents the funds available to our banking contract and $\text{sum}(s)$ represents the sum of all its stored balances. Thus, the formula requires that the difference between these two balances is bound by a certain value *bal*.

Now, we can formalize the properties thst we want to verify using the Hoare triple notation introduced in Sect. 3:

$$\{I\}\ \text{stmt}(\text{External}(\text{Address}(\text{ad}), \text{``deposit''}, [], val), env, cd)\ \{I\}\{E\}$$
$$\{I\}\ \text{stmt}(\text{External}(\text{Address}(\text{ad}), \text{``withdraw''}, [], val), env, cd)\ \{I\}\{E\}$$

where $I((a, \_, \_, s)) \stackrel{\text{def}}{=} iv(bal, s(ad), \lceil a(ad) \rceil)$, $E(e) \stackrel{\text{def}}{=} e = \text{Gas} \vee e = \text{Err}$, and address(*env*) $\neq$ ad.

6.4   Verification

As discussed in Sect. 3.2, Solidity implicitly triggers the execution of a so-called fallback method whenever money is transferred to a contract. In particular, if another contract calls `withdraw`, the transfer statement in Ln. 11 of Listing 1.2 triggers the execution of the callee's fallback method. Thus, as we do not know all potential contracts that call `withdraw`, we need to verify the invariant for all possible implementations.

To evaluate our approach, we verified the above property twice: from its semantics without using the calculus [28], and using our calculus [29]. Without the calculus, verifying the above property required ca. 3 250 lines of Isabelle/Isar code. Using the calculus reduced it to ca. 700 lines.

7   Related Work

Since Solidity is the most popular language for developing smart contracts there has been growing interest in formalizing its semantics. Bhargavan et al. [10], for example, provide a semantics of Solidity in F*. Crosara et al. [16] describe an operational semantics for a subset of Solidity. Hajdu and Jovanovic [21], provide a formalization of Solidity in terms of a simple SMT-based intermediate language. In addition, Zakrzewski [44] describes a big-step semantics of a small subset of Solidity and Yang and Lei [41] describe a formalization of a subset of Solidity in Coq [37]. Moreover, Jiao et al. [22,23], provide a formalization of Solidity in $\mathbb{K}$. Finally, Cassez et al. [11] provide an implementation of Solidity in Dafny. All of these works provide important contributions towards a better understanding of Solidity. The focus of our work was to provide a framework for the verification of smart contracts written in Solidity and while it is possible to verify them directly from the semantics it is often tedious and difficult.

Another line of research has focused on the development of automatic verification techniques for Solidity programs. For example, Mavridou et al. [31] provide an approach based on FSolidM [32], in which a Solidity smart contract is modeled as a state machine to support model checking of common security properties. In addition, Hajdu and Jovanovic [20] provide solc-verify, a modular verifier for Solidity smart contracts. Work in this area usually focuses on the automatic verification of different aspects of Solidity programs and can not be used to verify general *functional correctness*, which is the focus of our work.

Finally, some research has focused on the verification of functional correctness of Solidity programs. Early work in this area includes TinySol [7] and Feather-weight Solidity [15], two calculi formalizing some of the core features of Solidity. More recently, Ahrendt and Bubel described SolidiKeY [1], a formalization of a subset of Solidity in the KeY tool to verify data integrity for smart contracts. Similar to our work, research in this area can be used to verify the functional correctness of Solidity contracts. However, the above works differ from the work presented in this paper in two main aspects. First, the rules described above are provided in the form of axioms rather than being derived from a formal semantic, as is the case with our work. Second, the above works focus on a restricted subset of Solidity. For example, none of the works consider fixed-size integers, different types of stores with different semantics for assignments, or external vs. internal method calls, which are key features of Solidity addressed by our calculus.

8   Conclusion

In this paper, we presented a framework for the verification of Solidity smart contracts in Isabelle/HOL. To this end, we developed a calculus to reason about Solidity statements, formalized it in Isabelle, and mechanically verified its soundness. In addition, we developed a verification condition generator that automates the use of the calculus. To evaluate the approach, we used it to verify a basic token in Solidity, which showed that the calculus can significantly reduce the effort to verify Solidity smart contracts compared to a verification from its semantics.

While our calculus supports most of the important features of Solidity there are still some more advanced features of the language that are not yet supported. In particular, the calculus does not yet support inheritance, which seems to be an important feature for Solidity developers. Moreover, although our case study demonstrates the feasibility of our approach it is not clear how well it can be generalized to the verification of other contracts.

To address the above limitations, future work arises in two directions. First, future work should extend the calculus to support more advanced features of Solidity, such as inheritance. In addition, future work should also focus on conducting additional case studies in which the calculus is used for the verification of additional contracts.

Availability. Our formalisation and the evaluation results are available under BSD license (SPDX-License-Identifier: BSD-2-Clause) [29].

Acknowledgements. We would like to thank Achim Brucker for his support with Isabelle. Moreover, we would like to thank Wolfgang Ahrendt and Richard Bubel for inspiring discussions about the verification of Solidity contracts.

References

1. Ahrendt, W., Bubel, R.: Functional verification of smart contracts via strong data integrity. In: Margaria, T., Steffen, B. (eds.) ISoLA 2020. LNCS, vol. 12478, pp. 9–24. Springer, Cham (2020). https://doi.org/10.1007/978-3-030-61467-6_2
2. Almakhour, M., Sliman, L., Samhat, A.E., Mellouk, A.: Verification of smart contracts: a survey. Pervas. Mob. Comput. **67**, 101227 (2020). https://doi.org/10.1016/j.pmcj.2020.101227
3. Apt, K.R., de Boer, F., Olderog, E.R.: Verification of Sequential and Concurrent Programs, 3rd edn. Springer, London (2009). https://doi.org/10.1007/978-1-84882-745-5
4. Atzei, N., Bartoletti, M., Cimoli, T.: A survey of attacks on ethereum smart contracts (SoK). In: Maffei, M., Ryan, M. (eds.) POST 2017. LNCS, vol. 10204, pp. 164–186. Springer, Heidelberg (2017). https://doi.org/10.1007/978-3-662-54455-6_8
5. Azaria, A., Ekblaw, A., Vieira, T., Lippman, A.: Medrec: using blockchain for medical data access and permission management. In: 2016 2nd International Conference on Open and Big Data (OBD), pp. 25–30 (2016). https://doi.org/10.1109/OBD.2016.11
6. Bahrynovska, T.: History of Ethereum Security Vulnerabilities, Hacks and Their Fixes. https://applicature.com/blog/blockchain-technology/history-of-ethereum-security-vulnerabilities-hacks-and-their-fixes. Accessed 18 Apr 2023
7. Bartoletti, M., Galletta, L., Murgia, M.: A minimal core calculus for solidity contracts. In: Pérez-Solà, C., Navarro-Arribas, G., Biryukov, A., Garcia-Alfaro, J. (eds.) DPM/CBT -2019. LNCS, vol. 11737, pp. 233–243. Springer, Cham (2019). https://doi.org/10.1007/978-3-030-31500-9_15
8. Batra, G., Olson, R., Pathak, S., Santhanam, N., Soundararajan, H.: Blockchain 2.0: what's in store for the two ends? https://www.mckinsey.com/industries/industrials-and-electronics/our-insights/blockchain-2-0-whats-in-store-for-the-two-ends-semiconductors-suppliers-and-industrials-consumers. Accessed 18 Apr 2023
9. Berghofer, S., Wenzel, M.: Inductive datatypes in HOL — Lessons learned in formal-logic engineering. In: Bertot, Y., Dowek, G., Théry, L., Hirschowitz, A., Paulin, C. (eds.) TPHOLs 1999. LNCS, vol. 1690, pp. 19–36. Springer, Heidelberg (1999). https://doi.org/10.1007/3-540-48256-3_3
10. Bhargavan, K., et al.: Formal verification of smart contracts: short paper. In: Programming Languages and Analysis for Security, pp. 91–96. PLAS, ACM (2016). https://doi.org/10.1145/2993600.2993611
11. Cassez, F., Fuller, J., Quiles, H.M.A.: Deductive verification of smart contracts with dafny. In: Groote, J.F., Huisman, M. (eds.) Formal Methods for Industrial Critical Systems, pp. 50–66. Springer, Cham (2022). https://doi.org/10.1007/978-3-031-15008-1_5
12. Chavez-Dreyfuss, G.: Sweden tests blockchain technology for land registry. https://www.reuters.com/article/us-sweden-blockchain-idUSKCN0Z22KV. Accessed 18 Apr 2023
13. Clegg, P., Jevans, D.: Cryptocurrency crime and anti-money laundering report. Tech. rep, CipherTrace (2021)
14. Cock, D., Klein, G., Sewell, T.: Secure microkernels, state monads and scalable refinement. In: Mohamed, O.A., Muñoz, C., Tahar, S. (eds.) TPHOLs 2008. LNCS, vol. 5170, pp. 167–182. Springer, Heidelberg (2008). https://doi.org/10.1007/978-3-540-71067-7_16

15. Crafa, S., Di Pirro, M., Zucca, E.: Is solidity solid enough? In: Bracciali, A., Clark, J., Pintore, F., Rønne, P.B., Sala, M. (eds.) FC 2019. LNCS, vol. 11599, pp. 138–153. Springer, Cham (2020). https://doi.org/10.1007/978-3-030-43725-1_11

16. Crosara, M., Centurino, G., Arceri, V.: Towards an operational semantics for solidity. In: van Rooyen, J., Buro, S., Campion, M., Pasqua, M. (eds.) VALID, pp. 1–6. IARIA (2019)

17. Dijkstra, E.W.: Guarded commands, nondeterminacy and formal derivation of programs. Commun. ACM **18**(8), 453–457 (1975). https://doi.org/10.1145/360933.360975

18. Ethereum: Solidity. https://docs.soliditylang.org/. Accessed 24 May 2023

19. Gartner. Forecast blockchain business value, worldwide (2019). https://www.gartner.com/en/documents/3627117. Accessed 04 May 2023

20. Hajdu, Á., Jovanović, D.: SOLC-VERIFY: a modular verifier for solidity smart contracts. In: Chakraborty, S., Navas, J.A. (eds.) VSTTE 2019. LNCS, vol. 12031, pp. 161–179. Springer, Cham (2020). https://doi.org/10.1007/978-3-030-41600-3_11

21. Hajdu, Á., Jovanovic, D.: Smt-friendly formalization of the Solidity memory model. In: Müller, P. (ed.) ESOP. LNCS, vol. 12075, pp. 224–250. Springer, Cham (2020). https://doi.org/10.1007/978-3-030-44914-8_9

22. Jiao, J., Kan, S., Lin, S.W., Sanan, D., Liu, Y., Sun, J.: Semantic understanding of smart contracts: executable operational semantics of Solidity. In: SP, pp. 1695–1712. IEEE (2020)

23. Jiao, J., Lin, S.-W., Sun, J.: A generalized formal semantic framework for smart contracts. In: FASE 2020. LNCS, vol. 12076, pp. 75–96. Springer, Cham (2020). https://doi.org/10.1007/978-3-030-45234-6_4

24. Kelly, J.: Banks adopting blockchain 'dramatically faster' than expected: IBM. https://www.reuters.com/article/us-tech-blockchain-ibm-idUSKCN11Y28D (2016). Accessed 04 May 2023

25. Llama, D.: Tvl breakdown by smart contract language. https://defillama.com/languages (2022)

26. Marmsoler, D., Brucker, A.D.: A denotational semantics of solidity in Isabelle/HOL. In: Calinescu, R., Păsăreanu, C.S. (eds.) SEFM 2021. LNCS, vol. 13085, pp. 403–422. Springer, Cham (2021). https://doi.org/10.1007/978-3-030-92124-8_23

27. Marmsoler, D., Brucker, A.D.: Conformance testing of formal semantics using grammar-based fuzzing. In: Kovács, L., Meinke, K. (eds.) Tests and Proofs, pp. 106–125. Springer, Cham (2022). https://doi.org/10.1007/978-3-031-09827-7_7

28. Marmsoler, D., Brucker, A.D.: Isabelle/solidity: a deep embedding of solidity in isabelle/hol. Archive of Formal Proofs (2022). https://isa-afp.org/entries/Solidity.html. Formal proof development

29. Marmsoler, D., Thornton, B.: SSCalc - A Calculus for Solidity Smart Contracts (2023). https://doi.org/10.5281/zenodo.7846232

30. Matichuk, D., Wenzel, M., Murray, T.: An Isabelle proof method language. In: Klein, G, Gamboa, R. (eds.) ITP 2014. LNCS, vol. 8558, pp. 390–405. Springer, Cham (2014). https://doi.org/10.1007/978-3-319-08970-6_25

31. Mavridou, A., Laszka, A., Stachtiari, E., Dubey, A.: Verisolid: correct-by-design smart contracts for Ethereum. In: FC (2019)

32. Mavridou, A., Laszka, A.: Tool demonstration: FSolidM for designing secure ethereum smart contracts. In: Bauer, L., Küsters, R. (eds.) POST 2018. LNCS, vol. 10804, pp. 270–277. Springer, Cham (2018). https://doi.org/10.1007/978-3-319-89722-6_11

33. Nakamoto, S.: Bitcoin: A Peer-to-Peer Electronic Cash System (2008)
34. News, B.: Hackers steal $600m in major cryptocurrency heist (2021). https://www.securityweek.com/hackers-steal-over-600m-major-crypto-heist. Accessed 04 May 2023
35. Nipkow, T., Paulson, L.C., Wenzel, M.: Isabelle/HOL: A Proof Assistant for Higher-Order Logic (2002)
36. Perez, D., Livshits, B.: Smart contract vulnerabilities: vulnerable does not imply exploited. In: 30th USENIX Security Symposium (USENIX Security 21), pp. 1325–1341. USENIX Association (2021)
37. The COQ Development Team. The COQ proof assistant reference manual. LogiCal Project (2004). version 8.0
38. TNW. These are the top 10 programming languages in blockchain (2019). https://thenextweb.com/news/javascript-programming-java-cryptocurrency. Accessed 04 May 2023
39. Vogelsteller, F., Buterin, V.: "erc-20: token standard", ethereum improvement proposals, no. 20 (2015). https://eips.ethereum.org/EIPS/eip-20
40. Wadler, P.: Monads for functional programming. In: Broy, M. (ed.) Program Design Calculi, pp. 233–264. Springer, Heidelberg (1993). https://doi.org/10.1007/978-3-662-02880-3_8
41. Yang, Z., Lei, H.: Lolisa: Formal syntax and semantics for a subset of the solidity programming language in mathematical tool COQ. Math. Probl. Eng. **2020**, 6191537 (2020)
42. YCharts.com. Ethereum transactions per day (2022). https://ycharts.com/indicators/ethereum_transactions_per_day. Accessed 04 May 2023
43. Yurcan, B.: How blockchain fits into the future of digital identity (2016)
44. Zakrzewski, J.: Towards verification of Ethereum smart contracts. In: Piskac, R., Rümmer, P. (eds.) VSTTE. LNCS, vol. 11294, pp. 229–247. Springer, Cham (2018). https://doi.org/10.1007/978-3-030-03592-1_13

ATM: A Logic for Quantitative Security Properties on Attack Trees

Stefano M. Nicoletti[1](✉)(iD), Milan Lopuhaä-Zwakenberg[1](iD),
Ernst Moritz Hahn[1](iD), and Mariëlle Stoelinga[1,2](iD)

[1] Formal Methods and Tools, University of Twente, Enschede, the Netherlands
{s.m.nicoletti,m.a.lopuhaa,e.m.hahn,m.i.a.stoelinga}@utwente.nl
[2] Department of Software Science, Radboud University, Nijmegen, The Netherlands

Abstract. Critical infrastructure systems—for which high reliability and availability are paramount—must operate securely. Attack trees (ATs) are hierarchical diagrams that offer a flexible modelling language used to assess how systems can be attacked. ATs are widely employed both in industry and academia but—in spite of their popularity—little work has been done to give practitioners instruments to formulate queries on ATs in an understandable yet powerful way. In this paper we fill this gap by presenting ATM, a logic to express quantitative security properties on ATs. ATM allows for the specification of properties involved with *security metrics* that include "cost", "probability" and "skill" and permits the formulation of insightful what-if scenarios. To showcase its potential, we apply ATM to the case study of a CubeSAT, presenting three different ways in which an attacker can compromise its availability. We showcase property specification on the corresponding attack tree and we present theory and algorithms—based on binary decision diagrams—to check properties and compute metrics of ATM-formulae.

1 Introduction

Critical infrastructure systems—for which high reliability and availability are paramount—must operate securely. Attack trees (ATs) [54] are a flexible modelling language used to assess how systems can be attacked. They operate by decomposing the attacker's goal into intermediate elements and basic attack steps that a malicious actor can take to reach said objective. ATs are widely employed both in industry and academia but—in spite of their popularity—little work has been done to give practitioners instruments to formulate queries on ATs in an understandable yet powerful way. In this paper, we fill this gap by presenting a logic to express quantitative Metrics on ATs (ATM). ATM is a powerful language able to formulate structural queries on ATs that consider quantitative security properties, or *security metrics*, such as "cost" of an attack, "probability" of getting attacked and "skill" of a malicious actor. The ability to formulate these queries is essential to provide

---

This work was partially funded by the European Union's Horizon 2020 research and innovation programme under the Marie Skłodowska-Curie grant agreement No 101008233, and the ERC Consolidator Grant 864075 (*CAESAR*).

practitioners with an instrument to analyse what-if scenarios and to propel a more quantitatively-informed decision making process.

Attack Trees. Attack trees (ATs) are hierarchical diagrams that represent various ways in which a system can be compromised [42,54]. Due to their popularity, ATs are referred to by many system engineering frameworks, e.g. *UMLsec* [35] and *SysMLsec* [3,53], and are supported by industrial tools such as

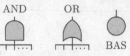

Fig. 1.   Nodes in an attack tree.

Isograph's *AttackTree* [31]. The root—or *top level event* (TLE)—of an AT represents the attacker's goal, and the leaves represent *basic attack steps* (BASes): actions of the attacker that can no longer be refined. Intermediate nodes are labeled with gates (see Fig. 1) that determine how basic actions of the attacker can propagate to reach higher-complexity elements in the attack. ATs that do not capture dynamic behaviours present only OR and AND gates—we call these *static attack trees* (SATs)—but many extensions exist to model more elaborate attacks. To build a solid and modular foundation for our framework, this paper focuses on SATs. It is important to note that—despite their name—ATs can be *directed acyclic graphs* (DAGs), i.e., graphs in which a node may have multiple parents. Them being DAGs or tree-structured has consequences on computations [42].

Example 1. Consider the AT in Fig. 2 (excerpt from Fig. 6). This AT represents different attacks to get access to the ground station database of a CubeSAT as admin. The TLE of this sub-tree is represented by the *ADA* AND-gate. For the attacker to reach *ADA*, they have to both gain access—the *GA* AND-gate — and escalate privileges—the *EP* OR-gate. Each of these gates is then refined by BASes: to gain access, an attacker must perform information gathering and a successful phishing attack—the *IGP* BAS—and login to the ground station database using phished credentials—the *LDG* BAS. In addition, they have to *either* leverage misconfigurations—the *LM* BAS—or exploit vulnerabilities—the *EV* BAS—to escalate privileges. Note that *IGP* is represented here as a BAS but is further refined as an additional sub-tree in Fig. 6.

Metrics on Attack Trees. ATs are often studied via *quantitative analysis*, during which they are assigned a wide range of security metrics [15,42]. Such metrics are key performance indicators that formalize how well a system performs in terms of security and are essential when comparing alternatives or making trade-offs. Typi-

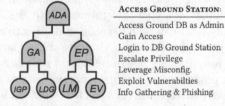

ACCESS GROUND STATION:

Access Ground DB as Admin	ADA
Gain Access	GA
Login to DB Ground Station	LDG
Escalate Privilege	EP
Leverage Misconfig.	LM
Exploit Vulnerabilties	EV
Info Gathering & Phishing	IGP

Fig. 2. AT modelling access to ground station DB of a CubeSAT (excerpt from Fig. 6).

cal examples of such metrics are the minimal time [5,38,39,43], minimal cost [4], or maximal probability [33] of a successful attack (see Table 1 for more examples).

1.1   Our Approach

A Logic for Attack Trees Metrics (ATM). To perform quantitatively informed decision making w.r.t. security of systems, practitioners need the ability to analyse their models in a meaningful and thorough way. As such, they must be able to formulate *meaningful queries* and meaningful *what-if scenarios*. To cater for this need, this paper presents ATM, a logic for general Metrics on Attack Trees. ATM is a flexible language used to specify properties that take metrics such as "cost", "skill" and "probability" into account directly on ATs. ATM is structured on four layers: these allow practitioners a) to reason about *successful/unsuccessful* attacks; b) to check whether metrics, such as the cost, are bounded by a given value on single attacks; c) to compute metrics for a class of attacks and d) to perform quantification.

Attack Trees in Practice. To offer a concrete example, we utilise ATM to specify some properties on the AT model of a CubeSAT [32,46] from the literature [22] (see Fig. 6). This model exemplifies the effect of a security threat for the availability of a system by showcasing three ways in which a malicious actor could attack a CubeSAT: performing a denial of service attack, tampering with data on the database of the ground station or killing radio communications on the satellite. Our logic can be used to specify properties on the corresponding AT and to check whether the system under examination exhibits desired characteristics. Is it necessary to leverage misconfigurations to perform a successful attack on CubeSAT's communications? Is there an attack that ensures successful access to the ground station database while keeping the cost under a certain threshold? Is there an attack that ensures data tampering without exploiting vulnerabilities in the ground station system? These are some of the properties that one could specify and check in the framework we present.

Model Checking Algorithms. In addition, we present model checking algorithms to check properties specified with ATM and to efficiently compute metrics that appear in these properties. In particular, we provide algorithms to a) check whether an AT and an attack satisfy a formula; b) compute all attacks that satisfy an AT and a formula; c) check whether the metric of a formula is bounded by a user-specified threshold; d) compute the metric value of formulae and e) check whether a quantified ATM-formula holds true. Building on previous work in the field [15,42,47,48], all these algorithms are based on construction and manipulation of binary decision diagrams (BDDs). This translation to BDDs constitutes a formal ground to address algorithmic procedures while integrating novel work presented in this paper with previously introduced frameworks.

Contributions. To summarize, in this work:
1. We develop ATM, a logic to reason about general metrics on ATs. ATM allows for the specification of metrics properties that include "cost", "proability" and "skill" and for the formulation of insightful what-if scenarios.
2. We showcase ATM by applying it to the case study of a CubeSAT and by exemplifying properties specification.
3. We propose novel algorithms based on BDDs to perform model checking and to compute metrics on properties specified using ATM.

1.2   Related Work

Numerous logics describe properties of state transition systems, such as labelled transition systems (LTSs) and Markov models, e.g., CTL [18], LTL [50], and their variants for Markov models, PCTL [28] and PLTL [49]. State-transition systems are usually not written by hand, but are the result of the semantics of high-level description mechanisms, such as AADL [12], the hardware description language VHDL [20] or model description languages such as JANI [14] or PRISM [41]. Consequently, these logics are not used to reason about the structure of such models (e.g. the placement of circuit elements in a VHDL model or the structure of modules in a PRISM model), but on the temporal behaviour of the underlying state-transition system. Similarly the majority of related work [9,11,55,56] on model checking on *fault trees* (FTs)—the safety counterpart of ATs—exhibits significant differences: these works perform model checking by referring to states in the underlying stochastic models, and properties are formulated in terms of these stochastic logics, not in terms of events in the given FT. In [57], the author provides a formulation of *Pandora*, a logic for the qualitative analysis of temporal FTs. In [27] the authors investigate how fault tree analysis (FTA) results can be linked to software safety requirements by proposing the same system model for both. They introduce a duration calculus based on discrete time interval logic (ITL) [45] to give FTs formal semantics. In [47,48] the authors present *BFL*—a logic on FTs that reasons about them in Boolean terms—and *PFL*—its probabilistic counterpart. Our work is aligned in intentions to the latter two, as we develop a logic directly on ATs. However, where they reason on FTs only in Boolean or probabilistic terms, our work exhibits a broader scope by allowing for more general queries on an ample class of security metrics. Regarding AT metrics, a seminal paper by Mauw & Oosdijk [44] shows that metrics can be computed for static ATs in a bottom-up fashion. Furthermore, [16,34] are among the first to model and compute the cost and probability of attacks. In [38,39] an attack is moreover characterised by the time it takes. In the related literature, most works are on static ATs, with the relevant exception of [5,15,25,33,42] which include sequential-AND gates. However, for static ATs the algorithmic spectrum remains broader [42]. Such algorithms range from classical BDD encodings for probabilities, and extensions to multi-terminal BDDs, to logic-based semantics that exploit DPLL, including an encoding of SATs as generalised stochastic Petri nets. Prominent contributions are [10] and [37, Alg. 1]: after computing so-called optional and necessary clones, computations are exponential on the number of shared BAS (only). A thorough analysis of the literature on metrics computation for ATs can be found in [15,42]. These two contributions provide efficient and general algorithms to compute security metrics on ATs. We choose to adhere to their perspective on metrics computations as it subsumes and generalizes most of the already available literature.

Structure of the Paper. Section 2 covers background on ATs, Sect. 3 presents syntax and semantics for ATM, Sect. 4 showcases an application of ATM to a CubeSAT AT, Sect. 5 presents model checking algorithms for ATM−formulae and Sect. 6 concludes the paper and discusses future work.

2   Attack Trees

Definition 1. *An* attack tree *(AT) T is a tuple (N, E, t) where (N, E) is a rooted directed acyclic graph, and $t \colon N \to \{\mathtt{OR}, \mathtt{AND}, \mathtt{BAS}\}$ is a function such that for $v \in N$, it holds that $t(v) = \mathtt{BAS}$ if and only if v is a leaf.*

Moreover, $ch \colon N \to \mathscr{P}(N)$ gives the set of *children* of a node and T has a unique root, denoted R_T. The subindex T is omitted if no ambiguity arises, e.g. an attack tree $T = (N, t, ch)$ defines a set $\mathrm{BAS} \subseteq N$ of basic attack steps. If $u \in ch(v)$ then u is called a *child* of v, and v is a *parent* of u. We let $v = \mathrm{AND}(v_1, \ldots, v_n)$ if $t(v) = \mathtt{AND}$ and $ch(v) = (v_1, \ldots, v_n)$, and analogously for OR, denoting $ch(v) = \{v_1, \ldots, v_n\}$. Furthermore, we denote the universe of ATs by $\mathscr{T}$ and call $T \in \mathscr{T}$ *tree-structured* if for any two nodes u and v none of their children is shared, else we say that T is *DAG-structured*. If only AND- and OR-gates (or their derivatives) are present we say that T is a *static attack tree* (SAT). In this paper we focus our attention on SATs and thus use the term ATs interchangeably to denote them. The semantics of a AT is defined by its successful attack scenarios, in turn given by its structure function. First, the notion of attack is defined:

Definition 2. *An* attack scenario, *or shortly an* attack, *of a static AT T is a subset of its basic attack steps: $A \subseteq \mathrm{BAS}_T$. We denote by $\mathscr{A}_T = 2^{\mathrm{BAS}_T}$ the universe of attacks of T. We omit the subscript when there is no confusion.*

The structure function $f_T(v, A)$ indicates whether the attack $A \in \mathscr{A}$ succeeds at node $v \in N$ of T. For Booleans we adopt $\mathbb{B} = \{1, 0\}$.

Definition 3. *The* structure function $f_T \colon N \times \mathscr{A} \to \mathbb{B}$ *of a static attack tree T is given by:*

$$
f_T(v, A) = \begin{cases}
1 & \textit{if } t(v) = \mathtt{OR} \quad \textit{and } \exists u \in ch(v).f_T(u, A) = 1, \\
1 & \textit{if } t(v) = \mathtt{AND} \quad \textit{and } \forall u \in ch(v).f_T(u, A) = 1, \\
1 & \textit{if } t(v) = \mathtt{BAS} \quad \textit{and } v \in A, \\
0 & \textit{otherwise.}
\end{cases}
$$

An attack A is said to *reach* a node v if $f_T(v, A) = 1$, i.e. it makes v succeed. If no proper subset of A reaches v, then A is a *minimal attack on* v. The set of minimal attacks on v is denoted $\llbracket v \rrbracket$.
We define $f_T(A) \doteq f_T(R_T, A)$, and attacks that reach R_T are called *succesful* w.r.t. T. Furthermore, the

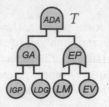

Given T, the set of its minimal attacks is
$\llbracket T \rrbracket = \{\{IGP, LDG, LM\},$
$\{IGP, LDG, EV\}\}$

Fig. 3. All minimal attacks for AT T modelling access to ground station DB of a CubeSAT (excerpt from Fig. 6).

minimal attacks on R_T (i.e. the minimal successful attacks) are called *minimal attacks*. ATs are *coherent* [6], meaning that adding attack steps preserves success: if A is successful then so is $A \cup \{a\}$ for any $a \in BAS$. Thus, the suite of successful attacks of an AT is characterised by its minimal attacks.

Definition 4. *The* semantics *of an AT T is its suite of minimal attacks $\llbracket T \rrbracket$.*

Example 2. Consider the AT in Fig. 3 representing ways to access the ground station database of a CubeSAT as admin: its suite of minimal attacks consists of $\{\{IGP, LDG, LM\}, \{IGP, LDG, EV\}\}$. That is, to mount a minimal attack a malicious actor needs to gain access performing information gathering and phishing IGP—a BAS that is further refined in Fig. 6—and by logging into the DB of the ground station; to then *either* leverage misconfigurations LM or exploit vulnerabilities EV in the DB software to gain admin privileges. A non-minimal attack on this AT would include both LM and EV.

2.1 Security Metrics for Attack Trees

Security metrics—such as the minimal time and cost among all attacks—are essential to perform quantitative analysis of systems and to support more informed decision making processes. To enable this, i.e. computing security metrics, we adopt the well-established *semiring* framework. Semirings have vast applicability potential [26] and have been successfully used to construct attribute domains on ATs [15,30,36,42]. In this paper, we formulate *linearly ordered unital semiring attribute domains* where V is the value domain, $\triangle$ is an operator to combine values of BASes in an attack, $\triangledown$ is an operator to combine values of different attacks and $\preceq$ is an order to compare values. These *linearly ordered unital semiring attribute domains* provide a convenient way to define an ample class of metrics including "min cost", "min time"—both with parallel or sequential attack steps—"min skill" and "discrete probability".

Definition 5. *A* linearly ordered unital semiring attribute domain *(simply* attribute domain *or* LOAD *from now on) is a tuple* $L = (V, \triangledown, \triangle, 1_\triangledown, 1_\triangle, \preceq)$ *where:*

- V *is a set;*
- $\triangledown, \triangle \colon V^2 \to V$ *are commutative, associative binary operations on V;*
- $\triangle$ *distributes over* $\triangledown$, *i.e.,* $x \triangle (y \triangledown z) = (x \triangledown y) \triangle (x \triangledown z)$ *for all $x, y, z \in V$;*

- ∇ *is absorbing w.r.t.* $\triangle$, *i.e.,* $x \nabla (x \triangle y) = x$ *for all* $x, y \in V$;
- 1_∇ *and* $1_\triangle$ *are unital elements, i.e.,* $1_\nabla \nabla x = 1_\triangle \triangle x = \dot{x}$ *for all* $x \in V$;
- $\preceq$ *is a linear order on* V.

As anticipated, many relevant metrics for security analyses on ATs can be formulated as attribute domains. Table 1 shows examples, where $\mathbb{N}_\infty = \mathbb{N} \cup \{\infty\}$ includes 0 and ∞.

Example 3. An example of a LOAD is $(\mathbb{N}_\infty, \min, +, \infty, 0, \leq)$. Indeed, min and $+$ are commutative, associative operations on $\mathbb{N}_\infty$. The distributive property amounts to the fact that $x + \min(y, z) = \min(x + y, x + z)$, while the absorbing property can be stated as $\min(x, x + y) = x$. The units are given by $1_{\min} = \infty$ and $1_+ = 0$, and $\leq$ is a linear order on $\mathbb{N}_\infty$. As we will discuss in Example 4, this LOAD corresponds to the *min cost* metric on ATs.

It is important to note that derived metrics such as stochastic analyses and Pareto frontiers can be represented by semirings. However, they do not fit in this framework not being LOADs [42]. Moreover, some meaningful metrics—like the cost to defend against all

Table 1. AT metrics with attribute domains.

METRIC	V	∇	$\triangle$	1_∇	$1_\triangle$	$\preceq$
min cost	$\mathbb{N}_\infty$	min	$+$	∞	0	$\leq$
min time (sequential)	$\mathbb{N}_\infty$	min	$+$	∞	0	$\leq$
min time (parallel)	$\mathbb{N}_\infty$	min	max	∞	0	$\leq$
min skill	$\mathbb{N}_\infty$	min	max	∞	0	$\leq$
discrete prob	$[0, 1]$	max	$\cdot$	0	1	$\leq$

attacks—do fall outside this category [42]. To render this framework functional, all BASes of ATs are enriched with attributes. More precisely, first an *attribution* α assigns a value to each BAS; then a *security metric* $\widehat{\alpha}$ assigns a value to each attack scenario; and finally the *metric* $\breve{\alpha}$ assigns a value to the set of minimal attacks. We then refer to LOADs to define AT metrics. Given a LOAD $(V, \nabla, \triangle, 1_\nabla, 1_\triangle, \preceq)$ we assign to each BAS a an *attribute value* $\alpha(a) \in V$. The operators $\nabla, \triangle$ are then used to define a metric value for T as follows:

Definition 6. *Let* T *be an AT and let* $L = (V, \nabla, \triangle, 1_\nabla, 1_\triangle, \preceq)$ *be a LOAD.*

1. *An attribution on* T *with values in* L *is a map* $\alpha : BAS_T \to V$;
2. *Given such* α, *define the* metric value *of an attack* A *by*

$$\widehat{\alpha}(A) = \bigwedge_{a \in A} \alpha(a);$$

3. *Given such* α, *define the* metric value *of* T *by*

$$\breve{\alpha}(T) = \bigvee_{A \in [\![T]\!]} \widehat{\alpha}(A) = \bigvee_{A \in [\![T]\!]} \bigwedge_{a \in A} \alpha(a).$$

Example 4. Consider L from Example 3 representing the metric *min cost*, and let T be the AT in Fig. 4. To each BAS we attach a cost value, given by the attribution $\alpha : BAS_T \to V$ given by $\{IGP \mapsto 15, LDG \mapsto 2, LM \mapsto 7, EV \mapsto 9\}$.

As in Example 2, T has two minimal attacks, $A_1 = \{IGP, LDG, LM\}$ and $A_2 = \{IGP, LDG, EV\}$. Since $\triangle = +$, We have $\widehat{\alpha}(A_1) = \alpha(IGP) + \alpha(LDG) + \alpha(LM) = 15 + 2 + 7 = 24$; this is the cost an attacker needs to spend to perform attack A_1. Similarly one finds $\widehat{\alpha}(A_2) = 15 + 2 + 9 = 26$. We then calculate $\breve{\alpha}(T) = \min(\widehat{\alpha}(A_1), \widehat{\alpha}(A_2)) = 24$. Indeed, the minimal cost incurred by an attacker to succesfully attack the system is by performing the cheapest minimal attack, which is A_1.

When computing multiple metrics on a given AT, one can resort to multiple LOADs and coherently chosen attributions over its BASes. We thus define such a tree as follows:

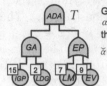

Given T and an attribution over BASes
$\alpha : \{IGP \mapsto 15, LDG \mapsto 2, LM \mapsto 7, EV \mapsto 9\}$,
then *min cost* for T is calculated as follows:

$\breve{\alpha}(T) = \widehat{\alpha}(\{IGP, LDG, LM\}) \triangledown \widehat{\alpha}(\{IGP, LDG, EV\})$
$= \widehat{\alpha}(\{IGP \triangle LDG \triangle LM\}) \triangledown \widehat{\alpha}(\{IGP \triangle LDG \triangle EV\})$
$= \min(15 + 2 + 7, 15 + 2 + 9) = \min(24, 26) = 24.$

Fig. 4. Computing *min cost* for T: AT for accessing a ground station DB of a CubeSAT (excerpt from Fig. 6).

Definition 7. *An* attributed AT *is a tuple* $\mathsf{T} = (T, \mathscr{L}, \mathfrak{a})$ *where: 1. T is an attack tree; 2. $\mathscr{L} = \{L_1, \ldots, L_l\}$ is a set of LOADs; 3. $\mathfrak{a} = \{\alpha_i\}_{i=1}^l$ is a set of attributions on T, where each α_i takes values in L_i.*

Although in this paper we calculate metrics by considering all *minimal* attacks—coherently with [15,42]—one could also simply consider all successful attacks. For metrics obtained from LOADs this does not make a difference: for example, the successful attack with minimal cost will always be a minimal attack, since adding BASes can only increase the cost. Therefore, in the calculation of min cost we may as well take the minimum over all successful attacks, rather than just minimal attacks.

3   A Logic for at General Metrics

3.1   Syntax of ATM

Below, we present ATM, a logic for general Metrics on Attack Trees. ATM shares the objective of developing a language directly on tree-shaped models with [47, 48]. However, it extends the scope of these works to the security domain and allows for property specification that consider a large class of security metrics. The syntax of ATM is structured on four layers. The first layer, ϕ, reasons about the status of elements in an AT. Atomic formulae e represent BASes and IEs in an AT and they can be combined with usual Boolean connectives. Furthermore, we can forcefully set the value of an element in a layer 1 formula to either 0 or 1 with $\phi[e \mapsto 0]$ and $\phi[e \mapsto 1]$. With $\mathrm{MA}(\phi)$ we can check whether an attack is a *minimal attack*, i.e., a minimal attack successful for a given ϕ. Layer two and three reason about metrics. Layer 2 formulae allow the user to check whether a given metric on a ϕ formula is bounded by m $(\mathbb{M}_k(\phi) \preceq_k m)$ and to forcefully

set the attribution of a given $e \in \psi$ to an appropriate value ν ($\psi[e \overset{k}{\mapsto} \nu]$).
Boolean connectives are also allowed. Layer 3 formulae also allow the setting of
attributions but simply return the *value* of a calculated metric ($\mathbb{V}_k(\phi)$). Note
that for the layer 1, layer 2 and layer 3 formulae we usually assign values with
$\mapsto$ to $e \in \mathsf{BAS}$. We can however assign values to IEs if 1. e is a module [21], i.e.,
all paths between descendants of e and the rest of the AT pass through e 2. and
none of the descendants of e. are present in the formula. If so, we prune that
(sub-)AT and treat occurring IEs as BASes. Finally, layer 4 formulae allow us to
perform quantification over layer 1 and layer 2 formulae. Given a set of LOADs
$\mathscr{L} = \{L_1, \dots, L_l\}$ with $L_k \in \mathscr{L}$ and $m \in V_k$ the syntax is defined as follows:

Layer 1: $\phi ::= e \mid \neg\phi \mid \phi \land \phi \mid \phi[e \mapsto 0] \mid \phi[e \mapsto 1] \mid \mathrm{MA}(\phi)$

Layer 2: $\psi ::= \neg\psi \mid \psi \land \psi \mid \mathbb{M}_k(\phi) \preceq_k m \mid \psi[e \overset{k}{\mapsto} \nu]$

Layer 3: $\xi ::= \mathbb{V}_k(\phi) \mid \xi[e \overset{k}{\mapsto} \nu]$

Layer 4: $\gamma ::= \neg\gamma \mid \exists(\phi \land \psi) \mid \forall(\phi \land \psi)$

Syntactic Sugar. We define the following derived operators, where formulae θ
are either layer 1 or layer 2 formulae.

$$\theta_1 \lor \theta_2 ::= \neg(\neg\theta_1 \land \neg\theta_2) \qquad \theta_1 \not\Leftrightarrow \theta_2 ::= \neg(\theta_1 \Leftrightarrow \theta_2)$$
$$\theta_1 \Rightarrow \theta_2 ::= \neg(\theta_1 \land \neg\theta_2) \qquad \mathrm{MD}(\phi) ::= \mathrm{MA}(\neg\phi)$$
$$\theta_1 \Leftrightarrow \theta_2 ::= (\theta_1 \Rightarrow \theta_2) \land (\theta_2 \Rightarrow \theta_1)$$

where $\mathrm{MD}(\phi)$ checks whether A is a *minimal defence* w.r.t. ϕ, i.e., a set that
guarantees that ϕ is not reached.

3.2 Semantics of ATM

The semantics for our logic reflect objects needed to evaluate the four syntactical
layers. For the first layer of ATM, formulae are evaluated on an attack A and on
a tree T. Atomic formulae e are satisfied by A and T if the structure function in
Definition 3 returns 1 with A and e as input. Formally:

$$
\begin{aligned}
&A, T \models e && \text{iff } f_T(e, A) = 1 \\
&A, T \models \neg\phi && \text{iff } A, T \not\models \phi \\
&A, T \models \phi \land \phi' && \text{iff } A, T \models \phi \text{ and } A, T \models \phi' \\
&A, T \models \phi[e_i \mapsto 0] && \text{iff } A', T \models \phi \text{ with } A' = \{a'_1, \dots, a'_n\} \text{ where} \\
&&& a'_i = 0 \text{ and } a'_j = a_j \text{ for } j \neq i \\
&A, T \models \phi[e_i \mapsto 1] && \text{iff } A', T \models \phi \text{ with } A' = \{a'_1, \dots, a'_n\} \text{ where} \\
&&& a'_i = 1 \text{ and } a'_j = a_j \text{ for } j \neq i \\
&A, T \models \mathrm{MA}(\phi) && \text{iff } A \in \llbracket\phi\rrbracket_T
\end{aligned}
$$

With $\llbracket\phi\rrbracket_T$ we denote the *minimal satisfaction set* of attacks for ϕ, i.e., the set
of minimal attacks that satisfy ϕ given T. We define $\llbracket\phi\rrbracket_T$ as follows: $\llbracket\phi\rrbracket_T = \{A \mid$

$A, T \models \phi \wedge \nexists A' \subseteq A . A', T \models \phi$}. It is important to note that—with semantics defined as we did—we allow for fairly granular reasoning over ATs. In particular, we can evaluate whether an attack compromises a particular sub-AT without *reaching* the TLE. Semantics for the second and third layer require *attributed trees* (see Definition 7). We can then define semantics for the second layer:

$$
\begin{aligned}
A, \mathsf{T} &\models \neg \psi & &\text{iff } A, \mathsf{T} \not\models \psi \\
A, \mathsf{T} &\models \psi \wedge \psi' & &\text{iff } A, \mathsf{T} \models \psi \text{ and } A, \mathsf{T} \models \psi' \\
A, \mathsf{T} &\models \mathbb{M}_k(\phi) \preceq_k m & &\text{iff } A, T \models \phi \wedge \widehat{\alpha}(A) \preceq_k m \\
A, \mathsf{T} &\models \psi[e_i \overset{k}{\mapsto} \nu] & &\text{iff } A, \mathsf{T}(\mathfrak{a}[\alpha_k(a_i) \overset{k}{\mapsto} \nu]) \models \psi
\end{aligned}
$$

For an attack A and an attributed tree T to satisfy $\mathbb{M}_k(\phi) \preceq_k m$, both the attack A and the tree T must satisfy the inner layer 1 formula and the security metric calculated on the attack must respect the given threshold. We let X_1 be the set of layer 1 formulae and we define a ϕ-*security metric* to attribute a value to a layer 1 formula:

Definition 8. *A ϕ-security metric is a function* $\breve{\alpha}^{\mathsf{T}} : X_1 \to V$ *defined as follows:*

$$
\breve{\alpha}^{\mathsf{T}}(\phi) = \bigvee_{A \in [\![\phi]\!]_T} \; \bigwedge_{a \in A} \alpha(a).
$$

Note that in Definition 8 some occurrences can lead to the application of the $\breve{\alpha}$ function to the empty set, i.e., when $[\![\phi]\!]_T = \varnothing$. To account for this, we resort to $1_\triangledown$ and $1_\triangle$ for $\triangledown$ and $\triangle$ (see Definition 5). Assuming the case in which $\breve{\alpha}^{\mathsf{T}}(\phi) \equiv \breve{\alpha}(\varnothing)$, we fix that $\breve{\alpha}^{\mathsf{T}}(\phi) = 1_\triangledown$; likewise for $\widehat{\alpha}$ and $1_\triangle$. Furthermore, with $\breve{\alpha}^{\mathsf{T}_k} : X_1 \to V_k$ we denote a ϕ-security metric whose domain and attribution are obtained appropriately from the k-est LOAD $L_k \in \mathscr{L}$. We then let $\mathfrak{a}[\alpha_k(a_i) \overset{k}{\mapsto} \nu]$ be the attribution on the element $a_i \in A$ via α_k to an arbitrary value ν, chosen appropriately from the domain V_k of L_k. Consequently, we define semantics for the third layer. Let $\mathsf{Val}_\mathsf{T} : X_3 \to V_k$ define an evaluation function of layer three formulae in X_3:

$$
\begin{aligned}
\mathsf{Val}_\mathsf{T}(\mathbb{V}_k(\phi)) &= \breve{\alpha}^{\mathsf{T}_k}(\phi) \\
\mathsf{Val}_\mathsf{T}(\xi[e_i \overset{k}{\mapsto} \nu]) &= \mathsf{Val}_{\mathsf{T}(\mathfrak{a}[\alpha_k(a_i) \overset{k}{\mapsto} \nu])}(\xi)
\end{aligned}
$$

Finally, we can define semantics for the fourth layer containing quantifiers:

$$
\begin{aligned}
\mathsf{T} &\models \neg \gamma & &\text{iff } \mathsf{T} \not\models \gamma \\
\mathsf{T} &\models \exists(\phi \wedge \psi) & &\text{iff } \exists A . A, T \models \phi \text{ and } A, \mathsf{T} \models \psi \\
\mathsf{T} &\models \forall(\phi \wedge \psi) & &\text{iff } \forall A . A, T \models \phi \text{ and } A, \mathsf{T} \models \psi
\end{aligned}
$$

4 Case Study: Attacking a CubeSAT

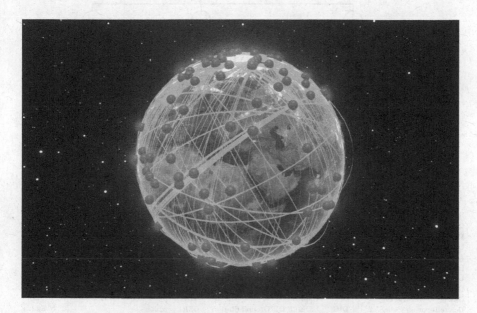

Fig. 5. Representation of orbiting CubeSATs.

CubeSATs are a type of *nanosatellite* typically used for academic and educational purposes [46]: they are usually built in units (or "U") of 10cm x 10cm x 10cm and can be combined to form larger satellites. They are relatively inexpensive to design, build, and launch compared to traditional, larger satellites and they are a popular choice among students, universities, technology pioneers, and crowd-sourced initiatives [32]. To give a sense of the importance of CubeSATs in our orbital ecosystem, we provide a representation of orbiting CubeSATs as of March 2023 in Fig. 5 and an animation in [23]. A total of 153 elements are plotted on the Earth, following data provided by the online database Celestrack [17]. The size of each sphere is exaggerated for visual purposes—a diameter of 500km for each element—and satellites are propagated using the Simplified General Perturbations 4 (SGP4) orbit propagator [29]. As CubeSATs are one of the platforms achieving more consensus in the context of the "New Space" [19,32], it is fundamental that security risks on these systems are not overlooked. To cater for this need, we showcase how ATM can be applied to specify useful properties on CubeSATs.

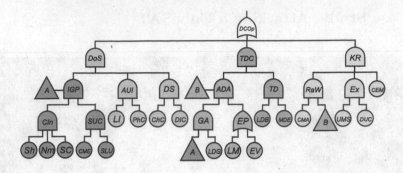

Fig. 6. An AT representing ways to attack a CubeSAT.

Table 2. Abbreviations for the AT in Fig. 6.

CubeSAT TLE:		Info Gathering + Phish:		Data Tampering:	
Disrupt CubeSAT Operations	DCOp	Info Gathering & Phishing	IGP	Tamper Data from CubeSAT	TDC
DoS Attack:		Collect Information	CIn	Tamper with Data	TD
Denial of Service	DoS	Shodan	Sh	Login to DB as Admin	LDB
Access CubeSAT UI	AUI	NMAP	Nm	Modify Database Entries	MDE
Locate Interfaces	LI	Scrape Credentials	SC	Kill Comms on CubeSAT:	
Login with Phished Creds	PhC	Access Ground Station:		Kill Radio on CubeSAT	KR
Disrupt Service	DS	Access Ground DB as Admin	ADA	Recon. and Weaponization	RaW
Change Config. Settings	ChC	Gain Access	GA	Create Malicious App	CMA
Delete Items on CubeSAT	DIC	Login to DB Ground Station	LDG	Exploit	Ex
Steal User Credentials	SUC	Escalate Privilege	EP	Upload Malware to Server	UMS
Craft Malicious Email	CME	Leverage Misconfig.	LM	Command for Upload	EV
Send as Legit User	SLU	Exploit Vulnerabilties	EV	SAT Gets & Exec. Malware	CEM

In Fig. 6, an AT represents three possible ways in which an attacker could compromise the availability of a CubeSAT. The scenario and the original ATs are taken from [22] and then slightly adapted to model a unique cohesive AT. The TLE in Fig. 6 represents the disruption of CubeSAT's operations—the *DCOp* OR-gate. This gate is detailed by three children: *DoS*—the indigo TLE of a sub-tree on the left presenting a denial of service attack—*TDC*—the violet TLE of the central sub-tree detailing a data tampering attack—and *KR*—the yellow TLE of the sub-tree on the right that presents an attack killing communications on the CubeSAT. For a denial of service to happen, the attacker must perform information gathering and a successful phishing attack—detailed by the red *IGP* AND-gate—and use gathered intel to access the CubeSAT UI and disrupt the service. On the other hand, to perform a data tampering attack, one must access the ground control database as admin—detailed by the green *ADA* AND-gate—then modify database entries and tamper with data. Finally, to kill communications on the CubeSAT an attacker must perform reconnaissance and weaponization, crafting a malicious app, and also conduct the exploit uploading the malware on the CubeSAT via the ground station: executing this code on the satellite would cause communications to go offline. Due to the increasing complexity of these three different attacks, the AT in Fig. 6 presents several sub-trees that are shared. The **red** sub-tree for information gathering and phishing is shared by the denial of service attack and by the sub-tree that models getting access to the database on the ground station. Furthermore, this **green** sub-tree is itself shared between the tampering data attack and the more complex malware-based communication killing attack.

Properties. ATM allows us to specify some properties on the AT in Fig. 6. As per semantics, properties 2 and 3 are evaluated w.r.t. a given attack. 1) What are all minimal attacks to achieve denial of service? $[\![DoS]\!]_T$; 2) Are the cost of data-tampering and info gathering and phishing respectively lower than 20 and at most 5? $\mathsf{Cost}(TDC) < 20 \wedge \mathsf{Cost}(IGP) \leq 5$; 3) Are the probability of successfully attacking the TLE and the parallel time of attack lower than 0.05 and 45 respectively? $\mathsf{Prob}(DCOp) < 0.05 \wedge \mathsf{ParTime}(DCOp) < 45$; 4) What is the min skill an attacker has to have to kill communications on the CubeSAT, assuming that one needs skill of 20 to perform info gathering and phishing? $\mathsf{Skill}(KR)[IGP \mapsto 20]$; 5) Is there an attack that ensures data tampering without exploiting vulnerabilities in the ground station system? $\exists(TDC[EV \mapsto 0])$; 6) Is it necessary to leverage misconfigurations to perform a successful attack on CubeSAT's communications? $\forall(KR \Rightarrow LM)$; 7) Is there an attack that ensures successful access to the ground station DB while keeping the cost under 20? $\exists(\mathsf{Cost}(ADA) < 20)$; 8) Do accessing the CubeSAT UI and disrupting service always imply that successful attacks to the TLE are strictly cheaper than 35 and strictly faster than 60 (when parallelized)? $\forall((AUI \wedge DS) \Rightarrow (\mathsf{Cost}(DCOp) < 35 \wedge \mathsf{ParTime}(DCOp) < 60))$ (Table 2).

5 Model Checking Algoritms

In this section we present model checking algorithms for ATM. As noted in [47, 48], some scenarios, especially in the Boolean domain, are trivial: e.g., checking if $A, T \models \phi$ holds is trivial if ϕ is a formula that does not contain a MA or MD operator. In that case, we can simply substitute the values of A in the atoms of ϕ and see if the Boolean expression evaluates to true. Non trivial scenarios arise if ϕ contains a MA or MD operator or if ATs are not tree-shaped. These require computations based on BDDs, introduced in Sect. 5.1: a coherent choice with the landscape of algorithms for FT logics [47,48] and AT computation [15,42]. In this section we build upon these results and present algorithms to: 1) Obtain BDDs from layer 1 formulae taking the structure of a given tree T into account (Sect. 5.2); 2) a) Check whether an attack A and a tree T satisfy a layer 1 formula and b) compute all the satisfying attacks A for a given tree T and layer 1 formula (Sect. 5.3); 3) Check whether an attack A and an attributed tree T satisfy a layer 2 formula (Sect. 5.4); 4) Compute the metric value of a given layer 3 formula (Sect. 5.5); 5) Check whether an attributed tree T satisfies a layer 4 formula (Sect. 5.6).

5.1   Binary Decision Diagrams (BDDs)

BDDs are directed acyclic graphs (DAGs) that compactly represent Boolean functions [2] by reducing redundancy. Depending on variable's ordering, BDD's size can grow linearly in the number of variables and at worst exponentially. In practice, BDDs are heavily used, including in AT analysis [15,42] and in their safety counterpart, FTs [7,47,48,52]. Formally, a BDD is a rooted DAG B_f that represents a Boolean function $f \colon \mathbb{B}^n \to \mathbb{B}$ over variables $Vars = \{x_i\}_{i=1}^n$. Each nonleaf w has two outgoing arrows, labeled 0 and 1, and a label $Lab(w) \in Vars$; furthermore, each leaf has a label 0 or 1. Given a b in $\mathbb{B}^n$, the BDD is used to compute $f(b)$ as follows: starting from the top, upon arriving at a node w with $Lab(w) = x_i$, one takes the 0-edge if $b_i = 0$ and the 1-edge if $b_i = 1$. The label of the leaf one ends up in, is then equal to $f(b)$. A function f can be represented by multiple BDDs, but has a unique *reduced ordered* representative, or ROBDD [8,13], where the x_i occur in ascending order, and the BDD is reduced as much as possible by removing irrelevant nodes and merging duplicates. This is formally defined below; we let $Low(w)$ (resp. $High(w)$) be the endpoint of w's 0-edge (resp. 1-edge) and let R_B be the BDD root.

Definition 9. *Let Vars be a set. A (RO)BDD over Vars is a tuple $B = (W, H, Lab, u)$ where (W, H) is a rooted directed acyclic graph, and $Lab \colon W \to Vars \sqcup \{0, 1\}, u \colon H \to \{0, 1\}$ are maps such that: 1. Every nonleaf w has exactly two outgoing edges h, h' with $u(h) \neq u(h')$, and $Lab(w) \in Vars$; 2. Every leaf w has $Lab(w) \in \{0, 1\}$. 3. Vars are equipped with a total order, B_f is thus defined over a pair $\langle Vars, < \rangle$; 4. the variable of a node is of lower order than its children, that is: $\forall w \in W_n. Lab(w) < Lab(Low(w)), Lab(High(w))$; 5. the children of nonleaf nodes are distinct nodes; 6. nodes are uniquely determined by their label, low child and high child.*

5.2   BDDs from ATs and Layer 1 Formulae

The first step to enable further computations is to obtain BDDs from layer 1 formulae taking the structure of a given tree T into account (for related procedures on FT logics see [47,48]). Following, operations between BDDs are represented by **bold** operands. e.g., $\boldsymbol{\wedge}$, $\boldsymbol{\vee}$. Where convenient notationally, we write B_T^ϕ for $B_T(\phi)$, i.e., the BDD B of ϕ, given T. Given a set of variables $Vars = \{x_i\}_{i=1}^n$ existential quantification can be defined as follows: $\exists x. B = \mathrm{RESTRICT}(B, x, 0) \boldsymbol{\vee} \mathrm{RESTRICT}(B, x, 1)$ and $\exists Vars. B = \exists x_1. \exists x_2. \dots \exists x_n. B$. Furthermore, we define a set of primed variables $Vars' = \{x_i'\}_{i=1}^n$ and let $B_T^\phi[Vars \curvearrowright Vars']$ be the BDD B_T^ϕ in which every variable $x_i \in Vars$ is renamed to its primed $x_i' \in Vars'$. Finally we let $Vars' \subset Vars \equiv (\bigwedge_i x_i' \Rightarrow x_i) \wedge (\bigvee_i x_i' \neq x_i)$. Algorithms to conduct typical BDD operations—such as $\mathrm{RESTRICT}$—can be found in [2,8].

Definition 10. *The translation function of an AT T is a function $\mathfrak{f}_T \colon E \to BDD$ that takes as input an element $e \in E$.*

$$\mathfrak{f}_T(e) = \begin{cases} B(e) & if\ e \in \mathtt{BAS} \\ \bigvee_{e' \in ch(e)} \mathfrak{f}_T(e') & if\ e \in \mathtt{IE}\ and\ t(e) = \mathtt{OR} \\ \bigwedge_{e' \in ch(e)} \mathfrak{f}_T(e') & if\ e \in \mathtt{IE}\ and\ t(e) = \mathtt{AND} \end{cases}$$

where $B(e)$ is a BDD with a single node w with $Low(w) = 0$ and $High(w) = 1$.

Algorithm 1 computes B_T^ϕ following semantics for layer 1 formulae:

Algorithm 1. Compute B_T^ϕ from T and ϕ

1: **Input:** AT T, formula ϕ
2: **Output:** BDD B_T^ϕ
3: **Method:**
4: **if** $\phi = e$ **then return** $\mathfrak{f}_T(e)$
5: **else if** $\phi = \neg\phi'$ **then return** $\neg\,(Algorithm\,1(T, \phi'))$
6: **else if** $\phi = \phi' \wedge \phi''$ **then return** $Algorithm\,1(T, \phi')\wedge Algorithm\,1(T, \phi'')$
7: **else if** $\phi = \phi'[e_i \mapsto 0]$ **then return** RESTRICT$(Algorithm\,1(T, \phi'), x_i, 0)$
8: **else if** $\phi = \phi'[e_i \mapsto 1]$ **then return** RESTRICT$(Algorithm\,1(T, \phi'), x_i, 1)$
9: **else** // $\phi = MA(\phi')$
10:     **return** $Algorithm\,1(T, \psi')\wedge(\neg\exists Vars'.(Vars' \sqsubset Vars)\wedge$
11:     $Algorithm\,1(T, \phi')[Vars \curvearrowright Vars'])$
12: **end if**

5.3 Model Checking Layer 1 Formulae

Is an Attack Successful w.r.t. ϕ? Algorithm 2 checks whether $A, T \models \phi$, given an attack A and a tree T. First, the BDD B_T^ϕ for ϕ given T is constructed via Algorithm 1. Then, the algorithm walks the BDD path representing values of BASes in A. If it ends up in the terminal 0, then $A, T \not\models \phi$, otherwise—if the terminal node is 1—$A, T \models \phi$.

Algorithm 2. Check if $A, T \models \phi$

1: **Input:** attack A, attack tree T, formula ϕ
2: **Output:** *true* iff $A, T \models \phi$; *false* otherwise.
3: **Method:**
4: $B_T^\phi \leftarrow Algorithm\,1(T, \phi)$; $w_i = R_{B_T^\phi}$
5: **while** $w_i \notin W_t$ **do:**
6:     **if** $a_i \in A = 0$ **then** $w_i = Low(w_i)$
7:     **else if** $a_i \in A = 1$ **then** $w_i = High(w_i)$
8:     **end if**
9: **end while**

10: **if** $Lab(w_i) = 0$ **then return** *false*
11: **else**   // $Lab(w_i) = 1$
12:     **return** *true*
13: **end if**

All Successful Attacks w.r.t. ϕ. Our ability to construct a BDD B_T^ϕ for layer 1 formulae granted by Algorithm 1 allows us to compute all attacks A such that $A, T \models \phi$. Algorithm 3 performs this computation by applying the ALLSAT [2] algorithm to B_T^ϕ: ALLSAT walks down the BDD and stores the paths that lead to the terminal node 1. These paths then represent satisfying attacks for ϕ given T. Note that Algorithm 3 can be used to compute all the minimal attacks of a given ϕ by simply calling it on $MA(\phi)$.

5.4   Model Checking Layer 2 Formulae

Algorithm 4 presented in this subsection checks if a layer 2 formula is satisfied, given an attack A and an attributed tree T. Boolean connectives are resolved as usual via case distinction. To check whether $A, T \models M_k(\phi) \preceq_k m$, first the BDD B_T^ϕ for the inner layer 1

Algorithm 3. Compute all A s.t. $A, T \models \phi$
1: **Input**: AT T, formula ϕ
2: **Output**: $\{A \mid A, T \models \phi\}$
3: **Method**:
4: $B_T^\phi \leftarrow$ *Algorithm* 1(T, ϕ); $w_i = R_{B_T^\phi}$
5: $\{A \mid A, T \models \phi\} \leftarrow$ ALLSAT(w_i)
6: **return** $\{A \mid A, T \models \phi\}$

---

formula is constructed and Algorithm 2 is emplyed to assess whether $A, T \models \phi$. If that is not the case, we return *false*. Otherwise, we compute the metric value for the given attack following the interpretation of $\triangle$ taken from the $k-$est LOSG L_k of our attributed tree T. We store this value in metr_val, and we return the result of the comparison with $\preceq_k m$. To handle the case in which we set evidence for a specific atom e_i in a layer 2 formula, we simply call the algorithm again and we make sure that the attribution α_k of the corresponding a_i is mapped to the chosen value ν.

Algorithm 4. Check if $A, T \models \psi$

1: **Input**: attack A, attributed AT T, formula ψ
2: **Output**: *true* iff $A, T \models \psi$; *false* otherwise.
3: **Method**:
4: **if** $\psi = \neg\psi'$ **then return not** *Algorithm* 4(A, T, ψ')
5: **else if** $\psi = \psi' \wedge \psi''$ **then return** *Algorithm* 4(A, T, ψ') **and** *Algorithm* 4(A, T, ψ'')
6: **else if** $\psi = M_k(\phi) \preceq_k m$ **then**
7:     **if** *Algorithm* 2(A, T, ϕ) returns *true* **then**   // $A, T \models \phi$
8:         metr_val $= \bigtriangleup_k \underset{a \in A}{} \alpha_k(a)$
9:         **return** metr_val $\preceq_k m$

```
10:     else  // A, T ⊭ φ
11:         return false
12:     end if
13: else  // ψ = ψ'[e_i ⟼ᵏ ν]
14:     return Algorithm 4(A, T(𝔞[α_k(a_i) ⟼ᵏ ν]), ψ')
15: end if
```

5.5 Compute Metrics for Layer 3 Formulae

This subsection showcases an algorithm to compute a metric value for a specified ξ-formula. If ξ equals $\mathbb{V}_k(\phi)$, one approach would be to directly use the formula of Definition 8. However, directly finding all minimal attacks on ϕ is computationally expensive [42]. Instead, we calculate metrics by applying the BDD-based method from [42]. This method exploits the fact that paths from the root

---
Algorithm 5. Compute metric for ξ-formula

```
1: Input: attributed ATT, formula ξ
2: Output: metric value for ξ.
3: Method:
4: if ξ = V_k(φ) then
5:     (W, H, Lab, u) ← Algorithm 1(T, φ)
6:     W_todo ← W
7:     while W_todo ≠ ∅ do
8:         Take w ∈ W_todo without children in W_todo
9:         if Lab(w) = 0 then v(w) ← 1_∇
10:        else if Lab(w) = 1 then v(w) ← 1_Δ
11:        else
12:            v(w)←v(Low(w))∇(v(High(w))Δα(Lab(w)))
13:        end if
14:        W_todo ← W_todo \ {w}
15:    end while return v(R_{W,H,Lab,u})
16: else  // ξ = ξ'[e_i ⟼ᵏ ν]
17:     return Algorithm 5(T(𝔞[α_k(a_i) ⟼ᵏ ν]), ξ')
18: end if
```
---

to 1 in a BDD encode succesful attacks, and 1-labeled edges on such a path represent the BAS of these attacks. Assigning weight $\alpha(Lab(w))$ to an edge $(w, High(w))$, the metric value can then be computed by a variant of the shortest path algorithm for DAGs. Note that the method in [42] is defined only for $\phi = e$, but the result readily generalizes. If $\xi = \xi'[e_i \overset{k}{\mapsto} \nu]$, the algorithm is called again on ξ' and the attribution α_k on the corresponding a_i is set to ν.

5.6 Model Checking Layer 4 Formulae

We present an algorithm to check whether an attributed tree T satisfies a layer 4 formula. The non-trivial cases of Algorithm 6 check whether $\mathsf{T} \models \exists(\phi \wedge \psi)$ and $\mathsf{T} \models \forall(\phi \wedge \psi)$. In the former case, for each attack A_i in the set of satisfying attacks for $\phi - \{A \mid A, T \models \phi\} \leftarrow Algorithm\ 3(T, \phi)$—we check whether $A_i, \mathsf{T} \models \psi$. If we find a fitting A_i, we return it alongside *true*. Otherwise, we return *false*. In the latter case, for each A_i in the set of all attacks for $T\ \mathscr{A}_T$ we check whether either $A_i, T \not\models \phi$ or $A_i, \mathsf{T} \not\models \psi$. If we find a counterexample A_i, we return it alongside *false*. Otherwise, we return *true*.

Algorithm 6. Check if $\mathsf{T} \models \gamma$

1: **Input**: set of all attacks $\mathscr{A}_T$, attributed ATT, formula γ
2: **Output**: *true* iff $\mathsf{T} \models \gamma$; *false* otherwise; (counter)example A_i.
3: **Method:**
4: **if** $\gamma = \neg\gamma'$ **then return not** *Algorithm* $6(A, \mathsf{T}, \gamma')$
5: **else if** $\gamma = \exists(\phi \wedge \psi)$ **then**
6:      **for** $A_i \in \{A \mid A, T \models \phi\} \leftarrow$ *Algorithm* $3(T, \phi)$ **do**
7:          **if** *Algorithm* $4(A_i, \mathsf{T}, \psi)$ returns *true* **then return** *true*, A_i
8:          **end if**
9:      **end for**
10:     **return** *false*
11: **else if** $\gamma = \forall(\phi \wedge \psi)$ **then**
12:     **for** $A_i \in \mathscr{A}_T$ **do**
13:         **if** *Algorithm* $2(A_i, T, \phi)$ returns *false* $\vee$ *Algorithm* $4(A_i, \mathsf{T}, \psi)$ returns *false* **then**
14:             **return** *false*, A_i
15:         **end if**
16:     **end for**
17:     **return** *true*
18: **end if**

---

6   Conclusions

We presented ATM, a logic for general metrics on ATs that enables the construction of complex queries and insightful what-if scenarios. We showcased its usefulness with an application of ATM to the case study of a CubeSAT. Specified properties can then be checked and metrics computed via model checking algorithms that we presented. Our work opens several relevant perspectives for future research. First, it would be interesting to extend ATM to consider timed behaviours: this would allow to further extend quantitative analysis capabilities. This step could be achieved by extending ATM to dynamic ATs that consider the sequential nature of attack steps. To handle dynamic gates in dynamic ATs it would be very natural to have a logic that can express temporal properties, moving more in the direction of LTL [50] or CTL [18] or their timed variants TLTL [51] and TCTL [1]. Another notable extension of ATM could express and calculate Pareto fronts between metrics [42]. Moreover, it is foreseeable to extend the proposed framework to safety-security variants of ATs and FTs, e.g., to attack-fault trees (AFTs) [40], and to graphs that consider more general safety-security *risks*, in the sense of *probability* × *impact* [24]. Lastly, implementing this logic could further propel usability of ATM by providing hands-on feedback from domain experts acquainted with threat modelling and vulnerability analysis.

Acknowledgements. The authors would like to thank Dr. Juan A. Fraire(0000-0001-9816-6989) (Inria, CONICET and Saarland University) for the insightful discussions about routing in space and for propagating and visualizing orbiting CubeSATs, resulting in Fig. 5 and in the animation in [23].

References

1. Alur, R., Courcoubetis, C., Dill, D.: Model-checking in dense real-time. Inf. Comput. **104**(1), 2–34 (1993)
2. Andersen, H.R.: An intro. to binary decision diagrams. Lecture notes, available online, IT University of Copenhagen, p. 5 (1997)
3. Apvrille, L., Roudier, Y.: SysML-sec: a sysML environment for the design and development of secure embedded systems. In: APCOSEC (2013)
4. Arnold, F., Guck, D., Kumar, R., Stoelinga, M.: Sequential and parallel attack tree modelling. In: Koornneef, F., van Gulijk, C. (eds.) SAFECOMP 2015. LNCS, vol. 9338, pp. 291–299. Springer, Cham (2015). https://doi.org/10.1007/978-3-319-24249-1_25
5. Arnold, F., Hermanns, H., Pulungan, R., Stoelinga, M.: Time-dependent analysis of attacks. In: Abadi, M., Kremer, S. (eds.) POST 2014. LNCS, vol. 8414, pp. 285–305. Springer, Heidelberg (2014). https://doi.org/10.1007/978-3-642-54792-8_16
6. Barlow, R.E., Proschan, F.: Statistical theory of reliability and life testing: probability models. In: International Series in Decision Processes, Holt, Rinehart and Winston (1975)
7. Basgöze, D., Volk, M., Katoen, J., Khan, S., Stoelinga, M.: BDDs strike back - efficient analysis of static and dynamic fault trees. In: NFM, vol. 13260, pp. 713–732 (2022)
8. Ben-Ari, M.: Mathematical Logic for Computer Science. Springer, Heidelberg (2012). https://doi.org/10.1007/978-1-4471-4129-7
9. Bieber, P., Castel, C., Seguin, C.: Combination of fault tree analysis and model checking for safety assessment of complex system. In: EDCC, vol. 2485, pp. 19–31 (2002)
10. Bossuat, A., Kordy, B.: Evil twins: handling repetitions in attack–defense trees. In: Liu, P., Mauw, S., Stølen, K. (eds.) GraMSec 2017. LNCS, vol. 10744, pp. 17–37. Springer, Cham (2018). https://doi.org/10.1007/978-3-319-74860-3_2
11. Boudali, H., Crouzen, P., Stoelinga, M.: Dynamic fault tree analysis using input/output interactive markov chains. In: DSN, pp. 708–717 (2007)
12. Bozzano, M., Cimatti, A., Katoen, J., Nguyen, V.Y., Noll, T., Roveri, M.: Safety, dependability and performance analysis of extended AADL models. Comput. J. **54**(5), 754–775 (2011)
13. Brace, K.S., Rudell, R.L., Bryant, R.E.: Efficient implementation of a BDD package. In: 27th ACM/IEEE Design Automation Conference, pp. 40–45 (1990)
14. Budde, C.E., Dehnert, C., Hahn, E.M., Hartmanns, A., Junges, S., Turrini, A.: JANI: quantitative model and tool interaction. In: Legay, A., Margaria, T. (eds.) TACAS 2017. LNCS, vol. 10206, pp. 151–168. Springer, Heidelberg (2017). https://doi.org/10.1007/978-3-662-54580-5_9
15. Budde, C.E., Stoelinga, M.: Efficient algorithms for quantitative attack tree analysis. In: CSF, pp. 1–15 (2021)
16. Buldas, A., Laud, P., Priisalu, J., Saarepera, M., Willemson, J.: Rational choice of security measures via multi-parameter attack trees. In: Lopez, J. (ed.) CRITIS 2006. LNCS, vol. 4347, pp. 235–248. Springer, Heidelberg (2006). https://doi.org/10.1007/11962977_19
17. Celestrack: Orbiting CubeSATs (2023). https://celestrak.org/NORAD/elements/gp.php?GROUP=cubesat&FORMAT=tle. Accessed Mar 2023

18. Clarke, E.M., Emerson, E.: Design and synthesis of synchronisation skeletons using branching time temporal logic. In: Logic of Programs, Proceedings of Workshop, LNCS, vol. 31, pp. 52–71 (1981). Springer, Heidelberg. https://doi.org/10.1007/bfb0025774

19. CORDIS, European Commission: MISSION (2023). https://cordis.europa.eu/project/id/101008233

20. Déharbe, D., Shankar, S., Clarke, E.M.: Model checking VHDL with CV. In: Gopalakrishnan, G., Windley, P. (eds.) FMCAD 1998. LNCS, vol. 1522, pp. 508–514. Springer, Heidelberg (1998). https://doi.org/10.1007/3-540-49519-3_33

21. Dutuit, Y., Rauzy, A.: A linear-time algorithm to find modules of fault trees. IEEE Trans. Reliab. **45**(3), 422–425 (1996)

22. Falco, G., Viswanathan, A., Santangelo, A.: Cubesat security attack tree analysis. In: SMC-IT, pp. 68–76 (2021)

23. Fraire, J.: All active CubeSATS as of 2023 (according to Celestrak). https://www.youtube.com/watch?v=PIkwxOvPLTw. Accessed Aug 2023

24. Fumagalli, M., et al.: On the semantics of risk propagation. In: International Conference on Research Challenges in Information Science, pp. 69–86. Springer, Heidelberg (2023). https://doi.org/10.1007/978-3-031-33080-3_5

25. Gadyatskaya, O., Jhawar, R., Kordy, P., Lounis, K., Mauw, S., Trujillo-Rasua, R.: Attack trees for practical security assessment: ranking of attack scenarios with ADTool 2.0. In: Agha, G., Van Houdt, B. (eds.) QEST 2016. LNCS, vol. 9826, pp. 159–162. Springer, Cham (2016). https://doi.org/10.1007/978-3-319-43425-4_10

26. Golan, J.S.: Semirings and their Applications. Springer, Heidelberg (2013). https://doi.org/10.1007/978-94-015-9333-5

27. Hansen, K.M., Ravn, A.P., Stavridou, V.: From safety analysis to software requirements. IEEE Trans. Softw. Eng. **24**(7), 573–584 (1998)

28. Hansson, H., Jonsson, B.: A logic for reasoning about time and reliability. Formal Aspects Comput. **6**(5), 512–535 (1994)

29. Hejduk, M.D., Casali, S.J., Cappellucci, D.A., Ericson, N.L., Snow, D.: A catalogue-wide implementation of general perturbations orbit determination extrapolated from higher order orbital theory solutions. In: Proceedings of the 23rd AAS/AIAA Space Flight Mechanics Meeting, pp. 619–632 (2013)

30. Horne, R., Mauw, S., Tiu, A.: Semantics for specialising attack trees based on linear logic. Fund. Inf. **153**(1–2), 57–86 (2017)

31. Isograph: AttackTree. https://www.isograph.com/software/attacktree/. Accessed Mar 2023

32. Jet Propulsion Laboratory NASA: CubeSATs and SmallSATs. https://www.jpl.nasa.gov/topics/cubesats. Accessed Mar 2023

33. Jhawar, R., Kordy, B., Mauw, S., Radomirović, S., Trujillo-Rasua, R.: Attack trees with sequential conjunction. In: Federrath, H., Gollmann, D. (eds.) SEC 2015. IAICT, vol. 455, pp. 339–353. Springer, Cham (2015). https://doi.org/10.1007/978-3-319-18467-8_23

34. Jürgenson, A., Willemson, J.: Computing exact outcomes of multi-parameter attack trees. In: Meersman, R., Tari, Z. (eds.) OTM 2008. LNCS, vol. 5332, pp. 1036–1051. Springer, Heidelberg (2008). https://doi.org/10.1007/978-3-540-88873-4_8

35. Jürjens, J.: UMLsec: extending UML for secure systems development. In: UML 2002 – The Unified Modeling Language, vol. 2460, pp. 412–425 (2002)

36. Kordy, B., Pouly, M., Schweitzer, P.: Probabilistic reasoning with graphical security models. Inf. Sci. **342**, 111–131 (2016)

37. Kordy, B., Wideł, W.: On quantitative analysis of attack–defense trees with repeated labels. In: Bauer, L., Küsters, R. (eds.) POST 2018. LNCS, vol. 10804, pp. 325–346. Springer, Cham (2018). https://doi.org/10.1007/978-3-319-89722-6_14
38. Kumar, R., Ruijters, E., Stoelinga, M.: Quantitative attack tree analysis via priced timed automata. In: Sankaranarayanan, S., Vicario, E. (eds.) FORMATS 2015. LNCS, vol. 9268, pp. 156–171. Springer, Cham (2015). https://doi.org/10.1007/978-3-319-22975-1_11
39. Kumar, R., et al.: Effective analysis of attack trees: a model-driven approach. In: Russo, A., Schürr, A. (eds.) FASE 2018. LNCS, vol. 10802, pp. 56–73. Springer, Cham (2018). https://doi.org/10.1007/978-3-319-89363-1_4
40. Kumar, R., Stoelinga, M.: Quantitative security and safety analysis with attack-fault trees. In: HASE, pp. 25–32 (2017)
41. Kwiatkowska, M., Norman, G., Parker, D.: PRISM 4.0: verification of probabilistic real-time systems. In: Gopalakrishnan, G., Qadeer, S. (eds.) CAV 2011. LNCS, vol. 6806, pp. 585–591. Springer, Heidelberg (2011). https://doi.org/10.1007/978-3-642-22110-1_47
42. Lopuhaä-Zwakenberg, M., Budde, C.E., Stoelinga, M.: Efficient and generic algorithms for quantitative attack tree analysis. IEEE TDSC **20**, 4169–4187 (2022)
43. Lopuhaä-Zwakenberg, M., Stoelinga, M.: Attack time analysis in dynamic attack trees via integer linear programming. arXiv e-prints arXiv:2111.05114 (2021)
44. Mauw, S., Oostdijk, M.: Foundations of attack trees. In: Won, D.H., Kim, S. (eds.) ICISC 2005. LNCS, vol. 3935, pp. 186–198. Springer, Heidelberg (2006). https://doi.org/10.1007/11734727_17
45. Moszkowski, B.: A temporal logic for multi-level reasoning about hardware. STANFORD UNIV CA, Technical report (1982)
46. NASA: CubeSATs Overview. https://www.nasa.gov/mission_pages/cubesats/overview. Accessed Mar 2023
47. Nicoletti, S., Hahn, E., Stoelinga, M.: BFL: a logic to reason about fault trees. In: DSN, pp. 441–452 (2022)
48. Nicoletti, S.M., Lopuhaä-Zwakenberg, M., Hahn, E.M., Stoelinga, M.: Pfl: a probabilistic logic for fault trees. In: FM 2023, pp. 199–221 (2023)
49. Ognjanovic, Z.: Discrete linear-time probabilistic logics: completeness, decidability and complexity. J. Log. Comput. **16**(2), 257–285 (2006)
50. Pnueli, A.: The temporal logic of programs. In: FOCS, pp. 46–57 (1977)
51. Raskin, J.F.: Logics, automata and classical theories for deciding real time. Ph.D. thesis (1999)
52. Rauzy, A.: New algorithms for fault trees analysis. RESS **40**(3), 203–211 (1993)
53. Roudier, Y., Apvrille, L.: SysML-Sec: a model driven approach for designing safe and secure systems. In: MODELSWARD, pp. 655–664. IEEE (2015)
54. Schneier, B.: Attack trees. Dr. Dobb's J. **24**(12), 21–29 (1999)
55. Thums, A., Schellhorn, G.: Model checking FTA. In: FME, vol. 2805, pp. 739–757 (2003)
56. Volk, M., Junges, S., Katoen, J.: Fast dynamic fault tree analysis by model checking techniques. Trans. Ind. Inf. **14**(1), 370–379 (2018)
57. Walker, M.D.: Pandora: a logic for the qualitative analysis of temporal fault trees. Ph.D. thesis, The University of Hull (2009)

Refactoring of Multi-instance BPMN Processes with Time and Resources

Quentin Nivon(✉) and Gwen Salaün

University of Grenoble Alpes, CNRS, Grenoble INP, Inria, LIG, F-38000 Grenoble,
France
quentin.nivon@inria.fr

Abstract. Business process optimisation is a strategic activity in organisations because of its potential to increase profit margins and reduce operational costs. In this paper, we focus on a specific technique used for process optimisation known as process refactoring. In this work, a process is described using BPMN extended with quantitative aspects for modelling execution times and resources associated with tasks. A process is not executed once but multiple times, and multiple concurrent executions of a process compete for using the shared resources. In this context, we propose a refactoring approach whose goal is to reduce the total execution time of the process and optimise the usage of the shared resources. To do so, we first analyse the given process in terms of task dependency and resource usage, and then rely on these results to restructure the process and return an optimal version of it. This process refactoring technique is fully automated by a tool that we implemented and applied on several examples for validation purposes.

1 Introduction

Context. Process optimisation is a strategic activity in companies and organisations because it is a source of improvement in terms of throughput, resource usage and associated costs. However, this is a difficult task, which requires a precise description and understanding of these processes. Process optimisation can be achieved in different ways. A first option is to compute metrics of interest or precise recommendations to effectively change and improve manually the aforementioned processes. Another option is to automatically compute a new version of the process, which is an improved version of the original process. In both cases, optimisation focuses on time or several specific criteria (execution time, costs, resource usage, carbon footprint, etc.).

In this paper, we assume that processes are described using BPMN 2.0 (BPMN, as a shorthand, in the rest of this paper). BPMN was published as an ISO/IEC standard in 2013 and is nowadays extensively used for modelling and developing business processes. Additional quantitative information is required to be able to precisely analyse and then optimise the process given as input. Therefore, in this work, the process model also includes time as a duration associated to tasks and an explicit description of the resources required to execute

C. Ferreira and T. A. C. Willemse (Eds.): SEFM 2023, LNCS 14323, pp. 226–245, 2023.
https://doi.org/10.1007/978-3-031-47115-5_13

each task. It is also worth noting that a process is not executed once but multiple times resulting in multiple instances. For each execution/instance, each task needs to acquire the required (globally shared) resources to be able to execute.

Motivation. When considering processes with time and resources, the two main optimisation criteria are execution time/throughput and better usage of resources (usually resulting in a reduction of associated costs). Operational research offers several techniques to solve such optimisation problems. However, they are difficult to apply in this context, due to the expressiveness of the model and the multiple instances of the process running in parallel, which would increase a lot the operational cost of such techniques. Another solution to this problem is *resource optimisation*, see e.g. [6,8], but this solution usually implies some flexibility in terms of budget because the solution may propose to increase the number of certain resources so as to obtain better results. If the number of resources is fixed and cannot be updated, an alternative solution is to change the organisation of the tasks within the process. This solution is usually called *process refactoring*, and aims at restructuring the process to optimise the aforementioned criteria.

Refactoring a process manually is however a very difficult task. A naive solution could be to increase the level of parallelism, but this solution does not systematically work in the case of multiple executions of a process, which may increase the competition (thus time) to acquire the resources. Therefore, there is a need for automated refactoring techniques in order to optimise a process. Such techniques can be used in different contexts, for improving an existing process or at design time for optimising a new process before effectively deploying it.

Approach. Given a BPMN process model, we propose new optimisation techniques that aim at automatically restructuring the given process. These refactoring techniques generate a different process which has the shortest execution time in the best case, or is close to the shortest otherwise. This new process is said to be optimal or close to optimal, given a number of shared resources. The main idea is to adjust the structure of the process to avoid competition of resources and bottlenecks, to obtain smoother executions of multiple instances of the process. More precisely, in a first step, the approach transforms the process into an optimal version, structurally speaking, by putting as many tasks in parallel as possible. This intermediate process is optimal as it has the shortest execution time possible. We then compute the pool of resources needed by the process to execute without having concurrency issues while accessing resources. If this pool of resources is smaller than the actual number of shared resources, we return this process. If not, more resources would be required, but in this work we do not want to change the number of shared resources. Therefore, we change again the structure of the process to decrease the degree of parallelism of certain tasks and thus remove the identified competition on some specific resources. As a result, we return a refactored process whose execution time is close to optimal, or optimal in the best case. The whole approach is fully automated by a tool that we implemented. Even though the overall complexity of the approach is exponential, the experimental results obtained on several real-world and handcrafted examples were satisfactory, as none of the execution exceeded a few seconds.

Structure. Section 2 introduces the languages and models used in this paper. Section 3 presents the different steps of the refactoring approach proposed in this paper. Section 4 describes the tool support and some experimental results to assess the performance of the approach. Section 5 compares our solution to related work and Sect. 6 concludes this paper.

2   Models

BPMN with Time and Resources. In this paper, we focus on BPMN activity diagrams including the constructs related to control-flow modeling and behavioural aspects. Beyond those constructs, execution time and resources are also associated with tasks.

More precisely, the node types *event*, *task*, and *gateway*, and the edge type *sequence flow* are considered. Start and end events are used, respectively, to initialise and terminate processes. A task represents an atomic activity that has exactly one incoming and one outgoing flow. A sequence flow describes two nodes executed one after the other in a specific execution order. A task may have a duration or delay, expressed by default in *units of time* (UT). Resources are explicitly defined at the task level. A task can thus include, as part of its specification, the required resources. In such a case, it means that the task needs those resources to be able to execute. Once the resources are acquired, the task is going to execute for the specified duration. The acquisition of a resource is achieved in a "first-come-first-served" strategy. If a task needs more replicas of one or several resources than those available, it remains in a waiting state until the release of a sufficient number of replicas of the required resources.

Gateways are used to control the divergence and convergence of the execution flow. We consider in this work the two main kinds of gateways used in activity diagrams, namely, *exclusive* and *parallel* gateways. The difference between them is that only one outgoing flow of an exclusive gateway is executed (choice), while all the outgoing flows of a parallel gateway are executed. Data-based conditions for exclusive split gateways are modelled using probabilities associated to outgoing flows.

Example. Figure 1 shows an example of BPMN process enhanced with time and resources. Each task has a duration and makes use of resources. For example, task *Vaccination* takes 7 units of time (days here) to execute in average and requires one replica of resources *doctor* and *user*.

Dependencies Between Tasks. In BPMN, tasks are naturally ordered by the sequence flows that are connecting them. Thus, two tasks connected by a sequence flow are dependent, as one must be executed before the other. In this approach, we perform a restructuring of the process. Thereby, there is no guarantee regarding the final position of a task in the resulting process compared to its position in the original one. Nonetheless, some tasks may have to remain in a specific order to preserve the meaning of the process (e.g., some product should

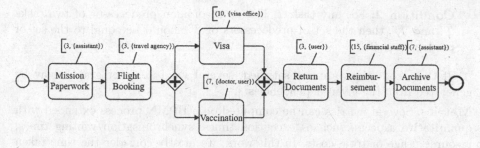

Fig. 1. Example of "Trip Organisation" process in BPMN [9]

be packaged before its delivery). Providing these dependencies is required in this work and is an information complementary to the BPMN process. They can be given by the user or computed by analysing the data-flow graph corresponding to the BPMN process [5, 10].

In the rest of this paper, a dependency or *partial order* between two tasks T_1 and T_2 is written as a pair (T_1, T_2). Two tasks are said to be dependent if they belong to a pair of dependencies, and non-dependent otherwise. T_1 is said to be a *predecessor* of T_2, and T_2 a *successor* of T_1. When there are several dependencies, they can be concisely represented using a *dependency graph*, which is a directed acyclic graph where each node corresponds to a task and each edge to a dependency between two tasks.

Example. Figure 1 shows an example of trip organisation process. In this example, the order of some tasks must not be changed by the refactoring techniques. For example, documents have to be returned by the user before being archived. Thus, task *Return Documents* must be executed before task *Archive Documents*.

Abstract Graphs. An abstract graph is an internal representation of a BPMN process that we use in this work as an intermediate format. It was originally introduced in [11] where the authors propose first to generate an abstract graph from a set of dependencies between tasks and then to generate the BPMN process corresponding to this abstract graph. It worth noting that this representation has the same expressiveness as the subset of BPMN that is supported in this work.

Definition 1. *(Abstract Graph) An abstract graph is a (hierarchical) directed graph (S_N, S_E) where S_N is a set of nodes and S_E a set of directed edges connecting these nodes. A node $n \in S_N$ is defined as a pair (S_T, S_G) where S_T is a set of tasks and S_G a set of abstract (sub-)graphs.*

Given a set of dependencies, an abstract graph can be generated if and only if the two following conditions are satisfied:

- **Condition 1:** For any task T'', if T'' is a common successor of two tasks T and T', then the set of successors of T should be equal to the set of successors of T'.

- **Condition 2:** For any task T, if T is a common predecessor of two tasks T' and T''', then the set of predecessors of T' should be equal to the set of predecessors of T'''.

If these conditions are not satisfied, several valid abstract graphs may be generated from the given dependencies.

Metrics. Several metrics can be computed on a BPMN process extended with quantitative aspects, such as execution times, synchronisation/waiting times, resource usage or total costs. In this work, we mostly consider the time taken by a process to execute since it is our main optimisation goal. The *execution time* of a process corresponds to the difference between the timestamp at which the last token has reached an end event and the timestamp at which the initial token has left the start event. This time varies depending on the structure of the process, the use of gateways or loops, but it is always finite if the process is syntactically well-formed (i.e., if each execution scenario eventually ends up with an end event). This approach considers two notions of execution times. The first one, called *worst-case execution time*, corresponds to the longest time taken by a BPMN process to complete its execution. Indeed, conditional structures, such as loops or choices, may lead to several different execution times for a single process.

Definition 2. *(Worst-Case Execution Time) Let B be a BPMN process and $S_{ET} = \{ET_1, ET_2, ..., ET_n\}$ the set of all possible execution times of B. The worst-case execution time of B is defined as $WCET_B = \max(S_{ET})$.*

The second execution time considered, called *average execution time*, is only relevant in a multi-instance context. It represents the time taken by each instance of the process to complete its execution, on average.

Definition 3. *(Average Execution Time) Let B be a BPMN process executed n times and $\{ET_{B_1}, ET_{B_2}, ..., ET_{B_n}\}$ the execution times of each instance of B. The average execution time of B is defined as $AET_B = \frac{1}{n} \sum_{i=1}^{n} ET_{B_i}$.*

These execution times can be computed using simulation techniques [7]. These simulation techniques and the resulting execution times highly depends on the *workload* of a process, which is a couple (N, R) where N represents the number of instances of the process being executed and R the rate at which each process execution is started. This rate is also known as *inter-arrival time* (IAT).

It is worth noting that synchronisation times play an important role in this work. The synchronisation time to merge parallel gateways corresponds to the time elapsed between the arrival of the first token through one of its incoming flows and the arrival of the last token (thus resulting in the activation of that merge). These merge gateways are often seen as bottlenecks because they induce additional delays. On the other hand, adding more parallelism to a process may also speed up its execution. The solution proposed in this paper takes particularly care of this issue by adding parallelism when it does not induce such bottlenecks and by avoiding parallelism when it results in additional delays.

Optimality. The main goal of this work is to improve the average execution time of the original process by applying refactoring techniques to it. The final process, returned to the user, is in the best case *optimal*.

Definition 4. *(Optimal Process) Let B be a BPMN process, S_D the set of dependencies of B, and $S_{B_D} = \{B_1, B_2, ..., B_n\}$ the set of processes generated from B and satisfying S_D. $\exists B_i \in S_{B_D}$, B_i is optimal if and only if $\min(AET_{B_1}, AET_{B_2}, ..., AET_{B_n}) = AET_{B_i}$.*

3 Refactoring

Overview. The approach proposed in this paper aims at automatically restructuring a BPMN process in order to minimise its average execution time. It takes as input a BPMN process with duration and used resources for each task, a pool of shared resources and an IAT. We recall that in this work, a process is executed multiple times, the beginning of execution of each instance being separated from the previous one by the IAT. Our refactoring technique does not change the tasks themselves, but the way they are organised within the process. The main idea behind our approach is that we increase the parallelism of the process as much as possible but not systematically. For instance, if adding parallelism results in the increase of resource competition or bottlenecks coming from synchronisation delays (at merge gateways), we prefer to keep a sequential organisation of tasks. At the end, the approach returns a new BPMN process whose average execution time is optimal or close to the optimal. It is worth noting that, except for the position of the tasks, the semantics of the process is preserved (i.e., a task that is not necessarily executed (choice), or that is possibly repeated (loop) has the same behaviour in the final process).

Figure 2 gives an overview of the mains steps of the approach. Beyond the previously mentioned inputs, our approach also needs as input a set of task dependencies. These dependencies correspond to some strong ordering of tasks that cannot be changed by our refactoring approach and thus must be preserved in the final process. They can be given by the user or computed by analysing the data-flow graph corresponding to the BPMN process [5,10]. The first step (1) aims at computing an abstract graph corresponding to the given dependencies. This abstract graph is an intermediate format which is used throughout this work to simplify computations and restructuring that will finally lead to the resulting process. In some cases however, as explained in the previous section, the abstract graph cannot be generated because some conditions on the dependencies are not satisfied. Concretely, this means that several abstract graphs satisfy the given dependencies. Since the goal here is to generate an optimal process, we need to choose, among the possible graphs satisfying the conditions, the one that is optimal with respect to our goal. To do so, we explore all possible additional dependencies for which the conditions become true, and among all these solutions we keep the one making the resulting abstract graph exhibit the shortest execution time.

The next step (2) takes into account the shared resources and verifies whether they are sufficient to execute the current abstract graph smoothly, that is, without resource competition or synchronisation delays at merge gateways. If this is the case, the resulting BPMN is synthesised and is optimal. If the shared resources are not sufficient, two more steps are performed in the approach. Step (3) analyses the current abstract graph, identifies the different sources of competition/synchronisation issues, and rate them using a scoring system. Repeatedly, the task identified as the highest issue is removed from its parallel structure and put in sequence, until the shared resources allow a smooth execution of the process-to-be. Step (4) aims at refining the organisation of tasks within the abstract graph in order to find the best structure between the tasks that should be put in sequence and the others. When Steps (3) and (4) need to be applied, the resulting BPMN process may not be optimal, but is close to the optimal solution.

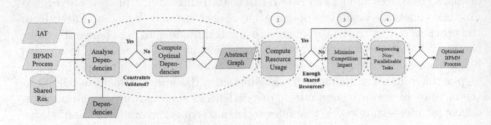

Fig. 2. Overview of the Approach

The rest of this section gives additional details on each step of the approach.

Computing Abstract Graph from Dependencies. The first step of this approach consists of computing the abstract graph corresponding to the process dependencies. This can be done using the algorithm proposed in [11], when the conditions stated by the authors are respected. These conditions ensure the uniqueness of the generated abstract graph. Thus, several abstract graphs respecting the dependencies of the process may exist when the conditions are not satisfied. Since our main concern is to generate an optimal abstract graph in terms of execution time, we need to pick the one with the shortest execution time. To do so, our idea is to iteratively add new dependencies to the initial ones, until obtaining a set of dependencies that satisfies the conditions. By doing so, we obtain all the possible abstract graphs satisfying the dependencies. Then, we keep the one with the shortest execution time.

This computation is performed by Algorithm 1. This algorithm takes as input the dependency graph built from the initial dependencies of the process, which is moved in the set of pending graphs S_{CB}. Then, for each pending graph, we iterate over its tasks (i.e., nodes) and add a new dependency between this task

---

Algorithm 1 Optimal Dependencies Finding

      Inputs: $G = (G_V, G_E)$ (Dependency graph built from the initial dependencies)
      Output: G_O (Optimal dependency graph validating the conditions)

1: $S_{CB} \leftarrow \{G\}$; $S_{NB} \leftarrow \emptyset$; $S_{PO} \leftarrow \emptyset$
2: **while** $S_{CB} \neq \emptyset$ **do**   ▷ Are there pending graphs?
3:     **for** $G_C \in S_{CB}$ **do**   ▷ Yes, iterate over each of them
4:        **for** $n \in G_{C_V}$ **do**   ▷ Then over each node of the current graph
5:            $S_{ND} \leftarrow findNonAlreadyDependentNodesOf(n)$
6:            **for** $nd \in S_{ND}$ **do**   ▷ Then over each non already dependent node
7:                $G'_C \leftarrow G_C.copy()$; $G'_C.addDependencyBetween(n, nd)$
8:                $G'_C.removeShortestPathBetweenNodes(n, nd)$
9:                **if** $conditionsSatisfied(G'_C)$ **then** $S_{PO} \leftarrow S_{PO} \cup \{G'_C\}$
10:               **else** $S_{NB} \leftarrow S_{NB} \cup \{G'_C\}$
11:              **end if**
12:         **end for**
13:       **end for**
14:     **end for**
15:     $S_{CB} \leftarrow S_{NB}$; $S_{NB} \leftarrow \emptyset$
16: **end while**
17: **return** $findOptimalGraph(S_{PO})$

---

and another task that is not already dependent nor transitively dependent of the current task (line 7). As this new dependency may generate a path (i.e., a (transitive) dependency) between two nodes that were already connected, the shortest path between these nodes is removed (i.e., the edges composing it are removed) in order to avoid the duplication of dependencies, while preserving the original ones (line 8). If this new dependency makes the constraints be satisfied, the current graph is added to the set of possibly optimal graphs S_{PO}. Otherwise, it is added to the set of new pending graphs S_{NB}. At the end of an iteration, S_{NB} is put in S_{CB} and if it is not empty, a new iteration starts. When the while loop finishes (line 16), each set of dependencies validating the conditions has been built and put in the set of possibly optimal dependencies S_{PO}. Then, the algorithm generates the abstract graph corresponding to each possibly optimal set of dependencies and computes its worst-case execution time. The one with the shortest execution time is returned. The corresponding abstract graph is finally generated, and all the non-dependent tasks are put in parallel with it. Since we do not consider the resources in this step, this abstract graph is an optimal version of the original process in terms of execution time, as tasks have been put as much as possible in parallel. However, as this algorithm explores all possible combinations of dependencies, its complexity is exponential. Nonetheless, real-world BPMN processes are usually small, thus even smaller are their dependencies. Consequently, the execution time of this algorithm is rather short in practice.

Example. Let us consider the trip organisation process shown in Fig. 1. According to the user, the dependencies that should be preserved by the approach are the ones shown in Fig. 3(a). As the reader can see, these dependencies do not validate the conditions stated previously, because for example, task *Reimbursement* has two predecessors (*Flight Booking* and *Return Documents*) that do not have the same successors.

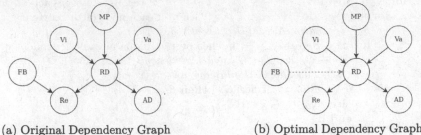

(a) Original Dependency Graph   (b) Optimal Dependency Graph

Fig. 3. Evolution of the Dependency Graph of the "Trip Organisation Process"

The result of the execution of Algorithm 1 on this dependency graph is shown in Fig. 3(b). As the reader can see, a new dependency has been added between tasks *Flight Booking* and *Return Documents*. The dependency between tasks *Flight Booking* and *Reimbursement* has been removed because these tasks are now transitively dependent through task *Return Documents*. These dependencies now validate the conditions, and the corresponding abstract graph is optimal, as it has the shortest worst-case execution time possible, that is 28UT.

Computation of Resource Usage. In the previous step, we have built an abstract graph that is an optimal representation of our initial process satisfying the dependencies that may exist between tasks. Nonetheless, this optimal graph has been built without considering the resources required by the tasks composing it to execute. Even if the execution time of the abstract graph may not vary a lot in a single instance context, it may drastically increase in the multi-instance context that we are dealing with, due to resource competition and synchronisation delays. The goal of this step is then to verify whether our optimal abstract graph can execute without such delays. To do so, we compute the resources needed by a single instance of the abstract graph to execute without resource competition. From this computation, we are able to compute the resources needed by multiple instances of the abstract graph to execute without resource competition. Then, we compare these resources to the shared ones. If the pool of computed resources is smaller than the pool of shared resources, the optimal abstract graph can execute without resource competition nor synchronisation delays. The corresponding BPMN process is then synthesised and returned to the user as optimal version of the original process. Otherwise, steps 3 & 4 of Fig. 2 are performed to limit the delays induced by the resource competition. In the latter case, the BPMN process returned to the user is close to the optimal one.

The first part of this step consists of transforming the current abstract graph into a *tasks execution flow*. A tasks execution flow is a representation in which each task of the abstract graph is pictured as a box, for which the length represents the duration. Tasks are put one after the other if they are executed sequentially, and one above the other if they are executed in parallel, along the time axis. In case of choices or loops, their probability of execution is also indicated. From this representation, we know exactly which task is executed at each moment. The resource usage at any time is then computed directly, by considering the resource usage of each currently executing task. Nonetheless, we recall that we are dealing with several instances of the abstract graph executing at the same time. Thus, we are interested in computing the global resource usage of the abstract graph. To do so, the idea is to count the maximum number of instances running at the same time. This is feasible because the worst-case execution time of the abstract graph and the IAT are known. Once the maximum number of instances running at the same time has been computed, the instances are divided into three blocks. The first block contains the pivot instance, that is the middle one. In other words, this instance is the instance for which the number of instances that started before it is equal to the number of instances that will start after it. The second block contains the instances that were already running before the beginning of the pivot instance. The third block contains the instances that started running after the beginning of the pivot instance. Then, each instance in block 2 & 3 is shifted by a precise number of IAT in order to represent the progression of its execution compared to the one of the pivot instance. Thus, instances belonging to the second block are shifted by a negative number of IAT, while instances belonging to the third block are shifted by a positive number of IAT. Finally, the tasks execution flow of each running instance is traversed, and the tasks executing at their relative instant of time compared to the pivot instance are retrieved. Then, we know precisely which tasks are executing at any instant of time of the execution. The global resource usage of the abstract graph (i.e., for multiple instances) is deduced by considering the maximum usage of each resource over the execution.

Algorithm 2 Multi-Instances Resource Computation

Input: T_S (Tasks executing per instant of time (single instance))
Output: R_G (Global resource pool needed by the abstract graph)

1: $T_M \leftarrow \emptyset$ ▷ List of tasks executing per unit of time
2: $NI \leftarrow \lceil \frac{WCET}{IAT} \rceil - 1$ ▷ Number of instances already running
3: **for** t = 0; t < WCET; t++ **do**
4:     $T_t \leftarrow \emptyset$ ▷ List of tasks executing at time t
5:     **for** i = -NI; i ≤ NI; i++ **do**
6:        $t_r \leftarrow i \times IAT + t$ ▷ Relative time of instance i
7:        **if** $0 \leq t_r <$ WCET **then**   ▷ Check that current instance is executing
8:           $T_t \leftarrow T_t \cup T_S.get(t_r)$ ▷ Add the tasks executing at $t = t_r$
9:        **end if**
10:    **end for**
11:     $T_M \leftarrow T_M \cup T_t$
12: **end for**
13: **return** $R_G \leftarrow extractGlobalPool(T_M)$

Algorithm 2 performs this computation. It takes as input the list of tasks executing per instant of time for a single instance. Then, it starts by computing the number of instances that were already running before the start of the pivot instance (line 2). By symmetry, it computes the number of instances that started executing after the beginning of the pivot instance. For each instant of time in the abstract graph execution, it iterates over the running instances. For each instance, it computes its relative instant of time t_r, that is its instant of time from the point of view of the pivot instance. Then, it verifies that this relative instant of time corresponds to an instant of time in which the current instance is running (i.e., has started and has not yet terminated). If this is the case, the tasks executing at this instant of time are added to the list of all tasks executing at this instant of time. This algorithm performs in linear time as it only traverses the list of tasks executing at each instant of time once.

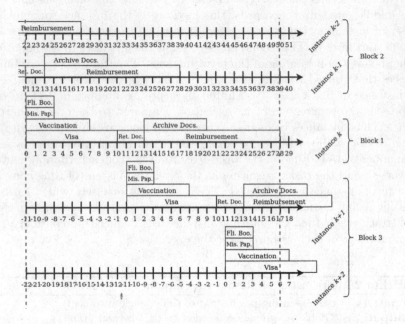

Fig. 4. Tasks Execution Flows of the Trip Organisation Process

Theorem 1. *(Optimality of BPMN Generation) Let A be the abstract graph generated from the original dependencies of the process, B the BPMN process synthesised from A, R_A the pool of available resources and R_C the pool of resources computed by Algorithm 2. Then, $R_C \leq R_A \implies B$ is optimal.*

Proof (Sketch). In a first time, A is generated from the given set of dependencies, without considering the resources. Either the dependencies validate the conditions stated in Sect. 2, in which case A is optimal according to [11], or not, in which case the optimal dependencies are computed using Algorithm 1. Then,

Algorithm 2 precisely computes the tasks executed at each instant of time of the execution of the multiple instances of B. It returns the maximum number of resources used at any instant of time, that we call R_C. If $R_A > R_C$, none of the instances will wait/compete to access a resource and execute a task, thus no delay will increase the execution time of the instances. Consequently, the execution time of B, which is the shortest execution time possible, is the same for each instance of B, i.e., $ET_{B_1} = ET_{B_2} = ... = ET_{B_n}$. By construction, the AET of B is then necessarily optimal: $AET_B = \frac{1}{n} \sum_{i=1}^{n} ET_{B_i} = ET_{B_1} = ET_{B_2} = ... = ET_{B_n}$ □

Example. Now, let us illustrate this computation on an example. Figure 4 shows the tasks execution flows corresponding to all the instances of the optimal trip organisation process running at the same time. The process has a worst-case execution time of 28UT, and is ran with an IAT of 11UT. The number of instances already executing when the pivot instance started is then $\lceil \frac{WCET}{IAT} \rceil - 1 = 2$. By symmetry, the same number of instances started executing after the pivot instance. Then, by progressing through the execution of the pivot instance (i.e., instance k), we are able to compute the tasks executed by all the running instances of the abstract graph. For example, at time $t = 10$, the pivot instance starts executing the task *Return Documents*. The corresponding relative time for instance $k - 1$ is $t = 21$, as this instance started executing 11UT ($1 \times$ IAT) before the pivot instance. Thus, it is executing task *Reimbursement*. By repeating this procedure for each instance, we obtain the list of tasks executing at each instant of time for multiple instances. From this list, we compute the global pool of resources needed by the process to execute without waiting times, that is 2 *assistants*, 1 *doctor*, 2 *financial staffs*, 1 *travel agency*, 2 *users* and 1 *visa office*.

Minimising Resource Competition Impact. At this point of the approach, we have computed the resource usage of our optimal abstract graph, and found that the shared resources were not sufficient to avoid resource competition and synchronisation delays. This step consists of verifying whether the lack of certain resources will strongly impact the average execution time of the abstract graph or not, and, if it is the case, to identify all the tasks that should be removed from their parallel constructs and put in sequence. Such tasks are called *non-parallelisable tasks*. To do so, we compute for each insufficient resource a value called *absorbance*. This value is the ratio between the amount of time at which the usage of the resource is lower than the number of available replicas of the resource, and the amount of time at which the usage of the resource is greater than this number. If this value is below a certain threshold, we conclude that the lack of the resource will not impact the average execution time of the abstract graph. If this is the case for each insufficient resource, the abstract graph does not need any modification. Thus, it is mapped to its equivalent BPMN representation [11] and returned to the user. Otherwise, some tasks have to be removed from their parallel constructs and put in sequence to limit the resource competition and the synchronisation delays. To do so, a score is assigned to each task, according to its duration and its resource usage: the longer the duration the smaller the score, and the higher the cost the higher the score. Then, the task with the highest score is put in sequence, and the absorbance of the new abstract graph is computed. If it is below the threshold, the computation stops, and the current task is put in the set of non-parallelisable tasks. Otherwise, the second task with highest score is put in sequence, and so on. This computation finishes either when the absorbance of the abstract graph reaches a value lower than the threshold for each lacking resource, or when all the tasks using a lacking resource have been put in sequence.

Algorithm 3 Find Non-Parallelisable Tasks

    Inputs: P_O, P_S, G, T (Optimal resource pool, shared resource pool, abstract graph, set of tasks of the abstract graph)

    Output: S_{NP} (Set of non-parallelisable tasks)

1: $computeScores(T)$
2: $P_L \leftarrow computeLackingResources(P_O, P_S)$; $modified \leftarrow True$; $S_{NP} \leftarrow \emptyset$
3: **while** $modified = True$ **do**   ▷ Iterate until fix point
4:     $modified \leftarrow False$
5:     **for** $r \in P_L$ **do**   ▷ Iterate over each lacking resource
6:         $\delta_O \leftarrow computeWeightedOverUsageTimeOf(r, G)$
7:         $\delta_U \leftarrow computeWeightedUnderUsageTimeOf(r, G)$
8:         $A \leftarrow \frac{\delta_O}{\delta_U} \times 100$ ▷ Compute absorbance of r
9:         **if** $A > Threshold$ **then**
10:            $T_{HS} \leftarrow getTaskWithHighestScore(r, T)$
11:            $T \leftarrow T \setminus \{T_{HS}\}$; $S_{NP} \leftarrow S_{NP} \cup \{T_{HS}\}$; $modified \leftarrow True$
12:            $putInSequence(T_{HS}, G)$
13:         **end if**
14:     **end for**
15: **end while**
16: **return** S_{NP}

Algorithm 3 performs this computation. It takes as input the optimal pool of resources P_O, the pool of shared resources P_S, the abstract graph G, and the set of tasks of the abstract graph T. First, it assigns a score to each task (line 1). Then, it computes the set of lacking resources (line 2). For each lacking resource r, it computes its absorbance A (lines 6, 7, 8). If A exceeds the threshold, the task with the highest score using this resource T_{HS} is put in sequence and added to the list of non-parallelisable tasks S_{NP}, and a new iteration starts. When the algorithm reaches a fix point (i.e., no tasks were put in sequence in the previous iteration), the while loop breaks, and the list of non-parallelisable tasks S_{NP} is returned. In this work, according to a study made on many examples (real-world and handcrafted), we found that the threshold giving the best results was 100. Thus, this threshold is used as default threshold in the approach. Nonetheless, the user can still specify his own threshold as input. This algorithm runs in linear time as it performs at most $|T|$ iterations before finishing.

Example. Now, let us consider the optimal abstract graph of the trip organisation process to illustrate this step. In this example, we consider that the shared

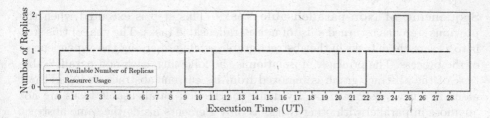

Fig. 5. Usage of Resource *assistant* Over Time

resources contain only one replica of the resource *assistant*, instead of the two required by the abstract graph to execute without resource competition. This means that tasks *Mission Paperwork* and *Archive Documents* will possibly be put in sequence, as they both require one replica of resource *assistant* to execute. Figure 5 shows the usage of the resource *assistant* over the execution time of the abstract graph. As the reader can see, the usage exceeds the total number of replicas by one between times 2 & 3, 13 & 14, and 24 & 25. Conversely, the usage is lower than the total number of replicas by one between times 9 & 11 and 20 & 22. The rest of the time, the replica is accessed without competition. The absorbance of resource *assistant* is then $\frac{1\times1+1\times1+1\times1}{2\times1+2\times1} = \frac{3}{4} = 75$. As this absorbance is lower than 100 (default threshold), the tasks *Mission Paperwork* and *Archive Documents* can remain in parallel. As no other resource is lacking, none of the tasks of the optimal abstract graph needs to be put in sequence. Thus, the BPMN process can directly be generated, as shown in Fig. 6. As the reader can see, as no non-parallelisable tasks have been found, this process is optimal as it has the highest degree of parallelism while respecting the original dependencies.

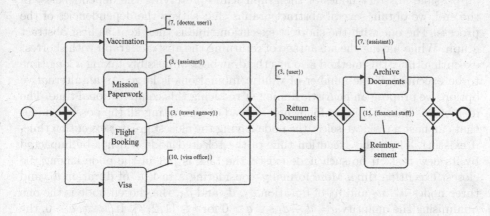

Fig. 6. Optimal Version of the Trip Organisation Process

Sequencing of Non-parallelisable Tasks. This step is executed when the previous step has returned a list of non-parallelisable tasks. The goal of this step is to *isolate* these tasks in the abstract graph, while preserving the dependencies of the process. The principle of isolation is the following: each non-parallelisable task of the abstract graph is removed from its current abstract node, and put alone in a new abstract node. By doing so, the non-parallelisable tasks are not anymore in parallel with other tasks, as only elements inside the same abstract node are parallelised. This new abstract node is then added to the set of abstract nodes of the abstract graph. As the dependencies of the process must be preserved by our approach, we split this step in two cases. In the first case, none of the non-parallelisable tasks belong to the dependencies of the process. Thereby, each non-parallelisable task can simply be put in a new abstract node, which is connected either to the first or last node of the abstract graph (i.e., it becomes either the first or the last abstract node of the abstract graph). By doing so, the non-parallelisable tasks are kept all together in sequence while ensuring the highest level of parallelism for the rest of the abstract graph, and thus the shortest execution time.

In the second case, some non-parallelisable tasks belong to the dependencies of the process. Thus, they cannot simply be put at the beginning or at the end of the abstract graph, as such restructuring may no longer satisfy the dependencies. Instead of removing these tasks from their nodes as we do in the first case, we extract all the tasks that should have been put in parallel with them. By doing so, the non-parallelisable tasks now belong to isolated nodes that will no longer be parallelised. Nonetheless, we still have to manage the tasks that we have just extracted. These tasks may be put at several different places of the abstract graph while preserving the dependencies of the process. As the main concern of this approach is to minimise the execution time, we propose to compute all the places where these tasks can be put. To do so, we try to put these tasks in all possible abstract nodes of the graph while preserving the dependencies. In the end, we obtain several abstract graphs that satisfy the dependencies of the process. The one with the shortest execution time is then kept as best abstract graph. While having the advantage of returning the abstract graph with shortest execution time, this method also has the drawback of possibly taking a long time to be executed, if the number of valid combinations is large. As an alternative option, we propose an heuristic aiming at reducing this computational time. The idea of this heuristic is the following: instead of computing all the possible nodes that can host a task, we select the node having the closest greater execution time, if existing. Thus, the execution time of the selected node will not be impacted by its new task. If no such node exists, the task is put in the node having the closest execution time. More formally, considering a task T of duration d_t, and three nodes n_1, n_2 and n_3 of duration d_1, d_2 and d_3, the chosen node is the one minimising the quantity $q = d_i - d_t$ s.t. $q > 0$ for $i \in \{1, 2, 3\}$. If $\nexists i$ s.t. $q > 0$, the chosen node is the one minimising the quantity $|d_i - d_t|$ for $i \in \{1, 2, 3\}$. This heuristic runs in linear time, but may generate an abstract graph that does not have the shortest execution time possible. Finally, the generated abstract graph is transformed into its equivalent BPMN process and returned to the user.

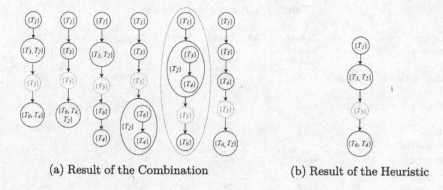

(a) Result of the Combination   (b) Result of the Heuristic

Fig. 7. Generation of Abstract Graph with Non-Parallelisable Tasks

Example. Let us consider a BPMN process with six tasks $T_1, T_2, T_3, T_4, T_5,$ T_6 in sequence, and the following dependencies: $(T_1, T_2), (T_1, T_3), (T_3, T_4),$ $(T_3, T_5), (T_5, T_6)$. Each task respectively has a duration of 6UT, 12UT, 10UT, 2UT, 7UT, 1UT. Finally, T_5 has been marked as non-parallelisable during Step 3. Figure 7 shows the abstract graphs generated after this step, both for the combination method and the heuristic. Figure 7(a) shows the six different abstract graphs generated by the combination method. All of them have task T_5 in sequence in an isolated node, and respect the initial dependencies. According to the duration of each task, the fifth abstract graph (circled) has the shortest worst-case execution time (26UT), and is the one returned by the combination method. Figure 7(b) shows the abstract graph generated by the heuristic. As the reader can see, T_2 is now in parallel with T_3 and T_4 in parallel with T_6. The resulting abstract graph has an execution time of 27UT, which is close to the best one, but not the best.

4   Tool and Experiments

The approach has been fully implemented in Java. It consists of approximately 10,000 lines of code, and the tool is available online [16]. It has been tested on various handcrafted and real-world examples found in the literature. The experiments allowed us to evaluate our approach both in terms of usefulness and performance, by considering the gain of the optimised process in terms of AET and the time taken by the tool to execute. The number of instances for each process tested vary between 20 and 100.

Table 1 summarises these experiments. Column 1 gives the name of the process. Columns 2, 3 & 4 show several characteristics of the process (number of nodes, flows, types of resources, replicas of resources, IAT). Columns 5 & 6 provide respectively the AET of the initial process and of the optimised process. Column 7 shows the gain that was obtained by optimising the process. Column 8 states whether the available pool of resources is sufficient to execute the opti-

Table 1. Experimental results

BPMN process	Nodes/ Flows	Types/ Number of Resources	IAT	Initial AET (UT)	Final AET (UT)	Gain	Sufficient Resources	Time (ms)
Perish. Goods Tran. [21]	24/26	9/17	6	26	14	46.2%	✓	563
Employee Hiring [4]	19/21	7/12	3	30	18	40.0%	✓	607
Trip Organisation [9]	11/11	6/11	7	41	28	31.7%	✓	588
Patient Diagnosis [1]	14/15	4/12	20	61	46	24.6%	✓	624
Shipment Process [12]	16/18	5/10	5	46	42	8.70%	✓	531
Evisa Application [19]	11/11	3/7	5	84	71	15.5%	✗	797
Employee Recruit. [11]	14/14	7/11	5	92	80	13.0%	✗	873
Account Opening [17]	22/25	6/17	8	67	63	5.97%	✗	732
Goods Delivery [3]	11/12	6/16	1	78	77	1.28%	✗	696

mal version of the process or not. Column 9 gives the time taken by the tool to execute.

The results can be split in two parts: the processes having enough resources to execute the optimal version of the process, and the others. In the first case, the AET of the generated process is optimal, and is generally a significant improvement of the initial one (up to 46% for the first process). A lower gain only indicates that the initial process was already syntactically close to its optimal form, not that the approach does not perform well. In the second case, the gain is lower than in the first case (up to 15.5%), due to the decrease of parallelism induced by the sequencing of some tasks. Overall, the tool executes in less than 1 s on real-world processes, which is satisfactory as this approach is executed at design time.

5   Related Work

In this section, we focus on existing works on process refactoring. [20] presents six common mistakes made by developers when modelling with BPMN. For each problem, the authors present best practices for avoiding these issues. As an example, the authors propose to use explicit gateways instead of using multiple incoming/outgoing sequence flows. [2] presents a technique for detecting refactoring opportunities in process model repositories. The technique works by first computing activity similarity and then computing three similarity scores for fragment pairs of process models. Using these similarity scores, four different kinds of refactoring opportunities can be systematically identified. As a result, the approach proposes to rename activities or to introduce subprocesses. IBUPROFEN, a business process refactoring approach based on graphs, is presented in [13,18]. IBUPROFEN defines a set of 10 refactoring algorithms grouped into three categories: maximisation of relevant elements, fine-grained granularity reduction, and completeness. These works mostly focus on syntactic issues and propose syntactic improvements of the process by, for instance, removing unreachable nodes or by merging consecutive gateways of the same type. They do not aim at providing any kind of optimisation regarding the process being designed as we do. Moreover, they do not consider rich models as we do (including, e.g., time and resources).

In [15], the authors present an approach for optimising the redesign of process models. It is based on capturing process improvement strategies as constraints in a structural-temporal model. Each improvement strategy is represented by a binary variable. An objective function that represents a net benefit function of cost and quality is then maximised to find the best combination of process improvements that can be made to maximise the objective. The BPMN subset used in [15] is similar to the one we use in this paper in terms of expressiveness. However, the approach is rather different since they compute optimal redesigns with respect to some constraints, thus resulting in a change in the number or execution of tasks (e.g., by splitting a task into several ones, or by executing one task or another instead of these two tasks in sequence). In contrast, we do not change the semantics of the application but only the structure of the process (the order in which the tasks are executed).

[11] proposes a semi-automated approach for helping non-experts in BPMN to model business processes using this notation. Alternatively, [14] presents an approach which combines notes taking in constrained natural language with process mining to automatically produce BPMN diagrams in real-time as interview participants describe them with stories. In this work, we tackle this issue from a different angle since we assume that an existing description of the process exists and that we want to automatically optimise it by updating its structure. In [9], the authors propose a refactoring procedure whose final goal is to reduce the total execution time of the process given as input. This solution relies on refactoring operations that reorganise the tasks in the process by taking into account the resources used by those tasks. This work assumes that processes are executed only once (single executions) and that only one replica of each resource is avalaible. In contrast, our approach applies refactoring techniques on processes that are executed multiple times, and for which several replicas of each resource can be available (no contraints on the number of resources).

6 Concluding Remarks

In this paper, we have proposed a solution to the optimisation of business processes using refactoring techniques. Processes are described using BPMN extended with time and resources, and are executed multiple times. The final goal of this approach is to restructure the tasks within the process in order to reduce the execution time and optimise the resource usage while avoiding bottlenccks. To do so, the approach applies several successive steps. The first steps aim at analysing the dependencies between tasks and the resources usage. From these first results, the approach determines whether some tasks have to be put in sequence to limit eventual bottlenecks, or if all the tasks can be put in parallel. Finally, it returns a process that is either optimal or close to the optimal. The whole approach is fully automated by using a tool we implemented, and was applied to a set of real-world processes in order to evaluate its usefulness and performance. The experiments show satisfactory results both in terms of optimisation and computation time. The main perspective of this work is to consider non-fixed IATs, such as IATs defined using probabilistic functions.

References

1. Bazhenova, E., Zerbato, F., Oliboni, B., Weske, M.: From BPMN process models to DMN decision models. Inf. Syst. **83**, 69–88 (2019)
2. Dijkman, R.M., Gfeller, B., Küster, J.M., Völzer, H.: Identifying refactoring opportunities in process model repositories. Inf. Softw. Technol. **53**(9), 937–948 (2011)
3. Durán, F., Falcone, Y., Rocha, C., Salaün, G., Zuo, A.: From static to dynamic analysis and allocation of resources for BPMN processes. In: Rewriting Logic and Its Applications: 14th International Workshop, WRLA 2022, Munich, Germany, 2–3 April 2022, Revised Selected Papers, pp. 3–21. Springer, Cham (2022). https://doi.org/10.1007/978-3-031-12441-9_1
4. Durán, F., Rocha, C., Salaün, G.: Computing the parallelism degree of timed BPMN processes. In: Mazzara, M., Ober, I., Salaün, G. (eds.) STAF 2018. LNCS, vol. 11176, pp. 320–335. Springer, Cham (2018). https://doi.org/10.1007/978-3-030-04771-9_24
5. Durán, F., Rocha, C., Salaün, G.: Symbolic specification and verification of data-aware BPMN processes using rewriting modulo SMT. In: Rusu, V. (ed.) WRLA 2018. LNCS, vol. 11152, pp. 76–97. Springer, Cham (2018). https://doi.org/10.1007/978-3-319-99840-4_5
6. Durán, F., Rocha, C., Salaün, G.: A rewriting logic approach to resource allocation analysis in business process models. Sci. Comput. Program. **183** (2019)
7. Durán, F., Rocha, C., Salaün, G.: A rewriting logic approach to resource allocation analysis in business process models. Sci. Comput. Program. **183** (2019)
8. Durán, F., Rocha, C., Salaün, G.: Resource provisioning strategies for BPMN processes: specification and analysis using maude. J. Log. Algebraic Methods Program. **123**, 100711 (2021)
9. Durán, F., Salaün, G.: Optimization of BPMN processes via automated refactoring. In: Troya, J., Medjahed, B., Piattini, M., Yao, L., Fernández, P., Ruiz-Cortés, A. (eds.) Service-Oriented Computing: 20th International Conference, ICSOC 2022, Seville, 29 November– 2 December 2022, Proceedings, pp. 3–18. Springer, Cham (2022). https://doi.org/10.1007/978-3-031-20984-0_1
10. Eshuis, R., Gorp, P.V.: Synthesizing data-centric models from business process models. Computing **98**(4), 345–373 (2016)
11. Falcone, Y., Salaün, G., Zuo, A.: Semi-automated modelling of optimized BPMN processes. In: Proceedings of SCC'21, pp. 425–430. IEEE (2021)

12. Falcone, Y., Salaün, G., Zuo, A.: Probabilistic model checking of BPMN processes at runtime. In: ter Beek, M.H., Monahan, R. (eds.) Integrated Formal Methods: 17th International Conference, IFM 2022, Lugano, Switzerland, 7–10 June 2022, Proceedings, pp. 191–208. Springer, Cham (2022). https://doi.org/10.1007/978-3-031-07727-2_11

13. Fernández-Ropero, M., Pérez-Castillo, R., Piattini, M.: Graph-based business process model refactoring. In: Proceedings of the 3rd Intenational Symposium on Data-Driven Process Discovery and Analysis, vol. 1027 of CEUR Workshop Proceedings, pp. 16–30 (2013)

14. Ivanchikj, A., Serbout, S., Pautasso, C.: From text to visual BPMN process models: design and evaluation. In: Proceedings of MoDELS'20, pp. 229–239. ACM (2020)

15. Kumar, A., Liu, R.: Business workflow optimization through process model redesign. In: Proceedings of TEM'22, LNCS, pp. 3068–3084. Springer, Cham (2022)

16. Nivon, Q.: Automated Tool for Multi-Instance BPMN Processes Optimisation (2023). https://github.com/KyriuDev/MultiInstancesRefactoring

17. Nivon, Q., Salaün, G.: Debugging of BPMN processes using coloring techniques. In: Tapia Tarifa, S.L., Proença, J. (eds.) Formal Aspects of Component Software: 18th International Conference, FACS 2022, Virtual Event, 10–11 November 2022, Proceedings, pp. 90–109. Springer, Cham (2022). https://doi.org/10.1007/978-3-031-20872-0_6

18. Pérez-Castillo, R., Fernández-Ropero, M., Piattini, M.: Business process model refactoring applying IBUPROFEN: an industrial evaluation. J. Syst. Softw. **147**, 86–103 (2019)

19. Salaün, G.: Quantifying the similarity of BPMN processes. In: Proceedings of APSEC'22, pp. 1–10 (2022)

20. Silingas, D., Mileviciene, E.: Refactoring BPMN models: from 'Bad Smells' to best practices and patterns. In: BPMN 2.0 Handbook, pp. 125–134 (2012)

21. Valderas, P., Torres, V., Serral, E.: Modelling and executing IoT-enhanced business processes through BPMN and microservices. J. Syst. Softw. **184**, 111139 (2022)

Verified Scalable Parallel Computing with Why3

Olivia Proust and Frédéric Loulergue

Univ Orléans, INSA CVL, LIFO EA 4022, Orléans, France
olivia.proust@etu.univ-orleans.fr, frederic.loulergue@univ-orleans.fr

Abstract. BSML is a pure functional library for the multi-paradigm language OCaml. BSML embodies the principles of the Bulk Synchronous Parallel (BSP) model, a model of scalable parallel computing. We propose a formalization of BSML primitives with WhyML, the specification language of Why3 and specify and prove the correctness of most of the BSML standard library. Finally, we develop and verify the correctness of a small BSML application.

Keywords: scalable parallel computing · functional programming · deductive verification · interactive theorem proving

1 Introduction

High-level approaches to big data analytics such as Hadoop MapReduce [26] or Apache Spark [1] are often inspired by bulk synchronous parallelism (BSP) [25] a model of scalable parallel computing. In this context, scalable means that the number of processors of the parallel machines running BSP programs could range from a few to several thousand cores or more. Bulk Synchronous Parallel ML (BSML) [19] is a pure functional library for the multi-paradigm language OCaml[1]. BSML embodies the principles of the BSP model, at a higher level than libraries such as the BSPlib library [14] and can easily express patterns [13,17] (or algorithmic skeletons [4]) of frameworks such as MapReduce or Spark.

Why3 [2,3] is a framework for the deductive verification of programs. It provides a specification and programming language named WhyML which can be used directly or as an intermediate language for other tools to verify C [15], Java [9], Ada or Rust [7] programs. The framework itself also provides mini-C and mini-Python front-ends. Why3 generates verification conditions to be verified by external provers. A strong point of Why3 is that it targets a large variety of provers including Alt-Ergo [5], Z3 [21] and CVC5. Correct-by-construction OCaml code can be extracted from WhyML.

Our contributions are the formalization of BSML and its standard library in WhyML and its use in the specification and verification of a scalable parallel function for the maximum prefix sum problem, using map and reduce skeletons.

---

[1] https://ocaml.org.

C. Ferreira and T. A. C. Willemse (Eds.): SEFM 2023, LNCS 14323, pp. 246–262, 2023.
https://doi.org/10.1007/978-3-031-47115-5_14

The remainder of the paper is organized as follows. In Sect. 2, we give an overview of Why3 and WhyML, including its limitations when dealing with higher-order functions. We introduce functional bulk synchronous parallel programming with BSML in Sect. 3. Section 4 is devoted to the formalization of the primitives of BSML and its application to the specification and verification of the BSML standard library. We consider the specification, development and verification of a small application: a parallel function that solves the maximum prefix sum problem in Sect. 5. We discuss related work in Sect. 6 and conclude in Sect. 7.

The set of Why3 modules is called WhyBSML and is available at:

$$\text{https://doi.org/10.5281/zenodo.8166092.}$$

2   An Overview of Why3

2.1   Specifying and Verifying Functional Programs with Why3

Why3 is often use in the verification of imperative programs. As BSML is purely functional and BSML applications mostly used the functional features of OCaml, we focus here on the verification of functional programs. This focus is also a necessity as we will explain in the next subsection.

In addition to its core features, Why3 provides a standard library with data structures such as lists and arrays, as well as basic arithmetic logic with integers and reals. We illustrate this short introduction with the example of Fig. 1. Note that this figure presents a pretty-printed version of the actual code, for example /\ is rendered as ∧, -> as →, 'a as α, etc.

WhyML developments are organized in *modules*. The example defines two modules: Max (lines 1–8) and MaxList (lines 10-32). Defined modules can be used in other modules with the use keyword. We use some modules of the Why3 standard library: int.Int about integer arithmetic (lines 2 and 11) and list.List, list.Length, list.NthNoOpt for basic definitions and facts about lists (lines 12–14).

The module Max is devoted to the specification and definition of a function max which returns the larger of two integers. This function does not have any pre-condition but its post-conditions are introduced by the keyword ensures.

Assuming the file maximum.mlw contains only the module Max, verifying that max satisfies its preconditions using the prover Alt-Ergo can be done with the following command:

```
why3 prove --prover alt-ergo maximum.mlw
```

and the tool answers max indeed satisfies its contract:

```
File maximum.mlw:
Goal max'vc.
Prover result is: Valid (0.00s, 8 steps).
```

```
1   module Max
2      use int.Int
3
4      let max (x : int) (y : int) : int
5         ensures { result = x ∨ result = y }
6         ensures { result ≥ x ∧ result ≥ y }
7      = if x < y then y else x
8   end
9
10  module MaxList
11     use int.Int
12     use list.List
13     use list.Length
14     use list.NthNoOpt
15     use Max
16
17     function ([]) (l : list α) (i : int) : α= nth i l
18
19     let rec maximum (l : list int) : int
20        requires { length l > 0 }
21        ensures { ∀ i:int. 0 ≤ i < length l →result ≥ l[i] }
22        ensures { ∃ i:int. 0 ≤ i < length l ∧ l[i] = result }
23        variant { l }
24     = match l with
25     | Nil → absurd
26     | Cons h Nil →h
27     | Cons h t →
28        let _ = assert { ∀ i:int. 0 ≤ i < length t →
29                                   l[i+1] = t[i] } in
30        max h (maximum t)
31     end
32  end
```

Fig. 1. A WhyML Example

In our example, most of the functions to verify are recursive and often manipulate lists. Lines 19–31 are an example of a recursive function that takes a list of integers and returns the highest value the list contains.

To write the contract of function `maximum`, we use the notation l[i] to access the ith element of list l. This notation is defined as a binary function in line 17 and is actually an alias for the nth function of the standard library. Note that this definition is introduced by the keyword `function` instead of the keyword `let` (as in line 4). The purpose of ([]) is to be used only in specifications while `max` is code that is meant to be executed. Pure functions may be used in both roles if they are defined using both keywords. In this example, `max` cannot be used in assertions while the bracket notation cannot be used in programs.

For `maximum`, we have a larger contract with new clause types. We add a pre-condition (following the keyword `requires`) to this contract, due to the fact that our function is not defined on empty lists. To ensure termination, we define a `variant`, which must be decreasing with each recursive call. The recursive call in line 30 is indeed call on the tail of the input list, thus this call is made on a strictly smaller argument than l. The variant can be a term of any type as long as this type comes with a well-founded order relation. It can even be a sequence of terms: in this case, lexicographic ordering is used.

We need quantifiers to express our post-conditions. The maximum value must be contained in the list (line 22 using ∃), and must be greater than or equal to all the values in the list (line 21 using ∀).

The definition of the function follows in lines 24–30. It proceeds by pattern matching on the input list. The case of the empty list (constructor `Nil`) is `absurd` as the pre-condition specifies the input list should not be empty (expressed as a fact on its length in line 20). If the list is a singleton (case `(Cons h Nil)`), the result is of course the only element of the list. Otherwise — and let us ignore lines 28–29 for the moment — the result is the maximum of the head and the recursive call on the tail (line 30). Without lines 28–29, the execution of the tool now answers:

```
File maximum.mlw:
Goal max'vc.
Prover result is: Valid (0.00s, 8 steps).
File maximum.mlw:
Goal maximum'vc.
Prover result is: Timeout (5.00s).
```

Using Z3 or CVC5, or increasing the timeout, or changing the proof strategy does not change the outcome. It is possible to apply transformations to the goals. Using the Why3 IDE, just splitting the verification condition for `maximum` gives five verification conditions: one for verifying the empty case is indeed absurd, one to check that the recursive call is indeed decreasing, one to check the pre-condition of the recursive call and one for each post-conditions. All these sub-goals are valid except for the one corresponding to the post-condition in line 22 remain unknown. To help the provers, we added lines 28–29 which relate elements of l with elements of its tail via `nth`. This assertion is easily verified and then eases the verification of the post-condition. The answer of the tool changes to:

```
Prover result is: Valid (0.09s, 749 steps).
```

2.2   Limitations with Higher-Order Functions

To show the limitations of Why3 in handling higher-order functions, let us consider the example of Fig. 2. Intuitively, `option` α extends the type α with a value `None` and all the other values are encapsulated in the constructor `Some`.

In lines 1–10, we define a module `Concrete` containing the definition of a function `remove_option` that extracts the value encapsulated in an optional value assuming this value is not `None`. In the module `Failure`, we apply this function but through a higher-order function `apply` that just applies a function

```
1   module Concrete
2     use export option.Option
3
4     let remove_option (opt : option α) : α
5       requires { opt ≠None } ensures { (Some result) = opt }
6   = match opt with
7     | Some x → x
8     | None → absurd
9     end
10  end
11  module Failure
12    use Concrete
13    let apply (f:α→β)(a:α) : β= f a
14
15    let test_KO (c: option α) : α(* CANNOT BE VERIFIED *)
16      requires { c ≠None } ensures { Some(result) = c }
17  = apply remove_option c
18  end
19  module Abstract
20    use export option.Option
21
22    val function remove_option(opt: option α) : α
23    axiom remove_option: ∀ x: α. remove_option(Some x) = x
24  end
25  module Success
26    use Abstract
27    let apply (f:α→β)(a:α) : β= f a
28
29    let test_OK (c: option α) : α
30      requires { c ≠None } ensures { Some(result) = c }
31  = apply remove_option c
32  end
```

Fig. 2. Limitations with Higher-Order Functions

to a value. The tool fails to verify the function test_KO which intuitively does exactly the same as remove_option. Note that if remove_option was performing side effects or was partial because it may raise exceptions, Why3 would reject the program with an error. Here the problem is less visible. Indeed, the arguments of a higher-order function must be purely functional and *total* functions. In our case remove_option is not total as its pre-condition excludes None. The manifestation of the problem can be seen in a sub-verification condition generated by Why3: $\forall$ opt:option α. opt $\neq$None, which is impossible to prove.

Still, as most BSML primitives are higher-order functions, and we need to use functions such as remove_option, a work-around was needed. Our solution is shown in module Abstract (lines 19–24). Instead of writing a concrete implementation of remove_option, we *declare* a function remove_option without defining it, and we only give its semantics (with an axiom) when the pre-condition is met.

It looks like a total function but if its application does not satisfy the precondition then it is impossible to reason about the result of the application. If the overall verification of a client code works despite an incorrect application of remove_option, it means the result of the incorrect application was not used. In module Success, the same client code as module Failure uses module Abstract instead of module Concrete and the verification succeeds.

3   Functional Bulk Synchronous Parallelism

The OCaml language is a versatile programming language that combines functional, imperative and object-oriented paradigms. BSML [19] (Bulk Synchronous Parallel ML) is an OCaml-based library that embodies the principles of the BSP [25] (Bulk Synchronous Parallel) model. It provides a range of constants and functions to facilitate BSP programming. The BSP machine, viewed as a homogeneous distributed memory system with a point-to-point communication network and a global synchronization unit, serves as the underlying architecture for BSML. BSP programs, composed of consecutive super-steps, run on this kind of machine. The execution of each super-step follows a distinct pattern, starting with the computation phase where each processor-memory pair performs local computations using data available locally. This phase is followed by the communication phase, during which processors can request and exchange data with other processors. Finally, the synchronization phase concludes the super-step, synchronizing all processors globally.

With its collection of four expressive functions and constants like bsp_p representing the number of processors in the BSP machine, BSML empowers developers to create BSP algorithms. While OCaml supports imperative programming and BSML can exploit it [16], in this paper we only consider the pure functional aspects of OCaml and BSML. Indeed, the four BSML functions are higher-order functions but Why3 does not handle non-pure function arguments. This deliberate focus differentiates it from the imperative counterparts provided by libraries such BSPlib for C [14]. The types and informal semantics of BSML primitives are listed in Fig. 3.

Let us consider a function f that maps integers to values of type α (denoted as f: int$\rightarrow\alpha$ in OCaml). The BSML primitive mkpar f produces a *parallel vector* of type α par when applied to function f. Within this parallel vector, each processor, identified by the index value i within the range $0 \leq i <$ bsp_p ,stores the computed value of f i . For instance, employing the expression mkpar(fun i$\rightarrow$i) yields a parallel vector denoted as $\langle 0, \ldots,$ bsp_p $- 1\rangle$ of type int par . Throughout subsequent discussions, we shall refer to this parallel vector as this . Additionally, the function replicate possesses the type $\alpha \rightarrow \alpha$ par and can be defined as follows: let replicate $=$ fun x $\rightarrow$ mkpar(fun i $\rightarrow$ x) . By employing the expression replicate x, the value x becomes uniformly available across all processors within the parallel vector. Parallel vectors always have size bsp_p .

To apply a parallel vector of functions (which is not a function) to a parallel vector of values, one has to use the primitive apply . Both mkpar and apply

$$\texttt{bsp\_p} : \texttt{int}$$
$$\texttt{bsp\_p} = p$$

$$\texttt{mkpar} : (\texttt{int} \to \alpha) \to \alpha\,\texttt{par}$$
$$\texttt{mkpar}\ f = \langle f\,0,\ \ldots,\ f\,(p-1)\rangle$$

$$\texttt{proj} : \alpha\,\texttt{par} \to (\texttt{int} \to \alpha)$$
$$\texttt{proj}\ \langle v_0,\ \ldots,\ v_{p-1}\rangle = \texttt{function}\,0 \to v_0 \mid \ldots \mid p-1 \to v_{p-1}$$

$$\texttt{apply} : (\alpha \to \beta)\texttt{par} \to \alpha\,\texttt{par} \to \beta\,\texttt{par}$$
$$\texttt{apply}\ \langle f_0,\ \ldots,\ f_{p-1}\rangle\ \langle v_0,\ \ldots,\ v_{p-1}\rangle = \langle f_0\ v_0,\ \ldots,\ f_{p-1}\ v_{p-1}\rangle$$

$$\texttt{put} : (\texttt{int} \to \alpha)\texttt{par} \to (\texttt{int} \to \alpha)\texttt{par}$$
$$\texttt{put}\ \langle tosend_0,\ \ldots,\ tosend_{p-1}\rangle = \langle received_0,\ \ldots,\ received_{p-1}\rangle$$
$$\text{where for all } src,\ dst$$
$$0 \le src,\ dst < p \Rightarrow received_{dst}\ src = tosend_{src}\ dst$$

Fig. 3. BSML primitives

are executed within the pure computation phase of a super-step. For communications and an implicit synchronization barrier, the last two primitives $\texttt{proj}$ and $\texttt{put}$ should be applied. $\texttt{proj}$ is essentially an inverse of $\texttt{mkpar}$ but the resulting function is partial and only defined on the domain [0, p-1] . As the first constant constructor of any inductively defined type is considered as the empty message, $\texttt{put}$ allows to program any communication pattern of a BSP super-step. In the input vector of $\texttt{put}$, each function encodes the message to be sent to other processors by the processor holding it. In the result vector, each function represents the message received from other processors by the processor holding the function.

Figure 4 presents a small BSML example using its primitives and $\textbf{parfun}$ which is part of its standard library. $\texttt{List.map}$ and $\texttt{List.fold\_left}$ are part of the OCaml standard library and are sequential map and reduce functions.

At lines 4–5, we define a function $\texttt{list\_of\_par}$ which converts a parallel vector into a list. This function requires a full super-step for its execution because it needs data exchanges. Also part of the BSML standard library, $\texttt{procs}$ has type $\texttt{int list}$ and is the list [0;...;bsp_p-1] .

At lines 7–8, we define an algorithmic skeleton: a parallel map that operates on a distributed list (represented here as a value of type α list par). This function also requires the computation phase of a super-step and does not need any data exchange or synchronization.

From line 10 to 13, we define the $\textbf{reduce}$ algorithmic skeleton, using a binary associative operation $\texttt{op}$ and a neutral element $\texttt{e}$, it "sums" a distributed list into a single value. It proceeds in two steps. First, each processor compute a partial "sum" of the list it holds locally. Second, this vector of partial sums is transformed into a list which is finally summed up. As we call $\texttt{list\_of\_par}$, a full super-step is required.

Finally, in lines 15–18, we implement a parallel function to solve the maximum prefix sum problem. The goal is to compute the maximum value among the sums of the prefixes of a list. Computing at the same time the maximum prefix sum and the sum of a list (in a pair) can be implemented using map and reduce . For example, on a machine with at least 4 processors, the value of mps (mkpar(function|0→[1;2]|1→[-1;2]|2→[-1;3]|3→[-4]|_→[])) is 6. Indeed, the argument of mps is a distributed version (on 4 processors) of the list [1;2;-1;2;-1;3;-4] and its prefix with the largest sum is the list without its last element. We specify and prove the correctness of mps in Sect. 5.

```
1   open Bsml
2   open Stdlib.Base
3
4   let list_of_par (v: α par) : α list =
5     List.map (proj v) procs
6
7   let map : (α→β) → α list par → β list par =
8     fun f v → parfun (List.map f) v
9
10  let reduce : (α→α→α) → α → α list par → α =
11    fun op e v →
12      let locally_reduced =parfun (List.fold_left op e) v in
13      List.fold_left op e (list_of_par locally_reduced)
14
15  let mps : int list par → int =
16    let op (xm, xs) (ym, ys) = (max 0 (max xm (xs+ym)), xs+ys) in
17    let f x = (max 0 x, x) in
18    fun v → fst (reduce op (0, 0) (map f v))
```

Fig. 4. A BSML Example

4   Formalization of BSML Core and Standard Library

To be able to specify and write BSML programs, we need BSML primitives in WhyML. BSML primitives are implemented in parallel on top of MPI [23] called through OCaml's Foreign Function Interface (FFI). Therefore, we cannot provide BSML in WhyML as an implementation. We need to give a BSML *theory*: a set of constant, axioms and function declarations. The axiomatization of BSML primitives can be found in Fig. 5. The semantics of functions mkpar, apply, proj and put are expressed in their contract (lines 12–24) while the strict positivity condition on bsp_p is given as an axiom on line 4. The type of parallel vector is abstract. Still we need to be able to observe parallel vectors. That is the role of logic function get which is a ghost function: it can only be used in specifications. A parallel vector is fully defined by the values all the processors hold as expressed by the axiom **extensionality** in lines 9-10. The axiomatization is very close to the informal semantics of Fig. 3. Instead of

```
1   theory BSML
2     use int.Int
3     val constant bsp_p : int
4     axiom at_least_one_processor : bsp_p > 0
5
6     type par α
7     val ghost function get (_ : par α) (_ : int) : α
8     axiom extensionality:
9       ∀ v v': par α.
10        (∀ i: int. 0≤i<bsp_p →get v i = get v' i) →v = v'
11
12    val mkpar (f : int →α ) : par α
13      ensures { ∀i:int. 0 ≤ i < bsp_p → get result i = f i }
14
15    val apply (f : par (α →β)) (v : par α) : par β
16      ensures { ∀i:int. 0 ≤ i < bsp_p →
17                         get result i = (get f i) (get v i) }
18
19    val proj (v : par α) (x : int) : α
20      ensures { result = get v x }
21
22    val put (v : par (int →α)) : par (int →α)
23      ensures { ∀s d:int. 0 ≤ s < bsp_p → 0 ≤ d < bsp_p →
24                         (get result d) s = (get v s) d }
25  end
```

Fig. 5. BSML Theory in WhyML

considering the parallel vectors globally with the notation $\langle v_0, \ldots, v_{p-1}\rangle$, we consider each value v_i denoted by get v i.

It is possible to realize this theory by a sequential implementation, for example implementing parallel vectors with sequential lists or arrays. This ensures the consistency of this theory.

To illustrate the use of this theory, we now specify, implement and verify several of the functions provided in the BSML standard library. The first one is replicate:

```
let replicate (x: α) : par α
  ensures { ∀ i:int. 0 ≤ i < bsp_p → get result i = x }
= mkpar(fun _ → x)
```

This verified function has only one post-condition: the result of replication is parallel vector which contains the same value everywhere.

In Sect. 3, we mentioned the function parfun without defining it. Its implementation and specification follows, as well as the definition of function parfun2:

```
let parfun (f : α → β) (v: par α) : par β
  ensures { ∀ i:int. 0 ≤ i < bsp_p →
                     get result i = f (get v i) }
```

```
= apply (replicate f) v
let parfun2 (f : α → β → γ) (u : par α) (v : par β) : par γ
  ensures { ∀ i:int. 0 ≤ i < bsp_p →
                        get result i = f (get u i) (get v i) }
= apply (parfun f u) v
```

It shows how to use the `apply` primitive. There is also a `parfun3` function omitted here.

Next, we use the communication primitive `proj`. As we wrote in Sect. 3, `proj` is essentially the inverse of `mkpar`. This function allows us to obtain the value of a vector `v` at a given processor `i`. However, it should not be used for such individual vector access, otherwise the performances would be extremely poor. Indeed, a call to `proj` requires a communication phase that is a total exchange and a global synchronization barrier. The use of `proj` should thus be thought as a collective operation. Note that `proj` and `get` have the same semantics. However, the intent is very different: `get` is written only in specifications, can be thought as an indexed array access, and is used for *local* reasoning, while `proj` is used only in programs and requires a full super-step to execute. `proj` should rather be thought as a *global* (i.e. concerning and involving all the processors) conversion of a parallel vector into a function.

To illustrate `proj`, we define `list_of_par`. As we mentioned before this function requires a complete super-step to run. Again it should be seen as a *global* conversion from parallel vectors to lists:

```
let function list_of_par (v : par α) : list α
  ensures { ∀ i:int. 0 ≤ i < bsp_p → result[i] = get v i }
  ensures { length result = bsp_p }
= map (proj v) (procs())
```

As in the BSML/OCaml version we call `procs` – which needs to be a function for Why3 to accept the code. `procs` returns the list of all processor identifiers. The definition of `procs` relies on a function `from_to` itself implemented using a `init` function. Our contribution does also contain a library of sequential functions, mostly on lists, as well as verified lemmas stating their properties. These functions can in most cases be used both in programs and in specifications.

Finally, the `put` primitive is illustrated to implement a broadcast function. This data exchange (and implicit global synchronization) function is more precise than `proj`, in the sense that with `proj` each processor sends the same value to all processors, while with `put` each processor can send a different value to each destination processor. Also, as some values are considered as empty messages, this makes possible to reduce exchange costs. We remind the reader that after a `put`, for all processors `d` and `s`, the result function at destination processor `d`, applied to the identifier of source processor `s` returns the value of the input function at source processor `s` applied to destination processor `d`.

The definition of the `bcast_direct` function of the standard library follows. This function is used to broadcast a value from a `root` processor to all other processors. To do so, first, we prepare a function vector for the processors to make the messages to send to each other (local definitions `make_msg` and `to_send`). It is clear that only the `root` processor will send data. The other processors' message is `None` which is interpreted by the BSML/OCaml implementation as an empty message. Second, the local definition `received` proceeds with the data exchange and ends the super-step. `received` is a parallel vector of functions. What we are interested in is the value sent by processor `root`. That is why the local definition `optional_result` then applies this parallel vector of functions to the replicated value `root`. Of course, the obtained message is encapsulated in a `Some` constructor. Therefore, all the processors finally apply `remove_option` to yield the final result. The broadcast is meaningless if `root` is not a valid processor identifier. In this case, the exception `Bcast` is raised:

```
let bcast_direct (root : int) (v : par α)
  ensures { 0 ≤ root < bsp_p →
             ∀ i:int. 0 ≤ i < bsp_p →
                       get result i = get v root }
  raises { Bcast }
= if (0 ≤ root) && (root < bsp_p )
  then
    let make_msg src load = fun _ →
        if src = root then Some load else None in
    let to_send  = apply (mkpar make_msg) v in
    let received = put to_send in
    let optional_result = apply received (replicate root) in
    parfun remove_option optional_result
  else raise Bcast
```

Our BSML theory allows us to write BSML programs and their specifications and is expressive enough for the Why3 framework to verify that they indeed satisfy their specifications.

We only presented a sub-set of the functions of the BSML standard library we implemented, and we refer to the companion artifact for the complete set of functions. For example, we also provide the `shift` , `shift_right` and `shift_left` communication functions, which offer a different communication pattern than `bcast_direct`: Each data item is shifted by a certain number of processors.

5   Verified Scalable Maximum Prefix Sum

To exercise the formalization presented in the previous section, we specify and verify an implementation of the maximum prefix sum informally presented in Sect. 3. As in the BSML implementation, the implementation with WhyML relies on algorithmic skeletons. The skeleton `par_map` is defined in lines 1–6 of Fig. 6. The only difference with its BSML/OCaml counterpart is the post-conditions including one expressed as a correspondence with the sequential `map`. Given a distributed list `dl` (of type `par(list α)`), one obtains the same result by either applying `map_par` then transforming the obtained distributed list into a list

```
1   let map_par (f: α→β) (dl: par (list α)) : par (list β)
2     ensures { ∀ i:int. 0 ≤ i < bsp_p →
3                         get result i = map f (get dl i) }
4     ensures { to_list result = map f (to_list dl) }
5   = let ghost _ = flatten_map f (list_of_par dl) in
6     parfun (map f) dl
7
8   let reduce_par (ghost inv: α→bool)
9     (op: α→α→α) (e: α) (dl: par(list α)) : α
10    requires { associative inv op }
11    requires { neutral inv op e }
12    requires { preserves inv op }
13    requires { inv e }
14    requires { ∀ i:int. 0 ≤ i < bsp_p →
15                        satisfies inv (get dl i) }
16    ensures { result = fold_left op e (to_list dl) }
17  = let ghost _ = fold_left_flatten inv op e (list_of_par dl) in
18    let reduce_seq l = fold_left op e l in
19    let partial_reductions = parfun reduce_seq dl in
20    reduce_seq (list_of_par partial_reductions)
```

Fig. 6. Verified Algorithmic Skeletons in WhyML

```
1   predicate associative (inv: α→bool) (op: α→α→α) =
2     ∀ x y z:α. inv x →inv y → inv z →
3       op x (op y z) = op (op x y) z
4
5   predicate neutral (inv: α→bool) (op: α→α→α) (e: α) =
6     (∀ x:α. inv x →op x e = x) ∧
7     (∀ x:α. inv x →op e x = x)
8
9   predicate preserves (inv: α→bool) (op: α→α→α) =
10    ∀ x y : α. inv x →inv y → inv (op x y)
11
12  predicate satisfies (inv: α→bool) (l: list α) =
13    ∀ i:int. 0 ≤ i < length l →inv (nth i l)
```

Fig. 7. Algebra Concepts

with to_list, or applying the sequential map to the sequentialization of the distributed list. Line 5 is just a hint for the provers: an application of lemma flatten_map that basically commutes map and flatten.

The implementation (lines 8-20) of the parallel reduction reduce_par is also very close to its BSML/OCaml counterpart of Fig. 4. As expected, the postcondition on line 16 is expressed with respect to the sequential reduction here implemented with the usual fold_left function. As the result is already a sequential value there is no need to sequentialize it. However, this correspondence is true only if op is associative and e is its neutral element which are two pre-conditions stated lines 10–11. There are two additional pre-conditions and a ghost argument, i.e. an argument only used in the contract (and possible annotations) of the function. The reason is again to deal with a form of partial functions. op is a total function, but it may not have the desired properties (associativity, neutral element) on all the values of its input type. Indeed, the OCaml version of op for mps that we will also use in the WhyML version of mps, is not associative if we consider all pairs of integers. In the maximum prefix sum problem, the first component of such a pair represents the maximum prefix sum, it is therefore positive, and the second component the sum of the list, thus it is lower or equal to the first component. The ghost argument inv expresses such properties on the values manipulated during the reduction. This is an invariant: op should preserve the property (line 12) and the input values e and dl should satisfy this property (line 13). The predicates associative, neutral, preserves and satisfies are defined in Fig. 7. Such definitions work also well when there is no need for an invariant: in this case we simply use the constant boolean function always returning true.

With these skeletons, it is possible to implement a parallel function to compute the maximum prefix sum of a distributed list as we did in Sect. 3. First, we define a *specification* as an inefficient function but direct translation of the informal specification: the mps_spec function on lines 1–2 of Fig. 8. We also define op (lines 7–8) and f (line 10) which are the arguments to map and reduce as in the BSML/OCaml example of Fig. 4. This time they are not local definitions because we need to state and verify some lemmas about them and because we have two versions of mps: mps_seq and map_par. The invariant explained above is defined lines 12–13. We need an auxiliary function to verify the correctness of our functions with respect to the specification: ms (line 4–5) is the tupling of mps_spec and sum. The rest of the code in Fig. 8 is the definitions of the sequential and parallel versions of the maximum prefix sum computation. Both of them are expressed as a composition of map and reduce.

The proof that mps_seq indeed implements the specification mps_spec proceeds by using the first homomorphism theorem. This theorem states that a homomorphic function can be implemented as a composition of map and reduce. A function f is homomorphic when there exists a binary operation $\odot$ such that: $\forall$ l1 l2: list α. f(l1++l2) = (f l1) $\odot$ (f l2) where ++ denotes list concatenation. mps_spec is not homomorphic but ms is. Two lines of annotations are necessary to guide the provers in the sequential case (lines 17–18). The parallel case does need any annotation: basically the contracts of map_par and reduce_par state their correspondence with their sequential counterpart thus the correspondence of the parallel mps_par with the sequential mps_seq, and mps_seq satisfies mps_spec.

The full development is about 600 lines of WhyML with about 45% of specifications and 55% of code. It generates 74 goals, 100% of which are proved. Their verification produces 37 sub-goals. The strategy Auto level 2 is used: it tries the provers CVC4, Alt-Ergo, CVC5 and Z3 with a short timeout (1 s). If the goal is not proved then it splits the goal and tries on the sub-goals with the

```
1    let function mps_spec (l: list int) : int
2    = maximum (map sum (prefix l))
3
4    function ms (l: list int) : (int,int)
5    = (mps_spec l, sum l)
6
7    let function op (x: (int,int)) (y: (int,int)) : (int, int)
8    = (max (max 0 (fst x)) ((snd x)+(fst y)), (snd x)+(snd y))
9
10   let function f (x : int) = (max 0 x, x)
11
12   predicate mps_sum_inv (x: (int,int))
13   = 0 ≤ fst x ∧ fst x ≥ snd x
14
15   let function mps_seq (l: list int) : int
16     ensures { result = mps_spec l }
17   = let ghost _ = first_homomorphism_theorem ms op l in
18     assert { fold_left op (0, 0) (map f l) = ms l };
19     fst (fold_left op (0, 0) (map f l))
20
21   let mps_par (dl: par(list int)) : int
22     ensures { result = mps_spec (to_list dl) }
23   = let mapped = map_par f dl in
24     fst (reduce_par mps_sum_inv op (0, 0) mapped)
```

Fig. 8. Verified Maximum Prefix Sum in WhyML

same timeout and finally if necessary tries with a larger timeout (10 s). Alt-Ergo version 2.4.3 proved 11 goals taking between 0.02 s and 0.56 s (when successful) and CVC4 version 1.6 proved 91 goals taking between 0.04 s and 2.45 s. Several sub-goals can contribute to a goal to be proved. For example the verification condition of mps_seq is split in 3 sub-goals. In the number of the goals proved by CVC4 and Alt-Ergo the root goals verified because their sub-goals are proved are not counted. In our case, only 9 goals needed to be split to achieve their proofs.

All the parts of the WhyML development that need to use BSML functions include use bsml.BSML. When we extract the code however, the module BSML cannot be extracted: there is no implementation for this module. For compiling the OCaml code obtained by extraction of the other modules of our WhyML development, we simply use the handwritten implementation of BSML in OCaml (which uses OCaml's FFI to call MPI C functions). This is done via a very simple Why3 custom extraction driver: each BSML type or value is written using the OCaml qualified identifier notation. For example, if the WhyML development contains mkpar then the extracted code will contain Bsml.mkpar where Bsml is the module containing the handwritten BSML parallel library.

6 Related Work

BSP-WHY [10,11] also uses (a previous version of) WHY to verify bulk synchronous parallel programs. However, the two approaches are very different. BSP-WHY considers BSP programs written in an imperative style close to BSPlib [14]. The verification proceeds by transforming well-formed programs — a sub-class of what has been formally defined later by Dabrowski as textually aligned programs [6] — into sequential simulating programs that are then verified using WHY. The BSP-WHY code cannot be run on parallel machines.

The work closest to ours is the specification, verification and extraction of BSML programs using the Coq proof assistant. Early contributions started with the work of Gava [12]. A formalization of BSML primitives in a style very close to the Why3 formalization presented in this paper was proposed by Tesson and Loulergue [24] and used in a framework, named SYDPACC, for the verification of BSP functional programs [8,20]. The two main differences with our work is that: (1) proofs are much less automated in Coq than in Why3 but (2) the framework leverages the type-class resolution mechanism of Coq to automatically parallelize programs. For example in this framework, the user does not need to write the code for `mps_seq` and `mps_par`, but only needs to write `mps_spec` and to prove that its tupling with `sum` is leftwards and rightwards (i.e. can be written as calls to `fold_left` and `fold_right`) and exhibits a weak right inverse. The framework would then use transformation theorems to automatically obtain `mps_seq` and then verified correspondences as expressed in the post-conditions of `map_par` and `reduce_par` to automatically produce `mps_par` [18].

Ono et al. [22] employed Coq to verify Hadoop MapReduce programs and extract Haskell code for Hadoop Streaming or directly write Java programs annotated with JML, utilizing Krakatoa [9] to generate Coq lemmas. The first part of their work is functional and therefore closest to our work. However, it is limited to MapReduce which is more general than the `map_par` and `reduce_par` skeletons but is less expressive than BSML. The second part of their work is more imperative.

7 Conclusion and Future Work

We were able to formalize the primitives of the parallel programming library BSML with WhyML and leverage Why3 for verifying a large part of the BSML standard library as well as an application written in BSML. We plan to experiment the extracted code more thoroughly and on larger parallel machines with a few thousand cores.

WhyML offers exceptions and references, thus allows to write imperative programs. However, such programs cannot be passed as arguments to higher-order functions. It therefore limits the usage of imperative features with BSML as all primitives are higher-order functions. The code outside BSML primitives can be imperative thus the sequencing of BSP super-steps could be imperative. It is also possible to use imperative features to implement pure functions passed as arguments to BSML primitives. Also, it is possible to deal with partial functions as we did with `remove_some` . We plan to explore all these possibilities in the future.

Acknowledgment. The authors thank the anonymous reviewers for their helpful comments.

References

1. Armbrust, M., et al.: Scaling spark in the real world: performance and usability. PVLDB **8**(12), 1840–1851 (2015). https://www.vldb.org/pvldb/vol8/p1840-armbrust.pdf
2. Bobot, F., Filliâtre, J.C., Claude, M., Melquiond, G., Paskevich, A.: The Why3 platform (2023). https://why3.lri.fr
3. Bobot, F., Filliâtre, J.-C., Marché, C., Paskevich, A.: Let's verify this with Why3. Int. J. Softw. Tools Technol. Transfer **17**(6), 709–727 (2014). https://doi.org/10.1007/s10009-014-0314-5
4. Cole, M.: Algorithmic skeletons: structured management of parallel computation. MIT Press (1989)
5. Conchon, S., Coquereau, A., Iguernlala, M., Mebsout, A.: Alt-Ergo 2.2. In: SMT Workshop: International Workshop on Satisfiability Modulo Theories. Oxford, United Kingdom (2018). https://inria.hal.science/hal-01960203
6. Dabrowski, F.: A denotational semantics of textually aligned SPMD programs. J. Log. Algebraic Methods Program. **108**, 90–104 (2019). https://doi.org/10.1016/j.jlamp.2019.02.010
7. Denis, X., Jourdan, J., Marché, C.: CREUSOT: a foundry for the deductive verification of rust programs. In: Riesco, A., Zhang, M. (eds.) Formal Methods and Software Engineering. ICFEM 2022. LNCS, vol. 13478. Springer, Cham (2022). https://doi.org/10.1007/978-3-031-17244-1_6
8. Emoto, K., Loulergue, F., Tesson, J.: A verified generate-test-aggregate Coq library for parallel programs extraction. In: Klein, G., Gamboa, R. (eds.) ITP 2014. LNCS, vol. 8558, pp. 258–274. Springer, Cham (2014). https://doi.org/10.1007/978-3-319-08970-6_17
9. Filliâtre, J.-C., Marché, C.: The Why/Krakatoa/Caduceus platform for deductive program verification. In: Damm, W., Hermanns, H. (eds.) CAV 2007. LNCS, vol. 4590, pp. 173–177. Springer, Heidelberg (2007). https://doi.org/10.1007/978-3-540-73368-3_21
10. Fortin, J., Gava, F.: BSP-WHY: an intermediate language for deductive verification of BSP programs. In: 4th workshop on High-Level Parallel Programming and applications (HLPP), pp. 35–44. ACM (2010). https://doi.org/10.1145/1863482.1863491
11. Fortin, J., Gava, F.: BSP-Why: a tool for deductive verification of BSP algorithms with subgroup synchronisation. Int. J. Parallel Prog. **44**(3), 574–597 (2015). https://doi.org/10.1007/s10766-015-0360-y
12. Gava, F.: Formal proofs of functional BSP programs. Parall. Process. Lett. **13**(3), 365–376 (2003)
13. Gava, F., Garnier, I.: New implementation of a BSP composition primitive with application to the implementation of algorithmic skeletons. In: 23rd IEEE International Symposium on Parallel and Distributed Processing (IPDPS 2009), APDCM workshop, pp. 1–8. IEEE (2009). https://doi.org/10.1109/IPDPS.2009.5160876

14. Hill, J.M.D., et al.: BSPlib: the BSP programming library. Parallel Comput. **24**, 1947–1980 (1998)
15. Kirchner, F., Kosmatov, N., Prevosto, V., Signoles, J., Yakobowski, B.: Frama-C: a software analysis perspective. Formal Aspects Comput. **27**(3), 573–609 (2015). https://doi.org/10.1007/s00165-014-0326-7
16. Loulergue, F.: A BSPlib-style API for bulk synchronous parallel ML. Scalable Comput.: Pract. Exp. **18**, 261–274 (2017). https://doi.org/10.12694/scpe.v18i3.1306
17. Loulergue, F.: Implementing algorithmic skeletons with bulk synchronous parallel ML. In: Parallel and Distributed Computing, Applications and Technologies (PDCAT), pp. 461–468. IEEE (2017). https://doi.org/10.1109/PDCAT.2017.00079
18. Loulergue, F., Bousdira, W., Tesson, J.: Calculating parallel programs in Coq using list homomorphisms. Int. J. Parallel Prog. **45**(2), 300–319 (2016). https://doi.org/10.1007/s10766-016-0415-8
19. Loulergue, F., Gava, F., Billiet, D.: Bulk synchronous parallel ML: modular implementation and performance prediction. In: Sunderam, V.S., van Albada, G.D., Sloot, P.M.A., Dongarra, J.J. (eds.) ICCS 2005. LNCS, vol. 3515, pp. 1046–1054. Springer, Heidelberg (2005). https://doi.org/10.1007/11428848_132
20. Loulergue, F., Robillard, S., Tesson, J., Légaux, J., Hu, Z.: Formal derivation and extraction of a parallel program for the all nearest smaller values problem. In: ACM Symposium on Applied Computing (SAC), pp. 1577–1584. ACM, Gyeongju, Korea (2014). https://doi.org/10.1145/2554850.2554912
21. de Moura, L., Bjørner, N.: Z3: an efficient SMT solver. In: Ramakrishnan, C.R., Rehof, J. (eds.) TACAS 2008. LNCS, vol. 4963, pp. 337–340. Springer, Heidelberg (2008). https://doi.org/10.1007/978-3-540-78800-3_24
22. Ono, K., Hirai, Y., Tanabe, Y., Noda, N., Hagiya, M.: Using Coq in specification and program extraction of Hadoop MapReduce applications. In: Barthe, G., Pardo, A., Schneider, G. (eds.) SEFM 2011. LNCS, vol. 7041, pp. 350–365. Springer, Heidelberg (2011). https://doi.org/10.1007/978-3-642-24690-6_24
23. Snir, M., Gropp, W.: MPI the complete reference. MIT Press (1998)
24. Tesson, J., Loulergue, F.: A verified bulk synchronous parallel ML heat diffusion simulation. In: International Conference on Computational Science (ICCS), pp. 36–45. Elsevier, Singapore (2011). https://doi.org/10.1016/j.procs.2011.04.005
25. Valiant, L.G.: A bridging model for parallel computation. Commun. ACM **33**(8), 103 (1990). https://doi.org/10.1145/79173.79181
26. White, T.: Hadoop - The Definitive Guide. O'Reilly, 2nd edn. (2010)

Exact and Efficient Bayesian Inference
for Privacy Risk Quantification

Rasmus C. Rønneberg[1]($\boxtimes$), Raúl Pardo[2], and Andrzej Wąsowski[2]

[1] Karlsruhe Institute of Technology, Karlsruhe, Germany
rasmus.ronneberg@kit.edu
[2] IT University of Copenhagen, Copenhagen, Denmark
{raup,wasowski}@itu.dk

Abstract. Data analysis has high value both for commercial and research purposes. However, disclosing analysis results may pose severe privacy risk to individuals. Privug is a method to quantify privacy risks of data analytics programs by analyzing their source code. The method uses probability distributions to model attacker knowledge and Bayesian inference to update said knowledge based on observable outputs. Currently, Privug uses Markov Chain Monte Carlo (MCMC) to perform inference, which is a flexible but approximate solution. This paper presents an exact Bayesian inference engine based on multivariate Gaussian distributions to accurately and efficiently quantify privacy risks. The inference engine is implemented for a subset of Python programs that can be modeled as multivariate Gaussian models. We evaluate the method by analyzing privacy risks in programs to release public statistics. The evaluation shows that our method accurately and efficiently analyzes privacy risks, and outperforms existing methods. Furthermore, we demonstrate the use of our engine to analyze the effect of differential privacy in public statistics.

Keywords: Privacy risk analysis · Bayesian inference · Probabilistic Programming

1 Introduction

Data anonymization methods gain legal importance [5] as data collection and analysis are expanding dramatically in data management and statistical research. Yet applying anonymization, or understanding how well a given analytics program hides sensitive information, is non-trivial [20]. Contemporary anonymization algorithms, such as differential privacy [18], require calibration to balance between reducing risks and preserving the utility of data. To assess the risks, data scientists need to assess the flow (leakage) of information from sensitive data fields to the output of analytics.

Work partially supported by funding from the topic Engineering Secure Systems of the Helmholtz Association (HGF), the KASTEL Security Research Labs and the Danish Villum Foundation through Villum Experiment project No. 0002302.

Measuring the information leakage is a useful technique to quantify how much an attacker may learn about the sensitive information a program processes. Many methods have been proposed in this domain [4, 8, 9, 12, 14, 15, 29, 32, 34]. Privug is a recent one [32]. It relies on Bayesian inference to quantify privacy risks in data analytics programs. The attacker's knowledge is modeled as a probability distribution over program inputs, and it is then conditioned on the disclosed program outputs. Then, Bayesian probabilistic programming is used to compute the posterior attacker knowledge, i.e., the updated attacker knowledge after observing the outputs in the program. One of the advantages of Privug is that it works on the program source code, and can be extended to compute most information leakage metrics [4]. However, Privug currently relies on approximate Bayesian inference such as Markov Chain Monte Carlo [33]. These methods can be used to analyze arbitrary programs, but may be computationally expensive and may produce imprecise results. In quantifying privacy risks, precision is critical, as under-estimation of risks may result in an illegal disclosure of personal information.

We present a new *exact* and *efficient* Bayesian inference engine for Privug targeting attackers modeled by multivariate Gaussian distributions. Even though not all standard program statements can be mapped to operations on Gaussian distributions (and thus not all programs can be analyzed using our new engine), multivariate Gaussian distributions are a good candidate for a semantic domain of attacker's knowledge for several reasons: (i) Multivariate Gaussians are closed under many common operations and they can be computed efficiently; (ii) The Gaussian distribution is a *maximum entropy* distribution under common conditions [27, 30] that allows modeling prior attacker knowledge with minimum assumptions; (iii) Gaussians are commonly used in probabilistic modeling of engineering systems to represent uncertainty of measurement.

This work constitutes a new point in the study of expressiveness vs performance in quantification of privacy risks by means of Bayesian inference. Specifically, our contributions are:

1. A probabilistic programming language for exact Bayesian inference using multivariate Gaussians. The language is a subset of Python (Sect. 3).
2. A definition of a sound (Sect. 3.2) Bayesian inference engine (Sect. 3.1) using multivariate Gaussian distributions.
3. A proof-of-concept implementation of the inference engine as a library that can be applied to analyze our subset of Python.
4. An application of the inference engine to a case study of privacy risk quantification in public statistics (Sect. 4), with and without differential privacy [18].
5. An evaluation of the scalability of the inference engine, and a comparison with existing inference methods for privacy risk quantification (Sect. 5). The evaluation shows that our engine can analyze large systems involving thousands of individuals, and also that we greatly outperform existing tools for the programs supported in our language.

The code to reproduce the evaluation and case study in this paper is available at [35]. The proof-of-concept implementation of the exact inference engine is an open source project available at https://github.com/itu-square/gauss-privug.

2 Background

2.1 Privug: A Data Privacy Debugging Method

Let $\mathbb{I}, \mathbb{O}$ denote sets of *inputs* and *outputs*, respectively. We use $\mathcal{D}(\mathbb{I})$ to denote a space of distributions; in this case over inputs. Let $d \in \mathcal{D}(\mathbb{I})$ denote a distribution over inputs, $I \sim \mathcal{D}(\mathbb{I})$ denotes a random variable distributed according to d.

Privug [32] is a method to explore information leakage on data analytics programs. The method combines a probabilistic model of attacker knowledge with the program under analysis to quantify privacy risks. This process is summarized in the following steps:

(1) Prior. We first model the *prior* knowledge of an attacker as a distribution over program inputs. This distribution represents the input values of a program that the attacker finds plausible. For example, consider a program that takes as input a real number A representing the age of an individual ($\mathbb{I} \triangleq \mathbb{R}$). A possible prior knowledge of the attacker could be: $A \sim \mathcal{U}(0, 120)$ (all ages between 0 and 120 are equally likely for the attacker) or $A \sim \mathcal{N}(\mu = 42, \sigma = 2)$ (the attacker believes that the age of 42 and values nearby are most likely ages). We write $P(I)$ for the distribution of prior attacker knowledge.

(2) Probabilistic Program Interpretation. The second step is to interpret a target program $\pi : \mathbb{I} \to \mathbb{O}$ using the attacker prior knowledge. To this end, we lift the program to run on distributions $\mathcal{D}(\mathbb{I})$ instead of concrete inputs $\mathbb{I}$. This corresponds to the standard lifting to the probability monad [24]; $lift : (\mathbb{I} \to \mathbb{O}) \to (\mathcal{D}(\mathbb{I}) \to \mathcal{D}(\mathbb{O}))$. For example, consider the following program that computes the average age of a list of ages (in Python):

```
1 def average_age(ages: List[float]): return sum(ages)/len(ages)
```

The lifted version of the program is (Python allows retaining the same body):

```
1 def average_age(ages: Dist[List[float]] ): return sum(ages)/len(ages)
```

where `Dist[List[float]]` denotes a distribution over lists of floats, $\mathcal{D}(\mathbb{R}^n)$. The lifted program yields the distribution $P(O|A)$. In general, the combination of prior attacker knowledge with the lifted program yields a joint distribution on inputs and outputs, $P(O|I)P(I) = P(O, I)$.

(3) Observations. It is possible to analyze privacy risks for concrete outputs of the program. To this end, one may add observations to the probabilistic model. In the average example above, we could check how the knowledge of the attacker changes when the attacker observes that the average is 44. This step yields the posterior distribution $P(I|O = 44)$. In general, the probabilistic lifting of the program π defines a likelihood function on the joint distribution of input and output, $P(E|I, O)$ with some predicate E on the joint distribution.

(4) Posterior Inference. The next step is to apply Bayesian inference to obtain a posterior distribution on the input variables.

$$P(I, O|E) = P(E|I, O)P(O|I)P(I)/P(E) \tag{1}$$

It is usually intractable to compute a symbolic representation of $P(E)$. Therefore, it is not possible to get analytical solutions for the posterior distributions. The current implementation of Privug uses Markov Chain Monte Carlo (MCMC) [33] to tackle this issue. But MCMC methods are approximate and do not always converge. As mentioned above, the subject of this paper is to provide an exact inference method to efficiently and precisely compute the posterior distribution.

(5) Posterior Analysis. We query the posterior and prior distributions (attacker knowledge) to measure how much the attacker has learned. This can be done by applying different techniques such as computing probability queries, plotting visualizations of probability distributions, computing information theoretic metrics (e.g., entropy or mutual information), and metrics from *quantitative information flow* [4] such as Bayes vulnerability.

For example, Fig. 1 compares the prior and posterior distributions of the average age program above. We analyze the case where the output of the program is 44. The green line shows the prior attacker knowledge on the victim's age $P(A)$ and the blue line the posterior knowledge $P(A|O = 44)$ when observing that the program output is 44. The prior attacker knowledge is $A \sim \mathcal{N}(35, 2)$ for the victim's age and also for the rest. The figure clearly shows that the attacker now believes that higher ages are more plausible.

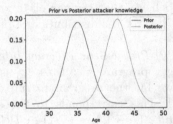

Fig. 1. Prior vs Posterior ages

In other words, the attacker prior knowledge has been corrected towards more accurate knowledge on the victim's age.

2.2 Multivariate Gaussian Distributions

In this paper, we use capital Greek letters for matrices, and bold font for column vectors. Small letters a and b are reserved for selecting subvectors (as in $\boldsymbol{\mu}_a$) and pairs of them for selecting submatrices (as in Σ_{ba}). Matrix and vector literals are written in brackets. We write $supp(X)$ for the support of the random variable X.

A *multivariate Gaussian distribution*, denoted $\boldsymbol{X} \sim \mathcal{N}(\boldsymbol{\mu}, \Sigma)$, defines a probabilistic model composed of n normally distributed random variables, $\boldsymbol{X} = [X_1, X_2, \dots, X_n]^{\mathsf{T}}$. The distribution is parameterized by a vector $\boldsymbol{\mu}$ of n means, and a symmetric $n \times n$ *covariance* matrix Σ, so $\Sigma_{ij} = \mathrm{cov}[X_i, X_j]$ gives the covariance between X_i and X_j, Σ_{kk} gives the variance of X_k. We assume that the covariance matrix is positive definite. The probability density function is:

$$P(\boldsymbol{x}) = ((2\pi)^n |\Sigma|)^{-1/2} \exp\left(-2^{-1}(\boldsymbol{x} - \boldsymbol{\mu})^{\mathsf{T}} \Sigma^{-1}(\boldsymbol{x} - \boldsymbol{\mu})\right) \tag{2}$$

where $|\Sigma|$ denotes the determinant of the matrix Σ. We recall standard properties of multivariate Gaussian distributions [10, 19, 28].

Theorem 1. *Let* $\begin{bmatrix} X_a \\ X_b \end{bmatrix} \sim \mathcal{N}(\mu, \Sigma)$ *with* $\mu = \begin{bmatrix} \mu_a \\ \mu_b \end{bmatrix}$ *and* $\Sigma = \begin{bmatrix} \Sigma_{aa} & \Sigma_{ab} \\ \Sigma_{ba} & \Sigma_{bb} \end{bmatrix}$. *The marginal distributions are* $X_a \sim \mathcal{N}(\mu_a, \Sigma_{aa})$, $X_b \sim \mathcal{N}(\mu_b, \Sigma_{bb})$, *and* $X_i \sim \mathcal{N}(\mu_i, \Sigma_{ii})$ *for* $i = 1 \ldots a + b$.

The covariance matrix identifies independent random variables:

Theorem 2. *Let* $[X_1, \ldots, X_n]^\mathsf{T} \sim \mathcal{N}(\mu, \Sigma)$, *two marginals* X_i, X_j *with* $i \neq j$ *are independent iff* $\Sigma_{ij} = \mathrm{cov}[X_i, X_j] = 0$.

The space of Gaussian distributions is closed under affine transformations:

Theorem 3. *Let* $X \sim \mathcal{N}(\mu, \Sigma)$ *and* $Y = \mathrm{A}X + b$ *be an affine transformation with* $\mathrm{A} \in \mathbb{R}^{m \times n}$ *a projection matrix and* $b \in \mathbb{R}^{n \times 1}$ *a column vector. Then,* $Y \sim \mathcal{N}(\mathrm{A}\mu + b, \mathrm{A}\Sigma\mathrm{A}^\mathsf{T})$ *holds.*

We use $Y | X_1, X_2, \ldots, X_n$ to denote a random variable Y that is distributed conditionally with respect to $X_1, X_2, \ldots, X_n$. Linear combinations of random variables can be used to define hierarchical probabilistic models consisting of dependent random variables, such as Gaussian Bayesian networks [28].

Theorem 4. *Let* $X \sim \mathcal{N}(\mu, \Sigma)$ *and* $Y | X \sim \mathcal{N}(a^\mathsf{T} X + b, \sigma^2)$, *where* $a \in \mathbb{R}^{n \times 1}$ *is a vector,* $b \in \mathbb{R}$ *and* $\sigma^2 > 0$. *Then* $[X^\mathsf{T}, Y]^\mathsf{T} \sim \mathcal{N}([\mu^\mathsf{T}, a^\mathsf{T}\mu + b]^\mathsf{T}, \Sigma')$ *with*

$$\Sigma'_{1..n, 1..n} - \Sigma, \quad \Sigma'_{(n+1)(n+1)} = \sigma^2 + a^\mathsf{T}\Sigma a, \quad \Sigma'_{i(n+1)} = \mathrm{cov}[X_i, Y] = \sum_{j=1}^{n} a_j \Sigma_{ij} .$$

Example 1. We present an example of a Gaussian Bayesian network [28]. Let $X_1 \sim \mathcal{N}(50, 2)$, $X_2 | X_1 \sim \mathcal{N}(2X_1 - 5, 1)$, and $X_3 | X_2 \sim \mathcal{N}(X_2 - 10, 4)$. Here the distribution of X_2 is conditioned on X_1, and of X_3 on X_2. The model defines a joint multivariate Gaussian probability distribution $[X_1, X_2, X_3]^\mathsf{T} \sim \mathcal{N}(\mu, \Sigma)$. Theorem 4 allows to compute the mean, variance, and covariance of this joint distribution:

$$\mu = \begin{bmatrix} 50 \\ 2 \cdot \mu_1 - 5 \\ 1 \cdot \mu_2 - 10 \end{bmatrix} = \begin{bmatrix} 50 \\ 95 \\ 85 \end{bmatrix}, \quad \Sigma = \begin{bmatrix} 2 & 2 \cdot \Sigma_{11} & 0 + 1 \cdot \Sigma_{12} \\ & 1 + 2 \cdot \Sigma_{11} \cdot 2 & 0 + 1 \cdot \Sigma_{22} \\ & & 4 + 1 \cdot \Sigma_{22} \cdot 1 \end{bmatrix} = \begin{bmatrix} 2 & 4 & 4 \\ & 9 & 9 \\ & & 13 \end{bmatrix}$$

As the matrices are symmetric, we only show the upper-right part. Note that, even tough X_3 does not directly depend on X_1, it still has a non-zero covariance. The reason for this is the indirect dependence through X_2. $\qquad\square$

We use *conditioning* to model observations on values of random variables.

Theorem 5. *Let* $X \sim \mathcal{N}(\mu, \Sigma)$ *be split into two sub-vectors so that*

$$X = \begin{bmatrix} X_a \\ X_b \end{bmatrix}, \quad \mu = \begin{bmatrix} \mu_a \\ \mu_b \end{bmatrix}, \quad \Sigma = \begin{bmatrix} \Sigma_{aa} & \Sigma_{ab} \\ \Sigma_{ba} & \Sigma_{bb} \end{bmatrix} \text{ and } x_b \in supp(X_b).$$

The conditioned distribution is $X_a | (X_b = x_b) \sim \mathcal{N}(\mu', \Sigma')$ *with* $\mu' = \mu_a + \Sigma_{ab}\Sigma_{bb}^-(x_b - \mu_b)$ *and* $\Sigma' = \Sigma_{aa} - \Sigma_{ab}\Sigma_{bb}^-\Sigma_{ba}$, *where* Σ^- *is the generalized inverse.*

Example 2. Consider the multivariate distribution of Example 1. We condition X_3 to be 85. By Thm. 5 the posterior of $X_1, X_2 | X_3 = 85$ is $\mathcal{N}(\boldsymbol{\mu}', \Sigma')$ with

$$\boldsymbol{\mu}' = \begin{bmatrix} 50 \\ 95 \end{bmatrix} + \begin{bmatrix} 4 \\ 9 \end{bmatrix} [13]^-(85-85) = \begin{bmatrix} 50 \\ 95 \end{bmatrix} \text{ and } \Sigma' = \begin{bmatrix} 2 & 4 \\ 4 & 9 \end{bmatrix} - \begin{bmatrix} 4 \\ 9 \end{bmatrix} [13]^- [4\,9] = \begin{bmatrix} {}^{10}/_{13} & {}^{16}/_{13} \\ {}^{16}/_{13} & {}^{36}/_{13} \end{bmatrix}$$

$\square$

3   Exact Inference Engine for Privug

Our inference engine is an interpreter of a probabilistic programming language that corresponds to a subset of Python. We include variable assignments, bounded for-loops, binary operators, sequencing, *probabilistic assignments*, and *observations* (conditioning). Let $v_r \in \mathbb{R}$ be real values, $x, y, z, \dots$ denote (deterministic) variables, $X, Y, Z, \dots$ be (Gaussian) random variables, and $\boldsymbol{X}$ a vector of random variables. Let $\oplus \in \{+, -, *, /\}$. The syntax of well-formed programs is generated by the rule p below.

(Expressions)	e ::=	$v_r \mid x \mid e \oplus e$
(Distributions)	d ::=	$\mathtt{Normal}(e, e) \mid \mathtt{Normal}(e * X + e, e)$
(Statements)	s ::=	$X = d \mid X = Y \oplus e \mid X = Y + Z \mid \mathtt{condition}(X, e) \mid$
		$x = e \mid s;\ s \mid \mathtt{for}\ x\ \mathtt{in}\ \mathtt{range}\ v_r\ s$
(Programs)	p ::=	$s;\ \mathtt{return}\ \boldsymbol{X}$

We admit (e) constants expressions, references to deterministic program variables, and binary operations. Two ways of defining normal distributions (d) are supported: an independent Gaussian distribution, or a linear transformation of random variables. Statements (s) are: probabilistic assignments (a normal, a transformed distribution, a sum of two random variables), an observation (conditioning), deterministic assignment, sequencing, and a limited for-loop. We define no expressions over random variables, only statements, to simplify introduction of changes to the state (the probabilistic model) in the semantics for each sub-expression (Sect. 3.1). The for-loops are only a convenience construct for repetitive statements. A program (p) terminates returning a random variable (return). The distribution of the returned variable is the marginal of the posterior joint probability distribution that we want to reason about.

Although the language appears restrictive, we show in Sect. 4 that it can be used in realistic case studies; e.g., for the study of privacy risks in database reconstruction attacks using public statistics. Furthermore, this syntax ensures soundness and termination (Sect. 3.2) of a highly scalable (Sect. 5) inference engine.

3.1   Semantics

The formal semantics is defined in the small-step style, over terms of multivariate Gaussian distributions (Sect. 2.2). It provides a sound and efficient inference engine to track attacker knowledge in Privug (cf. Sect. 2.1).

A *state* $\mathcal{S}$ is a tuple $\langle \boldsymbol{\mu}, \Sigma, \sigma \rangle$. The first two elements define a multivariate Gaussian distribution $\mathcal{N}(\boldsymbol{\mu}, \Sigma)$ over n random variables. Let $\mathcal{V}$ denote the set of deterministic variables, $\sigma : \mathcal{V} \to \mathbb{R}$ maps variables to values. We use $\Sigma_{[X,X]}$ to denote the variance of marginal variable X, and $\Sigma_{[X,.]}$, $\Sigma_{[.,X]}$ to denote the covariance vectors of X with other variables in the state's multivariate Gaussian distribution. Similarly, $\Sigma_{[\mathbf{X},\mathbf{X}]}$, and $\Sigma_{[\mathbf{X},\mathbf{Y}]}$ denote the covariance matrix of the sub-vector $\mathbf{X}$ of a multivariate Gaussian, and the covariance matrix between sub-vectors $\mathbf{X}, \mathbf{Y}$ of a multivariate Gaussian, respectively. We use μ_X to denote the mean of X, and $\boldsymbol{\mu_X}$ for the mean vector of $\mathbf{X}$.

Definition 1 (Semantics). *The semantics is given by the relations $\to_e$: $e \times S \to \mathbb{R}$, $\to_s$: $s \times S \to S$ and $\to_p$: $p \times S \to \mathbb{R}^{n \times 1} \times \mathbb{R}^{n \times n}$ for expressions e, statements s, and programs p, respectively, as defined in Fig. 2.*

The rules for expressions, (deterministic) assignments, sequence of statements, and for-loops are standard, and they do not change the state's multivariate Gaussian distribution. We omit their details. Programs finish with a return instruction. It returns the mean-vector $\boldsymbol{\mu_a}$ and covariance matrix Σ_{aa} of the specified sub-vector of the state's multivariate Gaussian. In what follows, we focus on the rules manipulating the state's multivariate Gaussian distribution.

There are two types of probabilistic assignments: independent and linearly dependent. In both cases the multivariate Gaussian distribution in the state is extended with a new variable, and consequently the mean vector ($\boldsymbol{\mu}$) and covariance matrix (Σ) increase their dimension. Independent assignments (P-ASG-IND) add to the mean vector the mean of the distribution. The covariance matrix is also updated with two $\mathbf{0}$ vectors indicating the new variable is not correlated with existing variables, and the variable's variance is added to the diagonal of the matrix. Dependent assignments (P-ASG-DEP) add to the mean vector a mean computed as a linear combination with the mean of the dependent random variable Y. The covariance matrix is extended with two vectors computed from the covariance of the dependent variable with other variables, $\Sigma_{[Y,.]}$, $\Sigma_{[.,Y]}$. This is because the new variable depends on Y and consequently on all the variables that Y depends on. The variance of the new variable is added to the diagonal of the matrix as a linear combination with the variance of Y.

Example 3. Consider the program $X = \mathtt{Normal}(15,2)$; $Y = \mathtt{Normal}(20,1)$; $Z = \mathtt{Normal}(2X,1)$. The first assignment results in state $\mu = [15]$ and $\Sigma = [2]$. The second assignment updates the state into,

$$\mu' = \begin{bmatrix} 15 \\ 20 \end{bmatrix} \quad \Sigma' = \begin{bmatrix} 2 & 0 \\ 0 & 1 \end{bmatrix}$$

Note the zeros in the covariance coefficients as these variables are independent. Finally, the last probabilistic statement results in

$$\mu'' = \begin{bmatrix} 15 \\ 20 \\ 2 \cdot 15 \end{bmatrix} = \begin{bmatrix} 15 \\ 20 \\ 30 \end{bmatrix} \quad \Sigma'' = \begin{bmatrix} 2 & 0 & 2 \cdot 2 \\ 0 & 1 & 2 \cdot 0 \\ 2 \cdot 2 & 2 \cdot 0 & 2^2 \cdot 2 + 1 \end{bmatrix} = \begin{bmatrix} 2 & 0 & 4 \\ 0 & 1 & 0 \\ 4 & 0 & 9 \end{bmatrix}$$

Here we observe that the covariance between Z and X is updated with a non-zero value due to the dependency between variables, but the coefficients of Y, Z are 0 as these variable remain independent. □

$$(\text{V-Exp}) \ \frac{\sigma(x) = c}{\langle x, \mathcal{S}\rangle \to_e c} \qquad\qquad (\text{O-Exp}) \ \frac{\langle e_0, \mathcal{S}\rangle \to_e c_0 \quad \langle e_1, \mathcal{S}\rangle \to_e c_1}{\langle e_0 \oplus e_1, \mathcal{S}\rangle \to_e c_0 \oplus c_1}$$

$$(\text{C-Exp}) \ \frac{}{\langle c, \mathcal{S}\rangle \to_e c} \qquad\qquad (\text{D-Asg}) \ \frac{e \to_e c}{\langle x = e, \mathcal{S}\rangle \to_s \langle \mu, \Sigma, \sigma[x \mapsto c]\rangle}$$

$$(\text{P-Asg-Ind}) \ \frac{\langle e_i, \mathcal{S}\rangle \to_e c_i \text{ for } i = 1,2 \quad \mu' = \begin{bmatrix}\mu\\c_1\end{bmatrix} \quad \Sigma' = \begin{bmatrix}\Sigma' & 0\\0 & c_2\end{bmatrix}}{\langle X = \texttt{Normal}(e_1, e_2), \mathcal{S}\rangle \to_s \langle \mu', \Sigma', \sigma\rangle} \ c_2 > 0$$

$$(\text{P-Asg-Dep}) \ \frac{\langle e_i, \mathcal{S}\rangle \to_e c_i \text{ for } i = 1..3 \\ \mu' = \begin{bmatrix}\mu\\c_1\mu_Y + c_2\end{bmatrix} \quad \Sigma' = \begin{bmatrix}\Sigma & c_1\Sigma_{[.,Y]}\\c_1\Sigma_{[Y,.]} & c_1^2\Sigma_{[Y,Y]} + c_3\end{bmatrix}}{\langle X = \texttt{Normal}(e_1 * Y + e_2, e_3), \mathcal{S}\rangle \to_s \langle \mu', \Sigma', \sigma\rangle} \ c_3 > 0$$

$$(\text{P-Cond}) \ \frac{\langle e, \mathcal{S}\rangle \to_e c \quad \mu = \begin{bmatrix}\mu_a\\\mu_X\end{bmatrix} \quad \Sigma = \begin{bmatrix}\Sigma_a & \Sigma_{[.,X]}\\\Sigma_{[X,.]} & \Sigma_{[X,X]}\end{bmatrix} \\ \mu' = \mu_a + (c - \mu_X)/\Sigma_{[X,X]}\Sigma_{[.,X]} \quad \Sigma' = \Sigma_a - 1/\Sigma_{[X,X]}\Sigma_{[.,X]}\Sigma_{[X,.]}}{\langle \texttt{condition}(X, e), \langle\mu, \Sigma, \sigma\rangle\rangle \to_s \langle\mu', \Sigma', \sigma\rangle}$$

$$(\text{Seq}) \ \frac{\langle s_0, \mathcal{S}\rangle \to_s \mathcal{S}'' \quad \langle s_1, \mathcal{S}''\rangle \to_s \mathcal{S}'}{\langle s_0; \ s_1, \mathcal{S}\rangle \to_s \mathcal{S}'} \qquad (\text{Ret}) \ \frac{\langle s, \mathcal{S}\rangle \to_s \langle\begin{bmatrix}\mu_X\\\mu_Y\end{bmatrix}, \begin{bmatrix}\Sigma_{[X,X]}\Sigma_{[X,Y]}\\\Sigma_{[Y,X]}\Sigma_{[Y,Y]}\end{bmatrix}, \sigma\rangle}{\langle s; \texttt{return } X, \mathcal{S}\rangle \to_p (\mu_X, \Sigma_{[X,X]})}$$

$$(\text{For-B}) \ \frac{v_r \le 0}{\langle \texttt{for } x \texttt{ in range } v_r \ s, \mathcal{S}\rangle \to_s \mathcal{S}} \qquad (\text{For-I}) \ \frac{v_r > 0 \quad \langle s', \mathcal{S}\rangle \to_s \mathcal{S}' \\ s' = s; x = x{+}1; \texttt{ for } x \texttt{ in range } v_r{-}1 \ s}{\langle \texttt{for } x \texttt{ in range } v_r \ s, \mathcal{S}\rangle \to_s \mathcal{S}'}$$

$$(\text{P-Sum}) \ \frac{\mu' = \begin{bmatrix}\mu\\\mu_Y + \mu_Z\end{bmatrix} \quad \Sigma' = \begin{bmatrix}\Sigma & \Sigma_{[.,Y]} + \Sigma_{[.,Z]}\\\Sigma_{[Y,.]} + \Sigma_{[Z,.]} & \Sigma_{[Y,Y]} + \Sigma_{[Z,Z]} + \Sigma_{[Y,Z]} + \Sigma_{[Z,Y]}\end{bmatrix}}{\langle X = Y + Z, \mathcal{S}\rangle \to_s \langle\mu', \Sigma', \sigma\rangle}$$

$$(\text{P-Op-PM})$$
$$\oplus \in \{+, -\} \quad \langle e, \mathcal{S}\rangle \to_e c$$
$$\mu' = \begin{bmatrix}\mu\\\mu_Y \oplus c\end{bmatrix} \quad \Sigma' = \begin{bmatrix}\Sigma & \Sigma_{[.,Y]}\\\Sigma_{[Y,.]} & \Sigma_{[Y,Y]}\end{bmatrix}$$
$$\frac{}{\langle X = Y \oplus e, \mathcal{S}\rangle \to_s \langle\mu', \Sigma', \sigma\rangle}$$

$$(\text{P-Op-MD})$$
$$\oplus \in \{*, /\} \quad \langle e, \mathcal{S}\rangle \to_e c$$
$$\mu' = \begin{bmatrix}\mu\\\mu_Y \oplus c\end{bmatrix} \quad \Sigma' = \begin{bmatrix}\Sigma & c \oplus \Sigma_{[.,Y]}\\c \oplus \Sigma_{[Y,.]} & c^2 \oplus \Sigma_{[Y,Y]}\end{bmatrix}$$
$$\frac{}{\langle X = Y \oplus e, \mathcal{S}\rangle \to_s \langle\mu', \Sigma', \sigma\rangle}$$

Fig. 2. Operational Semantics rules; $\mathcal{S}$ stands for a tuple $\langle\mu, \Sigma, \sigma\rangle$.

Two rules (P-OP-PM) and (P-OP-MD) define binary operations between random variables and values. These rules always produce a random variable that is added to the state's multivariate Gaussian. This is why the statement is combined with an assignment.

When a value is added/subtracted to a random variable (P-OP-PM), a new random variable is added with its mean updated accordingly. The new variable inherits the variance an covariances of Y. For multiplication and division (P-OP-MD), the mean is updated as before, but also the variance of the random variable, and the covariances with the dependent random variables.

Example 4. Consider the program $X = \mathtt{Normal}(1,1)$; $Y = X + 2$; $Z = Y * 2$. After the first statement we have the state $\mu = [1]$ and $\Sigma = [1]$. The second statement updates the state such that,

$$\mu' = \begin{bmatrix} 1 \\ 3 \end{bmatrix} \quad \Sigma' = \begin{bmatrix} 1 & 1 \\ 1 & 1 \end{bmatrix}$$

The last statements updates the state into

$$\mu'' = \begin{bmatrix} 1 \\ 3 \\ 6 \end{bmatrix} \quad \Sigma'' = \begin{bmatrix} 1 & 1 & 2 \cdot 1 \\ 1 & 1 & 2 \cdot 1 \\ 2 \cdot 1 & 2 \cdot 1 & 2^2 \cdot 1 \end{bmatrix} = \begin{bmatrix} 1 & 1 & 2 \\ 1 & 1 & 2 \\ 2 & 2 & 4 \end{bmatrix}$$

Sum of Random Variables. The sum of two Gaussian random variables (P-SUM) adds a new random variable to the multivariate Gaussian. The mean of the new random variable is the sum of the means of the operands. The covariance of the resulting random variable is the sum of the covariances of the operands with other variables, i.e., the new variable depends on all the variables that the operands depend on. The variance is the sum of the variances of the operands, and the covariances of the operands.

Example 5. Consider the program $X = \mathtt{Normal}(15,2)$; $Y = \mathtt{Normal}(2,1)$; $Z = X + Y$. After the second assignment we have

$$\mu' = \begin{bmatrix} 15 \\ 2 \end{bmatrix} \quad \Sigma' = \begin{bmatrix} 2 & 0 \\ 0 & 1 \end{bmatrix}$$

Thus, the third assignment updates the state's multivariate Gaussian into

$$\mu'' = \begin{bmatrix} 15 \\ 2 \\ 15+2 \end{bmatrix} = \begin{bmatrix} 15 \\ 2 \\ 17 \end{bmatrix} \quad \Sigma'' = \begin{bmatrix} 2 & 0 & 2+0 \\ 0 & 1 & 0+1 \\ 2+0 & 0+1 & 2+1+0+0 \end{bmatrix} = \begin{bmatrix} 2 & 0 & 2 \\ 0 & 1 & 1 \\ 2 & 1 & 3 \end{bmatrix}$$

Conditions. For conditioning (P-COND), we use Thm. 5 introduced in Sect. 2.2. As a result of conditioning, the observed variable is removed from the mean vector and covariance matrix. Note that, despite P-COND applying to the newest random variable, we may perform an affine transformation using a permutation matrix that swaps the order of random variables. Thus, conditions may refer to any variable in the multivariate Gaussian.

Example 6. Let μ'', and Σ'' be those in the final state of the program in Example 5. Suppose that we extend the program with the statement $\texttt{condition}(Z, 1)$. The resulting multivariate Gaussian is updated as

$$\mu''' = \begin{bmatrix} 15 \\ 2 \end{bmatrix} + \frac{1-17}{3} \cdot \begin{bmatrix} 2 \\ 1 \end{bmatrix} = \begin{bmatrix} 15 \\ 2 \end{bmatrix} + \begin{bmatrix} -32/3 \\ -16/3 \end{bmatrix} = \begin{bmatrix} 13/3 \\ -10/3 \end{bmatrix}$$

$$\Sigma''' = \begin{bmatrix} 2 & 0 \\ 0 & 1 \end{bmatrix} - \frac{1}{3} \cdot \begin{bmatrix} 2 \\ 1 \end{bmatrix} \cdot [2\ 1] = \begin{bmatrix} 2 & 0 \\ 0 & 1 \end{bmatrix} - \frac{1}{3} \cdot \begin{bmatrix} 4 & 2 \\ 2 & 1 \end{bmatrix} = \begin{bmatrix} 8/3 & -2/3 \\ -2/3 & 2/3 \end{bmatrix}$$

Recall that covariances may be negative as the covariance matrix is positive definite (cf. Sect. 2.2).

3.2 Soundness and Termination

In what follows, we show that the semantics rules in Fig. 2 are *sound*, and that the inference engine always *terminates* for well-formed programs.

We establish *soundness* of our engine by ensuring that all program statements perform a closed-form transformation on the state's multivariate Gaussian distribution. Lemmas (1-5) assert the soundness of each of the rules in $\rightarrow_s$ (cf. Fig. 2). For example, below we show the proof of the lemma for sum of random variables (i.e., P-SUM) whose soundness is based on the affine transformation property of multivariate Gaussian distributions (cf. Thm. 3). The lemma asserts that the distribution resulting from executing the program statement is a well-formed multivariate Gaussian and also that the newly introduced variable is distributed as the sum of the operands. We refer interested readers to the extended version of the paper [36] for the proofs of the remaining lemmas. Again, we omit the soundness details of deterministic statements and expressions as they are standard. The soundness of the RET rule follows from lemmas (1-5) and Thm. 1.

Lemma 1 (Sum random vars.). *Let $[X_1, X_2, \ldots]^\mathsf{T} \sim \mathcal{N}(\mu, \Sigma)$. For all states $\mathcal{S} = \langle \mu, \Sigma, \sigma \rangle$, if $\langle Y = X_i + X_j, \mathcal{S} \rangle \rightarrow_s \langle \mu', \Sigma', \sigma \rangle$ and $[X_1, X_2, \ldots, X_i + X_j]^\mathsf{T} \sim \mathcal{N}(\mu'', \Sigma'')$, then $[X_1, X_2, \ldots, Y]^\mathsf{T} \sim \mathcal{N}(\mu', \Sigma')$ and $\mathcal{N}(\mu', \Sigma') = \mathcal{N}(\mu'', \Sigma'')$.*

Proof. Let A be a $m \times n$ projection matrix where $A_n = I_n$ where I_n is a $n \times n$ identity matrix, $A_{n+1}[i] = A_{n+1}[j] = 1$ and $A_{n+1}[k] = 0$ for $i, j \neq k$. Let $\boldsymbol{b} = \mathbf{0}$. Then, by matrix multiplication $[X_1, X_2, \ldots, X_i + X_j]^\mathsf{T} = A X + \boldsymbol{b}$. By Thm. 3, $[X_1, X_2, \ldots, X_i + X_j]^\mathsf{T} \sim \mathcal{N}(A\mu + \boldsymbol{b}, A\Sigma A^\mathsf{T})$. By matrix multiplication

$$eA\mu + \boldsymbol{b} = \begin{bmatrix} \mu \\ \mu_{X_i} + \mu_{X_j} \end{bmatrix}$$

$$A\Sigma A^\mathsf{T} = \begin{bmatrix} \Sigma & \Sigma_{[.,X_i]} + \Sigma_{[.,X_j]} \\ \Sigma_{[X_i,.]} + \Sigma_{[X_j,.]} & \Sigma_{[X_i,X_i]} + \Sigma_{[X_j,X_j]} + \Sigma_{[X_i,X_j]} + \Sigma_{[X_j,X_i]} \end{bmatrix} \tag{3}$$

By definition 1 and Eq. 3 we have that $\mu' = A\mu + \boldsymbol{b}$ and $\Sigma' = A\Sigma A^\mathsf{T}$. Thus, $[X_1, X_2, \ldots, Y]^\mathsf{T} \sim \mathcal{N}(\mu', \Sigma')$ and $\mathcal{N}(\mu', \Sigma') = \mathcal{N}(A\mu + \boldsymbol{b}, A\Sigma A^\mathsf{T})$. $\qquad\square$

Lemma 2 (Independent assignment). *Let* $[X_1, X_2, \ldots]^\top \sim \mathcal{N}(\mu, \Sigma)$. *For all states* $\mathcal{S} = \langle \mu, \Sigma, \sigma \rangle$, *if* $\langle Y = \texttt{Normal}(e_1, e_2), \mathcal{S} \rangle \rightarrow_s \langle \mu', \Sigma', \sigma \rangle$ *and* $\langle \mathcal{S}, e_i \rangle \rightarrow_e c_i$, *then* $[X_1, X_2, \ldots; Y]^\top \sim \mathcal{N}(\mu', \Sigma')$ *and* $Y \sim \mathcal{N}(c_1, c_2)$ *and* Y, X_i *are independent.*

Lemma 3 (Dependent assignments). *Let* $[X_1, X_2, \ldots]^\top \sim \mathcal{N}(\mu, \Sigma)$. *For all states* $\mathcal{S} = \langle \mu, \Sigma, \sigma \rangle$, *if* $\langle Y = \texttt{Normal}(e_1 * X_i + e_2, e_3), \mathcal{S} \rangle \rightarrow_s \langle \mu', \Sigma', \sigma \rangle$ *and* $\langle \mathcal{S}, e_i \rangle \rightarrow_e c_i$, *then* $[X_1, X_2, \ldots, Y]^\top \sim \mathcal{N}(\mu', \Sigma')$ *and* $Y \mid X_i \sim \mathcal{N}(c_1 X_i + c_2, c_3)$.

Lemma 4 (Binary operations with values). *Let* $[X_1, X_2, \ldots]^\top \sim \mathcal{N}(\mu, \Sigma)$ *and* $\oplus \in \{+, -, *, /\}$. *For all states* $\mathcal{S} = \langle \mu, \Sigma, \sigma \rangle$, *if* $\langle Y = X_i \oplus e, \mathcal{S} \rangle \rangle \rightarrow_s \langle \mu', \Sigma', \sigma \rangle$ *and* $\langle \mathcal{S}, e \rangle \rightarrow_e c$ *and* $[X_1, X_2, \ldots, X_i \oplus c]^\top \sim \mathcal{N}(\mu'', \Sigma'')$, *then* $[X_1, X_2, \ldots, Y]^\top \sim \mathcal{N}(\mu', \Sigma')$ *and* $\mathcal{N}(\mu', \Sigma') = \mathcal{N}(\mu'', \Sigma'')$.

Lemma 5 (Conditioning). *Let* $[X_a^\top, Y]^\top \sim \mathcal{N}(\mu, \Sigma)$. *For all states* $\mathcal{S} = \langle \mu, \Sigma, \sigma \rangle$, *if* $\langle \mathcal{S}, e \rangle \rightarrow_e c$ *and* $\langle \texttt{condition}(Y, c), \mathcal{S} \rangle \rightarrow_s \langle \mu', \Sigma', \sigma \rangle$, *then* $X' \sim \mathcal{N}(\mu', \Sigma')$ *and* $X' = X_a \mid Y = c$.

Readers familiar with semantics of probabilistic programs will note that these lemmas define the cases of a pushfoward measure semantics *à la* Kozen [7] on the program statements in our language. A standard induction on the structure of well-formed programs establishes soundness of our inference engine.

We also establish termination of our inference engine.

Lemma 6 (Termination). *Given a well-formed program, the process of computing the resulting multivariate Gaussian always terminates.*

Proof. Well-formed programs are unbounded but finite sequences of program statements. Thus, to prove termination, it suffices to prove that each program statement is evaluated in finite time. Expressions (V-EXP, C-EXP, O-EXP) and deterministic statements (D-ASG, SEQ) can be resolved in constant time. For-loops (FOR-B,FOR-I) are bounded and can be unfolded in linear time in the number of iterations. Probabilistic assignments (P-ASG-IND, P-ASG-DEP) extend the mean vector with one element and the covariance matrix with a row and column vectors. Both operations can be performed in linear time in the number of variables of the program. Binary operations between random variables and values (P-OP-PM, P-OP-MD), summation of random variables (P-SUM) and conditioning (P-COND) are computed as a sequence of matrix multiplication operations. All these operations can be computed in polynomial time in the size of the program state, which is never larger than quadratic in the number of variables in the program. Return (RET) performs a lookup in the mean vector and covariance matrix, which can be computed in constant time.

Our inference engine not only terminates for all well-formed programs, but, most importantly, it is *very* efficient. In Sect. 5, we study the scalability of the inference engine, and we show that it can efficiently analyze systems with thousands of random variables. Moreover, we show that our method scales much better than existing tools for the family of programs captured by our language.

Table 1. *Left*: Incomes pr. year in DKK for different age groups and genders. The numbers have been scaled down by a factor of 1000. *Right*: Priors used in the experiments. The means are scaled down by a factor of 1000.

Age group	Males		Females	
	500	480	470	410
	460	430	420	450
21-30	490	510	460	410
	440	480	510	310
	520	410	370	440
	550	410	450	500
	490	580	520	530
31-40	530	420	510	600
	590	400	620	390
	680	510	550	390
	600	540	590	640
	640	590	540	580
41-50	580	620	740	540
	340	510	140	830
	620	660	540	740
	700	680	690	680
	740	640	720	780
51-60	590	650	680	580
	770	630	590	730
	540	840	640	980

Age group	Males		Females	
	$\mathcal{N}(480,100)$	$\mathcal{N}(490,100)$	$\mathcal{N}(450,100)$	$\mathcal{N}(430,100)$
	$\mathcal{N}(440,100)$	$\mathcal{N}(420,100)$	$\mathcal{N}(410,100)$	$\mathcal{N}(430,100)$
21-30	$\mathcal{N}(490,100)$	$\mathcal{N}(490,100)$	$\mathcal{N}(470,100)$	$\mathcal{N}(400,100)$
	$\mathcal{N}(520,100)$	$\mathcal{N}(490,100)$	$\mathcal{N}(490,100)$	$\mathcal{N}(330,100)$
	$\mathcal{N}(470,100)$	$\mathcal{N}(400,100)$	$\mathcal{N}(350,100)$	$\mathcal{N}(400,100)$
	$\mathcal{N}(500,100)$	$\mathcal{N}(410,100)$	$\mathcal{N}(400,100)$	$\mathcal{N}(450,100)$
	$\mathcal{N}(470,100)$	$\mathcal{N}(490,100)$	$\mathcal{N}(490,100)$	$\mathcal{N}(480,100)$
31-40	$\mathcal{N}(500,100)$	$\mathcal{N}(410,100)$	$\mathcal{N}(500,100)$	$\mathcal{N}(550,100)$
	$\mathcal{N}(540,100)$	$\mathcal{N}(410,100)$	$\mathcal{N}(590,100)$	$\mathcal{N}(350,100)$
	$\mathcal{N}(500,100)$	$\mathcal{N}(400,100)$	$\mathcal{N}(510,100)$	$\mathcal{N}(360,100)$
	$\mathcal{N}(580,100)$	$\mathcal{N}(530,100)$	$\mathcal{N}(550,100)$	$\mathcal{N}(490,100)$
	$\mathcal{N}(590,100)$	$\mathcal{N}(510,100)$	$\mathcal{N}(520,100)$	$\mathcal{N}(500,100)$
41-50	$\mathcal{N}(560,100)$	$\mathcal{N}(590,100)$	$\mathcal{N}(650,100)$	$\mathcal{N}(480,100)$
	$\mathcal{N}(280,100)$	$\mathcal{N}(500,100)$	$\mathcal{N}(150,100)$	$\mathcal{N}(790,100)$
	$\mathcal{N}(580,100)$	$\mathcal{N}(600,100)$	$\mathcal{N}(510,100)$	$\mathcal{N}(700,100)$
	$\mathcal{N}(680,100)$	$\mathcal{N}(570,100)$	$\mathcal{N}(680,100)$	$\mathcal{N}(670,100)$
	$\mathcal{N}(620,100)$	$\mathcal{N}(610,100)$	$\mathcal{N}(690,100)$	$\mathcal{N}(700,100)$
51-60	$\mathcal{N}(600,100)$	$\mathcal{N}(570,100)$	$\mathcal{N}(630,100)$	$\mathcal{N}(570,100)$
	$\mathcal{N}(700,100)$	$\mathcal{N}(600,100)$	$\mathcal{N}(500,100)$	$\mathcal{N}(670,100)$
	$\mathcal{N}(520,100)$	$\mathcal{N}(770,100)$	$\mathcal{N}(600,100)$	$\mathcal{N}(770,100)$

4   Case Study: Privacy Risks in Public Statistics

We analyze a program computing statistics on a database containing incomes for different genders and age groups. The purpose of this case study is to demonstrate the applicability of our approach in a real-life example. Average incomes are available through public national statistics banks [1–3], which makes information available to attackers. Leakage of private information and database reconstruction attacks are known issues (e.g., in US census data [21]). We use our inference engine to quantify the increase of attacker knowledge, as she gradually obtains statistics from a database. We also analyze a differentially private [18] mechanism in this setting. The case study uses a small database, but in Sect. 5 we show that our inference engine scales to databases with thousands of individuals.

Releasing Public Statistics. Consider a data analyst that releases average statistics on population income for different age groups and genders. An attacker with access to the statistics attempts to learn the income of an individual in the database. We consider the synthetic data shown in Tbl. 1 (left). The table shows the income for 40 individuals in different age groups and genders. We consider 3 different cases. *Case* 1) the attacker obtains the average income for males in the age group 21–30. *Case* 2) the attacker also obtains the average income for all people in the age group 21–30. *Case* 3) the attacker also obtains the average income for all males. In all cases the attacker attempts to learn the income of the first male in database in the age group 21–30. We note that the observations made by the attacker are independent, so it does not matter in which order the attacker obtains the observations.

To understand the privacy risks for these 3 cases we use the Privug method described in Sect. 2. In the following code snippet we show how to model the steps for case 1 using our inference engine. We model the program using our syntax (step 2).

```
1 def agg():
2     male_21_30 = [Normal(480_000, 100), ....]
3     male_21_30_total = male_21_30[0] + male_21_30[1] ...
4     male_21_30_average = male_21_total/10
5     condition("male_21_30_average", 472_000)
6     return male_21_30[0]
```

The array in line 2 contains the priors of the income for the individuals in the database—Tbl. 1 (right) shows the complete list—denoted as $P(I_i)$. They represent the possible incomes that the attacker considers possible before making any observations (step 1). The victim is the first male in the 21–30 age group, $P(I_1)$. In lines 2–3, we compute the average income of this each group, which defines $P(O|I_i)$. In line 5, we add the attacker observation in the condition statement (step 3). Finally, in line 6 we return the posterior distribution of the victim $P(I_1|O)$, which represents the updated attacker knowledge (step 4). Note that, for brevity, we omit the repetitive parts of the code. Also, arrays are syntactic sugar. We refer interested readers to [35] for the complete source code.

Figure 3 shows how attacker knowledge is updated in the 3 cases above, and how close it is to real victim data (vertical line). We plot the prior attacker knowledge $P(I_1)$, and for each case we plot the posterior distribution after conditioning on the output $P(I_1|O)$. The left plot shows the updated attacker knowledge without differential privacy. As the plot shows, the attacker knowledge gets closer to the actual income when obtaining more information. The most accurate attacker knowledge is case 3 where the attacker obtains several average statistics.

Releasing Public Statistics with Differential Privacy. Given the above results, the data analyst decides to use a differentially private mechanism [18] to protect the individuals' privacy. Differential Privacy (DP) is used in realistic settings for the release of public statistics. Notably, it was used in the 2020 US Census as a result of privacy issues in previous US Census editions [21]. Intuitively, if the privacy protection mechanism satisfies differential privacy, then the impact of an individual on the output of the program is negligible. More precisely, differential privacy states that: a randomized mechanism $\mathcal{M} : \mathbb{I} \to \mathbb{O}$ is (ϵ, δ)-differentially private if for all $\mathcal{O} \subseteq \mathbb{O}$, and neighboring inputs $i_1, i_2 \in \mathbb{I}$, the following holds

$$P(\mathcal{M}(i_1) \in \mathcal{O}) \leq \exp(\epsilon)P(\mathcal{M}(i_2) \in \mathcal{O}) + \delta.$$

The neighboring relation between inputs depends on the input domain ($\mathbb{I}$). For instance, when it applies to datasets of n natural numbers, $\mathbb{N}^n$, it is usually defined as the first norm $||i_x - i_y||_1$. The parameter ϵ is often referred to as the

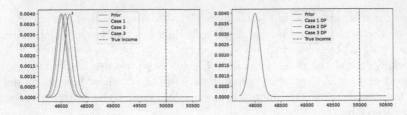

Fig. 3. Updated attacker knowledge after adding observations. Incomes are scaled down by a factor of 10. *Left*: Public stats. *Right*: Public stats with DP.

privacy parameter, and it is used to specify the required level of privacy. The parameter δ is the probability of failure. This parameter relaxes the definition of differential privacy. It is used to specify the probability that pure differential privacy (i.e., with $\delta = 0$) does not hold. This parameter may be used to, e.g., enable high utility gains while keeping a good level of privacy. Both ϵ and δ are often determined empirically [17].

We analyze a differentially private mechanism for the 3 cases presented above. To this end, we apply the Gaussian mechanism [18], which adds Gaussian noise to the observable output (o) as $o + \mathcal{N}(0, \sigma^2)$. The parameter σ^2 is calculated as follows: $\sigma^2 = 2\Delta^2 \log(1.25/\delta)/\epsilon^2$. The sensitivity $\Delta \in \mathbb{R}$ denotes how much o changes if computed in two datasets differing in at most 1 entry. In our setting, it is $\Delta = (max_{income} - min_{income})/size_{DB}$. We set $\delta = 1/size_{DB}^2$—as usual for this query [18]. We set ϵ to 0.9—this is an arbitrary value, but it is common to use values < 1 in practice [17]. Adding Gaussian noise is proven to satisfy (ϵ, δ)-differential privacy [18]. We remark that our method can be used to determine the values of ϵ and δ that satisfy high level privacy requirements. For instance, privacy requirements specified as probability queries for a given individual or using quantitative information flow metrics [32]. The program implementing the Gaussian mechanism is shown in the following listing

```
1  def agg_dp():
2      ...
3      noise = Normal(0, 1442533240)
4      male_21_30_average_dp = male_21_30_average + noise
5      condition("male_21_30_average_dp", 472_000)
6      return male_21_30[0]
```

We only show lines that change namely: line 3 where the noise distribution is defined, and line 6 where we add the noise to the output. The variance σ^2 of the noise distribution is calculated using the equation above.

The right plot in Fig. 3 shows the updated attacker knowledge in the 3 cases. We observe a decrease in privacy risks when using differential privacy; as the change in attacker knowledge is insignificant for all cases. The plot shows that the impact of the victim's data on the released statistics is minuscule compared to the non-differentially private version of the output.

Table 2. *Left*: KL-divergence between prior and posterior attacker knowledge on secret. *Right*: Mutual information between secret and output random variables.

	KL divergence			Mutual information		
	Case 1	Case 2	Case 3	Case 1	Case 2	Case 3
Public stats	312.762	3621.29	14374.13	4.17e-04	6.25e-05	7.81e-06
Diff. Priv	1.55e-12	1.72e-12	1.81e-12	5.00e-12	3.14e-13	2.16e-14

Information Leakage Metrics. In addition to inspecting the distributions of attacker knowledge in Fig. 3, we show for demonstration how to compute two metrics for information leakage: KL-divergence and mutual information [16]. Let $[P,Q]^\intercal \sim \mathcal{N}(\boldsymbol{\mu}, \Sigma)$. KL-divergence is $KL(P,Q) = \log_2(\Sigma_{[Q,Q]}^{1/2}/\Sigma_{[P,P]}^{1/2}) + (\Sigma_{[P,P]} + (\mu_P - \mu_Q)^2)/2\Sigma_{[Q,Q]} - 1/2$, and mutual information is $I(P,Q) = 1/2 \log_2(\Sigma_{[P,P]}\Sigma_{[Q,Q]}/|\Sigma|)$.

Table 2 shows the results. The left shows the KL-divergence between prior and posterior attacker knowledge on the secret. Intuitively, this is commonly understood as *information gain* [11]. We observe an increase in information gain from case 1 to 3 (both with and without differential privacy). However, with differential privacy, information gain is virtually 0 for all cases. Tbl. 2 (right) shows mutual information between attacker knowledge on the secret and the output. When mutual information between two random variables is 0, it means that the variables are independent. Thus, a value of mutual information close to 0 indicates that the amount of information shared between secret and output is low. We observe that mutual information decreases from case 1 to 3 (both with and without differential privacy). This is due to the output containing information for a larger set of individuals (which minimizes the effect of the secret on the output). As expected, mutual information is lower with differential privacy. Admittedly, these metrics are hard to interpret in practice, but we remark that more important than the concrete values is their relative distance—it provides a quantitative mean to compare information leakage in different settings.

5 Scalability Evaluation

We evaluate the scalability of our exact inference engine proof-of-concept implementation. The scalability of Bayesian inference engines mainly depends on the number of random variables. Thus, we consider two synthetic benchmark programs with increasing number of variables. The first computes the sum over an increasing number of variables $O = \sum_{i=1}^{n} X_i$. We choose this benchmark as it was originally used to measure the scalability of Privug [32]. We compare the scalability of our engine to Privug MCMC using the NUTS [26] sampler and the exact inference engine PSI [23]—PSI is the leading inference engine supporting the features of our language (cf. Sect. 6). We instruct NUTS to draw 10000 samples in 2 chains—this number of samples produces an accurate posterior in

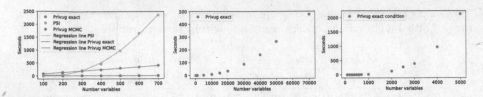

Fig. 4. Execution time for our engine (privug-exact), Privug NUTS (privug-mcmc) and PSI. *Left*: privug-mcmc, privug-exact, and PSI on $O = \sum_i^n X_i$. *Middle*: privug-exact on $O = \sum_i^n X_i$. *Right*: privug-exact on $\text{condition}(O, c)$.

this benchmark, see [32]. The second program performs the same computation but adds a condition statement $\text{condition}(O, c)$. The purpose is to evaluate the scalability of our engine in more realistic settings for the case study in Sect. 4. The evaluation run on a 4×2.80GHz cores machine with 16 GB RAM.

Figure 4 (left) shows the measured times for the first program. Execution time does not increase significantly when going from 100 to 700 variables using our engine. On the other hand, PSI takes approximately 40 min when summing 700 variables. Most notably, our engine greatly outperforms PSI—in this experiment, it was more than 40.000 times faster than PSI for 700 variables. Privug MCMC exhibits better results, but our engine scales better. As the number of variables increases, we observe a bigger gap between our engine and Privug MCMC— with our engine 6 times faster for 700. It is noteworthy that our exact engine outperforms an approximate inference method.

Figure 4 (middle,right) focus on the scalability for larger systems. The middle plot, shows that our engine can handle the first program with 70000 variables more efficiently that PSI for 700. Figure 4 (right) mimics the case study (Sect. 4). We observe that the condition statement notably degrades the performance of our engine. However, the running time for 5000 individuals is less than 40min. We omitted PSI in this benchmark as conditioning would only decrease its performance, and the previous experiment showed its lower scalability w.r.t. our engine. Privug MCMC is also omitted as a fair comparison requires determining the number of samples to draw to obtain an accurate posterior.

6   Related Work

The majority of existing methods to estimate privacy risks use sampling based techniques [12–15,32,34]. In [32], Privug made use of MCMC algorithms to perform Bayesian inference, e.g., *Metropolis-Hastings* or *Hamiltonian Monte Carlo* [6,25,26]. Other sampling based methods target specific quantitative information flow metrics [4]—these metrics are supported by Privug [32], and hence by our engine. LeakWatch/Leakiest [14,15] use program samples to estimate mutual information between secret inputs and public outputs. Cherubin et al. and Romanelli et al. [12,34], use machine learning to compute metrics from the g-leakage family [4]. These methods treat programs as black-boxes, so they can analyze any program, as opposed to our method that targets a subset of Python programs. However, their accuracy guarantees are proven in the limit, i.e., assuming an infinite size sample. In practice, samples are finite and it is often difficult to ensure that results are accurate; specially for programs with large number of variables (such as the ones in Sect. 5). On the contrary, our inference engine produces exact results. This is crucial as a under-approximations could miss important privacy breaches. Furthermore, the scalability evaluation shows that the inference engine scales better than MCMC-based Privug, which is one of the most scalable methods for this type of systems [32].

There exist several works that use exact inference in the context of privacy risk analysis. SPIRE [29] uses the exact inference engine PSI [22,23] to model attacker knowledge and synthesize privacy enforcers. PSI computes a symbolic representation of the joint probability distribution of a given program. It can handle continuous and discrete random variables. It targets a more expressive programming language than the subset of Python that our engine supports. However, PSI scales poorly compared to our engine for programs that our engine supports (cf. Sect. 5). Hakaru [31] and SPPL [37] are exact inference engines—not used for privacy risk analysis. We did not consider them in our evaluation because they do not handle some features of our language. Hakaru cannot handle conditioning probability-zero events (as in lemma 5). SPPL does not support linear combination and sum of Gaussians (as in lemmas 3, 1). QUAIL [9] computes mutual information between input and output variables. It performs forward state exploration of a program to construct a Markov chain, which is then used to compute mutual information. QUAIL works on discrete random variables. Instead, our inference engine works on Gaussian (continuous) random variables and computes the posterior distribution that can be used to compute mutual information (cf. Sect. 4) and other quantitative information flow metrics [4,32].

Stein and Staton proposed a Gaussian-based semantics to study exact conditioning through the lens of category theory [38]. They do not study the use of the semantics for privacy risks quantification on a subset of Python programs, or evaluate the efficiency of the semantics.

7 Conclusion

We have presented an exact Bayesian inference engine for quantifying privacy risks in a subset of Python. We have proven that our inference engine is sound. We have presented an application of our engine to analyze privacy risks on public statistics; a realistic case study for national statistics agencies where privacy risks analysis is crucial. We have also analyzed the impact of differential privacy on data release. In the scalability evaluation, we have shown that our engine can analyze systems with thousands of random variables, and that it greatly outperforms existing tools. All in all, this work provides a new point in the study of expressiveness vs performance. Future work includes adapting our engine with underlying probabilistic models that capture more Python program statements, for instance Gaussian mixtures or the exponential family of probability distributions.

References

1. Statistics Denmark. www.dst.dk/en Accessed 23 June 2023
2. Statistics New Zealand. www.stats.govt.nz/ Accessed 23 June 2023
3. US Census Bureau. www.census.gov/ Accessed 23 June 2023
4. Alvim, M.S., Chatzikokolakis, K., McIver, A., Morgan, C., Palamidessi, C., Smith, G.: The Science of Quantitative Information Flow. Springer, Cham (2020)
5. Article 29 Data Protection Working Party: Opinion 05/2014 on Anonymisation Techniques (2014). www.pdpjournals.com/docs/88197.pdf
6. Avi Pfeffer: Practical probabilistic programming. Manning Publications Co. (2016)
7. Barthe, G., Katoen, J.P., Silva, A. (eds.): Foundations of Probabilistic Programming. Cambridge University Press (2020)
8. Biondi, F., Kawamoto, Y., Legay, A., Traonouez, L.: Hybrid statistical estimation of mutual information and its application to information flow. Formal Aspects Comput. **31**(2), 165–206 (2019)
9. Biondi, F., Legay, A., Traonouez, L.-M., Wąsowski, A.: QUAIL: a quantitative security analyzer for imperative code. In: Sharygina, N., Veith, H. (eds.) Computer Aided Verification, pp. 702–707. Springer, Berlin, Heidelberg (2013). https://doi.org/10.1007/978-3-642-39799-8_49
10. Bishop, C.M.: Pattern Recognition and Machine Learning. Information science and statistics, Springer, New York (2006)
11. Burnham, K.P., Anderson, D.R.: Model Selection and Multimodel Inference: A Practical Information-Theoretic Approach. Springer, New York (2002)
12. Cherubin, G., Chatzikokolakis, K., Palamidessi, C.: F-BLEAU: fast black-box leakage estimation. In: SP'19, pp. 835–852. IEEE (2019)
13. Chothia, T., Guha, A.: A statistical test for information leaks using continuous mutual information. In: CSF'11, pp. 177–190. IEEE (2011)
14. Chothia, T., Kawamoto, Y., Novakovic, C.: A tool for estimating information leakage. In: Sharygina, N., Veith, H. (eds.) Computer Aided Verification, pp. 690–695. Springer, Berlin, Heidelberg (2013). https://doi.org/10.1007/978-3-642-39799-8_47
15. Chothia, T., Kawamoto, Y., Novakovic, C.: LeakWatch: Estimating Information Leakage from Java Programs. In: Kutyłowski, M., Vaidya, J. (eds.) ESORICS 2014. LNCS, vol. 8713, pp. 219–236. Springer, Cham (2014). https://doi.org/10.1007/978-3-319-11212-1_13
16. Cover, T.M., Thomas, J.A.: Elements of information theory (2. ed.). Wiley (2006)
17. Dwork, C., Kohli, N., Mulligan, D.: Differential privacy in practice: Expose your epsilons! J. Privacy Confidentiality **9**(2) (2019)
18. Dwork, C., Roth, A.: The algorithmic foundations of differential privacy. Found. Trends Theor. Comput. Sci. **9**(3–4), 211–407 (2014)
19. Eaton, M.: Multivariate Statistics: A Vector Space Approach. Lecture notes-monograph series, Institute of Mathematical Statistics (2007)
20. Elliot, M., Mackey, E., O'Hara, K., Tudor, C.: The Anonymisation Decision - Making Framework. University of Manchester, UKAN (2016)
21. Garfinkel, S.L., Abowd, J.M., Martindale, C.: Understanding database reconstruction attacks on public data. Commun. ACM **62**(3), 46–53 (2019)
22. Gehr, T., Misailovic, S., Vechev, M.T.: PSI: exact symbolic inference for probabilistic programs. In: CAV'16. LNCS, vol. 9779, pp. 62–83 (2016)
23. Gehr, T., Steffen, S., Vechev, M.: λPSI: exact inference for higher-order probabilistic programs. In: PLDI'20, pp. 883–897. ACM (2020)

24. Gordon, A.D., Henzinger, T.A., Nori, A.V., Rajamani, S.K.: Probabilistic programming. In: FOSE'14, pp. 167–181. ACM (2014)
25. Greenberg, S.C.E.: Understanding the Metropolis-Hastings Algorithm p. 10
26. Homan, M.D., Gelman, A.: The no-u-turn sampler: Adaptively setting path lengths in Hamiltonian monte carlo. J. Mach. Learn. Res. **15**(1), 1593–1623 (2014)
27. Jaynes, E.T.: Probability Theory: The Logic of Science. Cambridge University Press, Cambridge (2003)
28. Koller, D., Friedman, N.: Probabilistic Graphical Models - Principles and Techniques. MIT Press (2009)
29. Kucera, M., Tsankov, P., Gehr, T., Guarnieri, M., Vechev, M.T.: Synthesis of probabilistic privacy enforcement. In: CCS'17, pp. 391–408. ACM (2017)
30. McElreath, R.: Statistical rethinking: A Bayesian course with examples in R and Stan. CRC Press (2020)
31. Narayanan, P., Carette, J., Romano, W., Shan, C., Zinkov, R.: Probabilistic Inference by Program Transformation in Hakaru (System Description). In: Kiselyov, O., King, A. (eds.) FLOPS 2016. LNCS, vol. 9613, pp. 62–79. Springer, Cham (2016). https://doi.org/10.1007/978-3-319-29604-3_5
32. Pardo, R., Rafnsson, W., Probst, C.W., Wąsowski, A.: Privug: Using Probabilistic Programming for Quantifying Leakage in Privacy Risk Analysis. In: Bertino, E., Shulman, H., Waidner, M. (eds.) ESORICS 2021. LNCS, vol. 12973, pp. 417–438. Springer, Cham (2021). https://doi.org/10.1007/978-3-030-88428-4_21
33. Robert, C.P., Casella, G.: Monte Carlo Statistical Methods. Springer, New York, NY (2004)
34. Romanelli, M., Chatzikokolakis, K., Palamidessi, C., Piantanida, P.: Estimating g-leakage via machine learning. In: CCS'20. ACM (2020)
35. Rønneberg, R.C., Pardo, R., Wąsowski, A.: Exact and Efficient Bayesian Inference for Privacy Risk Quantification (Accompanying Artifact). www.doi.org/10.5281/zenodo.8173905
36. Rønneberg, R.C., Pardo, R., Wąsowski, A.: Exact and efficient Bayesian inference for privacy risk quantification (extended version). arXiv:2308.16700 (2023)
37. Saad, F.A., Rinard, M.C., Mansinghka, V.K.: SPPL: Probabilistic programming with fast exact symbolic inference. In: PLDI'21, pp. 804–819. ACM (2021)
38. Stein, D., Staton, S.: Compositional semantics for probabilistic programs with exact conditioning. In: LICS'21, pp. 1–13. IEEE (2021)

A Formalization of Heisenbugs and Their Causes

Sarah Sallinger(✉), Georg Weissenbacher, and Florian Zuleger

TU Wien, Vienna, Austria
{sarah.sallinger,georg.weissenbacher,florian.zuleger}@tuwien.ac.at

Abstract. The already challenging task of identifying the cause of a bug becomes even more cumbersome if those bugs disappear or change their behavior under observation. Such bugs occur in a range of contexts including elusive concurrency bugs as well as unintended system alterations during debugging and—as a pun on the name of Werner Heisenberg—are often referred to as Heisenbugs. Heisenbugs can be caused by various sources of nondeterminism on different system levels, many of which developers and testers might not even be aware of. This paper provides formal foundations for rigorously reasoning about causes of Heisenbugs. It provides a formal definition of Heisenbugs in terms of a hyperproperty and introduces a framework for determining the causality of Heisenbugs in presence of multiple candidate causes based on said hyperproperty. We analyze the properties of causes and the implications on practical causal analyses.

1 Introduction

Bugs which change their behavior under observation are notoriously difficult to detect and fix. Inspired by Heisenberg's uncertainty principle such bugs are often referred to as *Heisenbugs*. Depending on the context, the term Heisenbug has been used to describe slightly different concepts. In the software engineering community, the term is used mostly for bugs whose analysis is hampered by the probe effect, i.e., an unintended alteration of the system behavior during debugging [18]. In the formal methods community, the term has been used to refer to elusive faults arising from executions that exhibit nondeterminism, in particular in the context of concurrent software [30]. In the context of automated testing, the term flaky test is used for inconsistently failing test cases [31], i.e. manifestations of Heisenbugs. As will become apparent in this paper, all the mentioned phenomena can be formalized in a uniform manner. In the rest of the paper, we hence use the term Heisenbug to refer to all the mentioned categories[1].

---

[1] In the literature, sometimes the term Mandelbug is used as an umbrella term for the mentioned categories. However, Mandelbugs additionally include complex faults where there is "a delay between the fault activation and the final failure occurrence",

© The Author(s), under exclusive license to Springer Nature Switzerland AG 2023
C. Ferreira and T. A. C. Willemse (Eds.): SEFM 2023, LNCS 14323, pp. 282–300, 2023.
https://doi.org/10.1007/978-3-031-47115-5_16

A Formalization of Heisenbugs. The first contribution of this paper is a formal definition of Heisenbugs. The unifying characteristic of Heisenbugs in the above-mentioned categories is the existence of at least two system executions where one execution is correct and the other exhibits a bug. In terms of testing, the same test case sometimes succeeds and sometimes fails. We formalize this definition in terms of a hyperproperty [7], which checks for the existence of two terminating executions with equal inputs but deviating outcomes for a final assertion that is part of the system specification. Our definition accommodates deviations caused by nondeterminism in a single program, e.g. due to concurrency, as well as deviating behavior of different versions of the program, e.g. due to changes for debugging.

Debugging Challenges. Previous studies have shown that Heisenbugs are prevalent even in mature software systems and that the bug fixing process takes significantly longer than for ordinary bugs [9]. Furthermore, Heisenbugs significantly complicate automated testing techniques, as they lead to flaky tests [31].

A major step in the debugging process is the identification of the bug's root causes [35]. Developers reported this step to be particularly difficult for Heisenbugs [11] (referred to as flaky tests in this study). One reason for the complexity is that Heisenbugs can be caused by *mechanisms* (i.e., sources of nondeterminism or system alterations) located on all system levels ranging from the hardware level to the user program. The following examples illustrate some possible causes:

Example 1 (Concurrency). We first present an example for a Heisenbug stemming from system internal nondeterminism. The Therac-25 incident [24,37], which resulted in the death of several cancer patients, is a notorious instance of an atomicity violation [27]. Listing 1.1 illustrates the problem, which is caused by the concurrent execution of two routines: the `userInterface` routine allows the operator to choose between high energy x-ray therapy (`isXray`) and a lower energy electron beam therapy (`!isXray`) and to set the intensity of the radiation (`isHigh`). The assume statement in line 6 prevents a selection of high-intensity electron therapy. The `setup` routine then processes these inputs: a failed assertion represents the case where the patient is exposed to excessive radiation. Assume that the user changes the initial configuration from high-intensity x-ray treatment (`isXray=true, isHigh=true`) to low-energy electron therapy (`isXray=false, isHigh=false`) in lines 4 and 7. If a context switch occurs right after executing line 5, the assertion in line 13 will fail. When `userInterface` is executed atomically, however, the assertion always holds.

```
1  bool isXray = true;
2  bool isHigh = true;
3  void *userInterface(void *a) {
4    isXray = read();
5    bool isHighTmp = read();
6    assume(isXray || !isHighTmp);
7    isHigh = isHighTmp;
8  }

9  void *setup(void *a) {
10   bool filter = isXray;
11   bool highEnergy = isHigh;
12 }
13 assert(filter || !highEnergy);
```

Listing 1.1. Illustration of Therac-25 atomicity violation

To sum up, there is a Heisenbug caused by different possible schedules, which is an example for the category of Heisenbugs arising from nondeterministic systems. Even if the scheduler might in fact be deterministic, its internal steps are not observable for the programmer (which we model using nondeterminism).

Example 2 (Floating Point Precision).   A prominent example for unintented system alterations are debugging statements that inadvertently change program outcomes. Consider Listing 1.2 (following [28]), which computes the square of 10^{308} and is expected to cause an overflow given the double-precision floating-point representation. When compiled with optimization level -O3 and executed using x87 instructions, however, the computation results in 10^{308} rather than in an overflow, and the assertion fails. The reason is that the computation uses 80-bit floating point registers and performs rounding only once values are stored in 64-bit memory cells. Adding the printf statement in line 4 enforces such a write to memory, thus yielding the expected overflow, and the assertion holds.

```
1  double v = 1E308;
2  double y = 0;
3  y = v * v;
4  // printf("%g\n", y);
5  assert(isinf(y / v));
```

Listing 1.2. Floating-point computation overflows in case of printf-debugging

The failing and correct executions actually stem from two different system versions. In the considered execution model, the debugging statement changes the semantics of the program, introducing a probe effect which causes the Heisenbug.

Multiple Causes.   While the mechanisms causing the Heisenbugs in Example 1 and Example 2 can still be easily identified, such an analysis becomes more challenging for more complex systems where several such mechanisms interact in a non-trivial manner [33] (as in Example 3 below).

Example 3 (Weak Memory Models).   Listing 1.3 shows Peterson's mutual exclusion algorithm for two processes. Computer architectures with weak memory models relax the guarantees on the order in which variable assignments are observed across processor cores, causing the algorithm to fail. In particular, the synchronization fails if both processes set their flags in lines 5 and 15 but do not commit the modifications from cache to shared memory before lines 8 and 18 are executed, thus resulting in a Heisenbug (see [34]). Such a reordering, however, is effectively prevented if there are printf statements in lines 7 and 17 (as might be the case during development) and hence the bug only occurs once the printf statements are removed. Yet, the printf statements are not causally related to the Heisenbug (unlike in Example 2), as we will formally argue in Sect. 3.

Formal Causality Framework.   In order to rigorously determine which mechanisms cause a Heisenbug in settings with multiple candidate causes, we present a formal causality definition based on Lewis' counterfactuals [26] and the causality framework of Galles and Pearl [14]. In counterfactual reasoning, an event is a cause of an effect, if in an alternative world where the cause does not occur, the effect does also not occur. In a nutshell, in a setting with multiple candidate

```
1  int flagP0 = 0, flagP1 = 0;
2  int turn = 0;
3  int critical = 0, error = 0;
4  void *petersonP0(void *a) {
5    flagP0 = 1;
6    turn = 1;
7    //printf("barrier");
8    while (flagP1 && (turn == 1));
9    critical++;
10   if (critical != 1) error++;
11   critical--;
12   flagP0 = 0;
13 }
```

```
14  void *petersonP1(void *a) {
15    flagP1 = 1;
16    turn = 0;
17    //printf("barrier");
18    while (flagP0 && (turn == 0));
19    critical++;
20    if (critical != 1) error++;
21    critical--;
22    flagP1 = 0;
23  }
24  assert(error == 0);
```

Listing 1.3. Peterson's algorithm occasionally fails on weak memory models

mechanisms, a subset of the mechanisms is a cause of a Heisenbug if there are correct as well as failing executions which agree on the behavior of all other given mechanisms. This is formalized by means of a hyperproperty resembling our formal definition of Heisenbugs.

Note that our formal definition of causes refers to alternative scenarios for counterfactual reasoning. This requires the sources of nondeterminism to be made explicit in the underlying model (or controllable in the system under test, respectively). In practice, however, identifying and controlling all possible sources of nondeterminism is hardly feasible. Therefore, we prove that our causal analysis yields sound results even if some sources of nondeterminism remain unknown or uncontrollable: the result of evaluating our causality hyperproperty in a nondeterministic system is always a subset of a cause identified in the corresponding determinized system in which all sources are made explicit and controllable.

Based on these results, we present an iterative refinement methodology for causal analysis and discuss practical challenges. We showcase how the methodology can be applied for analyses based on model checking and testing.

Main Contributions. The paper presents:

- A formal definition of Heisenbugs in reactive systems in terms of a hyperproperty, in presence of system-internal nondeterminism and/or unintended system alternations (Sect. 2).
- A hyperproperty-based approach for defining the causality of Heisenbugs in the presence of several potential causes and nondeterminism (Sect. 3).
- A methodology for causal analysis based on iterative refinement (Sect. 4).

2 A Formalization of Heisenbugs

This section provides our system model and a formal definition of Heisenbugs.

2.1 System Model

In the following, the term *formula* refers to a first-order formula with a background theory that fixes the interpretations of predicates and function symbols.

Definition 1. *A* Symbolic Transition System *(STS) is a tuple* $(X, I, \text{init}, \text{final}, T)$, *where* X *and* I *are disjoint sets of* system *and* input *variables, respectively, the* initial condition init *is a formula over* $X \cup I$, *the* final condition final *is a formula over* X, *and the* transition relation T *is a formula over* $X \cup I \cup X'$, *where the variables* X' *denote primed copies of the variables* X.

Let Val *be a domain of* values. *Following [38], we assume* Val *to contain a special value* τ *that represents* quiescence, *i.e., the absence of an input. A* configuration c *of an STS is a mapping of the variables in* $(X \cup I)$ *to values in* Val. *A state* s *is a mapping of the variables in* X *to values in* Val. *An input* i *is a mapping of the variables in* I *to values in* Val. *The state* $c|_X$ *resp. input* $c|_I$ *of a configuration* c *is the restriction of the mapping to variables in* X *resp.* I. *We write* $c(v)$ *for the value of a variable* $v \in (X \cup I)$ *in configuration* c *(and we use the same notation for states and inputs).*

For a formula φ *and a mapping* m *of variables to values we write* $m \models \varphi$ *if* φ *evaluates to true under* m. *A configuration* c *is* initial *if* $c \models$ init. *A state* s *is* final *if* $s \models$ final. *A configuration* c *is* final *if* $c|_X$ *is final. A state* $s : X \to$ Val *is* successor state *of configuration* c *if* $\langle c, s' \rangle \models T$, *where* $s' : X' \to$ Val *is the function that maps each primed variable* $x' \in X'$ *to* $s(x)$ *and* $\langle \cdot, \cdot \rangle$ *denotes the union of two mappings with disjoint domains. We call* c_{i+1} *a* successor configuration *of* c_i *if* $c_{i+1}|_X$ *is a successor state of* c_i. *We require that* final configurations *do not have successor configurations.*

A (finite or infinite) trace *of an STS is a sequence of configurations* $c_0, \dots, c_n$ *where* $c_0 \models$ init, *and* c_{i+1} *is a successor of* c_i *for all* $i \geq 0$. *An* execution *of an STS is a finite trace* $c_0, \dots, c_n$ *such that* c_n *is a final configuration.*

It is straightforward to represent programs such as the examples from the introduction as symbolic transition systems:

Example 4. Listing 1.1 can be modeled as an STS with $I = \{\text{input}_1, \text{input}_2\}$ and $X = \{\text{isXray}, \text{isHigh}, \text{isHighTmp}, \text{filter}, \text{highEnergy}, \text{pc}_0, \text{pc}_1\}$, where the variables pc_0 and pc_1 model the program counters of the two threads. The initial condition is $(\text{isXray} \wedge \text{isHigh} \wedge \text{pc}_0 = 4 \wedge \text{pc}_1 = 10)$. The final condition is $(\text{pc}_0 = 8 \wedge \text{pc}_1 = 12)$ and describes that both traces have reached their final program location. The transition relation T shown in Fig. 1 is a disjunctive partitioning that represents a case split over all possible combinations of program locations, where the thread to be executed in each step is chosen nondeterministically.

While Example 4 illustrates the case of nondeterminism in a single system version, we next exemplify how to model system alterations in our formal model: the original and the altered system can be combined in one STS with an initial nondeterministic choice between two disjuncts of the transition relation.

control flow	data flow
$(pc_0 = 4 \wedge pc_0' = 5) \wedge (pc_1' = pc_1)$	$\wedge \; (\bigwedge_{var \in X \setminus \{isXray, pc_0, pc_1\}} var' = var) \wedge (isXray' = input_1)$
$\vee \quad (pc_0 = 5 \wedge pc_0' = 7) \wedge (pc_1' = pc_1)$	$\wedge \; (\bigwedge_{var \in X \setminus \{isHighTmp, pc_0, pc_1\}} var' = var) \wedge$
	$(isHighTmp' = input_2) \wedge (isXray' \vee \neg isHighTmp')$
$\vee \quad (pc_0 = 7 \wedge pc_0' = 8) \wedge (pc_1' = pc_1)$	$\wedge \; (\bigwedge_{var \in X \setminus \{isHigh, pc_0, pc_1\}} var' = var) \wedge (isHigh' = isHighTmp)$
$\vee \quad (pc_1 = 10 \wedge pc_1' = 11) \wedge (pc_0' = pc_0)$	$\wedge \; (\bigwedge_{var \in X \setminus \{filter, pc_0, pc_1\}} var' = var) \wedge (filter' = isXray)$
$\vee \quad (pc_1 = 11 \wedge pc_1' = 12) \wedge (pc_0' = pc_0)$	$\wedge \; (\bigwedge_{var \in X \setminus \{highEnergy, pc_0, pc_1\}} var' = var) \wedge$
	$(highEnergy' = isHigh)$

Fig. 1. Transition relation for Listing 1.1

Example 5. The floating point program from Listing 1.2 can be modeled as an STS where $X = \{v, y, pc, print\}$, $I = \emptyset$, the initial condition is ($pc = 3 \wedge v = 10^{308} \wedge y = 0$), the final condition is $pc = 5$, and the transition relation is defined as ($pc = 3 \wedge pc' = 5 \wedge y' = v * v \wedge v' = v \wedge \neg print \wedge print' = print) \vee (pc = 3 \wedge pc' = 5 \wedge y' = \mathsf{convert64}(v * v) \wedge v' = v \wedge print \wedge print' = print$) where convert64 is a function producing the 64 bit representation of the number. The initial condition does not constrain print, i.e., the initial value of print can be arbitrary; this initial (nondeterministic) choice then fixes the respective disjunct of the transition relation depending on whether the `printf`-statement is present or not.

In the following, we formally define a number of useful properties of STSs.

Definition 2 (Termination). *An STS is* terminating *if the STS does not have infinite traces.*

Definition 3 (Input Determinism). *An STS is* input-deterministic *if 1) for every input i there is at most one state s such that $\langle s, i \rangle \models$ init, and 2) for every state s and every input i there is at most one successor state. Otherwise, it is* nondeterministic.

Definition 4 (Input-enabled). *An STS is* input-enabled *if 1) for every input i there is at least one state s such that $\langle s, i \rangle \models$ init, and 2) every configuration that is not final has at least one successor. In case 2) is violated, we call the transition relation* partial.

We next define assertions as well as succeeding and failing executions:

Definition 5 (Assertions, Succeeding and Failing Executions). *An assertion is a formula φ over the system variables X. An execution $\pi \stackrel{\text{def}}{=} c_0, \ldots, c_n$ succeeds with respect to φ if $c_n|_X \models \varphi$. Similarly, π fails if $c_n|_X \models \neg \varphi$. Abusing our notation, we write $\pi \models \varphi$ if π succeeds and $\pi \not\models \varphi$ if π fails.*

We note that without input-enabledness, which we do not require in general, traces can get stuck at non-final configurations: For example, in Fig. 1, any state with $pc_0 = 5, pc_1 = 12, isXray = false, input_2 = true$ does not have a successor. For such traces, it is not meaningful to argue whether they satisfy an assertion.

This is why Definition 5 quantifies over executions, i.e., traces that end in a final configuration. Moreover, Definition 5 disregards infinite traces, as we limit ourselves in this paper to Heisenbugs that are observable in a finite amount of time; we leave the extension to non-terminating traces to future work.

Example 6. Figures 2 and 3 show executions of the STS from Example 4. For $\varphi \stackrel{\text{def}}{=} (\text{filter} \vee \neg\text{highEnergy})$ (the assertion in line 13), we have $\pi_1 \models \varphi$ and $\pi_2 \not\models \varphi$.

control flow		inputs		states				
pc_0	pc_1	$input_1$	$input_2$	isXray	isHigh	isHighTmp	filter	highEnergy
4	10	F	τ	T	T	F	F	F
5	10	τ	F	F	T	F	F	F
7	10	τ	τ	F	T	F	F	F
8	10	τ	τ	F	F	F	F	F
8	11	τ	τ	F	F	F	F	F
8	12	τ	τ	F	F	F	F	F

Fig. 2. Execution π_1 of Fig. 1

control flow		inputs		states				
pc_0	pc_1	$input_1$	$input_2$	isXray	isHigh	isHighTmp	filter	highEnergy
4	10	F	τ	T	T	F	F	F
5	10	τ	F	F	T	F	F	F
7	10	τ	τ	F	T	F	F	F
7	11	τ	τ	F	T	F	F	F
7	12	τ	τ	F	T	F	F	T
8	12	τ	τ	F	F	F	F	T

Fig. 3. Execution π_2 of Fig. 1

We presume that a system contains a bug if it has at least one failing execution (i.e., we assume that the assertion φ correctly encodes desired behavior of the program):

Definition 6. *Let* $(X, I, \text{init}, \text{final}, T)$ *be an STS and the assertion* φ *be a formula over* X. *The STS contains a* bug *with respect to* φ *if there exists a failing counterexample execution:*

$$\exists \pi_c . \pi_c \not\models \varphi.$$

A violation of the property φ in Definition 6, however, does not necessarily constitute a Heisenbug.

2.2 Formal Definition of Heisenbugs

Heisenbugs are special bugs which occur only on some, but not on all executions. We express this in terms of a hyperproperty [7]. Unlike properties over single executions (such as Definition 6), hyperproperties relate sets of traces, allowing us to characterize Heisenbugs by juxtaposing the behavior of two executions. In particular, we require at least one succeeding and one failing execution induced by the same input (as deviating behavior is to be expected for differing inputs). To express this requirement for reactive systems, we define the projection of a trace to its corresponding sequence of inputs that are not quiescent (i.e., not τ):

Definition 7. *Let π be a trace of the STS $(X, I, \text{init}, \text{final}, T)$, and let $J \subseteq I$ be some subset of the input variables. The input sequence $J(\pi)$ is defined inductively:*

$$J(\varepsilon) = \varepsilon, \qquad J(c \cdot \pi) = \begin{cases} J(\pi), & \text{if } \forall i \in J : c(i) = \tau \\ c|_J \cdot J(\pi) \text{ otherwise} \end{cases}$$

where ε is the trace of length zero and $\cdot$ represents concatenation.

Example 7. The traces from Figs. 2 and 3 have the same inputs $\langle \text{input}_1 \mapsto \text{false}, \text{input}_2 \mapsto \tau \rangle \cdot \langle \text{input}_1 \mapsto \tau, \text{input}_2 \mapsto \text{false} \rangle$ for $J = I = \{\text{input}_1, \text{input}_2\}$.

Heisenbugs can be characterized using a hyperproperty asserting the existence of two executions with matching inputs, one of which violates the assertion while the other fulfills it:

Definition 8. *An STS $(X, I, \text{init}, \text{final}, T)$ contains a* Heisenbug *with respect to an assertion φ if*

$$\exists \pi_c, \pi_w . I(\pi_c) = I(\pi_w) \land \pi_c \not\models \varphi \land \pi_w \models \varphi.$$

The execution π_c is the counterexample *execution, π_w is the* witness *execution.*

We emphasize that the definition is expressed in terms of a hyperproperty stating that the inputs of the two traces must match. This condition cannot be expressed as a simple trace property. Moreover, we remark that Definition 8 is amenable to hyperproperty model checking (e.g., [13]).

Example 8. The Therac-25 example contains a Heisenbug with counterexample execution π_2 from Fig. 3 and witness execution π_1 from Fig. 2.

3   Causality

In this section, we extend the hyperproperty from Definition 8 to counterfactually reason about the causality of Heisenbugs. We first present a refinement step for making potential causes explicit in the model and then introduce formal definitions of causality in deterministic as well as nondeterministic systems.

3.1   Modeling Sources of Nondeterminism

For the purpose of causality analysis, the sources of nondeterminism (which we call *mechanisms*) need to be made explicit. Nondeterminism can be due to incomplete observability, incomplete modeling or to inherent stochasticity in the modeled system, as is the case for example in quantum mechanics [15, Section 3.1]. Nondeterminism stemming from incomplete observability and modeling can be eliminated by refining the model with the relevant information. Even true nondeterminism can—at least in principle—be accounted for by means of prophecy variables [1].

To formalize this idea, we introduce refinements of a transition system:

Definition 9 (Refinement). *Let $S \overset{\text{def}}{=} (X, I, \text{init}, \text{final}, T)$ be an STS. We say an STS $S_{\text{ref}} = (X \uplus X_{\text{ref}}, I \uplus I_{\text{ref}}, \text{init}_{\text{ref}}, \text{final}_{\text{ref}}, T_{\text{ref}})$ is a refinement of S iff*

1. *for every $\langle\langle s, s_{\text{ref}}\rangle, \langle i, i_{\text{ref}}\rangle, \langle s', s'_{\text{ref}}\rangle\rangle \models T_{\text{ref}}$ we have that $\langle s, i, s'\rangle \models T$, and for every state $\langle s, s_{\text{ref}}\rangle$ of S_{ref} and transition $\langle s, i, s'\rangle \models T$ there are mappings $i_{\text{ref}}, s'_{\text{ref}}$ of I_{ref} and X'_{ref} to values such that $\langle\langle s, s_{\text{ref}}\rangle, \langle i, i_{\text{ref}}\rangle, \langle s', s'_{\text{ref}}\rangle\rangle \models T_{\text{ref}}$,*
2. *for every $\langle\langle s, s_{\text{ref}}\rangle, \langle i, i_{\text{ref}}\rangle\rangle \models \text{init}_{\text{ref}}$ we have $\langle s, i\rangle \models \text{init}$, and for every $\langle s, i\rangle \models \text{init}$ there are mappings $i_{\text{ref}}, s_{\text{ref}}$ of I_{ref} and X_{ref} to values such that $\langle\langle s, s_{\text{ref}}\rangle, \langle i, i_{\text{ref}}\rangle\rangle \models \text{init}_{\text{ref}}$, and*
3. *for every $\langle s, s_{\text{ref}}\rangle \models \text{final}_{\text{ref}}$ we have $s \models \text{final}$, and for every $s \models \text{final}$ and every mapping s_{ref} of the variables X_{ref} to values we have $\langle s, s_{\text{ref}}\rangle \models \text{final}_{\text{ref}}$.*

We note that the above definition preserves executions: Let S_{ref} be a refinement of some STS S. Then every execution of S_{ref} gives rise to an execution of S by projecting away the additional state and input variables. On the other hand, the conditions in the refinement definition ensure that every execution of S can be extended to an execution of S_{ref} by choosing suitable values for the additional state and input variables. We note that refinements can be thought of as adding additional information to the STS under analysis, and the requirements in our definition ensure that executions are preserved. If *all* mechanisms (i.e., sources of nondeterminism) are explicit, refinement yields a deterministic system:

Definition 10 (Determinization). *We say that an STS S_{det} is a determinization of some STS S, if S_{det} is a refinement of S and is input-deterministic.*

Example 9. The Therac-25 transition system from Example 4 can be refined by setting $I_{\text{ref}} = \{\text{thread}\}$, where thread is a Boolean variable selecting which thread takes a step. The refined transition relation is shown in Fig. 4.

schedule	control flow	data flow
	$\neg$thread $\wedge (pc_0 = 4 \wedge pc_0' = 5) \wedge (pc_1' = pc_1)$ $\wedge$	...
$\vee$	$\neg$thread $\wedge (pc_0 = 5 \wedge pc_0' = 7) \wedge (pc_1' = pc_1)$ $\wedge$	...
$\vee$	$\neg$thread $\wedge (pc_0 = 7 \wedge pc_0' = 8) \wedge (pc_1' = pc_1)$ $\wedge$	...
$\vee$	thread $\wedge (pc_1 = 10 \wedge pc_1' = 11) \wedge (pc_0' = pc_0)$ $\wedge$	...
$\vee$	thread $\wedge (pc_1 = 11 \wedge pc_1' = 12) \wedge (pc_0' = pc_0)$ $\wedge$	...

Fig. 4. Deterministic transition relation for Listing 1.1

Example 10. The floating point transition system from Example 5 can be extended to a deterministic system by setting $I_{\text{ref}} = \{\text{debug}\}$ and considering the refined initial condition $(pc = 3 \wedge v = 10^{308} \wedge y = 0 \wedge (\text{debug} \Leftrightarrow \text{print}))$, and leaving the transition relation unchanged. We point out that the initial value of the input variable debug fixes the value of print, which in turn fixes the transition relation reflecting the presence of the `printf`-statement.

For Example 9 and Example 10 we have $X_{ref} = \emptyset$. In the Peterson example below, the refinement contains a state variable reflecting whether the cache state has been propagated to main memory.

Example 11. Peterson's algorithm (Listing 1.3) can be modeled as a deterministic STS. In this example we present the final refinement that makes all involved mechanisms explicit. Alternatively, the mechanisms could be made explicit in successive refinement steps. Figure 5 shows the part of the transition relation that models P0. Let $X = \{pc_0, pc_1, flagP0, flagP0c, flagP1, flagP1c,$ $turn, critical, error, print\}$ where flagP0c and flagP1c represent the locally cached versions of the flags. We have $I = \emptyset$ and $I_{ref} = \{thread, debug, reorder\}$, where thread indicates whether P0 or P1 takes a step (thread is omitted in Fig. 5). Let $X_{ref} = \{delay\}$, and let $init_{ref}$ imply $(print = debug \land delay = reorder)$. The variable print indicates that the program version with `printf`-debugging is executed, and delay is true if the modifications of the flags flagP0 and flagP1 are only committed to shared memory after entering the critical section (to avoid clutter, we assume only two possible points for committing the modification of flagP0). We use $(print \Rightarrow \neg delay)$ to model the interplay between two mechanisms where the `printf` instruction prevents reordering because of the added barrier, resulting in a partial transition relation. Moreover, $init_{ref}$ ensures that $flagP0 = flagP0c = flagP1 = flagP1c = turn = critical = error = 0$ and $pc_0 = 5$ and $pc_1 = 15$, and $final_{ref}$ is $pc_0 = 13 \land pc_1 = 23$.

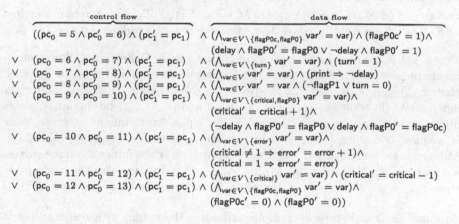

Fig. 5. A part of T_{ref} for Listing 1.3 (where $V \stackrel{\text{def}}{=} (X \cup X_{ref}) \setminus \{pc_0, pc_1\}$)

Note that the processor running the original nondeterministic version of Peterson's algorithm already has micro-architectural features that facilitate instruction reordering (not modeled in Example 11); the auxiliary input reorder and variable delay merely make this mechanism observable.

3.2 Defining Causes

In the following, we provide a formal definition of causes inspired by Lewis'
counterfactuals [26] and the causality framework of Galles and Pearl [14].

Definition 11 (Cause). *Let* $S \overset{\text{def}}{=} (X, I \cup M, \text{init}, \text{final}, T)$ *be a deterministic
STS, where* I *and* M *are disjoint sets of inputs, and let* φ *be an assertion. Let*
$M = M_C \uplus M_N$. *We say that* M_C *is a* cause *with respect to* M *and* φ *and iff*

$$\exists \pi_c, \pi_w \, . \, I(\pi_c) = I(\pi_w) \wedge M_N(\pi_c) = M_N(\pi_w) \wedge \pi_c \not\models \varphi \wedge \pi_w \models \varphi \qquad (1)$$

and M_C *is a minimal subset of* M *with this property.*

We note that in the above definition we require the inputs I to agree on the
executions π_c and π_w, while only the inputs M may differ. The rationale is that
we want to apply this definition for studying the causes of Heisenbugs: We are
given some (nondeterministic) STS with inputs I, which has a Heisenbug. We
now consider some determinization of the STS to which we have added inputs
M, modelling the *mechanisms* responsible for the nondeterminism. The above
definition then allows to study the cause among the modelled mechanisms: A
subset $M_C \subseteq M$ is a cause of a Heisenbug, if the Heisenbug still occurs when
the inputs M_N agree in the deviating executions π_c and π_w.

Proposition 1 (Existence of a Cause). *Let* $S \overset{\text{def}}{=} (X, I, \text{init}, \text{final}, T)$ *be a
nondeterministic STS with a Heisenbug (Definition 8) with respect to an asser-
tion* φ *and let* $S_{\text{det}} \overset{\text{def}}{=} (X \cup X_{\text{det}}, I \cup M, \text{init}_{\text{det}}, \text{final}_{\text{det}}, T_{\text{det}})$ *be a determinization
of* S. *Then there exists a cause* M_C *with respect to* M *and* φ.

Proof. Let π_c and π_w be executions of S that satisfy Definition 8. Since refinements preserve executions, there must be executions $\pi_{c\text{det}}$ and $\pi_{w\text{det}}$ of S_{det} such
that $\pi_{c\text{det}}|_{(I \cup X)} = \pi_c$ and $\pi_{w\text{det}}|_{(I \cup X)} = \pi_w$. Now assume that $\pi_{c\text{det}}$ and $\pi_{w\text{det}}$
agree on M (in addition to I). Let $\langle s_c, s_{c\text{det}} \rangle$ and $\langle s_w, s_{w\text{det}} \rangle$ be the initial states
of $\pi_{c\text{det}}$ and $\pi_{w\text{det}}$, respectively. Since S_{det} is input-deterministic, however, there
is at most one state $\langle \langle s, s_{\text{det}} \rangle, \langle i, m \rangle \rangle \models \text{init}_{\text{det}}$, hence $\langle s_c, s_{c\text{det}} \rangle = \langle s_w, s_{w\text{det}} \rangle$.
Moreover, for every state $\langle s, s_{\text{det}} \rangle$, each input $\langle i, m \rangle$ determines a unique succes-
sor state $\langle s', s'_{\text{det}} \rangle$. Since $\pi_{c\text{det}}|_{(I \cup M)} = \pi_{w\text{det}}|_{(I \cup M)}$, this violates the assumption
that $\pi_{c\text{det}} \not\models \varphi$ and $\pi_{w\text{det}} \models \varphi$. Hence, $\pi_{c\text{det}}$ and $\pi_{w\text{det}}$ must deviate on M. □

Example 12. The Peterson example contains a Heisenbug with respect to $\varphi \overset{\text{def}}{=}$
(error = 0). Here, {reorder} and {thread} are causes, but {debug} is not: The set
{reorder} is a cause because of two executions which both have debug = false and
the same schedule interleaving the critical sections, but only one execution sets
reorder = true and hence exhibits the bug. The set {thread} is a cause because
of two executions which both have debug = false and reorder = true where
one execution uses a sequential schedule of the two processes and the second
execution uses a schedule interleaving the critical sections. Only the second execution exhibits the bug. However, the set {debug} is not a cause because any two

executions would either both have to set reorder = false, making the bug impossible or both set reorder = true. In this case, by counterposition the constraint (print $\Rightarrow$ ¬delay) enforces debug = false, yielding a bug on both executions if the schedule interleaves the critical sections or on no execution otherwise.

3.3   Causes and Nondeterminism

By introducing the notion of a *contributing cause* below, we show that even in the presence of nondeterminism we can still provide guarantees.

Definition 12 (Contributing Cause). *Let $S \overset{\text{def}}{=} (X, I \cup M, \text{init}, \text{final}, T)$ be a (potentially nondeterministic) STS, where I and M are disjoints set of inputs, and let φ, $M = M_C \uplus M_N$ satisfy the conditions in Definition 11. We call M_C a contributing cause of a Heisenbug.*

We argue that any contributing cause must be a subset of a cause in a corresponding determinization:

Theorem 1. *Let $S \overset{\text{def}}{=} (X, I \cup M, \text{init}, \text{final}, T)$ be a nondeterministic STS and let $S_{\text{det}} \overset{\text{def}}{=} (X \cup X_{\text{det}}, I \cup M \cup J, \text{init}_{\text{det}}, \text{final}_{\text{det}}, T_{\text{det}})$ be a determinization of S. Let M_C be a contributing cause in S with respect to M and assertion φ. Then, there exists a cause C in S_{det} with respect to $M \cup J$ and φ such that $M_C \subseteq C \setminus J$.*

Proof. Consider two executions π_c and π_w satisfying Definition 12 for S. Since refinement preserves executions, there must be executions $\pi_{c\text{det}}$ and $\pi_{w\text{det}}$ in S_{det} such that $\pi_{c\text{det}}|_{(I \cup M \cup X)} = \pi_c$ and $\pi_{w\text{det}}|_{(I \cup M \cup X)} = \pi_w$ and $\pi_{c\text{det}} \not\models \varphi$ and $\pi_{w\text{det}} \models \varphi$. By Definition 12, for $M_N = M \setminus M_C$ it holds that $\pi_c|_{(I \cup M_N)} = \pi_w|_{(I \cup M_N)}$ and hence also $\pi_{c\text{det}}|_{(I \cup M_N)} = \pi_{w\text{det}}|_{(I \cup M_N)}$. Hence (following an argument similar to the one for Proposition 1) we argue that $\pi_{c\text{det}}$ and $\pi_{w\text{det}}$ must deviate on a subset of $M_C \cup J$, i.e., there exists a cause C satisfying Definition 11 such that $C \subseteq M_C \cup J$. Now assume that $M_C \not\subseteq C$. Then M_C is not minimal, since $(M_C \cap C)$ also constitutes a contributing cause. Thus, we must have $M_C \subseteq C \setminus J$. $\square$

Example 13. The refined STS in Example 9 is nondeterministic as the initial values of filter and highEnergy are unconstrained. Following Definition 12, {thread} is a contributing cause. Consider a further refinement with $I_{\text{ref}} = \{\text{initF}, \text{initH}\}$ and init = (filter = initF∧highEnergy = initH∧isXray∧isHigh∧$\text{pc}_0 = 4 \wedge \text{pc}_1 = 10$). As the initial values are never read, the cause is again {thread}.

We provide a condition under which contributing causes are also causes:

Definition 13 (Cause in Presence of Nondeterminism). *Consider a (potentially nondeterministic) STS $S \overset{\text{def}}{=} (X, I \cup M, \text{init}, \text{final}, T)$ such that for all traces π, π' of S with $\pi|_{I \cup M} = \pi'|_{I \cup M}$ we have that*

1. *π ends in a final state if and only if π' ends in a final state,*
2. *$\pi \models \varphi$ if and only if $\pi' \models \varphi$ (in case both traces end in a final state).*

Let φ, $M = M_C \uplus M_N$ satisfy the conditions in Definition 11. We say that M_C is a cause in presence of nondeterminism *with respect to* M *and* φ.

We will next state a justification for the introduction of the above definition. We first establish that input-enabled determinizations always exist:

Proposition 2. *Let* $S \stackrel{\text{def}}{=} (X, I, \text{init}, \text{final}, T)$ *be an input-enabled STS. Then, a deterministic input-enabled refinement* S_{ref} *always exists.*

Proof. We set $I_{\text{ref}} = \{\text{oracle}\}$ for a single variable oracle, whose values are mappings of configurations to successors, i.e., oracle fixes a successor state s' for every configuration $\langle s, i \rangle$ such that $\langle s, i, s' \rangle \models T$ (note that at least one successor state s' always exists because of our assumption that S is input-enabled). We then adopt T_{ref} from T as the transition relation that moves to the successor state fixed by the oracle variable. Likewise, we adopt the initial condition init_{ref}.   □

We next establish that no matter the input-enabled determinization S' of an STS S, a cause in the presence of nondeterminism in S is always a cause in S'. Together with Proposition 2, which guarantees the existence of an input-enabled determinization at least in theory, we obtain that a cause in presence of nondeterminism can indeed by considered as a cause.

Theorem 2. *Let* M_C *be a cause in presence of nondeterminism with respect to mechanisms* M *in an STS* $S \stackrel{\text{def}}{=} (X, I \cup M, \text{init}, \text{final}, T)$. *Let* $S_{\text{det}} \stackrel{\text{def}}{=} (X \cup X_{\text{det}}, I \cup M \cup J, \text{init}_{\text{det}}, \text{final}_{\text{det}}, T_{\text{det}})$ *be an input-enabled determinization of* S. *Then* M_C *is also a cause in* S_{det} *with respect to* $(I \cup J)$.

Proof. Let π_c and π_w be executions of S that satisfy Definition 13. Since refinements preserve executions, there must be an execution π_{cdet} of S such that $\pi_{\text{cdet}}|_{(I \cup M \cup X)} = \pi_c$. In particular, we have $\pi_{\text{cdet}} \not\models \varphi$. Because S_{det} is input-enabled we can obtain a trace π of S_{det} such that $\pi|_J = \pi_{\text{cdet}}|_J$ and $\pi|_{I \cup M} = \pi_w|_{I \cup M}$. Note that π induces a trace π' of S with $\pi' = \pi_{w\text{det}}|_{I \cup M \cup X}$. Hence, by the assumptions stated in Definition 13, the trace π' is in fact an execution (i.e., ends with a final configuration), and we have $\pi' \models \varphi$. Thus, we also get that π is an execution and that we have $\pi \models \varphi$.   □

Example 14. The nondeterministic refinement of the Therac-25 STS in Example 9 satisfies the properties in Definition 13. The refinement in Example 13 is input-enabled and deterministic and the contributing cause is indeed a cause.

3.4   Testing and Causal Analysis

In the context of testing, an evaluation of Definition 11 and Definition 12, respectively, is limited to the subset of the executions induced by a given test suite. Lemma 1 characterizes the results that can be drawn by analyzing a subset of the executions of an STS:

Lemma 1. *Let π_c and π_w be executions satisfying Eq. 1 in Definition 11 (or Definition 12, respectively) and let M_C be the inputs deviating in π_c and π_w. Then M_C is a superset of a cause (or contributing cause, respectively).*

Proof. Note that M_C is a cause according to Definition 11 (or a contributing cause according to Definition 12) if it is minimal with respect to Eq. 1. Otherwise, there must be a cause that is a subset of M_C.   □

Lemma 1 provides guarantees even if an exhaustive analysis is infeasible. If, in addition, the conditions in Definition 13 are met (i.e., we can control or at least observe the relevant mechanisms), then Proposition 2, Theorem 2, and Lemma 1 guarantee that each overapproximation of a cause identified by testing includes a *non-empty* (contributing) cause.

4   Analysis Methodology and Challenges

We sketch an (iterative) methodology for practical analyses based on the formalization above and showcase two possible instantiations and their challenges:

① **Task:** Starting from a Heisenbug (Definition 8), identify candidate mechanisms M (e.g., consulting surveys [31]).
   Challenge: The accuracy of the analysis is contingent on identifying the relevant mechanisms.
② **Task:** Pick a mechanism $m \in M$ and adapt (or refine according to Definition 9) the model or system to make m controllable (or at least observable).
   Challenge: The system may be inherently uncontrollable or unobservable, or attempts to control/observe it potentially introduce a probe effect.
③ **Task:** Identify (contributing) causes by finding witnesses that deviate in as few mechanisms as possible (i.e., satisfy Eq. 1 in Definition 11).
   Challenge: Testing will yield over-approximations only (cf. Lemma 1).
④ **Task:** Check a stopping criterion to determine whether further mechanisms or refinement steps are required (steps ① and ②).
   Challenge: Assessing whether all causes have been correctly identified is challenging and may amount to fixing the bug and re-verifying the system.

Causal Analysis Based on Model Checking. We built a NuSMV [5] model of Peterson's algorithm (Listing 1.3). We use self-composition [3], which composes two copies S_w and S_c of the STS S, to reduce the existence of a counterexample trace and a witness trace (which is a hyperproperty) to the existence of a single trace in the composed model. NuSMV can then construct the trace as a counterexample to an LTL property over the composed model. As NuSMV usually considers infinite traces, final conditions are accounted for in the property. The existence of a Heisenbug can be confirmed by checking that NuSMV finds a counterexample to the property $\psi := G(\mathsf{final}_c \wedge \mathsf{final}_w \Rightarrow (\varphi_w \Rightarrow \varphi_c))$ for final and φ as in Example 11 and Example 12 (where subscripted predicates range over the matching variable set).

```
1   bool flag0 = false;
2   bool flag1 = false;
3   spinlock_t lock0, lock1;
4   void *thread0(void*) {
5     spin_lock(lock0);
6       flag0 = true;
7       assert (!flag1);
8       yield();
9       spin_lock(lock1);
10        flag0 = false;
11      spin_unlock(lock1);
12      yield();
13    spin_unlock(lock0);
14  }
```

```
15  void *thread1(void*) {
16    spin_lock(lock1);
17      flag1 = true;
18      assert (!flag0);
19      yield();
20      spin_lock(lock0);
21        flag1 = false;
22      spin_unlock(lock0);
23      yield();
24    spin_unlock(lock1);
25  }
```

Listing 1.4. An assertion fails if (and only if) a deadlock occurs.

In step ①, we pick the fact whether the print statements are executed and model it adding variables print_w and print_c to the model (step ②). In step ③, we invoke NuSMV on the property $G(\text{print}_w \Leftrightarrow \text{print}_c) \Rightarrow \psi$. As there is a counterexample, we identify the empty set as a contributing cause.

We start another refinement iteration, pick concurrency as mechanism (step ①) and model it by variables thread_w and thread_c (step ②). We check the property $G((\text{print}_w \Leftrightarrow \text{print}_c) \wedge (\text{thread}_w \Leftrightarrow \text{thread}_c)) \Rightarrow \psi$ (step ③). Again, there is a counterexample and the empty set is a contributing cause.

In the next refinement iteration, we pick the weak memory behavior (step ①) we model it by variables delay_w and delay_c and reflect the fact that $\text{print} \implies \neg\text{delay}$ (cf. Example 11) (step ②). Checking property $G((\text{print}_w \Leftrightarrow \text{print}_c) \wedge (\text{thread}_w \Leftrightarrow \text{thread}_c) \wedge (\text{delay}_w \Leftrightarrow \text{delay}_c)) \Rightarrow \psi$ returns true, hence we have now found a non-empty cause superset and can start cause minimization. A counterexample to $G((\text{print}_w \Leftrightarrow \text{print}_c) \wedge (\text{thread}_w \Leftrightarrow \text{thread}_c)) \Rightarrow \psi$ witnesses that delay is a cause, similarly a counterexample to $G((\text{print}_w \Leftrightarrow \text{print}_c) \wedge (\text{delay}_w \Leftrightarrow \text{delay}_c)) \Rightarrow \psi$ witnesses that thread is a cause. As the model satisfies $G((\text{delay}_w \Leftrightarrow \text{delay}_c) \wedge (\text{thread}_w \Leftrightarrow \text{thread}_c)) \Rightarrow \psi$, print is not a cause. This concludes step ③. As we identified a non-empty cause, no more refinement steps are needed.

Test-Based Causal Analysis. Consider the code in Listing 1.4, which might deadlock because of a faulty locking discipline. The assertions in lines 7 and 18 fail when a deadlock, caused by a specific (combination of) context switche(s), occurs: a context switch at line 8 to thread1 (or, symmetrically, from line 19 to thread0) causes both threads to wait for a lock held by the other thread.

In step ①, we identify concurrency (limited to the context switches marked by yield for simplicity) as potential cause. Following the approach of KISS [32], we control the scheduler (step ②) by sequentializing the concurrent program and simulating the execution of a large subset of its interleavings. In KISS, threads can be started and terminated nondeterministically at any point during the execution. Using closures to save the local state of a thread, we add the capability to *re-enter* a thread after its interruption by `yield`. The execution of `thread0` (`thread1`, respectively) can be interrupted at lines 8 and 12 (19 and 23, respectively). Our sequentialization enables us to explicitly control these four context switches, inducing 2^4 potential schedules. Random (or systematic) exploration of these schedules then yields executions that terminate normally or violate an assertion. Failing executions deviate from the non-failing ones by performing a context switch at lines 8 or 19, at least one of which must constitute (part of) the candidate cause(s) we identify in step ③.

Testing merely provides an over-approximation of the cause M_C (Lemma 1). Due to the minimality requirement in Definition 11 and Definition 12, however, removing one element from M_C (by controlling the mechanism accordingly) eliminates the entire cause. Assume for now, that `thread0` in Listing 1.4 always executes first, in which case the context switch at line 8 is a unique cause for the deadlock. Consider an over-approximation comprising of two context switches at lines 8 and 19. Blocking the context switch at line 8 eliminates the Heisenbug, while blocking the one at line 19 doesn't. By individually blocking the context switches and checking whether subsequent testing provides sufficient confidence that the bug has been eliminated, we obtain a stopping criterion in step ④.

If, however, executions may start with `thread0` or `thread1`, the context switches at lines 8 and 19 form two independent (non-intersecting) causes (due to the symmetry in Listing 1.4). Consequently, *both* context switches must be identified to eliminate all causes of the bug (cf. Sect. 3.4). Blocking individual context switches (as suggested above) does not provide a reliable stopping criterion. Despite this limitation, testing-based analysis can help the developer to narrow down the set of candidate causes significantly.

5   Related Work

Terminology and Definition of Heisenbugs. The first paper mentioning Heisenbugs [17] uses the term for transient software bugs which disappear under observation. In [18], bugs are classified into Bohrbugs (bugs manifesting consistently), Mandelbugs (bugs with complex error propagation), and Heisenbugs (bugs manifesting differently under the probe effect). In contrast to this informal classification, our definition is formal, covering Heisenbugs which stem from the probe effect as well as from nondeterminism. The term is frequently (and informally) used in the context of concurrency [30], where it exclusively refers to bugs caused by control-flow nondeterminism. In the context of testing, the notion of flaky tests [31] resembles the notion of Heisenbugs. The comparison of failing and non-failing executions is used in several lines of research with goals orthogonal to the definition of bug classes. Differential assertion checking [21] compares failing and non-failing executions to define relative correctness of different program versions. In the context of diagnosability, the notion of critical pairs of failing and non-failing executions with equivalent observations is used to check whether faults can be detected at runtime [6].

Causality. Our definition of causality is inspired by Lewis' counterfactuals [25]. The negation of Definition 11 mirrors the definition of causal irrelevance in [14] and Definition 11 corresponds to its dual notion of causality between variables [12]. A core difference is that our interventions are restricted to inputs that represent nondeterministic mechanisms rather than affecting arbitrary points of the transition relation (or the causal model). Moreover, causal models have a fixed propagation depth, while we consider an arbitrary number of unwindings of the transition relation. Halpern and Pearl [19,20] provide a widely accepted definition of "actual" causes based on counterfactuals, where contingencies are used to control interference between interventions. Several lines of work reason about the origin of system faults [2,4,10,16,23] using Halpern and Pearl's notion of causality. In [8], actual causality is used to explain violations of hyperproperties. It formalizes causes for violations of (arbitrary) universally quantified hyperproperties as a hyperproperty with quantifier alternation, which can then be checked with a model checker such as [13]. We formalize causes for Heisenbugs (a specific hyperproperty) in terms of an existentially quantified hyperproperty.

Several approaches exist for automatically detecting causes of flaky tests. The RootFinder tool [22] collects passing and failing executions and correlates their differences with a specific cause. In [39] the authors present a tool for finding code locations that lead to differences between succeeding and failing executions. Identifying what happens in these locations is left to the developer. In [29,36] the system is repeatedly executed under different configurations to check which configuration influences the manifestation of the bug. All of these approaches are based on computing correlations rather than performing rigorous causal inference. In contrast, our framework is based on a formal causal analysis accounting for interactions of multiple potential causes. [31] provides a taxonomy of causes relevant in the context of automated testing.

6   Conclusion

While the term Heisenbug is widely used, its exact meaning often depends on the context. We provide a formal definition that unifies the notion of Heisenbugs caused by a system alteration and those caused by nondeterminism. Furthermore, we present a hyperproperty-based framework for determining which mechanisms cause the manifestation of a Heisenbug. In particular, our approach allows the identification of causes in the presence of multiple mechanisms that could trigger a Heisenbug and gives guarantees for results of a causal analysis even in presence of nondeterminism. Building on this result, we sketch a methodology for causal analysis based on iterative refinement.

Acknowledgements. This work was partially supported by ERC CoG ARTIST 101002685, by the FWF project W1255-N23, by a netidee scholarship, and by the Vienna Science and Technology Fund (WWTF) [10.47379/VRG11005].

References

1. Abadi, M., Lamport, L.: The existence of refinement mappings. In: LICS (1988)
2. Baier, C., et al.: From verification to causality-based explications. In: ICALP (2021)
3. Barthe, G., Crespo, J.M., Kunz, C.: Relational verification using product programs. In: FM (2011)
4. Beer, I., Ben-David, S., Chockler, H., Orni, A., Trefler, R.: Explaining counterexamples using causality. In: CAV (2009)
5. Climatti, A., et al.: NuSMV 2: an opensource tool for symbolic model checking. In: Brinksma, E., Larsen, K.G. (eds.) CAV 2002. LNCS, vol. 2404, pp. 359–364. Springer, Heidelberg (2002). https://doi.org/10.1007/3-540-45657-0_29
6. Cimatti, A., Pecheur, C., Cavada, R.: Formal verification of diagnosability via symbolic model checking. In: IJCAI (2003)
7. Clarkson, M.R., Schneider, F.B.: Hyperproperties. J. Comput. Secur. 18(6), 1157–1210 (2010)
8. Coenen, N., et al.: Explaining hyperproperty violations. In: CAV (2022)
9. Cotroneo, D., Grottke, M., Natella, R., Pietrantuono, R., Trivedi, K.S.: Fault triggers in open-source software: an experience report. In: ISSRE (2013)
10. Dubslaff, C., Weis, K., Baier, C., Apel, S.: Causality in configurable software systems. In: ICSE (2022)
11. Eck, M., Palomba, F., Castelluccio, M., Bacchelli, A.: Understanding flaky tests: the developer's perspective. In: ESEC/FSE (2019)
12. Eiter, T., Lukasiewicz, T.: Complexity results for structure-based causality. Artif. Intell. 142(1), 53–89 (2002)
13. Finkbeiner, B., Rabe, M.N., Sánchez, C.: Algorithms for model checking HyperLTL and HyperCTL*. In: CAV (2015)
14. Galles, D., Pearl, J.: Axioms of causal relevance. Artif. Intell. 97(1–2), 9–43 (1997)
15. Goodfellow, I.J., Bengio, Y., Courville, A.C.: Deep Learning. Adaptive Computation and Machine Learning. MIT Press (2016)
16. Gössler, G., Stefani, J.B.: Causality analysis and fault ascription in component-based systems. Theor. Comput. Sci. 837, 158–180 (2020)
17. Gray, J.: Why do computers stop and what can be done about it? Tech. Rep. 85.7, PN87614, Tandem Computers (1986)
18. Grottke, M., Trivedi, K.S.: A classification of software faults. In: ISSRE (2005)
19. Halpern, J.Y.: A modification of the halpern-pearl definition of causality. In: IJCAI (2015)
20. Halpern, J.Y., Pearl, J.: Causes and explanations: a structural-model approach: part 1: causes. British J. Philos. Sci. 56 (2005)
21. Lahiri, S.K., McMillan, K.L., Sharma, R., Hawblitzel, C.: Differential assertion checking. In: ESEC/FSE (2013)
22. Lam, W., Godefroid, P., Nath, S., Santhiar, A., Thummalapenta, S.: Root causing flaky tests in a large-scale industrial setting. In: ISSTA (2019)
23. Leitner-Fischer, F., Leue, S.: Causality checking for complex system models. In: VMCAI (2013)
24. Leveson, N., Turner, C.: An investigation of the Therac-25 accidents. IEEE Comput. 26(7), 18–41 (1993)
25. Lewis, D.: Causation. J. Philos. 70(17), 556–567 (1974)
26. Lewis, D.: Counterfactuals. Wiley-Blackwell (2001)
27. Lu, S., Tucek, J., Qin, F., Zhou, Y.: AVIO: detecting atomicity violations via access-interleaving invariants. IEEE Micro 27(1), 26–35 (2007)

28. Monniaux, D.: The pitfalls of verifying floating-point computations. TOPLAS **30**(3), 1–41 (2008)
29. Moran, J., Augusto Alonso, C., Bertolino, A., de la Riva, C., Tuya, J.: FlakyLoc: flakiness localization for reliable test suites in web applications. J. Web. Eng. **19**(2), 267–296 (2020)
30. Musuvathi, M., Qadeer, S., Ball, T., Basler, G., Nainar, P.A., Neamtiu, I.: Finding and reproducing heisenbugs in concurrent programs. In: OSDI (2008)
31. Parry, O., Kapfhammer, G.M., Hilton, M., McMinn, P.: A survey of flaky tests. TOSEM **31**(1), 1–74 (2021)
32. Qadeer, S., Wu, D.: KISS: keep it simple and sequential. In: PLDI (2004)
33. Ratliff, Z.B., Kuhn, D.R., Kacker, R.N., Lei, Y., Trivedi, K.S.: The relationship between software bug type and number of factors involved in failures. In: ISSRE Wksp (2016)
34. Senftleben, M.: Operational Characterization of Weak Memory Consistency Models. Master's thesis, University of Kaiserslautern (2013)
35. Sommerville, I.: Software Engineering, 9 edn. Addison-Wesley (2010)
36. Terragni, V., Salza, P., Ferrucci, F.: A container-based infrastructure for fuzzy-driven root causing of flaky tests. In: ICSE (2020)
37. Thomas, M.: The story of the therac-25 in lotos. High Integr. Syst. J. **1**(1), 3–15 (1994)
38. Tretmans, J.: Test generation with inputs, outputs, and quiescence. In: Margaria, T., Steffen, B. (eds.) TACAS 1996. LNCS, vol. 1055, pp. 127–146. Springer, Heidelberg (1996). https://doi.org/10.1007/3-540-61042-1_42
39. Ziftci, C., Cavalcanti, D.: De-Flake your tests : automatically locating root causes of flaky tests in code at google. In: ICSME (2020)

Verifying Read-Copy Update Under RC11

Mikhail Semenyuk[1], Mark Batty[2], and Brijesh Dongol[1]($\boxtimes$)

[1] University of Surrey, Guildford, UK
b.dongol@surrey.ac.uk
[2] University of Kent, Canterbury, UK

Abstract. Read-Copy Update (RCU) is a key lock-free synchronisation mechanism that is used extensively in the Linux kernel. One use of RCU is safe memory reclamation in languages such as C/C++ that do not support garbage collection. Correctness of RCU is, however, difficult to verify, even when assuming sequentially consistent (SC) memory. In this paper, we develop and verify an RCU implementation under RC11 (a restricted version of C11 weak memory model, which includes relaxed and release-acquire accesses), increasing the verification challenge. Our proof technique is based on a notion of ownership, which we use to systematically track each thread's read/write capabilities to each memory location. In our proof, we extend a recent Owicki-Gries logic for RC11, which we combine with our ownership model to show correctness. All our proofs have been mechanised in the Isabelle/HOL theorem prover.

Keywords: Owicki-Gries · ownership · RCU · verification · C11 · weak memory

1 Introduction

Over the years, many non-blocking concurrent algorithms [12] have been developed to exploit the parallelism possibilities in multi-core architectures. Unlike lock-based algorithms (which restrict access to critical regions), non-blocking programs rely on atomic test-and-set primitives (e.g., compare-and-swap) to ensure consistency of the object being implemented. Non-blocking algorithms generally yield better performance (i.e., are more scalable) than their lock-based counterparts, and by design, avoid problems such as priority inversion and deadlock. However, a key problem faced by such algorithms is that of safe *memory reclamation*, particularly in languages such as C/C++, which do not provide garbage collection. Here, since multiple threads may access the same memory location concurrently, prior to freeing a memory location, one must make sure that no other concurrent thread has a reference to that location. Otherwise this may lead to memory access violations via the ABA problem [9,10].

Semenyuk is supported by VeTSS. Batty is supported by EPSRC grants EP/X021173/1, EP/V000470/1, and EP/X015076/1. Dongol is supported by EPSRC grants EP/X037142/1, EP/X015149/1, EP/V038915/1, and EP/R025134/2.

C. Ferreira and T. A. C. Willemse (Eds.): SEFM 2023, LNCS 14323, pp. 301–319, 2023.
https://doi.org/10.1007/978-3-031-47115-5_17

There have been many proposals for safe memory reclamation such as epoch-based reclamation [8], hazard pointers [19] and RCU [17]. Prior works have considered verification of hazard pointers for particular algorithms (e.g., [16, 22,28]) and specialised separation logics that have been shown to work across several memory reclamation schemes [9]. However, these works have assumed a strong memory model of sequential consistency (SC), which is not supported by modern multi-processor systems. In this paper, we assume a more realistic *concurrency model* based on the RC11 weak memory model [14,15], which models both relaxed and release-acquire accesses as present in RC11.

Our main case study is RCU [17], which is one of the most widely used memory reclamation schemes. Although RCU has been proven correct under SC [9], its main memory reclamation property fails under RC11 using relaxed accesses[1]. There are two options to addressing this issue: (1) introduce additional weak memory synchronisation within the RCU library itself, or (2) ensure adequate weak memory synchronisation in a client and use RCU without change. Although the latter introduces additional programmer overhead, it is much more desirable from a performance point of view, since the RCU library itself can fully benefit from the parallelisation possibilities from weak memory.

Thus, our solution is not to modify the RCU original algorithm, but to show how it can be safely used by a client program, even when all memory operations within the RCU library are relaxed. The main thrust of our work is a formal proof of correctness that extends a recent Owicki-Gries logic [3] for RC11.[2] We extend RC11 logic in two ways. The first introduces a new type of assertion that captures the *message passing paradigm* in RC11 through the last write in memory. This assertion is particularly effective for reasoning about locations that are only ever updated through read-modify-write operations.[3] Second, we use a systematic ownership discipline [25] to simplify reasoning about the read/write capabilities that threads have on each memory location.

Contributions. This paper comprises three main contributions. (1) We present a method of using RCU under RC11, where the RCU algorithm contains only relaxed accesses, and weak-memory synchronisation is relegated to the client. (2) We extend the RC11 semantics with a model of pointers and a systematic model of ownership. Additionally, we extend an existing Owicki-Gries logic for RC11 with a new type of assertion. This extended model is used to prove correctness of our example program. (3) Our entire development, including our RC11

---

[1] The RC11 model has been extensively studied [14,15] as a strengthening of the C11 memory model [1,23,32] that offers operations such as releasing writes and acquiring reads (that enable inter-thread synchronisation) as well as relaxed reads and writes that are unsynchronised.

[2] Note that developments in weak memory include logics (e.g., [26,31,33]) for the full C/C++ model with relaxed dependencies [1,13,23]. However, these models and logics are currently still too difficult to use in practice for programs such as RCU, which require reasoning about an unbounded number of threads. We consider verification of such programs to be part of future work.

[3] Such locations are common in non-blocking algorithms, e.g., the top pointer of the Treiber Stack [29].

```
 1  int *C = new int(0);
 2  int inc() {
 3      int v, *s, *n;
 4      n = new int;
 5      do {
 6          s = C;
 7          v = *s;
 8          *n = v+1;
 9      } while(!CAS(&C,s,n));
10      free(s);
11      return v;}
```

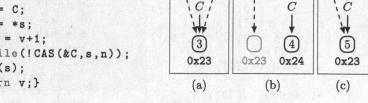

Fig. 1. Shared counter

Fig. 2. ABA problem for the shared counter in Fig. 1

semantics, logic and proof of RCU, has been mechanised in the Isabelle/HOL proof assistant to provide a high level of assurance.

Auxiliary Material. The Isabelle/HOL proofs corresponding to this submission may be found here [24].

2 Motivation

In this section we present some background and motivation for our work. This includes the ABA problem in the context of memory reclamation (Sect. 2.1), McKenney's RCU algorithm for solving ABA (Sect. 2.2), and the changes needed for correctness of RCU under RC11 (Sect. 2.3).

2.1 ABA Problem During Memory Reclamation

High-performance lock-free algorithms, such as the Treiber stack [29] and the Michael-Scott queue [20], use non-blocking atomic read-modify-write operations (e.g., CAS) to synchronise threads. A CAS-based implementation typically takes a snapshot of a shared location, and computes a new value based on this local snapshot, before updating the shared location using a CAS. We illustrate the essence of the approach using a shared counter (Fig. 1) with an increment operation inc on a shared location C, implemented using a typical lock-free pattern. The executing thread takes a snapshot of C at Line 6, calculates a new value for the contents of the location C at Lines 7 and 8, and attempts to update C to point to the new value at Line 9. Note that the CAS will fail, if the value of C does not match value the local snapshot, which occurs when there is interference from another thread. Further note that there is some subtlety with the implementation in that, after a successful execution of the CAS (Line 9), C points to a new location containing the updated value.

The question of memory reclamation is typically not the focus of such algorithms, and is left up to the implementer to deal with. However, extra attention

```
1   bool rcu[N] = {0};
2   rcu_enter() {rcu[tid]=1;}
3   rcu_exit() {rcu[tid]=0;}
4   sync() {
5     bool r[N+1] = {0};
6     for(int i = 0; i < N; i++)       21  int inc() {
7       r[i] = rcu[i];                  22    int v, *n, *s;
8     for(int i = 0; i < N; i++)       23    n = new int;
9       if(r[i]) {                     24    rcu_enter();
10        while(rcu[i]);}}             25    do {
11                                     26      rcu_exit();
12  int *C = new int(0);               27      rcu_enter();
13  Set det[N] = {∅};                  28      s = FAA^RA(C,0);
14                                     29      v = *s;
15  void reclaim(int* s) {             30      *n = v+1;
16    insert(det[tid], s);             31      r = CAS^RA(&C,s,n);
17    if (nondet()) return;            32    } while !r;
18    sync();                          33    rcu_exit();
19    while !isEmpty(det[tid])         34    reclaim(s);
20      free(pop(det[tid])); }         35    return v; }
```

Fig. 3. Safe use of RCU in RC11

must be paid to avoid the occurrence of a common phenomenon known as the ABA problem [12], where the value of a location changes from "A" to "B" the back to "A". A thread that takes a snapshot from the first "A" may not notice that the value has changed if it compares its snapshot with the second "A".

Example 1. Consider the following execution of Fig. 1 as depicted in Fig. 2. In Fig. 2(a), assume that threads t_1 and t_2 have both taken snapshots of the shared pointer C, and stored the value 3 (located in memory address 0x23), in their local copies of v (i.e., both t_1 and t_2 have executed Line 7 of Fig. 1). Suppose t_2 continues execution so that it completes the inc operation. This gives rise to the state depicted in Fig. 2(b), where the address 0x23 is freed, and C points to a new location 0x24 with value 4. Suppose that another thread t_3 (not shown) completes an entire inc operation, picking the freed location 0x23, updating the value to 5, and swinging the pointer C to 0x23. Now if t_1 continues execution, its CAS can succeed, which will cause the value of C to be updated to 4 (since t_1's local value of v is 3).

2.2   An RCU-Based Solution

An RCU-based solution to safe memory reclamation is presented in Fig. 3. It assumes N threads and a shared array of RCU flags, rcu, initialised to an array of 0s. We assume that t is the thread identifier of the calling thread (where $0 \leq t \leq N-1$). The RCU flag for thread t is therefore rcu[t]. Each thread sets and unsets its RCU flag by calling rcu_enter and rcu_exit, respectively.

Thread 1	Thread 2
x := 1 ;	r := y ;
y := 1 ;	s := x ;
$\{r, s \in \{0, 1\}\}$	

Thread 1	Thread 2
x := 1 ;	r :=^{A} y ;
y :=^{R} 1 ;	s := x ;
$\{r = 1 \longrightarrow s = 1\}$	

Fig. 4. Message passing

A thread that is about to free a location must first call sync to ensure no other thread is accessing that location. In sync, the calling thread first takes a local snapshot r of rcu, then iterates through r. If r[i] is found to be set, then it waits until rcu[i] is unset.

Correct use of RCU prevents threads from performing reclamation on addresses that other threads could reference. The addition of calls to rcu_enter and rcu_exit outlines a *critical region*. When threads are outside of this region, they have no opportunity to cause the ABA problem, because they must read a *new* value of C to successfully execute their CAS. This principle makes reclamation *safe* — during RCU synchronisation (i.e., execution of sync), threads that are about to perform reclamation are forced to wait for competing threads to leave the critical region, before proceeding to memory deallocation. To cope with weak memory, the program in Fig. 3 uses an atomic *fetch-and-add* operation (FAA) without any increment when reading the value of C (unlike the simple read in Fig. 1). This is discussed in more detail in Sect. 2.3.

Note that rcu[i] may be set by thread t_i *after* the syncing thread, say t has read rcu[i] as being unset. This is however not a problem. When using RCU, the client program must ensure that when t_i calls rcu_enter, the location that t_i is trying to protect is different from the location that t is trying to free via its sync operation. Conversely, a sync operation executed by thread t may be in progress *before* rcu[i] is set. In this case, t will be forced to wait for t_i to call rcu_exit, but this is an example of a false-negative, and does not violate safety.

The counter from Fig. 1 modified to use RCU is given in Fig. 3. Prior to accessing the shared location C, the executing thread, say t, must first call rcu_enter (Line 27). Upon successfully performing its operation, t calls rcu_exit (Line 33). Note that t must also exit rcu_exit when its CAS fails, and the only opportunity to do this is at Line 26. This is matched by an earlier call to rcu_enter at Line 24. Following [9], we perform a reclaim operation, which uses a *detached list*, det, to improve the efficiency of memory reclamation. At Line 16, t inserts the freed location into its detached list, then non-deterministically decides, whether to perform reclamation at Line 17 or not. If it decides to perform reclamation, it first executes sync (Line 18), and once this is complete, frees all of the locations in its detached list (Line 19).

2.3   Execution Under RC11 Memory

A difference between the program in Fig. 1 and Fig. 3 is that we assume the latter executes under RC11 with relaxed and release-acquire accesses. Unlike

SC, where reads always read from the last write, RC11 allows threads to access stale writes (i.e., writes that have been overwritten). The difference between relaxed and release-acquiring operations is best explained using the message passing example [1,3,15] (see Fig. 4). Assuming all variables are instantiated with the value 0, the program on the left can only guarantee $r, s \in \{0, 1\}$ when it terminates since thread 2 is allowed to read a stale value for x even if it reads the new value for y written by thread 1. In contrast, the program on the right can guarantee the stronger property $r = 1 \longrightarrow s = 1$ upon termination since thread 2 can only set r to 1 if it reads from thread 1's write to y. This induces a *release-acquire* synchronisation, which ensures that thread 2 can only read the value 1 for x (written by thread 1) when it later updates s.

Example 2. To see the importance of the release and acquire flags on FAA and CAS, consider an execution of the program in Fig. 3, where these flags are omitted. Suppose a thread t_1 executes Line 28 (having set rcu[t_1] to 1 in rcu_enter). Suppose another thread t_2 executes inc, successfully performing its CAS. Due to RC11's weak memory effects, t_2 may continue with its execution and miss that rcu[t_1] has been set to 1 since weak memory allows t_2 to read *stale*, i.e., overwritten values, when the program is improperly synchronised.

To prevent the issues described in Example 2, we require *acquire/release* annotations on FAA and CAS, to ensure relaxed updates (e.g., to rcu) are correctly propagated. Namely, we must replace the simple read of C in Fig. 1 with a fetch-and-add (FAA) at Line 28 in Fig. 3. Additionally, this FAA, as well as the CAS, must be both releasing and acquiring.

Note that RC11 provides an opportunity for parallelisation that would not be possible under SC. Namely, under SC, the RCU algorithm forces a synchronising thread t_1 (i.e., a thread executing sync) to wait until rcu[t_2] is set to 0 for thread t_2 regardless of whether t_2 has references to addresses in the detached list of t_1. Under RC11, another thread t_2 setting rcu[t_2] to 1 can be missed by t_1, since t_1 is able to read stale values. Note that t_1 can only miss t_2 entering its RCU (i.e., setting rcu[t_2] to 1), when it is impossible for t_2 to access the locations in the detached list of t_1. Thus, this behaviour is safe and provides an opportunity for improved performance.

3   Background

In this section, we first present our modelling language and semantics for RC11-RAR, which is RC11 restricted to relaxed and release-acquire accesses (Sect. 3.1). For simplicity, we write RC11 to mean RC11-RAR. In Sect. 3.2, we present the Owicki-Gries proof rules. Our presentation combines prior works on Owicki-Gries for weak memory [2,3]. In Sect. 3.3, we present the two weak-memory assertions from [3] that we use in our proof.

3.1 Syntax and RC11 Semantics

Syntax. Our formal modelling language is unstructured and defined in terms of a mapping from labels (of type *Label*) to commands (of type *Com*). Let *Loc* and *Val* be the set of all locations and values, respectively. We assume *Loc* is partitioned into local Loc_L, global Loc_G and auxiliary Loc_A locations. Suppose $r \in Loc_L$, $x \in Loc_G$, $m, n \in Val$, $i, j, k \in Label$, $\hat{a} \in Loc_A$ and $\alpha \in Com$. Moreover, let Exp_L be expressions over Loc_L and $BExp_L \ni B$ be boolean-valued expressions over Loc_L, and suppose $\hat{e}$ be an expression over both Loc_L and Loc_A.

$$Com ::= r := Exp_L \mid x :=^{[R]} Exp_L \mid r \leftarrow^{[A]} x \qquad LabAux ::= i \mid \langle i, \hat{a} := \hat{e} \rangle$$
$$\mid r := \mathtt{FAA}^{[R][A]}(x, n) \mid r := \mathtt{CAS}^{[R][A]}(x, m, n)$$
$$LCom ::= \alpha \text{ goto } LabAux \mid \text{if } B \text{ goto } j \text{ else to } k$$

Here, we use $[X]$ to mean that the annotation X is optional. Thus, $\mathtt{CAS}^{[R][A]}(x, m, n)$ denotes either a relaxed CAS ($\mathtt{CAS}(x, m, n)$), a releasing CAS ($\mathtt{CAS}^R(x, m, n)$), an acquiring CAS ($\mathtt{CAS}^A(x, n)$) or a release-acquiring CAS ($\mathtt{CAS}^{RA}(x, m, n)$).

Let *Tid* be the set of all thread identifiers. A program is a function of type $(Tid \times Label) \rightharpoonup LCom$ that maps a thread id (of type *Tid*) and a label to the command to be executed.

The operational semantics for our language is defined in three parts: the program semantics, the memory semantics and the combined semantics that brings the program and memory semantics together.

Program Semantics. The program semantics (Fig. 5) assumes three state components: the *local state*, $lst \in Tid \rightarrow (Loc_L \rightharpoonup Val)$, the *auxiliary state*, $ast \in Tid \rightarrow (Loc_A \rightharpoonup Val)$ and the *program counter state*, $pct \in Tid \rightarrow Label$, where $\rightharpoonup$ denotes a partial function. Figure 5 defines the steps $(P, lst, ast, pct) \xRightarrow{a}_t (P, lst', ast', pct')$ that the thread t of concurrent program P can take, where a is either a memory action or a silent action τ. Note that we assume that the local variables of different threads are disjoint, i.e., if $t \neq t'$, then $\mathsf{dom}(lst(t)) \cap \mathsf{dom}(lst(t')) = \emptyset$.

We write $[\![E]\!]_s$ for the value of E evaluated in the state s and define $f[x \mapsto v] = \lambda i. \text{ if } i = x \text{ then } v \text{ else } f(i)$ for functional override.

RC11-RAR Memory Semantics. The *memory semantics* (given in Fig. 6) defines transitions over the RC11 state (denoted by σ). We assume that the write and RMW actions are of type W and can be read by a read or an RMW action (of type $\mathbb{R}$). We let $\mathsf{W_R}$ and $\mathbb{R}_A$ be the set of releasing write actions and acquiring read actions, respectively.

Each global write or RMW is represented by a *write event* (a, q), where a is a write or RMW action, and q is a rational number that we use as a *timestamp* (c.f., [3]). For $w = (a, q)$, we denote w's timestamp by $tst(w) = q$. We also use *wrval* to denote the value written by an action (if any). The memory state contains the following components:

- *writes* $\subseteq \mathsf{W} \times \mathbb{Q}$ recording the set of all writes that have occurred in the execution thus far.

Atomic statements (selected)

$$\frac{a = rmw^{[R][A]}(x, m, n) \quad m, n \in Val}{(r := CAS, ls) \xrightarrow{a} ls[r \mapsto true]} \qquad \frac{a = rd(x, m') \quad m' \in Val}{(r := CAS, ls) \xrightarrow{a} ls[r \mapsto false]}$$

Auxiliary variables (a step with no auxiliary variables (left) and a step with auxiliary variables (right))

$$\frac{}{(i, ls, as) \xrightarrow{aux} (as, i)} \qquad \frac{n = [\![\hat{e}]\!]_{ls \cup as} \quad n \in Val}{(\langle i, \hat{a} := \hat{e} \rangle, ls, as) \xrightarrow{aux} (as[\hat{a} \mapsto n], i)}$$

Control flow (selected)

$$\text{STEP} \frac{(\alpha, ls) \xrightarrow{a} ls' \quad (l, ls', as) \xrightarrow{aux} (as', i)}{(\alpha \text{ goto } l, ls, as) \xRightarrow{a} (ls', as', i)} \qquad \text{BR1} \frac{[\![b]\!]_{ls}}{(IF, ls, as) \xRightarrow{\tau} (ls, as, j)}$$

Parallel composition

$$\text{PAR} \frac{(P(t, pct(t)), lst(t), ast(t)) \xRightarrow{a} (ls', as', i)}{(P, lst, ast, pct) \xRightarrow{a}_t (P, lst[t \mapsto ls'], ast[t \mapsto as'], pct[t \mapsto i])}$$

Fig. 5. Selected program semantics, assuming $ls, ls' \in Loc_L \rightharpoonup Val$ and $as, as' \in Loc_A \rightharpoonup Val$ and defining $IF = \text{if } b \text{ goto } j \text{ else to } k$ and $CAS = \text{CAS}^{[R][A]}(x, m, n)$

- $tview_t \in Loc_G \to writes$ recording the *viewfront* of thread t. Thread t can read from any write to location x whose timestamp is at least $tst(tview_t(x))$.
- $mview_w \in Loc_G \to writes$ recording the *viewfront* of write w, which is set to be the viewfront of the thread that executed w at the time of w's execution. We use $mview_w$ to compute a new value for $tview_t$ if a thread t *synchronizes* with w, i.e., if $w \in W_R$ and another thread executes an $e \in \mathbb{R}_A$ that reads from w (see Fig. 6).
- $covered \subseteq writes$ recording the set of writes that cannot be seen by modifying actions wr and rmw. This is used to maintain atomicity of existing rmw actions. Since an rmw with a write a is introduced immediately after (in timestamp order) the write, say w, that it reads from, later modifications to the state must not introduce a write between w and the write corresponding to the rmw. Doing so would violate atomicity of the rmw action (see [3] for further details).

Combined Semantics. The program semantics is combined with the memory semantics as follows, where $LS = (lst, ast, pct)$

$$\frac{(P, LS) \xRightarrow{\tau}_t (P, LS')}{(P, LS, \sigma) \Longrightarrow (P, LS', \sigma)} \qquad \frac{(P, LS) \xRightarrow{a}_t (P, LS') \quad \sigma \xrightarrow{a}_t \sigma'}{(P, LS, \sigma) \Longrightarrow (P', LS', \sigma')}$$

The full state of a program in RC11 is denoted Σ, where each state of Σ is a pair of the form (LS, σ).

$$\text{READ} \frac{\begin{array}{c} a \in \{rd(x,n), rd^{\mathsf{A}}(x,n)\} \quad (w,q) \in OW_\sigma(t,x) \quad wrval(w) = n \\ TV = \begin{cases} \sigma.tview_t \otimes \sigma.mview_{(w,q)} & \text{if } (w,a) \in \mathsf{W_R} \times \mathbb{R}_{\mathsf{A}} \\ \sigma.tview_t[x := (w,q)] & \text{otherwise} \end{cases} \end{array}}{\sigma \overset{a}{\rightsquigarrow}_t \sigma[tview_t := TV]}$$

$$\text{WRITE} \frac{\begin{array}{c} a \in \{wr(x,n), wr^{\mathsf{R}}(x,n)\} \quad (w,q) \in OW_\sigma(t,x) \setminus \sigma.covered \quad fresh_\sigma(q,q') \\ WR = \sigma.writes \cup \{(a,q')\} \qquad TV = \sigma.tview_t[x := (a,q')] \end{array}}{\sigma \overset{a}{\rightsquigarrow}_t \sigma[tview_t := TV, mview_{(a,q')} := TV, writes := WR]}$$

$$\text{RMW} \frac{\begin{array}{c} a = rmw^{\mathsf{RA}}(x,m,n) \quad (w,q) \in OW_\sigma(t,x) \setminus \sigma.covered \quad wrval(w) = m \\ fresh_\sigma(q,q') \quad WR = \sigma.writes \cup \{(a,q')\} \quad CO = \sigma.covered \cup \{(w,q)\} \\ TV = \begin{cases} \sigma.tview_t[x := (a,q')] \otimes \sigma.mview_{(w,q)} & \text{if } w \in \mathsf{W_R} \\ \sigma.tview_t[x := (a,q')] & \text{otherwise} \end{cases} \end{array}}{\sigma \overset{a}{\rightsquigarrow}_t \sigma[tview_t := TV, mview_{(a,q')} := TV, writes := WR, covered := CO]}$$

Fig. 6. Selected transition relations of the memory semantics, where $OW_\sigma(t,x) = \{(a,q) \in \sigma.writes \mid var(a) = x \wedge tst(\sigma.tview_t(x)) \leq q\}$ define the observable writes, $(v_1 \otimes v_2)(x) = \text{if } tst(v_2(x)) \leq tst(v_1(x)) \text{ then } v_1(x) \text{ else } v_2(x)$ returns the maximal timestamp and $fresh_\sigma(q,q') = q < q' \wedge \forall w' \in \sigma.writes. q < tst(w') \Rightarrow q' < tst(w')$ returns a fresh timestamp after q

3.2 Owicki-Gries Reasoning

The proof outline of a program is a triple: $(init, ann, I)$, where $init \in 2^\Sigma$ defines the initial state, $ann \in Tid \times Label \rightarrow 2^\Sigma$ and $I \in 2^\Sigma$ is a global invariant. This definition can be extended to handle termination, but, given that our main example is non-terminating, we omit this detail for simplicity. We assume programs start execution such that $pct(t) = \iota$ for all $t \in Tid$, where $\iota \in Label$ is a special label denoting the initial label.

Definition 1 (Valid proof outline). *A proof outline $(init, ann, I)$ is valid for a program P iff the following hold:*

Initialisation. *For all $t \in Tid$, $init \longrightarrow I \wedge ann(t, \iota)$.*
Local correctness. *For all $t \in Tid$ and $i \in Label$, either:*
- $P(t,i) = \alpha$ goto j *and* $\{I \wedge ann(t,i)\} \; \alpha \; \{I \wedge ann(t,j)\}$
- $P(t,i) = \alpha$ goto $\langle j, \hat{a} := \hat{e} \rangle$ *and* $\{I \wedge ann(t,i)\} \; \alpha \; \{(I \wedge ann(t,j))[\hat{e}/\hat{a}]\}$
- $P(t,i) = \text{if } B \text{ goto } j \text{ else to } k$ *and both*
  - $I \wedge ann(t,i) \wedge B \longrightarrow ann(t,j)$ *and*
  - $I \wedge ann(t,i) \wedge \neg B \longrightarrow ann(t,k)$ *hold.*
Stability. *For all $t_1, t_2 \in Tid$ such that $t_1 \neq t_2$ and $i_1, i_2 \in Label$:*
- *if* $P(t_1, i_1) = \alpha$ goto j, *then*
  $\{I \wedge ann(t_2, i_2) \wedge ann(t_1, i_1)\} \; \alpha \; \{ann(t_2, i_2)\}$;
- *if* $P(t_1, i_1) = \alpha$ goto $\langle j, \hat{a} := \hat{e} \rangle$, *then*
  $\{I \wedge ann(t_2, i_2) \wedge ann(t_1, i_1)\} \; \alpha \; \{ann(t_2, i_2)[\hat{e}/\hat{a}]\}$.

3.3   View-Based Assertions

Prior works [3,4] have defined several view-based assertions, that enable reasoning about weak memory behaviours. In the proof of RCU, we have found that many of these are not needed. On the other hand, we have identified a new type of assertion that we call *conditional-on-last* that greatly simplifies reasoning, which we introduce in Sect. 4.2.

Definite Observation. This is denoted $[x =_t u]$ and means that thread t *must* observe the value u for x if it reads x. For a set of writes W, let W_x be the writes in W that write to location x. The last write to x in W is denoted $last(W, x)$, where $last(W, x) = w \Leftrightarrow w \in W_x \land (\forall w' \in W_x.\ tst(w') \le tst(w))$. Then, we obtain:

$$[x =_t n]\ =\ \lambda\sigma.\ \sigma.tview_t(x) = last(\sigma.writes, x) \land wrval(last(\sigma.writes, x)) = n$$

The first conjunct ensures that the viewfront of t for x is the last write to x in σ (thus t can only read this last write to x). The second conjunct ensures that the value written by the last write is n.

Covered Write. When a location x is only modified using RMW operations, it is often convenient to reason about them using the covered write assertion [3–5], denoted $\mathbf{C}_x^n$. This states that all writes to variable x except the last write are covered, and that the last write to x has value n. Formally we have:

$$\mathbf{C}_x^n\ =\ \lambda\sigma.\ \forall w \in \sigma.writes_x.\ w \notin \sigma.covered \longrightarrow$$
$$wrval(w) = n \land w = last(\sigma.writes_x, x)$$

4   Extensions to Semantics and Logic

To prove correctness of our RCU example, we require two extensions to the semantics and logic. First, in Sect. 4.1, we extend our RC11 model with a simple model of pointers. Second, in Sect. 4.2, we extend the assertion language (Sect. 3.3) with a new type of assertion that simplifies reasoning about message passing over covered writes.

4.1   Allocation Model

One of the first challenges in verifying RCU (Sect. 5) is adapting an adequate representation of the allocation functions **new** and **free** called in Lines 23 and 20 of Fig. 3. In practice, C programs assume one of two schemes based on *provenance* (the origins of the value of each pointer), whose models require intricate considerations depending on how aliasing is to be handled [18]. Our RCU implementation relies on only allocation functions **new** and **free**, and thus, use a simple allocation map, $A : \Pi \longrightarrow Loc$ that maps a *pointer identifier* (of type Π) to a location. This mapping is inspired by provenance mappings [18], but is much simpler. On every allocation, we choose a fresh pointer identifier i (that is unique across the entire execution). The following transitions handle allocations and freeing of pointers, where $A[i \mapsto \bot]$ denotes that the mapping $i \mapsto \_$ is removed from A:

$$\text{ALLOC}\frac{a = alloc(i,l) \quad i \notin dom(A) \quad l \notin ran(A)}{A \overset{a}{\hookrightarrow} A[i \mapsto l]} \qquad \text{KILL}\frac{a = kill(i) \quad i \in dom(A)}{A \overset{a}{\hookrightarrow} A[i \mapsto \bot]}$$

The resulting Isabelle model is lightweight and guarantees that no two objects with different pointer identifiers values share the same location in memory.

$$\forall\, i, j \in dom(A).\ i \neq j \ \longrightarrow\ A(i) \neq A(j) \tag{1}$$

Full Allocation Semantics. The next step is to link this allocation semantics with the program semantics from Sect. 3.1. Recalling that $LS = (lst, ast, pct)$, we have two transitions depending on whether or not the transition in question modifies the allocation mapping:

$$\frac{(P, LS, \sigma) \Longrightarrow (P', LS', \sigma')}{(P, LS, \sigma, A) \Longrightarrow (P', LS', \sigma', A)} \qquad \frac{(P, LS) \overset{a}{\Rightarrow}_t (P', LS') \quad A \overset{a}{\hookrightarrow} A'}{(P, LS, \sigma, A) \Longrightarrow (P', LS', \sigma, A')}$$

Note that the second rule only applies when a is an *alloc* or *kill* action. The first premise of the rule uses PAR in Fig. 5 to reduce to a step of thread t, which in turn reduces to a step transition $(\overset{a}{\rightarrow})$. Then, using the rule STEP (assuming no auxiliary variables are modified) reduces to an execution of some program syntax. Here we assume two atomic statements `r := new X` (which performs an allocation) and `free(l)` (which frees the location l). The behaviours of these statements are defined by the following rules:

$$\frac{a = alloc(\_, l)}{(\texttt{r := new X}, ls) \overset{a}{\rightarrow} ls[r \mapsto l]} \qquad \frac{a = kill(l)}{(\texttt{free(l)}, ls) \overset{a}{\rightarrow} ls}$$

4.2 Extending the Assertion Language

In prior works [3–5], message-passing, as enabled by release-acquire synchronisation in RC11 programs, is achieved by an assertion known as *conditional observation*. This assertion states that synchronising on a particular write to a location, say x, guarantees that the reading thread's view advances sufficiently on another location, say y, such the reading thread no longer sees stale writes to y. For the purposes of our verification, this assertion is insufficient because it inherently assumes that threads synchronise on a unique *value*. Instead, we define a new type of assertion that we call *conditional-on-last*, which does not have a uniqueness requirement: it only requires that the reading thread sees the *last write* to the synchronising variable (i.e., x in the discussion above). We show that this assertion is sufficient for verifying our example, but conjecture that it could also apply to other examples such as non-blocking data structures (e.g., the Treiber stack [29]), where all updates to a shared global pointer occurs through a read-modify-write instruction.

Conditional-on-Last Observation. This is denoted $[\![x = u]\!](y = v)$ and means that if the last write to location x has value u, then x is a releasing write (or RMW) such that synchronising on x is guaranteed to advance the reading thread's view on y such that it definitely observes y to have the value v. Formally,

$$[\![x = u]\!](y = v)$$
$$\equiv \lambda\sigma.\ \mathbf{let}\ last(\sigma.writes, x) = w, last(\sigma.writes, y) = w'\ \mathbf{in}$$
$$wrval(w) = u\ \longrightarrow\ w \in \mathbb{W}_{\mathsf{R}} \wedge \sigma.mview_w(y) = w' \wedge wrval(w') = v$$

Like with other assertions in the proof (see [3–5]), we verify a number of pre/postcondition axioms describing the interaction between the conditional-on-last observation assertions and the atomic program statements.

For example, a weak memory read by any thread t preserves the *conditional-on-last observation*. Similarly, provided the location of a weak memory write does not affect x or y, the *conditional-on-last observation* is preserved, recalling that [X] means that the annotation X is optional.

$$\frac{X = [\![x = u]\!](y = v)}{\{X\}\ r \leftarrow^{[A]} z\ \{X\}} \qquad \frac{z \notin \{x, y\}\quad X = [\![x = u]\!](y = v)}{\{X\}\ z :=^{[R]} n\ \{X\}}$$

The next rule shows how conditional-on-last observations can be used to synchronise on another location through a release-acquire CAS:

$$\overline{\{\mathbf{C}_x^u \wedge [\![x = u]\!](y = v)\}\ r := \mathsf{CAS}^{\mathsf{RA}}(x, u, n)\ \{r \longrightarrow [y =_t v]\}}$$

Lastly, we show how information can be relayed through the assertion, when using a release-acquire CAS, provided that the CAS succeeds:

$$\overline{\{\mathbf{C}_x^m \wedge [y =_t v]\}r := \mathsf{CAS}^{\mathsf{RA}}(x, m, u)\{r \longrightarrow [\![x = u]\!](y = v)\}}$$

5　Proof of Correctness

Our strategy for showing that ABA cannot occur in our algorithm is by tracking each thread's reads and writes to each location. We introduce a notion of ownership of memory locations within Owicki-Gries proofs [25] to track the read and write capabilities of each thread. Threads may only dereference a pointer if they have at least a *read capability* on the pointer value. Similarly, a pointer can be de-allocated only by the thread which holds *write capabilities* over it.

5.1   Ownership and Capabilities

We differentiate between read/write capabilities over addresses by introducing two ownership types:

$$own_{rd} \in Loc \longrightarrow 2^T \qquad\qquad own_{wr} \in Loc \longrightarrow T \cup \{\bot\}$$

where own_{rd} is an auxiliary map tracking ownership of *read capabilities* over addresses, and own_{wr} is an auxiliary map tracking *write capabilities*. Note that multiple threads may have read capability to each location, whereas at most one thread has write capability.

To enable tracking changes in the mapping of read and write capabilities, we introduce the following auxiliary functions:

$$\mathcal{O}_{rd}^A(\mathtt{x},\mathtt{t}) \equiv own_{rd} := own_{rd}[x \mapsto own_{rd}(x) \cup \{t\}]$$
$$\mathcal{O}_{rd}^R(\mathtt{x},\mathtt{t}) \equiv own_{rd} := own_{rd}[x \mapsto own_{rd}(x) \setminus \{t\}]$$
$$\mathcal{O}_{wr}^A(\mathtt{x},\mathtt{t}) \equiv own_{wr} := own_{wr}[x \mapsto t]$$
$$\mathcal{O}_{wr}^R(\mathtt{x},\mathtt{t}) \equiv own_{wr} := own_{wr}[x \mapsto \bot]$$

where $\mathcal{O}^A$ and $\mathcal{O}^R$ stand for *Acquire* and *Release*, respectively.

We incorporate these auxiliary functions in our model, as shown in Fig. 7. Note that we also add another auxiliary variable `repeat`, initially false, that is set to true the first time the `CAS` at Line 31 is executed. This is to accommodate the special case, where `rcu_exit` is spuriously called at Line 26 at the first execution of the loop.

At Line 23, thread t acquires both *read* and *write* capabilities over the address that it allocates. When performing a `FAA` call, Line 28, the thread acquires *read* capability on the location, to which the shared pointer `C` points. The next change in ownership occurs at Line 31, but this change is conditional and only occurs if the `CAS` is successful. If the `CAS` is successful, i.e., `r` is set to true, the executing thread releases write capability on `n` (the new value of `C`), while acquiring write capability on `s` (the old value of `C`). The former is because the thread publishes `n` for shared access and relinquishes its rights to de-allocate the address. The latter is essential for the thread to be able to free the memory at location `s` at a later stage of the algorithm. If the `CAS` fails, the executing thread returns to Line 26 after having set `repeat` to true. Here it relinquishes its read capabilities of the address pointed to by the local `s`, before it is set to the new value of the shared pointer, `C`.

5.2   Invariants and Proof Outlines

The proof of correctness relies on several invariants, which we describe below. We first describe the main invariant that we wish to preserve. Subsequently, we describe the mechanisms that help preserve the main invariant from the point of view of executing threads. We discuss how the assumption of the *weak memory model* affects our proof, and incorporate semantics, which demonstrate how the

RCU synchronisation method helps preserve the main invariant. This section utilises a mix of global invariants and proof outlines to demonstrate the general strategy of the Isabelle/HOL proof.

Main Correctness Property. The main correctness property is straightforward to state: We require that if a location is free, then no thread has read capability on that location. Formally, we have the following, where we assume $isFree(l) = \forall i \in dom(A). \; A(i) \neq l$:

$$\forall u. \quad isFree(u) \; \longrightarrow \; own_{rd}(u) = \{\} \tag{2}$$

Since a thread relinquishes its own read/write capabilities on any location it frees, a consequence of (2) is that a thread is only ever able to de-allocate a memory location if no other thread has read or write capability on that location. Note that (3) below ensures that we also have $own_{wr}(u) = \bot$ as a consequence of (2).

Global Properties on Read and Write Capabilities. We maintain the following properties relating read and write capabilities on memory locations. First, if a thread has write capability on a location, then it must also have read capability on that location. Second, given that n_t is the value of the pointer **n** of thread t, allocated at Line 23 in Fig. 3, and that t holds the write capability on n_t, t must also be the only thread with read capability on the location.

$$\forall u, t. \quad own_{wr}(u) = t \; \longrightarrow \; t \in own_{rd}(u) \tag{3}$$

$$\forall t. \quad own_{wr}(n_t) = t \; \longrightarrow \; own_{rd}(n_t) = \{t\} \tag{4}$$

The key difference between invariant assertions (3) and (4) is that thread t, which has performed its pointer allocation on Line 23, is the only thread with *read* capabilities over the referenced address. Here, the read ownership mapping of location n_t should consist only of the allocating thread t.

Global Weak Memory Properties. From a weak-memory perspective, as discussed in Sect. 2.3, the main property we must guarantee is that a thread that can free a location, say u, must see that any thread that has read capability on u has executed `rcu_enter`. This is challenging due to the fact that `rcu_enter` is a relaxed write, under RC11, without adequate synchronisation, a thread may see stale updates to `rcu`. To show that this is not the case (i.e., that the program is well synchronised), we maintain the following invariant:

$$\forall u, t, t'. \; t \neq t' \wedge u \in ran(det_t) \wedge t' \in own_{rd}(u) \; \longrightarrow \; [rcu(t') =_t 1] \tag{5}$$

which states that for any location in thread t's detached list, if another thread t' has read capability on that location, then t must see that $rcu(t')$ has been set to 1. This means that t, when executing its `sync` operation, will wait for $rcu(t')$ to be unset (i.e., for t' to execute `rcu_exit`).

Thread-local proof obligations. We establish (5) via *message passing* the information about updates to `rcu` through release-acquire synchronisation on the shared counter C. Message passing is proved in two steps and expressed as thread-local proof obligations as shown in Fig. 7.

First, $\mathsf{preCAS_{ok}}(t)$ (defined below) is used to establish that, prior to executing the CAS, the executing thread can be sure that it will see that $rcu(t')$ is 1 for any thread t' that has read capability on C, if the CAS is successful. This is guaranteed by the consequent $[\![C = u]\!](rcu(t') = 1)$ of $\mathsf{preCAS_{ok}}(t)$. The execution of a successful CAS by thread t under precondition $\mathsf{preCAS_{ok}}(t)$ establishes $\mathsf{postCAS_{ok}}(t)$ below, which states that for any other thread t' that has read

$$\{\neg repeat \ \wedge W_t(det_t) \ \wedge \ R_t(det_t) \ \wedge \ \mathsf{preCAS_{ok}}(t)\}$$
$$\cdots$$

23: $\langle \texttt{n = new int}; \ \mathcal{O}^A_{rd}(\texttt{n,t}); \ \mathcal{O}^A_{wr}(\texttt{n,t})\rangle$
$$\{\neg repeat \ \wedge \ W_t(det_t \mathbin{+\!\!+} n_t) \ \wedge \ R_t(det_t \mathbin{+\!\!+} n_t) \ \wedge \ n_t \neq \bot \ \wedge \ \mathsf{preCAS_{ok}}(t)\}$$
   `rcu_enter();`
$$\{\neg repeat \ \wedge W_t(det_t \mathbin{+\!\!+} n_t) \ \wedge \ R_t(det_t \mathbin{+\!\!+} n_t) \ \wedge \ n_t \neq \bot \ \wedge \ [rcu(t) =_t 1] \ \wedge \ \mathsf{preCAS_{ok}}(t)\}$$
   `do {`
$$\left\{ \begin{aligned} &W_t(det_t \mathbin{+\!\!+} n_t) \ \wedge \ n_t \neq \bot \wedge [rcu(t) =_t 1] \wedge \mathsf{preCAS_{ok}}(t) \ \wedge \\ &(repeat \longrightarrow s_t \neq \bot \ \wedge \ R_t(det_t \mathbin{+\!\!+} n_t \mathbin{+\!\!+} s_t)) \ \wedge \ (\neg repeat \longrightarrow R_t(det_t \mathbin{+\!\!+} n_t)) \end{aligned} \right\}$$
26:    $\langle \texttt{rcu\_exit(); repeat?} \ \mathcal{O}^R_{rd}(\texttt{s,t})\rangle$
$$\{ R_t(det_t \mathbin{+\!\!+} n_t) \ \wedge \ W_t(det_t \mathbin{+\!\!+} n_t) \ \wedge \ n_t \neq \bot \ \wedge \ [rcu(t) =_t 0] \ \wedge \ \mathsf{preCAS_{ok}}(t)\}$$
   `rcu_enter();`
$$\{ R_t(det_t \mathbin{+\!\!+} n_t) \ \wedge \ W_t(det_t \mathbin{+\!\!+} n_t) \ \wedge \ n_t \neq \bot \ \wedge \ [rcu(t) =_t 1] \ \wedge \ \mathsf{preCAS_{ok}}(t)\}$$
28:    $\langle \texttt{s = FAA}^{\mathsf{RA}}\texttt{(C,0)}; \ \mathcal{O}^A_{rd}(\texttt{C,t})\rangle$
$$\left\{ \begin{aligned} &R_t(det_t \mathbin{+\!\!+} n_t \mathbin{+\!\!+} s_t) \ \wedge \ W_t(det_t \mathbin{+\!\!+} n_t) \ \wedge \ n_t \neq \bot \wedge \ s_t \neq \bot \ \wedge \\ &[rcu(t) =_t 1] \ \wedge \ \mathsf{preCAS_{ok}}(t) \end{aligned} \right\}$$
31:    $\langle \texttt{r = CAS}^{\mathsf{RA}}\texttt{(\&C,s,n); repeat := true, r?} \ (\mathcal{O}^R_{wr}(\texttt{n,t}); \ \mathcal{O}^A_{wr}(\texttt{s,t}))\rangle$
$$\left\{ \begin{aligned} &repeat \ \wedge \ R_t(det_t \mathbin{+\!\!+} n_t \mathbin{+\!\!+} s_t) \ \wedge \ W_t(det_t \mathbin{+\!\!+} s_t) \ \wedge \ n_t \neq \bot \ \wedge \ s_t \neq \bot \ \wedge \\ &[rcu(t) =_t 1] \ \wedge \ (r \longrightarrow \mathsf{postCAS_{ok}}(t)) \ \wedge \ (\neg r \longrightarrow \mathsf{preCAS_{ok}}(t)) \end{aligned} \right\}$$
   `} while !r;`
$$\left\{ \begin{aligned} &R_t(det_t \mathbin{+\!\!+} n_t \mathbin{+\!\!+} s_t) \ \wedge \ W_t(det_t \mathbin{+\!\!+} s_t) \ \wedge \ n_t \neq \bot \ \wedge \ s_t \neq \bot \ \wedge \\ &[rcu(t) =_t 1] \ \wedge \ \mathsf{postCAS_{ok}}(t) \end{aligned} \right\}$$
33: $\langle \texttt{rcu\_exit(); } \ \mathcal{O}^R_{rd}(\texttt{n,t})\rangle$
$$\{ R_t(det_t \mathbin{+\!\!+} s_t) \ \wedge \ W_t(det_t \mathbin{+\!\!+} s_t) \ \wedge \ s_t \neq \bot \ \wedge \ [rcu(t) =_t 0] \ \wedge \ \mathsf{postCAS_{ok}}(t)\}$$
$$\cdots$$
   `reclaim(s);`
$$\{ det_t \neq [\,] \longrightarrow R_t(det_t) \ \wedge \ W_t(det_t) \}$$
$$\cdots$$
   `return v`
$$\{ det_t \neq [\,] \longrightarrow R_t(det_t) \ \wedge \ W_t(det_t)\}$$

Fig. 7. Proof outline for the RCU algorithm for thread t with highlighted assertions denoting the changes from the previous statement and $X \mathbin{+\!\!+} x$ denoting a list X appended with the element x.

capability on the newly freed location s_t, thread t has a definite observation that $rcu(t')$ is 1.

$$\mathsf{preCAS_{ok}}(t) = \forall\, u, t'.\; t \neq t' \wedge \mathbf{C}_C^u \wedge t' \in own_{rd}(u) \;\longrightarrow\; \llbracket C = u \rrbracket (rcu(t') = 1)$$
$$\mathsf{postCAS_{ok}}(t) = \forall\, t'.\; t \neq t' \;\wedge\; t' \in own_{rd}(s_t) \;\longrightarrow\; [rcu(t') =_t 1]$$

Note that $\mathsf{postCAS_{ok}}(t)$ is used later in the precondition of 16 in Fig. 8 to establish (5), i.e., when the location s_t is inserted into the t's detached list.

```
      {R_t(det_t + s_t) ∧ W_t(det_t + s_t) ∧ s_t ≠ None ∧ postCAS_ok(t)}
16: insert(det[t], s);
      {R_t(det_t) ∧ W_t(det_t)}
17: if (nondet()) return;
      {R_t(det_t) ∧ W_t(det_t)}
18: sync();
      {R_t(det_t) ∧ W_t(det_t) ∧ (∀ u ∈ ran(det_t). own_rd(u) = {t})}
19: while !isEmpty(det[t])
      {R_t(det_t) ∧ W_t(det_t) ∧ (∀ u ∈ ran(det_t). own_rd(u) = {t})}
20:    ⟨free(pop(det[t])); O_rd^R(head(det[t]),t); O_wr^R(head(det[t]),t));
      {det_t = [ ]}
```

Fig. 8. Proof outline the `reclaim` method for thread t. The proof of `sync()`, which is non-atomic, is straightforward, following from the discussion in Overview 5.2, and hence elided

Along with some minor book-keeping assertions, the final thread-local predicates we require are the following:

$$R_t(LocSeq) = \forall\, x \in ran(LocSeq).\; t \in own_{rd}(x)$$
$$W_t(LocSeq) = \forall\, x \in ran(LocSeq).\; own_{wr}(x) = t$$

where $R_t(LocSeq)$ holds iff t has read capability on all the locations in the set of locations $LocSeq$. Similarly, $W_t(LocSeq)$ for write capabilities.

Overview. Having introduced all the necessary invariants, we recap the main steps of the proof. We observe that to ensure condition (2), we require the precondition of Line 20 shown in Fig. 8. This follows specifically from the assertion $(\forall u.\; u \in ran(det_t) \longrightarrow own_{rd}(u) = \{t\})$, which is in turn guaranteed after completion of `sync`, via (5). The latter is preserved after execution of Line 16 in Fig. 8, following from the assumption of $\mathsf{postCAS_{ok}}(t)$. Finally, $\mathsf{postCAS_{ok}}(t)$ is established from a successful execution of `CAS`, Line 31, in Fig. 7 using the $\mathsf{preCAS_{ok}}(t)$ statement in its precondition. Note that $\mathsf{preCAS_{ok}}(t)$ holds until the `CAS` succeeds, as shown in Fig. 7.

6   Related and Future Work

We build on our previous work [25], specifically with the use of *ownership* to aid verification of *interference freedom*. The notion of *ownership* is well studied and work related to *ownership* is discussed at length in our earlier paper.

The closest related work to this paper is that of Tassarotti et al. [27], where they verify correctness of an implementation of RCU under the release-acquire memory model, using a specialised separation logic called GPS [30]. Like us, they use ownership over read and write capabilities to help guarantee absence of data races. Under their model of ownership, having neither *full* nor *partial* permission to access a location, makes it impossible for a thread to read that location, while another is augmenting it's contents. The transfer of these access rights is also defined very similar to us, and occurs, for example, upon gaining a reference to a location or during the *compare-and-swap* operation. However, unlike our work, their proofs are (a) not mechanised and (b) over a stronger memory model, where all writes are releasing and all reads are acquiring.

The topic of safe memory management in sequentially consistent models is discussed at length in works by Dechev et al. [6,7], Herlihy et al. [11] and Hart et al. [10]. More specifically, they introduce approaches to safely handle and reason about memory reclamation, while evaluating their results based on performance of implemented algorithms. The general approach to safe memory management involves monitoring for competing threads on either the shared locations by monitoring for competing threads inside critical regions, which encompass the shared locations in question. The RCU method is of the latter type of approach. To this end, we believe our ownership based approach could be used to help verify these algorithms.

Another approach to solving ABA is that of *hazard pointers* (HP) [21]. HP is a direct counterpart to the RCU method, offering management of accesses directly, by observing that competing threads have access to the to-be-reclaimed addresses. What is interesting, is that during verification of our ownership model, we rely on the very same mechanism to guarantee interference freedom, alongside ABA-freedom. It would be interesting to see how our verification approach can be adapted to verify an algorithm using HPs in the context of RC11.

7 Conclusions

This paper uses a previously discussed notion of ownership [25] to facilitate verification of a solution to the ABA problem. Moreover, we propose an improvement on the original algorithm in the form of relaxing the memory model and adding release/acquire annotations. We make use of and extend the operational semantics for the RC11 weak memory model to help demonstrate correctness of the augmented algorithm. We show that the proposed RCU solution to the ABA problem can be implemented in RC11 with minimal changes to the source code. The idea of ownership could be readily extended to help reason about interference.

We verified the RCU solution to be ABA free under the assumption of a weak memory model in Isabelle/HOL. This paper uses the notion of ownership over capabilities to make the formal and subsequently *high-level* proofs easy to understand. It was natural to implement the operational semantics, and they helped to further preserve the concise nature of our proof.

References

1. Batty, M.J.: The C11 and C++11 concurrency model. Ph.D. thesis, University of Cambridge, UK (2015). https://ethos.bl.uk/OrderDetails.do?uin=uk.bl.ethos.708458
2. Bila, E.V., Dongol, B., Lahav, O., Raad, A., Wickerson, J.: View-based owicki-gries reasoning for persistent x86-tso. In: Sergey, I. (ed.) ESOP. LNCS, vol. 13240, pp. 234–261. Springer (2022). https://doi.org/10.1007/978-3-030-99336-8_9
3. Dalvandi, S., Doherty, S., Dongol, B., Wehrheim, H.: Owicki-Gries reasoning for C11 RAR. In: Hirschfeld, R., Pape, T. (eds.) ECOOP. LIPIcs, vol. 166, pp. 11:1–11:26. Dagstuhl (2020). https://doi.org/10.4230/LIPIcs.ECOOP.2020.11
4. Dalvandi, S., Dongol, B.: Implementing and verifying release-acquire transactional memory in C11. Proc. ACM Program. Lang. 6(OOPSLA2), 1817–1844 (2022). https://doi.org/10.1145/3563352
5. Dalvandi, S., Dongol, B., Doherty, S., Wehrheim, H.: Integrating Owicki-Gries for C11-style memory models into Isabelle/HOL. J. Autom. Reason. 66(1), 141–171 (2022). https://doi.org/10.1007/s10817-021-09610-2
6. Dechev, D.: The ABA problem in multicore data structures with collaborating operations. In: CollaborateCom, pp. 158–167 (2011). https://doi.org/10.4108/icst.collaboratecom.2011.247161
7. Dechev, D., Pirkelbauer, P., Stroustrup, B.: Understanding and effectively preventing the ABA problem in descriptor-based lock-free designs. In: ISORC, pp. 185–192 (2010). https://doi.org/10.1109/ISORC.2010.10
8. Fraser, K.: Practical lock-freedom. University of Cambridge, Computer Laboratory, Tech. rep. (2004)
9. Gotsman, A., Rinetzky, N., Yang, H.: Verifying concurrent memory reclamation algorithms with grace. In: Felleisen, M., Gardner, P. (eds.) ESOP. LNCS, vol. 7792, pp. 249–269. Springer (2013). https://doi.org/10.1007/978-3-642-37036-6_15
10. Hart, T.E., McKenney, P.E., Brown, A.D., Walpole, J.: Performance of memory reclamation for lockless synchronization. J. Parallel Distributed Comput. 67(12), 1270–1285 (2007). https://doi.org/10.1016/j.jpdc.2007.04.010
11. Herlihy, M., Luchangco, V., Martin, P., Moir, M.: Nonblocking memory management support for dynamic-sized data structures. ACM Trans. Comput. Syst. 23(2), 146–196 (2005). https://doi.org/10.1145/1062247.1062249
12. Herlihy, M., Shavit, N., Luchangco, V., Spear, M.: The art of multiprocessor programming. Newnes (2020)
13. Kang, J., Hur, C., Lahav, O., Vafeiadis, V., Dreyer, D.: A promising semantics for relaxed-memory concurrency. In: Castagna, G., Gordon, A.D. (eds.) POPL, pp. 175–189. ACM (2017). https://doi.org/10.1145/3009837.3009850
14. Lahav, O., Giannarakis, N., Vafeiadis, V.: Taming release-acquire consistency. ACM SIGPLAN Notices 51(1), 649–662 (2016)
15. Lahav, O., Vafeiadis, V., Kang, J., Hur, C., Dreyer, D.: Repairing sequential consistency in C/C++11. In: Cohen, A., Vechev, M.T. (eds.) PLDI, pp. 618–632. ACM (2017). https://doi.org/10.1145/3062341.3062352
16. Lowe, G.: Analysing lock-free linearizable datatypes using CSP. In: Gibson-Robinson, T., Hopcroft, P.J., Lazic, R. (eds.) Concurrency, Security, and Puzzles - Essays Dedicated to Andrew William Roscoe on the Occasion of His 60th Birthday. LNCS, vol. 10160, pp. 162–184. Springer (2017). https://doi.org/10.1007/978-3-319-51046-0_9

17. McKenney, P.E.: Exploiting deferred destruction: an analysis of read-copy-update techniques in operating system kernels. Oregon Health & Science University (2004)
18. Memarian, K., et al.: Exploring C semantics and pointer provenance. Proc. ACM Program. Lang. **3**(POPL), 67:1–67:32 (2019). https://doi.org/10.1145/3290380
19. Michael, M.M.: Safe memory reclamation for dynamic lock-free objects using atomic reads and writes. In: Ricciardi, A. (ed.) PODC, pp. 21–30. ACM (2002). https://doi.org/10.1145/571825.571829
20. Michael, M.M., Scott, M.L.: Simple, fast, and practical non-blocking and blocking concurrent queue algorithms. In: Burns, J.E., Moses, Y. (eds.) Proceedings of the Fifteenth Annual ACM Symposium on Principles of Distributed Computing, Philadelphia, Pennsylvania, USA, 23–26 May 1996, pp. 267–275. ACM (1996). https://doi.org/10.1145/248052.248106, https://doi.org/10.1145/248052.248106
21. Michael, M.: Hazard pointers: safe memory reclamation for lock-free objects. IEEE Trans. Parallel Distrib. Syst. **15**(6), 491–504 (2004). https://doi.org/10.1109/TPDS.2004.8
22. Parkinson, M.J., Bornat, R., O'Hearn, P.W.: Modular verification of a non-blocking stack. In: Hofmann, M., Felleisen, M. (eds.) POPL, pp. 297–302. ACM (2007). https://doi.org/10.1145/1190216.1190261
23. Paviotti, M., Cooksey, S., Paradis, A., Wright, D., Owens, S., Batty, M.: Modular relaxed dependencies in weak memory concurrency. In: Müller, P. (ed.) ESOP. LNCS, vol. 12075, pp. 599–625. Springer (2020). https://doi.org/10.1007/978-3-030-44914-8_22
24. Semenyuk, M., Dongol, B.: Isabelle/HOL files for Verifying Read-Copy Update under RC11 (2022). https://doi.org/10.5281/zenodo.8099415
25. Semenyuk, M., Dongol, B.: Ownership-based Owicki-Gries reasoning. In: Proceedings of the 38th ACM/SIGAPP Symposium on Applied Computing, pp. 1685–1694 (2023)
26. Svendsen, K., Pichon-Pharabod, J., Doko, M., Lahav, O., Vafeiadis, V.: A separation logic for a promising semantics. In: Ahmed, A. (ed.) ESOP. LNCS, vol. 10801, pp. 357–384. Springer (2018). https://doi.org/10.1007/978-3-319-89884-1_13
27. Tassarotti, J., Dreyer, D., Vafeiadis, V.: Verifying read-copy-update in a logic for weak memory. SIGPLAN Not. **50**(6), 110–120 (2015). https://doi.org/10.1145/2813885.2737992
28. Tofan, B., Schellhorn, G., Reif, W.: Formal verification of a lock-free stack with hazard pointers. In: Cerone, A., Pihlajasaari, P. (eds.) ICTAC. LNCS, vol. 6916, pp. 239–255. Springer (2011). https://doi.org/10.1007/978-3-642-23283-1_16
29. Treiber, R.K.: Systems programming: Coping with parallelism. Thomas J. Watson Research, International Business Machines Incorporated (1986)
30. Turon, A., Vafeiadis, V., Dreyer, D.: GPS: navigating weak memory with ghosts, protocols, and separation. In: Black, A.P., Millstein, T.D. (eds.) OOPSLA, pp. 691–707. ACM (2014). https://doi.org/10.1145/2660193.2660243
31. Wright, D., Batty, M., Dongol, B.: Owicki-Gries reasoning for C11 programs with relaxed dependencies. In: Huisman, M., Pasareanu, C.S., Zhan, N. (eds.) FM. LNCS, vol. 13047, pp. 237–254. Springer (2021). https://doi.org/10.1007/978-3-030-90870-6_13
32. Wright, D., Dalvandi, S., Batty, M., Dongol, B.: Mechanised operational reasoning for C11 programs with relaxed dependencies. Formal Aspects Comput. **35**(2), 10:1–10:27 (2023). https://doi.org/10.1145/3580285
33. Wright, D., Dalvandi, S., Batty, M., Dongol, B.: Mechanised operational reasoning for C11 programs with relaxed dependencies. Form. Asp. Comput. (2023). https://doi.org/10.1145/3580285, just Accepted

QNNREPAIR: Quantized Neural Network Repair

Xidan Song[1] (iD), Youcheng Sun[1](✉)(iD), Mustafa A. Mustafa[1,2](✉)(iD),
and Lucas C. Cordeiro[1,3](✉)(iD)

[1] Department of Computer Science, The University of Manchester, Manchester, UK
{xidan.song,youcheng.sun,mustafa.mustafa,lucas.cordeiro}@manchester.ac.uk
[2] COSIC, KU Leuven, Leuven, Belgium
[3] Federal University of Amazonas, Manaus, Brazil

Abstract. We present QNNRepair, the first method in the literature
for repairing quantized neural networks (QNNs). QNNRepair aims to
improve the accuracy of a neural network model after quantization. It
accepts the full-precision and weight-quantized neural networks, together
with a repair dataset of passing and failing tests. At first, QNNRepair applies a software fault localization method to identify the neurons that cause performance degradation during neural network quantization. Then, it formulates the repair problem into a MILP, solving
neuron weight parameters, which corrects the QNN's performance on
failing tests while not compromising its performance on passing tests.
We evaluate QNNRepair with widely used neural network architectures
such as MobileNetV2, ResNet, and VGGNet on popular datasets, including high-resolution images. We also compare QNNRepair with the state-
of-the-art data-free quantization method SQuant [22]. According to the
experiment results, we conclude that QNNRepair is effective in improving the quantized model's performance in most cases. Its repaired models
have 24% higher accuracy than SQuant's in the independent validation
set, especially for the ImageNet dataset.

Keywords: neural network repair · quantization · fault localization ·
constraints solving

1 Introduction

Nowadays, neural networks are often used in safety-critical applications, such
as autonomous driving, medical diagnosis, and aerospace systems [61]. In such
applications, often quantized (instead of full precision) neural network models are
deployed due to the limited computational and memory resources of embedded
devices [23]. Since the consequences of a malfunction/error in such applications
can be catastrophic, it is crucial to ensure that the network behaves correctly
and reliably [47].

Quantized neural networks [23] use low-precision data types, such as 8-bit
integers, to represent the weights and activations of the network. While this

reduces the memory and computation requirements of the network, it can also lead to a loss of accuracy and the introduction of errors in the network's output. Therefore, it is important to verify that the quantization process has not introduced any significant errors that could affect the safety or reliability of the network.

To limit the inaccuracy in a specific range, various neural network model verification methods [14,25,30,31,56] have been proposed. Neural network verification [26,44,48] aims to provide formal guarantees about the behavior of a neural network, ensuring that it meets specific safety and performance requirements under all possible input conditions. They set constraints and properties of the network input and output to check whether the model satisfies the safety properties. However, neural network verification can be computationally expensive, especially for large, deep networks with millions of parameters. This can make it challenging to scale the verification process to more complex models. While the majority of the neural network verification work is on full precision models, many verification techniques focus on quantized models as well [4,19,25,60].

Other researchers improve the performance and robustness of the trained neural network models by repair [6,20,50,54,59]. These methods can be divided into three categories: retraining/refining, direct weight modification, and attaching repairing units. There are also quantized aware training (QAT) techniques [8,21,34], a method to train neural networks with lower precision weights and activations, typically INT8 format. QAT emulates the effects of quantization during the training process. QAT requires additional steps, such as quantization-aware back-propagation and quantization-aware weight initialization, making the training process more complex and time-consuming. Quantized-aware training methods require datasets for retraining, which consume a lot of time and storage. However, for Data-free quantization like SQuant [22], which does not require datasets, the accuracy after quantization is relatively low.

In QNNREPAIR, we use the well-established software fault localization methods to identify suspicious neurons in a quantized model corresponding to the performance degradation after quantization. We then correct these most suspicious neurons' behavior by MILP, in which the constraints are encoded by observing the difference between the quantized model and the original model when inputs are the same. The main contributions of this paper are three-fold:

- We propose, implement and evaluate QNNREPAIR – a new method for repairing QNNs. It converts quantized neural network repair into a MILP (Mixed Integer Linear Programming) problem. QNNREPAIR features direct weight modification and does not require the training dataset.
- We compare QNNREPAIR with a state-of-the-art QNN repair method – Squant [22], and demonstrate that QNNREPAIR can achieve higher accuracy than Squant after repair. We also evaluate QNNREPAIR on multiple widely used neural network architectures to demonstrate its effectiveness.
- We have made QNNREPAIR and its benchmark publicly available at: https://github.com/HymnOfLight/QNNRepair

2   Related Work

2.1   Neural Network Verification

The first applicable methods supporting the non-linear activation function for neural network verification can be traced back to 2017, R. Ehlers et al. [14] proposed the first practicable neural network verification method based on SAT solver (solve the Boolean satisfiability problem) [13]. They present an approach to verify neural networks with piece-wise linear activation functions. Guy Katz et al. [31] presented Marabou, an SMT(Satisfiability modulo theories) [11]-based tool that can answer queries about a network's properties by transforming these queries into constraint satisfaction problems. However, implementing SMT-based neural network verification tools is limited due to the search space and the scale of a large neural network model, which usually contains millions of parameters [18]. The SMT-based neural network verification has also been proved as an NP-complete problem [30]. Shiqi Wang et al. develop β-CROWN [56], a new bound propagation-based method that can fully encode neuron splits via optimizable parameters β constructed from either primal or dual space. Their algorithm is empowered by the α,β-CROWN (alpha-beta-CROWN) verifier, the winning tool in VNN-COMP 2021 [5]. There are also some quantized neural network verification methods. TA Henzinger et al. [25] proposed a scalable quantized neural network verification method based on abstract interpretation. However, due to the search-space explosion, it has been proved that SMT-based quantized neural network verification is a PSPACE-hard problem [25].

2.2   Neural Network Repair

Many researchers have proposed their full-precision neural network repairing techniques. These can be divided into three categories: Retraining, direct weight modification, and attaching repairing units.

In the first category of repair methods, the idea is to retrain or fine-tune the model for the corrected output with the identified misclassified input. DeepRepair [59] implements transfer-based data augmentation to enlarge the training dataset before fine-tuning the models. The second category uses solvers to get the corrected weights and modify the weight in the trained model directly. These types of methods, including [20] and [54], used SMT solvers for solving the weight modification needed at the output layer for the neural network to meet specific requirements without any retraining. The third category of methods repairs the models by introducing more weight parameters or repair units to facilitate more efficient repair. PRDNN [50] introduces a new DNN architecture that enables efficient and effective repair, while DeepCorrect [6] corrects the worst distortion-affected filter activations by appending correction units. AIRepair [49] aims to integrate multiple existing repair techniques into the same platform. However, these methods only support the full-precision models and cannot apply to quantized models.

2.3 Quantized Aware Training

Some researchers use quantized-aware training to improve the performance of the quantized models. Yuhang Li et al. proposed a post-training quantization framework by analyzing the second-order error called BRECQ(Block Reconstruction Quantization) [34]. Ruihao Gong et al. proposed Differentiable Soft Quantization (DSQ) [21] to bridge the gap between the full-precision and low-bit networks. It can automatically evolve during training to gradually approximate the standard quantization. J Choi et al. [8]proposed a novel quantization scheme PACT(PArameterized Clipping acTivation) for activations during training - that enables neural networks to work well with ultra-low precision weights and activations without any significant accuracy degradation. However, these methods require retraining and the whole dataset, which will consume lots of computing power and time to improve tiny accuracy in actual practices. In addition, there is a method called Data-free quantization, which quantizes the neural network model without any datasets. Cong Guo et al. proposed SQuant [22], which can quantize networks on inference-only devices with low computation and memory requirements.

3 Preliminaries

3.1 Statistical Fault Localization

Statistical fault localization techniques (SFL) [37] have been widely used in software testing to aid in locating the causes of failures of programs. During the execution of each test case, data is collected indicating the executed statements. Additionally, each test case is classified as passed or failed.

This technique uses information about the program's execution traces and associated outcomes (pass/fail) to identify suspicious program statements. It calculates four suspiciousness scores for each statement based on the correlation between its execution and the observed failures. We use the notation $C^{af}, C^{nf}, C^{as}, C^{ns}$. The first part of the superscript indicates whether the statement was executed/"activated" (a) or not (n), and the second indicates whether the test is a passing/successful (s) or failing (f) one. For example, C^{as} is the number of successful tests that execute a statement C. Statements with higher suspiciousness scores are more likely to contain faults. There are many possible metrics that have been proposed in the literature. We use Tarantula [29], Ochiai [2], DStar [57], Jaccard [3], Ample [9], Euclid [17] and Wong3 [58], which are widely used and accepted in the application of Statistical fault localization, in our ranking procedure. We discuss the definition and application in our method of these metrics in Sect. 4.1. In addition, SFL has been also used for analyzing and explaining neural networks [16,51].

3.2 Neural Network and Quantization

A neural network consists of an input layer, an output layer, and one or more intermediate layers called hidden layers. Each layer is a collection of nodes, called neurons. Each neuron is connected to other neurons by one or more directed edges [15].

Let $f : \mathcal{I} \to \mathcal{O}$ be the neural network N with m layers. In this paper, we focus on a neural network for image classification. For a given input $x \in \mathcal{I}$, $f(x) \in \mathcal{O}$ calculates the output of the DNN, which is the classification label of the input image. Specifically, we have

$$f(x) = f_N \left(\ldots f_2 \left(f_1 \left(x; W_1, b_1 \right); W_2, b_2 \right) \ldots ; W_N, b_N \right) \tag{1}$$

In this equation, W_i and b_i for $i = 1, 2, \ldots, N$ represent the weights and bias of the model, which are trainable parameters. $f_i \left(z_{i-1}; W_{i-1}, b_{i-1} \right)$ is the layer function that maps the output of layer $(i - 1)$, i.e., z_{i-1}, to the input layer i.

Quantization. As one of the general neural network model optimization methods, model quantization can reduce the size and model inference time of DNN models and their application to most models and different hardware devices. By reducing the number of bits per weight and activation, the model's storage requirements and computational complexity can be significantly optimized. Jacob et al. [28] report benchmark results on popular ARM CPUs for state-of-the-art MobileNet architectures, as well as other tasks, showing significant improvements in the latency-vs-accuracy tradeoffs. In the following formula, r is the true floating point value, q is the quantized fixed point value, Z is the quantized fixed point value corresponding to the 0 floating point value, and S is the smallest scale that can be represented after quantization of the fixed point. The formula for quantization from floating point to fixed point is as follows:

$$r = S(q - Z)$$
$$q = \text{round} \left(\tfrac{r}{S} + Z \right) \tag{2}$$

Currently, Google's TensorFlow Lite [10] and NVIDIA's TensorRT [55] support the INT8 engine framework.

3.3   Solvers for Mixed Integer Linear Optimization

MILP (Mixed Integer Linear Programming) is an extension of linear programming in which some or all of the decision variables are restricted to integers. In this type of problem, the objective function and all constraints are linear, but due to the presence of integer constraints, the solution space becomes discrete, making the problem more complex and challenging.

All state-of-the-art solvers for MILP employ one of many existing variants of the well-known branch-and-bound algorithm of [33]. This class of algorithm searches a dynamically constructed tree (known as the search tree).

The state-of-the-art MILP solvers include Gurobi [41], which is a commercial solver widely used for linear programming, integer programming, and mixed integer linear programming. According to B. Meindl and M. Templ's [36] Analysis of commercial and free and open source solvers for linear optimization problems, Gurobi is the fastest solver and can solve the largest number of problems.

Another reason for choosing Gurobi was primarily in the area of neural network robustness, and other approaches, such as alpha-beta-crown in the area of neural network verification, use Gurobi as their backend. Hence we use Gurobi as the backend to solve the neural network repairing problem.

Other MILP solver include: CPLEX [39], GLPK (GNU Linear Programming Kit) [35]. Python external library Scipy [7] also provides some functions for MILP.

4   QNNRepair Methodology

The overall workflow of QNNRepair is illustrated in Fig. 1. It takes two neural networks, a floating-point model and its quantized version for repair, as inputs. There is also a repair dataset of successful (passing) and failing tests, signifying whether the two models would produce the same classification outcome when given the same test input.

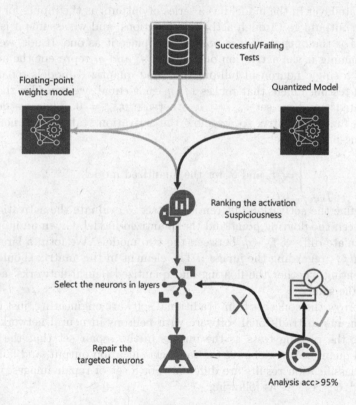

Fig. 1. The QNNRepair Architecture.

The passing/failing tests are used by QNNRepair to evaluate each neuron's importance and localize these neurons to repair for improving the quantized model's performance (Sect. 4.1). The test cases can be generated by by dataset augmentation [45] or various neural network testing methods [40,42,52,53]. In QNNREPAIR, the neural network repair problem is encoded into a Mixed Integer Linear Programming problem for solving the corrected neuron weights (Sect. 4.2). It then replaces the weights with corrected weights, which QNNRE-PAIR evaluates the performance of the quantized model by testing its classification accuracy. If the quantized model's performance is good enough w.r.t. the floating point one after repair, the model is ready for deployment. Otherwise, QNNREPAIR continues by selecting other parameters to repair. More detailed information is presented in Algorithm 1 (Sect. 4.3).

4.1   Ranking the Importance of the Neurons

QNNREPAIR starts with evaluating the importance of the neurons in the neural network for causing the output difference between the quantized model and the floating point one. When conducting an inference·procedure on an image, the intermediate layer in the model has a series of outputs as the inputs for the next layer. The outputs go through activation functions, and we assume it is a ReLU function. For the output, if it is positive, we place it as one. If not, we place it as zero, naming it the activation output. Let f_i and q_i represent the activation output of a single neuron in full-precision and quantized models separately. If there is a testing image that makes (f_i, q_i) not equal, we consider the neuron as "activated", and we set $v_{mn} = 1$, otherwise $v_{mn} = 0$. Then we define the activation function matrix to assemble the activation status of all neurons for the floating-point model:

$$\begin{pmatrix} f_{11} & \cdots & f_{1n} \\ \vdots & \ddots & \vdots \\ f_{m1} & \cdots & f_{mn} \end{pmatrix} = f_i \text{ and } q_i \text{ for the quantized model.}$$

We define the activation differential matrix to evaluate the activation difference between the floating point and the quantized model. Given an input image i, we calculate $\text{diff}_i = f_i - q_i$ between the two models. We form a large matrix of these $diff_i$ regarding the image i. The element in this matrix should be 0 or 1, representing whether the floating and quantized neural networks' activation status is the same.

We borrow the concepts from traditional software engineering, just replacing the statements in traditional software with neurons in neural network models. We define the passing tests as the images in the repair set that the floating-point and quantized model have the same classification output, and failing tests as their classification results are different. For a set of repair images, we define $< C_n^{\text{af}}, C_n^{\text{nf}}, C_n^{\text{as}}, C_n^{\text{ns}} >$ as following:

- C_n^{af} is the number of "activated" neurons for failing tests.
- C_n^{nf} is the number of "not activated" neurons for failing tests.
- C_n^{as} is the number of "activated" neurons for passing tests.
- C_n^{ns} is the number of "not activated" neurons for passing tests.

We borrow the concepts from traditional software fault localization: Tarantula [29], Ochiai [2], DStar [57], Jaccard [3], Ample [9], Euclid [17] and Wong3 [58] and defined the indicators of neuronal suspicion in Table 1. Note that in DStar, * represents the n square of C_n^{af}.

Table 1. Importance (i.e., fault localization) metrics used in experiments

Tarantula: $\dfrac{C_n^{af}/(C_n^{af}+C_n^{nf})}{C_n^{af}/(C_n^{af}+C_n^{nf})+C_n^{as}/(C_n^{as}+C_n^{ns})}$ Euclid: $\sqrt{C_n^{af}+C_n^{ns}}$

Ochiai: $\dfrac{C_n^{af}}{\sqrt{(C_n^{af}+C_n^{as})(C_n^{af}+C_n^{nf})}}$ DStar: $\dfrac{C_n^{af^*}}{C_n^{as}+C_n^{nf}}$

Ample: $\left|\dfrac{C_n^{af}}{C_n^{af}+C_n^{nf}}-\dfrac{C_n^{as}}{C_n^{as}+C_n^{ns}}\right|$ Jaccard: $\dfrac{C_n^{af}}{C_n^{af}+C_n^{nf}+C_n^{as}}$

Wong3: $C_n^{af}-h$ $h=\begin{cases} C_n^{as} & \text{if } C_n^{as}\leq 2 \\ 2+0.1(C_n^{as}-2) & \text{if } 2<C_n^{as}\leq 10 \\ 2.8+0.01(C_n^{as}-10) & \text{if } C_n^{as}>10 \end{cases}$

We then rank the quantitative metrics of these neurons from largest to smallest based on certain weights, with higher metrics indicating more suspicious neurons and the ones we needed to target for repair.

4.2 Constraints-Solving Based Repairing

After the neuron importance evaluation, for each layer, we obtain a vector of neuron importance. We rank this importance vector. The neuron with the highest importance is our target for repair as it could have the greatest impact on the corrected error outcome.

The optimization problem for a single neuron can be described as follows:

Minimize: M
Subject to:
$M \geq 0$
$\delta_i \in [-M, M] \quad \forall i \in \{1, 2, \ldots, n\}$

If floating model gives the result 1 and quantized model gives 0:

$\forall x_i \text{ in TestSet } X : \sum_{i=1}^{m} w_i x_i < 0 \text{ and } \sum_{i=1}^{m}(w_i+\delta_i)x_i > 0$

If floating model gives the result 0 and quantized model gives 1:

$\forall x_i \text{ in TestSet } X : \sum_{i=1}^{m} w_i x_i > 0 \text{ and } \sum_{i=1}^{m}(w_i+\delta_i)x_i < 0$

$$(3)$$

In the formula, m represents the number of neurons connected to the previous layer of the selected neuron, and we number them from 1 to m. We add incremental δ to the weights to indicate the weights that need to be modified all the way to m. M is used to make $\delta_1...\delta_i$ are sufficiently small. The value $\delta_1...\delta_i$ are encoded as the non-deterministic variables, and our task is to use Gurobi to solve these non-deterministic based on the given constraints.

We assume that in the full-precision neural network, this neuron's activation function gives the result 1, and the quantized gives 0. The corrected neuron in the quantized model result needs to be greater than 0 for the output of the activation function to be 1. If in the full-precision neural network, this neuron's activation function gives the result 0, and the quantized gives 1. The corrected neuron in the quantized model result needs to be smaller than 0 for the output of the activation function to be 0. In this case, we make the distance of the repaired quantized neural network as close as possible to that of the original quantized neural network.

The inputs to our algorithm are a quantized neural network Q that needs to be repaired, a set of data sets X for testing, and the full-precision neuron network model F to be repaired. We use Gurobi [41] as the constraint solver to solve the constraint and then replace the original weights with the result obtained as the new weights.

4.3 QNNRepair Algorithm

Our repair method is formulated in Algorithm 1. The input to our algorithm is the full-precision model F, the quantized model Q. The repair set X, the validation set V, and the number of neurons that need to be repaired N (Line 1). Firstly, we initialize arrays to store the activation states of the floating and quantized model, the values of the neuron importance, and four arrays $C^{as}[]$, $C^{af}[]$, $C^{ns}[]$ and $C^{nf}[]$ mentioned in Sect. 4.1 (Line 1). For these six arrays, we set all elements to 0.

Next, in lines 3–4, for each input in the test set $x \in \mathcal{X}_n$, we perform the inference process once obtain the neurons' activation states in the corresponding model layers and store them in the activation states of the floating and quantized model. In line 5, if $x[i]$ is a failing test, then we add the difference of activation status between the float model and quantized model to $C^{as}[i]$, and vice versa. In line 11 and 12, we calculate $C^{ns}[]$ and $C^{nf}[]$ according to the definition in Sect. 4.1. We calculate the importance (here we use DStar as an example) for each neuron regarding seven importance metrics and sort them in descending order then store them in set $I_n[]$ in line 14.

Then, we pick the neuron in $I_n[]$, according to the neuron's weights and the corresponding inputs from the previous layer, we create and solve the LP problem we discussed in Sect. 4.2, get the correction of each neuron, and update their weights. When it arrives at the maximum number of neurons to repair, the loop breaks and we have corrected all the neurons. These are implemented at lines 17-24 in Algorithm 1.

Algorithm 1: Repair algorithm

Input: Floating-point model F, Quantized model Q, Repair set X, Validation set V, Number of neurons to be repaired N

Output: Repaired model Q', Repaired model's accuracy Acc

1 Initialize $F_a[][], Q_a[][], I_n[], C^{as}[], C^{af}[], C^{ns}[], C^{nf}[]$
2 **foreach** X **do**
3      $F_a[][i] = \text{getActStatus}(F, x_i)$
4      $Q_a[][i] = \text{getActStatus}(Q, x_i)$
5   **if** $x[i]$ *is a failing test* **then**
6          $\mid \quad C^{af}[i] = C^{af}[i] + |F_a[][i] - Q_a[][i]|$
7   **else**
8          $\mid \quad C^{as}[i] = C^{as}[i] + |F_a[][i] - Q_a[][i]|$
9   **end**
10 **end**
11 $C^{nf}[] = C^{nf}[] - C^{af}[]$
12 $C^{ns}[] = C^{ns}[] - C^{as}[]$
13 $I_n[] = \text{DStar}(C_n^{as}[], C_n^{as}[], C_n^{as}[], C_n^{as}[])$
14 $I_n[] = \text{sort}(I_n[])$ // In descending order
15 Initialize weight of neurons $w[][]$ and the increment $\delta[][]$
16 **foreach** $neuron[i] \in I_n[]$ **do**
17   **foreach** $edge[j][i] \in neuron[i]$ **do**
18          $\mid \quad w[j][i] = \text{getWeight}(edge[j][i])$
19   **end**
20      $\delta[][i] = \text{solve}(X, w[][i])$ // Solve LP problem 3
21   **foreach** $edge[j][i] \in neuron[i]$ **do**
22          $\mid \quad edge[j][i] = \text{setWeight}(w[j][i] + \delta[j][i])$
23          $\mid \quad Q' = \text{update}(Q, edge[j][i])$
24   **end**
25   **if** $i >= N$ **then**
26          $\mid$ break
27   **end**
28 **end**
29 $Acc = \text{calculateAcc}(Q', V)$
30 **return** Q'

Finally, we evaluate the classification accuracy of the corrected quantized model. If it satisfies our requirements, then the model is repaired. Otherwise, try other combinations of parameters like important metrics or the maximum number of neurons needed to repair and repeat the LP solving and correction process. The output for this algorithm is the repaired model with updated weight.

5 Experiment

5.1 Experimental Setup

We conduct experiments on a machine with Ubuntu 18.04.6 LTS OS Intel(R) Xeon(R) Gold 5217 CPU @ 3.00GHz and two Nvidia Quadro RTX 6000 GPUs. The experiments are run with TensorFlow2 + nVidia CUDA platform. We use the Gurobi [41] as the linear program solver and enable multi-thread solving (up to 16 cores). We apply QNNREPAIR to repair a benchmark of five quantized neural network models, including MobileNetV2 [43] on ImageNet datasets [12], and ResNet-18 [24], VGGNet [46] and two simple convolutional models trained on CIFAR-10 dataset [32]. The details of these models are given in Table 2.

Table 2. The baseline models. Parameters include the trainable and non-trainable parameters in the models; the unit is million (M). The two accuracy values are for the original floating point model and its quantized version, respectively.

Model	Dataset	#Layers	#Params	Accuracy	
				floating point	quantized
Conv3	CIFAR-10	6	1.0M	66.48%	66.20%
Conv5	CIFAR-10	12	2.6M	72.90%	72.64%
VGGNet	CIFAR-10	45	9.0M	78.67%	78.57%
ResNet-18	CIFAR-10	69	11.2M	79.32%	79.16%
MobileNetV2	ImageNet	156	3.5M	71.80%	65.86%

We obtained the full-precision MobileNetV2 directly from the Keras library, whereas we trained the VGGNet and ResNet-18 models on the CIFAR-10 dataset. We also defined and trained two smaller convolutional neural networks on CIFAR-10 for comparison: Conv3, which contains three convolutional layers, and Conv5, which contains five convolutional layers. Both models have two dense layers at the end. The quantized models are generated by using TensorFlow Lite (TFlite) [1] from the floating point models. In TFLite, we chose dynamic range quantization, and the weights are quantized as 8-bit integers. The quantized convolution operation is optimized for performance, and the calculations are done in the fixed-point arithmetic domain to avoid the overhead of de-quantizing and re-quantizing tensors.

For repairs of the quantized model's performance, we use a subset of ImageNet called ImageNet-mini [27], which contains 38,668 images in 1,000 classes. The dataset is divided into the repair set and the validation set. The repair set contains 34,745 images, and the validation set contains 3,923 images. The CIFAR-10 dataset contains 60,000 images in 10 classes in total. 50,000 of them are training image, and 10,000 of them are test set. We use 1,000 images as the repair set. We use the repair set to identify suspicious neurons, generate LP constraints, apply corrections to the identified neurons, and use the validation set to evaluate the accuracy of the models. We repeat the same experiment ten times for random neuron selection and get the average to eliminate randomness in repair methods.

5.2   Repair Results on Baselines

In this part, we apply QNNREPAIR to these baseline quantized models, except for MobilenetV2, in Table 2. In our experiments, MobileNetV2 is trained on ImageNet while other models are trained on CIFAR-10, and it contains more layers. The results for MobileNetV2 are reported in Sect. 5.5. For each model, we perform a layer-by-layer repair of its last dense layers. We name these dense layers dense-3 (the third last layer), dense-2 (the second last layer), and dense-1 (the output layer).

Table 3. QNNREPAIR results on CIFAR-10 models. The best repair outcome for each model, w.r.t. the dense layer in that row, is in **bold**. We further highlight the best result in $\boxed{blue}$ if the repair result is even better than the floating point model and in red if the repair result is worse than the original quantized model. Random means that we randomly select neurons at the corresponding dense layer for the repair, whereas Fault Localization refers to the selection of neurons based on important metrics in QNNREPAIR. In All cases, all neurons in that layer are used for repair. 'n/a' happens when the number of neurons in the repair is less than 100, and '-' is for repairing the last dense layer of 10 neurons, and the result is the same as the All case.

| | Random | | | | Fault Localization | | | | - |
#Neurons repaired	1	5	10	100	1	5	10	100	All
Conv3_dense-2	63.43%	64.74%	38.90%	n/a	66.26%	**66.36%**	62.35%	n/a	57.00%
Conv3_dense-1	65.23%	66.31%	-	n/a	66.10%	66.39%	-	n/a	**66.46%**
Conv5_dense-2	72.49%	72.55%	72.52%	72.52%	72.56%	72.56%	72.56%	72.56%	72.54%
Conv5_dense-1	72.51%	72.52%	-	n/a	72.58%	72.56%	-	n/a	72.56%
VGGNet_dense-3	78.13%	78.44%	78.20%	78.38%	$\boxed{\textbf{78.83\%}}$	78.82%	78.78%	78.66%	78.60%
VGGNet_dense-2	78.36%	78.59%	78.44%	78.22%	78.55%	$\boxed{\textbf{78.83\%}}$	78.83%	78.83%	78.83%
VGGNet_dense-1	78.94%	67.75%	-	n/a	$\boxed{\textbf{79.29\%}}$	69.04%	-	n/a	74.49%
ResNet_dense_1	78.90%	78.92%	-	n/a	79.08%	**79.20%**	-	n/a	78.17%

The QNNREPAIR results are reported in Table 3. We ranked the neurons using important metrics and chose the best results among the seven metrics. We also run randomly picked repairing as a comparison. We have chosen Top-1, Top-5, Top-10, Top-100, and all neurons as the repairing targets. For most models, the repair improves the accuracy of the quantized network, and in some cases, even higher than the accuracy of the floating-point model.

The dense-2 layer only contains 64 neurons in the Conv3 model. Hence we selected 30 neurons as the repair targets. In the dense-1 layer of Conv3, the effect of repairing individual neurons is not ideal, but as the number of repaired neurons gradually increases, the more correct information the Conv3 quantization model obtains from the floating-point model, so the accuracy gradually improves until it reaches 66.46% (which does not exceed the accuracy of the floating-point Conv3 neural network, but it gets very close to it: 66.48%, see Table 2). This is because all the repair information in the last layer comes from the original floating-point neural network. Note that because of the simple structure of the Conv3 neural network, the floating-point version of Conv3 itself is inaccurate, and the quantized and repaired neural network does not exceed the accuracy. In the dense-2 layer of Conv5, applying importance metrics to repair this layer is slightly better than random selection, only 0.01% regarding randomly selecting 5 neurons compared with using fault localization to select Top-5 neurons. Compared to the quantized model before repair, whose accuracy is 72.64%, the repairing only gets an accuracy of 72.56%, which does not improve the model's accuracy. In the dense-1 layer of Conv5, the best result is using fault localization to pick the Top-1 neuron and repair at 72.58% accuracy, and this is not better than the quantized model before repair.

For VGGNet and ResNet-18 neural networks, the dense-1 layer is a good comparison. Both VGGNet and ResNet-18 have relatively complex network structures, and the accuracy of the original floating-point model is close to 80%. In the dense-1 layer of ResNet-18, only some of the neurons were repaired with accuracy close to their original quantized version, but all of them did not exceed the exact value of the floating-point neural network after the repair. However, unlike ResNet-18, correcting a single neuron randomly in the dense-1 layer of VGGNet make it more accurate than the quantized version of VGGNet. Using the importance metric and correcting a single neuron make the accuracy even higher than the floating-point version of VGGNet. However, repairing dense-1 of VGGNet was unsatisfactory, especially when 5 neurons are selected for repair; it suffered a significant loss of accuracy, even below 70%, which was regained if all ten neurons in the last layer were repaired. In the dense-2 layer of VGGNet, the overall accuracy is higher than 78%. When the importance metric is applied, the accuracy reaches 78.83%, noting that this accuracy is also achieved if all neurons in this layer are repaired. For the dense-3 layer of VGGNet, repairing 5 or 10 neurons using importance metrics will achieve the highest accuracy at 78.83%, the same as repairing the dense-2 layer.

Table 4. QNNREPAIR results on ImageNet model.

#Neurons repaired	Random		Fault Localization		–
	10	100	10	100	All
MobileNetV2_dense-1	70.75%	70.46%	**70.77%**	70.00%	68.98%

ImageNet. We also conducted repair on the last layer for MobileNetV2 trained on the ImageNet dataset of high-resolution images. Using Euclid as the importance metric and picking 10 neurons as the correct targets achieve the best results, at 70.77%, improving the accuracy the quantized model.

5.3 Comparison with Data-Free Quantization

We tested SQuant [22], a fast and accurate data-free quantization framework for convolutional neural networks, employing the constrained absolute sum of error (CASE) of weights as the rounding metric. We tested SQuant two quantized models, the same as our approach: MobileNetV2 trained on ImageNet and ResNet-18 on CIFAR-10. We made some modifications to the original code to support MobileNetV2, which is not reported in their experiments.

In contrast, to complete data-free quantization, our constraint solver-based quantization does not require a complete dataset but only some input images for repair. Despite taking much more time than SQuant because it uses Gurobi and a constrained solution approach, MobileNetV2 – a complex model trained on ImageNet – QNNREPAIR achieves much higher accuracy.

Table 5. QNNREPAIR vs SQuant

	MobileNetV2		ResNet-18	
	Accuracy	Time	Accuracy	Time
SQuant [22]	46.09%	1635.37 ms	70.70%	708.16 ms
QNNREPAIR	**70.77%**	~15 h	**79.20%**	~9 h

5.4 Repair Efficiency

The constraints-solving part contributes to the major computation cost in QNNREPAIR. For other operations, such as importance evaluation, modification of weights, model formatting, etc., it takes only a few minutes to complete. Thereby, Table 6 measures the runtime cost when using the Gurobi to solve the values of the new weights for a neuron for our experiments on the VGGNet model. It is shown in Table 6 that 75% of the solutions were completed within 5 min, and less than 9% of the neurons could not be solved, resulting in a total solution time of 9 h for a layer of 512 neurons.

Table 6. The Gurobi solving time for constraints of each neuron in the dense-2 layer of the VGGNet model. There are 512 neurons in total.

Duration	<=5 mins	5–10 mins	10–30 mins	30 mins-1 h	No solution
Percentage	75%	8.98%	5.27%	1.76%	8.98%

5.5 Comparison Between Fault Localization Metrics in QNNREPAIR

We let the model and the layer stay the same. We use MobileNetV2 and the last layer as our target. We compare seven representative important metrics mentioned in Sect. 5.5. In these experiments, we used 1,000, 500, 100, and 10 jpeg images as the repair sets to assess the performance of different importance assessment methods.

Firstly, we rank the neurons in the last layer using seven different representative important metrics, which are Tarantula [29], Ochiai [2], DStar [57], Jaccard [3], Ample [9], Euclid [17] and Wong3 [58]. As shown in Fig. 2, for the last fully connected layer of MobileNetV2, the important neurons are mainly concentrated at the two ends, those neurons with the first and last numbers. The evaluation metrics results are relatively similar for different neurons.

We selected the 100 neurons (for Conv3, it is 30 neurons) with the highest importance and could be solved by MILP solvers according to different importance measures. The deltas are obtained according to Eq. 3, and we apply the deltas to the quantized model. After that, we use the validation sets from ImageNet, which contains 50,000 jpeg images, to test the MobileNetV2 model. We

Table 7. The results regarding importance metrics, including 7 fault localization metrics and 1 random baseline. The number of images indicates how many inputs are in the repair set.

Model+Repair Layer	#Images	Tarantula	Ochiai	DStar	Jaccard	Ample	Euclid	Wong3	Random
MobileNetV2_dense-1	1000	70.61%	69.76%	69.73%	69.73%	69.72%	**70.70%**	69.73%	69.56%
	500	68.99%	69.01%	69.05%	69.05%	68.99%	**69.46%**	69.06%	69.00%
	100	69.50%	69.42%	69.46%	69.46%	69.53%	69.98%	69.46%	**70.12%**
	10	70.62%	70.15%	70.12%	70.12%	70.17%	**70.73%**	70.12%	70.18%
VGGNet_dense-3	1000	78.64%	78.64%	78.64%	78.64%	78.65%	**78.66%**	**78.66%**	78.22%
VGGNet_dense-2	1000	**78.83%**	**78.83%**	**78.83%**	**78.83%**	**78.83%**	**78.83%**	**78.83%**	78.38%
Conv3_dense	1000	**59.50%**	**59.50%**	**59.50%**	**59.50%**	59.27%	59.27%	59.27%	32.42%

also use the validation sets from CIFAR-10, which contains 10,000 png image files, to test VGGNet and Conv5 after the repair. As a comparison, we also randomly picked 100 neurons to apply to repair and tested their accuracy. We give the results of the top 100 important neurons after selection and repair, as shown in Table 7.

We pick Tarantula and plot the scatter plots based on the importance distribution of the different neurons. We rank the importance of those neurons and draw line plots as illustrated in Fig. 2.

The figures give scatter plots of neuron importance and ranked line plots for the last dense layer of MobileNetV2. The horizontal coordinates of these plots are the serial numbers of the neurons. For the last layer in the MobileNetV2 model, few neurons have the highest importance. More than 300 neurons had an importance measurement of 0, and another large proportion had an importance of 0.5 or less. Based on the ranking of the importance of neurons, all the evaluation metrics except Tarantula and Euclid considered 108, 984, 612, 972 to be the four most important neurons in this layer, and among the 5th-10th most important neurons, 550, 974, 816, 795 and 702, just in a different order. This is reflected in the importance distribution graphs as spikes at the ends and as spikes at the ends of the graphs. Hence Ochiai, Dstar, Jaccard, Ample, and Wong3 have similar performance regarding the accuracy evaluation, and Euclid and Tarantula achieve better accuracy on ImageNet validation sets.

Table 7 shows that the Euclid importance assessment method is highly effective, achieving relatively good results from restoration with 500 images to restoration with ten images and achieving only weaker accuracy than the Tarantula method in a restoration scenario with 1,000 images. A random selection of neurons can achieve good restoration results, especially when we select 100 images as restoration images, it has a validation accuracy higher than 70%. Also, in Table 7, our methods work well with the models containing fewer neurons. In experiments with Conv3_dense, our approach achieves more than 20% higher accuracy than random selection. When it comes to large models, although it is not as obvious as smaller models, but still has higher accuracy than random selection in most cases, even if random selection is better than importance ranking, which is only a little bit better (0.14%). Considering the successful and failing tests used for repair, i.e., the repair images, in our experiments, the repair results of using 10 repair images were slightly better than using 1,000 repair images. For the Euclid method that produces the best repair results, the accuracy of using 10 images is 0.03% higher than using 1,000 repairing images.

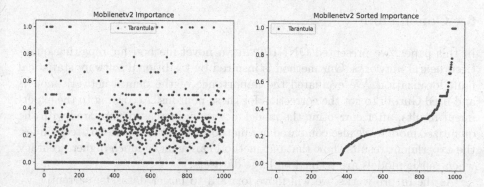

Fig. 2. Importance distribution regarding certain importance metrics on MobileNetV2.

For the VGGNet model, for the same reason as MobileNetV2 regarding the neuron importance ranking, the Tarantula, Ochiai, DStar, Jaccard, Euclid, and Wong3 give the same results when selecting 100 top important neurons to repair. As a comparison, the accuracy of random selection in dense-2 layer and dense-3 has a slight drop, at 78.38% and 78.22%. For Conv3 model, the seven importance metrics give the same results, and randomly selected 30 neurons suffered a great accuracy loss, at 32.42%. But compared to the results in Table 3, repairing 30 top neurons also suffered accuracy drops. For the dense layer of conv3, the best repair is still to select one neuron for repair based on Tarantula sorting at 66.10%, and if random selection is taken into account, then selecting five neurons for repair would give the best result at 64.74%.

We also conducted a side-by-side comparison of the number of images required for the repair on MobileNetV2. It shows that the best results are obtained using 1,000 images for repair and 10 images for the repair, but given the amount of time required to generate constraints for the repair using 1,000 images and to solve the constraints using Gurobi, we recommend using a smaller set of repair images for the model.

Euclid demonstrates that it has the highest accuracy most of the time, and repairing with importance evaluation is more accurate than repairing randomly selected neurons.

5.6   Limitations

According to Nemhauser and Wolsey [38], the MILP problem is NP-Hard. There is no known polynomial time algorithm that can solve all MILP instances. Therefore, for very large or structurally complex problems, the solver may take a very long time to find the optimal solution or an acceptable approximate solution. Hence, selecting more repairing images for correction will have a greater likelihood of Gurobi being unable to solve the MILP problem, reflected in the limitation of improving accuracy.

6 Conclusion

In this paper, we presented QNNREPAIR, a novel method for repairing quantized neural networks. Our method is inspired by traditional software statistical fault localization. We evaluated the importance of the neural network models and used Gurobi to get the correction for these neurons. According to the experiment results, after correcting the model, accuracy increased compared with the quantized model. We also compared our method with state-of-the-art techniques; the experiment results show that our method can achieve much higher accuracy when repair models are trained on large datasets.

As the future works, we will move forward to larger datasets; currently, we support MobileNetV2 trained on ImageNet. In the future, we will test our tool and make it scalable for larger models and not limited to classification tasks like GPT and stable diffusion. For these large networks, due to the complexity of the model itself, repairing them will require a lot of computational resources, and we will find a balance between improving accuracy and computing time.

For some of the repairing problems, Gurobi was not able to solve them in the given time limit, so in the future, we intend to optimize the encoding of the neural network repair problem to increase the speed of the repair solution and to solve some of the repair problems that were not previously solved. We will also try more problem solvers in the future, such as SMT solvers, to solve these problems that Gurobi cannot solve.

Acknowledgements. This work is funded by the EPSRC grants EP/T026995/1, EP/V000497/1, EU H2020 ELEGANT 957286, Soteria project awarded by the UK Research and Innovation for the Digital Security by Design (DSbD) Programme, and Cal-Comp Electronic by the R&D project of the Cal-Comp Institute of Technology and Innovation.

References

1. TensorFlow Lite. https://www.tensorflow.org/lite
2. Abreu, R., Zoeteweij, P., Van Gemund, A.J.: On the accuracy of spectrum-based fault localization. In: Testing: Academic and industrial conference practice and research techniques-MUTATION (TAICPART-MUTATION 2007). IEEE (2007)
3. Agarwal, P., Agrawal, A.P.: Fault-localization techniques for software systems: a literature review. ACM SIGSOFT Softw. Eng. Notes **39**(5), 1–8 (2014)
4. Amir, G., Wu, H., Barrett, C., Katz, G.: An SMT-based approach for verifying binarized neural networks. In: TACAS 2021. LNCS, vol. 12652, pp. 203–222. Springer, Cham (2021). https://doi.org/10.1007/978-3-030-72013-1_11

5. Bak, S., Liu, C., Johnson, T.: The second international verification of neural networks competition (vnn-comp 2021): Summary and results. arXiv preprint arXiv:2109.00498 (2021)
6. Borkar, T.S., Karam, L.J.: Deepcorrect: correcting dnn models against image distortions. IEEE Trans. Image Process. **28**(12), 6022–6034 (2019)
7. Bressert, E.: Scipy and numpy: an overview for developers (2012)
8. Choi, J., Wang, Z., Venkataramani, S., Chuang, P.I.J., Srinivasan, V., Gopalakrishnan, K.: Pact: parameterized clipping activation for quantized neural networks. arXiv preprint arXiv:1805.06085 (2018)
9. Dallmeier, V., Lindig, C., Zeller, A.: Lightweight bug localization with ample. In: Proceedings of the Sixth International Symposium on Automated Analysis-Driven Debugging, pp. 99–104 (2005)
10. David, R., Duke, et al.: Tensorflow lite micro: Embedded machine learning for tinyml systems. Proc. Mach. Learn. Syst. (2021)
11. de Moura, L., Bjørner, N.: Z3: an efficient SMT solver. In: Ramakrishnan, C.R., Rehof, J. (eds.) TACAS 2008. LNCS, vol. 4963, pp. 337–340. Springer, Heidelberg (2008). https://doi.org/10.1007/978-3-540-78800-3_24
12. Deng, J., Dong, W., Socher, R., Li, L.J., Li, K., Fei-Fei, L.: Imagenet: a large-scale hierarchical image database. In: 2009 IEEE Conference on computer vision and Pattern Recognition, pp. 248–255. IEEE (2009)
13. Eén, N., Sörensson, N.: An extensible SAT-solver. In: Giunchiglia, E., Tacchella, A. (eds.) SAT 2003. LNCS, vol. 2919, pp. 502–518. Springer, Heidelberg (2004). https://doi.org/10.1007/978-3-540-24605-3_37
14. Ehlers, R.: Formal verification of piece-wise linear feed-forward neural networks. In: D'Souza, D., Narayan Kumar, K. (eds.) ATVA 2017. LNCS, vol. 10482, pp. 269–286. Springer, Cham (2017). https://doi.org/10.1007/978-3-319-68167-2_19
15. Elboher, Y.Y., Gottschlich, J., Katz, G.: An abstraction-based framework for neural network verification. In: Lahiri, S.K., Wang, C. (eds.) CAV 2020. LNCS, vol. 12224, pp. 43–65. Springer, Cham (2020). https://doi.org/10.1007/978-3-030-53288-8_3
16. Eniser, H.F., Gerasimou, S., Sen, A.: DeepFault: fault localization for deep neural networks. In: Hähnle, R., van der Aalst, W. (eds.) FASE 2019. LNCS, vol. 11424, pp. 171–191. Springer, Cham (2019). https://doi.org/10.1007/978-3-030-16722-6_10
17. Galijasevic, Z., Abur, A.: Fault location using voltage measurements. IEEE Trans. Power Delivery **17**(2), 441–445 (2002)
18. Gehr, T., Mirman, M., Drachsler-Cohen, D., Others: Ai2: safety and robustness certification of neural networks with abstract interpretation. In: 2018 IEEE Symposium on Security and Privacy (SP), pp. 3–18. IEEE (2018)
19. Giacobbe, M., Henzinger, T.A., Lechner, M.: How many bits does it take to quantize your neural network? In: TACAS 2020. LNCS, vol. 12079, pp. 79–97. Springer, Cham (2020). https://doi.org/10.1007/978-3-030-45237-7_5
20. Goldberger, B., et al.: Minimal modifications of deep neural networks using verification. In: LPAR, p. 23rd (2020)
21. Gong, R., et al.: Differentiable soft quantization: bridging full-precision and low-bit neural networks. In: Proceedings of the IEEE/CVF International Conference on Computer Vision. pp. 4852–4861 (2019)
22. Guo, C., et al.: Squant: on-the-fly data-free quantization via diagonal hessian approximation. arXiv preprint arXiv:2202.07471 (2022)
23. Guo, Y.: A survey on methods and theories of quantized neural networks. arXiv preprint arXiv:1808.04752 (2018)

24. He, K., et al.: Deep residual learning for image recognition. Proceedings of the IEEE conference on computer vision and pattern recognition pp. 770–778 (2016)

25. Henzinger, T.A., Lechner, M., et al.: Scalable verification of quantized neural networks. In: Proceedings of the AAAI Conference on Artificial Intelligence (2021)

26. Huang, X., Kwiatkowska, M., Wang, S., Wu, M.: Safety Verification of Deep Neural Networks. In: Majumdar, R., Kunčak, V. (eds.) CAV 2017. LNCS, vol. 10426, pp. 3–29. Springer, Cham (2017). https://doi.org/10.1007/978-3-319-63387-9_1

27. ifigotin: Imagenetmini-1000.   https://www.kaggle.com/datasets/ifigotin/imagenetmini-1000 (2021), (Accessed 4 April 2023)

28. Jacob, B., et al.: Quantization and training of neural networks for efficient integer-arithmetic-only inference. In: Proceedings of the IEEE Conference on Computer Vision and Pattern Recognition, pp. 2704–2713 (2018)

29. Jones, J.A., Harrold, M.J.: Empirical evaluation of the tarantula automatic fault-localization technique. In: Proceedings of the 20th IEEE/ACM International Conference on Automated Software Engineering, pp. 273–282 (2005)

30. Katz, G., Barrett, C., Dill, D.L., Julian, K., Kochenderfer, M.J.: Reluplex: an efficient SMT Solver for verifying deep neural networks. In: Majumdar, R., Kunčak, V. (eds.) CAV 2017. LNCS, vol. 10426, pp. 97–117. Springer, Cham (2017). https://doi.org/10.1007/978-3-319-63387-9_5

31. Katz, G., et al.: The marabou framework for verification and analysis of deep neural networks. In: Dillig, I., Tasiran, S. (eds.) CAV 2019. LNCS, vol. 11561, pp. 443–452. Springer, Cham (2019). https://doi.org/10.1007/978-3-030-25540-4_26

32. Krizhevsky, A., Hinton, G.: CIFAR-10 (canadian institute for advanced research). Tech. rep., University of Toronto (2009). https://www.cs.toronto.edu/kriz/cifar.html

33. Land, A.H., Doig, A.G.: An automatic method for solving discrete programming problems. In: Jünger, M., et al. (eds.) 50 Years of Integer Programming 1958-2008, pp. 105–132. Springer, Heidelberg (2010). https://doi.org/10.1007/978-3-540-68279-0_5

34. Li, Y., et al.: Brecq: pushing the limit of post-training quantization by block reconstruction. arXiv preprint arXiv:2102.05426 (2021)

35. Makhorin, A.: Glpk (gnu linear programming kit). http://www.gnu.org/s/glpk/glpk.html (2008)

36. Meindl, B., Templ, M.: Analysis of commercial and free and open source solvers for linear optimization problems. Eurostat and Statistics Netherlands within the project ESSnet on common tools and harmonised methodology for SDC in the ESS 20 (2012)

37. Naish, L., Lee, H.J., Ramamohanarao, K.: A model for spectra-based software diagnosis. ACM Trans. Softw. Eng. Methodol. (TOSEM) **20**(3), 1–32 (2011)

38. Nemhauser, G.L., Wolsey, L.A.: Integer and combinatorial optimization john, vol. 118. Wiley & Sons, New York (1988)

39. Nickel, S., Steinhardt, C., Schlenker, H., Burkart, W.: Ibm ilog cplex optimization studio-a primer. In: Decision Optimization with IBM ILOG CPLEX Optimization Studio: A Hands-On Introduction to Modeling with the Optimization Programming Language (OPL), pp. 9–21. Springer (2022). https://doi.org/10.1007/978-3-662-65481-1_2

40. Odena, A., Olsson, C., Andersen, D., Goodfellow, I.: Tensorfuzz: Debugging neural networks with coverage-guided fuzzing. In: ICML, pp. 4901–4911. PMLR (2019)

41. Optimization, G.: Inc. gurobi optimizer reference manual, version 5.0 (2012)

42. Pei, K., Cao, Y., Yang, J., Jana, S.: Deepxplore: automated whitebox testing of deep learning systems. In: Proceedings of the 26th Symposium on Operating Systems Principles, pp. 1–18 (2017)
43. Sandler, M., et al.: Mobilenetv 2: inverted residuals and linear bottlenecks. In: Proceedings of the IEEE Conference on Computer Vision and Pattern Recognition (2018)
44. Sena, L.H., Song, X., da S. Alves, E.H., Bessa, I., Manino, E., Cordeiro, L.C.: Verifying quantized neural networks using smt-based model checking. CoRR abs/arXiv: 2106.05997 (2021)
45. Shorten, C., Khoshgoftaar, T.M.: A survey on image data augmentation for deep learning. J. Big Data **6**(1), 1–48 (2019)
46. Simonyan, K., Zisserman, A.: Very deep convolutional networks for large-scale image recognition. arXiv preprint arXiv:1409.1556 (2014)
47. Song, C., Fallon, E., Li, H.: Improving adversarial robustness in weight-quantized neural networks. arXiv preprint arXiv:2012.14965 (2020)
48. Song, X., et al.: Qnnverifier: a tool for verifying neural networks using smt-based model checking. CoRR abs/ arXiv: 2111.13110 (2021)
49. Song, X., Sun, Y., Mustafa, M.A., Cordeiro, L.: Airepair: a repair platform for neural networks. In: ICSE-Companion. IEEE/ACM (2022)
50. Sotoudeh, M., Thakur, A.V.: Provable repair of deep neural networks. In: PLDI (2021)
51. Sun, Y., Chockler, H., Huang, X., Kroening, D.: Explaining image classifiers using statistical fault localization. In: Vedaldi, A., Bischof, H., Brox, T., Frahm, J.-M. (eds.) ECCV 2020. LNCS, vol. 12373, pp. 391–406. Springer, Cham (2020). https://doi.org/10.1007/978-3-030-58604-1_24
52. Sun, Y., Huang, X., Kroening, D., Sharp, J., Hill, M., Ashmore, R.: Structural test coverage criteria for deep neural networks. ACM Trans. Embedded Comput. Syst. (TECS) **18**(5s), 1–23 (2019)
53. Sun, Y., Wu, M., Ruan, W., Huang, X., Kwiatkowska, M., Kroening, D.: Concolic testing for deep neural networks. In: Proceedings of the 33rd ACM/IEEE International Conference on Automated Software Engineering, pp. 109–119 (2018)
54. Usman, M., Gopinath, D., Sun, Y., Noller, Y., Păsăreanu, C.S.: NNREPAIR: constraint-based repair of neural network classifiers. In: Silva, A., Leino, K.R.M. (eds.) CAV 2021. LNCS, vol. 12759, pp. 3–25. Springer, Cham (2021). https://doi.org/10.1007/978-3-030-81685-8_1
55. Vanholder, H.: Efficient inference with tensorrt. In: GPU Technology Conference, vol. 1, p. 2 (2016)
56. Wang, S., Zhang, H., Xu, K., Others: Beta-crown: efficient bound propagation with per-neuron split constraints for neural network robustness verification. In: Advances in Neural Information Processing Systems 34 (2021)
57. Wong, W.E., Debroy, V., Gao, R., Li, Y.: The dstar method for effective software fault localization. IEEE Trans. Reliab. **63**(1), 290–308 (2013)
58. Wong, W.E., Qi, Y., Zhao, L., Cai, K.Y.: Effective fault localization using code coverage. In: COMPSAC, vol. 1, pp. 449–456. IEEE (2007)
59. Yu, B., et al.: Deeprepair: style-guided repairing for deep neural networks in the real-world operational environment. IEEE Trans. Reliability (2021)
60. Zhang, Y., et al.: Qvip: an ilp-based formal verification approach for quantized neural networks. In: ASE. IEEE/ACM (2022)
61. Zhang, J., Li, J.: Testing and verification of neural-network-based safety-critical control software: a systematic literature review. Inf. Softw. Technol. **123**, 106296 (2020)

Timeout Prediction for Software Analyses

Nicola Thoben[(✉)], Jan Haltermann, and Heike Wehrheim

Department of Computing Science, University of Oldenburg, Oldenburg, Germany
{nicola.thoben,jan.haltermann,heike.wehrheim}@uol.de

Abstract. Software verification tools automatically prove the correctness of programs with respect to user supplied specifications. Today, such tools implement a range of different types of analyses. As different analyses are good at different sorts of verification tasks, state-of-the-art tools often employ *sequential compositions* of analyses in which every analysis gets a fixed time slot assigned for verification. As a consequence, however, one analysis might consume parts of the overall available time although it does not finish within its time slot.

In this paper, we propose *timeout prediction* as a way to determine when an analysis should get its full time slot and when to prematurely stop it. Our technique for timeout prediction employs machine learning to predict whether a given analysis will terminate on a given verification task (within a time limit) or will time out. To this end, we develop *static* as well as *dynamic* features of verification tasks and analyses. Values of static features can be statically determined for tasks; dynamic features are determined while an analysis is already running. Our experimental evaluation shows that we can predict timeouts with a high accuracy.

Keywords: Software verification · sequential compositions · timeout prediction

1 Introduction

Although software verification is a challenging problem, the field has made enormous progress in the past years by developing and adopting new tools and techniques, among others visible in the annual verification competitions such as SV-COMP[1] or VerifyThis [16]. In practice (and in these competitions), tools use a plethora of different techniques like predicate analysis, bounded model checking, value analysis, or k-induction. Each of these techniques has its individual strengths and weaknesses, while none of it is superior to the others. To enhance the performance, it is common to employ a combination of conceptually different techniques, e.g., in SV-COMP 2023 19 out of 52 participants used a portfolio-based approach. These combinations either make use of a parallel [3,7,23] or a sequential composition [3,8,9,13,15,20,21,25,26] of different approaches. In the former, the approaches are executed in parallel as a portfolio, and the available computing resources are split among them, whereas in the latter case full resources are given to each approach but the overall available execution time is split. Nearly

---

[1] https://gitlab.com/sosy-lab/benchmarking/sv-benchmarks/-/tree/svcomp23

© The Author(s), under exclusive license to Springer Nature Switzerland AG 2023
C. Ferreira and T. A. C. Willemse (Eds.): SEFM 2023, LNCS 14323, pp. 340–358, 2023.
https://doi.org/10.1007/978-3-031-47115-5_19

all implementations of such sequential compositions employ hand-crafted strategies assigning fixed time budgets to each analysis. One of the main reasons is that an apriori prediction of the expected run time for a technique on a given task is extremely challenging. Thus, if a certain analysis within a sequence does not succeed in computing a correct answer to the verification problem, it usually still consumes the full-time budget assigned to it.

In this paper, we present a technique for *predicting timeouts* of analyses during their execution, allowing for a fast reallocation of resources to other, more promising analyses that may solve the task correctly. The main idea of our approach is to use machine learning to predict at runtime whether the analysis will succeed within the assigned time limit. For this, we first designed a set of 29 different features for CEGAR-based [10] (CEGAR = Counter Example Guided Abstraction Refinement) predicate analyses. This feature set contains *static* features of programs like the size of the control-flow graph, as well as *dynamic* features, partially dependent on the analysis, like the elapsed CPU time, the number of conducted CEGAR iterations, or the number of variables within the discovered predicates. We reduced this set to eight features using feature selection to prevent overfitting and to speed up the prediction. In addition, a third feature set consists of the static features alone (out of the 29 features). Next, we built a method for extracting the data of these features for analyses implemented in the tool CPACHECKER [4] for usage as the training and test sets. Using this data, we employed a random forest classifier, after evaluating various machine learning techniques for this use case, and trained a predictor. We integrated the prediction within a sequential composition of analyses in order to abort one analysis in case a timeout is predicted. More precisely, in our evaluation we employed a sequential combination of predicate analysis with k-induction.

Our evaluation on SV-COMP benchmarks shows in particular that the small set of eight features suffices to predict timeouts with an accuracy of 86%. Employed within the sequential composition, performing first predicate analysis with the prediction followed by k-induction, 15 new tasks get solved instead of reaching the time limit, compared to the sequence without a prediction. The computation time of complex tasks is reduced by 74% in the median.

2 Background

We start by giving some notations on programs and explaining predicate analysis and the concept of CEGAR to which we later apply timeout prediction.

2.1 Programs and Control Flow Automata

In software verification, programs are checked for errors. The goal is to show whether a program is correct, or not, with respect to a certain specification. In this paper, we propose timeout prediction for verification of programs written in C and specifications given by error locations, which together are also referred

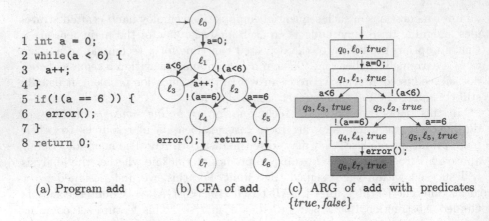

(a) Program add

(b) CFA of add

(c) ARG of add with predicates {*true, false*}

Fig. 1. Example program add, the corresponding CFA and an ARG.

to as *(verification) task* in the further course. In that, a program is correct if no error location is reachable.

Programs and their error locations can be represented as *control flow automata (CFAs)* [2] which are directed graphs. The edges of these graphs are labeled with the operations of the respective program and connect control flow locations. A CFA $A = (L, \ell_0, G, L_E)$ consists of a set of program locations L, an initial location $\ell_0 \in L$ and a set of edges $G \subseteq (L \times Ops \times L)$, with $op \in Ops$ (the set of operations) being either an assignment, an assume operation (for boolean conditions of if or loop statements) or a function call or return. The CFA also contains all error locations L_E of the program, which are defined as the locations with an incoming transition $\xrightarrow{error()}$. In CFAs we mark these in red.

Locations are reachable if a program path $\sigma = \ell_0 \xrightarrow{op_0} \ell_1 \xrightarrow{op_1} \ldots$ to these locations exists that is feasible, i.e., concrete values for the program variables exist to reach an error location via execution of operations $op_0, op_1, \ldots$ [5,18]. The exact semantics of CFAs is of no importance for our approach, so we elide it here.

Figure 1a shows an example C program add in which the variable a is assigned to 0 and then incremented by 1 in each iteration within a while loop until a is no longer less than 6. After the loop, an if statement is used to check whether a is unequal to 6. If this is the case, the error location $l_7 \in L_E$ is reached by calling error(). This will however never occur since a is always 6 when the while loop is exited. In Fig. 1b the CFA corresponding to program add can be found.

2.2 Predicate Analysis

One widely used analysis technique for software verification is *predicate analysis* [17], a technique that examines the reachability of specific locations within a program via abstract interpretation [11]. Instead of using concrete program states, assigning concrete values to the variables of a program, the states in a

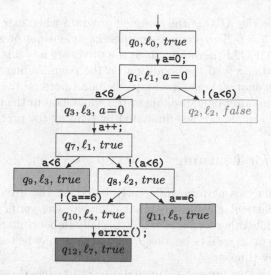

Fig. 2. ARG for example program `add` with predicates $\{a = 0, true, false\}$

predicate analysis are abstractly described by predicates. All (currently) employed predicates are kept in a set π called the *precision*.

During predicate analysis, an abstraction of the concrete program execution is build and the CFA thereby gets unrolled into an *abstract reachability graph* (ARG). Every state in the ARG is related to a CFA location ℓ and abstractly describes a set of concrete states. Predicate analysis aims at proving non-reachability of error locations on such ARGs. Figure 1c shows an ARG of program `add` using precision $\pi = \{true, false\}$. We see a path from q_0 to q_6 which is related to the CFA error location ℓ_7 (a potential *counterexample*). On the ARG, location ℓ_7 thus seems reachable. In this example, the predicate analysis would next *refine* the precision by a technique called *counterexample guided abstraction refinement* (CEGAR).

2.3   CEGAR

CEGAR [10] is a technique for computing precisions, e.g. the sets of predicates, for analysis. CEGAR works iteratively and starts with a very coarse precision (e.g., with $\pi = \{true, false\}$). Within one pass, it first builds an abstract model of the program executions using this precision. On this model, the reachability of abstract states representing error locations is checked. If a path to an error location is found, this is a potential counterexample. Counterexamples next need to be checked for feasibility. If feasible, an error is indeed found and CEGAR stops. If the counterexample is not feasible, the level of abstraction as defined by the precision is too coarse and needs to be refined. There are different techniques for refining precisions which are however of no importance for our technique of timeout prediction. Once a new precision is computed, the iteration starts anew with the next pass.

In Fig. 2 we see the ARG of the example program when extending the precision by predicate $a = 0$. The previous counterexample is not present in the ARG anymore. In this CEGAR iteration, since the predicate $a = 0$ is true at state q_1 due to the operation $\mathtt{a = 0}$ the condition on the edge leading to q_2 cannot be true. Nonetheless, another counterexample is found because the predicate $a = 0$ is not true anymore after one unrolling of the while loop in the program. Again, this new counterexample can be eliminated by refining the precision.

3   Features for Learning

Since different analyses perform differently based on the given program, it is possible that a particular analysis cannot complete the verification in a given period of time, while other analyses can. Especially in benchmark settings, when many verification tasks need to be solved, a lot of time may be wasted by analyses running until they timeout.

To prevent this, we present a timeout prediction based on machine learning here. The prediction is used to abort a running analysis when the machine learning model predicts that it will not compute a result in time. Here, we will only present models that are trained to abort predicate analyses. Similar models could be trained for other types of analyses, e.g. for value analysis, in particular when they also employ CEGAR techniques. We train two sorts of models, one for predicting at the beginning of every analysis whether the analysis should be started at all, and the second for predicting at each CEGAR iteration whether to continue the analysis or not.

In order to be able to train such models, we first need *features* (of programs or analysis runs). The chosen features can be split into two groups:

1. *Static* features that describe the program and remain unchanged during the analysis, and
2. *dynamic* features which change throughout the analysis.

Static features have been used before in related work for selection of verification tools or analyses [1,14]. In our case, they describe the size of the program as well as some properties of loops within programs. The performance of CEGAR depends on both and thus can be partially predicted by this kind of features. In particular, if the analysis were to perform one CEGAR refinement per loop iteration, it would most likely timeout.

Dynamic features are less often used in related work. We employ them here to enable the learned model to predict whether the analysis is making good progress. One reason for an analysis not coming to an end with a conclusive result is the fact that CEGAR techniques do not necessarily compute predicates which are helpful for verification. Because of this, our dynamic features examine predicates in detail so that the model can learn about connections between specific sorts of predicates and timeouts of the analysis. Other dynamic features examine the runtime of the analysis, the number of CEGAR iterations, and the structure of the ARG to infer whether time is wasted by unrolling loops.

Table 1. All features

Index	Description	Type
s1	no. of all loops in program	static
s2	no. of endless loops	static
s3	no. of loops nested in another loop	static
s4	estimated no. of max. loop iterations of all loops in program	static
s5	no. of arrays in program	static
s6	no. of CFA nodes	static
p1	time from start of analysis to begin of current iteration	dynamic
p2	index of current iteration	dynamic
arg1	current no. of all ARG states	dynamic
arg2	no. of new ARG states in current iteration	dynamic
arg3	no. of abstraction locations (e.g. loop heads) in path to ARG state with the highest index	dynamic
arg4	no. of new abstraction locations	dynamic
arg5	most often occurring CFA location in ARG	dynamic
pred1	no. of predicates used since previous iteration	dynamic
pred2	no. of predicates with $=$ operator	dynamic
pred3	no. of new predicates with $=$ operator	dynamic
pred4	no. of predicates with $<$ operator	dynamic
pred5	no. of new predicates with $<$ operator	dynamic
pred6	no. of predicates with $+$ operator	dynamic
pred7	no. of predicates with $/$ operator	dynamic
pred8	no. of predicates with $*$ operator	dynamic
pred9	no. of predicates with $\%$ operator	dynamic
pred10	no. of predicates with only one operator	dynamic
pred11	no. of predicates with multiple operators	dynamic
pred12	highest no. of different variables in one predicate	dynamic
pred13	no. of predicates with the most occurring variable	dynamic
pred14	no. of predicates that include more than one variable	dynamic
pred15	no. of predicates with constants increasing by 1	dynamic
pred16	highest no. of boolean operations in a single predicate	dynamic

To train models, we next require training data (i.e., data instances with values of features) which we first need to collect. The values of all features are collected within CPACHECKER [4] through the available ARG, CFA, and general statistics.

For the models that will be used in every CEGAR iteration, the data must also be *collected* in each iteration. Thus, each row of data in these datasets (one instance) corresponds to the values of features of one such iteration and the number of data rows per analysis represents the number of iterations the analysis runs in total. For the model used at the beginning of an analysis, we only use static features.

In the following, we describe three feature sets (FS1, FS2 and FS3) for which we later provide results of experimental evaluations. We have made further experiments with different subsets of FS1 (see [30]) which we – due to lack of space – can however not describe here.

A total of 29 features has been selected for the first feature set FS1 (see Table 1). To speed up the prediction and avoid overfitting, we then used the feature selection technique *Select from Model*[2] (see also Sect. 4) to reduce the feature set giving FS2 ={s1, s6, p1, p2, arg1, arg2, arg3, arg5}. A third feature set FS3={s1, s2, s3, s4, s5, s6} consists of all static features of FS1 only. Table 1 shows the type of each feature as well as a short description.

We next explain all features of the reduced feature set FS2 in more detail because the evaluation showed that it performs better than FS1 and FS3 (see Sect. 5). First, we have two general features. The CPU time from the point on when the analysis starts is tracked by feature p1. Every time the feature extraction starts in an iteration, the time that has elapsed so far will be stored for this feature. It is possible that after a certain time the probability of the analysis finding a result decreases and this is detected by the trained model. Feature p2 stores the current CEGAR iteration in which the feature extraction is called. CEGAR is working iteratively, so the value of this feature will always start at 0 in the first data line and increases with every following iteration. The value of this feature in the last gathered data line of an analysis, therefore, describes how many CEGAR iterations are done until the analysis is stopped due to a timeout or termination. A strongly increasing, high number of iterations could possibly indicate that it is unlikely that the analysis computes a result before the timeout.

Static Features in FS2. The two static features in FS2 are s1 and s6. They do not change during the running analysis. s1 counts the number of for or while loops within the C program to be analyzed. Since the unrolling of loops is often the reason for a high number of CEGAR iterations and additionally for timeouts, the number of loops can be an indicator of the performance of the analysis. The program seen in Fig. 1a contains one while loop, so the value for this feature is 1 for the entire analysis.

Feature s6 counts the number of CFA nodes. As described in Sect. 2.1, a single CFA node describes a specific location ℓ of the program to be analyzed. A high number of nodes can therefore be used to conclude that a program is large and more likely to be more difficult to analyze than a short program. In the example Fig. 1b the CFA consists of eight nodes, so the value for s6 is 8 throughout every iteration of the analysis.

ARG-Related Features in FS2. Feature arg1 counts all the states in the ARG when the CFA gets unrolled. The value for arg1 is 7 for the ARG in Fig. 1c and 9 for the one in Fig. 2. For arg2 the number of ARG states in both the current and previous iterations are compared to determine the difference. Which of the new

---

[2] https://scikit-learn.org/stable/modules/generated/sklearn.\discretionary-feature_ selection.SelectFromModel.html.

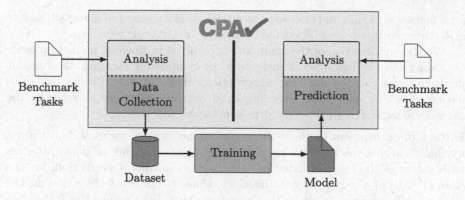

Fig. 3. Overview of data collection, training and prediction steps.

states have been in the previous set of states is not relevant for this feature. In Fig. 1c the ARG consists of seven states and in the following CEGAR iteration of nine states, as seen in Fig. 2. This makes the value of arg2 to be 2 in the current iteration.

Feature arg3 takes a look at every ARG state on the path to the last explored state and counts the abstraction locations. An abstraction location is telling us where to perform an abstraction, which is by default at every loop head in the CFA but can also be set to every node or whenever multiple paths get merged. The number of loop heads in the example Fig. 2 in the path leading to q_{12} is 2 because the loop head ℓ_1 appears twice.

Feature arg5 determines the CFA location occurring most often in the ARG. Every ARG state belongs to a CFA location. If a loop gets unrolled or a method is called often, a CFA location present in this loop or method can appear multiple times on the ARG. Loop unrolling can possibly cause many CEGAR iterations and may result in a timeout. In Fig. 2 the most often occurring locations are ℓ_1 and ℓ_3, both being in the ARG twice, so the value of this feature is 2 in this iteration.

Predicate-Related Features in FS2. Surprisingly, the feature selection technique *Select from Model* did not keep any of the predicate-related features in FS2. Predicate-related features (pred1 to pred16) store values about precisions in predicate analyses, like the number of predicates or the number of certain operators in predicates. In conclusion, then, the properties of the predicates do not have a strong influence on the predictions of the model.

4 Timeout Prediction

An overview of the components of our implementation and their interaction can be found in Fig. 3. We realized all components except for the training within the software verification tool CPACHECKER. All processes related to machine learning, such as preparing the data, splitting the data into training and test sets, feature selection and training the model, are implemented using SKLEARN[3] in Python, so these are realized independently of CPACHECKER.

We shortly describe all the components involved in timeout prediction next. Our approach requires a set of tasks to learn from. After learning, the timeout prediction can then be used for a (potentially different) set of tasks. For evaluation of our approach, we have employed over 10 000 tasks taken from the category ReachSafety of the SV-COMP benchmark collection.

Data Collection. For implementing timeout prediction, we must first train a machine learning model. This requires a data set consisting of data instances with values of the features listed in Sect. 3 plus the correct prediction, i.e. the class (1 or 0) of a particular data instance. Class 1 represents the case that the analysis will return a result (within the given time limit) and class 0 the case when it times out.

As one model has to make a prediction at the start of the predicate analysis and the other models in each CEGAR iteration, we run predicate analysis twice on every task: once for the model using FS3, not collecting data throughout CEGAR iterations, and then again for the other models (FS1 and FS2) collecting also data of dynamic features.

Training. Before actually training, we first need to choose a particular *classifier*. For this we have chosen a *random forest classifier* which turned out to perform best in experimental evaluations (compared to decision trees, SVMs and logistic regression). Random forests consist of multiple decision trees whose leaves represent the classes (0 or 1) to which data points can be assigned. All inner nodes of the trees (i.e., nodes which are not leaves) contain *decisions* consisting of thresholds that examine the values of the features to then determine the path to the next node accordingly.

Since the benchmark tasks in category ReachSafety are divided into different subcategories according to their structure, the training and test set is divided in such a way that 25% of each subcategory is randomly selected for the test set (used in the evaluation) and the rest for the training set. This avoids bias to certain program structures.

Feature Selection. The overall feature set FS1 presented in Sect. 3 is reduced by feature selection to speed up the prediction and to avoid overfitting. SKLEARN provides different feature selection methods. Since there is no ideal method to select the best features for training, the results of three methods were compared: *Select from Model, Select k Best* and *Sequential Feature Selection*.

Select from Model calculates the importance of each feature based on an already trained model. The importance of a feature indicates how relevant it is for the predictions of this model. The most important features are then selected for the reduced set. *Select from Model* was applied to the model trained with FS1 and performed better than the alternatives. The resulting feature set is FS2.

Prediction. The trained models can be called from within the predicate analysis in the CPACHECKER by using a script that passes the relevant data to the model

[3] https://github.com/scikit-learn/scikit-learn.

and returns the result of the prediction. This input data consists of values for the same features as for the previous data collection. The script is called in each CEGAR iteration, or in case of the model trained only on static features, at the beginning of the analysis.

The prediction predicts whether the analysis will produce a result before the specified time limit or not. In case of a negative prediction, the running analysis is stopped without providing any results. Alternatively, the analysis is left running until either (1) a result is found, (2) it reaches the timeout or (3) a prediction in the following CEGAR iterations aborts the analysis.

5 Evaluation

As explained in the previous section, we have implemented all components necessary for timeout prediction. In the evaluation, we were interested in several aspects of our approach: (a) the choice of feature sets and how they compare to each other with respect to the quality of predictions and their required time, (b) the usage of machine learning and whether the involved machinery pays off compared to simple heuristics, and (c) the usefulness of timeout predictions in sequential compositions of analyses.

We have formulated the following three research questions for the evaluation of these aspects.

RQ1 Comparing static features to dynamic ones, which feature set leads to a better-performing model?
RQ2 Can a machine learning model outperform simple heuristics?
RQ3 Does a sequential composition benefit from a timeout prediction?

5.1 Evaluation Setup

The evaluation is done on Intel Xeon E3-1230 v5 @ 3.40 GHz (8 cores) machines, 33 GB of memory, and Ubuntu 22.04 LTS with Linux kernel 5.15.0. BenchExec [6] is used for the execution of all runs to ensure reproducibility. To make sure the setup matches that of the SV-Comp, the analyses are limited to 15 GB of memory, 4 CPU cores, and 15 min of CPU time.

5.2 Metrics

In order to evaluate the different models, the ground truth (= correct prediction) must be known first. This has already been determined during data collection. We then employ the ground truth and the actual predictions to calculate values of standard metrics for the models. The metrics are computed from the model's values of *true positives* (TP), *true negatives* (TN), *false positives* (FP), and *false negatives* (FN).

The TPs state that the prediction of the model has been positive and also agrees with the ground truth. In this case, the prediction correctly states that the analysis will not reach a timeout. TNs also make a correct prediction, but this time a negative one. This means the analysis does not provide a result before the timeout and the model predicts the timeout before it occurs. So these two values represent the number of correct predictions about whether the analysis will terminate before the timeout or not. The FPs and the FNs each indicate the number of incorrect predictions, i.e., when the model indicates that the analysis will terminate before timeout when it does not, and vice versa.

The values of TPs, TNs, FPs, and FNs are used to compute the standard metrics. The first is *Accuracy* to indicate how many of the predictions are correct in total.

$$Accuracy = \frac{TP + TN}{TP + TN + FN + FP} \tag{1}$$

The *Precision* indicates how high the number of correctly predicted positive predictions is in relation to all positive predictions. If the priority is, that timeouts do not remain undetected, care should be taken to ensure that the Precision is high. With a low Precision, more time is consumed by analyses that could have been aborted.

$$Precision = \frac{TP}{TP + FP} \tag{2}$$

For the *Recall*, the number of correctly detected positive predictions is again considered, but now in proportion to all results that are actually positive by the ground truth. A high Recall is desirable when all positive results have to be recognized as such. A low value in the context of timeout predictions means that many analyses are incorrectly aborted and the verification results can no longer be determined.

$$Recall = \frac{TP}{TP + FN} \tag{3}$$

The structure of *Specificity* is similar to that of Recall, but focuses on negative instead of positive predictions. Therefore, if it is important that the actual negative objects are also recognized as negative, the Specificity should contain a high value. A high Specificity in this case means that timeouts are recognized as such, i.e. the analyses are not incorrectly allowed to continue.

$$Specificity = \frac{TN}{TN + FP} \tag{4}$$

In order to combine the recall and the precision into one value and to make models comparable by a single value, the *F1 Score* is calculated. It makes it easier to see the overall performance at a glance.

$$F1\ Score = \frac{2 * Precision * Recall}{Precision + Recall} \tag{5}$$

Depending on the goal of the user of the models, the metrics can be of different importance. With regard to the motivation to run several analyses in sequences until a result is found, a high specificity makes sense. If an analysis is incorrectly aborted, one of the following analyses may still be able to determine a result.

Table 2. Results of the evaluation, measured by presented metrics

	Accuracy	Recall	Specificity	Precision	F1-Score
FS1	**0.88**	0.85	**0.94**	**0.95**	**0.90**
FS2	0.86	0.81	**0.94**	**0.95**	0.87
FS3	**0.88**	**0.89**	0.86	0.90	**0.90**

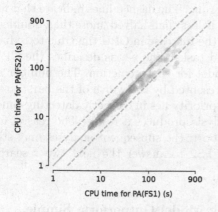

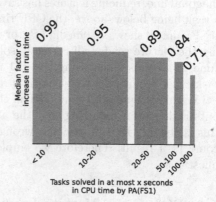

(a) Scatterplot of CPU time comparing FS1 and FS2

(b) Comparison of CPU time: FS1 and FS2

Fig. 4. Comparison of computation time of predicate analysis using FS1 and FS2.

5.3 RQ1: Comparing Static Features to Dynamic Ones, Which Feature Set Leads to a Better Performing Model?

In Sect. 3, the three feature sets are presented. Two of these sets, FS1 and FS2, contain both dynamic and static features, a third one (FS3) consists of static features only. The values of the metrics allow the different feature sets to be compared with each other.

In Table 2, it can be seen that FS1 achieves the best values except for Recall. The static feature set achieves the highest recall value with 89% and is therefore the best at predicting that an analysis will not reach the timeout. With respect to Specificity (94%) and Precision (95%), i.e. the correct detection of timeouts, FS1 and FS2 perform better. With respect to Accuracy (88%) and the F1 Score (90%), the static model and the one that also used dynamic features for training do not differ.

FS2 has been reduced to eight features to avoid overfitting and to save time. By reducing the size of the feature set, the computation time of the analyses of the majority of the tasks can actually be reduced. This is visualized by Fig. 4. In Fig. 4a, the CPU time needed by the predicate analysis to solve a task correctly is shown on the x-axis for FS1 and on the y-axis for FS2. For all tasks below the

Table 3. Evaluation results of simple heuristics, measured by presented metrics.

	Accuracy	Recall	Specificity	Precision	F1-Score
FS2	**0.86**	0.81	**0.94**	**0.95**	**0.87**
Heuristics	0.61	**0.99**	0.06	0.61	0.75

diagonal line, reducing features has saved time. The dashed lines indicate that for a task being below/above, the CPU time is less than halved/more than doubled.

Figure 4b shows the median factor of the increase in CPU time due to reducing the feature set for all correctly solved tasks. The x-axis describes the CPU time in seconds when using the FS1 model for the prediction. The number of tasks that require the time shown is represented by the width of the bars.

Within a sequential composition, the priority lies in correctly detecting timeouts rather than detecting that the analysis produces a result. The reason for this is the fact that in case of a wrong abort, the subsequent analyses may still come to a result. Therefore we employ FS2 to answer the next two research questions.

5.4   RQ2: Can a Machine Learning Model Outperform Simple Heuristics?

An alternative to predictions via machine learning would be to employ simple heuristics. This would in particular significantly decrease the overhead of the prediction. For comparison with our own approach, we therefore designed and implemented a very simple heuristics, namely counting the number of CEGAR iterations and stopping the analysis after the 50th iteration. We have also made experiments with more complicated heuristics involving values of features s4, s6, arg1 and arg5, but these have performed worse.

For the evaluation of the heuristics, we used the same set of tasks as in the experiments for RQ1.

In Table 3 we show the result of the comparison between the heuristics and the reduced feature set FS2. It can be seen that heuristics achieve a very high Recall value of 99% and, in contrast, a low Specificity value of 6%. These values result from the fact that very few analyses are aborted overall and that the heuristics barely takes action, so they are less significant. Since the test set contains more solved tasks than timeouts, the accuracy is still at 61%, since most tasks are correctly not aborted. It can be said that this simple heuristics, chosen by intuition, does not outperform the machine learning model.

5.5   RQ3: Does a Sequential Composition Benefit from a Timeout Prediction?

In software verification, sequential compositions in which several different analyses are executed one after another are often used. An analysis in a sequence

Table 4. Evaluation results of prediction in a sequential composition.

	# Solved	# Unsolved	# Add. Solved
Without Prediction	1164	945	154
With Prediction	997	1112	**15**

is started when the previous analysis does not return a result within a certain time limit. If individual analyses in a sequence do not produce a result, they however still use all the time attributed to them. Since a time limit is also set for the entire sequence, this wastes time that may be better used by the following analyses.

To evaluate whether a sequence can benefit from our timeout prediction, we investigated a sequence that occurs as a subsequence in [1]: Predicate Analysis, with 450 seconds maximum run time, followed by k-induction [32]. The entire sequence is given a timeout of 900 seconds. This configuration is used on all tasks that were also used to answer RQ1 and RQ2.

While running the analyses on these tasks, we check in each CEGAR iteration of the predicate analysis whether the analysis should be aborted. If the prediction is negative before the predicate analysis has reached 450 seconds runtime or the task gets solved, k-induction is started early. It then has more time than the usual 450 seconds, depending on the time of abort, until the total time limit of 900 seconds is reached. For the prediction, the reduced feature set FS2 is used, due to the mentioned reasons of overfitting and time savings.

In Table 4 we show the effect of prediction on the number of tasks that can be solved (i.e., for which verification is successfully completed). In summary, out of the 2 109 tasks of our test set prediction can ensure that 15 additional tasks are solved (which could not be solved before due to timeouts of the two analyses). Unfortunately, due to incorrect aborts of the predicate analysis, this also entails that 154 tasks are no longer solved, although they are solved in a configuration without timeout prediction.

Figure 5a shows the effect of prediction on the computation time. The x-axis of the scatterplot shows the CPU time of the sequence without prediction, the y-axis shows the CPU time of the sequence with prediction. We see that the time for tasks that can be solved quickly increases when using prediction. However, the time is significantly shortened for tasks where the verification takes more time. The tasks in the plot in Fig. 5b are summarized by CPU Time of the sequence without prediction. The y-axis again shows the median factor of the increase in time by adding the prediction to the sequence. Here it can be seen more easily how much faster the analyses of the complex tasks are due to the prediction. The tasks taking more than 100 seconds of CPU time only need 26% of the original time with prediction in the median.

So while the overall CPU time for solving complex verification tasks is reduced, we unfortunately also have less correctly solved tasks. For a successful application of timeout prediction within a sequence of two analyses, we require

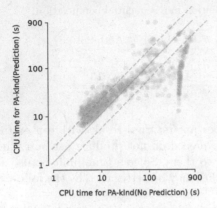
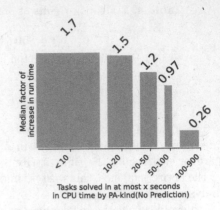

(a) Scatterplot of CPU time comparing Predicate Analysis + k-induction with and without prediction

(b) Comparison of CPU time: Predicate Analysis + k-induction with and without prediction

Fig. 5. Comparison of computation time of predicate analysis + k-induction without and with prediction.

a setting (a choice of analyses and their order) in which the second analysis in the sequence can actually make use of the additional time it gets and solve tasks on which the first analysis times out. Such a setting could be found by doing experiments with lots of different pairs of analyses. This is left for future work.

6 Related Work

Closest related to our own approach are works on *selecting* analysis or algorithms during software verification. Selecting the best-performing analysis or configuration for a given task is in general a challenging endeavor. Therefore, heuristics [1,28] or algorithm selectors [3,12,14,21,25,26,31] are used. Their task is to either select the best configuration for a single tool [28], the most promising analysis [3,14] or a sequence of analyses [1,12,26,31]. To be able to employ these methods, the program needs to be represented as a feature vector. Many make use of hand-crafted, syntactic features such as program size, and the presence of specific language features like arrays or enumerations [1,14,28]. Instead of using just a selected set of program features, the full program can also be used as input to the algorithm selectors. For this, the program is transformed, e.g. using Contextualized Syntax Trees [27], Abstract Syntax Trees [21], or a combination of multiple graphs [12,25,26]. In contrast to our approach, these techniques predict the analysis or the sequence of analyses *offline*, hence only using static program features, whereas we predict timeouts during the running analysis, allowing the use of dynamic features. These techniques can be seen as an orthogonal line of work, and we reused static features computed by the analysis within our approach.

The majority of software verification techniques internally make use of SAT- or SMT-solvers. Hence, using the best solver for a given query is one key to success. There are therefore several algorithm selection approaches for such solvers which predict their performance for a given query [19, 22, 24, 29].

The approaches of Scott et al. [29] and Leeson et al. [22] work directly on the abstract syntax tree of the query, in [19] a fixed feature set is used. All three approaches predict the best solver in advance. In contrast, Luo et al. [24] present an approach to predict the remaining execution time of an SMT-Solver for a given query in symbolic execution, allowing to steer the exploration of paths. For prediction, operands occurring in the remaining sub-formulae of the query are used as features. Unlike our approach, Luo et al. perform the prediction once in the analysis. Also, regression techniques are selected for the adaptive machine learning and a time value in the form of seconds is predicted in opposite to a class. Again, we could reuse the features for formulae in our approach.

7   Conclusion

In this paper, we presented a timeout prediction for predicate analysis in the tool CPACHECKER which employs machine learning for prediction. The goal was to detect whether a running predicate analysis, performed on an individual verification task, still returns a result before a specified time limit is reached. When it is predicted that a timeout will be reached, the analysis is aborted early. In sequential compositions, in which different analyses try to solve a task one after the other, resources could then be given to the following analyses after the predicate analysis is aborted.

For this purpose, three feature sets were first defined and then employed for training multiple machine learning models. A collection of data of these features built a dataset that was subsequently used for training and evaluation. The evaluation on the tasks of the SV-COMP benchmarks compared all generated models and showed that a small feature set consisting of eight features, which are both static and dynamic, achieves an accuracy of 86%. Applied in a sequential composition, consisting of predicate analysis and k-induction, 15 tasks could be solved that were not solved without the prediction. With the prediction, the sequential composition needs only 26% of the original time to solve complex tasks.

As future work, we see potential in finding sequential compositions other than predicate analysis plus k-induction in which our trained models can be more useful. This requires determining sequences of analyses in which the later analysis actually needs the additional time after an abort of the predicate analysis. This is likely to happen when combining two complementary analyses. Moreover, the application of timeout prediction is not limited to predicate analysis and the features presented here. Our dynamic features could also easily be adapted to other CEGAR-based analyses and the static features are anyway applicable to all analyses. Finally, combining machine learning and handcrafted heuristics into a hybrid approach might prove to be useful as well.

References

1. Beyer, D., Dangl, M.: Strategy selection for software verification based on boolean features. In: Margaria, T., Steffen, B. (eds.) ISoLA 2018. LNCS, vol. 11245, pp. 144–159. Springer, Cham (2018). https://doi.org/10.1007/978-3-030-03421-4_11
2. Beyer, D., Henzinger, T.A., Théoduloz, G.: Configurable software verification: concretizing the convergence of model checking and program analysis. In: Damm, W., Hermanns, H. (eds.) CAV 2007. LNCS, vol. 4590, pp. 504–518. Springer, Heidelberg (2007). https://doi.org/10.1007/978-3-540-73368-3_51
3. Beyer, D., Kanav, S., Richter, C.: Construction of verifier combinations based on off-the-shelf verifiers. In: FASE 2022. LNCS, vol. 13241, pp. 49–70. Springer, Cham (2022). https://doi.org/10.1007/978-3-030-99429-7_3
4. Beyer, D., Keremoglu, M.E.: CPACHECKER: a tool for configurable software verification. In: Gopalakrishnan, G., Qadeer, S. (eds.) CAV 2011. LNCS, vol. 6806, pp. 184–190. Springer, Heidelberg (2011). https://doi.org/10.1007/978-3-642-22110-1_16
5. Beyer, D., Keremoglu, M.E., Wendler, P.: Predicate abstraction with adjustable-block encoding. In: FMCAD 2010, pp. 189–197. IEEE (2010)
6. Beyer, D., Löwe, S., Wendler, P.: Reliable benchmarking: requirements and solutions. STTT **21**(1), 1–29 (2019)
7. Chalupa, M., Henzinger, T.A.: BUBAAK: runtime monitoring of program verifiers. In: Sankaranarayanan, S., Sharygina, N. (eds.) Tools and Algorithms for the Construction and Analysis of Systems. TACAS 2023. LNCS, vol. 13994, pp. 535–540. Springer, Cham (2023). https://doi.org/10.1007/978-3-031-30820-8_32
8. Chalupa, M., Mihalkovič, V., Řechtáčková, A., Zaoral, L., Strejček, J.: SYMBIOTIC 9: string analysis and backward symbolic execution with loop folding. In: TACAS 2022. LNCS, vol. 13244, pp. 462–467. Springer, Cham (2022). https://doi.org/10.1007/978-3-030-99527-0_32
9. Chalupa, M., Strejcek, J., Vitovská, M.: Joint forces for memory safety checking revisited. Int. J. Softw. Tools Technol. Transf. **22**(2), 115–133 (2020). https://doi.org/10.1007/s10009-019-00526-2
10. Clarke, E., Grumberg, O., Jha, S., Lu, Y., Veith, H.: Counterexample-guided abstraction refinement. In: Emerson, E.A., Sistla, A.P. (eds.) CAV 2000. LNCS, vol. 1855, pp. 154–169. Springer, Heidelberg (2000). https://doi.org/10.1007/10722167_15
11. Cousot, P., Cousot, R.: Abstract interpretation: a unified lattice model for static analysis of programs by construction or approximation of fixpoints. In: ACM 1977, pp. 238–252. ACM (1977). https://doi.org/10.1145/512950.512973
12. Czech, M., Hüllermeier, E., Jakobs, M., Wehrheim, H.: Predicting rankings of software verification tools. In: SWAN@ESEC/SIGSOFT FSE 2017, pp. 23–26. ACM (2017). https://doi.org/10.1145/3121257.3121262
13. Dangl, M., Löwe, S., Wendler, P.: CPACHECKER with support for recursive programs and floating-point arithmetic. In: Baier, C., Tinelli, C. (eds.) TACAS 2015. LNCS, vol. 9035, pp. 423–425. Springer, Heidelberg (2015). https://doi.org/10.1007/978-3-662-46681-0_34
14. Demyanova, Y., Pani, T., Veith, H., Zuleger, F.: Empirical software metrics for benchmarking of verification tools. Formal Methods Syst. Des. **50**(2), 289–316 (2017). https://doi.org/10.1007/s10703-016-0264-5

15. Ernst, G.: KORN–software verification with horn clauses (Competition Contribution). In: Sankaranarayanan, S., Sharygina, N. (eds) Tools and Algorithms for the Construction and Analysis of Systems. TACAS 2023. LNCS, vol. 13994, pp 559–564. Springer, Cham (2023). https://doi.org/10.1007/978-3-031-30820-8_36

16. Ernst, G., Huisman, M., Mostowski, W., Ulbrich, M.: VerifyThis – verification competition with a human factor. In: Beyer, D., Huisman, M., Kordon, F., Steffen, B. (eds.) TACAS 2019. LNCS, vol. 11429, pp. 176–195. Springer, Cham (2019). https://doi.org/10.1007/978-3-030-17502-3_12

17. Graf, S., Saidi, H.: Construction of abstract state graphs with PVS. In: Grumberg, O. (ed.) CAV 1997. LNCS, vol. 1254, pp. 72–83. Springer, Heidelberg (1997). https://doi.org/10.1007/3-540-63166-6_10

18. Hajdu, Á., Micskei, Z.: Efficient strategies for CEGAR-based model checking. J. Autom. Reason. **64**(6), 1051–1091 (2020). https://doi.org/10.1007/s10817-019-09535-x

19. Healy, A., Monahan, R., Power, J.F.: Predicting SMT solver performance for software verification. In: F-IDE@FM 2016, EPTCS, vol. 240, pp. 20–37 (2016). https://doi.org/10.4204/EPTCS.240.2

20. Heizmann, M., Hoenicke, J., Podelski, A.: Software model checking for people who love automata. In: Sharygina, N., Veith, H. (eds.) CAV 2013. LNCS, vol. 8044, pp. 36–52. Springer, Heidelberg (2013). https://doi.org/10.1007/978-3-642-39799-8_2

21. Leeson, W., Dwyer, M.B.: Graves-CPA: a graph-attention verifier selector (Competition Contribution). In: TACAS 2022. LNCS, vol. 13244, pp. 440–445. Springer, Cham (2022). https://doi.org/10.1007/978-3-030-99527-0_28

22. Leeson, W., Dwyer, M.B., Filieri, A.: Sibyl: improving software engineering tools with SMT selection. In: Proceedings of ICSE (2023)

23. Luckow, K., et al.: JDART: a dynamic symbolic analysis framework. In: Chechik, M., Raskin, J.-F. (eds.) TACAS 2016. LNCS, vol. 9636, pp. 442–459. Springer, Heidelberg (2016). https://doi.org/10.1007/978-3-662-49674-9_26

24. Luo, S., Xu, H., Bi, Y., Wang, X., Zhou, Y.: Boosting symbolic execution via constraint solving time prediction (experience paper). In: ISSTA 2021, pp. 336–347. ACM (2021). https://doi.org/10.1145/3460319.3464813

25. Richter, C., Hüllermeier, E., Jakobs, M., Wehrheim, H.: Algorithm selection for software validation based on graph kernels. Autom. Softw. Eng. **27**(1), 153–186 (2020). https://doi.org/10.1007/s10515-020-00270-x

26. Richter, C., Wehrheim, H.: PeSCo: predicting sequential combinations of verifiers. In: Beyer, D., Huisman, M., Kordon, F., Steffen, B. (eds.) TACAS 2019. LNCS, vol. 11429, pp. 229–233. Springer, Cham (2019). https://doi.org/10.1007/978-3-030-17502-3_19

27. Richter, C., Wehrheim, H.: Attend and represent: a novel view on algorithm selection for software verification. In: ASE 2020, pp. 1016–1028. IEEE (2020). https://doi.org/10.1145/3324884.3416633

28. Saan, S. et al.: GOBLINT: autotuning thread-modular abstract interpretation. In: Sankaranarayanan, S., Sharygina, N. (eds.) Tools and Algorithms for the Construction and Analysis of Systems. TACAS 2023. LNCS, vol. 13994, pp. 547–552. Springer, Cham (2023). https://doi.org/10.1007/978-3-031-30820-8_34

29. Scott, J., Niemetz, A., Preiner, M., Nejati, S., Ganesh, V.: MachSMT: a machine learning-based algorithm selector for SMT solvers. In: TACAS 2021. LNCS, vol. 12652, pp. 303–325. Springer, Cham (2021). https://doi.org/10.1007/978-3-030-72013-1_16

30. Thoben, N.: Online Performance Prediction of Software Verification using Machine Learning. Master's thesis, University of Oldenburg, Department of Computer Science (2023)
31. Tulsian, V., Kanade, A., Kumar, R., Lal, A., Nori, A.V.: MUX: algorithm selection for software model checkers. In: MSR 2014, pp. 132–141. ACM (2014). https://doi.org/10.1145/2597073.2597080
32. Wahl, T.: The k-induction principle (2013). http://www.ccs.neu.edu/home/wahl/Publications/k-induction.pdf

Tool Papers

PMC-VIS: An Interactive Visualization Tool for Probabilistic Model Checking

Max Korn[1]([⊠]) , Julián Méndez[2]([⊠]) , Sascha Klüppelholz[1]([⊠]) ,
Ricardo Langner[2]([⊠]) , Christel Baier[1]([⊠]) , and Raimund Dachselt[2]([⊠])

[1] Institute of Theoretical Computer Science, TU Dresden, Dresden, Germany
{max.korn,sascha.klueppelholz,christel.baier}@tu-dresden.de
[2] Interactive Media Lab Dresden, TU Dresden, Dresden, Germany
{julian.mendez2,ricardo.langner,raimund.dachselt}@tu-dresden.de

Abstract. State-of-the-art Probabilistic Model Checking (PMC) offers multiple engines for the quantitative analysis of Markov Decision Processes (MDPs), including rewards modeling cost or utility values. Despite the huge amount of internally computed information, support for debugging and facilities that enhance the understandability of PMC models and results are very limited. As a first step to improve on that, we present the basic principles of PMC-VIS, a tool that supports the exploration of large MDPs together with the computed PMC results per MDP-state through interactive visualization. By combining visualization techniques, such as node-link diagrams and parallel coordinates, with quantitative analysis capabilities, PMC-VIS supports users in gaining insights into the probabilistic behavior of MDPs and PMC results and enables different ways to explore the behaviour of schedulers of multiple target properties. The usefulness of PMC-VIS is demonstrated through three different application scenarios.

1 Introduction

Probabilistic model checking (PMC) is a well-established technique used in the field of formal verification to analyze and assess the behavior of probabilistic systems. Sources of probabilistic behavior include randomized algorithms as well as stochastic assumptions about the external use of the system (i.e., the system environment) and error probabilities. PMC combines concepts from probability theory and model checking to provide quantitative insights into the reliability and performance of such systems on various types of stochastic models. It is applicable at all stages of the life cycle of a system (i.e., in the design phase, at runtime, and at inspection time) for the evaluation of system properties, such as reliability, safety, and various cost and performance metrics.

State-of-the-art probabilistic model checkers, such as PRISM [23], Storm [15], and MRMC [20], have successfully been applied in various application fields,

---

M. Korn and J. Méndez—Authors contributed equally.

© The Author(s) 2023
C. Ferreira and T. A. C. Willemse (Eds.): SEFM 2023, LNCS 14323, pp. 361–375, 2023.
https://doi.org/10.1007/978-3-031-47115-5_20

including computer science, engineering, robotics, and biology [2,7]. Neverthe-less, understanding, debugging, and using computed results for a given general goal often involves a laborious manual process that is only supported by hand-written and tailored software scripts in combination with general-purpose tools for handling large datasets. Existing model checkers provide rather limited sup-port for *(re)configuration* tasks (i.e., calibrating systems before or at runtime to complete set objectives under possibly multiple criteria) that involve sys-tematically exploring and understanding (1) complex system behavior and (2) metrics returned by PMC processes. While there exist model checkers for PMC that provide graphical user-interfaces to inspect the model and its results, like PRISM [23], they do not incorporate advanced visualization techniques.

From the application viewpoint, the missing visual tool support for using computed PMC results has already been recognized in some domains, such as DNA sequencing [7] and automated driving [13]. The tools proposed in these fields provide support for solving concrete problems in their respective domains, yet they do not transfer to more domain-independent general goals such as (re)configuration. To the best of our knowledge, no PMC tool fully harnesses interactive visualization to support the exploration and facilitate the under-standing of large models and their (functional or non-functional) properties.

In response, we set to create PMC-VIS, a visual tool that explicitly supports understanding the above-mentioned system behavior (1) and metrics (2) while remaining independent from a concrete application field. PMC-VIS connects the PRISM model checker on the backend side with a visualization frontend. Our focus is on *Markov Decision Processes* (MDPs) as operational models, in which the initial states stand for design alternatives (*configurations*) and the nondeter-ministic choices stand for possible *reconfiguration* steps. Metrics in this setting are of a quantitative nature and include probabilities and expectations of random variables, standing for either costs or gained rewards. The backend of our tool PMC-VIS consists of a simple API shell around PRISM that allows for calls to the model checker at runtime and a database wrapper for efficient data-exchange to the frontend. The frontend consists of a web-based application that enables *exploration of large MDPs* including features for comparing metrics computed by PMC attached to MDP states, actions and schedulers, while additionally sup-porting *finding suitable configurations* in families of MDPs and *reconfiguration in adaptive systems* modeled as MDPs. The current version of PMC-VIS, usage scenarios, and performance experiments are available at imld.de/pmc-vis.

2   Background and Related Work

Markov Decision Processes (MDP) are formal, stochastic models used to describe systems that exhibit both controllable and uncontrollable behaviour [3]. MDPs are typically represented as directed graphs with *states* as vertices and *actions* (also referred to as *transitions*) as edges. Edges can additionally express uncer-tainty, or in other words, the same action may lead to different states according to a probability distribution. We will use the term *PMC results* to refer to the output of the PMC, including probabilities of temporal events and expectations of random variables. Apart from the sole purpose of evaluation by means of a quantitative analysis, the computed PMC results can be used to decide on different design alternatives, determine appropriate values for system parameters (i.e., parameter synthesis for configuration) and to synthesize suitable adaptation policies (i.e., strategy synthesis for reconfiguration in adaptive systems) by examining *schedulers*, the functions that resolved the non-determinism during computation.

Visual Tools for Model Checking. HMMEditor [7] and TraceVis [13] exemplify the usage of PMC results for specific application scenarios which do not transfer to domain-independent (re)configuration tasks. On the other hand, tools like Palette [19] and Theseus [11] visualize model checking outcomes, but not the model or its inherent behaviour. Another example of this is MDPVis [25], which provides insights for debugging through a succinct overview of MDPs of arbitrary size, yet it does not visualize individual decisions nor the model itself, making it quite abstract for understanding the model behavior. Some model checking toolboxes in adjacent fields, such as mCRL2 [5], CADP [10] and UPPAAL [4] already contain capabilities to create visual support for understanding their models by visualizing them in graph form. In the field of MDPs, this also has been partially addressed for learning scenarios [27] as well as for the understanding of model checking counterexamples [17], using multiple coordinated views. But all these tools were evaluated on relatively small graphs, making scaling to large MDPs remain an open challenge.

Degree-Of-Interest for Large Decision Graphs. Large graphs are typically handled using aggregation and clustering methods [12], (e.g., ZAME [8] and ASK-GraphView [1] and HybridVis [24]), or focus+context techniques [6,30]. However, noting that a complete graph overview may not be necessary for decision graphs (as the interest is typically on a few decisions at a time), we make use of Degree-Of-Interest (DOI) graphs [14] instead. This approach for large graph exploration shows only an initial set of nodes and delegates to the user the responsibility of revealing, on-demand, the neighbors of nodes of interest. In this way, the graph is revealed progressively. This is fitting for MDPs as we can expand by discreet time steps of the model. However, while visual clutter and subsequently, cognitive load, start low, they increase as the graph is expanded in this approach. To overcome this limitation, we take further inspiration from concepts for iterative graph exploration on sequential views [16,29].

Parallel Coordinates Plots for Multivariate Graphs and Decision-Making. The surveys on multivariate network visualization [21,26] present various approaches fitting to our challenge of joining per-state PMC results to MDPs. Most prominently, multiple coordinated view setups featuring *Parallel Coordinates Plots* (PCPs) [18] are used to effectively display and explore the attributes alongside or within the graph view. A PCP consists of a set of n parallel lines axes for each of the dimensions or attributes of n-dimensional data. The data points are then represented as polylines connecting the axes at the values of each data

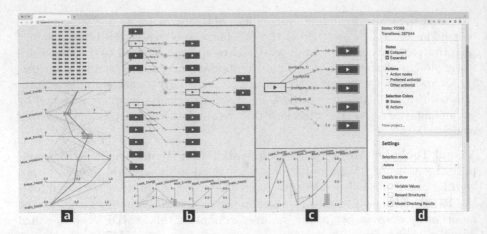

Fig. 1. Screenshot of PMC-VIS, illustrating three *panes* (a, b, c), each showing a different part of the MDP. The settings sidebar is visible on (d).

point's attributes. By organizing the data in such a way, it is possible to detect patterns and correlations between attribute values. PCPs typically incorporate interaction techniques such as axes re-ordering, brushing and highlighting. By brushing on an axis x, the user selects the set of data points where the value for x is within the range determined by the brushed area. Multiple brushes can be specified simultaneously on different axes, which is why PCPs are employable for multi-criteria decision-making (e.g., Parasol [28]). HybridVis [24] also exemplifies the usage of a PCP alongside a graph view. Using the before-mentioned abstraction approaches, this graph view scales, although visually cluttered, to a few thousand nodes. The PCP encodes the multi-variate nodes of the graph, which in turn allows coordinated filtering and highlighting in both views.

3   PMC-VIS: Visualising Probabilistic Model Checking

As an interdisciplinary team, bridging the visualization and formal verification communities, we designed and developed PMC-VIS, a tool that integrates visualization techniques and efficient retrieval methods. A screenshot of PMC-VIS can be seen in Fig. 1. PMC-VIS consists of two web servers, *Backend* and *Frontend*. Our architecture decouples the heavy probabilistic model checking computations done in the *Backend* from the visualization and interaction service provided by the *Frontend*. The Frontend can request data for states or subgraphs of interest from Backend, and uses this data to populate interactive visualizations.

Backend: The Backend server manages instances of the model checker PRISM [23], using its publicly available API[1]. As opposed to retrieving the data from resulting log files, we extract and store it in a database while it is generated during the stages of the PMC process. *Before model checking*, we extract structural information from the model input: existence of variables and their domains

---

[1] github.com/prismmodelchecker/prism-api

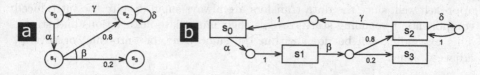

Fig. 2. Representation of MDPs. Version (a) is a more typical, compact version, with edges for actions and vertices for states. We propose version (b) for PMC-VIS, with a more stretched but explicit representation of actions versus outcomes.

(i.e., possible values they can take), labels for the states, parameters for experiments, and reward functions. *After model construction*, we create two tables, for (1) reachable states in the model, together with information about variables, labels and rewards, and (2) reachable actions, along with their labels and possible outcomes. *After model checking a property*, the computed PMC results are extracted for every reachable state of the MDP and stored in the above-mentioned tables, along with the scheduler actions taken or possibly taken.

Frontend: The Frontend of PMC-VIS is a web-based application that visualizes MDPs and their conjunct PMC results through sequential *panes*. Each pane has two sub-panes, for a *graph view* and an *attribute view*. Every graph view uses the Degree-Of-Interest (DOI) [14] approach to reveal the MDP on demand, and every attribute view uses configurable Parallel Coordinates Plots (PCPs) [18] to navigate through the PMC results related to selections within the graph view. Both panes and sub-panes are re-sizable, and the content within them adapts to the available space. For example, Fig. 1a shows a vertical PCP to better use the height of the sub-pane, whereas the PCPs in Fig. 1b and c are horizontal. PMC-VIS uses both traditional context menus and direct interactions (e.g., shift+click, double click) to support both novices and experienced users.

DOI MDPs: We designed a representation of MDPs, visible in Fig. 2b. For the *states*, we use rectangular nodes. For the edges, instead of overloading their meaning to indicate both *actions* and probabilistic *outcomes* (as shown in edge β of Fig. 2a), we explicitly separate these meanings by introducing handle nodes for the actions as label-less circles. This allows the user to more easily scan and parse the edges, since an outgoing edge from a state will always carry the action name (e.g., α, β, γ), and any outgoing edge from a handle node shows the probability of reaching the state that it points to. For example, when only glancing over Fig. 2a one could mistakenly get the impression that there are two outgoing actions from s_1 (as opposed to just β). This effect worsens when, (e.g., for each state) there are several outgoing actions, each with several probable outcomes. In reconfiguration tasks, where the user needs to decide between several actions, the handle nodes also simplify the selection of actions by area (e.g., using rectangle or lasso selections over the circle nodes instead of edges). The labels of the states are provided by the Backend as either text or icons. The scheduler choices are represented as solid edges, with the sub-optimal choices shown as dashed edges. Our proposed representation suits the implementation of an incremental DOI approach well, since the data transfers are always small despite the introduced components. Expanding states reveals their immediate next actions and states. This expanding can be done within the same pane, or onto one, or several, adjacent panes.

PMC Results via PCPs: Alongside each DOI graph, a PCP is shown in each pane to explore the additional PMC results. The PCPs in our PMC-VIS tool support axes re-ordering and brushing for selections, hovering to preview selections, and other miscellaneous options for numerical, boolean and nominal data. The data that is shown on the PCP of a pane is linked to the selection of nodes on its respective graph view, meaning that states (blue) and actions (orange) can be loaded onto the PCP for filtering based on the shown PMC results, which in turn can refine the selection made on the graph view through e.g., axes brushing. The PCPs can be seen at the bottom of the panes visible in Fig. 1a–c. Additionally, details for each state on the DOI graph can be shown on-demand via tooltips.

Settings: PMC-VIS has a sidebar on the right with several options to modify the shown attributes of the PMC results, as well as several graph layout options (e.g., force-directed, hierarchical) that can be applied to each *pane* individually. Understanding the part of the MDP shown in each pane may be easier using different graph layout options for particular cases, and this flexibility in configuration supports varying user preferences within each individual pane. The settings sidebar is visible in Fig. 1d.

Multi-pane Possibilities: Our multi-pane approach allows the users to expand as much as desired and to create structural "check-points" by expanding a selection of states from the MDP onto new panes. Doing so creates multiple work spaces within the same MDP, enhancing the scalability of the DOI approach by turning the model exploration into a task that can be distributed and completed asynchronously. Furthermore, a pane can be cloned onto a neighbor pane, for comparison and to save previous states. This approach also supports backtracking to previous states and work spaces, to re-evaluate decisions and explore branching paths of the MDP. Lastly, the content of any pane can be exported/imported, allowing users to completely off-load their progress from a browser tab and start directly from any state or state selection that they had reached before.

Implementation: The Backend uses *dropwizard*[2] to establish a RESTful web-server that wraps PRISM and manages an SQL-lite database. The Frontend of PMC-VIS uses the *Cytoscape.js*[3] library (v3.25.0 [9]) for the graph views, enhanced through several of its add-ons (e.g., for graph layouts), alongside the well-established *D3.js*[4] library (v7.8.4) to construct the PCPs. This selection of libraries and frameworks ensures efficient loading and rendering times.

---

[2] dropwizard.io.

[3] js.cytoscape.org.

[4] d3js.org.

4   Usage Scenarios and Performance

To illustrate the capabilities of PMC-VIS, we provide four example models and several performance measurements on the accompanying artifact [22] and website imld.de/pmc-vis. In the following, we exemplify the usage of PMC-VIS for three individual usage scenarios on the model of a server management system (SMS). This model, consisting of 93,588 states, describes how a number of *tasks* is distributed to a number of *servers*. The usage scenarios are further illustrated in the Appendix of this paper.

Scenario 1 (Configuration) deals with the model configuration, in which the user is interested in finding a good server setup. In order to do this, a selection over the initial 84 states must be made. Using the PCP, the user can refine a selection that satisfies some criteria of interest. For example, by brushing the axis for $PrMaxHappy$ near value 1, the user ensures that only states that maximize the probability of successfully completing all tasks are selected. After similarly brushing over the lowest values of maximum and minimum energy consumption ($MostEnergy$ and $LeastEnergy$), a selection of only 3 states is achieved and can be expanded on an adjacent pane. Other patterns can be seen in the PCP that may inform different selections, for which the user can simply go back to the original pane to change the selection.

Scenario 2 (Exploration) explains how through the exploration of the MDP in different panes, it is possible for the user to distinguish 3 *phases* the model goes through, which helps construct a visual understanding of the model behavior while using PMC-VIS: (1) generating tasks, (2) re-configuring, and (3) assigning work. These phases repeat until some termination criteria is reached (e.g., a fixed number of phases have been completed). The split between these different phases also highlights the value of using different panes to make sure that no partial work is lost, which in systems with a single view is often not possible.

Lastly, **Scenario 3 (Strategic Exploration)** describes the additional means by which the users of PMC-VIS can construct *strategies* while navigating the MDP, informed by the accompanying PMC results. These strategies are essentially a list of choices that must be made in order to find certain paths in the MDP, that fulfill the goals of the SMS. Users can discover strategies by comparing per-node tooltips, PCPs in different panes (for both states and actions within the MDP), and MDPs with different highlighted schedulers. Schedulers, and particularly, the comparison of multiple scheduler options, helps the user understand how non-determinism is solved for maximum and minimum PMC results. Thus, the flexible exploration and comparison facilities of PMC-VIS aid in making sense of schedulers over multiple properties without the need to trigger new model checking computations. Ultimately, the creation of a strategy may span many panes, and disconnected, asynchronous work, which is why PMC-VIS also provides a feature to export a collection of marked nodes, which can be loaded onto a pane to explore gaps until a complete strategy has been developed.

Performance Experiment: Our goal was to provide both fast build time and smooth interaction with the MDP regardless of its total size. Thus, we measured the build and response times of multiple models of similar structure but exponentially increasing size (measured in number of states of the MDP), all solved for the same properties. With respect to the **model computation times,** our experiment shows that the overhead introduced by the creation and initial insertion into the database, compared to only executing the PMC procedures, is mainly bound to the database writing speed, where we perform around 40–50 operations per millisecond. However, all operations scale similarly with respect to model size, meaning we can compute PMC results normally with PRISM. Likewise, with regards to the **model exploration**, the Frontend performance is influenced by the response times of the Backend, which we kept under a second for small requests (1 to 5 states) or within a few seconds for large (10 queried states) requests, even on a model with 10^7 states. Beyond this, on a laptop with Intel(R) Core(TM) i7-7500U CPU and 16 GB of RAM, and using a Chromium 114.0.5735.133 browser, a single pane continues to operate smoothly with over 500 nodes. However, we do not foresee users working with large requests often, nor with that much content on a single pane.

5   Conclusion

We contributed PMC-VIS to support exploration of MDPs and PMC configuration and reconfiguration tasks. Our solution incorporates DOI graphs and PCPs on a multi-pane approach that, making use of efficient model checking and retrieval methods, supports users in understanding model behaviour and conjunct PMC results. We discussed how PMC-VIS can be used to answer various formal verification questions, especially in regard to the (re)configuration tasks. We foresee that further formal model and verification methods would benefit from extensions of our approach. Thus, we look forward to further generalizing PMC-VIS in various directions towards an IDE for automata-based operational models, model checking of functional and nonfunctional properties and functionalities for various synthesis questions, including further features for what-if analysis.

Data-Availability Statement. PMC-VIS, the used models, scenarios and performance experiment are open source and available on our supplementary web page at imld.de/pmc-vis and in the accompanying artifact at Zenodo [22]. Further figures of PMC-VIS can be found in the Appendix of this paper.

Acknowledgements. This work was supported by the Deutsche Forschungsgemeinschaft (DFG, German Research Foundation) under Germany's Excellence Strategy: EXC-2068, 390729961 - Cluster of Excellence "Physics of Life" and EXC 2050/1, 390696704 - Cluster of Excellence "Centre for Tactile Internet" (CeTI) of TU Dresden, by DFG grant 389792660 as part of TRR 248 – CPEC (see https://cpec.science) and by the German Federal Ministry of Education and Research (BMBF, SCADS22B) and the Saxon State Ministry for Science, Culture and Tourism (SMWK) by funding the competence center for Big Data and AI "ScaDS.AI Dresden/Leipzig".

Appendix

The following illustrations are appended to the paper for the interested reader to have a deeper look at PMC-VIS and our results. (See Figs. 3, 4, 5, 6, 7 and 8).

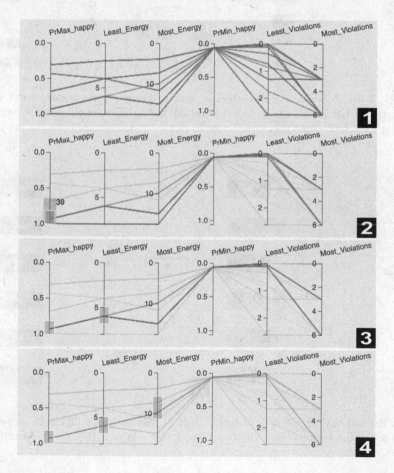

Fig. 3. Related to Scenario 1 described in Sect. 4. Axes brushing on the parallel coordinates plot. The numbers (1) through (4) represent the order of the brushing steps to reach a selection of 3 states out of the initial 84.

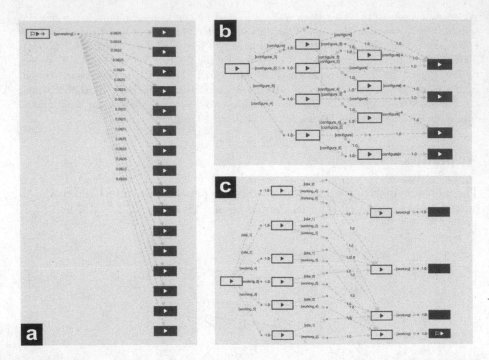

Fig. 4. Related to Scenario 2 described in Sect. 4. Three phases of our model shown as patterns in the graph views: (a) Generating tasks, (b) re-configuring servers, (c) assigning work to each server.

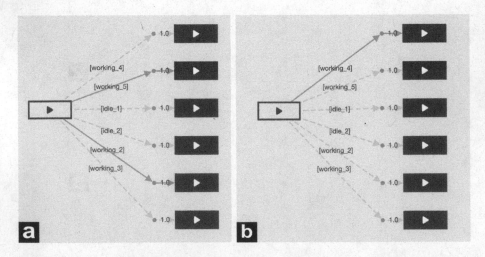

Fig. 5. Related to Scenario 3 described in Sect. 4. Different edge highlights depending on the selected scheduler. (a): $PrMax\_Happy$ was selected. (b): $Least\_Energy$ was selected.

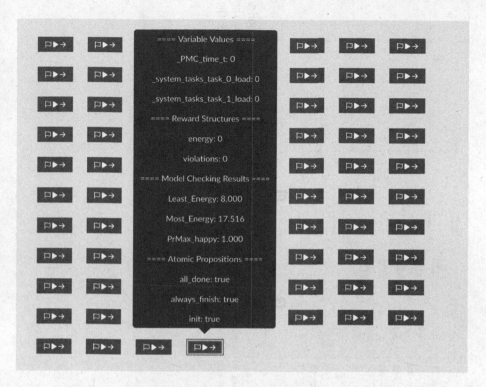

Fig. 6. Related to Scenario 3 described in Sect. 4. Shift+click on a state (with blue border) shows a tooltip, detailing all properties selected in the settings sidebar. (Color figure online)

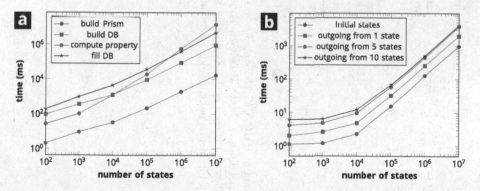

Fig. 7. Related to the experiment described in Sect. 4. (a): Times for single model computation. (b): Average response time (gathered over 10,000 responses). These experiments were carried out on a server with Intel(R) Xeon(R) L5630 CPUs with in total 8 physical cores and 189 GB of DDR3 RAM.

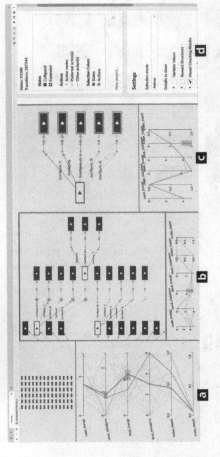

Fig. 8. Screenshot of PMC-VIS, showing 3 *panes* (a, b, c). Pane (a) shows the initial states of the MDP (as a grid of unconnected nodes above, and as polylines in the PCP below). Pane (b) shows a set of selected actions (in blue). Pane (c) shows a selection over the possible outcomes of a chosen action (in orange). Pane (c) shows a selection over the possible outcomes of a chosen action, currently linked to pane (b) as indicated by the green border on top of this pane. (Color figure online)

References

1. Abello, J., van Ham, F., Krishnan, N.: ASK-GraphView: a large scale graph visualization system. IEEE TVCG **12**(5), 669–676 (2006). https://doi.org/10.1109/TVCG.2006.120

2. Baier, C., Hermanns, H., Katoen, J.-P.: The 10,000 facets of MDP model checking. In: Steffen, B., Woeginger, G. (eds.) Computing and Software Science. LNCS, vol. 10000, pp. 420–451. Springer, Cham (2019). https://doi.org/10.1007/978-3-319-91908-9_21

3. Baier, C., Katoen, J.-P.: Principles of Model Checking. MIT Press, Cambridge (2008)

4. Bengtsson, J., Larsen, K., Larsson, F., Pettersson, P., Yi, W.: UPPAAL — a tool suite for automatic verification of real-time systems. In: Alur, R., Henzinger, T.A., Sontag, E.D. (eds.) HS 1995. LNCS, vol. 1066, pp. 232–243. Springer, Heidelberg (1996). https://doi.org/10.1007/BFb0020949

5. Bunte, O., et al.: The mCRL2 toolset for analysing concurrent systems. In: Vojnar, T., Zhang, L. (eds.) TACAS 2019. LNCS, vol. 11428, pp. 21–39. Springer, Cham (2019). https://doi.org/10.1007/978-3-030-17465-1_2 ISBN 9783030174651

6. Card, S.K., Shneiderman, B., MacKinlay, J.D.: Readings in Information Visualization-Using Vision to Think. Series in Interactive Technologies. Morgan Kaufmann Publishers (1999). ISBN 1-55860-533-9

7. Dai, J., Cheng, J.: HMMEditor: a visual editing tool for profile hidden Markov model. BMC Genom. **9**(1), S8 (2008). https://doi.org/10.1186/1471-2164-9-S1-S8. ISSN 1471–2164

8. Elmqvist, N., et al.: ZAME: interactive large-scale graph visualization. In: 2008 IEEE PacificVis, pp. 215–222 (2008). https://doi.org/10.1109/PACIFICVIS.2008.4475479

9. Franz, M., et al.: Cytoscape.js 2023 update: a graph theory library for visualization and analysis. Bioinformatics **39**(1) (2023). https://doi.org/10.1093/bioinformatics/btad031. ISSN 1367–4811

10. Garavel, H., et al.: CADP 2011: a toolbox for the construction and analysis of distributed processes. STTT **15**(2), 89–107 (2013). https://doi.org/10.1007/s10009-012-0244-z. ISSN 1433–2787

11. Goldsby, H., Cheng, B.H.C., Konrad, S., Kamdoum, S.: A visualization framework for the modeling and formal analysis of high assurance systems. In: Nierstrasz, O., Whittle, J., Harel, D., Reggio, G. (eds.) MODELS 2006. LNCS, vol. 4199, pp. 707–721. Springer, Heidelberg (2006). https://doi.org/10.1007/11880240_49

12. Görke, R., Hartmann, T., Wagner, D.: Dynamic graph clustering using minimum-cut trees. In: Dehne, F., Gavrilova, M., Sack, J.-R., Tóth, C.D. (eds.) WADS 2009. LNCS, vol. 5664, pp. 339–350. Springer, Heidelberg (2009). https://doi.org/10.1007/978-3-642-03367-4_30 ISBN 978-3-642-03367-4

13. Gros, T.P., Groß, D., Gumhold, S., Hoffmann, J., Klauck, M., Steinmetz, M.: TraceVis: towards visualization for deep statistical model checking. In: Margaria, T., Steffen, B. (eds.) ISoLA 2020. LNCS, vol. 12479, pp. 27–46. Springer, Cham (2021). https://doi.org/10.1007/978-3-030-83723-5_3

14. van Ham, F., Perer, A.: Search, show context, expand on demand: supporting large graph exploration with degree-of-interest. IEEE TVCG **15**(6), 953–960 (2009). https://doi.org/10.1109/TVCG.2009.108

15. Hensel, C., et al.: The probabilistic model checker storm (2020). arXiv: 2002.07080 [cs.SE]

16. Horak, T., Dachselt, R.: Hierarchical graphs on mobile devices: a lane-based approach. In: CHI MobileVis Workshop (2018)
17. Horak, T., et al.: Visual analysis of hyperproperties for understanding model checking results. IEEE TVCG **28**(1), 357–367 (2022). https://doi.org/10.1109/TVCG.2021.3114866. ISSN 1941–0506
18. Johansson, J., Forsell, C.: Evaluation of parallel coordinates: overview, categorization and guidelines for future research. IEEE TVCG **22**(1), 579–588 (2016). https://doi.org/10.1109/TVCG.2015.2466992
19. Kamhi, G., Fix, L., Binyamini, Z.: Symbolic model checking visualization. In: Gopalakrishnan, G., Windley, P. (eds.) FMCAD 1998. LNCS, vol. 1522, pp. 290–302. Springer, Heidelberg (1998). https://doi.org/10.1007/3-540-49519-3_19 ISBN 9783540495192
20. Katoen, J.-P., et al.: The ins and outs of the probabilistic model checker MRMC. IPerform. Eval. **68**(2), 90–104 (2011). https://doi.org/10.1016/j.peva.2010.04.001. ISSN 0166–5316
21. Kerren, A., Purchase, H.C., Ward, M.O. (eds.): Multivariate Network Visualization. LNCS, vol. 8380. Springer, Cham (2014). https://doi.org/10.1007/978-3-319-06793-3
22. Korn, M., et al.: Interactive Visualization Meets Probabilistic Model Checking Artifact (2023). https://doi.org/10.5281/zenodo.8172531
23. Kwiatkowska, M., Norman, G., Parker, D.: PRISM 4.0: verification of probabilistic real-time systems. In: Gopalakrishnan, G., Qadeer, S. (eds.) CAV 2011. LNCS, vol. 6806, pp. 585–591. Springer, Heidelberg (2011). https://doi.org/10.1007/978-3-642-22110-1_47
24. Liu, Y., et al.: HybridVis: an adaptive hybrid-scale visualization of multivariate graphs. JVLC **41**, 100–110-(2017). https://doi.org/10.1016/j.jvlc.2017.03.008. ISSN 1045–926X
25. McGregor, S., et al.: Facilitating testing and debugging of Markov Decision Processes with interactive visualization. In: IEEE VL/HCC 2015, pp. 53–61 (2015). https://doi.org/10.1109/VLHCC.2015.7357198
26. Nobre, C., et al.: The state of the art in visualizing multivariate networks. CGF **38**(3), 807–832 (2019). https://doi.org/10.1111/cgf.13728
27. Pfannkuch, M., Budgett, S.: Markov processes: exploring the use of dynamic visualizations to enhance student understanding. JSE **24**(2), 63–73 (2016). https://doi.org/10.1080/10691898.2016.1207404
28. Raseman, W.J., Jacobson, J., Kasprzyk, J.R.: Parasol: an open source, interactive parallel coordinates library for multi-objective decision making. EMS **116**, 153–163 (2019). https://doi.org/10.1016/j.envsoft.2019.03.005
29. Tan, Y.-Q., et al.: VecRoad: point-based iterative graph exploration for road graphs extraction. In: 2020 IEEE/CVF CVPR, pp. 8907–8915 (2020). https://doi.org/10.1109/CVPR42600.2020.00893
30. Wang, Y., et al.: Structure-aware fisheye views for efficient large graph exploration. IEEE TVCG **25**(1), 566–575 (2019). https://doi.org/10.1109/TVCG.2018.2864911

Author Index

C. Ferreira and T. A. C. Willemse (Eds.): SEFM 2023, LNCS 14323, pp. 377–378, 2023.
https://doi.org/10.1007/978-3-031-47115-5

Printed in the United States
by Baker & Taylor Publisher Services